The Institute of Chartered Accountants in England and Wales

AUDIT AND ASSURANCE

For exams in 2019

Question Bank

www.icaew.com

Audit and Assurance
The Institute of Chartered Accountants in England and Wales

ISBN: 978-1-50972-019-4
Previous ISBN: 978-1-78363-705-8

First edition 2007
Twelfth edition 2018

The content of this publication is intended to prepare students for the ICAEW examinations, and should not be used as professional advice.

British Library Cataloguing-in-Publication Data
A catalogue record for this book is available from the British Library

Originally printed in the United Kingdom on paper obtained from traceable, sustainable sources.

Contents

The following questions are exam-standard. Unless told otherwise, these questions are the style, content and format that you can expect in your exam.

Question Bank topic finder

Set out below is a guide showing the Audit and Assurance syllabus learning outcomes, topic areas, and related questions in the Question Bank for each topic area. If you need to concentrate on certain topic areas, or if you want to attempt all available questions that refer to a particular topic, you will find this guide useful.

Topic area	Syllabus learning outcome(s)	Question number(s)	Study Manual chapter(s)
Accepting engagements	1b, 1o	10, 11, 13, 22, 23, 38, 56, 61, 64, 74, 77	6
Audit approach	2h, 2j	41, 57, 68	10
Audit completion	3a, 3b, 3c, 3d, 3g, 3h	70	12
Audits of different types of entity	2m, 2n, 2o	34	11
Comparing audit with other assurance	1b	12, 16, 19, 29, 49, 54, 58, 60	1
Going concern	3b	17, 34, 41, 62, 68	12
Other assurance engagements	1b, 2j, 3d, 3e, 3f, 3g	6, 7, 8, 9, 10, 12, 14, 16, 19, 24, 28, 29, 30, 39, 49, 54, 58, 65	14
Planning	2h, 2i, 2o	18, 24, 37, 44, 52, 60, 76	7
Professional ethics	1a, 1c, 1e, 1k	3, 11, 13, 22, 38, 42, 45, 48, 53, 56, 61, 62, 68, 69, 72, 77	4
Professional standards	1l, 1m, 1p	73	3
Quality control	1d, 1f, 1g, 1h, 1l, 1j	4, 17, 66	5
Reporting	3e, 3f, 3i, 3j	3, 17, 31, 32, 33, 34, 35, 39, 46, 48, 50, 52, 58, 62, 66, 71, 74, 78	13
Reporting to those charged with governance	3f	23, 32, 33, 34, 46, 50, 57, 64, 72, 76	13
Responsibilities	1a, 1e, 1k, 1n, 1q, 2l	2, 41, 73	2
Risk assessment	2a, 2b, 2c, 2d, 2e, 2f, 2g, 2k, 2p	18, 23, 26	8, 9
Risks and procedures	2g, 2j, 2p	20, 21, 25, 37, 44, 48, 52, 56, 60, 64, 68, 72	9, 10

Exam

Your exam will consist of

Part one	6 short-form questions	20 marks
Part two	3 questions	80 marks
Pass mark		55
Exam length		2.5 hours

The ACA student area of our website includes the latest information, guidance and exclusive resources to help you progress through the ACA, Find everything you need, from exam webinars, past exams, marks plans, errata sheets and the syllabus to advice from the examiners at icaew.com/exams.

Question Bank

Audit and Assurance: Question Bank

Section 1: Legal and other professional regulations, ethics, accepting and managing engagements and current issues

... le Ltd has approached your firm and requested a second ... which its current auditors are proposing to give on the ... ended 31 July 20X7. The proposed auditor's report ... ue to disagreement over the accounting policies adopted in

... ay arise for your firm and state, with reasons, how your firm

(4 marks)

... company or group of companies constitute a substantial ... f an audit firm, a self-interest threat is likely to arise so as to

... ould use to recognise this threat and the procedures

(2 marks)

... sportsresults-a-minute.com. ... company has overdue fees of £15,000, being the previous year's audit fee.

Explain the threat to your firm's independence and state the action your firm should take in respect of this matter.

(3 marks)

... g the audit of Cairn Ltd, the audit senior discovered that some of the company's ... mers had paid invoices twice. The overpayments had not been refunded and had ... credited to the statement of profit or loss. The managing director told the audit senior ... hese customers, which are government bodies, periodically pay the same invoice ... . He also told the audit senior that he has no intention of repaying the money unless ... ustomers ask for it to be repaid.

... , with reasons, the action the audit senior should take in respect of this matter.

(3 marks)

... raud has recently been discovered, involving the chief buyer in the purchasing ... partment of Rodney Ltd and a purchase ledger clerk in the accounts department over a ... riod of two years. The managing director of Rodney Ltd has written to the company's ... ditors claiming that they had a responsibility to detect frauds during the course of their ... dits, and requesting an explanation as to how they could have missed it.

... hat points should the auditors make in response to the managing director? **(2 marks)**

1.6 Dimension Ltd is a software company providing e-commerce solutions to business. It was incorporated on 1 April 20X8 and revenue has doubled each year. Rapid expansion is expected to continue for the next few years.

This growth requires heavy investment in working capital, particularly work in progress and receivables, and the company will be seeking a substantial increase in the borrowing facility from its bankers when the present facility is due for annual review in September 20X1.

The increase in revenue in the year ended 31 March 20X1 has taken the company over the exemption threshold, and it is obliged to have a statutory audit for the first time.

List the benefits that the company may obtain from the statutory audit. **(2 marks)**

1.7 You have been invited to tender for the audit of Data plc, a company that owns and operates 35 hotels in the south west of England. You have not previously acted for Data plc, but you are the current auditors of Lodge Ltd, a company that owns and operates hotels in 30 out of the 35 towns in which Data plc operates. The hotels operated by each company offer similar facilities to each other at a similar price.

Identify and explain the principal ethical issue that you may need to consider when deciding whether or not to tender for the audit of Data plc, and state the procedures you may need to implement in the event that your tender was successful. **(3 marks)**

1.8 You are the auditor of Royale Ltd, a manufacturer of fireworks. Following a disappointing last three months of trading, the company has requested an extension to its overdraft facility from its bankers. The bank has in turn asked your firm to provide a report on the company's working capital, focusing on the recoverability of trade receivables and inventory.

Explain the benefits and limitations to both the bank and Royale Limited of obtaining the working capital report. **(4 marks)**

1.9 Mrs Wallace is the audit partner in her firm for Racdale Ltd. She has just been appointed a trustee of the Racdale Family Trust, which owns 20% of the shares in Racdale Ltd. She replaces the family solicitor who has just retired.

In addition, Mr Netwater, the audit manager for Racdale Ltd, has given one month's notice that he will be leaving the firm to become finance director of the company.

State the threats to independence that these situations pose, and the safeguards that the firm should employ to maintain objectivity. **(3 marks)**

1.10 The following is an extract from an independent accountant's unmodified report on a profit forecast:

'Based on our examination of the evidence supporting the assumptions, nothing has come to our attention which causes us to believe that these assumptions do not provide a reasonable basis for the forecast.'

Describe the level of assurance provided by this statement and explain how and why it differs from the level of assurance provided by an auditor's report on annual historical financial statements. **(4 marks)**

1.11 Your firm acts as auditor to Columbus Ltd, a retail car dealer. During the course of your audit for the year ended 30 June 20X5, you discover that the company's sales manager, helped by the accounts clerk, has deliberately falsified details of the value of vehicles sold in order to increase his monthly bonus payments.

Set out your responsibilities in respect of the above matter and contrast these with the responsibilities of the management of Columbus. **(3 marks)**

1.12 Your firm's largest client is Count Ltd (Count), a non-listed company. The statutory audit fee amounts to £468,000 per annum. In addition your firm provides tax services to Count worth £179,000 per annum. Your firm's total fee income for the current year is estimated at £6,200,000 including all the fees from Count described above.

Outline the ethical issues and state how your firm should address these issues. **(3 marks)**

1.13 Your firm is the external auditor of Kerry Ltd (Kerry) for the year ended 31 May 20X9. Following a due diligence investigation by your firm, Kerry acquired in January 20X9 the trade and assets of Blue Ltd from the liquidator. These assets are included in Kerry's statement of financial position at 31 May 20X9.

Identify and explain the principal threat to your firm's objectivity in respect of the audit of the financial statements of Kerry for the year ended 31 May 20X9 and state the safeguards that should be applied. **(2 marks)**

1.14 Explain why an external auditor of a company should be objective and independent. **(2 marks)**

1.15 Your firm has been the external auditor of Moose Ltd (Moose) for a number of years. Adam Flayman has been the engagement partner for four years. Moose is in the process of becoming a listed company and its directors have requested that Adam Flayman continue as the engagement partner once the company is listed.

Discuss the ethical issues arising and any safeguards that your firm should adopt in respect of the directors' request. **(4 marks)**

1.16 Describe the role of the ethics partner within an external audit firm. **(3 marks)**

1.17 During the external audit of Kipper Ltd (Kipper), an employee of the company informed the audit senior that the managing director of Kipper had instructed the employee not to record a transaction in the accounting records as it had nothing to do with Kipper's business. The transaction involved a cash deposit which was paid into the company's bank account and a week later the same amount was paid by Kipper, via direct transfer, into a bank account in the name of David Hake, a friend of the managing director. The amount is not material in the context of any of the key figures in the financial statements.

State, with reasons, how the audit senior should deal with this matter. **(2 marks)**

1.18 Explain the fundamental principle of professional competence and due care and provide **two** examples of how a firm of chartered accountants can identify whether its partners and staff are complying with this principle. **(4 marks)**

1.19 During the external audit of Milk Ltd (Milk) you discover that the directors have accounted for research costs inappropriately resulting in a material misstatement in Milk's financial statements. Your firm plans to issue a modified audit opinion if the misstatement is not corrected. During a conversation with your firm's audit partner, Milk's managing director, Hazel Blue, indicated that it is the directors' intention to seek the removal of your firm as external auditors if your firm issues a modified audit opinion in respect of this matter.

Explain the actions that your firm should consider taking in response to the conversation between Hazel Blue and your firm's audit partner. **(3 marks)**

1.20 Your firm has received notice from Pisces plc (Pisces), a listed company, that it will not be re-appointed as external auditor when its term of office expires as the audit committee of Pisces has recommended the appointment of another firm.

Set out the rights and responsibilities of your firm, including those under the Companies Act 2006, relating to the change in appointment. **(4 marks)**

1.21 Your firm has been approached by Snipe Ltd to accept appointment as external auditor for the year ending 30 June 20X6. In the auditor's report on the financial statements for the year ended 30 June 20X5, the previous auditor issued a qualified opinion, due to disagreement over the accounting policy for inventory valuation. This matter was cited by the previous auditor in response to your firm's letter requesting information that might influence your firm's decision as to whether to accept the engagement. In addition, the previous auditor stated that the audit fees due for the year ended 30 June 20X5 remain unpaid.

Identify and explain the ethical issues arising from the above and identify any actions your firm should take in respect of this matter before deciding whether it should accept the appointment as external auditor. **(3 marks)**

1.22 Explain why external audit firms are required to monitor the length of time that audit engagement partners serve as members of the engagement team for each audit. **(3 marks)**

1.23 Your firm, which has 25 offices throughout the UK, is planning to open a new UK office in the town of Milton Keynes. The managing director of Robinia plc (Robinia), a property company with numerous properties throughout the UK, has suggested that your firm leases one of Robinia's vacant properties in Milton Keynes at the market rate. Your firm is the external auditor of Robinia.

State with reasons, whether it is appropriate for your firm to lease this property from Robinia. **(3 marks)**

1.24 Your firm has informed its external audit client, Lion Ltd (Lion), that it will not be seeking reappointment at the end of its term of office because of a disagreement with Lion's directors over the treatment of an accounting item. Charn LLP (Charn), a firm of auditors, has recently written to your firm requesting information that might influence its decision to accept appointment as external auditor of Lion.

State your firm's responsibilities in relation to Charn's request, as set out in the ICAEW *Code of Ethics*. **(3 marks)**

1.25 During the course of the external audit of Wood Ltd (Wood), the audit junior identified a payment in the cash book, described as 'commission', for which there was no supporting documentation. On enquiry of the management of Wood, the audit junior was informed that the payment was made to a government official in another country to facilitate the progress of a contract Wood was undertaking in that country.

State, with reasons, the action to be taken by the audit junior. **(2 marks)**

1.26 During your firm's external audit of Long Ltd (Long), a chemical manufacturer, you were told by an employee of Long that the company frequently fails to provide its factory workers with the legally required protective clothing when working with hazardous chemicals.

Explain why this information should be considered by your firm during the external audit. **(4 marks)**

1.27 Your firm has received a request for information from Blonde LLP, a firm of auditors, in respect of its prospective external audit client Auburn Ltd (Auburn). Auburn is currently audited by your firm but, after discovering that Auburn's manufacturing process includes unethical labour practices in its overseas supply chain, your firm decided not to seek reappointment.

State, with reasons, the actions that your firm should take with respect to the request for information from Blonde LLP. **(4 marks)**

1.28 While reviewing the post year-end purchase invoices of Builda Ltd (Builda), a construction company, the audit senior discovered an invoice for two designer watches costing £5,000 each. On enquiry, the audit senior was informed that the watches were given, by the directors of Builda, to the managing director of Deluxe Developments Ltd (DD) and his wife. DD is a property development company to which Builda regularly submits tenders for construction projects.

State, with reasons, the action to be taken by the audit senior. **(2 marks)**

1.29 The FRC stated recently that its reviews of audits would give particular consideration as to whether appropriate professional scepticism has been applied in specific areas. Two of these areas are asset impairments and related parties.

State what is meant by professional scepticism and explain why it is fundamental to the audit of asset impairments and related parties. **(4 marks)**

1.30 Mullet LLP (Mullet) is the external auditor of Bream plc (Bream), which is a listed company. The directors of Bream have requested that Mullet undertakes an engagement to revalue a class of the company's assets which amount to 12% of total assets.

Explain why Mullet should refuse this request. **(4 marks)**

1.31 Grover Ltd (Grover) has headquarters in London and is an external audit client of Tyler LLP (Tyler), an ICAEW firm of chartered accountants. Tyler has received a telephone call from the City of London Police requesting that the firm discloses information about transactions undertaken by Grover in order to help the Police with their enquiries.

State, with reasons, the actions to be taken by Tyler. **(4 marks)**

1.32 Describe **two** procedures that an assurance firm should have in place to ensure that members of an audit team act with objectivity and independence. **(2 marks)**

1.33 You are the manager responsible for the engagement to review the financial information of Riff Ltd (Riff) on behalf of an external audit client, Alto plc (Alto), a listed company. Alto requested the review as it intends to acquire the share capital of Riff. The audit junior currently working with you on the review engagement told you that, yesterday, he purchased shares in Alto because he believes its share price will rise when the acquisition of Riff is announced. He also told you that he has informed his parents about the acquisition and has advised them to purchase shares in Alto.

Explain the ethical issues arising in this situation and state the actions you and your firm should take. **(4 marks)**

1.34 You are the senior responsible for the external audit of Bass Ltd (Bass). During the audit, the managing director of Bass requested that you complete the audit work as quickly as possible. As an incentive, he has offered you the company's holiday villa for your personal use for no charge if you ensure the audit work is completed to his deadline.

Explain the ethical issues arising in this situation. **(4 marks)**

1.35 Your firm sets its senior employees targets for generating fees from their external audit clients, including fees for non-audit services. One of the criteria for progression within the firm is achieving these targets.

Identify and explain the threat to the objectivity of the senior employees and state, with reasons, whether or not these arrangements are appropriate. **(3 marks)**

1.36 Your firm is the external auditor of Googly Ltd (Googly). The directors of Googly have requested that your firm provides a member of staff to help in the preparation of its annual financial statements.

Explain the threats to your firm's objectivity arising from the above and describe the safeguards, if any, which should be put in place to mitigate those threats. **(4 marks)**

1.37 The ICAEW *Code of Ethics* identifies circumstances where an auditor is or may be required to disclose, to third parties, confidential information obtained during the course of an external audit.

List, with examples, the circumstances in which the disclosure of confidential information, without the client's permission, is or may be required. **(4 marks)**

1.38 Coniston LLP (Coniston) has tendered for the external audit of Windermere plc. Coniston has proposed a fee below the market rate in the hope that the firm will subsequently be awarded more lucrative advisory work.

Identify and explain the ethical issues posed by Coniston's proposal. **(4 marks)**

1.39 Your audit firm, which has several listed clients in its portfolio, has a policy prohibiting partners and staff from owning shares in client companies.

Outline the procedures that your firm should have in place to ensure that partners and staff comply with this policy. **(3 marks)**

2 Criticisms of auditors

Following high profile corporate failures, auditors have been criticised by various interested parties in connection with:

(1) their responsibility for the detection of fraud
(2) the provision of non-audit services to their audit clients
(3) the period of time for which they can act as auditors for a client

Requirement

Outline the current regulatory and professional requirements in respect of the matters identified in (1) to (3) above and state how they might be further changed by the UK regulatory bodies. Set out the case for and against changes to the current regulatory and professional requirements.

Total: 15 marks

3 Kristoff Ltd, Reindeer Ltd, Pabbie Group plc

Described below are three situations which have arisen at three unrelated audit clients of your firm. The year end in each case is 31 December 20X4.

Kristoff Ltd (Kristoff)

Kristoff has made payments to a trust fund set up for the benefit of Anna Oaken, the niece of Hans North, Kristoff's managing director and majority shareholder. Your firm has concluded that the payments should be disclosed as a related party transaction in Kristoff's financial statements. Hans has refused to include the necessary disclosures as he considers the payments to be of a sensitive nature and does not wish the rest of his family to be aware of them. He has threatened your firm with removal from office if it pursues this issue any further.

Reindeer Ltd (Reindeer)

Reindeer has included a note in its financial statements disclosing a possible tax liability of £22 million. HMRC (the UK tax authority) claims Reindeer has evaded taxes on some of its overseas activities. Reindeer plans to appeal against the claim before an appeals tribunal but the outcome of the tribunal will not be determined until after the auditor's report has been signed. The directors have assessed that it is possible, but not probable, that the claim will be upheld by the tribunal and your firm agrees with this assessment. A provision has not been included in Reindeer's financial statements in respect of the claim. Your firm has concluded that a provision is not required and that the note, describing the uncertainty, in Reindeer's financial statements is adequate. The directors of Reindeer have requested that your firm provides a team of tax experts to support them through the appeals tribunal.

The total assets of Reindeer at 31 December 20X4 are £450 million and the profit before tax for the year ended 31 December 20X4 is £18 million.

Pabbie Group plc (Pabbie)

Pabbie is your firm's largest listed audit client. On 31 October 20X4, Pabbie expanded by acquiring a significant overseas subsidiary, Queen SARL (Queen). Your firm is the group auditor, but Queen's financial statements for the year ended 31 December 20X4 have been audited by an overseas auditor, Blizzard. Your firm planned to rely on Blizzard's work. However, during the audit Blizzard refused to cooperate. Your firm has no alternative audit procedures it can perform in respect of Queen's financial statements. Queen's results are highly material to a large number of items in Pabbie's group financial statements. The directors of Pabbie have requested that your firm accepts appointment as external auditor of Queen for the year ending 31 December 20X5 in order to avoid this issue arising next year. Your firm estimates the total fee for the 20X5 audit of the Pabbie group will be £1.4 million and your firm's total annual fee income is likely to be £20 million.

Requirements

For each of the situations outlined above:

3.1 identify and explain the threats to your firm's objectivity and state the steps that your firm should take to address them. **(12 marks)**

3.2 state whether you would modify the audit opinion. Give reasons for your conclusions and describe the modification(s), if any, to each auditor's report. **(8 marks)**

Total: 20 marks

4 Financial Reporting Council

The Financial Reporting Council (FRC) has recently undertaken reviews of the quality control procedures at your firm including the inspection of a sample of external audit files. It has reported the following matters to be addressed by your firm.

(1) External audit partners and staff are set targets for selling non-audit services to their audit clients and, as an incentive, are given credit in their annual pay review when the target is met or exceeded.

(2) Shane Smith has been the audit engagement partner for Garfield plc, a listed company, since 20X2. It is now 20X9. No further documentation relating to this issue was available on the files reviewed.

(3) One external audit file did not show any evidence that work performed by junior members of the audit team was reviewed by more senior members.

(4) Kapil LLP (Kapil), a firm of consultants, was verbally instructed to act for your firm as an auditor's expert providing valuations of property included in the financial statements of a number of audited entities. Your firm intends to continue to use Kapil but has not formalised the arrangement.

Requirements

4.1 (a) Describe how the FRC promotes improvements in the quality of auditing. **(3 marks)**

(b) Explain why matters (1) to (4) above have been reported to your firm and describe the actions that your firm should take in respect of each matter. **(10 marks)**

4.2 (a) In respect of quality control procedures undertaken by audit firms, outline the differences between:

- an engagement quality control review (hot review); and
- a review as part of the firm's monitoring procedures (cold review). **(5 marks)**

(b) Set out the attributes required of an individual who is appointed by an audit firm to undertake engagement quality control reviews. **(2 marks)**

Total: 20 marks

4.1 (a) issues ISAs and ethical standards. Have power to take disciplinary action. Monitor compliance. Findings are available to the public. Investigate misconduct.

(b) 1.

5 Short form questions

5.1 A prospective auditor is required to write to the client's existing auditor to seek information which could influence his decision as to whether he may accept the auditor appointment.

Give examples of relevant matters which could be within this letter and which would influence the prospective auditor's decision to accept the audit appointment.   **(2 marks)**

5.2 Certain rights are conferred on an auditor by the Companies Act when a company proposes to remove him from office.

State the rights the auditor has in these circumstances.   **(2 marks)**

5.3 Your firm has been engaged to undertake a review of the cash flow forecast prepared by Yale Ltd in support of its request for a loan from its bank.

Identify the points specific to the review of a cash flow forecast that your firm should include in its engagement letter and explain why their inclusion is important.   **(4 marks)**

5.4 You are the senior in charge of the external audit of Hairsay Ltd which operates a chain of hair-dressing salons. While undertaking audit work at one of the salons, you observed the cashier, Jane, placing cash received from a customer in an envelope with the managing director's name, Robert Stone, on it and placing the envelope in the safe. The transaction was not recorded in the till. Jane then crossed through the customer's name in the appointments diary and wrote 'cancelled'. She informed you that Robert had instructed her to do this once a week. Robert collects the envelope on his weekly visit to the salon.

Explain your and your firm's responsibilities in respect of this matter.   **(4 marks)**

5.5 You are responsible for supervising the junior staff on the audit of Sole Ltd (Sole) for the year ended 30 November 20X9. An audit junior performed direct confirmations on a sample of trade receivables balances and has reconciled the balance on one customer's reply to Sole's receivables ledger balance as follows:

	£
Balance owing per reply from customer	32,624
(1) Payment per customer 29 Nov 20X9 not on Sole's ledger	15,056
(2) Prompt payment discount per customer 21 Oct 20X9 not on Sole's ledger	378
(3) Sales invoice 25 Nov 20X9 not accepted by customer as goods were returned because the wrong items were delivered	7,920
Balance owing per Sole's receivables ledger	55,978

State the information you would require for each of the reconciling items (1) to (3) above in order to draw a conclusion on the accuracy of the balance due from this customer.

      (3 marks)

...dit senior with responsibility for directing, supervising and reviewing the
...ior members of the engagement team during the external audit of Plain Ltd.

...u would discharge these responsibilities **before** and **during** the audit

(4 marks)

...d why the planned procedures for an engagement to review financial
...ld differ from the planned procedures for an audit required under the
...2006.

(4 marks)

...e engagement partner responsible for the external audit of Snipe plc
(Snipe), a listed company. Erica is due to be rotated off the audit team as she has been in
...t for the last five years. Following recent substantial changes in the structure of the
...ss, the audit committee of Snipe has requested that Erica continues to act
...artner for the next two years.

...s, whether it is appropriate for Erica to comply with the audit committee's

(2 marks)

...r a recurring audit, that indicate that it may be appropriate for an external
...e the terms of an audit engagement or remind a client of existing terms.

(3 marks)

5.10 Your firm has been the external auditor of Pharma plc (Pharma) for a number of years.
...any operating in the pharmaceutical sector, has recently listed on the
...change. Consequently, the audit work undertaken by your firm will be
...engagement quality control review.

...utes required of the individual who is appointed to undertake the
...lity control review.

(3 marks)

...s are required to consider the integrity of key management before
...gement with a new client.

...dures to be undertaken by an audit firm to assess the integrity of key
...prospective client. For each procedure, explain how it helps with the
...integrity of management.

(4 marks)

...sked by a partner in your firm to help with the preparation of a tender for
...f Petro plc (Petro), a multi-national company operating in the oil and gas
...r has asked you to prepare the section of the tender document that sets
...e calculation of the audit fee.

...s that will affect the basis of the calculation of the audit fee to be included
...ument to be submitted to Petro.

(2 marks)

5.13 The finance director of Iron Ltd (Iron) has prepared profit and cash flow forecasts, which are to be submitted to the company's bank in support of an application for funding. Iron's board of directors would like your firm to examine and provide an assurance report on the forecasts.

List the matters, in respect of the **purpose and scope** of your firm's work, to be included in the engagement letter relating to the examination of the profit and cash flow forecasts.

(4 marks)

5.14 Your firm has been invited by Tony Divot, the managing director and majority shareholder of Wedge Ltd (Wedge), to accept appointment as external auditor. Your firm's client acceptance procedures have identified a recent newspaper article, which reported details of court proceedings relating to a fraud committed by Tony Divot.

Explain why this matter should be considered when deciding whether or not to accept the appointment as external auditor of Wedge.

(4 marks)

5.15 In respect of quality control procedures, distinguish between:

(a) an engagement quality control review (hot review); and
(b) a review as part of the firm's monitoring procedures (cold review). **(4 marks)**

5.16 Animal Sanctuary is a not-for-profit entity, which derives some of its income from donations received through the mail.

Identify **two** internal controls that should be exercised by the entity in respect of donations received through the mail and, for each internal control identified, describe how you would test the effectiveness of that internal control. **(4 marks)**

5.17 For the first time, Moose Ltd (Moose) is required to have its financial statements audited under the Companies Act 2006. Your firm has accepted the audit engagement and has sent a draft engagement letter to Moose's directors. The directors have queried why they need to sign an engagement letter when the requirements of an audit are already set out by law and in auditing standards.

List points for inclusion in your firm's response to the directors' query. **(4 marks)**

5.18 Your firm is tendering for the external audit of Macaw Ltd (Macaw). The directors of Macaw have requested that your firm's tender document includes a section on the procedures that your firm will adopt to ensure that the quality of work performed by the engagement team is of a high standard.

List points for inclusion in your firm's tender document for the external audit of Macaw to address the directors' request. **(4 marks)**

5.19 You are the audit senior responsible for supervising the external audit of King Ltd (King) for the year ended 30 June 20X3. You and a team of three junior members of your audit firm are currently working at King's premises performing the planned audit procedures.

Explain your responsibilities as the audit senior for quality control over the audit of King's financial statements. **(4 marks)**

5.20 Sing Ltd (Sing) is not required to have an audit. However, Sing's bank has requested that an independent firm of accountants reviews and reports on its year-end financial statements. Sing's directors have requested that your firm performs the review and provides the report.

Contrast your firm's report for this review engagement with a report issued in respect of an external audit, of an unlisted company, carried out under the Companies Act 2006. **(4 marks)**

5.21 Snoe plc (Snoe) has four factories in the UK and one in Poland. It is required to prepare a greenhouse gas (GHG) statement, which discloses information about the company's GHG emissions, in accordance with specific industry regulations. Your firm, which has offices in the UK, has been appointed by Snoe to perform a reasonable assurance engagement, in respect of the GHG statement, and report its findings.

List the factors your firm should consider when planning how to **resource** this assurance engagement. **(4 marks)**

5.22 Your firm has recently accepted appointment as external auditor of Herring Ltd (Herring), a competitor of Hake Ltd (Hake). Your firm has acted as external auditor of Hake for a number of years. Both companies have provided your firm with informed consent to act.

Outline the procedures that your firm should implement to address any potential conflicts of interest arising out of this appointment. **(3 marks)**

5.23 An audit firm may be subject to claims for damages arising out of professional negligence after providing an inappropriate audit opinion on financial statements.

Outline the steps a firm should take to reduce its exposure to such claims. **(4 marks)**

5.24 You are the audit senior responsible for the external audit of Krill Ltd (Krill). The engagement partner has requested that you undertake a review of the work recently performed by the audit junior during the audit of Krill's financial statements.

List the purposes of the review requested by the engagement partner. **(3 marks)**

6 Sparkleen Ltd

The directors of Sparkleen Ltd (Sparkleen) are planning to reorganise the business as a result of recent significant growth in revenue. The reorganisation will involve relocation of the business premises, the acquisition of additional delivery vehicles and an upgrade of the IT infrastructure for which quotes have been obtained from suppliers. The directors are negotiating with the company's bank to fund the reorganisation with a loan and have prepared cash flow forecasts for the three years ending 31 March 20X3 in support of the request for funding. The company's bank requires the cash flow forecasts to be examined and reported on by independent accountants and the board of directors has requested that your firm undertakes this work.

The company's principal activity is the sale and distribution of cleaning materials to customers in the retail, industrial and service sectors. All sales are on a credit basis and Sparkleen's terms of trading require payment within 30 days of invoice date. However, some of the company's smaller customers tend to take longer than this to pay. Sparkleen offers an early payment discount but only a few customers take advantage of this facility.

The goods are purchased from a number of suppliers based in the UK and overseas. Two of the company's main suppliers operate a rebate scheme under which Sparkleen receives a rebate, which is paid quarterly in arrears, when it purchases a specified volume of products.

The significant growth experienced in the current year is due to Sparkleen being awarded two three-year contracts to supply two government bodies with all their cleaning materials. This has resulted in Sparkleen having to expand its range of products and increase the level of inventory held at any point in time. As a result, the company has outgrown its own warehouse facilities and is temporarily renting additional premises to supplement its existing facilities. Sparkleen is required to give three months' notice of its intention to vacate the temporary premises.

The directors plan to sell the warehouse, which the company owns, and move all of Sparkleen's operations to a larger purpose-built warehousing facility. This is a leasehold property and rent is payable quarterly in advance. The directors will use the proceeds of the sale of the existing warehouse to pay off the outstanding loan on that warehouse and reduce the company's overdraft.

Requirements

6.1 (a) Describe the matters to be included in your firm's engagement letter for the examination of the cash flow forecasts in respect of:

- management's responsibilities
- the purpose and scope of your firm's work
- limiting your firm's liability

bridge expectations gap

(b) Explain why these matters should be included. *limit the amount of damages* **(8 marks)**
avoid liability.

6.2 From the information provided in the scenario, identify the key **receipts** and **payments** that you would expect to be included in the cash flow forecasts prepared by the directors of Sparkleen. For each receipt and payment, identify the specific matters you would consider when reviewing the reasonableness of the assumptions underlying that receipt or payment.

(12 marks)

Total: 20 marks

7 Bambi Ltd

Your firm has been engaged by the management of Bambi Ltd (Bambi) to undertake a review of and provide an assurance report on the interim financial information of Bambi for the six months ended 30 November 20X2. The terms of the engagement are restricted to making enquiries of management and applying analytical procedures to the financial information. The business was started 12 years previously and has grown steadily with no outside investors. Management wishes to increase the rate of expansion and has identified a potential investor who has asked for assurance on the interim financial information.

Historically, the principal activity of Bambi has been the retailing of high quality and stylish children's clothing. However, in July 20X2, the company launched a new range of up-market accessories which includes children's chairs, prams, cots and bedding. The company holds a limited amount of inventory of the most expensive accessories, but guarantees delivery of any item ordered within six weeks of the order date. The clothing is sourced from suppliers in the UK and more recently Portugal. The accessories are sourced from suppliers in Germany.

Sales are made through the company's eight retail outlets, by mail order and over the internet. Seven of the retail outlets are in the UK and one, which was opened in April 20X2, is in Paris, France. Revenue has grown steadily at between 4% and 6% per annum over the five years ended 31 May 20X2.

To help management with its objective to increase the rate of expansion, the company entered into a contract, in October 20X2, to lease a purpose-built warehouse facility and, in November 20X2, it upgraded its IT infrastructure.

The following is an extract from Bambi's financial information.

Statement of profit or loss	Six months ended 30 November	
	20X2 £'000	20X1 £'000
Revenue	6,716	6,064
Cost of sales	(3,761)	(3,517)
Gross profit	2,955	2,547
Operating expenses	(1,947)	(1,394)
Profit from operations	1,008	1,153

Statement of financial position	As at 30 November	
	20X2 £'000	20X1 £'000
Current assets		
Inventories	1,780	1,388
Current liabilities		
Trade payables	701	771

Your preliminary analytical procedures have identified the following as matters of significance to discuss with management:

	Six months ended 30 November	
	20X2	20X1
Increase in revenue	10.8%	6%
Gross profit margin	44%	42%
Operating margin	15%	19%
Inventory days	86 days	72 days
Trade payables days	34 days	40 days

V 6 days

Requirements

7.1 Prepare briefing notes on the matters which you wish to discuss with the management of Bambi in respect of the information provided in the scenario. Your notes should include reference to the results of your preliminary analytical procedures. **(12 marks)**

   Note: You are **not** required to calculate any additional ratios.

7.2 Identify the financial information, in addition to the interim financial information, that would be useful when undertaking analytical procedures in respect of Bambi's performance for the six months ended 30 November 20X2. **(4 marks)**

7.3 Comment on the level of assurance provided by the report on the financial information of Bambi and explain how and why it differs from the level of assurance provided by an auditor's report on annual financial statements. **(4 marks)**

Total: 20 marks

8 Paradise Ltd

Your firm has accepted an appointment to examine prospective financial information included in a business plan prepared by Paradise Ltd (Paradise). Paradise specialises in the sale of holidays in Venezuela. The company's directors are currently negotiating investment in Paradise by a venture capitalist, Squirrel Ventures (Squirrel). The investment is required in order to fund the company's growth plans, which include the acquisition of a competitor, Russell Ltd (Russell). Squirrel has requested a copy of Paradise's business plan along with a report by independent accountants on their examination of the prospective financial information included in the business plan. Your firm is not the external auditor of either Paradise or Russell.

Paradise's business plan includes prospective financial information for the next three years including statements of financial position, statements of profit or loss and cash flow forecasts. The prospective financial information is based on the assumption that full investment is received from Squirrel and that Russell is successfully acquired and integrated into Paradise's operations. Consequently, the prospective financial information includes information relating to Russell.

Your firm is currently finalising its terms of engagement with Paradise. Carl Fredrickson, Paradise's managing director, has asked for an explanation of the following phrases used in the draft engagement letter:

(1) 'We will conduct our examination in accordance with International Standard on Assurance Engagements 3400 *The Examination of Prospective Financial Information*.'

(2) '...plan and perform the examination so as to obtain a moderate level of assurance...'

(3) 'As part of our examination process we will request from management written confirmation concerning representations made to us in connection with the examination.'

(4) 'Our report based on our examination of the prospective financial information included in the business plan is for the sole use of Paradise Ltd and Squirrel Ventures and may not be distributed to any other parties without our prior written consent.'

(5) 'Our liability is limited to Paradise Ltd and Squirrel Ventures and in aggregate shall not exceed the higher of 5 times the aggregate fees paid and payable or £1 million.'

Requirements

8.1 Explain the practical implications **and** purposes of including phrases (1) to (5) in the engagement letter for the examination of Paradise's business plan. **(8 marks)**

8.2 Outline, with reasons, any action that your firm should take with respect to Paradise's external auditor. **(2 marks)**

8.3 Describe the procedures that your firm should plan to perform to reach a conclusion on its examination of the prospective financial information included in Paradise's business plan.

(10 marks)

Total: 20 marks

9 Pampered Pooches Ltd

Your firm has been engaged by Pampered Pooches Ltd (PP) to undertake a review of, and provide an assurance report on, the interim financial information of PP for the six months ended 31 October 20X2. The terms of engagement include making enquiries of management and applying analytical and other review procedures to the financial information.

PP commenced trading 10 years previously and has grown steadily without outside investment. The management of PP wishes to increase the rate of expansion and has identified a potential investor who has asked for assurance on the interim financial information.

The principal activity of PP is the manufacture and retailing of high quality pet-related products. The manufactured product range includes protective coverings for car seats and furniture, pet beds and harnesses, all of which are made in the company's factory in the UK. PP also sells a range of bought-in accessories for pets, some of which are imported from overseas suppliers. Historically, 90% of PP's sales were made to the public through mail order and over the internet and 10% to independent retailers of pet-related products. Sales to the independent retailers are on 30-day credit terms.

In March 20X2 the company opened two retail outlets. This was funded by a loan from the managing director and an increase in the overdraft facility. Following the success of the retail outlets, management intends to open five additional retail outlets and is seeking outside investment to fund the expansion.

In May 20X2 PP entered into a contract to manufacture and supply pet beds to a national chain store, Animal Accessories (AA), which has over 200 stores throughout the UK. AA is increasingly switching from overseas to UK suppliers due to rising transport costs. The pet beds manufactured for AA are sold under the AA brand and are of a lower specification than those sold under the PP brand.

The following is an extract from PP's financial information.

Statement of profit or loss

	Six months ended 31 October	
	20X2	20X1
	£'000	£'000
Revenue: to public for cash	5,157	4,664
to other retailers on credit	1,207	519
	6,364	5,183
Cost of sales	(4,575)	(3,638)
Gross profit	1,789	1,545
Operating expenses	(890)	(622)
Profit from operations	899	923

Statement of financial position

	As at 31 October	
	20X2	20X1
	£'000	£'000
Current assets		
Inventories	1,680	1,217
Trade receivables	364	88
Current liabilities		
Trade payables	487	293

Your preliminary analytical procedures have identified the following as matters of significance to discuss with management:

| | Six months ended 31 October | |
	20X2	20X1
Increase in revenue:		
To public	10.6%	6.0%
To retailers	132.6%	7.0%
Gross profit margin	28.1%	29.8%
Operating margin	14.1%	17.8%
Inventory turnover	67 days	61 days
Trade receivables collection period	55 days	31 days
Trade payables payment period *	38 days	30 days

* Based on credit purchases of £2,336,000 (20X2) and £1,780,000 (20X1).

Requirements

9.1 Describe the matters to be included in your firm's letter of engagement in respect of:

   (a) the purpose and scope of your firm's work; and

   (b) limiting your firm's liability. **(5 marks)**

9.2 Using the information provided in the scenario and the results of your preliminary analytical procedures, identify:

   (a) the enquiries you should make of the management of PP that will help your review of the financial information; and

   (b) any documentary information that should be requested from the management of PP that would be useful for your review procedures.

Note: You are **not** required to calculate any additional ratios. **(15 marks)**

Total: 20 marks

10 Giza Science Group plc

Your firm has recently been invited to tender for the provision of audit and assurance services to Giza Science Group plc (Giza), a listed scientific research company. Giza requires the following services to be provided:

- Review of and report on Giza's interim financial information for the six months ending 31 March 20X4.

- External audit of Giza's financial statements for the year ending 30 September 20X4.

- Examination of and report on the financial information of Minion Ltd (Minion), a medical research company, identified by Giza's board of directors as an acquisition target. The directors require your firm's service to include helping to determine an appropriate valuation of the shares in Minion.

Agnes Baker, the partner in charge of considering your firm's response to the invitation to tender, has asked you to help her and has provided you with the following additional information:

- Giza provides scientific research services to the pharmaceutical, veterinary and food industries and is subject to a number of laws and regulations. In 20X2, three employees were suspended after serious breaches of animal protection laws were identified by a UK current affairs TV programme.

- Giza controls subsidiaries operating in Europe, the US and Japan and is seeking to expand the group through the acquisition of the share capital of Minion.

- Giza's directors have invited your firm to tender due to its experience in providing external audit, assurance and advisory services to a number of companies operating in the scientific research sector. Marlena Sato, the finance director of SciRay plc (SciRay), a supplier to Giza, has also recommended your firm to Giza's directors. SciRay is one of your firm's largest external audit clients.

- Giza's existing external auditors resigned from office after completing the external audit for the year ended 30 September 20X3.

Requirements

10.1 Identify and explain the matters your firm should consider before deciding to tender for the services required by Giza. **(18 marks)**

10.2 Describe the differences between the scope of the review of Giza's interim financial information for the six months ending 31 March 20X4 and the scope of the external audit of the financial statements for the year ending 30 September 20X4. Give reasons for these differences. **(5 marks)**

Total: 23 marks

11 Pytch Ltd

unsure on opening balance.
unprofessional competence + due care.

Your firm has recently been invited to accept appointment as external auditor of Pytch Ltd (Pytch) for the year ending 31 December 20X4. The audit partner considering the invitation has asked you to gather information about Pytch and its directors to help him reach a decision on whether to accept the appointment.

You have documented the following relevant information:

unfamiliar industry

Pytch is a research and development company operating in the cosmetics industry. It carries out research and development projects to create consumer products for skin and hair such as make-up and hair colourant. Once a product is developed and fully tested, the rights to manufacture and market the product are sold to a third party manufacturer. Industry data shows that up to 60% of research and development projects, of the type undertaken by Pytch, will fail to reach the stage at which a saleable product is developed.   *capitalisation*   *substantive approach.*

The audit opinion on the financial statements for the year ended 31 December 20X3 was qualified by the previous auditor due to an inability to obtain sufficient appropriate audit evidence over the labour costs attributed to a number of research and development projects. The issue arose due to deficiencies in internal controls over Pytch's project costing system and the recording of labour costs. The previous auditor resigned shortly after issuing the qualified opinion.   *Why? fees, intimidation, integrity &*   *laws + reg.*   *is limitation of scope.*

In June 20X4 the press reported the withdrawal from shops of a new type of hair colourant sold by Perfect Ltd (Perfect). Perfect had purchased the rights to manufacture and sell the hair colourant from Pytch in January 20X4. The press reported that severe allergic reactions were experienced by many consumers using the new hair colourant. Industry experts expressed concerns that insufficient time was spent in the testing phase of the product development process because Pytch wanted to ensure that the new hair colourant beat competitors' products to the market.   *Bad Rep?*   *Inherent risk.*   *is manager's integrity.*   *loss in direction?*

Pytch's founder and managing director, Aubrey Swanson, owns 100% of the share capital of Pytch and has led the company and provided its main source of finance since its incorporation in 20X4. Aubrey wishes to sell his shares and retire in 20X5 and the other two members of Pytch's board of directors have each agreed to purchase 20% of Aubrey's shares in Pytch. In addition, Aubrey is negotiating the sale of the remaining 60% of his shares to Club Ltd (Club), a research and development company.   *is conflict of interest?*

The directors of Pytch have also requested that your firm undertakes non-audit engagements to advise the following:

(1) Pytch on the replacement of its project costing system; and

(2) Aubrey on an appropriate valuation of his shares for their sale to the other directors of Pytch and Club.

Your firm has been the external auditor of Club for a number of years.

Requirements

11.1 Explain the relevance of each item of information, documented in the box above, to your firm's decision on whether to accept appointment as Pytch's external auditor for the year ending 31 December 20X4. **(13 marks)**

11.2 Prepare a list of questions your firm should ask the directors of Pytch before making a decision to accept appointment as external auditor for the year ending 31 December 20X4. **(4 marks)**

11.3 Assuming your firm accepts appointment as external auditor of Pytch, identify and explain the principal threats to your firm's independence and objectivity which may arise if it also accepts the additional non-audit engagements requested by the directors.

Note: You are **not** required to list safeguards to mitigate those threats. **(6 marks)**

Total: 23 marks

12 University of Downtown

The University of Downton (the University) has recently bought a disused freehold factory adjacent to its campus. The University wants to expand and has received planning permission to demolish the factory and construct an engineering workshop and classrooms for teaching purposes.

Rob Grantham, the University's finance director, has prepared cash flow forecasts in respect of the expansion plans for the five years ending 31 December 20X9, which are to be submitted to the University's bank in support of a loan to finance the project. The University has requested that your firm examines and provides an assurance report on the cash flow forecasts.

Rob has provided the following additional information about the project:

- Three firms have submitted tenders for the demolition and site clearance work and these are awaiting evaluation by the University.

- Tenders have not yet been invited for the building contract but the build cost has been estimated by the University's director of estates at £2,500 per square metre.

- Landscaping works are expected to be minimal as the new building will occupy the whole of the site.

- The University currently has no engineering provision, therefore all equipment for the workshops and classrooms will be purchased.

- The whole project will be managed on behalf of the University by Crawley and Co, a firm of quantity surveyors.

- The University is applying for a government grant to help with the building cost. The grant amounts to 40% of the building cost and is payable to the University on completion of the build. However, the grant is conditional on the workshop and classrooms being in use by 1 September 20X6.

- To help finance the project the University is planning to sell playing fields, identified by the University's estates strategy as being surplus to requirements, to a property developer.

- Investment appraisals show that, once completed, the project is expected to generate additional cash inflows from student fees which will be in excess of the additional running costs incurred.

Your firm is currently finalising its terms of engagement with the University for the review of the cash flow forecasts. Rob has asked for an explanation of the following phrases used in your firm's draft engagement letter:

(1) 'We will request from management written confirmation concerning representations made to us in connection with the examination.'

(2) 'The level of assurance will not be the same as for an external audit.'

Requirements

12.1 From the information provided in the scenario, identify the key **receipts** and **payments** that you would expect to be included in the cash flow forecasts for the five years ending 31 December 20X9 in respect of the expansion plans. For each receipt and payment, you should identify the specific matters you would consider when reviewing the reasonableness of the assumptions underlying that receipt or payment. **(12 marks)**

12.2 Draft a response to Rob which:

(a) lists the general representations that should be obtained from management as part of the assurance work on the cash flow forecasts and explains why such representations are required; and

(b) explains how and why the level of assurance provided by the report on the cash flow forecasts differs from the level of assurance provided by an auditor's report on annual financial statements. **(8 marks)**

Total: 20 marks

13 Clymene Ltd, Dusky Ltd, Risso Ltd, Irrawaddy Ltd

Your firm is considering whether to accept the following four unrelated prospective engagements:

Clymene Ltd (Clymene)

Your firm has been the external auditor of Clymene for a number of years. Clymene has recently reduced the number of employees working in its accounts department to save costs. The directors have asked your firm to accept reappointment as external auditor for the year ending 31 December 20X5 and have requested that your firm prepares the year-end financial statements in addition to the audit. Your firm has not prepared the financial statements in previous years. The engagement partner has estimated that your firm's current fee from Clymene, of £600,000, would increase by 25% as a result of providing the additional service. Your firm's gross annual fee income, **excluding** amounts received from Clymene, is £6.4 million.

Dusky Ltd (Dusky)

Your firm's report to management and those charged with governance, prepared during the external audit of Dusky for the year ended 30 September 20X4, identified a number of significant internal control deficiencies in Dusky's inventory system. In March 20X5, the company modified its inventory system to address the deficiencies identified in your firm's report. The directors of Dusky have requested that your firm accept an engagement to evaluate the design and operation of the system and confirm in an assurance report that the system is now free from any control deficiencies.

Risso Ltd (Risso)

Risso is a marine biology research and development company. The directors of Risso have approached your firm to provide a second opinion on the application of an accounting standard to Risso's financial statements. The audit opinion on Risso's financial statements for the year ended 31 March 20X5 was modified by Risso's external auditors due to a disagreement over the application of the accounting standard.

Irrawaddy Ltd (Irrawaddy)

The directors of Irrawaddy have requested that your firm accepts an engagement to examine and report on prospective financial information for the three years ending 30 June 20X8, prepared by the company in support of a loan application. The independent examination and report has been requested by Irrawaddy's bank. Irrawaddy's external auditor is currently performing audit work on the financial statements for the year ended 30 June 20X5 but has not been offered the engagement to examine the prospective financial information.

Requirement

For each of the four prospective engagements, identify the matters that your firm should consider, including any professional and ethical issues arising, and any steps it should take **before** deciding whether to accept the engagement.

Total: 25 marks

14 Tasty Sauces Ltd

Tasty Sauces Ltd (TSL) was incorporated three years ago. TSL produces a range of branded sauces which are exceptionally popular, especially in the warmer months when they are bought for barbeques. The directors are planning to reorganise the business as a result of a forecast rapid growth in revenue. This will involve outsourcing all manufacturing, relocation of the business premises and development of new products.

The growth will be funded by equity finance from Denzil Dragon (Denzil), proceeds from the disposal of TSL's manufacturing unit and an increase in the bank overdraft facility. Denzil is a wealthy individual who specialises in providing finance for rapidly expanding businesses in return for a minority shareholding in the business. The directors have prepared profit and cash flow forecasts for the three years ending 31 December 20X8 in support of the request for the overdraft facility. The company's bank requires the cash flow forecasts to be examined and reported on by independent accountants and the directors have requested that your firm performs this examination.

The directors have provided the following additional information:

- The significant growth experienced since incorporation was due to a two-year contract with Terose, a supermarket with stores across the south of England. The contract specifies that TSL cannot supply any other supermarket during the period of the contract. The contract is due to expire in June 20X6. Credit terms are 75 days after delivery. The contract specifies that if Terose purchases a specified volume of sauces over the period of the contract, TSL has to pay Terose a rebate at the end of the contract.

- TSL is in negotiations with five other large supermarkets, with stores across the UK and Europe, which want to purchase TSL's sauces when the contract with Terose expires in June 20X6. The directors are seeking four-year contracts with each supermarket with credit terms of 30 days.

- TSL will cease its own production and has agreed with Mixit Ltd (Mixit), a specialist manufacturer, that Mixit will manufacture TSL's sauces from July 20X6 onwards. Mixit has requested payment in advance each month, for 12 months, until a trading relationship is established after which it will give 30 days credit.

- TSL will sell its manufacturing unit, which it owns, as it will then be surplus to requirements. The manufacturing unit will take six months to decommission and all equipment will be scrapped. A property developer has expressed interest in the site and TSL is currently applying for permission to change the use of the site from industrial to residential.

- TSL proposes to rent a new combined warehouse, office and research facility from July 20X6. Rent is payable quarterly in advance with a rent-free period for the first six months. TSL plans to develop new products such as soups and curries at this facility. It is expected that soups will take one year to develop and curries two years before they can be sold to supermarkets.

- Denzil will provide equity funding in equal tranches in March 20X6 and June 20X6. Half of Denzil's investment will be repurchased by TSL once TSL achieves a specified level of profit. TSL has a policy of paying cash dividends equivalent to one quarter of its annual profits.

You are the senior responsible for planning the examination of the cash flow forecasts and the engagement partner has identified the following items included in the cash flow forecasts as being significant:

(1) Receipts from and payments to supermarkets for the sale of products
(2) Payments to Mixit
(3) Proceeds from the disposal of the manufacturing unit
(4) Payments for the rented warehouse, office and research facility
(5) Receipts from and payments to Denzil Dragon

Requirements

14.1 (a) Identify the matters to be included in your firm's engagement letter for the examination of the cash flow forecasts in respect of:

- management's responsibilities;
- the purpose and scope of your firm's work; and
- limiting your firm's liability.

 (b) Explain why these matters should be included. **(8 marks)**

14.2 For the items listed (1) to (5), identify the specific matters you would consider when reviewing the reasonableness of the assumptions underlying each receipt or payment.

(10 marks)

14.3 State **four** key differences you would expect to see between the items included in the profit forecasts and the receipts and payments included in the cash flow forecasts prepared by the directors of TSL. **(4 marks)**

Total: 22 marks

Section 2: Planning engagements

15 Short form questions

15.1 You are the manager in charge of the external audit of Kerry Ltd ('Kerry') for the year ending 31 December 20X7. Kerry operates a chain of retail outlets throughout England. In January 20X7 Kerry introduced an internal audit function, consisting of a chief internal auditor and five assistants, to undertake monitoring procedures at head office and the retail outlets. You have made a preliminary assessment of the internal audit function and intend to use its work.

State the matters that you would consider when evaluating the work of Kerry's internal audit function. **(3 marks)**

15.2 Your firm is the group auditor of Narberth Group plc. The financial statements of one of the components which will be included in the financial statements of Narberth Group plc has been audited by another firm of auditors who have modified their auditor's report on the component's financial statements.

State the matters that should be considered, in respect of the above issue, by the group auditor when reporting on the financial statements of Narberth Group plc. **(2 marks)**

15.3 You have conducted analytical procedures on the draft accounts of Blunt Ltd for the year ended 31 October 20X1. Two of your findings are as follows:

(1) The gross profit margin has decreased from 29% for the previous year to 23% for this year.

(2) The current ratio has decreased from 1.6 at the previous year end to 1.2 at this year end.

The directors had expected a decrease in both these measures but not by as much as shown above.

Indicate what errors might be incorporated within the draft accounts to produce these unexpected variations, and in which areas you would carry out extra audit work in order to reach a conclusion. **(3 marks)**

15.4 During the course of the audit of your client Sloth plc you notice a balance within receivables entitled 'advances against directors' expenses'. The company's managing director, who is familiar with the concept of materiality, has questioned your need to audit this balance, which at the year end stands at £12,500. The company's retained profit for the year is £1.3 million.

Prepare brief notes to the managing director explaining your audit approach in respect of this item. **(2 marks)**

15.5 Your client, Neral Ltd, is a family owned and run haulage business. The managing director's brother runs a manufacturing business, Jaron Ltd, which uses Neral Ltd for its distribution requirements.

You are planning the audit of Neral Ltd. Identify the audit risks in respect of this relationship between the two companies and state how you would plan to address these risks. **(3 marks)**

15.6 When planning to use the work of experts and in assessing the results of the work of experts, to what matters should the auditor pay attention? **(3 marks)**

15.7 During the planning of the audit of Milten Textiles Ltd, the financial controller asked to have a quiet word with you. She tells you that she suspects the payroll clerk is defrauding the company, as she is regularly going on exotic holidays, buying new cars and spending substantial sums of money on home improvements. There is only one payroll clerk who manages the single monthly payroll run.

What would be the impact on your audit approach in respect of the information provided by the financial controller? **(3 marks)**

15.8 You have completed the tests of controls in your audit. The only deviations found were that there was no evidence that one particular control had been operated in three cases out of 25 tested.

Explain what considerations will determine whether you are able to reduce the substantive procedures in the area of this control. **(2 marks)**

15.9 At the audit planning meeting for the year ended 28 February 20X4 with the finance director of Malbec Ltd, you ascertained that payroll processing, which had been outsourced for a number of years, was brought back in-house in December 20X3.

Management was not satisfied with the performance of the service provider and repudiated the contract. The service provider had been responsible for making payments to the employees and the monthly remittances to HMRC. Two of Malbec Ltd's accounts clerks have been trained in payroll processing.

Identify the audit risks in respect of the above matter for the year ended 28 February 20X4 and state how you would address these risks. **(4 marks)**

15.10 Your firm has been appointed as external auditor to Supreme Limos Ltd (Supreme) for the year ended 31 May 20X9. Supreme's principal activity is the hiring out of limousines. The company commenced trading on 1 June 20X8 and, although the company's revenue and assets are below the thresholds for statutory audit purposes, the company's bank requires the financial statements to be subject to a full audit. Your initial enquiries reveal that an off-the-shelf computer package is used to maintain the accounting records. These records are maintained by a part-qualified accountant who is helped by a part-time payroll clerk.

State, with reasons, an appropriate approach to the audit of Supreme, which addresses the extent of tests of control and substantive procedures, including analytical procedures.

(4 marks)

15.11 Your firm is the external auditor of Musicdigit Ltd (Musicdigit). The principal activity of the company is the retail sale of music equipment such as radios and MP3 players. The company provides a free one-year warranty with all items sold. In addition, customers can purchase an extended warranty for either a further two or five years. In the case of the one-year warranty, Musicdigit agrees to replace items found to be faulty. In the case of extended warranties, Musicdigit agrees to either repair or replace items found to be faulty. Musicdigit includes a warranty provision in its financial statements to reflect the future cost of fulfilling its obligations under existing warranties.

Outline the audit procedures that you would plan to undertake as part of your firm's audit of the warranty provision at the year end.

(4 marks)

15.12 Your firm is the external auditor of GreenEat, a charity established to promote the protection of the environment. GreenEat raises income from the sale of food and drink in cafés located in city centres and from donations made by individuals. The cafés are managed and staffed by unpaid volunteers. Donations are made to GreenEat through collection boxes located in each café and by post to GreenEat's headquarters.

Identify and explain **three** key audit risks associated with your firm's audit of GreenEat's income.

(3 marks)

15.13 External auditors have to consider the implications of any breaches, by their clients, of employment and social security legislation which may come to their attention.

State why external auditors should consider these implications and provide two examples of such breaches.

(3 marks)

15.14 When a group engagement team plans to request a component auditor to perform work on the financial information of a component, the team is required to obtain an understanding of the component auditor.

State the matters to be considered by the group engagement team when obtaining an understanding of a component auditor.

(3 marks)

15.15 Explain why it is necessary for the external auditors of companies to have an understanding of the laws and regulations which impact on their clients' operations.

(3 marks)

15.16 You are the audit senior planning the external audit of Dark Ltd (Dark) for the year ended 31 August 20X2. The following extracts are from the draft financial statements of Dark:

	Draft year ended 31 August 20X2 £'000	Actual year ended 31 August 20X1 £'000
Extracts from statement of profit or loss		
Loss on sale of plant	(450)	–
Depreciation charge for the year	(380)	(758)
Extract from statement of financial position		
Non-current assets		
Property, plant and equipment	4,165	3,789

On 1 September 20X1, freehold land was revalued by £1,000,000 and £850,000 was received from the sale of plant. Dark also made additions of £1,056,000 to property, plant and equipment during the year. All amounts are material to the financial statements of Dark.

Identify the risks of misstatement in the financial statements of Dark for the year ended 31 August 20X2 in respect of the audit of property, plant and equipment. **(4 marks)**

15.17 During your planning meeting for the external audit of Leo Ltd (Leo), the finance director informed you that the managing director, who owns all of the shares in Leo, is planning to sell his shares in the business. He has been negotiating with a prospective purchaser who has agreed in principle to purchase the shares. The purchase consideration will be calculated as a multiple of the current year's profit before tax.

Explain how this matter will affect the overall audit strategy. **(3 marks)**

15.18 You are planning the audit of Scorpio plc (Scorpio) for the year ending 31 December 20X0. Scorpio's principal activity is the manufacture of a range of electrical appliances. In today's newspapers, there are headlines about Scorpio recalling one of its most popular products due to electrical faults which, in a number of cases, have caused fires.

Explain why this matter should be considered when planning the audit of Scorpio for the year ending 31 December 20X0. **(2 marks)**

15.19 Your firm has been engaged by the management of Divot plc (Divot) to undertake a review of and provide an assurance report on the interim financial information of Divot for the six months ended 31 May 20X1. The terms of the engagement include applying analytical procedures to the interim financial information. Divot operates in the textile sector and has a comprehensive system for reporting financial results to the board of directors, including comparison against budget.

Outline how you should use analytical procedures when reviewing the interim financial information and state the limitations of using analytical procedures as a source of evidence.

(4 marks)

15.20 Animal Welfare is a not-for-profit entity which derives some of its income from donations made by the public through collecting boxes in retail outlets and restaurants. Following a number of thefts of cash collected through collecting boxes and, in some cases, theft of the collecting boxes, the trustees of Animal Welfare have requested that your firm undertakes a comprehensive review of the internal controls exercised over the collection, custody and recording of cash donated through collecting boxes.

Describe **four** internal control procedures that should be exercised over the system of cash donations received through collecting boxes.

(4 marks)

15.21 During the external audit of Albatross Ltd for the year ended 31 March 20X1, it was discovered that a sales credit note, relating to a large pre-year-end delivery of inventory, was issued to a customer on 21 April 20X1.

Explain why the external audit team should investigate this matter.

(2 marks)

15.22 Your firm is the external auditor of Dust Ltd (Dust), an industrial cleaning company. Dust has recently applied to its bank for a loan to fund the replacement of all its cleaning equipment. If the application is successful Dust will dispose of its existing cleaning equipment which is included in the statement of financial position as tangible non-current assets. As part of its application, Dust has submitted profit and cash flow forecasts to the bank for the three years ending 30 June 20X4. The bank has requested that the forecasts are examined and reported on by independent accountants and Dust has appointed your firm to undertake this examination.

In respect of the purchase and disposal of the cleaning equipment, identify the key items that you would expect to be included in:

- the profit forecasts; and
- the cash flow forecasts.

For each item identified, state the specific matters you would consider when reviewing that item for reasonableness.

(4 marks)

15.23 An engagement to review financial statements provides a moderate level of assurance that the financial statements are free from material misstatement, whereas an external audit engagement provides a reasonable level of assurance that the financial statements are free from material misstatement.

State how the planned procedures for an engagement to review financial statements, and provide a moderate level of assurance, would differ from those planned for an external audit engagement, to provide reasonable assurance, in respect of cash at bank. **(4 marks)**

15.24 You are the supervisor on the external audit of Plummer Ltd (Plummer) for the year ended 31 December 20X1. While performing the planned audit procedures in the week commencing 12 March 20X2, the audit team noted the following issues in the schedule of unadjusted errors:

(1) The balance on a trade receivable account, totalling £435,000, remains unpaid and is in dispute. No allowance against the receivable has been made.

(2) Goods despatched and delivered to a customer on 2 January 20X2 were included at £260,000 in both revenue and trade receivables at 31 December 20X1. A member of the engagement team attended the year-end inventory count and obtained a copy of the count records.

The draft financial statements of Plummer for the year ended 31 December 20X1 show profit before tax of £11.3 million.

Explain why further audit procedures are required and, for each of the issues, identify **one** relevant audit procedure to address the issue noted. **(4 marks)**

15.25 Glossy Ltd (Glossy) operates a national chain of hair salons in the UK. It plans to engage BuildaWeb Ltd (BuildaWeb) to design and build a new website and online appointment system. Design will commence on 2 January 20X3 and the new website and online appointment system will be available to customers from 1 June 20X3. In addition, BuildaWeb will host and maintain the website for a fixed monthly fee plus a charge for each online appointment made.

Glossy has applied to its bank for a loan to fund the new website and online appointment system. The bank has requested a cash flow forecast for the year ending 30 September 20X3 and an independent examination of and report on the cash flow forecast. Your firm has agreed to perform the independent examination and prepare the report.

Identify the **key payments to BuildaWeb** that you would expect to be included in the cash flow forecast for the year ending 30 September 20X3. For each payment identified, state the specific matters you would consider when reviewing that item for reasonableness.
(4 marks)

15.26 You are responsible for planning the audit of payroll as part of the external audit of Geese Ltd (Geese) for the year ended 31 December 20X2. You have been provided with the following information:

	Year ended 31 December	
	20X2 (draft)	20X1 (audited)
Employees' total gross pay (£'000)	2,189	2,175
Average number of employees in year	85	91
Company-wide pay rise (effective 1 January)	2%	3.5%
Amounts deducted from gross pay in respect of payroll taxes (employees' income taxes and NI) (£'000)	548	652
Profit before tax (£'000)	1,088	1,081

Using analytical procedures, identify factors which may indicate a risk of misstatement in the payroll of Geese for the year ended 31 December 20X2. **(4 marks)**

15.27 You are planning the external audit of Canary Ltd (Canary) for the year ended 28 February 20X3. During a meeting with Canary's finance director she told you that the payroll function had been outsourced to Cockatoo Ltd, a payroll service organisation, on 1 June 20X2.

State the implications of the above for the audit of the financial statements of Canary for the year ended 28 February 20X3.

(3 marks)

15.28 You are responsible for the audit of Petro plc (Petro), a company engaged in oil refining. Given the potentially hazardous nature of the company's activities, compliance with health and safety at work regulations is central to Petro's operations. Consequently, management has strict procedures, including monitoring, in place to ensure compliance.

Identify the business risks to which accidental breaches of these regulations could expose Petro and the implications for the financial statements in the event of such breaches.

(4 marks)

15.29 You are planning the audit of Homeco Ltd (Homeco), which operates a chain of retail stores selling household goods. Customers pay by cash or credit card. The company has standardised operating procedures in all stores including the use of electronic point of sale systems which record the sale of an item and update the inventory records. The inventory records are checked through periodic counting by store staff. In order to reduce the number of visits to stores by your firm, the audit plan requires the evaluation of the internal control procedures exercised by the head office of Homeco over operations at its stores.

Outline the internal control procedures that you would expect to see exercised by **head office** over operations at the stores.

(4 marks)

15.30 Garfield Educational (Garfield) is a-not-for-profit entity whose objective is to support 18 to 21 year old students in full-time education in London with their academic studies. Garfield awards non-repayable grants to students for items such as personal computers and books or for expenses such as travelling to their place of study. Students apply to Garfield for support and, if their application is successful, the grant is paid by electronic bank transfer into the students' bank accounts.

State **four** internal control procedures that should be exercised over the awarding and payment of grants to students.

(4 marks)

15.31 The directors of Madison Ltd (Madison) have prepared an insurance claim for loss of profits following a fire at one of Madison's factories. The directors have engaged your firm to review the claim and provide an assurance report, as the directors believe that this will accelerate the processing of the claim.

Identify the points, specific to the review of the claim, that your firm should include in its engagement letter and explain why their inclusion is necessary.

(4 marks)

15.32 Contrast the purposes of walk-through tests with the purposes of tests of controls when considering the internal controls of an external audit client. **(3 marks)**

15.33 Your firm has been engaged by Queen Ltd (Queen) to undertake a review of, and provide assurance on, the interim financial information for the six months ended 31 July 20X3. Queen produces a range of sausages which it sells to supermarkets in the UK and the rest of Europe. Supermarkets are invoiced in their local currency. In the six months to 31 July 20X3, Queen opened a number of its own retail outlets in the UK selling directly to the public and has increased sausage production using spare capacity in its factory. Your preliminary analytical procedures have identified the following as matters of significance to discuss with management:

	Six months ended 31 July	
	20X3	**20X2**
Increase in revenue	16%	5%
Gross profit **margin**	32%	26%
Operating **margin**	12%	19%

Using the information above, identify the enquiries you should make of the management of Queen that will help your review of the financial information. **(4 marks)**

15.34 Your firm is the external auditor of Magpies Ltd (Magpies) for the year ended 30 November 20X4. On 15 November 20X4, the directors of Magpies engaged a firm of expert property valuers to provide an independent valuation of the company's freehold land and buildings. The directors intend to recognise freehold land and buildings at this valuation in the financial statements for the year ended 30 November 20X4.

State the audit procedures that your firm should plan to undertake to determine whether the valuation provided by the firm of expert property valuers can be used.

(3 marks)

15.35 Your subsequent events review, performed during the audit of Ice Ltd for the year ended 31 December 20X4, included reading the minutes of board meetings held after the year end. Minutes of the board meeting held on 16 February 20X5 identified that the company failed a routine health and safety inspection performed by industry regulators in January 20X5.

Outline the further audit procedures you should perform in respect of this matter. **(3 marks)**

15.36 The risk of management override of internal controls is present in all audited entities.

State **three** procedures that should be included in external audit plans to address this risk.

(3 marks)

15.37 You are responsible for planning the external audit of Squid Ltd (Squid) for the year ending 30 September 20X5. Today, you read a newspaper article stating that Squid, a manufacturer of dried food products, has recalled its leading baby milk powder from supermarkets due to a number of batches being contaminated with substances that may be harmful to babies.

Briefly explain the matters you should consider, as part of your audit planning, as a result of reading the newspaper article. **(4 marks)**

15.38 Becker LLP has been invited to tender for the external audit of Laver plc (Laver) a listed entity. The principal activity of Laver is the retailing of food, clothing and household goods through its 500 UK stores and its e-commerce platform. The audit committee at Laver has requested that the tender document includes a section on how the external auditor will use data analytics in the course of the audit.

List **four** matters in respect of the use of data analytics routines to be included in the tender document. **(4 marks)**

15.39 During the external audit of Murray plc (Murray), your firm is planning to use data analytics routines to gain assurance that revenue is fairly stated in the financial statements for the year ended 31 May 20X6. The principal activity of Murray is the retailing of discounted branded goods, including designer clothing, beauty products and household goods, at up to 60% off their recommended retail prices. Sales are made through Murray's 25 retail outlets, located in cities throughout the UK, and through its website. All retail outlets use electronic point of sale (EPOS) systems and the website has online ordering and payment facilities.

List **four** data analytics routines that your firm could perform on data from Murray's information systems. **(4 marks)**

15.40 During the course of the audit of Novak Ltd (Novak) it was discovered that the company does not routinely update its anti-malware software.

In respect of this internal control deficiency, draft points for inclusion in your firm's report to those charged with governance and management at Novak. You should outline the possible consequence(s) of the deficiency and provide recommendations to address it. **(4 marks)**

15.41 During the year ended 31 May 20X6, Federa Ltd (Federa) outsourced its payroll processing to a service organisation which provides Federa with monthly payroll information relating to its employees. Federa uses this information to pay the wages and salaries directly into its employees' bank accounts and the relevant payroll taxes to the tax authorities.

Identify the business risks arising out of Federa outsourcing its payroll processing and explain the implications for the financial statements. **(4 marks)**

15.42 During the year ending 30 November 20X6, the audit committee of Baikal plc (Baikal) is scheduled to meet three times. One of the terms of reference of the audit committee of Baikal is to monitor the effectiveness of the outsourced internal audit function.

List the matters that should be considered by the audit committee at its meetings during the year ending 30 November 20X6 that will help it to meet this term of reference.

(3 marks)

16 Styleco Ltd

The directors of Styleco Ltd (Styleco), an external audit client of your firm, are planning to expand the business. The expansion is to be funded by borrowings and the directors have been negotiating with the company's bankers in order to increase borrowings. The directors have prepared profit and cash flow forecasts for the three years ending 31 March 20X2 in support of the request for funding. The company's bankers require this information to be reviewed and reported on by independent accountants and the board of directors has requested that your firm undertakes this review.

Styleco designs and sells high quality home accessories and clothing which are sold by mail order and over the internet. Customers pay for goods at the time of order and the company operates a policy whereby customers who are not satisfied with any purchase are entitled to a full refund if they return the product, undamaged, within three months of receipt. In recent years the level of returns has been approximately 8% of revenue. All products are made exclusively for Styleco by suppliers based in the United Kingdom and overseas. It is company policy to pay all suppliers 10 working days following the week of delivery of the goods.

The company currently operates from a warehouse in the south of England, but the directors wish to expand the business by opening retail outlets in cities throughout England so that customers can see and touch the products they are buying. The directors have identified three potential properties, in the premier shopping areas of London, Bath and Chester. These are leasehold properties with rent payable quarterly in advance. The directors intend to have the properties fitted out to a very high standard in line with the company's corporate image and will use specialist contractors to undertake this work. There will be electronic point-of-sales systems and customers will be able to pay by cash, credit or debit cards.

Each outlet will be run by a manager helped by a mixture of full and part-time staff. One of the company's objectives is to provide a high level of service and knowledgeable advice to its customers and the company aims to reflect this in the staffing levels and remuneration of its employees. All outlet staff, including managers, will be paid at rates above those paid by other companies in the retail sector and will be eligible for an annual bonus linked to the performance of the outlet.

Requirements

16.1 From the information provided above, identify the specific matters you would consider when reviewing the reasonableness of the assumptions underlying the receipts and payments included in the cash flow forecast for the three years ending 31 March 20X2.

(13 marks)

16.2 Compare the purpose and scope of a review of the profit and cash flow forecasts for the three years ending 31 March 20X2 with that of a statutory external audit. **(7 marks)**

Total: 20 marks

17 Dunlec Ltd

Your firm is the external auditor of Dunlec Ltd (Dunlec) for the year ended 31 October 20X1. The company is owned by members of the Dunlop family, none of whom is involved in running the business. Dunlec's principal activity is the installation of electrical systems for customers in the retail, construction and industrial sectors in the UK. The company operates from premises in London and six freehold regional depots throughout the UK.

All contracts are fixed-price. Customers pay 95% of the contract price on completion of the work and withhold 5% of the contract price for up to six months from the date of completion in case remedial work is required. The materials and components used by Dunlec are bought from UK suppliers who require payment within 30 days of the invoice date.

Dunlec made an operating loss during the year ended 31 October 20X1. This was mainly due to a substantial bad debt in respect of a company which went into liquidation in July 20X1, with insufficient funds to pay unsecured creditors. As a result, Dunlec experienced severe cash flow problems. In August 20X1, to ease its cash flow problems, Dunlec sold its London freehold premises and leased new premises. Dunlec used the proceeds to:

- pay a loan instalment on the due date in September 20X1 (final instalment due in September 20X2);
- pay its overdue tax and related penalties; and
- reduce the company's overdraft.

During the year ended 31 October 20X1, Dunlec suffered a fall in demand for its services in the construction sector. The directors have undertaken a strategic review of operations and have decided to reduce the company's cost base by:

- closing two of the regional depots and putting both premises up for sale. Contracts in those regions will be serviced by the nearest existing depot; and
- making 25% of the company's employees redundant.

The closures and redundancies were announced on 12 November 20X1 and the premises were immediately put up for sale.

As part of their assessment of the company's ability to continue as a going concern, the directors have prepared cash flow forecasts. These show that the company can operate within its current overdraft facility for the two years ending 31 October 20X3.

Requirements

17.1 From the information provided in the scenario, identify the specific matters you would consider when reviewing the assumptions underlying the **receipts and payments** included in the cash flow forecasts for the two years ending 31 October 20X3. **(8 marks)**

17.2 Discuss the implications for your firm's auditor's report in each of the following two circumstances:

    (a) Dunlec is not a going concern.
    (b) There is a significant uncertainty about the going concern status of Dunlec. **(7 marks)**

17.3 Identify the parties to whom your firm may be liable for damages if an inappropriate opinion is provided on the financial statements of Dunlec for the year ended 31 October 20X1 and state the circumstances under which those parties may be successful in claiming **such** damages against your firm. **(5 marks)**

Total: 20 marks

18 Paravel Gardens Ltd

Your firm has recently been appointed as the external auditor of Paravel Gardens Ltd (Paravel) for the year ending 31 March 20X2.

Paravel operates a chain of 45 retail garden centres throughout the UK, supplying customers with trees and plants as well as related gardening products such as lawn mowers, tools and pesticides. Customers pay for purchases using cash or debit/credit cards. The business has been highly successful due to the popularity of gardening in the UK and, in August 20X1, the directors commenced a programme of building works to increase the size of its garden centres.

As a result of the highly seasonal nature of the business, the directors obtained a bank loan on 31 October 20X1 to ensure sufficient cash was available to continue the building works during the winter months, November 20X1 to March 20X2. The bank loan is repayable over three years with interest payable quarterly in arrears. Part of the loan was also used to make a lump-sum payment of £2 million to Miraz Events Ltd (Miraz) for a two-year sponsorship deal. Miraz organises gardening shows in the UK and invited Paravel to become its lead sponsor for all shows for the two years ending 31 December 20X3. Paravel's brand will be used by Miraz when promoting its gardening shows throughout the sponsorship period.

Employees at each garden centre include permanent gardening staff, who maintain the trees and plants available for sale, and permanent retail and customer services staff. In addition, a large number of temporary staff are employed between April and September due to the increased volume of sales in this period.

Plants and trees are purchased, ready for sale, from a variety of specialist suppliers in the UK and overseas. Overseas suppliers invoice Paravel in their local currency. Paravel requires a licence to import plants and trees into the UK and is regularly inspected by the licensing authority to ensure that it is complying with the terms of the licence. Paravel plans to undertake a full inventory count at each garden centre on 31 March 20X2.

The engagement partner has provided you with the following extracts from the financial statements for the full year to 31 March:

	20X2 (estimated) £'000	20X1 (audited) £'000
Statement of profit or loss		
Revenue	156,960	116,888
Cost of sales	(99,544)	(81,822)
Gross profit	57,416	35,066
Finance cost	(103)	(100)
Statement of financial position		
Current assets		
Inventories	9,545	5,604
Current liabilities		
Trade payables	8,434	8,141

The directors are planning to diversify the business by introducing, in September 20X2, a gourmet food hall and gift shop into each garden centre. The directors believe that this will help to reduce the impact of seasonality as these products will be more popular with customers from October to December each year. In order to fund the proposed diversification, a new loan application has been submitted to the company's bank. The bank wishes to examine the audited financial statements for the year ended 31 March 20X2 together with the profit and cash flow forecasts in respect of the proposed diversification, for the three years ending 31 March 20X5.

The bank requires an independent examination of and a report on the profit and cash flow forecasts and Paravel's directors have requested that your firm perform this engagement.

Paravel's finance director, Edmund Lewis, has proposed, in respect of this engagement, that:

(1) the responsibilities of your firm include making recommendations to the directors as to how best to prepare and present the profit and cash flow forecasts to increase the likelihood of the bank agreeing to Paravel's application; and

(2) your firm's fee for the examination of and report on the profit and cash flow forecasts will only be paid once the bank agrees to provide the finance to Paravel with no fee payable should Paravel's bank decline the new loan application.

If the loan is approved by the bank, Paravel will invest the funds in refrigeration units and shelving in each garden centre and in an initial purchase of inventories of gourmet foods and gifts. In addition, an upgrade to the computerised tills at each garden centre will be performed by Caspian Ltd, Paravel's technology provider. As the upgrade represents an enhancement to the current tills, the directors propose to include the cost of the upgrade as an addition to computer equipment within non-current assets.

Requirements

18.1 From the information provided, identify the areas of audit risk in respect of the financial statements of Paravel for the year ending 31 March 20X2. For each audit risk explain the factors which have led you to identify that risk. **(20 marks)**

18.2 From the information provided, identify the key receipts and payments that you would expect to be included in the cash flow forecast prepared by the directors of Paravel in respect of the diversification plans for the three years ending 31 March 20X5. For each key receipt and payment, identify the specific matters you would consider when reviewing the reasonableness of the assumptions in forecasting that receipt or payment. **(10 marks)**

18.3 State the key differences you would expect to see between the items included in the profit forecasts and the receipts and payments included in the cash flow forecasts prepared by the directors of Paravel. **(4 marks)**

18.4 Explain the professional issues for your firm raised by Edmund's proposals in (1) and (2). **(6 marks)**

Total: 40 marks

19 Luxstove Ltd

Your firm has been engaged by the management of Luxstove Ltd (Luxstove) to undertake a review of, and provide an assurance report on, the interim financial information of Luxstove for the six months ended 31 May 20X2. The terms of the engagement are restricted to making enquiries of management and applying analytical and other review procedures to the financial information.

The business was started 12 years ago and grew steadily for the first 10 years without outside investment. However, during the last year, the company has experienced a significant increase in demand for its products. The management wishes to increase the rate of expansion to meet this demand and has identified a potential investor who has asked for assurance on the interim financial information.

The principal activity of Luxstove has been the manufacture of a range of high quality wood burning and multi-fuel stoves, which are used for heating residential properties. However, in October 20X0, the company introduced a luxury range of fireside accessories including handmade furniture. All stoves and accessories are manufactured by hand at the company's factory in the UK. Raw materials and components are sourced from suppliers based in the UK and overseas.

The company sells its products through independent retailers throughout the UK. The retailers do not hold inventory, only demonstration items, but as soon as a customer places an order, the retailer informs Luxstove which aims to deliver the item to the retailer within 21 days of order. Retailers are invoiced on delivery and are required to pay Luxstove within 30 days of invoice date. In September 20X1, Luxstove opened a showroom adjacent to its factory and commenced selling stoves and accessories directly to the public in addition to retailers. The showroom was converted from redundant buildings which were refurbished to a high standard and designed to display the company's products in a stylish atmosphere. Showroom customers are required to pay in full when they place an order.

The following is an extract from Luxstove's financial information:

Statement of profit or loss

	Six months ended 31 May	
	20X2	20X1
	£'000	£'000
Revenue	5,938	5,108
Cost of sales	(4,022)	(3,587)
Gross profit	1,916	1,521
Operating expenses	(1,377)	(918)
Profit from operations	539	603

Statement of financial position

	As at 31 May	
	20X2	20X1
	£'000	£'000
Current assets		
Inventories	999	815
Trade receivables	987	766
Current liabilities		
Trade payables	306	328

Your preliminary analytical procedures have identified the following as matters of significance to discuss with management:

	Six months ended 31 May	
	20X2	20X1
	£'000	£'000
Increase in revenue	16.2%	8.0%
Gross profit margin	32.3%	29.8%
Operating margin	9.1%	11.8%
Inventory turnover	45.3 days	41.5 days
Trade receivables collection period *	34.2 days	27.4 days
Trade payables payment period **	26.6 days	30.3 days

*   Based on credit sales of £5,263,000 (20X2)

**   Based on credit purchases of £2,103,000 (20X2) and £1,977,000 (20X1).

Requirements

19.1 (a) Using the information provided in the scenario and the results of your preliminary analytical procedures, set out the enquiries you should make of the management of Luxstove that will help your review of the financial information; and

(b) Identify any documentary information that should be requested from the management of Luxstove that would be useful for your review procedures. **(15 marks)**

19.2 Describe the differences between the **conclusion** expressed following an engagement to review financial information and the **opinion** expressed in an auditor's report on financial statements. Give reasons for these differences. **(5 marks)**

Total: 20 marks

20 Pyramid Event Structures Ltd

Your firm has recently been appointed external auditor of Pyramid Event Structures Ltd (PES) for the year ended 28 February 20X4.

PES provides a range of temporary structures which it hires to customers for sporting events, music concerts and exhibitions. Structures are hired to customers for events lasting from a few weeks to many months.

For each event, PES documents the customer's requirements and calculates a fixed contract price for approval by the customer. The contract price is based on the estimated direct labour costs to erect and dismantle the structure plus a standard mark-up of 60% to cover overheads and profit. Customers are required to pay 50% of the contract price on signing the contract, with the balance due at the end of the event. Revenue is recognised evenly over the duration of the event.

The components, such as pillars, wall panels and flooring, used in structures are purchased from suppliers around the world who invoice PES in the supplier's local currency. All the components are recorded in PES's financial statements as tangible non-current assets. The cost less any estimated residual value is depreciated on a straight-line basis over the estimated useful life of each asset. PES is renowned for offering its customers the latest structures and constantly seeks to improve or replace the structures it holds in its range.

PES has a product development team which works on research and design of new structures. Development costs are capitalised and amortised over the useful life of the structure and £1 million was included in intangible assets at 1 March 20X3. During the year ended 28 February 20X4, the product development team completed development of a new temporary flooring system, MezzSpace. PES intends to include the costs of developing MezzSpace in intangible assets in its financial statements for the year ended 28 February 20X4.

Margo Zavos, the finance director of PES, recently provided your firm with the following information:

- The accountant responsible for recording the costs associated with product development projects left PES on 31 December 20X3 and a replacement has not yet been recruited. Margo has requested that a member of the audit team be temporarily seconded to PES to calculate the figures, in respect of the development costs associated with MezzSpace, for inclusion in the financial statements for the year ended 28 February 20X4.

- On 28 February 20X4, Nefario Ltd (Nefario) closed its exhibition event early. PES had supplied structures to Nefario for the exhibition, which commenced on 1 January 20X4 and had been due to close on 31 May 20X4. Nefario closed the exhibition early due to financial difficulties and has informed PES that it is unable to pay the remainder of the contract price. Early termination is allowed under the terms of the contract however, no refund is required to be paid to Nefario. The following financial information relates to the Nefario contract (incurred in full by PES before 28 February 20X4).

	£'000
Total contract price	2,000
Cash received from Nefario in November 20X3	1,000
Costs to erect structures supplied to Nefario	1,300

- On 15 February 20X4 a viewing platform supplied by PES collapsed at a major sporting event, injuring a number of spectators. This platform was one of four new platforms acquired by PES in January 20X4. Initial investigations indicate that the collapse was caused by faulty materials used to manufacture the pillars which support the platform. The cost of each platform was £90,000.

You are the audit manager and the engagement partner has asked you to consider the following areas of audit risk:

(1) Revenue
(2) Intangible assets – development costs
(3) Property, plant and equipment
(4) The contract with Nefario

Relevant extracts from PES's financial statements are set out below:

Statement of profit or loss for the year ended 28 February

	20X4 (draft) £'000	20X3 (audited) £'000
Revenue	15,221	18,219
Cost of sales	(12,147)	(12,572)
Gross profit	3,074	5,647

Requirements

20.1 Identify and explain the principal threats to independence and objectivity arising from Margo Zavos's proposal to second a member of the audit team to PES and state how your firm should respond to the proposal. **(5 marks)**

20.2 Justify why the items listed by the engagement partner have been identified as areas of audit risk and, for each item, describe the procedures that should be included in the audit plan to address those risks. You should present your answer using the following subheadings:

(a) Revenue
(b) Intangible assets – development costs
(c) Property, plant and equipment
(d) The contract with Nefario **(24 marks)**

20.3 Identify and explain any additional areas of audit risk arising from the collapse of the viewing platform at the sporting event on 15 February 20X4 and describe the audit procedures to be undertaken in respect of this matter. **(8 marks)**

Total: 37 marks

21 Barden Metalwork Ltd

Your firm has recently been appointed as the external auditor of Barden Metalwork Ltd (Barden). You are the senior responsible for planning the external audit for the year ended 31 August 20X4 and the engagement partner has asked you to consider the following key areas of audit risk:

(1) Work in progress
(2) Trade receivables
(3) Trade payables

Barden supplies bespoke light fittings to hotels and restaurants. Customers commission Barden to design and construct light fittings to their specific requirements using specialist metals. When a customer commissions work, a Barden designer meets with the customer to draw the design and calculate a fixed price for the work. The customer is required to provide written approval of the design and price before the design is passed to the production team who order the metals required and construct the light fitting. Customers are invoiced and revenue is recognised when the light fittings are despatched, which may be many months after the date of the commission. Barden's credit terms are 30 days.

All direct costs (labour, metal and other materials) relating to each commission are recorded in Barden's job costing system. Each month these direct costs are manually transferred into the job costing system from the payroll and purchases systems. The direct costs recorded in the job costing system are used as a basis for the calculation of the work in progress figure to be included in the financial statements. The finance director adds 20% to the direct costs to cover overheads.

It is Barden's policy to order the metals required for a commission only when written approval of the design is received from the customer. Metals are purchased from suppliers around the world who invoice Barden in their local currency.

Barden's light fittings have recently become very fashionable and the volume of commissions has grown rapidly. As a result, Barden sourced its metals from a number of new suppliers during the year, to avoid production delays. However, it has experienced quality issues with metals from some of the new suppliers which have resulted in a number of customer complaints.

In April 20X4 Barden's finance director appointed an internal auditor, Howard Ng, as she was concerned that Barden's internal controls were inadequate for the increasing size of the business. She instructed Howard to undertake a review of Barden's internal controls over purchasing. Howard concluded that the internal controls were effective with the exception of the following internal control deficiencies:

- Supplier statements are not retained or reconciled with the payables ledger.

- Metals were ordered and work started on some commissions before written approval of the design and price were obtained from the customer.

Howard resigned and left his post as internal auditor in August 20X4 without completing his final report on the internal controls over purchasing.

The engagement partner has provided you with the following extracts from the financial statements of Barden which are to be used as part of your consideration of the key audit risks:

Statements of profit or loss for the year ended 31 August

	20X4 (draft) £'000	20X3 (audited) £'000
Revenue	8,997	6,128
Cost of sales	(6,468)	(4,413)
Gross profit	2,529	1,715

Statements of financial position as at 31 August

	20X4 (draft) £'000	20X3 (audited) £'000
Current assets		
Work in progress	1,015	587
Trade receivables	980	451
Current liabilities		
Trade payables	571	483

On 1 June 20X4, Barden acquired 100% of the ordinary share capital of Bellass Ltd (Bellass). Barden is required to prepare group financial statements for the year ended 31 August 20X4 and your firm will act as group auditor. Bellass' financial statements for the year ended 31 August 20X4 will be audited by another audit firm, Capella LLP. The financial statement extracts above exclude financial information relating to Bellass.

Requirements

21.1 Outline the matters your firm should consider in respect of whether it should use the work of:

    (a)   Howard Ng; and

    (b)   Capella LLP.   **(4 marks)**

21.2 Justify why the items listed by the engagement partner have been identified as key areas of audit risk and, for each item, describe the procedures that should be included in the audit plan in order to address those risks. You should present your answer using the following subheadings:

    (a)   Work in progress

    (b)   Trade receivables

    (c)   Trade payables   **(23 marks)**

21.3 For each of the two internal control deficiencies identified by Howard Ng, outline the possible consequence(s) of the deficiency and provide recommendation(s) to remedy each deficiency. You should present your answer under the following subheadings:

    (a)   Supplier statements not retained or reconciled with the payables ledger

    (b)   Metals ordered and work started before written approval of the design and price obtained from the customer.   **(13 marks)**

Total: 40 marks

22 Hyena Ltd

Your firm has recently been appointed as the external auditor of Hyena Ltd (Hyena), an unlisted company, which operates fitness clubs across the UK. The outgoing auditors did not seek re-appointment following the conclusion of the previous year's audit.

You are the senior responsible for planning the external audit for the year ended 30 November 20X4 and the engagement partner has asked you to consider the following key areas of audit risk:

(1)   Revenue

(2)   Payroll

(3)   Fitness equipment

The engagement partner has provided you with the following extracts from the financial statements and additional information to help with your analytical procedures:

Statement of profit or loss for the year ended 30 November

	20X4 (draft) £'000	20X3 (audited) £'000
Revenue	94,123	75,937
Profit before tax	15,522	10,188

Statement of financial position as at 30 November

Non-current assets		
Fitness equipment	11,749	9,049

Additional information to help with analytical procedures

	20X4 (draft)	20X3 (actual)
Number of fitness clubs (all operating for a full year)	150	135
Payroll		
Employees' total gross pay (£'000)	50,150	47,225
Average number of employees in year	2,959	2,685
Company-wide pay rise (effective 1 December 20X3)	2%	–
Fitness equipment		
Loss on sale of fitness equipment	(1,650)	–
Depreciation charge for fitness equipment	(1,941)	(1,890)

The engagement partner has also provided you with the following information:

Hyena's fitness clubs are of similar size and layout and are equipped with the latest fitness equipment. Revenue grew steadily at approximately 5% pa over the five years ended 30 November 20X3. However, the number of fitness clubs remained constant at 135 during this period. On 1 December 20X3 Hyena opened 15 new fitness clubs.

Customers pay by one of three methods:

- On a pay-per-session basis in cash or by debit card at the fitness club reception;

- By monthly subscription paid by direct debit into Hyena's head office bank account; or

- By payment in advance to head office for a discounted annual package. The annual package runs for 12 months from the date the package is paid for.

In September 20X4, the company launched a new online registration and subscription management system. Initially, Hyena suffered operational problems with the system resulting in some monthly subscriptions being paid twice. Management is confident that refunds have been made for all monthly subscriptions that were affected.

Reports by Hyena's internal audit function highlighted a number of deficiencies in the payroll system and this led to the directors outsourcing the management of the payroll to Zebra Ltd, a payroll service organisation, from 1 June 20X4. A follow up report by the internal audit function confirms that these deficiencies have now been addressed.

Hyena replaces the fitness equipment in each fitness club over a five-year period. The fitness equipment is imported from manufacturers in the USA who invoice Hyena in US dollars. All costs associated with setting up the equipment, including time spent by Hyena's employees, are capitalised. The cost less any estimated residual value is depreciated on a straight-line basis over the estimated useful life of the fitness equipment.

During a meeting with Hyena's finance director, she:

(1) requested that the engagement partner is appointed as a non-executive director and attends the audit committee's quarterly meetings so your audit firm can be made aware of any issues promptly;

(2) requested that your firm calculates the amounts to be included in respect of taxation in the financial statements; and

(3) offered members of the audit team a free one-year package to a fitness club of their choice.

The proposed fees for audit and non-audit services amount to 1% of the firm's annual fee income.

Requirements

22.1 State the responsibilities of an **outgoing** firm of external auditors relating to a change of appointment as set out in the ICAEW *Code of Ethics*. Give reasons for each of the responsibilities.

Note: You are **not** required to refer to the Companies Act 2006 provisions in respect of the auditor who has not sought re-appointment. **(6 marks)**

22.2 Justify why the items listed by the engagement partner have been identified as key areas of audit risk and, for each item, describe the procedures that should be included in the audit plan in order to address those risks. You should present your answer using the following subheadings:

(a) Revenue
(b) Payroll
(c) Fitness equipment

Note: Your answer should include reference to the results of your analytical procedures. **(26 marks)**

22.3 Explain the threats to objectivity of the audit firm arising from the matters listed as (1) to (3) in the scenario and describe the safeguards, if any, that should be put in place to mitigate those threats. **(8 marks)**

Total: 40 marks

23 Weselton plc

Your firm has recently been appointed as the external auditor of Weselton plc (Weselton) which is your firm's largest and only listed client. You are the senior responsible for planning the external audit for the year ended 28 February 20X5 and the engagement partner has asked you to consider the following key areas of audit risk:

(1) Work in progress
(2) Trade receivables

Weselton provides global relocation services to corporate customers. Services include project management of overseas relocation of offices and employees.

For each relocation project, Weselton estimates the cost of supplying services based on customer requirements and the locations in which the services will be supplied. An indicative price is provided to the customer equal to the estimated cost plus a mark-up of 35%. Actual costs incurred often vary from estimated costs due to changes in customer requirements during the relocation project or unforeseen issues resulting in higher than expected costs. On completion of each project, the customer is invoiced, in sterling, for actual costs incurred plus the 35% mark-up. Credit terms are 30 days.

Weselton employs a small team of project managers who manage multiple projects. However, the majority of costs billed by Weselton arise from the use of external suppliers and other third parties. Costs include payments to local employment agencies for temporary personnel who pack the items to be relocated, fees for overseas legal and HR advice, local visa and immigration costs, shipping and transport fees and insurance costs.

Temporary personnel submit timesheets to local employment agencies which invoice Weselton each month for the total hours worked at rates agreed with Weselton. Invoices may include hours relating to more than one relocation project. Other suppliers invoice Weselton for services at varying points during the relocation and some overseas suppliers invoice in their local currency. All costs incurred, including those of Weselton's own project managers, are recorded in the job costing system against a unique code for each relocation project. Any costs recorded for projects not completed at 28 February are included as work in progress in the year-end financial statements.

Weselton's financial controller, Olaf Cyro, has provided you with the following information:

- In July 20X4, the directors decided that the job costing system was outdated. A replacement system was implemented on 21 January 20X5 and use of the old system ceased immediately. A delay in training employees on the new system resulted in a backlog of costs to be recorded and some customers were invoiced before all the costs relating to their projects were included on the new system. Additional invoices in respect of the omitted costs, plus the 35% mark-up, were sent to customers in February or are due to be sent by 31 March 20X5.

- Bulda GmbH (Bulda), a customer, is refusing to pay its balance outstanding at 28 February 20X5 due to a disagreement over the amount invoiced in respect of its relocation project. The disagreement has arisen due to a significant variation between the indicative price and the actual amount invoiced. The balance due from Bulda at 28 February 20X5 is £1.8 million. The original indicative price provided was £1.3 million. Olaf believes all of the additional costs arose due to changes in Bulda's requirements during the relocation and that the full amount is recoverable.

- Weselton's previous auditors did not seek reappointment after completing the external audit for the year ended 28 February 20X4. During that audit, reliance was placed on the controls over the job costing system. Olaf requested that your firm also relies on those controls as he believes this will ensure the audit is conducted efficiently.

Olaf also provided you with the following extracts from the financial statements of Weselton to use as part of your consideration of the key audit risks:

Statement of profit or loss for the year ended 28 February

	20X5 (draft) £'000	20X4 (audited) £'000
Revenue	45,467	41,339
Cost of sales	(30,795)	(30,622)
Gross profit	14,672	10,717

Statement of financial position as at 28 February

	20X5 (draft) £'000	20X4 (audited) £'000
Work in progress	7,171	5,034
Trade receivables	5,481	3,741

Your discussion with Olaf also revealed the following internal control deficiencies:

(1) Customers are not required to provide written confirmation of changes to their requirements arising during a relocation project.

(2) Project managers do not monitor actual costs incurred to date compared with the estimated cost of each project.

Requirements

23.1 List the matters your firm should have considered and the procedures it should have performed before accepting appointment as external auditor of Weselton. **(10 marks)**

23.2 Justify why work in progress and trade receivables have been identified as key areas of audit risk and, for each one, describe the procedures that should be included in the audit plan in order to address those risks. You should present your answer using the following subheadings:

(a) Work in progress
(b) Trade receivables **(18 marks)**

23.3 Explain why reliance on controls over the job costing system, requested by Olaf, is unlikely to be appropriate in respect of the audit for the year ended 28 February 20X5. **(5 marks)**

23.4 For each internal control deficiency listed as (1) and (2) in the scenario, draft points for inclusion in your firm's report to those charged with governance and management at Weselton. For each deficiency, you should outline the possible consequence(s) of the deficiency and provide recommendations to address it.

(7 marks)

Total: 40 marks

24 Arendelle Ltd

Your firm has been the external auditor of Arendelle Ltd (Arendelle) for a number of years and has recently been engaged to perform a review of Arendelle's interim financial information for the six months to 31 January 20X5. Arendelle's bank has requested interim financial information in support of a loan application and requires the information to be reviewed and reported on by Arendelle's auditor. Your firm's review is to be conducted in accordance with ISRE 2410 and will consist of making enquiries and applying analytical and other review procedures.

Arendelle supplies boxes of fruit and vegetables to households and businesses in the east of the UK. Deliveries are spread evenly throughout the year and revenue is collected by direct debit on the day of delivery. Arendelle's delivery vehicles are currently fully utilised. The directors have requested the bank loan to invest in new delivery vehicles so the company can extend its service to other areas of the UK.

You are the senior responsible for the review engagement and you recently met with Arendelle's finance director, Elsa Duke, who provided you with the following information regarding events in the six months since 31 July 20X4:

- Arendelle contracted to supply 22 nursing homes. On average, each contract is worth £20,000 pa and supplies commenced on 1 August 20X4. Arendelle allowed 30-day credit terms on these specific contracts.

- To meet the increased demand from the nursing home contracts, Arendelle commenced purchasing fruit and vegetables from two new suppliers. The two new suppliers require payment on delivery in contrast to the 30-day credit terms allowed by Arendelle's four existing suppliers.

- On 1 September 20X4, Arendelle rented additional space adjacent to its existing storage facility for the purpose of fulfilling the new nursing home catering contracts.

- 20 of Arendelle's 40 delivery vehicles became fully depreciated on 1 August 20X4 but are still in use awaiting the outcome of the loan application.

- On 30 October 20X4, Arendelle paid Trolls Ltd £100,000 for a marketing campaign due to be launched in April 20X5 in the areas of the UK where Arendelle plans to extend its delivery service.

Elsa also provided you with draft interim financial information for the six months to 31 January 20X5 from which you have extracted the following key information for further review:

Statement of profit or loss for	Six months to 31 January 20X5 (draft) £'000	Full year to 31 July 20X4 (audited) £'000
Revenue	4,720	6,500
Cost of sales *	(3,446)	(5,120)
Gross profit	1,274	1,380
Operating expenses **	(650)	(638)
Profit from operations	624	742

Statement of profit or loss for	Six months to 31 January 20X5 (draft) £'000	Full year to 31 July 20X4 (audited) £'000
* Cost of sales includes:		
Warehouse rent paid	125	180
Depreciation of delivery vehicles	55	110
** Operating expenses include:		
Marketing expenses	196	192

Statement of financial position as at	31 January 20X5 (draft) £'000	31 July 20X4 (audited) £'000
Trade receivables	62	–
Trade payables	660	435

Elsa commented she is looking forward to your firm's guidance on how best to present the interim financial information to increase the likelihood of Arendelle's bank agreeing to provide the loan. She also indicated she anticipated Arendelle would be unwilling to pay your firm's fee for this engagement if the loan application was not successful.

You agreed with Elsa to meet with her again on 18 March 20X5 to discuss any questions you have arising from your initial review of the draft interim financial information.

Requirements

24.1 Explain the ethical issues arising from Elsa's comments in respect of:

(a) providing guidance on the presentation of Arendelle's interim financial information; and

(b) your firm's fee being contingent on Arendelle successfully receiving the loan from its bank.

(3 marks)

24.2 As part of your review of the interim financial information, perform analytical procedures on the information provided and prepare a list of questions which you wish to ask Elsa at your meeting on 18 March 20X5. You should present your answer using the following subheadings:

(a) Revenue
(b) Margins
(c) Warehouse rent
(d) Depreciation – delivery vehicles
(e) Marketing expenses
(f) Trade receivables
(g) Trade payables

(17 marks)

Total: 20 marks

25 Hutton plc

Your firm has recently been appointed as the external auditor of Hutton plc (Hutton), a listed company, for the year ending 30 June 20X5. The previous auditors did not seek re-appointment following the conclusion of the previous year's audit.

Hutton sells household products through a chain of retail stores in the UK and its own website. An extensive range of products is offered including the latest electronic equipment such as smart phones and soft furnishings such as curtains and carpets. Hutton has experienced many years of rapid growth but recent trading conditions have been difficult due to competitors offering comparable products at lower prices. In response to the difficult trading conditions, Hutton has developed a new website to replace the old website and is planning a reorganisation involving the closure of 50% of its stores.

You are the senior responsible for planning the external audit for the year ending 30 June 20X5 and the engagement partner has asked you to consider the following key areas of audit risk:

(1) Volume-based supplier rebates
(2) Inventory
(3) Intangible assets – website development costs

The engagement partner has provided you with the following extracts from the financial statements, to help with your analytical procedures:

Statement of profit or loss for the year ending 30 June

	20X5 (estimated) £m	20X4 (audited) £m
Revenue	2,329	2,784
Cost of sales (gross)	(1,434)	(1,489)
Supplier rebates	185	106

Statement of financial position as at 30 June	20X5 (estimated) £m	20X4 (audited) £m
Non-current assets		
Intangible assets – website development costs	31	11
Current assets		
Inventories	306	220

The engagement partner has also provided you with the following information:

Hutton has negotiated individual terms for supplier rebates, which range from 1% to 15% of purchases, with each of its 350 principal suppliers. The terms are set out in signed contracts, with each supplier, which typically run from one to three years. Rebates are paid in arrears to Hutton on the conclusion of the contract if Hutton exceeds the volumes of purchases stipulated in the contract. Hutton's sales managers prepare revenue forecasts for each product. The revenue forecasts are used by the accounts department to estimate the volume of purchases that will be placed with each supplier over the contract period. If the volume of estimated purchases exceeds that required in the contract to earn a rebate, a rebate is recognised in the financial statements. Spreadsheets are used to collate the information and calculate the rebate attributable to the current year.

The company has standard operating procedures in every store including electronic point of sales (EPOS) systems and maintains a perpetual inventory system, which records the quantities held and the cost price of inventory. Quantities in the perpetual inventory system are updated from goods received records, the EPOS systems, the company website and the results of inventory counts. The cost price of inventory is updated from purchase invoices. Where there is sufficient certainty that a supplier rebate relating to historical purchases will be received in the future, an adjustment is made to the cost of inventory. Overseas suppliers invoice in their local currency.

At each month end, the inventory system generates an inventory valuation listing and an aged inventory report. The valuation listing includes the cost and quantity on hand for each inventory item. The valuation listing at 30 June 20X5 will be used as the basis for the inventory value in the financial statements as no count will take place at the year end. Hutton carries out monthly inventory counts at all of its stores and the next inventory count is planned for 19 June 20X5. Your firm has not attended any inventory counts during the year but the internal auditors have attended inventory counts at a sample of stores throughout the year.

Employees from Hutton's IT department commenced work on the replacement website on 1 October 20X4 but were unable to resolve a technical issue arising on the interface between the new website and the perpetual inventory system. A contract was signed with Sweepweb, a website development company, to resolve this issue and the IT director has stated that the interface is now working properly. Internal costs are based on the IT director's estimate of time spent by Hutton's staff. The total costs of developing the replacement website are included as an intangible asset in the financial statements for the year ending 30 June 20X5 and are being amortised over 10 years.

Requirements

25.1 Set out the benefits and limitations of using analytical procedures at the planning stage of an external audit. **(5 marks)**

25.2 Justify why the items listed by the engagement partner have been identified as key areas of audit risk and, for each item, describe the procedures that should be included in the audit plan in order to address that risk. You should present your answer using the following subheadings:

(a) Volume-based supplier rebates
(b) Inventory
(c) Intangible assets – website development costs **(30 marks)**

Total: 35 marks

26 Haskett Ltd

Your firm has recently been appointed as the external auditor of Haskett Ltd (Haskett), a wholly-owned subsidiary of McCarthy Travel Group Ltd (MT Group). Your firm has been the external auditor of MT Group for a number of years. The group audit is performed by an audit team based in your firm's London office.

MT Group owns a number of subsidiaries that operate bus services in five regions of the UK. In July 20X4, MT Group was awarded a new contract, by a government body, to provide bus services in the east of England. On 1 August 20X4, MT Group created a new company, Haskett, to supply the bus services under the new contract. All revenue and costs relating to fulfilment of the contract are recorded in Haskett's own accounting records.

You are the audit senior responsible for the audit of Haskett's financial statements for the year ended 31 July 20X5 and you are based in your firm's office located in the east of England. Your responsibilities include preparing the audit plan and communicating with the group auditor in your firm's London office. The engagement partner for the Haskett audit, Mandy Winter, has asked you to consider the following key areas of audit risk:

(1) Revenue
(2) Property, plant and equipment – buses
(3) Legal claim against Haskett

Passengers can pay for journeys taken on Haskett's buses in the following ways:

- Purchase of a ticket using cash when boarding a bus.

- Electronic contactless card which the customer has pre-loaded with funds. Customers touch their contactless card on a card reader when boarding a bus and a single fare is deducted from the funds available on the card.

- Purchase of a season ticket, through Haskett's website, which allows unlimited travel on Haskett's bus routes for a period of 3, 6 or 12 months.

The contactless card system is operated by Dolphin Systems Ltd (Dolphin). Dolphin was formed in June 20X4 by Clay McCarthy who was appointed as managing director of Haskett in August 20X4. Clay owns 100% of the share capital of Dolphin.

Revenue from season ticket sales is recognised evenly over the relevant season ticket period. All other revenue is recognised on the day of travel. Haskett's customers load funds onto a contactless card through Dolphin's own website, payment is taken and the funds held by Dolphin until the customer makes a bus journey. Data from the Dolphin card reader on each bus are electronically transmitted to Dolphin's central computer at the end of each day. The central computer software calculates the amount due to Haskett and the funds are electronically transferred, on a daily basis, to Haskett's bank account, after deducting a 12% commission charge. No checks are made by Haskett regarding the amounts calculated and transferred by Dolphin. This is the first time any MT Group subsidiary has used a contactless card system on its buses.

Haskett operates a fleet of buses half of which consists of buses purchased at market value from other MT Group subsidiaries and refurbished by Haskett's own employees. The rest of the fleet consists of new buses purchased from EchoBus Ltd (EchoBus), a UK bus manufacturer. All costs associated with both purchasing and refurbishing the fleet have been recognised as property, plant and equipment in Haskett's financial statements. All buses are being depreciated over 10 years.

The east of England bus service contract runs for eight years and required Haskett to commence bus services on 1 February 20X5. However, due to delays in the manufacture of the new buses by EchoBus, a significantly reduced service commenced on 1 February 20X5 and the full service commenced on 1 April 20X5. The government body that awarded the contract has made a claim for damages against Haskett of £250,000 for breach of contract. The outcome of the claim will not be known until after the auditor's report on Haskett's financial statements is due to be signed. Haskett's directors do not wish to include a provision or make any disclosure in respect of the claim as they intend to make their own claim of £250,000 against EchoBus.

Mandy has provided you with the following draft extracts from the financial statements of Haskett and budget information, prepared by MT Group when tendering for the new contract, to be used as part of your consideration of the key audit risks. Mandy also informed you that Haskett's draft profit before tax for the year ended 31 July 20X5 is £538,000.

Statement of profit or loss for the year ended 31 July 20X5 (extract)

	Actual (draft) £'000	Budgeted £'000
Revenue	8,975	7,450
Cost of sales	(7,180)	(6,183)
Gross profit	1,795	1,267

Statement of financial position as at 31 July 20X5 (extract)

	Actual (draft) £'000	Budgeted £'000
Property, plant and equipment – buses	4,900	3,500

Requirements

26.1 Justify why the items listed by the engagement partner have been identified as key areas of audit risk and, for each item, describe the procedures that should be included in the audit plan in order to address those risks. You should present your answer using the following subheadings:

(a) Revenue
(b) Property, plant and equipment – buses
(c) Legal claim against Haskett

(25 marks)

26.2 Set out the matters you should consider, as part of your audit planning, arising from:

(a) the ownership of Dolphin by Clay McCarthy; and
(b) Haskett being a component of MT Group.

(10 marks)

Total: 35 marks

Section 3: Concluding and reporting on engagements

27 Short form questions

27.1 The new auditor of a company has concluded that a material amount in the preceding [...] was included within an incorrect current asset heading. The audit [...] nsibilities in relation to the current year's auditor's report.

(handwritten note: comparative form a part of FS. Itd no opinion on comparatives. Do affect on CY FS. If correctly adjusted, no modification of FS.)

(2 marks)

[...] d audit tests indicated that company policy requiring [...] only by the company's buying department was not adhered [...] examined.

[...] h in company policy, draft extracts suitable for inclusion in the [...] which set out the possible consequences and the [...] ould make.

(handwritten note: Us Consequence - duplicate of orders, breaches of budget, use of unauthorised supplies. Negative impact on cash flow. Recommendation - Training, disciplinary action. Management approval - signature. IT software)

(4 marks)

[...] recently been appointed as auditor to Donner Ltd for the year ending [...] 0X5. This is the first year of audit for Donner Ltd as it fell below the statutory [...] on limits for the year ended 31 October 20X4, which was the company's first [...] ling.

[...] ters to be considered in respect of the opening balances of Donner Ltd.

(handwritten note: Review working papers for PY. Check PY balances have correctly been b/f. Check for changes. Disclosure. Substantive. ISA 710 state not prev audited.)

(3 marks)

27.4 You have obtained external confirmations of receivables as part of your audit of Charnley Ltd for the year ended 31 October 20X0.

The following disagreements have been revealed:

(1) A customer disagreed with the balance because it had sent a cheque on 27 October 20X0.

(2) A customer had been promised a credit note against an invoice dated 5 October 20X0 [...] e had been charged, but this had not yet been issued.

[...] you require in order to conclude on the results of this test, and [...] mation?

(handwritten note: (1) Original invoicing. Amount of cheque, cheque received, banked and posted. To confirm acceptable timing difference.)

(3 marks)

(handwritten note: (2) @ y/e = acceptable timing diff not provided for = error isolated? Need to extrapolate)

27.5 The directors of two companies, Fletcher Ltd and Dervish Ltd, have each prevented their auditors from carrying out procedures considered necessary to verify the amount of inventories held by third parties of £250,000.

In the audit of Fletcher Ltd materiality has been set at £200,000, and in the audit of Dervish Ltd materiality has been set at £15,000.

State the effect this matter will have on the auditor's report of each company.   **(3 marks)**

27.6 The directors of Denzil Ltd are preparing the financial statements for the year ended 31 May 20X1, and have approached the auditors for advice because they are unsure whether the company can be considered a going concern.

State the importance of the going concern concept in the preparation of financial statements, and describe the effect on the financial statements if the company:

(1) is considered a going concern, although there are significant doubts about this.
(2) is not considered a going concern.   **(4 marks)**

27.7 During the course of the audit of Beacon Ltd for the year ended 30 November 20X2 you discovered that on 25 January 20X3 a liquidator was appointed at Gamlec Ltd, a major customer of Beacon Ltd. The balance due from Gamlec Ltd at 30 November 20X2 was £150,000.

Identify the matters to which you would direct your attention after the reporting period date.   **(3 marks)**

27.8 The directors of Pinot plc have included the following note in the accounts for the year ended 31 December 20X3.

'The company reached agreement with its lenders, in October 20X3, to extend the maturities of its debt facilities until September 20X4, waive all existing covenant breaches and reduce interest costs.

All preconditions contained in the facilities agreement have now been satisfied. The company is working on initiatives to significantly reduce its current debt levels and is to explore opportunities to raise further funds by September 20X4. Based on progress to date, the directors remain confident that the company will be successful in achieving its strategy. While there can be no certainty, the directors believe that the adoption of the going concern basis is appropriate in the preparation of the financial statements.

If adoption of the going concern basis was not appropriate, adjustments would be required to write down assets to their recoverable value, to reclassify non-current assets as current assets and to provide for any further liabilities that might arise.'

Describe, with reasons, the possible effects of this note on the auditor's report for the year ended 31 December 20X3.   **(4 marks)**

27.9 Siskin Ltd conducts all its sales on a cash basis. The managing director and majority shareholder of Siskin Ltd has provided a written representation in respect of the completeness of cash sales.

What additional matters would you consider in determining whether or not you would rely on this representation? **(3 marks)**

27.10 During the audit of Poplar Ltd for the year ended 31 January 20X3 you have been assigned the responsibility of checking the cash at bank figure in the statement of financial position. While checking the bank reconciliation you discovered that receipts from customers, listed as outstanding lodgements at the year end, were cleared through the bank on 14 February 20X3.

Explain why this matter should be investigated further. **(2 marks)**

27.11 You are the auditor of Bomburst Ltd (Bomburst). An extract from the directors' report states:

'The company always adheres to its policy to comply with the terms of payment agreed with suppliers.'

However, during your audit work on the year-end trade payables balance you found evidence of a number of suppliers requesting payment from Bomburst on overdue invoices.

State the actions you would take and outline the implications for your auditor's report. **(4 marks)**

27.12 Your firm has been engaged by the directors of Bilko Inc (Bilko), a company based overseas, to undertake a review of and provide an assurance report on the year-end financial information of its UK branch. The terms of the engagement include making enquiries of management, applying analytical procedures to the financial information and assessing whether the accounting policies and presentation have been consistently applied unless otherwise disclosed.

Outline the matters to be included in your firm's assurance report to the directors of Bilko to ensure that the purpose and scope of the engagement is clear. **(3 marks)**

27.13 Your firm has completed the external audit of the financial statements of Roses Ltd (Roses) for the year ended 31 December 20X9 and an unmodified auditor's report was signed by the engagement partner on 1 March 20X0. Your firm's auditor's report has been provided to the directors who plan to issue the financial statements and auditor's report to the shareholders on 30 March 20X0. While reading today's newspaper, 23 March 20X0, you discover that Meadow Ltd (Meadow), a major customer of Roses, went into liquidation on 15 March 20X0. You were the audit senior on the audit of Roses and you recall that Meadow owed a material amount to Roses, at 31 December 20X9, for goods purchased. This amount remained outstanding at the conclusion of the subsequent events review. You have informed the engagement partner of your discovery.

Discuss the issues arising as a result of the newspaper article and state what, if any, action your firm should take. **(4 marks)**

27.14 Describe the auditors' responsibilities, in the UK, with respect to forming and reporting their opinion on a directors' report which is included in a company's annual report containing financial statements. **(2 marks)**

27.15 You are the audit senior on the external audit of Dug Ltd (Dug) for the year ended 31 January 20X1. In January 20X1 Dug sold some office equipment to the wife of Dug's managing director. The audit junior has noted that the sale has not been disclosed in the note to the financial statements detailing related party transactions and has suggested the inclusion of an emphasis of matter paragraph in the auditor's report to highlight this issue.

Comment on the suitability or otherwise of the audit junior's suggestion. **(4 marks)**

27.16 During the external audit of Eagle Ltd (Eagle), the audit senior discovered that the company does not undertake periodic reconciliations of the plant and equipment register with the physical assets.

Prepare notes, in readiness for drafting the audit firm's report to the management of Eagle, which outline the possible consequences of this internal control deficiency and provide recommendations to remedy the deficiency. **(4 marks)**

27.17 Your firm is the external auditor of Weaver Ltd (Weaver), a marketing agency, for the year ended 30 June 20X1. During the audit of work in progress, you discover that 20% of the work in progress balance relates to completed marketing projects which were delivered to clients more than three months before the year end and had not yet been invoiced.

Prepare notes, in readiness for drafting your firm's report to the management of Weaver, which outline the possible consequences of this significant internal control deficiency and provide recommendations to remedy the deficiency. **(4 marks)**

27.18 Your firm is the external auditor of Dawn Ltd (Dawn), a manufacturer of office furniture. As part of your work on trade payables you discovered that the company does not keep a list of approved suppliers from which to purchase its raw materials.

Prepare notes, in readiness for drafting your firm's report to the management of Dawn, which outline the possible consequences of this significant internal control deficiency and provide recommendations to remedy the deficiency. **(4 marks)**

27.19 Putter Ltd, a manufacturer of electrical appliances, has included a provision for warranties in its financial statements.

List the procedures you would undertake between the year end and the date of the auditor's report in respect of the provision for warranties. **(2 marks)**

27.20 During the course of the external audit of Green Ltd (Green), it was discovered that, on a number of occasions, sales staff granted customer discounts in excess of authorised levels.

Prepare notes, in readiness for drafting the audit firm's report to the management of Green, which outline the possible consequences of this significant internal control deficiency and provide recommendations to remedy the deficiency. **(4 marks)**

27.21 Your firm is the external auditor of Brown plc (Brown). You have reviewed the chairman's statement to be included in Brown's annual report, with the audited financial statements, for the year ended 30 June 20X2. Your review has identified that key financial ratios contained in the chairman's statement are inconsistent with the audited financial statements.

Identify the actions that your firm should take to address this issue. **(3 marks)**

27.22 During the external audit of Stamp Ltd (Stamp) for the year ended 30 September 20X2, it was discovered that plant and equipment, included in the statement of financial position at £200,000, was sold for £150,000 on 5 October 20X2. The directors refuse to adjust this figure on the grounds that the item was sold after the year end. The draft financial statements for the year ended 30 September 20X2 show profit before tax of £450,000 and total assets of £980,000.

State, with reasons, whether or not you would modify the audit opinion on the financial statements of Stamp. **(3 marks)**

27.23 During the subsequent events review on the external audit of Mono Ltd (Mono) for the year ended 30 April 20X3, it was discovered that inventory, which was included in the statement of financial position at a cost of £100,000, was sold for £75,000 on 12 May 20X3.

The management of Mono has refused to make any adjustment to the financial statements in respect of this matter. The draft financial statements for the year ended 30 April 20X3 show a profit before tax of £225,000 and total assets of £490,000.

State, with reasons, the action which should be taken by the external auditor in respect of this matter. **(3 marks)**

27.24 Reporting accountants are required to obtain written representations from management when performing an engagement to examine prospective financial information.

List the representations that should be obtained and explain why they are required. **(4 marks)**

27.25 During the external audit of Guard Ltd (Guard), you discovered that company policy to obtain three quotes for capital expenditure in excess of £10,000 was not adhered to on a number of occasions.

Draft points for inclusion in your firm's report to the management of Guard, outlining the possible consequences of this deficiency and providing recommendations to remedy the deficiency. **(3 marks)**

27.26 List the key differences between the auditor's report issued in respect of an audit conducted under the Companies Act 2006 and an assurance report issued in respect of an engagement to examine prospective financial information. **(4 marks)**

27.27 During the external audit of Whinter Ltd your firm has identified a material inconsistency between the directors' report and the financial statements.

State the actions your firm should take and outline any potential implications for the auditor's report. **(3 marks)**

27.28 Your firm recently conducted the external audit of the financial statements of Oval Ltd (Oval) for the year ended 28 February 20X5. Oval's bank requested the audited financial statements before deciding whether to make a loan to Oval. Oval received the loan from its bank but has defaulted on its first quarterly loan repayment. Your firm's audit opinion was unmodified.

In respect of the bank having relied on the audited financial statements, explain the possible consequences for your firm if it has provided an inappropriate opinion in the auditor's report on Oval's financial statements. **(4 marks)**

27.29 You are the audit junior working on the external audit of Bouncer Ltd (Bouncer). The sales ledger clerk informed you that when he requested the payment of an overdue amount from Mr Wicket, a sole trader, he was told by Mr Wicket that the managing director of Bouncer had personally collected the overdue amount in cash. The managing director subsequently instructed the sales ledger clerk to write off the overdue amount as a bad debt. The amount is not material to the financial statements.

State, with reasons, the actions that should be taken by you and your firm in relation to this matter. **(3 marks)**

27.30 Your firm is concluding its audit of the financial statements of Turtle Ltd (Turtle) for the year ended 31 March 20X5. The audit work has identified a number of misstatements, which are individually immaterial, in transactions and account balances recorded in the statement of profit or loss and statement of financial position.

State the actions your firm should take in relation to the misstatements before reaching its audit opinion on the financial statements of Turtle. **(3 marks)**

27.31 Your firm is the external auditor of Trigg Ltd and the audit fieldwork has been completed. The engagement partner, Alfie Smith, is performing a review of the audit files and during his review identified that the financial statements show that the gross profit margin had fallen by 5% compared with the previous year.

State, with reasons, the additional steps Alfie Smith should take in respect of this issue before concluding his review of the audit. **(4 marks)**

27.32 External auditor's reports on the financial statements of listed companies (which are required to apply the UK Corporate Governance Code) have to provide additional information about the audit work performed in line with ISA (UK) 701 *Communicating Key Audit Matters in the Independent Auditor's Report*.

List the additional information required to be included in the auditor's report and state the benefits to the users of the financial statements of having this information. **(4 marks)**

28 Progear Inc

Your firm has been engaged by the directors of Progear Inc (Progear), a company based overseas, to undertake a review of and provide a limited assurance report on the financial information of its UK branch. The terms of the engagement include making enquiries of management and applying analytical procedures to the financial information. The review is to cover the financial information for the **six months** ended 30 September 20X9.

Progear manufactures specialist protective clothing which is used by organisations operating in the medical, research and energy sectors. All products sold by the branch are supplied by Progear and the branch normally sells them at a mark-up of 25% on cost to the branch. However, quantity discounts are available for orders above specified levels. All customers are required to pay within 30 days but customers are offered an early payment discount if they pay within seven days of invoice date. In the previous three years, branch sales have increased steadily at rates between 4% and 6% in the corresponding six-month period.

You are preparing for your planning meeting with the financial controller of the branch and have obtained, in advance of the meeting, a copy of the draft financial information for the **six months** ended 30 September 20X9. During your preliminary review, you identified the following extracts from the financial information of the branch as matters to discuss at that meeting.

Statement of profit or loss

	Six months ended 30 September	
	20X9	20X8
	£'000	£'000
Revenue	5,353	4,907
Cost of sales	(4,472)	(3,974)
Gross profit	881	933
Operating expenses	(747)	(646)
Profit from operations	134	287

Statement of financial position

	As at 30 September	
	20X9	20X8
	£'000	£'000
Current assets		
Inventories	994	951
Trade receivables	812	806

Requirements

28.1 Prepare briefing notes on the matters which you wish to discuss with the financial controller of the branch in respect of the information provided in the scenario. Your notes should refer to the results of your analytical procedures. **(13 marks)**

28.2 Describe the main contents of the limited assurance report to be issued following your firm's review of the financial information. **(7 marks)**

Note: You may assume that there are 180 days in a six-month period. **Total: 20 marks**

29 Gourmet Ltd

Gourmet Ltd (Gourmet), a client of your firm, is a fast-food chain, operating outlets in and around London selling ethically-sourced healthy food and drink to eat in or take away. The company opened its first outlet six years ago and, following its phenomenal success, it has opened 10 additional outlets. The directors wish to continue the company's expansion by opening two outlets outside London and introducing a delivery service.

The directors of Gourmet have been negotiating with the company's bankers in order to increase borrowings. In support of the request for funding, the directors have prepared profit and cash flow forecasts for the three years ending 31 December 20X4, on the basis of assumptions they have made about the future operations of the business. The company's bankers require this information to be examined and reported on by independent accountants. The directors have requested that your firm undertakes this examination.

In respect of the new outlets, the directors have identified two potential properties outside London. The properties are leasehold premises which will require extensive refurbishment to bring them up to the high standard of existing outlets.

The delivery service, for which a charge will be made, will only be available from the central London outlets and, if successful, will be extended to other outlets at a later date. This will require the acquisition of vehicles which the directors plan to purchase outright. The vehicles will be painted with the company's logo in order to raise the profile of the delivery service.

The majority of the ingredients used in the preparation of the food and the packaging are bought centrally on credit terms. Fruit and vegetables are purchased locally by the chef at each outlet and paid for at the time of purchase. All ingredients are sourced from within the UK to reduce the company's carbon footprint and all packaging used in the take-away business is made from recycled material. In addition, all employees are paid above the average wage for the industry sector and are entitled to a bonus based on the level of profit achieved by the company as a whole.

Requirements

29.1 From the information provided in the scenario, identify the key **receipts** and **payments** that you would expect to be included in the cash flow forecasts prepared by the directors of Gourmet. For each receipt and payment, identify the specific matters you would consider when reviewing the reasonableness of the assumptions in forecasting that receipt or payment. **(10 marks)**

29.2 Explain the role of written representations in the examination of and reporting on forecast information. **(3 marks)**

29.3 Describe the differences between the **conclusion** expressed in an assurance report on forecast information and the **opinion** expressed in an auditor's report on financial statements. Give reasons for these differences. **(7 marks)**

Total: 20 marks

30 Kipo Ltd

Kipo Ltd (Kipo) operates a chain of four restaurants each located inside UK shopping centres owned and operated by Retail Investment Organisation Ltd (RIO). Kipo leases each of its premises from RIO and is required by the terms of each lease to pay rent based on the level of revenue generated by each restaurant. Kipo is required to declare the revenue for each restaurant to RIO annually and RIO requires the revenue declared to be reviewed and reported on by an independent assurance provider. Kipo does not require a statutory audit under the Companies Act 2006.

Your firm has been engaged by Kipo to review and provide assurance on the restaurant revenues declared by Kipo to RIO for the year ended 31 December 20X2. The terms of the engagement are restricted to making enquiries of management and applying analytical and other review procedures. In addition, your firm is required to provide a report to the management of Kipo regarding any relevant matters, such as any deficiencies in internal control identified during the review.

During your firm's review you identified that one of the four restaurants, located in Cambridge, showed a decrease in revenue of 12% on the prior year compared with the other three restaurants, each of which showed a small increase. When you made enquiries of management regarding the decrease, you were told that the Cambridge restaurant operated a new discount voucher scheme for customers from 1 January 20X2. Vouchers are printed in the local newspaper and customers present the discount voucher on payment, reducing the final price of their meal by 5%. The net revenue figure, ie, after deducting customer discounts, is reported by the restaurant to Kipo's head office and recorded in the sales account in the nominal ledger. The terms of each lease require Kipo to declare the net revenue for each restaurant.

During discussions with the Cambridge restaurant manager you identified a number of internal control deficiencies in respect of the discount voucher scheme. After entering the full price of a meal into the cash till, staff members manually calculate and separately enter the 5% discount to give the final price of the customer's meal. Any member of staff may deduct a discount from a sale entered into the till without authorisation. There is no daily reconciliation between discounts deducted on the cash till and physical discount vouchers presented as the vouchers are discarded by restaurant staff on presentation by the customer.

Kipo's management is unable to offer any other explanations regarding the 12% decrease in revenue at the Cambridge restaurant. Your firm has identified no issues with the net revenue declared in respect of the other three restaurants.

Requirements

30.1 Draft points for inclusion in your firm's report to management at Kipo, outlining the possible consequences of the internal control deficiencies identified. You should provide recommendations to remedy the deficiencies. **(7 marks)**

30.2 Discuss the implications for your firm's assurance report on the restaurant revenues declared by Kipo to RIO and explain the nature of the report conclusion that you consider your firm should provide. **(8 marks)**

30.3 Outline the issues your firm should consider if the directors of Kipo request that your firm accepts the engagement to provide assurance on the revenue declared to RIO for the year ending 31 December 20X3. **(5 marks)**

Total: 20 marks

31 Hattie Ltd, Moon plc

31.1 Described below are situations which have arisen in respect of two unrelated external audit clients of your firm. The year end in each case is 31 December 20X3.

Hattie Ltd (Hattie)

The management of Hattie has refused to provide written representations that:

- it has provided the auditor with all the relevant information and access as agreed in the terms of the audit engagement; and

- all transactions have been recorded and reflected in the financial statements.

Vector Ltd (Vector)

On 23 January 20X4 Vector received a letter from the administrator of Perkins Ltd (Perkins), a customer of Vector. The letter notified Vector that Perkins had gone into administration on

17 January 20X4. At 31 December 20X3, Vector had an amount due from Perkins of £190,000 for goods supplied. The directors of Vector have refused to make any allowance against the amount due from Perkins as they are hopeful they will be able to recover the full amount. On examination of Perkins' financial statements you have identified that its assets are insufficient to meet the amounts owed to creditors.

Vector's draft financial statements for the year ended 31 December 20X3 show a profit before tax of £1.5 million and total assets of £8.7 million.

Requirements

(a) Explain the key purposes of obtaining written representations from management as part of an external audit engagement. **(5 marks)**

(b) For each of the two situations outlined above, state whether you would modify the audit opinion. Give reasons for your conclusions and describe the modifications, if any, to each auditor's report. **(9 marks)**

31.2 Moon plc (Moon)

Your firm is the external auditor of Moon's financial statements for the year ended 31 December 20X3. Gru Ltd (Gru), a customer, is suing Moon for breach of contract. Gru claims that, during 20X3, Moon supplied it with defective materials and is seeking £580,000 from Moon for a refund of the cost of the materials and compensation for loss of profits. Moon's directors dispute the claim but have included a note to the financial statements detailing the issue and amounts involved. The dispute is not due to be settled by the court until after your firm has signed its auditor's report.

Moon's draft financial statements for the year ended 31 December 20X3 show a profit before tax of £5.5 million and total assets of £49.3 million.

Requirement

Discuss the implications for your firm's audit opinion on the financial statements of Moon.

(6 marks)

Total: 20 marks

32 Mansard plc, Gable Ltd, Hip Ltd

32.1 Your firm has recently been appointed as the external auditor of Mansard plc (Mansard), a listed company, which sells pharmaceutical products. The company operates from a head office in London and eight offices in Europe. Trading conditions in Europe have been difficult and Mansard has recently opened a network of offices in Asia in a drive to increase business. Both European and Asian office managers are set targets for generating revenue for their office and they are paid bonuses when the targets are reached.

During the external audit for the year ended 31 March 20X4, you identified the following deficiencies in internal control to be reported to those charged with governance and management at Mansard:

(1) Mansard does not have any bribery prevention policies.

(2) References were not always obtained for all new employees.

(3) The Italian and German offices did not follow Mansard's accounting policies when preparing monthly accounting returns for submission to head office. Consequently revenue and profits were overstated.

Requirement

Draft points for inclusion in your firm's report to those charged with governance and management at Mansard. For each internal control deficiency identified above, you should outline the possible consequence(s) of the deficiency and provide recommendation(s) to address each deficiency. You should present your answer using the following subheadings:

(a) Bribery prevention policies
(b) Employee references
(c) Not following accounting policies

(13 marks)

32.2 Described below are situations which have arisen at two unrelated external audit clients of your firm. The year end in each case is 31 March 20X4.

Gable Ltd (Gable)

Gable is an international company operating in the construction sector. The financial statements for the year ended 31 March 20X4 include cranes disposed of during the year with a carrying amount of £220,000. Gable has accounted for the proceeds of the disposal in other income in the statement of profit or loss but has not removed the carrying amount of the disposed cranes from the statement of financial position. The directors refuse to amend the financial statements in respect of this matter because the buyer of the cranes has not yet collected the cranes which are still on Gable's premises.

Gable uses sub-contractors who are paid a variable daily rate depending on the location and complexity of the construction project. The system used to process the payments to sub-contractors developed a fault during the year and many sub-contractors were paid at incorrect daily rates. The directors estimate that £340,000 was overpaid and they have recorded a receivable for this amount at 31 March 20X4. At the time of completion of the audit, £25,000 had been received in respect of this balance. Your firm's enquiries during the audit revealed that Gable has not had any success in contacting any of the sub-contractors that are still to reimburse the company as they no longer undertake work for Gable. The directors refuse to include an allowance for doubtful debts in respect of the outstanding amount.

Gable's total assets at 31 March 20X4 are £42.3 million and profit before tax for the year then ended is £7.6 million.

Hip Ltd (Hip)

The managing director of Hip refused permission for your firm to contact Dome Ltd (Dome), a customer, to confirm the balance of £185,000 which was outstanding at 31 March 20X4. She claimed that the relationship between the two companies was particularly sensitive and that she did not want to upset that relationship. At the time of completion of the audit, £15,000 had been received in respect of the outstanding balance and the managing director is confident that Dome will pay all outstanding amounts. No alternative audit procedures were available to establish the existence of the debt.

Hip's total assets at 31 March 20X4 are £5.2 million and profit before tax for the year then ended is £1.5 million.

Requirement

For each of the situations outlined above, state whether or not you would modify the audit opinion. Give reasons for your conclusions and describe the modifications, if any, to each auditor's report.

(10 marks)

Total: 23 marks

33 Speedy Shifters plc, Letterbox Group Ltd

33.1 Speedy Shifters plc

You are responsible for the external audit of Speedy Shifters plc (Speedy), a haulage contractor operating from a head office and 65 depots throughout the UK. During the external audit for the year ended 30 November 20X4, you identified the following significant internal control deficiencies:

(1) Speedy does not keep a list of approved suppliers from which to purchase replacement parts for its fleet of trucks and vans.

(2) Speedy does not have a business continuity plan to enable it to recover its management information and finance systems quickly in the event of a systems failure.

(3) Drivers at some depots are regularly scheduled to exceed the legal limit for driving hours, because of a shortage of drivers.

(4) The audit committee has not complied with its own terms of reference which require it to:

- approve annual plans of work to be undertaken by the internal audit function; and

- monitor the effectiveness of the internal audit function through the use of performance measures.

Requirement

Draft points for inclusion in your firm's report to those charged with governance and management at Speedy. For each internal control deficiency identified above, you should outline the possible consequence(s) of the deficiency and provide recommendation(s) to address each deficiency. You should present your answer using the following subheadings:

(a) No approved supplier list
(b) No business continuity plan
(c) Truck drivers exceed legal limit for driving hours
(d) Internal audit plans and monitoring   **(14 marks)**

33.2 Letterbox Group Ltd

Your firm is the external auditor of Letterbox Group Ltd (Letterbox) for the year ended 30 November 20X4. Letterbox is an international trading group with a head office in London. On 1 November 20X4, Letterbox acquired 100% of the ordinary share capital of Pampas Holdings (Pampas), a company operating in South America, which is audited by Santos, another firm of external auditors.

Your enquiries have found that Santos will not grant your firm access to its external audit working papers nor provide any other information in respect of their audit of Pampas. The directors of Letterbox have stated that your firm will not be given access to the accounting records of Pampas and have refused to disclose further information about the activities of Pampas.

Letterbox's draft financial statements show consolidated profit before tax for the year ended 30 November 20X4 of £19.2 million. Included within this figure is profit before tax of £2.4 million in respect of one month's trading for Pampas.

Requirements

(a) Discuss the implications of the above for the auditor's report on the consolidated financial statements of Letterbox for the year ended 30 November 20X4.

(b) Discuss whether or not it is appropriate for your firm to continue to act as Letterbox's external auditor.   **(6 marks)**

Total: 20 marks

34 Rescue24

Rescue24 is a UK not-for-profit charity whose activities involve the rescue and veterinary treatment of injured wild animals. The charity is required to undergo an external audit in accordance with the constitution in its governing document and you are the audit senior responsible for the audit for the year ended 30 June 20X5.

Due to a reduction in government spending, Rescue24 has experienced a decline in the level of government grants available for its activities. It has also found it increasingly difficult to obtain financial donations through its traditional fundraising activities of street collections and telephone campaigns. In December 20X4, the trustees decided to meet a shortfall in Rescue24's funding using crowdfunding which is the practice of obtaining funding by raising monetary contributions via the internet. Rescue24 chose to raise funds through the crowdfunding website, crowdcause.com, and launched a campaign on the website in January 20X5. However, the trustees had no experience of this type of fundraising activity and failed to put in place any promotional or marketing support for the campaign. The lack of public awareness meant the campaign failed and no funds were received by Rescue24.

In March 20X5, the trustees negotiated an increase in Rescue24's overdraft facility and obtained a bank loan, secured on Rescue24's only premises, to meet the shortfall in funds and enable Rescue24 to continue its activities. However, the draft statement of financial activities for the year ended 30 June 20X5 shows that expenditure exceeded income for the year and the draft balance sheet at 30 June 20X5 shows a net liability position. As a result of the financial issues arising in the year, three of Rescue24's five trustees and its fundraising manager resigned from their positions.

During the audit, you identified the following internal control deficiencies:

(1) Collection boxes used during street collections were not sealed or numbered and collectors were responsible for counting and recording proceeds from their own collection boxes.

(2) Certain veterinary drugs were not stored in a secure lockable container, in contravention of the requirements of the Veterinary Medicines Directorate.

Requirements

34.1 For each internal control deficiency identified in above, draft points for inclusion in your firm's report to the trustees. For each deficiency, outline the possible consequence(s) of the deficiency and provide recommendations to address it. You should present your answer using the following subheadings:

    (a) Collection boxes
    (b) Veterinary drugs   **(7 marks)**

34.2 Identify and explain the factors which give rise to an uncertainty about the going concern status of Rescue24.   **(7 marks)**

34.3 Assuming your firm concludes there is an uncertainty about the going concern status of Rescue24, explain the potential implications for the audit opinion on the financial statements of Rescue24 for the year ended 30 June 20X5 if the trustees:

    (a) make appropriate disclosures; or
    (b) do not make any disclosures.

    Your answer should describe the effects, if any, on your firm's auditor's report in each situation.   **(6 marks)**

                                      Total: 20 marks

35 Mint Ltd, Coriander Ltd, Basil Ltd

Described below are three situations that have arisen at unrelated external audit clients of your firm, a firm of ICAEW Chartered Accountants. The year end in each case is 31 October 20X5.

Mint Ltd (Mint)

Your audit work concluded that the accounting records relating to cash sales were inadequate. Cash sales comprise 7% of Mint's recorded revenue.

Coriander Ltd (Coriander)

The financial statements of Coriander include inventory at cost of £1.3 million. The inventory was purchased on 1 October 20X5 in anticipation of fulfilling a large order for a customer. However, the customer went into liquidation on 5 November 20X5 and was unable to complete any part of the transaction with Coriander. On 30 November 20X5 Coriander sold the inventory for £1 million. The draft financial statements show that Coriander's profit before tax is £12.9 million and total assets are £39.1 million.

Basil Ltd (Basil)

The financial statements of Basil show the purchase of a motor vehicle from Saffron Ltd (Saffron), for £19,000, which has been appropriately included in non-current assets. While reviewing Basil's board minutes you discovered that Saffron is owned and managed by the husband of Basil's managing director. The directors of Basil refuse to disclose the transaction in the notes to the financial statements as they claim that the amount is too small to warrant disclosure. The draft financial statements of Basil show total assets of £7.5 million.

Requirements

35.1 For each of the situations outlined above, state whether or not you would modify the audit opinion. Give reasons for your conclusions and describe the modifications, if any, to each auditor's report. **(11 marks)**

35.2 Describe the possible consequences for your firm if an inappropriate audit opinion on financial statements is issued and outline the quality control procedures your firm should implement to reduce the risk of issuing an inappropriate audit opinion. **(7 marks)**

Total: 18 marks

March 2016 exam questions

36 Short form questions

36.1 During a recent external audit performed by your firm, a trainee ICAEW Chartered Accountant altered the sample of trade receivable balances initially selected for testing, at the request of the audited entity's financial controller, an ICAEW Chartered Accountant. The financial controller threatened the trainee that he would tell the audit engagement partner that the trainee was incompetent if he did not comply with the request. Therefore, the trainee replaced trade receivable balances for which no cash was received after the year end with balances for which cash had been received.

Identify and explain the ethical issues arising in this situation. **(4 marks)**

36.2 The directors of your firm's external audit client Gruber Ltd (Gruber), an accounting software company, have approached your firm with a proposal to sell Gruber's software to your firm's other external audit clients. Under the proposal Gruber would supply the software and your firm would be responsible for its implementation at each client. The directors of Gruber expect to increase software sales by 50% as a result of this arrangement.

State, with reasons, whether it is appropriate for your firm to accept the directors' proposal. **(4 marks)**

36.3 Padding LLP (Padding) has tendered for the external audit of Clyde plc. Padding has proposed a fee which is less than the market rate in the hope that the firm will subsequently be awarded the more lucrative tax and advisory work for Clyde plc.

Identify and explain the ethical issues posed by Padding's proposal. **(4 marks)**

36.4 State what is meant by 'performance materiality' and outline why this is set by external auditors. **(2 marks)**

36.5 During the external audit of Bushat Ltd it was discovered that, on a number of occasions, adjustments were made, by the payroll clerk, to standing data relating to employees on the payroll system on the oral authority of the human resources manager.

Outline the possible consequences of this internal control deficiency and provide recommendations to remedy the deficiency. **(3 marks)**

36.6 List the differences between a report prepared by a practitioner for an engagement to review financial statements and the report prepared by auditors for an external audit engagement. **(3 marks)**

37 Marmalade Ltd

Your firm has recently been appointed as the external auditor of Marmalade Ltd (Marmalade). You are the audit manager responsible for planning the external audit for the year ended 31 January 20X6. The engagement partner for the audit, Lucy Bond, has asked you to consider the following key areas of audit risk:

(1) Revenue
(2) Property, plant and equipment – freehold factory
(3) Inventory – finished goods

Marmalade designs and manufactures luxury luggage at its UK factory and sells its products through its website to customers around the world. Customers pay online in their local currency using a debit or credit card. Demand for Marmalade's luggage has increased following a recent rise in popularity amongst internet bloggers who like the fact that Marmalade frequently updates its luggage designs and colours.

To meet the increased demand, Marmalade expanded its production capacity during the current year by 25%, by converting the warehouse space in its freehold factory into additional manufacturing space. The conversion, along with repairs to the existing factory, was carried out by a building contractor, helped by some of Marmalade's employees. The conversion was completed at the end of August 20X5. Marmalade has included the associated costs in the cost of the freehold factory in property, plant and equipment.

In February 20X5, to compensate for the loss of warehouse space, Marmalade engaged a fulfilment company Pastuzo Ltd (Pastuzo), to store and operate the despatch of finished inventory to customers and subsequent returns. Marmalade despatches finished inventory directly from its factory to Pastuzo's warehouse and Pastuzo views customers' orders through an interface with Marmalade's website. Pastuzo maintains inventory records for finished goods on behalf of Marmalade and provides real-time reporting to Marmalade on inventory movements and quantities on hand. Marmalade has included the inventory quantities reported by Pastuzo on 31 January 20X6 in its draft financial statements at that date. Marmalade's employees performed an inventory count at Pastuzo's premises on 31 May 20X5 but no other counts have taken place. Pastuzo's own auditor is able to provide an assurance report regarding the adequacy of Pastuzo's controls over inventory managed on behalf of third parties.

Historically, Marmalade has recognised a provision for returns in its financial statements equal to 5% of website sales made in December and January. Since February 20X5, Marmalade has experienced an increase in the volume of returns due to Pastuzo despatching incorrect products to customers. However, Marmalade's directors believe this issue is now resolved and therefore propose to include the provision for returns on the same basis as in prior years.

In April 20X5, Marmalade won a contract to design and supply cabin crew luggage for TaxiDair Ltd (TaxiDair), a large commercial airline. The contract runs for two years from 1 May 20X5 and requires Marmalade to supply 4,500 units of luggage during the contract period. Under the terms of the contract, TaxiDair is required to make four six-monthly payments of £281,500 and the first payment was made on 1 May 20X5. Marmalade had completed and despatched 1,200 units by 31 January 20X6.

Lucy has provided you with the following draft extracts from the financial statements of Marmalade to be used as part of your consideration of the key areas of audit risk:

Statement of profit or loss for the year ended 31 January (extract)

	20X6 (draft) £'000	20X5 (audited) £'000
Revenue		
Website sales (net of provision for returns)	9,617	7,124
TaxiDair contract	563	–
	10,180	7,124
Cost of sales	(5,169)	(4,277)
Gross profit	5,011	2,847

Statement of financial position as at 31 January (extract)

	20X6 (draft) £'000	20X5 (audited) £'000
Property, plant and equipment		
Freehold factory (see note below)	6,330	3,240
Inventory – finished goods	1,797	850

Note: Freehold factory	20X6 (draft) £'000	20X5 (audited) £'000
Cost	7,800	4,500
Accumulated depreciation brought forward	(1,260)	(1,080)
Depreciation charge for the year	(210)	(180)
Carrying amount at 31 January	6,330	3,240

Requirements

37.1 State the purposes of performing analytical procedures when planning an external audit and when undertaking substantive procedures. **(4 marks)**

37.2 Justify why the items listed by the engagement partner have been identified as key areas of audit risk and, for each item, describe the procedures that should be included in the audit plan to address those risks. You should present your answer using the following subheadings:

(a) Revenue
(b) Property, plant and equipment – freehold factory
(c) Inventory – finished goods **(28 marks)**

37.3 Outline the key matters that should be discussed with the junior members of any audit team before performing the planned audit procedures. **(5 marks)**

Total: 37 marks

38 Underground Ltd

Your firm has recently been invited to accept appointment as external auditor of Underground Ltd (Underground) for the year ending 31 March 20X6. The audit has been requested by Underground's bank. The engagement partner considering the invitation has asked you to gather information about Underground and its directors to help her reach a decision on whether to accept the appointment.

You have documented the following relevant information:

Underground makes and supplies fresh sandwiches from its UK factory. The company was incorporated on 1 April 20X5 having previously traded as a partnership owned by Judy and Jonathan Bird, husband and wife. The trade and assets of the partnership were sold to Underground by Judy and Jonathan in exchange for shares in Underground. The value of the shares issued by Underground exceeded the value of the assets by £1.8 million and this has been included as goodwill in the financial statements of Underground. Judy and Jonathan are the only directors and shareholders of Underground.

Judy and Jonathan previously worked at Hill Snacks Ltd (Hill) where they were customer service managers. They left Hill and formed their business partnership in June 20X4 to supply sandwiches to the London stores of a large UK supermarket chain, Notting Ltd (Notting). Notting was previously a customer of Hill. However, Judy spent a number of months, while still working at Hill, persuading Notting's purchasing director to move Notting's business to them by promising to undercut Hill's prices.

Sandwiches are now supplied by Underground to Notting's stores throughout the UK under a three-year contract which commenced on 1 June 20X5. The contract specifies situations in which Notting may terminate the contract early, which include poor quality and failure to deliver quantities ordered. Underground has also won a few smaller contracts but supplies to Notting are expected to account for at least 70% of Underground's revenue while the contract is in force.

The growth in Underground's business has been funded by a bank loan. The loan covenant requires Underground to maintain a current ratio of 1.8:1.

Underground makes sandwiches from fresh ingredients which are delivered daily by its suppliers. The storage and production of fresh food is highly regulated in the UK. On 1 March 20X6 Underground received a warning after a routine inspection by the regulator identified that, due to a mechanical defect, Underground's refrigerator temperatures were too high. Underground has been told to correct the problem before 30 April 20X6, when a further inspection will take place.

At a meeting with Judy on 1 March 20X6, she told you that she has used spreadsheets to maintain Underground's accounting records. However, she has found that these have become increasingly inadequate due to the size of the business. She also confided that the setting up of Underground and the rapid growth in business has been very stressful for herself and Jonathan. Consequently, they have decided to divorce and Judy is considering leaving the business and selling her shares to Jonathan.

The directors of Underground have also requested that your firm undertakes a non-audit engagement to advise on an appropriate valuation of Judy's shares in Underground.

Requirements

38.1 Explain the relevance of each item of information, as documented in the box above, to your firm's decision on whether to accept appointment as Underground's external auditor for the year ending 31 March 20X6. **(18 marks)**

38.2 Assuming your firm accepts appointment as external auditor of Underground, explain the conflict of interest and self-interest threat which may arise if it also accepts the non-audit engagement requested by the directors. Outline the safeguards, if any, which should be put in place to mitigate those threats. **(7 marks)**

Total: 25 marks

39 Brown Ltd, Bear Ltd, Windsor Ltd, Peru Ltd

Described below are situations which have arisen at four unrelated clients of your firm.

Brown Ltd (Brown)

During the external audit of Brown for the year ended 31 December 20X5 you discover a letter dated 1 February 20X6 from the administrator of Duffel Ltd (Duffel), a customer of Brown. The letter informs Brown that Duffel is in administration and that the amounts due to Brown will not be paid. Brown's financial statements include a trade receivable due from Duffel of £750,000. The directors refuse to make an allowance against this because the administrator's letter was not received until after the year end. Brown's draft financial statements for the year ended 31 December 20X5 show profit before tax of £3.8 million and total assets of £29.6 million.

Bear plc (Bear)

During the external audit of Bear for the year ended 31 December 20X5 you have read the information contained in the Chairman's Statement which includes a statement that all Bear's products are fair trade certified. However, a number of new product lines introduced by Bear during 20X5 have not been certified by the independent fair trade body. The directors refuse to amend the Chairman's Statement as they claim they are currently in the process of obtaining certification and are concerned about the impact on the company's reputation if they do not include this statement.

Windsor Ltd (Windsor)

Your firm has been appointed as the external auditor of Windsor for the year ended 31 December 20X5. Windsor is required to have an audit of its financial statements for the first time as it had previously satisfied the criteria for exemption from mandatory audit. The financial statements for the year ended 31 December 20X4 were not audited. However, your firm has obtained sufficient appropriate evidence that the current year's financial statements and the opening balances do not contain material misstatements.

Peru Ltd (Peru)

Your firm has completed an engagement to review prospective financial information, prepared by the directors of Peru, for submission to the company's bank in support of a loan application. The bank requested an independent examination of the profit forecasts for the three years ending 31 December 20X8. Your firm has concluded that, while the prospective information is correctly prepared on the basis of management's assumptions, the assumptions made in respect of revenue growth are highly unrealistic.

Requirements

39.1 For each of the situations described above, outline, with reasons, the implications for your firm's audit or assurance reports. **(10 marks)**

39.2 Describe the caveat, concerning the achievability of results indicated by Peru's prospective financial information, that your firm should include in its assurance report and state the reasons for its inclusion. **(3 marks)**

39.3 Explain how audit and assurance firms can reduce their exposure to claims from unforeseen parties who rely on the firm's audit or assurance reports. **(5 marks)**

Total: 18 marks

June 2016 exam questions

40 Short form questions

40.1 Larch LLP (Larch) is a recently established firm of ICAEW Chartered Accountants specialising in audit and assurance work. Larch has three partners and 20 staff.

List the actions that Larch must take to comply with the Money Laundering Regulations.

(2 marks)

40.2 Your firm is the external auditor of Willow Aquatics Ltd (Willow) for the year ended 31 May 20X6. Willow is a retailer of a range of leisure boats. In recent years, Willow has sold an average of 200 boats each month. Customers pay 40% of the selling price when the order is placed and the balance on delivery of the boat. It is Willow's policy to recognise revenue on delivery of the boat to the customer.

Describe the audit procedures that should be included in the audit plan, for the year ended 31 May 20X6, to address the risk of revenue misstatement. **(4 marks)**

40.3 Fraudulent activities can be carried out through the use of journal entries.

State the characteristics of journal entries that external auditors should select for testing to identify fraudulent activities. **(3 marks)**

40.4 Your firm is the external auditor of Chestnut Ltd (Chestnut), a manufacturer of vacuum cleaners, for the year ended 31 May 20X6. Historically, all vacuum cleaners were sold with a two-year warranty against defective materials and workmanship. In June 20X5, Chestnut increased the warranty period to five years to match the warranties offered by its competitors. Chestnut includes a provision for such warranties in its financial statements. The provision is based on the finance director's assessment of future claims.

You have been provided with the following relevant extracts from the financial statements:

	20X6 (draft) £'000	20X5 (audited) £'000
Revenue	28,990	25,260
Non-current provision for warranty claims	289	253
Current provision for warranty claims	319	316

Explain the factors which could indicate that the provision for warranty claims may be materially misstated. **(4 marks)**

40.5 Your firm has received notice from Ash plc (Ash), a listed company, that your firm will not be re-appointed as external auditor when its term of office expires as the audit committee of Ash has recommended the appointment of another firm.

Set out the rights and responsibilities of your firm, including those under the Companies Act 2006, relating to the change in appointment. **(3 marks)**

40.6 During the audit of Elm Ltd, a building contractor, you discovered that references were not always obtained when new plumbers and electricians were employed.

Outline the possible consequences of this internal control deficiency and provide recommendations to remedy this deficiency. **(4 marks)**

41 Flint plc

Your firm is the external auditor of Flint plc (Flint), a listed company, for the year ending 31 July 20X6. Flint manufactures aeroplane engines and replacement spare engine parts in the UK. The spare parts are stored in Flint's UK warehouse and then shipped to its worldwide subsidiaries for installation in customers' engines.

You are planning the audit for the year ending 31 July 20X6. Susan Green, the engagement partner, has asked you to consider the following key areas of audit risk in Flint's individual company financial statements:

(1)   Going concern
(2)   Inventory of spare parts stored in the UK

Additionally, Susan said that she is concerned about the risk of material misstatement due to fraud.

She has provided you with the following information about the company:

- Flint agrees contracts with governments and customers in the aviation industry following a bidding process. In many of the countries where Flint operates, the use of commercial intermediaries (agents) in contract bidding is either required by law or is standard practice. The contract states a fixed price for the supply of new engines and a fixed price for the spare parts over the life of the engine which can be many years. Engines are manufactured to order once a contract is agreed.

- In 20X3, a competitor released a new generation of more efficient engines and, as a result, Flint has experienced a fall in demand for its engines and spare parts. Consequently, Flint has recently published a number of downward revisions to its profit forecasts during the year and there have been significant falls in its quoted share price. In response, Flint has invested heavily in the development of its own range of more efficient engines and it expects these to be ready by 20X8.

- The management of Flint is now seeking to increase the company's overdraft and loan facilities and the company's bank requires the audited financial statements to be available before considering Flint's request for the increased facilities. Flint's finance director has carried out an assessment of the company's ability to continue as a going concern, including preparation of profit and cash flow forecasts which indicate that the company can meet its debts as they fall due. The forecasts assume the bank facilities will be increased to the level requested.

- Components used in the manufacture of spare parts are sourced from around the world and suppliers invoice in their local currency. Flint operates a perpetual inventory system for spare parts which is checked by periodic sample counting throughout the year by Flint's employees. As a result, the company does not undertake a full inventory count at the year end.

- The inventory system is fully integrated with the cost accounting system. Spare parts are manufactured to a standard specification. The cost accounting system records the cost of components, labour and production overheads for each spare part. Each week, the inventory system generates an inventory valuation listing. The inventory valuation listing includes the cost and quantity on hand for each spare part.

- In December 20X5, the UK Serious Fraud Office commenced an investigation into bribery and corruption in Flint's worldwide activities. In March 20X6 an internal audit review found a number of payments to new customers and agents which were made before the contracts were awarded.

Susan has provided you with the following extracts from Flint's individual company financial statements:

Statement of profit or loss for the year ending 31 July (extract)

	20X6 (forecast) £m	20X5 (audited) £m
Revenue	4,850	6,277
Cost of sales	(3,900)	(4,632)
Gross profit	950	1,645
Loss before tax	(1,200)	(10)

Statement of financial position as at 31 July (extract)

	20X6 (forecast) £m	20X5 (audited) £m
Current assets		
Inventory of spare parts	1,050	858
Non-current liabilities		
Bank loan	0	990
Current liabilities		
Bank overdraft (facility £500 million)	475	10
Bank loan (repayable 30 September 20X6)	990	0
Net current liabilities	2,750	153

Flint is required to prepare group financial statements for the year ending 31 July 20X6 and your firm will also act as group auditor. Flint has five subsidiary companies operating overseas, with minimal supervision from UK management and with their own local external auditors. The subsidiaries are responsible for servicing the aeroplane engines, installing the spare parts in aeroplane engines and maintaining customer and agent relationships. Two of the subsidiary companies' external auditors were changed during the year following a tender exercise to reduce audit costs. Susan has asked that you draft instructions to be sent to the subsidiaries' auditors and draw up proposals for the review of their audit work. Each of the subsidiaries' financial statements are material to the group financial statements.

41.1 (a) Outline the responsibilities of those charged with governance and external auditors in relation to the prevention and detection of fraud.

(b) Identify the factors, in the scenario, that increase the risk of material misstatement due to fraud and, for each factor, explain why it is a concern for your firm. **(10 marks)**

41.2 Justify why the items listed by the engagement partner have been identified as key areas of audit risk and, for each item, describe the procedures that should be included in the audit plan to address those risks. You should present your answer using the following subheadings:

(a) Going concern
(b) Inventory of spare parts stored in the UK **(20 marks)**

41.3 In respect of the audit work of the subsidiaries' auditors:

(a) list **five** items that should be included in the instructions to be sent to the subsidiaries' auditors that are relevant to the planning of their audit work and for each item state, briefly, the reason why it should be included; and

(b) explain why your firm should evaluate the sufficiency and appropriateness of the audit evidence obtained by the subsidiaries' auditors and outline how your firm should undertake this evaluation. **(10 marks)**

Total: 40 marks

42 Shentan plc, Maxfield Ltd, Newbee Group plc

Your firm is a long-established firm of ICAEW Chartered Accountants and has six partners operating from two offices. Described below are situations which have arisen in respect of the provision of services by your firm to three external audit clients who are competitors within the same market sector.

Shentan plc (Shentan)

The engagement partner responsible for the audit of Shentan, a listed company, was rotated after five years and immediately became the relationship partner with responsibility for managing the firm's overall relationship with the client.

Maxfield Ltd (Maxfield)

Maxfield has requested that your firm provides a member of staff to help with the preparation of the annual financial statements.

Newbee Group plc (Newbee)

Your firm audits the financial statements of Newbee, a listed company, and its wholly-owned subsidiary Prospect Ltd (Prospect). The audit fees for Newbee and Prospect are £95,000 and £47,000 respectively. In addition, your firm undertakes an annual taxation engagement for both companies with fees totalling £45,000. During the current year the firm undertook a one-off consultancy engagement. The total fee for this engagement was £129,000. Your firm's total annual fee income from all its clients is £2,010,000.

Requirements

42.1 Explain why objectivity and independence are important principles in the context of an external audit engagement. **(3 marks)**

42.2 Identify and explain the threats to your firm's objectivity presented by each of the situations above and list the steps your firm should take to address those threats. **(10 marks)**

42.3 Explain the ethical issues arising within your firm caused by acting for all three competitor companies identified above, and outline the safeguards that your firm should have in place to address these issues. **(4 marks)**

Total: 17 marks

September 2016 exam questions

43 Short form questions

43.1 Explain how the use of separate engagement teams mitigates the threats to compliance with the fundamental principles, as set out in the ICAEW *Code of Ethics*, when an audit firm:

(a) provides non-audit services to an external audit client; and

(b) acts for competing clients. **(4 marks)**

43.2 Ronnie San, a trainee ICAEW Chartered Accountant, is working on the external audit of Persow Ltd (Persow). Ronnie previously worked on the external audit of Majin Ltd (Majin), a car fleet management company. Persow is searching for a new car fleet management supplier and Ronnie has proposed that his audit firm recommends Majin to Persow in return for a fee from Majin for the introduction.

Explain the ethical issues arising for the audit firm in respect of Ronnie's proposal. **(3 marks)**

43.3 Bobby Core is an employee of Mem Ltd (Mem), an external audit client of your firm. Bobby has informed the audit manager that some of Mem's employees, working in the retail division, are paid directly out of cash receipts. Bobby believes Mem's retail manager is making these cash payments to conceal the level of employee costs from senior management and to avoid paying payroll taxes in respect of these employees.

State the actions that should be taken by the audit manager in respect of the comments made by Bobby. **(4 marks)**

43.4 Your firm has been invited by Caul Ltd (Caul) to accept an engagement to examine and report on prospective financial information (PFI). The PFI has been prepared by Caul's directors to help in evaluating capital investment for its factory in India.

Identify the factors that will affect the calculation of your firm's fee for this engagement. **(3 marks)**

43.5 Emow Ltd (Emow), a national chain of estate agents, has applied to its bank for an increase in its overdraft facility. The bank has requested a cash flow forecast for the year ending 30 September 20X7 and an independent examination of and report on the cash flow forecast. Your firm has agreed to perform the independent examination and prepare the report.

Emow has 25 UK offices each of which charge customers a fee for selling their homes. The standard fee is 2% of the house sale price achieved but each office can agree discounts with individual customers. Customers pay fees to Emow on completion of each sale. House prices vary in the UK depending on location. The UK housing market is also seasonal with more houses available for sale between April and September compared with October to March.

For the independent examination of the cash flow forecast, state the specific matters you would consider when examining fee income for reasonableness. **(4 marks)**

43.6 The International Auditing and Assurance Standards Board (IAASB) included monitoring of 'the various applications of data analytics and the relationship to the audit' in its work plan for 2015/16.

Outline how data analytics might impact on the conduct of an external audit engagement.

(2 marks)

44 Thought Train Ltd

Your firm has recently been appointed as the external auditor of Thought Train Ltd (TT), a market research company. Its head office is in the UK with 12 other offices based in mainland Europe and Asia. Each TT office is run autonomously by a local management team.

You are the audit senior responsible for the audit of TT's financial statements for the year ended 31 July 20X6. Your firm has offices in all of the locations where TT operates. The engagement partner for the TT audit, Joy Anderson, has asked you to consider the following key areas of audit risk:

(1) Revenue
(2) Employee costs and external consultants' fees included in cost of sales
(3) Trade receivables

Each TT office maintains its own electronic accounting records in its local currency, including receivables and payables ledgers and payroll. These accounting records are integrated with accounting software managed by TT's UK head office. The accounting software automatically translates each office's transactions and balances using exchange rates determined and input by the UK financial controller. Original documents, such as sales and purchase invoices, are stored by each TT office.

Each TT office undertakes market research projects for corporate customers based on an agreed statement of work detailing the research to be undertaken. A fixed fee is agreed with each customer when the statement of work and a project plan are finalised and signed by the customer. Customers are invoiced the full fee, in their local currency, on completion of the project. Credit terms are 30 days. At the year end, a manager at each TT office calculates and notifies the UK financial controller of the amount of accrued revenue to be recognised in the financial statements. The accrued revenue calculations are based on each manager's estimate of the proportion of work completed for any projects in progress at 31 July. These calculations are not checked by the UK financial controller.

Employees in each office are paid a salary and an annual bonus based on the profit before tax generated by the office in which they work. In addition, TT uses a large number of external consultants to provide expertise for specific projects. Consultants invoice their local TT office for the time spent on a project. An estimate for accrued consultants' fees at 31 July is calculated by each TT office and notified to the UK financial controller for inclusion in the financial statements. TT employees are required to keep timesheets to allow TT office managers to monitor the progress of each project. However, no time records are maintained for external consultants who often submit invoices many months after the completion of a project.

Following a meeting with TT's UK financial controller, Joy Anderson has informed you that Jangles Ltd (Jangles), one of TT's major international customers, has refused to pay the invoice for its most recent project as it believes the work is of poor quality. The amount due from Jangles, included in trade receivables, is £725,000. The work was performed by TT's Hong Kong office, which was reorganised in March 20X6 due to the resignation of a number of its senior managers.

Joy has also provided you with the following draft extracts from the financial statements of TT, as prepared by the UK financial controller, and additional information relevant to your consideration of the key areas of audit risk:

Statement of profit or loss for the year ended 31 July (extract)

	20X6 (draft) £'000	20X5 (audited) £'000
Revenue	120,716	101,514
Cost of sales *	(52,154)	(50,899)
Gross profit	68,562	50,615

Note	20X6 (draft) £'000	20X5 (audited) £'000
* Cost of sales includes:		
Employee costs	20,700	21,965
External consultants' fees	20,125	19,800

Statement of financial position as at 31 July (extract)

	20X6 (draft) £'000	20X5 (audited) £'000
Trade receivables	14,883	9,291

Additional information

	Year ended 31 July 20X6	Year ended 31 July 20X5
Average number of employees in the year	312	308
Total number of market research projects in the year	1,290	1,245

Requirements

44.1 Set out the benefits and limitations of using analytical procedures at the planning stage of an external audit. **(5 marks)**

44.2 Set out the matters you should consider, as part of your audit planning, arising from TT operating offices outside the UK. **(5 marks)**

44.3 Justify why the items listed by the engagement partner have been identified as key areas of audit risk and, for each item, describe the procedures that should be included in the audit plan to address those risks. You should present your answer using the following subheadings:

(a) Revenue
(b) Employee costs and external consultants' fees
(c) Trade receivables **(25 marks)**

Total: 35 marks

45 Byng LLP

Byng LLP (Byng), a medium-sized audit and assurance firm, provides services to non-listed clients only. Byng's two largest clients are Wagon Ltd (Wagon) and Rocket Ltd (Rocket) from which Byng earns the following fee income:

	Wagon £'000	Rocket £'000
Annual external audit	920	880
Annual tax services	575	550
One-off engagements	560	145
Total	2,055	1,575

Byng's total annual fee income, including fees from Wagon and Rocket, is £16 million. Byng's other clients generate total annual fee income of less than £1 million each. Bing is currently completing the external audits of Wagon's and Rocket's financial statements.

Wagon's financial statements and auditor's report, for the year ended 31 July 20X6, are due to be signed on 12 September 20X6. However, audit procedures have identified a number of internal control issues relating to new accounting software implemented by Wagon during the year. The engagement partner, Riley Fritz, has advised the directors of Wagon that the auditor's report will not be signed before 30 September 20X6, to allow time for additional audit procedures. Wagon's directors have responded that the signing of the auditor's report cannot be delayed. This is because Wagon is required to present its audited financial statements to its bank, on 13 September 20X6, in support of a loan application. Wagon's directors have stated that any delay will result in your firm not being reappointed as external auditor at Wagon's next annual general meeting. Riley was unaware that Wagon's bank had requested the audited financial statements.

The financial controller of Rocket left the company suddenly during the course of the audit. The directors of Rocket have offered the role of financial controller to the audit manager who has informed the engagement partner that he intends to accept the offer.

Requirements

45.1 Set out Byng's responsibilities if it is not reappointed as external auditor at Wagon's next annual general meeting.   **(2 marks)**

45.2 Identify and explain the significant matters arising, including any professional and ethical issues, in relation to the services provided to Wagon and Rocket. State any steps Byng should take to address those matters.   **(13 marks)**

45.3 Identify the parties to whom Byng may be liable if an inappropriate audit opinion is provided on the audited financial statements of Wagon. Describe the methods available to Byng to limit its liability to such parties.   **(5 marks)**

Total: 20 marks

46 Sednass Ltd, Gustis Ltd, Raef Ltd

Described below are situations which have arisen at three unrelated clients of your firm.

Sednass Ltd (Sednass)

Your firm is the external auditor of Sednass for the year ended 30 June 20X6. Sednass maintains a perpetual inventory system and uses this to calculate the value of inventory for inclusion in its year-end financial statements. In July 20X6, a computer virus corrupted the data held on the inventory system resulting in the loss of records relating to the value of inventory at 30 June 20X6. Sednass' antivirus software was out of date and no recent back up of data were stored because the IT manager responsible for this process had been on extended leave. The directors have included an estimate for inventory of £1.8 million in the financial statements but your firm has been unable to corroborate this value.

The draft financial statements show that Sednass' profit before tax is £16.2 million.

Gustdis Ltd (Gustdis)

Your firm is the external auditor of Gustdis. The financial statements include a note relating to a significant uncertainty over going concern. The uncertainty has arisen because a major customer has threatened to terminate its contract early due to Gustdis failing to comply with service levels required by the contract. Contracted service levels are not regularly monitored by Gustdis. Your firm has concluded that the note included in the financial statements is appropriate and adequate.

Raef Ltd (Raef)

Your firm has been engaged to perform an independent review and to report on the financial statements of Raef for the year ended 30 June 20X6. Raef is not required to have an external audit under the Companies Act 2006 but Raef's bank has requested the review. Your firm identified payments made in July 20X6, totalling £120,000, which related to goods received in May 20X6. Invoices relating to these goods were posted to the payables ledger in July 20X6. Raef does not reconcile supplier statements and did not identify the invoices until after the year end. The directors of Raef have refused to include an accrual in the financial statements in respect of these invoices.

The draft financial statements show that Raef's profit before tax is £70,000.

Requirements

46.1 Explain the attributes of auditors' communications to those charged with governance that make such communications effective when reporting deficiencies in internal control identified during an audit.   **(4 marks)**

46.2 In each of the situations outlined above:

    (a)   identify the internal control deficiencies. For each deficiency, outline the possible consequence(s) of each deficiency and provide recommendation(s) to address it.

                                                                   (12 marks)

    (b)   state whether you would modify your firm's report. Give reasons for your conclusions and outline the modifications, if any, to each report.   **(9 marks)**

Total: 25 marks

December 2016 exam questions

47 Short form questions

47.1 Explain the benefits of the mandatory rotation of the appointment of audit firms. **(3 marks)**

47.2 Your firm is the external auditor of Storm Relief, a not-for-profit entity, whose main sources of revenue are cash donations received through the post and through collection boxes managed by volunteers.

List the internal controls that Storm Relief should have in place over cash donations received through the post and through collection boxes managed by volunteers. **(4 marks)**

47.3 Your firm has been the external auditor of both Langdon Ltd (Langdon) and Portdean Ltd (Portdean) for several years. Langdon has requested your assistance in determining an appropriate valuation for its business and has invited bids for its share capital. Portdean is considering making a bid for all of the share capital of Langdon and has also requested your assistance in valuing Langdon.

Identify and explain the principal threats to your firm's independence and objectivity which may arise from the situation described above.

Note: You are not required to list safeguards to mitigate those threats. **(3 marks)**

47.4 A cold review of the external audit file of one of your firm's clients identified that the audit documentation did not show any evidence that work performed by junior members of the audit team was reviewed by more senior members.

Explain why this deficiency was identified and describe the actions that your firm should take. **(3 marks)**

47.5 The managing director of Oldfield Ltd (Oldfield), an external audit client of your firm, has discovered that a warehouse manager made fictitious entries in Oldfield's inventory records to conceal the misappropriation of inventory costing £25,000. The managing director discovered the fraud as a result of an inventory count at which your firm was not present. He has contacted your firm to express his concern that the audit team did not discover this fraud during the external audit. The financial statements for the current year show revenue of £10 million and profit before tax of £1.5 million.

Explain why the managing director's expectation that the audit team should have discovered the fraud is unrealistic. **(4 marks)**

47.6 While reviewing the post year-end purchase invoices of Melchester Ltd (Melchester), an international engineering company, the audit senior discovered an invoice for a luxury cruise holiday costing £17,500. On enquiry, the audit senior was informed that the cruise was purchased for the managing director of Terino SpA (Terino). Terino is an Italian oil exploration company to which Melchester regularly submits tenders for work.

State, with reasons, the action to be taken by the audit senior. **(3 marks)**

48 United Cities Express plc

Your firm is the external auditor of United Cities Express plc (UCEP), a listed company.

UCEP's principal activity is the provision of parcel delivery services throughout the UK using its own fleet of lorries. The company operates a central distribution hub in the North of England and a network of 45 depots throughout the UK.

You are the audit senior and Julie Town, the engagement partner, has asked you to consider the following three key areas of audit risk:

(1) Going concern
(2) Provision for redundancy costs
(3) Non-current assets – lorries.

Julie has provided you with the following extracts from the draft financial statements:

Extract from draft statement of profit or loss for the year ended 30 November

	20X6 (draft) £'000	20X5 (audited) £'000
Revenue	106,502	112,998
Loss on sale of lorries	(1,200)	(875)
Depreciation charge for lorries	(2,312)	(2,350)
Loss before tax	(5,155)	(153)

Extract from draft statement of financial position as at 30 November

	20X6 (draft) £'000	20X5 (audited) £'000
Non-current assets		
Lorries	15,649	13,650
Non-current liabilities		
Bank loan	18,000	24,000
Current liabilities		
Overdraft (facility £20 million)	18,897	7,890
Bank loan	6,000	6,000
Provision for redundancy costs	3,000	–

In addition, Julie has provided you with the following information:

- Approximately 90% of revenue is generated from business customers. The remaining 10% comes from members of the public who send parcels from their local depot. Business customers have contracts that state the agreed price for delivering each size of parcel. The company's largest customer, WhiteNile, a popular internet retailer, generates 25% of UCEP's revenue and the contract between UCEP and WhiteNile is due to expire in May 20X7.

- Recent trading conditions have been difficult for UCEP. UCEP has not invested in the latest technology to sort and track parcels; it has lost business to its competitors who have invested in the latest technology and benefit from improved efficiency and reduced costs. Furthermore, internet-based retailers want to keep their costs low and are increasingly reluctant to pass on parcel delivery costs in full to their customers.

- UCEP has received extensive criticism in the media for failing to meet its well-publicised promise of delivering parcels within 24 hours. Existing machinery used to sort parcels is unable to deal with large parcels resulting in many of these parcels having to be sorted manually.

- On 31 October 20X6, UCEP's directors approved and announced a major reorganisation plan to return the company to profitable trading. The plan includes the closure of 25 depots and the rationalisation of the senior management team. Approximately 20% of the workforce will be made redundant over the next 12 months through a voluntary redundancy programme. The directors have requested that applications for voluntary redundancy are made by 31 December 20X6. Redundancy payments are calculated based on the employee's length of service and current salary. UCEP is offering an enhanced package with terms in excess of the statutory rates set by the UK government.

- The overdraft facility is due for review on 31 January 20X7 and the bank has requested audited financial statements by that date together with profit and cash flow forecasts for the three years ended 30 November 20X9. The bank loan is repayable in quarterly instalments of £1.5 million.

- In addition to routine maintenance, UCEP refurbishes its lorries every four years and replaces them every seven years. All costs associated with both purchasing and refurbishing the fleet of lorries, including time spent by UCEP's employees, is included in the cost of lorries in the non-current asset register. The cost less any estimated residual value is depreciated on a straight-line basis over the estimated useful life of the lorries.

During a meeting between Julie and the chairman of UCEP's audit committee, the chairman requested that:

(a) your firm assists with the recruitment of a new chief executive as UCEP's current chief executive is retiring in June 20X7

(b) your firm provides internal audit services for UCEP as the audit committee is unhappy with the performance of the firm currently providing these services; and

(c) Julie, who has been the engagement partner for five years, continues as the engagement partner.

The combined fee for the external audit and the services in (a) and (b) above will be less than 5% of your firm's total expected fee income.

Requirements

48.1 Justify why the items listed by the engagement partner have been identified as key areas of audit risk and, for each item, describe the procedures that should be included in the audit plan to address that risk. You should present your answer using the following subheadings:

(a) Going concern
(b) Provision for redundancy costs
(c) Non-current assets – lorries

(23 marks)

48.2 Explain the principal threats to the objectivity of your firm arising from the matters listed as (a) to (c) in the scenario and state how your firm should respond to those threats.

(11 marks)

48.3 Assuming your firm concludes that there is a significant uncertainty as to whether UCEP can continue as a going concern, state, with reasons, the implications for the auditor's report on UCEP's financial statements for the year ended 30 November 20X6 if the directors of UCEP:

(a) make adequate disclosures; or
(b) do not make any disclosures

in respect of the uncertainty.

(6 marks)

Total: 40 marks

49 Speedy Pedals Ltd

Your firm has been engaged by Speedy Pedals Ltd (SP) to undertake a review of and provide an assurance report on the interim financial information of SP for the six months ended 30 November 20X6. The terms of engagement include making enquiries of management and applying analytical and other review procedures to the financial information.

SP's principal activity is the manufacture of a range of affordable bicycles for children and adults. All bicycles are manufactured at the company's factory in the UK. Historically, raw materials and components were purchased from European suppliers. However, in July 20X6, SP started to buy the steel used in the bicycle frames from suppliers in China. All suppliers are paid in their local currency.

The range of bicycles available is updated each year to reflect current fashions. The bicycles are sold to independent retailers located throughout Europe who then sell them to the public. Retailers are invoiced in sterling on delivery and are required to pay SP within 30 days of invoice date. SP's revenue grew steadily at between 8% and 10% pa over the five years ended 30 November 20X5.

In June 20X6, SP launched a website which has e-commerce ordering and payment facilities. SP also launched a new range of high-specification bicycles, Super Speedys, targeted at the specialist cyclist. Super Speedys are assembled according to each customer's requirements. Customers can purchase the Super Speedys only through SP's website and are required to pay in full when they place their order.

In August 20X6, SP received notification of legal proceedings from a competitor claiming significant damages for an alleged infringement of the patent of the design of one of their children's bicycles. SP's patent lawyers are of the opinion that the claim has some merit.

The following is an extract from SP's interim financial information:

Extract from the statement of profit or loss for the six months ended 30 November

	Six months ended 30 November	
	20X6 £'000	20X5 £'000
Revenue		
Credit sales	8,858	8,235
Cash sales	817	0
	9,675	8,235
Cost of sales	(6,570)	(5,781)
Gross profit	3,105	2,454
Operating expenses	(2,193)	(1,649)
Profit from operations	912	805

Extract from the statement of financial position as at 30 November

	20X6 £'000	20X5 £'000
Current assets		
Inventories	1,923	1,314
Trade receivables	1,769	1,325
Current liabilities		
Trade payables	462	452

As part of your preliminary analytical procedures, you have calculated a number of ratios and have identified the following as matters of significance to discuss with SP's management:

	Six months ended 30 November	
	20X6 £'000	20X5 £'000
Increase in revenue	17.5%	8.5%
Gross profit margin	32.1%	29.8%
Operating margin	9.4%	9.8%
Inventory days	53.4 days	41.5 days
Trade receivables collection period	36.4 days	29.4 days
Trade payables payment period	27.9 days	32.0 days

Requirements

49.1 (a)   Using the information provided in the scenario, identify the enquiries you should make of the management of SP to ascertain the reasons for the changes in each of the ratios calculated as part of your preliminary analytical procedures.

(b)   List any documentation that should be requested from the management of SP that would be useful for your analytical and other review procedures.

Note: You are **not** required to calculate any additional ratios.   **(15 marks)**

49.2 Describe the differences between the **conclusion** expressed following an engagement to review financial information and the **opinion** expressed in an auditor's report on financial statements. Give reasons for these differences.   **(5 marks)**

Total: 20 marks

50   Classy Cars plc

Your firm has recently been appointed as external auditor of Classy Cars plc (Classy), a listed company, following the resignation of the previous auditor. Classy is a retailer of a range of new and used cars from sites in major UK cities. To secure the sale of a new car, Classy frequently takes a customer's used car in part exchange. The used car is then sold to another customer or is sent to an auction to be sold. This is your firm's first listed company client and its only client in the motor trade.

During the audit of the financial statements for the year ended 30 November 20X6, the following was discovered:

(a)   On a number of occasions, sales staff granted customer discounts in excess of authorised levels.

(b)   Classy publically claims that each used car is assessed against a checklist of 100 items to ensure that it is safe to drive. Workshop managers have stated that, because of insufficient time, some of these checks are rarely performed.

(c)   Inventories of used cars with a book value of £2.4 million at 30 November 20X6 were sold at auctions in December 20X6 for £0.9 million. The directors have refused to amend the financial statements as the amendment will cause the profit to fall below the level required for the payment of directors' bonuses.

The draft financial statements for the year ended 30 November 20X6 show profit before tax of £22.9 million and total assets of £121 million.

Requirements

50.1 Explain why the risk of expressing an inappropriate opinion may be higher in your firm's first audit of Classy's financial statements. Outline how your firm can mitigate this risk.

(8 marks)

50.2 In respect of the internal control deficiencies listed in (a) and (b), draft points for inclusion in your firm's report to those charged with governance and management of Classy. For each deficiency, you should outline the possible consequence(s) of the deficiency and provide recommendations to address it. You should present your answer using the following subheadings:

(a) Excessive discounts

(b) 100 item checklist

(8 marks)

50.3 In respect of the matter described in (c), state whether or not you would modify the audit opinion. Give reasons for your conclusion and outline the modifications, if any, to the auditor's report.

(4 marks)

Total: 20 marks

March 2017 exam questions

51 Short form questions

51.1 Your firm is the external auditor of Shan plc (Shan), a large listed entity. The directors of Shan have requested that your firm undertakes an additional engagement to value the company's investments for inclusion in the financial statements for the year ending 31 March 20X7. Shan's investments are a material proportion of the company's total assets.

State, with reasons, how your firm should respond to this request. **(3 marks)**

51.2 Explain the importance of professional scepticism in the context of an external audit engagement. **(3 marks)**

51.3 List the key purposes of:

- an engagement quality control review; and
- monitoring ('cold' audit file review). **(3 marks)**

51.4 Your firm is the external auditor of Munkee Ltd (Munkee) for the year ending 31 March 20X7. Jade Vachir, Munkee's sole shareholder and managing director, has informed the engagement partner that she intends to sell her shares after the year end and has started negotiations with a prospective buyer.

Explain why this information should be considered by the engagement partner for the external audit of Munkee for the year ending 31 March 20X7. **(4 marks)**

51.5 During the external audit of Martial Ltd (Martial) for the year ended 31 January 20X7, you discover a letter to Martial dated 15 February 20X7 from its largest customer, Artz Ltd (Artz). The letter threatens the early termination of Artz's contract with Martial due to issues over the quality of goods supplied.

Explain the relevance of this letter to the external audit of Martial for the year ended 31 January 20X7. **(3 marks)**

51.6 You are the audit senior responsible for the external audit of Crock Ltd (Crock) for the year ended 31 December 20X6. The directors of Crock have refused to provide a written representation that all transactions have been recorded and reflected in the financial statements. The audit junior has suggested that an emphasis of matter paragraph is included in the audit report to highlight to users of the financial statements that the written representation has not been provided by the directors.

State, with reasons, whether the audit junior's suggestion is appropriate and outline the impact on the auditor's report of the directors' refusal to provide the written representation. **(4 marks)**

52 Shifu Ltd

Your firm has recently been appointed as the external auditor of Shifu Ltd (Shifu). Shifu has developed Nodle, an online human capital management system which includes payroll processing, employee expense management and time tracking tools. Shifu contracts with corporate customers to supply access to Nodle over the internet. You are the audit senior responsible for planning the external audit for the year ended 31 January 20X7. The engagement partner has asked you to consider the following key areas of audit risk:

(1) Revenue – user licence fees and set-up fees
(2) Intangible assets – software development costs
(3) Compensation payable and receivable

Shifu charges customers an annual licence fee for Nodle based on the number of expected users within the customer's organisation. A user is any person at the customer's organisation that has access to Nodle. The expected full licence fee is payable by customers at the start of each 12-month period covered by the contract. At the end of each 12-month period, Shifu compares the number of actual users who have accessed Nodle with the expected number of users to determine any over- or under-usage by the customer. Customers pay additional licence fees to Shifu for over-usage and Shifu refunds customers for any under-usage. Shifu recognises revenue from licence fees evenly over each 12-month contract period. Revenue is adjusted for any anticipated over- or under-usage on contracts straddling the year end.

New customers are charged a fixed set-up fee, which must be paid before work commences on setting up Nodle for the organisation. Set-up takes between three and nine months to complete. On completion of the set-up customers are required to confirm in writing that Nodle has been satisfactorily set up. Set-up fees are recognised evenly over the set-up period.

Shifu has a reputation in the market for making continuous improvements to Nodle. Shifu's software developers make changes to Nodle to fix software problems (bugs), make improvements and release new features. Developers keep a record of the time spent working on each change. Each month Shifu's head of development uses these time records to calculate the amount of developers' costs relating to improvements and new features. These software development costs are capitalised and amortised over their estimated useful lives. Amortisation and developers' costs incurred to fix bugs are included in cost of sales.

Contracts between Shifu and its customers require Nodle to be available to users for 99.5% of the time. Shifu must pay compensation to its customers, at the rate agreed in each contract, for each month in which the 99.5% service level is not met. In January 20X7, Shifu did not meet the 99.5% service level due to a failure at the data centre where Nodle is hosted. The data centre is owned and operated by Mantis Ltd (Mantis). Shifu intends to claim compensation, under its contract with Mantis, for the costs incurred as a result of the failure at the data centre. Shifu's directors have estimated that the compensation due to its customers in respect of this failure is £920,000. No amounts for compensation payable or receivable have been included in the draft financial statements as the directors expect the compensation to be claimed from Mantis to exceed the amount due to Shifu's customers.

You have obtained the following information from Shifu's management to use in your consideration of the key areas of audit risk:

Year ended 31 January:	20X7	20X6
Average number of Nodle users	627,546	572,158
New customers	49	63

Statement of profit or loss for the year ended 31 January (extract)

	20X7 (draft) £'000	20X6 (audited) £'000
Revenue		
User licence fees	58,187	42,198
Set-up fees	11,997	12,480
	70,184	54,678
Cost of sales (note)	(35,051)	(34,454)
Gross profit	35,133	20,224

Note: Cost of sales for the year ended 31 January 20X7 includes costs of £899,000 incurred in fixing bugs (year ended 31 January 20X6: £1,678,000).

Extract from notes: Intangible assets – software development costs

	20X7 (draft) £'000	20X6 (audited) £'000
Carrying amount at 1 February	8,745	10,163
Additions	5,791	3,417
Amortisation in the year	(4,124)	(4,835)
Carrying amount at 31 January	10,412	8,745

Requirements

52.1 Justify why the items listed by the engagement partner have been identified as key areas of audit risk and, for each item, describe the procedures that should be included in the audit plan to address those risks. You should present your answer using the following subheadings:

(a) Revenue – user licence fees
(b) Revenue – set-up fees
(c) Intangible assets – software development costs
(d) Compensation payable and receivable   **(28 marks)**

52.2 Companies, such as Shifu, have a responsibility to put measures in place to protect their customers from loss of data and breaches of data security.

Identify and explain the audit risks that would arise if Shifu failed to meet these responsibilities.

(5 marks)

52.3 State, with reasons, the implications for the auditor's report if Shifu's directors do not make any changes to the financial statements for the year ended 31 January 20X7 in respect of the £920,000 compensation payable to Shifu's customers.   **(3 marks)**

Total: 36 marks

53 Oogway, Dragoon, Pand, Dymsum

Described below are four situations which have recently arisen at four unrelated firms of ICAEW chartered accountants.

Oogway Group plc (Oogway)

Jade LLP is the external auditor of Oogway. Li Ping was the engagement partner for the audit of Oogway, a listed company, for five years. In April 20X6 he was rotated off the audit engagement and replaced by Sarah Bao. On 6 March 20X7, whilst planning the audit for the year ended 28 February 20X7, Sarah became unwell and took an indefinite leave of absence from your firm.

The directors of Oogway have requested that Li immediately returns as engagement partner to complete the planning and ensure that the audit remains on schedule.

Dragoon Ltd (Dragoon)

Wok LLP is considering whether to accept appointment as external auditor of Dragoon for the year ending 30 June 20X7. Wok LLP has written to the previous auditor, Master LLP, requesting information which could influence its decision. Master LLP has responded that it did not accept reappointment because it identified irregularities in the recognition of revenue during the audit for the year ended 30 June 20X6. Master LLP considered the irregularities to be deliberate misstatements. When Wok LLP raised the matter with Dragoon's directors, they responded that the misstatements had been genuine errors which were corrected and that Master LLP had issued an unmodified auditor's report.

Pand Ltd (Pand)

Red LLP provides internal, but not external, audit services to Pand, a luxury holiday company. During a recent visit to Pand, Peony Meng, a member of the internal audit team, identified that two payments of the same amount were paid to the same supplier. Further investigation showed that only one transaction had taken place. Enquiries of the accounts department personnel produced unsatisfactory responses. A few days later Pand's finance director telephoned Peony. He offered her a free holiday to compensate for the additional work that she had to undertake due to this issue. He also requested that she keep the matter quiet so as not to make the accounts department appear incompetent.

Dymsum Group Ltd (Dymsum)

Shen LLP is the external auditor of Dymsum and its UK-based subsidiaries. Dymsum has recently acquired 100% of the share capital of Mei Ltd (Mei), a company incorporated and operating in China. The directors of Dymsum have requested that Shen LLP accepts appointment as external auditor of Mei and undertakes a one-off engagement to review and report on the adequacy of internal controls at Mei. Shen's annual audit fee is expected to rise to £998,400 if it accepts appointment as auditor of Mei. The fee to review and report on internal controls at Mei is expected to be £155,000. Your firm's total annual fee income is expected to be £7.2 million. None of the entities within the group is listed.

Requirements

53.1 Identify and explain the professional and ethical issues arising in each of the situations above. State any actions that each firm's partners or its other employees should take to address these issues. **(22 marks)**

53.2 List the specific matters, arising from the acquisition of Mei, that Shen LLP should consider when planning the audit of Dymsum. **(4 marks)**

Total: 26 marks

54 Viper Ltd

Your firm is performing an engagement to review and provide an assurance report on the financial statements of Viper Ltd (Viper) for the year ended 31 January 20X7. The review was requested by Po Bank plc (Po Bank) which is considering a loan application from Viper. Viper is not required to have an external audit under the Companies Act 2006.

The following matters arose when performing the planned procedures:

- When reviewing the accounting records for significant journal entries, it was noted that the year-end journal to record prepayments had been posted to the general ledger twice in error. The journal entries had not been authorised or reviewed and IT controls do not prevent the posting of journals with a reference number which is identical to an existing journal.

- Your firm's analytical procedures identified that trade receivables days had increased from 35, at 31 January 20X6, to 42 at 31 January 20X7. Viper's credit terms are 30 days. Enquiries of management revealed that trade receivables included an overdue balance of £152,000 in respect of Warrior Ltd (Warrior). Warrior has refused to pay the balance because it claims it did not receive the goods. Viper does not retain evidence that goods have been dispatched from its warehouse or received by its customers. The directors do not consider it necessary to make any adjustments to the financial statements in respect of this matter.

Viper's financial statements show profit before tax for the year ended 31 January 20X7 of £1.2 million.

Requirements

54.1 State the internal control deficiencies identified when performing the planned procedures. For each deficiency, outline the possible consequence(s) of the deficiency and provide recommendation(s) to remedy each deficiency. **(7 marks)**

54.2 List the differences between a report prepared by a practitioner for an engagement to review financial statements and the report prepared by auditors for an external audit engagement of an unlisted company. **(3 marks)**

54.3 In respect of Warrior's overdue balance, state whether you would modify your firm's assurance report. Give reasons for your conclusion and describe the modifications, if any, to the assurance report. **(4 marks)**

54.4 Outline the possible consequences for your firm of reaching an inappropriate conclusion following the review of the financial statements of Viper. Describe how firms can mitigate the impact of any financial consequences arising from an inappropriate conclusion. **(4 marks)**

Total: 18 marks

55 Short form questions

55.1 You are the audit senior on the external audit of Chance Ltd (Chance), a UK construction company. During a review of Chance's bank statements, you identified a large monthly receipt from an overseas company. The amount of the receipt is the same every month. You have also identified an identical monthly payment to another overseas company. No entries have been made in Chance's accounting records for any of these receipts and payments. Chance has not previously traded with any overseas company.

State, with reasons, the actions that you and your firm should take in respect of this matter.

(3 marks)

55.2 The testing of journal entries is one of the procedures used by external auditors to respond to the risk of fraud at audited entities.

List the characteristics of journal entries that external auditors should select for testing to identify any fraudulent activities.

(3 marks)

55.3 Circus Ltd (Circus) has outsourced its payroll function to Payco Ltd (Payco). Each month, Circus provides Payco with the hours worked by each employee. Payco calculates monthly payroll information by reference to employees' details held as standing data on Payco's IT system. Based on the information provided by Payco, Circus pays wages directly into its employees' bank accounts and pays payroll taxes to the authorities. Payco is responsible for the online filing of the monthly returns required by the tax authorities.

Identify the business risks to which Circus is exposed by outsourcing its payroll function to Payco and state the implications for the financial statements.

(4 marks)

55.4 Audit committees are responsible for monitoring the quality of the work of an internal audit function within an audited entity. One of the ways this can be achieved is by the use of agreed performance indicators.

List three performance indicators which could be used by audit committees to monitor the quality of an internal audit function.

(3 marks)

55.5 A firm sets its senior employees targets for generating non-audit fees from its external audit clients. One of the criteria for paying annual bonuses to senior employees is achieving these targets.

Identify and explain the threat to the objectivity of senior employees arising from this arrangement. State, with reasons, whether the arrangement is appropriate.

(3 marks)

55.6 Kent LLP (Kent) is an international external audit firm. Kent is considering transferring some external audit work relating to UK audited entities to an overseas office.

State how Kent could effectively manage audit quality if the work is transferred to an overseas office. **(4 marks)**

56 Top Hat and Boot Ltd

Top Hat and Boot Ltd (THB) is a retailer of designer clothing and a large range of accessories such as handbags and shoes. THB sells its products through its own website and stores located in major cities throughout the UK. It distributes its products from a warehouse located in Milton Keynes.

Your firm has recently been appointed as external auditor for the year ending 30 June 20X7 following a competitive tender. THB has applied for a bank loan to finance the expansion of the business. The bank requires the audited financial statements by 31 August 20X7 prior to considering the application. THB appointed your firm to act as auditor because of its reputation for providing professional services to companies operating in the retail sector. The previous auditor declined to submit a tender.

You are the audit senior and the engagement partner has asked you to consider the following two key areas of audit risk:

(1) Purchases and trade payables
(2) Inventory.

You have been provided with the following extracts from the financial statements:

Statement of profit or loss for the year ending 30 June

	20X7 (estimated) £'000	20X6 (audited) £'000
Revenue	120,500	110,233
Cost of sales (see note below)	(62,500)	(60,007)
Gross profit	58,000	50,226
Note: Purchases included in cost of sales	66,493	60,934

Statement of financial position as at 30 June

	20X7 (estimated) £'000	20X6 (audited) £'000
Current assets		
Inventory	12,300	8,307
Current liabilities	4,600	4,902
Trade payables		

In addition, the following information has also been provided:

- The company buys its products from suppliers based in Asia. All purchases are made on 30-day credit terms and are invoiced in the suppliers' local currency.

- Following media criticism about the quality of products sold, THB identified an issue with products bought from its largest supplier resulting in a significant amount of returns to that supplier in May and June 20X7. THB's accounts department had paid the invoices relating to these products as it had not been notified of the returns. The failure to notify the accounts department of the returns was not discovered until the supplier's credit notes arrived in the accounts department.

- THB maintains a perpetual inventory system, which records the quantities held and the cost price of inventory. The cost price of inventory is updated from purchase invoices.

- Recent monthly counts of a sample of inventory items at the warehouse identified inventory shortfalls where the physical quantities were significantly lower than those recorded in the records. As a result, the directors have instructed that a full inventory count is undertaken at the year end. Whitechapel LLP, a firm of professional inventory counters, will undertake the count on 30 June 20X7.

- At each month end, the inventory system generates an inventory valuation listing and an aged inventory report. The valuation listing includes the cost and the quantity held for each inventory item. The valuation listing at 30 June 20X7, with the quantity held updated for the results of the year-end inventory count, will be used as the basis for the inventory figure in the financial statements.

During a meeting with Tom Boot, THB's finance director, Tom requested that your firm provides:

(a) a member of staff to assist with the preparation of the annual financial statements to help THB meet the deadline for submission of the financial statements to the bank.

(b) a forensic specialist to assist THB in an investigation of the inventory shortfalls at the warehouse. A preliminary investigation by Tom has highlighted the theft of a significant amount of inventory by two warehouse employees as a possible cause. Tom has requested that the forensic specialist estimates the value of the inventory loss and acts as an expert witness in any resulting legal proceedings against the employees.

The proposed fees for audit and non-audit services together amount to 4% of the firm's annual fee income.

During the meeting with Tom, at which the audit assistant, a trainee ICAEW Chartered Accountant, was present, Tom advised that there is a promotion commencing on 1 July 20X7 in which a number of selected products will be for sale at £1 each to online customers. However, customers will have to search the website to find these offers and it is hoped, that when doing so, they will also buy full-price products. Tom showed you a list of products to be discounted in the sale. The audit assistant subsequently told you that she had informed her family of the discounted products as her family owns a store which retails clothes and accessories. She also told you that she had asked Tom to keep her informed of any products that will be discounted in the future.

Requirements

56.1 Identify and explain the matters that your firm should have considered before deciding to tender for THB's external audit. **(7 marks)**

56.2 Justify why the items listed by the engagement partner have been identified as key areas of audit risk and, for each item, describe the procedures that should be included in the audit plan in order to address those risks. Your answer should be presented using the following subheadings:

(a) Purchases and trade payables
(b) Inventory

Your answer should include examples of specific data analytics routines. **(20 marks)**

56.3 Identify and explain the principal threats to independence and objectivity which may arise from the provision of each of the non-audit services listed as (a) and (b) in the scenario and state how your firm should respond to each threat. **(9 marks)**

56.4 In respect of the audit assistant's actions, explain the ethical issues arising and state the actions that you and your firm should take. **(4 marks)**

Total: 40 marks

57 Ventnor Estates Ltd

Your firm is the external auditor of Ventnor Estates Ltd (VE) which owns and manages a portfolio of commercial properties from which it receives rental income. VE is responsible for repairs and maintenance of each property. In addition to properties, VE has non-current assets comprising vehicles, office equipment and high value tools used to carry out property repairs. Properties are purchased using bank loans which are repayable over periods of five to seven years and are subject to covenants. Funding to buy new properties is increasingly difficult to obtain because of recent falls in the market value of commercial property.

The audit plan in respect of the external audit of VE, for the year ended 31 March 20X7, requires the use of substantive analytical procedures to calculate expected rental income, using data independent of the current year's rental income figure. You have been asked to perform these procedures using the following information:

- Rental periods cover quarters ended 31 March, 30 June, 30 September and 31 December.

- Rental agreements in place on 1 April 20X6 increased by 2% on that date.

- The same rental agreements remained in place for the year ended 31 March 20X7 compared with the prior year except for:

  - a tenant paying rent of £250,000 per quarter, was placed into administration on 30 June 20X6. A revised rent of £150,000 per quarter was agreed with the administrator from that date.

  - a tenant vacated a property on 30 June 20X6 and there was a period of six months before the property was rented to a new tenant on 1 January 20X7, at the same rental of £75,000 per quarter. No rental income was received on the property during this six-month period.

  - a property was sold on 30 September 20X6. Rental income for that property was £400,000 per quarter.

- The draft financial statements for the year ended 31 March 20X7 include rental income of £15,151,000. Prior year audited rental income was £15,687,000.

During the audit for the year ended 31 March 20X7, you identified the following deficiencies in internal control:

(1) Comparison of the non-current asset register with physical assets was last undertaken in January 20X6. Company policy stipulates that an annual asset verification exercise must be performed.

(2) Directors are presented with management accounting information at their monthly board meetings. The management accounting information does not include cash flow forecasts nor details of whether VE complies with the bank covenants.

Requirements

57.1 Explain the purpose of performing substantive analytical procedures. **(3 marks)**

57.2 (a) Calculate the expected rental income, for the year ended 31 March 20X7, as required by the audit plan for VE. Show each step in your calculation.

(b) Identify the audit evidence that you would obtain to test the reliability of the data used at each step of your calculation.

(c) List the enquiries you would make based on the result of your analytical procedures in 8.2(a). Explain why you would make these enquires and identify any additional information that you would need to complete your audit work. **(10 marks)**

57.3 For each internal control deficiency identified, draft points for inclusion in your firm's report to those charged with governance and management at VE. For each internal control deficiency identified, you should outline the possible consequence(s) of the deficiency and provide recommendation(s) to address it. You should present your answer using the following subheadings:

(a) Asset verification

(b) Content of management accounting information

(7 marks)

Total: 20 marks

58 Bow, Euston, Oxford, Strand

Described below are situations which have arisen at four unrelated clients of your firm. The year end in each case is 31 March 20X7.

Bow Ltd (Bow)

Your firm is the external auditor of Bow. Your firm attended the inventory count at Bow's warehouse on 31 March 20X7, but was unaware that Bow also owned inventory held at a third party's premises on this date. Neither Bow nor the third party has retained any count records in respect of this inventory. Your firm has concluded that there are no other records from which the amount of inventory held by the third party can be substantiated. Bow's directors wish to include the inventory held at the third party's premises in the year-end financial statements at £550,000. The draft financial statements show that Bow's profit before tax is £5.2 million and total assets are £21.7 million.

Euston Ltd (Euston)

Your firm is the external auditor of Euston. A competitor has alleged that Euston has infringed patent rights and the competitor is threatening to claim damages of £5.0 million. Euston's independent legal advice is that the competitor's case is weak and, if the matter is pursued by the competitor, the case is unlikely to come to court for at least three years. For these reasons, no provision for any liability that may result has been made in the financial statements. Euston has made relevant disclosures in the financial statements. The engagement partner agrees with the accounting treatment and is satisfied that the note includes all the necessary information for the users of the financial statements to understand the situation. The draft financial statements show that Euston's profit before tax is £2.5 million.

Oxford plc (Oxford)

During the external audit of Oxford, a listed company, you read the strategic report to be included in Oxford's annual report. The strategic report contains a statement that "the company's expansion into China has been a success and is responsible for generating 20% of revenue". However, the notes to the financial statements disclose that only 10% of revenue originated from China. You are satisfied that the error is in the strategic report and not the financial statements. The directors have refused to amend the strategic report.

In addition, Oxford has not disclosed in the financial statements that one of its lenders has a floating charge over all of the company's assets as security for a long-term loan. The Companies Act 2006 requires this disclosure to be made.

Strand Ltd (Strand)

Your firm has completed an engagement to review and provide an assurance report on Strand's consolidated financial statements. This assurance engagement was requested by Strand's directors to support the acquisition of funding to grow the business. Strand has recently acquired a subsidiary Fleet Ltd (Fleet). Strand has not consolidated the financial statements of Fleet but has included it as an investment, at cost, in the consolidated financial statements. This accounting treatment is not in compliance with International Financial Reporting Standards. Had Fleet been consolidated, many elements in the financial statements would have been materially affected.

Requirements

58.1 For each of the situations described above, state, with reasons, the implications for your firm's audit or assurance reports. **(13 marks)**

58.2 Describe the differences between the conclusion expressed following an engagement to review financial statements and the opinion expressed in an external auditor's report on financial statements. Give reasons for these differences. **(4 marks)**

58.3 List three items of additional information to be included in the extended auditor's report on financial statements of listed companies. **(3 marks)**

Total: 20 marks

September 2017 exam questions

59 Short form questions

59.1 Your firm is the external auditor of Buddy Ltd (Buddy). The directors of Buddy discovered a fraud soon after the auditor's report on the financial statements for the year ended 30 June 20X7 was signed. Some of Buddy's employees had given unauthorised discounts on sales made to their friends and families, which is not allowed by Buddy's discount policy. The amounts were not material to the financial statements but Buddy's managing director has expressed concern that your firm did not discover this fraud during the audit.

Outline the responsibilities of your firm and Buddy's directors in respect of this fraud and reach a conclusion as to whether those responsibilities were met. **(4 marks)**

59.2 Your firm has identified that the total fees from the provision of audit and non-audit services to Dachshund plc (Dachshund), a listed company, is expected to amount to 6% of the firm's annual fee income in 20X7.

State, with reasons, the steps that the engagement partner of Dachshund should take, including any safeguards that might be necessary. **(3 marks)**

59.3 Sphynx plc (Sphynx) is an international engineering company. Your firm has accepted an engagement to provide a limited assurance report on safety performance indicators included in Sphynx's published corporate responsibility report. One such safety performance indicator is the number of workplace accidents by employees, per million working hours, at each of its international engineering plants.

List three procedures that your firm could perform in relation to the number of workplace accidents performance indicator. **(3 marks)**

59.4 You are working on the external audit of Snowball Ltd (Snowball) for the year ended 31 August 20X7. You are responsible for performing the planned procedures in respect of trade receivables. Your analytical procedures identified that receivables days have increased from 35 days at 31 August 20X6 to 43 days at 31 August 20X7. On enquiry, Snowball's financial controller explained: "The increase is due to a contract for the supply of goods to a new customer, Pets Ltd (Pets). The contract allows Pets 60 days' credit rather than our standard 30 days' credit. We despatched a large order to Pets 50 days before the year end."

Outline the additional audit procedures you would perform in respect of the financial controller's explanation. **(4 marks)**

59.5 During your firm's external audit of the financial statements of Sausage Ltd, the audit team has identified a number of misstatements. No individual misstatement is material.

Outline the actions that should be taken in respect of these misstatements before the auditor's report is signed. **(3 marks)**

59.6 The financial statements of Budgie Ltd (Budgie) include an investment in Viper Ltd (Viper) stated at £7.8 million. The external auditor has concluded that the investment in Viper should be recognised at £2 million. The directors of Budgie have refused to recognise the reduction in the value of the investment. The profit before tax of Budgie is £46.7 million and gross assets are £824 million.

State, with reasons, the implications for the auditor's report. **(3 marks)**

60 Gidget Ltd

Your firm is the external auditor of Gidget Ltd (Gidget) and you are the senior responsible for planning the audit for the year ended 31 August 20X7. Your firm performed an engagement to review Gidget's financial statements for the year ended 31 August 20X6 but Gidget is now required to have an external audit of its financial statements for the first time.

Gidget installs and operates charging points which are used to recharge the batteries in electric vehicles. Gidget earns revenue from (a) the sale and installation of charging points at customers' homes and (b) income from electric vehicle owners who use Gidget's network of charging points located in public car parks.

Gidget has experienced rapid growth due to an increase in electric vehicle ownership. The UK Society of Motor Manufacturers, which publishes industry data, reported that ownership of electric vehicles grew by 52% between August 20X6 and August 20X7. The engagement partner has asked you to consider the following key areas of audit risk:

(1) Revenue
(2) Rental expenses relating to charging points in public car parks
(3) Property, plant and equipment – charging points in public car parks.

The sales price of charging points, including installation at customer's homes, is £800. Customers can claim a £500 contribution towards this cost from the UK government's Office for Low Emission Vehicles (OLEV). Gidget manages the process to claim the contribution by providing claim forms to the customer for completion. The contribution is subject to the customer complying with a list of conditions specified on the claim form.

Gidget sends completed customer claim forms to OLEV and receives £500 directly from OLEV providing the claim form demonstrates compliance with the list of conditions. Customers pay Gidget the net amount of £300, online, prior to the installation. Gidget recognises £800 as revenue on the day of installation. It also records a receivable of £500 as Gidget does not receive the contribution from OLEV until several weeks after the installation has taken place.

Your firm visited Gidget in July 20X7 and identified two internal control deficiencies relating to claims for the £500 contribution from OLEV. Prior to sending customer claim forms to OLEV:

* the sequential numbering of the forms was not checked for gaps in the sequence
* not all claims were checked for compliance with the conditions required by OLEV

Gidget also owns charging points located in public car parks such as those at supermarkets. Owners of electric vehicles pay Gidget for each minute of charging. To use these charging points, owners of electric vehicles must register an account on Gidget's website and provide personal data including a credit card number. On registration, owners are sent a Gidget card which they insert into the charging point to recharge their car batteries. Owners add funds to their online accounts using a credit card. Usage data from each charging point is transmitted to Gidget's business information system and the amount due is deducted from the vehicle owner's account. Data from the business information system is used to update Gidget's nominal ledger accounts.

Gidget pays a fixed rent, quarterly in arrears, to the owners of the public car parks in which its charging points are located. Each rental agreement specifies a maximum number of total minutes of charging. If the maximum number of minutes is exceeded, then additional rent becomes payable to the car park owner. Any additional rent is payable each year on the anniversary of the rental agreement. Gidget accrues for the additional rent relating to agreements that straddle the year end. The accrual is calculated by multiplying the rate specified in the agreement with the estimated number of additional minutes used, for the months between the anniversary of the agreement and 31 August.

Charging points are assembled in Gidget's UK factory using components that are sourced from around the world. Suppliers invoice Gidget in their local currency.

Charging points located in public car parks are capitalised as property, plant and equipment and depreciated at 25% pa using the reducing balance method. The total costs capitalised include the cost of the components, labour costs and overheads. The capitalised overhead cost is estimated by Gidget's finance director, Jack Russell, and is based on a proportion of the total overhead costs recorded in the management accounts.

During 20X7, Gidget developed an app for smartphones which allows electric vehicle owners to register an account and use charging stations without a Gidget card. This development required Gidget to modify each of its charging points so they can be operated with the new app. The costs of the modifications have been capitalised and included in charging points in property, plant and equipment.

During your planning meeting Jack provided the following information.

Statement of profit or loss for the year ended 31 August (extract)

	20X7 (draft) £'000	20X6 (reviewed) £'000
Revenue		
Home charging point installations (Note 1)	10,205	4,277
Public car park charging point usage	8,976	3,122
	19,181	7,399
Cost of sales (Note 2)	(16,022)	(6,516)
Gross profit	3,159	883

Note to the financial statements for the year ended 31 August (extract) Property, plant and equipment – public charging points

	20X7 (draft) £'000	20X6 (reviewed) £'000
Carrying amount at 1 September	5,367	4,876
Additions	4,777	1,998
Depreciation charge	(1,932)	(1,507)
Carrying amount at 31 August	8,212	5,367

Notes

1   Includes amounts received and receivable from OLEV.

2   Includes rental payments and accrual for the year ended 31 August 20X7 of £4,917,000 (20X6: £2,988,000) and depreciation of public charging points.

Jack also suggested that your firm considers using the data available in Gidget's business information system as part of the audit:

Examples of data available in Gidget's business information system

- Date and location of each home charging point installation
- Daily usage minutes for each charging point in a public car park

- Faults recorded by each charging point in a public car park
- Customers' personal data

Requirements

60.1 Describe the differences between the scope of the review of Gidget's financial statements for the year ended 31 August 20X6 and the scope of the external audit of the financial statements for the year ended 31 August 20X7. Give reasons for these differences.

(6 marks)

60.2 For each of the key areas of audit risk listed by the engagement partner as (1) to (3), describe **one** data analytics routine which makes use of the data available in Gidget's accounting or business information systems. **(3 marks)**

60.3 Justify why the items listed by the engagement partner have been identified as key areas of audit risk and, for each item, describe the procedures that should be included in the audit plan to address those risks. You should present your answer using the following subheadings:

(a) Revenue
(b) Rental expenses relating to charging points in public car parks
(c) Property, plant and equipment – charging points in public car parks

Do **not** include the specific data analytics routines described in your answer to 87.2.

(25 marks)

60.4 Identify and explain the audit risks that might arise due to Gidget storing the personal data supplied by customers. **(5 marks)**

Total: 39 marks

61 Terrier, Pug, Tabby

Described below are three unrelated situations which have arisen at two external audit clients and a further prospective client of your firm.

Terrier Ltd (Terrier)

Your firm is concluding its external audit of Terrier for the year ended 30 June 20X7. Yesterday, the engagement partner discovered that a significant fee, for information security services provided to Terrier by your firm, is overdue. The fee has not been paid by Terrier due to a dispute over the quality of these services.

Pug plc (Pug)

Your firm is the auditor of Pug, a listed entity. The audit engagement partner has identified that the senior audit manager has been involved in the audit of Pug for each of the previous eight years.

Tabby Group plc (Tabby)

Tabby is a pharmaceutical research company listed on the London Stock Exchange. Your firm is tendering for the external audit of Tabby for the year ending 31 December 20X7. Tabby's previous auditor resigned due to a disagreement with Tabby's directors. Tabby has recently started a major restructuring of its business which includes the sale of several of its overseas subsidiaries. The partner in charge of the tender is keen to propose a low audit fee to win the audit and improve the firm's chances of winning future non-audit engagements related to the business restructuring.

Requirements

61.1 Identify and explain the threats to your firm's independence and objectivity presented by each of the situations above and list the steps your firm should take to address those threats. **(10 marks)**

61.2 Identify the specific factors relevant to the calculation of your firm's proposed audit fee to be included as part of its tender for the audit of Tabby. For each factor, explain why you consider it should influence the proposed audit fee. **(8 marks)**

Total: 18 marks

62 Redtail Ltd

SLP LLP (SLP) is the external auditor of Redtail Ltd (Redtail) which prepares financial statements to 30 September each year. Redtail assembles turbines, in its UK factory, for customers based in the UK and mainland Europe. Contracts with its customers are agreed many years in advance and prices are denominated in sterling.

Components for turbines are sourced from international suppliers. Redtail negotiates fixed-term, fixed-price contracts for the supply of components which are denominated in the supplier's local currency. Redtail's contract with Hawk Gmbh (Hawk), its largest supplier, expired in June 20X7. A new contract is being negotiated but Redtail and Hawk cannot agree on prices. Recent falls in the value of sterling make Hawk's products more expensive and Redtail is demanding a higher discount from Hawk to compensate for this. Redtail has been paying full list price for components purchased from Hawk since the contract expired. List prices are significantly higher than previous contract prices. Redtail's management accounts for the period June to August 20X7, show a fall in the gross profit margin from 23% to 18%. Redtail is unable to source some components, supplied by Hawk, from alternative suppliers.

Redtail is purchasing smaller quantities of components from Hawk whilst the new contract is negotiated. This has resulted in stockouts which have caused a significant delay in the supply of turbines to Tiberius SRL (Tiberius). Tiberius is threatening to action a penalty clause in its contract with Redtail due to the delay.

Redtail's directors have prepared a revised cash flow forecast to reflect the above issues. The revised forecast shows that Redtail expects to significantly exceed its overdraft limit in November 20X7. Redtail's directors have approached the company's bank to request an extension to its current overdraft facility. The bank has requested Redtail's audited financial statements for the year ending 30 September 20X7 before making a decision.

Redtail's finance director, Chloe Duke, has insisted that the audit is completed by 31 October 20X7. Resources for this year's audit have already been scheduled, in line with timetables for prior years, to allow the audit work to be completed by 16 December 20X7. Chloe also informed the engagement partner that Redtail is undertaking a large project which requires a tax adviser. She suggested that SLP's support in meeting the 31 October deadline would result in SLP being appointed as the tax adviser.

Requirements

62.1 Identify and explain the professional and ethical issues for SLP in relation to the audit of Redtail. **(5 marks)**

62.2 Identify and explain the factors which give rise to an uncertainty about the going concern status of Redtail. **(12 marks)**

62.3 Assuming SLP concludes there is an uncertainty about the going concern status of Redtail, explain the implications for the auditor's report on the financial statements of Redtail for the year ending 30 September 20X7 if the directors:

(a) make appropriate disclosures; or

(b) do not make any disclosures.

(6 marks)

Total: 23 marks

December 2017 exam questions

63 Short form questions

63.1 External audit firms handle large volumes of client data and have a responsibility to put internal controls in place to protect that data.

List the consequences that could arise if an audit firm failed to meet this responsibility and outline the internal controls that should be in place to mitigate the risk of failing to protect client data. **(4 marks)**

63.2 Wharfe Golf Club (Wharfe) is unincorporated and is not legally required to have an external audit. Wharfe's main sources of income are membership fees and sales of food and golf equipment.

List the benefits for Wharfe of voluntarily undergoing an external audit. **(3 marks)**

63.3 The risk of management override of internal controls is present in all organisations.

List **three** procedures that should be included in external audit plans to address this risk. **(3 marks)**

63.4 Swale Ltd's (Swale) external auditor is proposing to express an adverse opinion on the company's financial statements for the year ended 30 September 20X7. This is due to disagreement over a number of accounting policies applied in the preparation of the financial statements. Swale has approached your firm and requested a second opinion on the auditor's report

Identify and explain the ethical issues that may arise for your firm from this request and state how your firm should deal with this request. **(3 marks)**

63.5 Your firm is the external auditor of Aire Ltd (Aire) which operates a chain of retail stores selling household goods. Aire is wholly-owned by Sunwac Ltd (Sunwac) and is dependent on Sunwac to provide finance to continue operating.

The directors of Aire have provided your firm with an email from Sunwac's directors stating that Sunwac will continue to provide Aire with ongoing financial support. No audit work has been performed in respect of the email. The directors of Aire have prepared the financial statements on the going concern basis.

Comment on the reliability of the email as audit evidence and outline any audit work that should be undertaken in respect of the email confirmation. **(4 marks)**

63.6 Sue Ure is the engagement partner responsible for the external audit of Nidd plc (Nidd), a listed company. Sue is due to be removed from the audit team as she has been the engagement partner for the last five years. However, because of a recent major change in the structure of Nidd's business following the acquisition of a competitor, the audit committee has requested that Sue continues as engagement partner.

State, with reasons, how Sue's firm should respond to the audit committee's request.

(3 marks)

64 Lab Equipment Ltd

Your firm has recently been appointed as the external auditor of Lab Equipment Ltd (LEL) for the year ending 31 December 20X7. The previous auditors did not seek reappointment following the conclusion of the 20X6 audit.

You are the audit senior and the engagement partner asked you to consider the following two key areas of audit risk:

(1) Trade receivables
(2) Inventories.

You have been provided with the following extracts from the financial statements:

Statement of profit or loss for the year ending 31 December

	20X7 (estimated) £'000	20X6 (audited) £'000
Revenue	125,500	108,137
Cost of sales	(68,500)	(64,007)
Gross profit	57,000	44,130

Statement of financial position as at 31 December

	20X7 (estimated) £'000	20X6 (audited) £'000
Current assets		
Inventories	14,200	8,307
Trade receivables	15,500	9,222

In addition, the following information has been provided:

- LEL is a UK-based producer of scientific instruments, for use in hospitals and universities, which sells its instruments around the world. Each year, the range of instruments is updated and presented in an online catalogue which includes the selling prices. Customers either order directly from the catalogue or agree a contract with LEL. In some countries the use of commercial intermediaries (agents) to facilitate negotiations is standard practice.

- LEL invoices customers in Sterling and requires payment within 30 days of the invoice date. One overseas customer, Ruritania Education Consortium, is withholding payment of £1.3 million as it claims that the instruments it purchased are defective.

- Instruments are assembled, from bought-in components, to a standard specification produced by the in-house design team. Components are purchased from suppliers based in the UK and overseas who invoice LEL in their local currency. LEL operates a perpetual inventory system for components and finished instruments. Quantities recorded in the perpetual inventory system are checked by periodic counting throughout the year by the company's employees. The company does not undertake a full inventory count at the year end.

- The inventory system is fully integrated with the cost accounting system. The cost accounting system records the cost of components, labour and production overheads for each instrument.

- Each week, the inventory system generates an inventory valuation listing and an aged inventory report. The inventory valuation listing includes the cost and quantity on hand for each component and each instrument.

- During 20X7, LEL experienced quality problems with components purchased from one of its major suppliers, Partco Ltd (Partco). LEL terminated its contract with Partco on 30 September 20X7 and switched to a new supplier which charges higher prices for higher quality components. LEL has not passed on these costs to its customers.

- During 20X7, the chief buyer exceeded reorder limits in respect of a number of components.

The recent interim audit revealed the following internal control deficiencies:

(a)   The sales staff amend the prices in the online catalogue on the oral authority of the sales director. No check is made on the amendments.

(b)   LEL does not have any bribery prevention policies in place.

During the interim audit, the managing director of LEL requested that the audit team completes the audit by 28 February 20X8. The company requires the audited financial statements to support an application for a bank loan to finance the purchase of equipment. As an incentive to complete the audit to this deadline, the managing director offered the audit team and their close family free use of LEL's private box for a premier league football match. He also offered to pay for the costs of travelling and overnight accommodation at a luxury hotel following the football match.

Requirements

64.1 Outline the process set out by the ICAEW Code of Ethics that your firm should have undertaken to obtain professional clearance from LEL's previous auditors. List the reasons for this process.   **(6 marks)**

64.2 Justify why the items listed as (1) and (2) in the scenario have been identified as key areas of audit risk and, for each item, describe the procedures that should be included in the audit plan to address those risks. Your answer should include examples of specific data analytics routines that can be applied to the items listed as (1) and (2).

Present your answer in a two-column format using the headings:

- Justification; and
- Procedures to address each risk.   **(21 marks)**

64.3 For each internal control deficiency listed as (a) and (b) in the scenario, draft points for inclusion in your firm's report to those charged with governance and management at LEL. For each deficiency, you should outline the possible consequence(s) of the deficiency and provide recommendations to address it.   **(9 marks)**

64.4 Explain the ethical issues arising in respect of the offer of the free use of a private box at a premier league football match and paid travel and hotel costs.   **(4 marks)**

Total: 40 marks

65 Crystal Diamond Screens Ltd

Crystal Diamond Screens Ltd (CDS) is a cinema operator with 22 cinemas in large cities across the UK. The main source of income is ticket sales for admission to watch the films. The directors want to attract more customers by offering a greater choice of films. Each cinema currently has only one screen but CDS is planning to convert 20 of the 22 cinemas to multiplexes (ie. a cinema with at least five screens).

Arnie Flynn, CDS's finance director, has prepared profit and cash flow forecasts for the four years ending 31 December 20Y1, which are to be submitted to CDS's bank in support of a loan to finance the conversions. CDS has requested that your firm examines and provides an assurance report on the cash flow forecasts.

Arnie has provided the following additional information:

- 10 cinemas will be converted to multiplexes each year. During the conversions, which will each take one year to complete, the cinema being converted will not show any films. The first 10 conversions are planned to start on 1 January 20X9.

- There will be a 10% increase in ticket price once conversions are completed to reflect the improved facilities. Because the conversions allow more efficient use of space, the seating capacity of each cinema will increase by 5%.

- Three construction firms have submitted tenders for the conversion work and these are awaiting evaluation by CDS.

- New seating will be installed in the cinemas during the conversions. Tenders have not yet been invited for the seating but costs have been estimated, by the directors, at £150 per seat.

- The conversions will be managed on behalf of CDS by Monroe and Co, a firm of project managers.

- To help finance the conversions, two cinemas which are too small to be converted will be closed on 30 June 20X8 and sold. A property developer has expressed interest in both sites and CDS is currently applying for permission to change the use of the sites from a cinema to residential.

- CDS pays the film distribution company a rental fee, monthly in arrears, for each film shown. The fee is a percentage of the ticket sales for each film. CDS has negotiated a rent-free period for the first three months following the cinema conversions.

- Following each conversion, the directors plan to recruit six additional employees for each cinema who will be paid the minimum hourly wage. All employees are eligible for annual bonuses linked to profits made by the company as a whole.

Your firm is currently finalising its terms of engagement with CDS for the review of the cash flow forecasts. Arnie has asked for an explanation of the following phrases used in your firm's draft engagement letter:

- "We will request from management written confirmation concerning representations made to us in connection with the examination of the forecasts."

- "Our report will provide a moderate level of assurance as to whether the assumptions provide a reasonable basis for the preparation of the forecasts."

You are the senior responsible for planning the examination of the cash flow forecasts. The engagement partner has identified the following items included in the cash flow forecasts as being significant:

(1) Receipts from ticket sales
(2) Payments for the conversion of cinemas, new seating and project management fees

(3)   Proceeds from the sale of the two cinemas

(4)   Payments to the film distribution company

(5)   Payments to employees

(6)   Receipts from and payments to the bank.

Requirements

65.1 Draft a response to Arnie which:

   (a)   lists the general representations that should be obtained from management as part of the assurance work on the cash flow forecasts and explains why such representations are required; and

   (b)   explains the term moderate assurance and why a higher level of assurance cannot be provided as to whether the assumptions provide a reasonable basis for the preparation of the cash flow forecasts.   **(8 marks)**

65.2 For the items listed (1) to (6) in the scenario, identify the specific matters you would consider when reviewing the reasonableness of the assumptions underlying each receipt or payment.   **(12 marks)**

Total: 20 marks

66   FOPT

Described below are situations which have arisen at four unrelated external audit clients of your firm. The year end in each case is 30 September 20X7.

Foyle Ltd (Foyle)

In June 20X6, Foyle entered into a fixed-price contract with Mersey plc. The contract is due to be completed in January 20X8. Due to increases in the cost of the materials purchased by Foyle for the contract, the directors of Foyle estimate that the contract will make a total loss of £0.2 million. The directors of Foyle have refused to provide for this loss in the financial statements as they maintain that the loss on this contract will be offset by profits on other contracts in the year ending 30 September 20X8.

The draft financial statements show that Foyle's profit before tax is £9.7 million and total assets are £84.7 million.

Ogmore Ltd (Ogmore)

Your firm's evaluation of the directors' assessment of Ogmore's ability to continue as a going concern included an examination of the company's financial forecasts prepared by its directors for the two years ending 30 September 20X9. Your firm has concluded that there are significant doubts as to whether Ogmore can continue as a going concern. The directors of Ogmore prepared the financial statements on the going concern basis. The notes to the financial statements include adequate disclosures in respect of the uncertainty related to the going concern assumption.

Pattack plc (Pattack)

The brother of the managing director of Pattack owns Clyde Ltd (Clyde) a haulage business which Pattack uses for some of its distribution requirements. The total amount paid by Pattack to Clyde during the year was £0.4 million. The directors of Pattack have refused to disclose this transaction in the notes to the financial statements as they claim that the amount is too small to warrant disclosure.

The draft financial statements show that Pattack's profit before tax is £11.3 million and total assets are £88.0 million.

Tyne Ltd (Tyne)

The former engagement partner responsible for the audit of Tyne left your firm and joined Tyne on 1 September 20X7 as finance director. Your firm has determined that there is no significant threat to the audit team's integrity, objectivity and independence arising from this move and has decided to continue as external auditor. Tyne is a small entity as defined by the Companies Act 2006 and the firm has taken advantage of the exemptions of the FRC's Provisions Available for Small Entities.

Requirements

66.1 For each of the situations described above, explain the implications, if any, for the auditor's report.

(12 marks)

66.2 (a) Identify the parties to whom your firm may be liable for damages if an inappropriate audit opinion is issued.

(b) Outline the methods available to your firm to limit its liability to such parties.

(c) Outline the quality control procedures your firm should implement to reduce the risk of issuing an inappropriate audit opinion.

(8 marks)

Total: 20 marks

March 2018 exam questions

67 Short form questions

67.1 Your firm has recently undertaken monitoring (ie, a 'cold' review) of the external audit completed on the financial statements of JK Ltd. This identified that your firm's policies in respect of audit sampling had not been complied with.

State the steps that your firm should take in respect of this matter. **(3 marks)**

67.2 Fantastic Ltd (Fantastic) is a global retailer. It has stores in many countries and an online retail website. Fantastic has invited your firm to tender for its external audit.

List the key factors you believe Fantastic will consider when evaluating your firm's tender and explain why each factor will be important to Fantastic. **(4 marks)**

67.3 List the points specific to the examination of a profit forecast that should be included in an engagement letter for such an examination. Give the reason for including each point. **(4marks)**

67.4 Your firm has accepted an engagement to examine the profit forecast prepared by Beast Ltd (Beast) for the two years ending 31 March 20Y0. Beast owns 45 hotels throughout Europe. Beast's business is seasonal with higher occupancy of its hotel rooms during May to September. During the year ending 31 March 20X9, Beast plans to close 12 of its least profitable hotels and sell the properties to developers. Employees at these hotels will be offered the choice of transferring to another hotel or redundancy.

List the key variables which should be subjected to sensitivity analysis in the examination of Beast's profit forecast for the two years ending 31 March 20Y0. **(3 marks)**

67.5 You are responsible for planning the external audit of Tofind Ltd (Tofind), a mobile phone service provider. You see a news report that Tofind has suffered a cyber-attack resulting in the theft of some of its customers' personal data.

Outline the audit procedures you would plan to perform in relation to this cyber-attack. **(3 marks)**

67.6 Your firm has been the external auditor of Scamander Ltd (Scamander) for several years. You are responsible for planning the audit for the year ended 28 February 20X8. The engagement partner has identified payroll as a key area of audit risk. Scamander's employees work in eight different offices across the UK and the total workforce has grown by 6% during the year ended 28 February 20X8. On 1 March 20X7, Scamander awarded a company-wide pay increase of 2%.

List the analytical procedures, relevant to payroll, to be included in your audit plan. **(3 marks)**

68 Barebones Ltd

Your firm has recently been appointed as the external auditor of Barebones Ltd (BB) for the year ending 31 March 20X8. BB was incorporated on 1 April 20X6 and is owned equally by Nomaj Ltd (Nomaj) and Macusa Ltd (Macusa). BB was not required to have an audit for the year ended 31 March 20X7. Your firm has been the external auditor of Nomaj for many years but has no previous relationship with Macusa.

BB was formed to develop and manufacture sportswear which has wearable technology woven into the fabric. The technology monitors athletic performance by providing data, such as heart rate and distance travelled, to a smartphone. BB has successfully developed the technology and negotiated two contracts with large retailers to sell its new sportswear. The contracts commenced in July 20X7.

You are the senior responsible for planning the audit of BB. The engagement partner has asked you to consider the following key areas of audit risk:

(1) Going concern
(2) Intangible assets – development costs of wearable technology
(3) Trade payables

The development of the sportswear was funded by equity investment and loans from Nomaj and Macusa. During the year ending 31 March 20X8, BB received a bank loan and has also made use of an overdraft facility. The terms of the bank loan require BB to maintain an interest cover of 1.5 times or higher. BB has asked its bank for an additional loan to develop the use of its technology in baby clothing. The directors of BB wish to diversify into baby clothing because the wearable technology sportswear market is highly competitive. Similar sportswear has been launched by other companies. During contract negotiations retailers pushed down prices and demanded extended credit terms of over 60 days. BB's bank has requested a copy of the audited financial statements for the year ending 31 March 20X8 and will decide on the additional loan after it has reviewed them.

BB's management has provided you with the following financial information:

Forecast financial information from the statement of profit or loss for the year ending 31 March 20X8

	£'000
Cost of sales	(10,750)
Profit before interest and tax	2,984
Interest payable	(2,105)

Notes to the financial statements for the year as at 31 March (extracts)
Intangible assets – development costs

	20X8 (Forecast) £'000	20X7 (Unaudited) £'000
Carrying amount at 1 April 20X7	2,050	–
Additions	1,780	2,450
Amortisation charge	(430)	(400)
Carrying amount at 31 March 20X8	3,400	2,050

Current liabilities

	20X8 (Forecast) £'000	20X7 (Unaudited) £'000
Trade payables	1,325	250
Bank overdraft	750	–

Development costs include salaries of employees working in the product development team and materials used in the development process for the wearable technology. In addition, the product development team uses equipment classified as plant and equipment. The depreciation charge on this equipment is included in development costs. The product development director also estimates the relevant proportion of overheads to attribute to development costs.

Materials used in the product development and in the production processes are purchased from suppliers around the world. Suppliers invoice in their local currency. Credit terms are 30 days. The purchase ledger is currently being managed by Henry Shaw. Henry was seconded to BB from Nomaj to save costs. He set up a spreadsheet to manage the purchase ledger but the time taken to do this has resulted in a large backlog of suppliers' invoices that have not been processed.

Jacob Langdon, Nomaj's finance director and a board member of BB, requested that your firm undertakes an additional engagement, for Nomaj's board of directors. The engagement is to examine the five-year profit and cash flow forecasts of BB and prepare a report to the directors of Nomaj which recommends whether Nomaj should continue to support BB. Jacob requested that your firm does not mention this engagement to any of Macusa's representatives that are on BB's board of directors.

Requirements

68.1 Justify why the items listed by the engagement partner as (1) to (3) have been identified as key areas of audit risk and, for each item, describe the procedures that should be included in the audit plan to address those risks.

You should start each justification on a new line and present your answer in a two-column format using the headings:

- Going concern
- Intangible assets – development costs of wearable technology
- Trade payables **(28 marks)**

68.2 Assuming your firm concludes there is uncertainty over whether BB is a going concern, state, with reasons, the implications for the auditor's report on the financial statements of BB for the year ending 31 March 20X8. **(4 marks)**

68.3 Identify and explain the ethical issues arising in relation to the additional engagement requested by Jacob Langdon. **(4 marks)**

68.4 BB is a significant component of Macusa and financial information relating to BB will be included in Macusa's group financial statements for the year ending 31 March 20X8. Your firm has not yet received any communication from Macusa's auditor regarding its requirements.

List the requirements and information that you expect the external auditor of Macusa to include in its communication to your firm. **(3 marks)**

Total: 39 marks

69 NANN

The following situations have recently been referred to your firm's ethics partner by other partners in your firm.

Niffler plc (Niffler)

Your firm is the external auditor of Niffler, a UK listed company. In addition to the external audit, your firm provides recurring non-audit services that are permitted under the FRC's Revised Ethical Standard. Your firm expects to earn the following fees from Niffler during 20X8:

Audit services £'000	Non-audit services £'000
973	650

Your firm's total annual fee income in 20X8 is expected to be £32 million.

Auror Ltd (Auror)

Mary Graves is the audit engagement partner for the external audit of Auror. Frank Gellert, Mary's father, has recently been appointed as Auror's chief executive.

Nundu Ltd (Nundu)

The audit engagement partner has discovered that during the external audit of Nundu, for the year ended 31 December 20X7, a member of the engagement team accepted an expensive watch as a gift from Nundu for his hard work during the audit. The auditor's report for the year ended 31 December 20X7 has been published.

Newt Ltd (Newt)

Newt is a specialist scientific research company. Its directors have requested that your firm accepts an engagement to audit Newt's financial statements for the year ending 31 March 20X8. Newt recently submitted a loan application and its bank requires a copy of the auditor's report before it decides whether to provide the loan. Newt's finance director has also requested that your firm provides assistance with the preparation of some aspects of the financial statements.

Requirement

Identify and explain the threats to objectivity and independence, and the professional issues (if any), arising in each of the situations above. State any actions that your firm should take in respect of these matters.

Total: 20 marks

70 Billywig Ltd

Your firm is the external auditor of Billywig Ltd (Billywig) for the year ended 31 January 20X8. The audit fieldwork has been completed. The engagement partner, Percy Rowling, is performing a review of the audit files and Billywig's draft annual report, including its financial statements.

Billywig is a pest control company, eliminating pests, such as rodents and insects, from buildings. Billywig has large contracts with government bodies around the UK. It has had a difficult year because cuts in government spending have resulted in a reduction in contract prices. Weak sterling has also resulted in increased costs of the pesticides purchased from overseas suppliers.

Percy made the following observations during his review:

(1) The financial statements show that the gross profit margin increased from 28% in the year ended 31 January 20X7 to 32% in the year ended 31 January 20X8.

(2) The audit documentation in relation to 'plant and equipment' notes an error in the calculation of depreciation on some items in the sample tested. The audit junior who performed the test extrapolated the error across the population of plant and equipment. This resulted in an overall expected error of £52,985. Materiality for the audit was set at £82,000. The audit junior concluded the error was not material.

(3) The audit work on subsequent events included a review of the minutes of Billywig's board meetings held since 31 January 20X8. The audit senior carrying out the review highlighted that in the February board minutes there was discussion about a formal complaint from one of Billywig's largest customers. The customer claimed that Billywig had failed to meet its contractual obligations.

(4) The audit team performed a data analytics routine on journal entries. This highlighted that 18 journals were processed outside of normal office hours.

(5) The audit documentation in relation to trade payables notes that Billywig did not perform any supplier statement reconciliations during the year.

(6) The directors' report, included in the draft annual report, states that "Billywig's net profit has remained stable despite difficult trading conditions." However, the financial statements show that net profit fell by 12%.

Requirements

70.1 State, with reasons, the additional steps Percy Rowling should take in respect of each of his observations listed as (1) to (6) above before concluding his review of the Billywig audit.

(16 marks)

70.2 In respect of observation (5), outline the possible consequences of the internal control deficiency and provide recommendations to remedy the deficiency. (3 marks)

70.3 In respect of observation (6), state, with reasons, the possible implications for the auditor's report. You should describe any modifications to the auditor's report that you consider necessary. (2 marks)

Total: 21 marks

June 2018 exam questions

71 Short form questions

71.1 You are planning the external audit of Eustace plc (Eustace), a steel producer, for the year ending 30 September 20X8. During your review of internal audit reports, you read that some steel was incorrectly classified resulting in low quality steel being sold as high quality steel. The directors have informed the industry regulators and have taken action to rectify the matter.

Identify the business risks to which Eustace is exposed as a result of this matter and state the implications for the financial statements. **(4 marks)**

71.2 You have completed the controls testing on payroll during the external audit of Jenkins Ltd. You found that in two cases out of 30 tested there was no evidence that one particular control was operated.

State, with reasons, the actions that you would take in respect of this matter. **(3 marks)**

71.3 You are the audit senior on the external audit of Lawson plc. During the interim audit, the credit controller asks for a private interview with you. During this interview she informs you that she suspects the chief accountant of misappropriating company funds received from customers and altering the financial records.

List the actions that you would take to assess whether the credit controller's suspicions are valid. **(3 marks)**

71.4 Your firm has recently accepted appointment as external auditor of Healey Ltd, a competitor of Howe Ltd (Howe). Your firm has acted as external auditor of Howe for many years. Both companies have provided your firm with informed consent to act.

Outline the procedures that your firm should implement to address any potential conflicts of interest arising out of this appointment. **(3 marks)**

71.5 Explain why the level of assurance provided by a report on the examination of prospective financial information differs from the level of assurance provided by an auditor's report on annual financial statements. **(3 marks)**

71.6 Your firm is the external auditor of Dalton City Ltd (Dalton), a football club, for the year ended 31 May 20X8. On 30 April 20X8 Ron Osborne commenced legal proceedings against Dalton. Ron is the former team manager who was dismissed by Dalton on 31 March 20X8 and is claiming substantial damages for breach of contract. The directors of Dalton dispute the claim. If the claim is successful, the damages are likely to be material to the financial statements of Dalton for the year ended 31 May 20X8 but will not affect the going concern status of Dalton.

List the audit procedures that your firm should undertake in respect of the legal claim by Ron.   **(4 marks)**

72 Puskas plc

Your firm is the external auditor of Puskas plc (Puskas) for the year ending 30 June 20X8. The principal activity of the company is the design, manufacture and installation of electrical systems. Puskas has applied for a bank loan to finance the expansion of the business. The bank requires the audited financial statements by 31 July 20X8 prior to considering the application.

You are the audit manager and the engagement partner asked you to consider the following two key areas of audit risk:

- Work in progress
- Provision for warranty claims.

You have been provided with the following extracts from the financial statements:

Statement of profit or loss for the year ending 30 June (extract)

	20X8 (estimated) £'000	20X7 (audited) £'000
Revenue	652,000	564,137
Cost of sales	(384,000)	(360,007)
Gross profit	268,000	204,130

Statement of financial position as at 30 June (extract)

	20X8 (estimated) £'000	20X7 (audited) £'000
Current assets		
Work in progress	81,200	49,307
Current liabilities		
Provision for warranty claims	550	564
Non-current liabilities		
Provision for warranty claims	652	564

In addition, the following information has been provided:

- All work is carried out under short-term fixed-price contracts for customers operating in the UK construction industry. Puskas's employees design the systems to each customer's specification, buy in components from suppliers in mainland Europe and install the system. Overseas suppliers invoice Puskas in euro.

- The contract price is negotiated and agreed with the customer before commencement of any work by Puskas. It is company policy to recognise revenue once the customer confirms successful installation of the systems.

- Puskas maintains a computerised contract costing system. In the previous year's report to management, your firm identified that the contract costing system was unreliable. Puskas replaced the contract costing system in March 20X8.

- All direct costs relating to each contract are recorded in the contract costing system which is integrated with the purchases and payroll systems. The finance director uses the cost records to calculate the value of work in progress for the monthly management accounts and the year-end financial statements. For the valuation of work in progress, the financial controller, a new employee, adds a percentage to the direct costs to cover overheads. The percentage is determined by taking attributable overheads in the management accounts as a percentage of direct costs in the management accounts. Provision is made for contract losses where appropriate.

- Historically, Puskas provided a two-year warranty against defects in the design, manufacture or installation of its electrical systems. In July 20X7, Puskas increased the warranty period to three years to match the warranties offered by its competitors. Puskas includes a provision for such warranties in its financial statements. The provision is based on the finance director's assessment of future claims.

- An element of the directors' remuneration is based on audited profit before tax.

The recent interim audit revealed the following internal control deficiencies:

(a) References were not obtained for new employees recruited for the teams responsible for the installation of electrical systems and the accounts department.

(b) Puskas does not routinely update its anti-malware software on its contract costing, purchases and payroll systems.

The board of Puskas has decided to seek tenders for the appointment of the external auditor for the year ending 30 June 20X9. A number of firms have been invited to tender, including your firm. The engagement partner has sent you the following email:

'One of the former audit partners of our firm and a very good friend of mine, Jane Kopa, is a member of the audit committee of Puskas. She is always very supportive of our work and I would like Jane's advice before we submit our tender. Whilst you are at Puskas, please can you arrange to meet her and seek out her views on key issues facing the business so that our firm can include these in the formal tender. As a member of the audit committee, Jane is well placed to help us with the tendering process'.

Requirements

72.1 Justify why work in progress and provision for warranty claims have been identified as key areas of audit risk and, for each key area, describe the procedures that should be included in the audit plan to address those risks. You should present your answer using the following subheadings:

- Work in progress
- Provision for warranty claims   (23 marks)

72.2 For each internal control deficiency listed as (a) and (b) in the scenario, draft points for inclusion in your firm's report to those charged with governance and management at Puskas. For each deficiency, you should outline the possible consequence(s) of the deficiency and provide recommendations to address it.   (10 marks)

72.3 Explain the ethical issues arising in respect of the email from the engagement partner. State the actions that you should take.   (4 marks)

72.4 List three factors that could be used by the audit committee of Puskas to monitor the effectiveness of the external auditor.   (3 marks)

Total: 40 marks

73 Alonso Ltd

ICAEW has recently undertaken quality control reviews at your firm, including the inspection of a sample of external audit files. It has reported the following matters to be addressed by your firm.

(1) The recruitment section of your firm's website states that commission will be paid to employees for the successful generation of new business from audit and assurance clients.

(2) Your firm has no policies in place in respect of staff and partners holding shares in client companies.

(3) From March 20X6 to December 20X7, your firm seconded a senior manager to Alonso Ltd (Alonso) as Head of Internal Audit. The same individual is the senior manager responsible for the external audit of Alonso for the year ending 30 September 20X8.

(4) On several external audit files, there was no evidence that the planned audit approach, scope of the audit, ethical matters and timetable were communicated to those charged with governance at the audited entity.

The report noted that your firm fully complied with the Money Laundering Regulations.

Requirements

73.1 Describe how ICAEW promotes improvements in the quality of the audit and assurance work performed by its members. **(5 marks)**

73.2 Explain why matters (1) to (4) above have been reported to your firm and list the actions that your firm should take in respect of each matter. **(12 marks)**

73.3 List the actions that audit and assurance firms are required to take to comply with the Money Laundering Regulations. **(3 marks)**

Total: 20 marks

74 CKP

Described below are situations which have arisen at three unrelated external audit clients of your firm. The year end in each case is 31 March 20X8.

Chobe Ltd (Chobe)

The management of Chobe has refused to provide your firm with written representations regarding its responsibility for the preparation of the financial statements or the completeness of recorded transactions and information provided during the audit.

Kanye plc (Kanye)

Kanye recognised payments received from customers for one month after the year end on the statement of financial position at the year end, as cash at bank. Your firm's audit identified that, as a result, cash was overstated by £21 million and trade receivables understated by the same amount at the year end. The directors refuse to adjust the financial statements because the cash balance is one measure used by stakeholders to assess Kanye's financial performance.

The draft financial statements show that Kanye's total assets are £355 million.

Pula plc (Pula)

During the audit of Pula, a listed company, you read the strategic report to be included in Pula's annual report. The strategic report does not include a description of the risks and uncertainties facing Pula's business. The Companies Act 2006 requires the strategic report to disclose a description of such risks and uncertainties. The directors are refusing to include this information in the strategic report because it is too time-consuming and costly to produce this information.

Requirements

74.1 In respect of external audit engagements:

    (a) List the key purposes of obtaining written representations from management; and

    (b) Describe three confirmations relating to specific items in the financial statements that could be included in a management representation letter. **(6 marks)**

74.2 For each of the situations described above, explain the implications, if any, for the auditor's report. **(9 marks)**

74.3 Explain why the behaviour of the directors of Kanye should be considered by your firm when deciding whether to continue to act as external auditor for the year ending 31 March 20X9. **(5 marks)**

Total: 20 marks

September 2018 exam questions

75 Short form questions

75.1 Island Ltd (Island) and Flint Ltd (Flint) are both external audit clients of your firm. Each company has a year end of 30 September. In April 20X8, Flint contracted with Island for the provision of services. Flint is dissatisfied with the quality of services provided by Island and is currently taking legal action against Island. The outcome of the legal action will not be known before the conclusion of both external audits for the year ending 30 September 20X8.

Identify and explain the ethical issues arising from the situation outlined above and state how your firm should address these issues.　**(4 marks)**

75.2 Your firm is the external auditor of Blackett Ltd (Blackett), an unlisted company, and its wholly-owned subsidiary Coniston Ltd (Coniston). The audit fees for Blackett and Coniston are £4.2 million and £2.7 million respectively. Your firm also provides annual tax services to both companies for a total fee of £1.6 million. During the current year, your firm performed a one-off IT engagement for Blackett for a fee of £1.1 million. Your firm's total annual fee income from all its clients is £74.8 million.

Explain what is meant by the self-interest threat in relation to the fee income, arising from the circumstances outlined above, and state how your firm should address this threat.　**(4 marks)**

75.3 Your firm is the external auditor of Captain Ltd (Captain) for the year ending 31 December 20X8. Your firm plans to use data analytics routines relevant to the audit of inventory. Captain sells fashion goods from 3,000 retail stores located in 36 countries. The goods are purchased from around the world and are invoiced in each supplier's local currency.

Describe **three** data analytics routines relevant to the audit of Captain's inventory.　**(3 marks)**

75.4 Your firm has been the external auditor of Parrot Ltd (Parrot) for three years. You have performed preliminary analytical procedures whilst planning the audit for the year ended 30 June 20X8. Trade payables days have fallen to 24.9 days compared with 31.6 days at 30 June 20X7. Parrot's suppliers have credit terms of 30 days.

List the audit procedures you would include in the audit plan for the year ended 30 June 20X8 given the change identified in trade payables days.　**(3 marks)**

75.5 Outline how the planned procedures for an engagement to review financial statements will differ from the planned procedures in respect of an external audit performed under the Companies Act 2006. Give reasons for the differences.　**(2 marks)**

75.6 Your firm is the external auditor of Pirate Ltd (Pirate). During the current year, Pirate acquired 100% of the share capital of Oar Ltd (Oar), a company incorporated in the UK. The year end for both companies is 30 June 20X8. Oar's financial statements are being audited by Turner LLP (Turner) and your firm intends to use the audit evidence obtained by Turner for the group audit. Oar is a significant component of Pirate.

Outline the procedures that your firm should undertake because of its intention to use the audit evidence obtained by Turner for the year ended 30 June 20X8. **(4 marks)**

76 Ransome

Your firm is the external auditor of Ransome Guard Ltd (RG), a UK-based company, for the year ending 30 September 20X8. RG designs and sells wireless home security cameras to retailers.

Homeowners purchase RG's security cameras from a retailer, install them at their property and link them to their smartphones via a free mobile app. Homeowners receive alerts in the app when a camera detects motion at their property and they can also view video recordings made by the cameras. Some homeowners use RG's premium service. The premium service allows storage of larger volumes of video recordings in the app compared with the basic plan, which is free.

You are the audit senior responsible for planning the audit. The engagement partner has asked you to consider the following key areas of audit risk:

- Revenue from retailers and the premium service
- Inventory
- Going concern

RG has contracts to supply 32 major retailers in Europe and North America with its security cameras. Each contract with a retailer states the number of cameras to be supplied in the contract period and the price to be paid to RG for each camera, denominated in the retailer's local currency.

Homeowners who use the premium service pay RG on an annual basis in advance by entering their credit card details in the app. The annual cost is denominated in the homeowner's local currency.

RG's security cameras are assembled by Pemmican Ltd (Pemmican) a company based in Asia. Pemmican purchases components for the cameras, based on specifications set out in its contract with RG. Pemmican delivers the assembled cameras to a shipping company in Asia which then ships them to one of RG's 12 warehouses in Europe and North America. Ownership of the cameras passes to RG when Pemmican delivers them to the shipping company. In accordance with the contract, Pemmican invoices RG a fixed price, denominated in sterling, for each camera assembled.

RG maintains a perpetual inventory system at each of its 12 warehouses. Inventory at each warehouse is counted once a year with one warehouse being selected for counting each month. Year-end inventory included in the financial statements is based on the quantities recorded in the perpetual inventory system.

On 30 April 20X8, an audit junior attended the inventory count at RG's UK warehouse and noted the following issues:

(a) The movement of cameras to and from the warehouse continued throughout the count.

(b) There was a large quantity of one camera, the GrG-I model, which appeared to be old with damaged packaging. The UK warehouse manager said that he had not had time to review the aged inventory report for many months.

(c) There were several discrepancies identified between the perpetual inventory records and the quantity of physical inventory counted at the warehouse. The UK warehouse manager explained that adjustments are made to the perpetual inventory records for any discrepancies without further investigation.

As part of your planning for the year ending 30 September 20X8, you met with Susan Walker, RG's finance director, who provided you with the following information:

- RG is currently discussing quality issues with Pemmican. Pemmican has been sourcing cheaper components, which are inferior to those stipulated in its contract with RG, to improve Pemmican's profit margin.

- During the year, RG received a significant number of complaints about its cameras malfunctioning shortly after installation. In response to the resulting adverse media attention, RG has publicly promised refunds to all affected homeowners. RG's quality control team is currently investigating whether the malfunctions are due to the inferior components used by Pemmican.

- RG is currently renegotiating eight of its retail contracts which are due to expire by June 20X9. Susan is concerned that other retailers might exercise early termination clauses in their contracts if the quality issues are not resolved quickly.

- In August 20X8, RG was the victim of a cyber-attack which prevented RG from operating for two days. RG's IT security department is currently investigating whether any personal data of homeowners was stolen during the attack.

Susan also provided you with the following financial information:

Statement of profit or loss for the year ending 30 September (extract)

	20X8 (estimated) £'000	20X7 (audited) £'000
Revenue		
Contracts with retailers	132,750	124,120
Premium service	49,780	35,500
	182,530	159,620
Cost of sales	(98,710)	(97,770)
Gross profit	83,820	61,850
Profit before tax	15,470	30,925

Statement of financial position as at 30 September (extract)

	20X8 (estimated) £'000	20X7 (audited) £'000
Inventory	13,890	10,500

At the end of your planning meeting, Susan asked whether you would be interested in working for RG as financial controller. The position has been vacant for many months. You are very interested in the offer and intend to discuss this further with Susan.

Requirements

76.1 Justify why revenue, inventory and going concern have been identified as key areas of audit risk and, for each key area, describe the procedures that should be included in the audit plan to address those risks.

Present your answer using the following subheadings:

- Revenue from retailers
- Revenue from the premium service

- Inventory
- Going concern

(25 marks)

76.2 For each of the issues (a) to (c) noted by the audit junior, draft points for inclusion in your firm's report to those charged with governance and management at RG. For each issue, state the internal control deficiency, outline the possible consequence(s) and provide recommendations to address the deficiency.

(12 marks)

76.3 Identify and explain the threats to independence and objectivity arising from Susan's offer for you to become RG's financial controller. State any actions that you or the engagement partner should take.

(3 marks)

Total: 40 marks

77 Swallow

Your firm has been invited to tender for appointment as external auditor of Swallow Group Ltd (Swallow) for the year ending 31 December 20X8. The audit partner considering the invitation has documented the following information:

Swallow is a specialist engineering company which designs and manufactures precision equipment for industrial customers in Europe, Asia and Africa. Swallow operates through three subsidiaries, one based in each continent, and has manufacturing facilities in 20 countries.

Contracts for the design and manufacture of equipment for customers are fixed-price and are typically longer than 12 months. Swallow recognises revenue and costs based on the estimated stage of completion of each contract. Full provision is made for any anticipated losses on contracts.

In response to challenging market conditions during 20X7, Swallow undertook a business reorganisation in the first six months of 20X8. This included implementation of new IT systems and a redesign of its manufacturing processes to improve efficiency. This has resulted in difficult employee relations because employees working in the manufacturing facilities claim that the changes compromise health and safety standards. Swallow has experienced significant adverse publicity about this issue.

Swallow has also changed the way it remunerates the employees in its sales team to provide greater incentives to win new contracts. Since the changes were made, Swallow's fraud and anti-bribery confidential hotline has received increased calls about the sales practices in some regions.

Swallow's share capital is owned equally by three siblings, John, Nancy and Kitty Walker. John and Nancy are directors of Swallow. Kitty left her role as finance director in June 20X8 due to a disagreement and has not been replaced. The disagreement arose because John and Nancy wish to raise additional loan finance to enable Swallow to increase investment in research and development. Kitty disagreed with this because Swallow already invests significant amounts in research and development.

John and Nancy have requested a loan from Swallow's bank. The bank requires the audited financial statements for the year ending 31 December 20X8 before making a final decision on the loan. Swallow's invitation to tender document states: "The successful firm will be able to demonstrate its ability to complete the 20X8 audit on or before 31 January 20X9."

Swallow's invitation to tender document also requires your firm to include the following non-audit services in its tender response:

- Management of Swallow's payroll
- Assistance in recruiting a new finance director
- Representation of Swallow in a significant dispute with HMRC

Requirements

77.1 Using the information documented by the audit partner, identify and explain the factors that should be considered by your firm when deciding whether to submit a tender for appointment as Swallow's external auditor.

You do not need to consider the provision of the non-audit services in this part of the question. **(18 marks)**

77.2 Assuming your firm is appointed as external auditor of Swallow, explain the threats to independence and objectivity which may arise if your firm also provides the non-audit services requested. Outline the safeguards, if any, which should be put in place to mitigate those threats. **(8 marks)**

Total: 26 marks

78 AWLS

Described below are situations which have arisen at four unrelated clients of your firm.

AMA Zones Ltd (AMA)

Your firm is the external auditor of AMA for the year ended 30 June 20X8. AMA's financial statements show revenue of £54.8 million, of which £1.1 million relates to cash sales. During the audit, your firm identified that AMA had no system of internal control over cash sales. No other audit procedures were available to obtain assurance over cash sales. AMA's profit before tax is £9.5 million.

Wild Ltd (Wild)

Your firm is the external auditor of Wild for the year ended 30 June 20X8. In March 20X8, Wild sold a property to Holly James. Holly is Wild's managing director. Wild's directors have refused to disclose the sale of the property to Holly in the financial statements for the year ended 30 June 20X8.

Lake Ltd (Lake)

Your firm is performing an engagement to examine and provide assurance on Lake's cash flow forecast for the three years ending 30 September 20Y1. The forecast has been prepared by Lake's directors in support of a loan application. Lake's bank requires the forecast to be examined and reported on by independent accountants. The cash flow forecast has been prepared on the assumption that revenue will grow by 8% pa. Your firm believes this is highly unrealistic because current revenue growth for Lake and the industry in which it operates is 2% pa and 3% pa respectively.

Sail plc (Sail)

Sail is a listed company. Your firm has accepted an assurance engagement to provide an opinion on Sail's greenhouse gas (GHG) statement for the year ended 30 June 20X8. Sail has estimated the emissions figures for the period February to June 20X8 and is required to disclose this fact in the GHG statement. Your firm is satisfied with the basis of the estimate and that it has been appropriately disclosed by Sail. The inclusion of estimates is fundamental to users' understanding of the GHG statement.

Requirement

For each of the four situations above, state, with reasons, the implications for your firm's audit or assurance reports. **Total: 14 marks**

Answer Bank

Section 1: Legal and other professional regulations, ethics, accepting and managing engagements and current issues

1 Short form questions

1.1 Ethical issues and procedures

- May compromise the opinion of the existing auditor
- Client may be opinion shopping
- May be a threat to professional competence and due care, if not in possession of all the facts
- Audit firm may be tempted to give the opinion the client desires in order to obtain the audit in future
- Obtain client's permission to contact the existing auditor
- Notify auditor of the work to be undertaken
- So that your firm is in full possession of all the facts
- If client refuses permission, decline to act

1.2 Safeguards re fees

To recognise threat

- Regularly review situation as client profile changes

To offset threat

- Consider whether the firm could be open to criticism and either:
    - refuse appointment; or
    - introduce safeguards, including independent review and disclosure to ethics partner and those charged with governance.
- Do not accept the assignment if total fees regularly exceed 15% of annual fee income (or 10% for listed company), although it may be possible for another part of the firm to carry out the work.

1.3 Overdue fees

- Overdue fees constitute a self-interest threat to independence (ES S4)
- Issue of unmodified report this year may increase chance of collecting overdue fees
- Ideally arrange for settlement of the overdue fees
- Consider resigning from the engagement if not settled and fees are:
    - significant
    - in dispute
- If do not resign apply appropriate safeguards (eg, second partner review)
- And notify ethics partner

1.4 Actions

- Report to Money Laundering Reporting Officer (MLRO) within the firm
- Report to National Crime Agency (NCA)
- Avoid tipping off the client
- So as not to prejudice legal proceedings

- Recommend repayment to customers
- Ensure included as liability not income

Reasons

- Represents proceeds of crime/theft
- Criminal offence if auditor does not report

1.5 Points re fraud

- Duty is to report on financial statements

- No responsibility as such to detect fraud

- An audit conducted in accordance with ISAs obtains reasonable assurance that the financial statements are free from material misstatement whether caused by fraud or error

- Auditors may not find material frauds

- Frauds involving collusion harder to detect

- Responsibility set out in engagement letter

- Management is responsible for implementing and monitoring the system of control

1.6 Possible benefits

- Independent confirmation of profits earned/net assets
- Assurance of compliance with Companies Act
- Recommendations on systems via management letter
- Added credibility of accounts will help negotiations with bank
- Reliable financial information for business decisions

1.7 Principal ethical issue

Confidentiality

- Data and Lodge may perceive threat of disclosure/use of information
- Conflict of interest for audit firm
- Difficult to act in best interest of both clients

Procedures

- Ensure staff are aware of confidentiality issues
- Staff to certify they are aware of procedures
- Obtain informed consent of both clients/inform both clients
- Use different partners and teams
- Independent review of arrangements for ensuring confidentiality maintained
- Information barriers in place

1.8 Benefits

To the bank

- Reduces uncertainty as to reliability of the information/increases credibility
- Reduces the risk of management bias/independent
- Enables bank to determine risk in advancing more money to Royale

To Royale

Enables them to obtain the overdraft which may not be possible without the report

Limitations

To the bank

- Not all receivable and inventory balances will be looked at by your firm

- Possibility of collusion or misrepresentation

- Evidence likely to be persuasive rather than conclusive/assurance not absolute - reasonable or limited level of assurance depending on scope of work

- Report may not highlight full extent of problem/lack of sufficient information
- Inherent limitations of accounting system/integrity of data

1.9 Threats to independence and safeguards

Mrs Wallace

- Self-interest threat
- Trustee interest held by a person in a position to influence the audit is only allowed by ES S2 where:
  - Mrs Wallace not a beneficiary of the trust
  - the financial interest held by the trust in Racdale Ltd is not material to the trust
  - trust is not able to exercise significant influence over Racdale Ltd
  - Mrs Wallace does not have significant influence over investment decisions made by the trust
- Therefore transfer audit responsibility to another partner

Mr Netwater

- Familiarity/self-interest/intimidation threat
- Should be removed immediately from audit role
- Review of the audit work performed by Mr Netwater in the current year and, where appropriate, most recent audit
- Firm should reassess composition of audit team

1.10 Accountant's report on profit forecast

Comment

- Negative assurance which is limited assurance

How it differs

- Audit provides high level of assurance which is reasonable/not absolute assurance
- Opinion expressed in positive terms
  - Give a true and fair view/prepared in accordance with Companies Act/directors' report consistent

Why it differs

- Financial statements are based on fact as well as judgement
- Persuasive evidence available
- Often the delay between reporting date and auditor's report means that even items such as provisions/estimates can be substantiated
- Scope of work on forecasts is limited as forecasts are based on assumptions about the future and as such are subject to uncertainty

1.11 Responsibilities

Auditor responsibilities

- No responsibility to prevent fraud
- Responsibility to detect material misstatements in the financial statements whether due to fraud or error
- Must design audit procedures to obtain reasonable assurance that financial statements are free from material misstatement whether caused by fraud or error

- Must make report to relevant authority under money laundering regulations
- Must not tip-off sales manager or accounts clerk

Management responsibilities

- Responsible for preventing fraud
- Responsible for detecting fraud
- Must implement system of internal control suitable for the business and monitor such systems
- Responsible for safeguarding the assets of the company

1.12 Ethical issues

- Fee income from Count amounts to 10.44% of firm's total fee income
- This is above 10% 'review' limit in ES S4 for non-listed client
- But under 15% limit
- Self interest threat – firms objectivity may be impaired if fear losing major client
- Self review threat for tax work if numbers impact financial statements

How address

- Disclose fee % to ethics partner and those charged with governance at Count
- Internal independent quality control review by partner not connected with audit
- If likely to exceed 10% on regular basis should arrange external quality review
- Separate teams for audit and tax to counter self review threat
- Consider resignation from tax engagement

1.13 Threat

- Self review
- Audit team may be reluctant to identify impairments
- Audit team may rely too heavily on colleagues' work

Safeguards

- Members of the audit team should not have been involved in the due diligence investigation
- Independent partner or quality control review

1.14 Reasons why external auditors should be objective and independent

- Issues arising in the preparation of financial statements involve the use of judgement
- The auditor therefore needs to be unbiased in forming the audit opinion
- Directors may make biased or inappropriate judgements
- The auditor needs to adopt rigorous and robust approach to identify such bias or inappropriate judgement
- The audit opinion should be based only on the available audit evidence and no other factors
- Independence increases the likelihood that an auditor will be objective
- A lack of independence may reduce public confidence in the auditor's objective view
- Which would reduce the credibility and reliability of reports and opinions issued by auditors
- Objectivity and independence are required by Ethical Standard S1 and the Companies Act

1.15 Ethical issues and safeguards in respect of long association with a client who is in the process of becoming a listed company

- There is an issue of long association with Moose Ltd
- Which may lead to a familiarity threat
- The audit partner may be too trusting of the client or the client's representations
- Ethical Standard S3 guideline for rotation of unlisted company engagement partners is 10 years
- For listed companies the engagement partner must not act for more than five years
- Where the entity becomes listed the length of time the partner has already acted must be taken into account
- If the partner has served four years or more they may continue for no more than two years once listed
- Adam Flayman has served for four years and therefore may continue for a maximum of two years
- If Adam continues for two further years after listing safeguards will be required
- Such as independent partner review of the audit work
- Should communicate the maximum number of years to the client
- Document reasons for allowing Adam to continue
- Self interest threat may arise if fear losing client by failing to meet the directors' request
- Seek advice from ethics partner

1.16 Role of ethics partner within an external audit firm

- Responsible for adequacy of firms policies and procedures regarding integrity, objectivity and independence
- Responsible for firm's compliance with the FRC Ethical Standard
- Responsible for effectiveness of communication on ethical matters to partners and staff
- Provides ethical guidance and advice to individual partners and teams
- Gives consideration to whether policies and procedures are properly covered in training
- Provides guidance where difficult and objective judgement needs to be made or a consistent position reached
- Assesses implications of any breach of the FRC Ethical Standard
- Determines whether any safeguards can be put in place or whether there is a need to resign from engagement

1.17 Actions

- Report to firm's Money Laundering Reporting Officer (MLRO)
- Without tipping off
- There is suspected money laundering
- Appears to be disguising/transferring proceeds
- No *de minimis* where money laundering concerned

1.18 Professional competence and due care

- Maintain professional knowledge and skill at the level required to ensure that clients receive a professional service, based on current developments in practice, legislation and techniques

- Act diligently and in accordance with applicable technical and professional standards when providing professional services

Identify compliance

- On the job supervision of junior staff
- Review of juniors' and seniors' work by manager
- Hot/internal quality control reviews
- Cold reviews/monitoring
- Staff appraisals
- Staff training

1.19 Actions and explanation

- Discuss the issue with the directors and request that they amend the financial statements as the issue may be avoided if the directors understand the problem of incorrect accounting treatment.

- Reconsider other areas of the audit or undertake an independent internal quality review as the intimidation threat may have impaired objectivity on other aspects of the audit work.

- Seek legal advice or advice from the ethics partner in order to ensure that the firm's exposure to any risk is limited.

- Consider resignation as the directors' actions represent an intimidation threat and breakdown of trust as well as raising doubts about management's integrity.

1.20 Rights

Outgoing auditors may:

- make written representations and request directors to circulate to members
- attend and speak at general meeting

Responsibilities

- Prepare a statement of circumstances:

    - specifying reasons for ceasing to hold office

    - to be deposited at Pisces' registered office and copy to be sent to Registrar of Companies

- As Pisces is listed, there is no option to state there are no circumstances
- Obtain permission from client to reply to prospective auditor's communication
- Return promptly all books and records of the company
- Maintain client confidentiality after ceasing to act
- Maintain anti-money laundering identification records

1.21 Ethical issues

- The previous auditors appear not to have been reappointed due to giving a qualified opinion and the directors may now be opinion shopping

- This raises doubts over management's integrity and suggests a possible intimidation threat which may result in the firm issuing an inappropriate audit opinion

- Failure to pay fees could be further indication of an intimidation threat and also leads to self-interest threat if the firm fears non-payment of its own fees

- However, these issues do not preclude acceptance

Actions

- Review the prior year financial statements and auditor's report to establish the accounting policy for inventory valuation and ascertain the basis for the qualification

- Consider whether firm agrees with basis for qualification

- If the firm agrees, discuss with management whether they intend to change the accounting policy

- Ascertain from management the reason for the overdue fees in respect of prior year audit

- Consult firm's ethics partner

- Decline appointment if any suggestion that non-payment of previous auditors fees was linked to the qualification

- Carry out a background check on management

1.22 Audit firm is required, by Ethical Standard S3 (ES S3), to establish procedures and policies because a long association with the audit engagement may create threats to an auditor's objectivity and independence resulting from:

- Self-interest
- Self-review
- Familiarity

ES S3 sets out a mandatory requirement for the audit of listed companies where the engagement partner must be rotated every five years.

ES S3 also recommends that engagement partners for audits of non-listed companies be rotated every 10 years, however this requirement is not compulsory.

A firm may need to:

- apply safeguards to reduce any threats to an acceptable level; or
- resign from the audit if appropriate safeguards cannot be applied.

1.23 Business relationships are permitted under ES S2 as long as the arrangement is:

- in the ordinary course of business
- on an arms length basis
- not material to either party

Leasing properties is in the ordinary course of business for both parties

Market rate implies arms length basis

As both parties are large, transaction is unlikely to be material to either

Robinia has numerous properties and firm has 25 other offices therefore appropriate to accept

1.24
- Obtain authority from the company to discuss Lion's affairs with the new auditor

- Answer promptly the request for information

- Record in writing any discussions with Charn

- Confirm to Charn that there are matters about which they ought to be aware

- Explaining these matters meaningfully (honestly and unambiguously)

- This should include an explanation of the differences of opinion between the firm and Lion regarding the accounting treatment

- If Lion refuses to grant the firm permission to discuss the client's affairs, the firm should report that fact to Charn

1.25 **Action**

- Report to firm's MLRO/senior member of the engagement team

Reasons

- Bribery of foreign government official/inducement
- Is a criminal offence/illegal
- Under Bribery Act
- Also required to be reported under POCA
- Benefiting from criminal conduct

1.26 Firm required, by ISA (UK) 250A *Consideration of Laws and Regulations in an Audit of Financial Statements*, to consider non-compliance with laws and regulations

Failure to provide protective clothing may breach health and safety regulations and may indicate a lack of management integrity

There may be an impact on the financial statements due to:

- Fines for non-compliance with regulations
- Provisions/contingent liabilities arising from legal claims if employees suffer injuries
- Going concern issues if authorities close factory/suspend licence

Breaching law and regulations to save costs may be considered money laundering

1.27 Request written authority from Auburn to respond to Blonde

- Firm is bound by confidentiality until permission is received

If request is refused inform Blonde

- Blonde can evaluate impact on decision as to whether to accept appointment

Once authority is received should respond in writing as quickly as possible

- Allow Blonde to make a decision in the time available

Set out reasons in response as to why firm is not seeking reappointment

- So Blonde is in possession of all the facts before deciding to accept

1.28
- Report to firm's MLRO/senior member of engagement team/ethics partner
- Bribery/inducement
- Is a criminal offence
- Under Bribery Act 2010
- Excessive in value
- Also required to be reported under Proceeds of Crime Act
- Benefiting from criminal conduct
- Must not tip off client

1.29 Professional scepticism is an attitude that includes a questioning mind, being alert to conditions which may indicate possible misstatement due to error or fraud, and a critical assessment of audit evidence.

Asset impairments

- Involve estimates/assumptions/judgements about the future/discount factors/subject to uncertainty
- Assets more vulnerable to impairment in current economic climate
- Management may be reluctant to write down assets

Related parties

- Related party transactions may be used as vehicle for fraud
- Management may be reluctant to disclose/deliberately conceal
- Evidence not readily available/reliant on management to disclose

1.30 Reasons

- Not permitted by Ethical Standard S5
- Material to financial statements as greater than 2% of total assets
- Self review threat too great/no adequate safeguards
- May rely too heavily on valuations in subsequent audit
- May be reluctant to identify a misstatement in the valuation
- Management threat as may involve subjective judgement/making assumptions

1.31 Actions to be taken by Tyler

- Ask the police for more information/request to be in writing

- Firm owes a duty of confidentiality to the client

- Do not disclose any information, unless there is a court order or other legal duty

- Ask the client for permission to disclose

- If given, disclose the information to the police

- Consider whether:

    - money laundering is involved
    - a report should be made to NCA

- Re-review the audit work in the areas about which the police have requested information

- Consider the implications for audit work/risk assessment/audit opinion

- Consider future involvement/reputational risk

- Seek legal advice or contact the ICAEW helpline

Examiner's comments:

Answers to this question were very disappointing. The vast majority of candidates failed to appreciate that the audit firm should only disclose the information to the police if there was a legal duty to do so or if the client granted permission to disclose. Furthermore, a legal duty would apply only if the police had a court order. Although the majority of candidates considered the possibility of money laundering, many of these candidates stated, incorrectly, that this should be reported to the police thereby confusing the role of the police and the NCA. Few candidates considered the implications for the audit work and the appropriateness of continuing to act for the audited entity.

1.32 Marks were awarded for the **first two procedures given only** from the following list:

- Rotation of engagement partners – partners of listed clients must be rotated every five years/partners of non-listed clients should be considered for rotation every 10 years

- 'Fit and proper'/independence declarations – signed annually/at start of each audit

- Formal process in place for partners/employees to report family/personal relationships, financial interests in audited entity or decision to join audited entity – adequately communicated to employees

- Training/development/appraisal processes – including employees' understanding of how to identify threats to objectivity and independence and actions to take when threats identified

- Formal processes for considering appropriateness of appointment/reappointment – such as evaluation of client integrity, press/internet searches, obtaining references and discussion with directors/background checks

- Appointment of ethics partner – consulted on safeguards to ensure they are sufficient to address potential threats

- Requirement for engagement partners to be responsible for forming a conclusion on compliance with independence requirements for each engagement – includes identifying and evaluating circumstances/relationships that cause threats and taking action to eliminate them

- Engagement quality control reviewer – consider the adequacy of documentation of engagement partner's consideration of auditors' objectivity and independence

- Monitoring of compliance with firm's policies and procedures – periodic review, on a test basis, of audit engagement partners' documentation of consideration of objectivity and independence

Examiner's comments:

Answers to this question were of a mixed standard. Many candidates lost marks by only stating the procedure and failing to go on to describe the procedure. For example, rotation of engagement partners was a commonly cited procedure but candidates often failed to elaborate by providing additional information regarding the period of time for which an engagement partner may act for an audited entity. A major shortcoming was to cite objectives instead of procedures. For example, statements such as 'ensure members of an audit engagement team do not have financial interests in the audited entity', without specifying the procedure that would achieve this, were common. A significant number of candidates wasted time by providing more than two procedures as stipulated in the question.

1.33 Ethical issues

Breach of the fundamental principles of confidentiality and professional behaviour due to:

Improper disclosure of information

- Junior has given confidential information about the acquisition to his parents

Improper use of information

- Junior has acted on the information for his own personal advantage/insider trading
- ICAEW Code of Ethics: professional accountant should not deal in shares of a company in which he/she has a professional association

Self-interest threat

- Junior will want acquisition to take place to make a gain on the shares purchased
- Threat to professional competence and due care
- May not carry out work properly or fail to raise issues identified during review
- Could lead to inappropriate conclusion

Actions

- Remove junior from engagement team immediately
- Review/re-perform work of junior
- Notify engagement partner/ethics partner
- Disciplinary action/training of audit junior
- Obtain advice from ICAEW helpline

This question was very well answered as the majority of candidates identified that confidentiality had been breached by improper disclosure and improper use of information. Most of these candidates also recognised that there was a self-interest threat to professional competence and due care and that the junior's actions represented insider trading. Having identified the ethical threats, most candidates were also able to state appropriate actions to be taken by the manager and firm. The most common omission was to overlook the fact that the fundamental principle of professional behaviour had also been breached.

1.34 Ethical issues

Self-interest threat

- Senior may comply with MD's wishes to gain use of villa
- Use of villa likely to be considered excessive (not insignificant)
- Compromises objectivity/independence of senior

Offer may represent a bribe/inducement

- Could lead to improper performance by senior/finishing work too quickly/audit quality compromised
- Raises questions over management's integrity

Possible intimidation threat

- If managing director exerts pressure on senior
- Lack of professional competence and due care

Risk of unprofessional behaviour

Insufficient audit evidence may be obtained

Inappropriate opinion/material misstatement may not be detected

Examiner's comments:

This question was well answered. The majority of candidates identified the self-interest threat to objectivity, professional competence and due care and the intimidation threat. Most of these candidates provided plausible explanations of the self-interest threat. However, fewer candidates were able to explain the intimidation threat ie, pressure exerted by the managing director to complete the audit quickly. Weaker candidates strayed beyond the requirement and wasted time considering the actions that should be taken by the audit senior and the firm.

1.35 Setting targets to progress within a firm

Threat

- Self-interest threat
- Incentive for progression within the firm.

Explanation

- Senior employees may push services not required by the client/exaggerate the benefits of non-audit services
- Audit quality may suffer/errors may be overlooked/senior employees may be reluctant to raise contentious issues.

Is arrangement appropriate?

- Not appropriate

- No safeguards possible

- For each audited entity, ES S4 states that the audit firm shall establish a policy to ensure that:

    - objectives of the members of the team do not include selling non-audit services

    - criteria for evaluating performance or promotion of the members of the audit team do not include success in selling non-audit services

    - no specific element of remuneration of the members of the audit team is based on success in selling non-audit services.

Examiner's comments:

This question was generally well answered as the majority of candidates identified the self-interest threat to the objectivity of the senior employees within the firm and that the arrangements were inappropriate. Many of these candidates also appreciated that there was a risk to audit quality. However, the points most commonly overlooked were those relating to the risk of exaggerating the claims regarding the benefit of non-audit services and the promotion of services not required by the client. The requirement in the question was to identify 'the threat' implying that only one threat was required. However many candidates strayed beyond the requirement by listing a number of threats to the firm's objectivity in respect of the provision of non-audit services and the safeguards to such threats and scored no marks for these points. Disappointingly, a small number of candidates incorrectly stated that, with safeguards, the arrangement was appropriate.

1.36 Help with the preparation of financial statements

Explanation of threats to objectivity

- Management threat

    - Firm is expected to make decisions
    - Firm becomes too closely aligned with the views and interests of management

- Self-review threat

    - Results of a non-audit service are reflected in the amounts included or disclosed in the financial statements

    - Such as calculations

    - Audit team reluctant to identify shortcomings in their colleague's work or

    - May place too much reliance on that work

Safeguards

- Refer to ethics partner

- Not prohibited in UK as company is not listed

- Limit the length of time for which help is provided

- Informed management in place

    - Management makes all decisions requiring the exercise of judgement and
    - Has prepared the underlying accounting records

- Staff member does not initiate transactions or
- Make decisions
- Services provided are of a technical, mechanical, informative nature

- Audit documentation demonstrates that management has made all decisions

- Responsibilities set out in engagement letter

- Staff member must have no involvement in the audit of the financial statements

- Independent partner review of:
  - Audit work
  - Accounting services

Examiner's comments:

This question was generally well answered with a significant number of candidates scoring full marks. As in previous exams, many candidates cited incorrect threats. For example, many candidates cited the self-interest threat resulting from fee dependency and wasted time detailing the fee thresholds. There was no indication in the question that this was likely to be a recurring engagement and, in addition, one of the criteria to be satisfied for the engagement to be acceptable, is that it is for a short period of time. A significant minority of candidates stated, incorrectly, that information barriers would be required.

1.37 Circumstances requiring the disclosure of confidential information by auditors

- Required by law
  - Legal proceedings
  - Suspected terrorist activities
  - Suspected money laundering to the NCA
  - Suspected bribery

- Required to report to regulators
  - Such as FCA (financial services industry) and the Charity Commission (charities)
  - On regulatory breaches

- Required in the 'public interest'
  - Providing not contrary to law or regulations

- Professional duty to disclose
  - Comply with quality review by ICAEW or professional regulator
  - Respond to enquiry or investigation by ICAEW or regulatory body
  - To protect professional interests in legal proceedings
  - Comply with technical standards and ethics requirements

Examiner's comment

Answers to this question were often disappointing, particularly in light of the availability of relevant information in the Open Book. The majority of candidates identified that an auditor can disclose confidential information without clients' permission when it is required by law. These candidates also provided relevant examples such as money laundering and, to a lesser extent, terrorist activities and bribery. However, many candidates wasted time describing the actions to be taken if money laundering was suspected. This was not required and no marks were awarded for these points. Most candidates also identified that an auditor may disclose confidential information when there is a professional right or duty and also provided relevant examples. The circumstance most commonly overlooked was that in respect of reporting to a regulator and, consequently, examples of such circumstances.

1.38 Identify and explain the ethical threats of proposing a fee below market rates

- Proposal represents 'lowballing'

- Not prohibited by the Code of Ethics

- ES Part B S4 states that the audit fee must not be influenced by the provision of other services

- Threat to professional competence and due care
    - Audit quality may be jeopardised
    - Risk of audit failure/issuing an inappropriate audit opinion
    - Impaired scepticism

- Self-interest threat
    - Fear of not obtaining advisory work

If the advisory work is obtained there may be:

- Self-review threat
    - Over reliance on colleagues' work during the external audit
    - Reluctance to identify firm's errors to audited entity's management

- Management threat
    - May be expected to make decisions
    - Too closely aligned with management

Examiner's comment

This question was very well answered. Most candidates appreciated that the firm's policy represented lowballing and that such a policy has associated risks in respect of audit quality. However, many candidates failed to identify that this represented a threat to the fundamental principle of professional competence and due care. Although many candidates identified and explained the self-interest threat, a significant number overlooked the additional threats to objectivity that could arise if the audit firm succeeded in winning the lucrative advisory work. Weaker candidates wasted time writing at length about fee dependency and the fee thresholds. A minority of candidates wasted time citing safeguards for each of the threats which were not required.

1.39 Procedures to comply with firm's policy prohibiting partners and staff from owning shares in client companies

- Firm to maintain an up-to-date list of all clients

- Written confirmation by partners and staff of compliance with the firm's policies on independence

- Annual or more frequent confirmations

- New partners and staff required to provide confirmations on joining firm

- Regular training for partners and staff on the firm's policies and procedures on independence

- Monitoring of procedures

- Disciplinary action for breaches
- Procedures for prompt notification by partners and staff when shareholdings change
- Eg, shares inherited
- Eg, new client of the firm

Examiner's comment

This question was very well answered as many candidates identified that partners and staff should sign a declaration of compliance with the firm's policy and that the declaration should be made at least annually. In addition, most candidates identified the need for training, monitoring and disciplinary action for non-compliance. The points most commonly overlooked were those relating to the maintenance of an up-to-date list of listed clients and procedures for prompt notification of a change in circumstance in respect of share ownership for partners and staff within the firm. A minority of candidates failed to appreciate that the firm's policy prohibited all partners and staff within the firm from holding shares in client companies and wasted time listing irrelevant safeguards such as not using personnel who held shares in a client company on that company's audit.

2 Criticisms of auditors

			Marks
(1)	**Responsibility for detecting fraud**		
	Current situation	2	
	How it might be changed	1	
	Case for change	2	
	Case against change	3	
	Marks available	8	
	Maximum		5
(2)	**Provision of non-audit services**		
	Current situation	2	
	How it might be changed	½	
	Case for change	4	
	Case against change	4	
	Marks available	10½	
	Maximum		5
(3)	**Period of time for which auditors can act for a client**		
	Current situation	1	
	How it might be changed	2	
	Case for change	2	
	Case against change	2	
	Marks available	7	
	Maximum		4
	General		
	Confidence and credibility		1
Total marks available			15

(1) Responsibility for the detection of fraud

Current regulatory and professional requirements

Auditors are not responsible for the detection of all fraud – it is management's responsibility to detect fraud.

The auditors' responsibility is discharged by planning, performing and evaluating their work so that they obtain reasonable assurance that the financial statements are free from **material** misstatements due to fraud.

Possible changes

The auditors' responsibility for the detection of fraud could be extended by requiring them to perform specific (limited scope) procedures.

Case for change

This would narrow the expectation gap in respect of the auditors' duty in relation to fraud detection and this higher priority would be a greater deterrent to fraud.

Case against change

It would result in increased costs owing to additional work and also increased cost of professional indemnity insurance due to extended exposure to litigation.

It may also not be feasible/practicable due to the inherent limitations of an audit.

(2) Provision of non-audit services to audit clients

Current regulatory and professional requirements

Some non-audit services are permitted as long as objectivity would not be perceived to be impaired and safeguards are in place. However:

- fee levels must be appropriate
- financial statements must not be prepared for listed companies
- internal audit services may not be provided for listed companies
- auditors must advise only and not make management decisions

and certain non-audit services have effectively been banned by the FRC's Ethical Standard (ES), for example:

- internal audit services where heavy reliance would subsequently be placed on the work of internal audit

- valuations which have a material effect on the financial statements and involve a significant degree of judgement

Possible further changes

The provision of **all** non-audit services could be banned.

Case for change

This would negate the threats to objectivity, in particular:

- fear of losing fee
- reluctance to report adversely on own firm's work
- insufficient rigorous checking of colleagues' work

It would discourage lowballing – the practice of quoting a low audit fee in order to attract more lucrative consultancy work.

The use of a different firm may provide a different perspective/skill sets.

Case against change

Such action could result in:

- a lower quality of services (the auditor would not be in possession of the whole picture)
- increased costs due to a lack of pooling of background information
- a loss of convenience/one stop shop for clients
- a lack of comfort for clients from having services provided by a trusted source

It may also impair the ability of firms:

- to recruit high calibre personnel who value the broad-based training provided by firms undertaking a variety of services

- to audit tax and computer systems

- to draw upon the wider intellectual capital which currently exists in firms

(3) Period of time for which auditors can act for a client

Current regulatory and professional requirements

Auditors are appointed from the conclusion of the AGM to the conclusion of the next AGM with no limit on the number of reappointments.

There are professional requirements in ES S3 which do not allow the engagement partner or other key employees to act for a continuous period of:

- more than five years (listed clients)

- more than 10 years (non-listed clients) unless reasons for continuing are documented and facts communicated to those charged with governance

Possible further changes

Fixed-term appointments/mandatory rotation (of audit firms, as opposed to audit partners) could be introduced for all clients.

Case for change

There is currently a risk of familiarity/complacency – auditors who get too close to their clients may lose their independence, objectivity, scepticism and become complacent.

Rotation stimulates the auditors' courage and independence because there is no expectation of a long-term relationship and hence they do not fear dismissal.

Case against change

Recurring first-time audits are likely to:

- be disruptive to clients (process of selection/answering questions, etc)

- result in increased costs (introducing new auditors is costly to the client as the team builds detailed knowledge of the client, its business and the key issues in its financial statements)

However, the understanding and experience of long-term complex issues where the auditors' expertise is needed most is lost on rotation.

Rotation can discourage auditors from specialising to the required depth, thus limiting the choice of available alternatives.

However, there would be increased risk due to first time audits, as auditors may miss things due to their lack of experience with a particular client.

General

If users perceive auditors to be free from influence they will have more confidence in the audit process and financial information will have greater credibility.

This question was generally well answered by the majority of candidates.

The provision of non-audit services was the best answered part of the question, and the detection of fraud was the least well answered part. In relation to the detection of fraud, the most common omissions were the failure to consider the expectation gap and the increased exposure to litigation that would accompany an extension of auditors' responsibility and its likely impact on professional indemnity insurance. A minority of candidates wasted time writing about the responsibility for the **prevention** of fraud rather than the **detection** of fraud. A significant number of candidates were unable to distinguish between audit firm rotation and audit principal (partner) rotation and wrote, incorrectly, about an existing requirement to change audit **firms** every five years. A small number of candidates wasted time writing about the regulatory structure for auditors, while others wrote about the changes to the thresholds for statutory audit purposes. Strangely, in the current climate, a small number of candidates considered increasing the non-audit services audit firms could offer in order to gain more fees!

3 Kristoff Ltd, Reindeer Ltd, Pabbie Group plc (March 2015)

Marking guide

			Marks
3.1	Kristoff	6½	
	Reindeer	16½	
	Pabbie	6	
	General (awarded in any section but once only)	½	
	Marks available	29½	
	Maximum		12
3.2	Kristoff	4	
	Reindeer	6	
	Pabbie	5	
	Marks available	15	
	Maximum		8
Total marks available			20

3.1 Kristoff

Threats

Self-interest threat

The firm may be reluctant to modify its audit opinion for fear of losing the client/fees.

Intimidation threat

Hans appears to be aggressive and to be exerting pressure which may have influenced other areas of the audit work.

Steps

The firm should undertake an engagement quality control review and consider whether intimidation has affected work in other areas of the audit. More senior members of the firm should be included in the audit team and if the intimidation threat is too great the firm should consider resigning.

If the firm is removed it should use its legal right to circulate a written representation to the minority shareholders and to attend/speak at the general meeting where it would have been reappointed.

Reindeer

Self-review threat

The outcome of the work defending the claim may impact on future financial statements. The claim is 4.9% of gross assets and 122% of profit before tax and is therefore material to the financial statements. The audit team may place too much reliance on the work performed by the firm's tax experts or be reluctant to criticise the work if any deficiencies are found during the audit.

Management threat

The tax experts may be expected to make decisions on the best course of action and their views may become too closely aligned with management.

Advocacy threat

The firm may be perceived to be supporting a position held by management if it defends the company against HMRC. Ethical Standard S5 prohibits the provision of such tax services where the firm acts as an advocate before an appeals tribunal.

Self-interest threat

The firm may be reluctant to agree with HMRC's position if it indicates that there are misstatements in prior year financial statements that have been audited by the firm. This may impact adversely on the firm through adverse publicity arising from disciplinary action, fines/penalties and/or damages as a result of negligence.

Steps

Explain to management that the firm cannot act as an advocate at the tribunal but that it may be able to respond to management's specific requests for information in relation to the appeal. The firm must not make management decisions and should document the existence of informed management.

If the advocacy threat is too great it must decline the tax engagement. However, if services of tax experts are provided, these should be performed by employees not involved in the audit and an independent partner review should be performed on the audit team's conclusions on the accounting treatment of the amounts relating to the HMRC claim.

Pabbie

Self-interest threat

Ethical Standard S5 fee thresholds apply to fees earned from both an audited entity and its subsidiaries. The regular fee income from Pabbie group will represent 7% of the firm's total annual fee income which exceeds the 5% threshold for listed companies but does not exceed the 10% threshold. The firm may be reluctant to modify its opinion or challenge management for fear of losing the fees from its largest client.

Steps

The firm needs to consider the significance of the self-interest threat and whether safeguards are required. It should disclose the fee income to those charged with governance and perform an independent internal quality control review as part of the audit. The firm should regularly monitor the percentage of fees earned from Pabbie to ensure there is no risk of breaching the 10% threshold.

General

Consult the firm's ethics partner.

3.2 Kristoff

The audit opinion should be modified. Related party transactions are material by nature and the failure to disclose such transactions results in a material misstatement. The misstatement is not pervasive as it is isolated to one aspect of the financial statements therefore a qualified/except for opinion should be issued. A basis for qualified opinion paragraph should include the reasons and amounts relating to the qualification.

Reindeer

An unmodified opinion should be issued. The claim is 4.9% of total assets and 122% of profit before tax and represents a significant uncertainty. The auditor agrees with management's treatment and there is no limitation on scope. As a successful claim would turn Reindeer's profit into a loss the existence of the claim is fundamental to the users' understanding of the financial statements. Therefore, the auditor's report should be modified using an emphasis of matter paragraph which should draw the users' attention to the relevant disclosure note. This is included immediately after the basis for opinion paragraph and should indicate that the auditor's opinion is not modified in respect of this matter.

Pabbie

The audit opinion should be modified. The firm is unable to obtain sufficient appropriate audit evidence over Queen's financial statements. Queen affects a large number of areas of Pabbie's group financial statements and therefore appears to be pervasive to the group financial statements. A disclaimer of opinion should be issued stating that the firm does not express an audit opinion. A basis for disclaimer of opinion paragraph should include the reasons for the disclaimer of opinion. The firm should also report by exception under the Companies Act 2006 that it has not received all information and explanations required for the audit.

Examiner's comments

This was the best answered long-form question with the majority of candidates demonstrating good knowledge of both threats to the firm's objectivity and auditor's reports. It was pleasing to note that candidates coped well with the combination of these two syllabus areas within the same scenario.

Part 3.1 of the question was well answered. Candidates were able to identify and explain the threats to the firm's objectivity in each of the scenarios and recommend appropriate steps to be taken by the firm to address the threats. However, the answers to Kristoff and Pabbie were generally of a higher standard than the answers to Reindeer.

Kristoff

The majority of candidates identified the intimidation and self-interest threats and provided plausible explanations of these threats. However, many candidates were unable to state any appropriate steps to be taken to address the intimidation threat. Statements such as 'do not be intimidated' appeared often from weaker candidates who failed to consider whether more senior members of the firm should be included in the audit team. Few candidates considered that the intimidation threat might affect areas of the audit other than related party transactions. Although the majority of candidates considered the option of resigning, few candidates identified the steps to be taken by the auditor post-resignation or post-removal.

Reindeer

The majority of candidates identified the advocacy threat in respect of the support work relating to the tribunal. The point most commonly overlooked was in relation to the self-interest threat. Candidates failed to appreciate that agreeing with HMRC's position may indicate that misstatements exist in prior year financial statements audited by the firm and that if this came to light it may adversely affect the firm.

Pabbie

The vast majority of candidates identified the self-interest threat arising out of fee dependency and appreciated that Pabbie's fee, as a percentage of the firm's fee income, fell between the 5%-10% thresholds applicable to listed companies and consequently listed the appropriate safeguards. A minority of candidates quoted the fee thresholds applicable to unlisted entities. A number of candidates incorrectly identified a self-review threat in respect of Pabbie and went on to make inappropriate recommendations such as having separate teams and information barriers for the audit of the financial statements of the Pabbie Group and Queen.

Part 3.2 of the question was well answered with a significant number of candidates scoring maximum marks.

Kristoff

The majority of candidates correctly identified that related party transactions are material by nature and that the audit opinion should be modified due to a material misstatement. Furthermore, most candidates appreciated that it was not pervasive and therefore required a qualified opinion. However, a significant minority wasted time by considering the type of modification if the matter was pervasive.

Reindeer

The majority of candidates correctly identified that the opinion should be unmodified. A minority of candidates confused an emphasis of matter paragraph which deals with matters correctly stated in the financial statements, with an other matters paragraph, which is used by the auditor to communicate a matter other than those that are presented or disclosed in the financial statements. A small minority also incorrectly concluded that the absence of a provision in the financial statements meant the audit opinion should be qualified, in spite of the fact that the scenario stated that the firm had concluded a provision was not necessary and that disclosures in the financial statements were adequate.

Pabbie

The majority of candidates correctly identified that the circumstances represented a limitation on scope and strong candidates appreciated that the information given in the question in the form of 'highly material to a large number of items' deemed the matter to be persuasive warranting a disclaimer of opinion. However, a significant minority of those candidates who identified the issue as pervasive stated, incorrectly, that the opinion should be adverse. These candidates failed to appreciate that an adverse opinion relates to material misstatements. Some candidates incorrectly stated that the issue was not pervasive because it related to one area of a much larger group, and therefore proposed a qualified opinion rather than a disclaimer of opinion. However, the scenario clearly stated that the subsidiary is highly material to a large number of items in the group financial statements. Only a minority of candidates earned the marks available for identifying the matters to be reported by the exception under the Companies Act 2006.

4 Financial Reporting Council (June 2015)

				Marks
4.1	(a)	One mark per point well made		
		Marks available	8	
		Maximum		3
	(b)	Target setting	5	
		Actions	1½	
		Long association	4	
		Actions	7	
		Review of work	4	
		Actions	2	
		Use of an external expert	2	
		Actions	4	
		Marks available	29½	
		Maximum		10
4.2	(a)	Purpose of hot review	1	
		Elements of a hot review	3	
		Elements of a cold review	2½	
		Uses of hot and cold reviews	1½	
		Timing of reviews	1	
		Marks available	9	
		Maximum		5
	(b)	One mark per point well made		
		Marks available	4	
		Maximum		2
	Total marks available			20

4.1 (a) The FRC promotes improvements in the quality of auditing through issuing International Standards on Auditing (UK) (ISAs), the Ethical Standard (ES) and occasional briefing papers on key audit issues such as professional scepticism. The FRC monitors compliance with ISAs and the ES through reviews of audit firms' policies and procedures. The findings from these reviews are presented in reports, which are available to the public. The FRC also oversees the regulatory activities of the professional accountancy bodies and investigates matters of misconduct with the power to take disciplinary action against audit firms. Additional work includes influencing the development of ISAs and commissioning research on audit and assurance issues.

(b) **Target setting**

The scenario represents a self-interest threat. External audit partners and staff may promote services not required by the client or make exaggerated claims about the benefit of such services to receive credit in their annual pay review. There is a loss of objectivity and independence and audit quality may suffer if external audit partners and staff overlook errors or are reluctant to raise contentious issues. It is also a breach of ES S4 which requires firms to establish policies and procedures to ensure that:

- the objectives of the members of the engagement team do not include selling non-audit services to the audited entity;

- the criteria for evaluating performance or promotion of members of the engagement team do not include success in selling non-audit services to the audited entity; and

- no specific element of remuneration of members of the engagement team is based on their success in selling non-audit services to the audited entity.

Actions

The firm must remove the targets and break the link between sales of non-audit services and pay of audit partners and staff. Objectives should be set that include a link between audit quality and pay.

Long association

Shane Smith has worked continuously as the audit partner for Garfield plc for more than six years. The long association of Shane represents a familiarity threat as he may be too trusting and insufficiently sceptical of Garfield's financial statements. A reasonable and informed third party may consider or perceive the firm's independence and objectivity to be impaired. There is also a self-interest threat as Shane may fear losing the fees generated by this client. A self-review threat may arise as Shane will be reluctant to identify any errors or misstatements made in prior years' financial statements.

Actions

ES S3 requires that, for listed companies, the firm establishes procedures to ensure that no one shall act as audit engagement partner for more than five years and shall not subsequently participate in the audit engagement for a further five years. When it is necessary to safeguard the audit quality (because of, for example, a substantial change in the business or an unexpected change in senior management), the engagement partner can continue for a further two years. The firm must therefore review the effectiveness of its procedures to monitor the length of time engagement partners are associated with audited entities. If Shane has acted for six years, he can continue for up to one more year but the reasons must be disclosed to the shareholders and safeguards applied. These safeguards should include an expanded review of the audit work by the engagement quality control reviewer. If Shane has acted for seven years he must cease to act as engagement partner.

Review of work

The firm cannot demonstrate that it has complied with ISA requirements. ISA (UK) 220 requires that a review is undertaken of the work performed by junior members of the audit team and without a record of the review there is no evidence that it has taken place. Paragraph A13 of ISA (UK) 230 requires that reviews of audit files are documented to show what audit work was reviewed, who reviewed it and when it was reviewed. A review reduces the risk of material misstatements and the issue of an inappropriate opinion.

Actions

The firm's audit and quality control manuals should be checked and, if necessary, updated to ensure that the review procedure is adequately covered. Staff should be reminded of the procedure with training given, if appropriate. Partners should monitor that the procedure is undertaken and disciplinary action taken in the event of non-compliance.

Use of an external expert

The firm cannot demonstrate that it has complied with ES S2, which requires that the audit engagement partner shall be satisfied that any external consultant involved in the audit will be objective and shall document the reason for that conclusion. Paragraph 11 of ISA (UK) 620 requires that a number of matters are agreed between the auditor and auditor's expert. Without a formalised arrangement, there is no evidence that these matters have been considered.

Actions

The firm must obtain confirmation, in writing, of Kapil's objectivity and independence. They should also assess the competence and capabilities of Kapil. The arrangement should then be agreed with Kapil, in writing if appropriate. The agreement should cover the following:

- The nature, scope and objectives of Kapil's work
- The respective roles of Kapil and the audit firm
- The nature, extent and timing of communication and the form of Kapil's report
- The need to observe confidentiality requirements
- Access to Kapil's working papers

4.2 (a) A hot review is designed to provide an objective evaluation of the significant judgements made and conclusions reached in formulating an auditor's report. A cold review seeks to provide the firm with reasonable assurance that its system of quality control is operating effectively.

A hot review involves the following:

- Discussion of significant matters with the engagement partner

- Review of financial statements and proposed auditor's report

- Review of judgements

- Evaluation of conclusions

- Evaluation of the firm's independence

- Consideration of whether appropriate consultation has been undertaken on contentious matters

A cold review considers compliance with the following:

- Firm's procedures
- ISAs
- Ethical Standard
- Legislative requirements
- UK Audit Regulations

A hot review is mandatory for audits of listed entities and for other audits where the firm has determined a review is required, for example, those engagements where risk is assessed as high. A cold review is performed on a sample of audit files.

A hot review takes place on or before the date of the auditor's report whereas a cold review is performed after the date of the auditor's report.

(b) The reviewer should be a technically competent person with experience of the audited entity's industry and listed companies. The reviewer must be independent of both the engagement team and the audited entity and have the authority to evaluate objectively the judgements made and conclusions reached during the audit.

Examiner's comments:

This was the second highest scoring long-form question but was mainly due to a number of excellent answers on part 4.1 (b).

Answers to part 4.1 (a) of the question were disappointing with many candidates failing to score any marks by either not attempting the question or by discussing quality control procedures implemented by individual audit firms. Candidates who did score marks on this part of the question were able to identify that the FRC issued standards and briefing papers with a smaller number identifying that they also monitor compliance with standards through reviews of individual audit firms. The points most commonly overlooked were those relating to the oversight of the regulatory activities of the professional accountancy bodies, disciplinary powers and research on audit and assurance issues.

It was pleasing to note that the standard of answers to part 4.1 (b) of the question was particularly high. Most candidates were able to explain why each of the four matters had been reported and suggest some actions for the firm to take. There were some excellent answers in respect of the first two matters although the final two matters caused some issues for weaker candidates.

Target setting

Most candidates were able to identify that this matter presented a self-interest threat and consequently audit quality may suffer. These candidates then correctly identified the actions required to be taken by the firm. Stronger candidates covered the requirements of ES S4 in their answers. Disappointingly, a small minority of candidates thought that setting targets for selling non-audit services was either perfectly acceptable or acceptable provided that there were safeguards in place. A number of candidates incorrectly discussed low-balling when there was no evidence in the scenario that this had occurred and provided the fee income thresholds for listed and unlisted companies. A minority of candidates stated, incorrectly, that it is inappropriate for the audit firm to sell any non-audit service to its clients.

Long association

This matter was the best answered part of the question. The areas less frequently mentioned were the self-interest and self-review threats and the circumstances in which the length of time for which the engagement partner may act could be extended. Only stronger candidates correctly mentioned that the firm needs to review the effectiveness of its procedures to monitor the length of time engagement partners are associated with audit entities.

Review of work

Answers to this matter were of a mixed standard. Most candidates identified that the work of the junior staff should be reviewed by more senior members and suggested some actions for the firm to take. Only the stronger candidates identified that the firm was unable to demonstrate that it had complied with the requirements set out in ISA 220 (UK) and ISA (UK) 230. Many candidates assumed the review had not been done rather than the review may have been done but not documented hence restricting the number of marks available to them.

Use of an external expert

Answers to this matter were of a mixed standard. Most candidates identified the need for the agreement with Kapil to be formalised, preferably in writing. Stronger candidates who were familiar with ISA (UK) 620 were able to identify the contents of the agreement. Very few candidates considered non-compliance with ES S2 and that the firm must obtain written confirmation from Kapil of its independence from, or connections with, the audited entity. A number of candidates wasted time listing the audit procedures that should be performed when auditing a property valuation included in the financial statements of an audited entity. This was not within the scope of the question and no marks were awarded for these points.

Answers to part 4.2 (a) of the question were of a mixed standard. Most candidates identified that engagement quality control reviews are mandatory for listed companies and that cold reviews are undertaken on a sample of files. Most candidates also correctly identified when the reviews should take place although some candidates thought that cold reviews are undertaken before the hot reviews. Only the stronger candidates were then able to identify some of the procedures undertaken on each review. Weaker candidates confused the engagement quality control review with that of the supervisory review that is required on all audit engagements.

Part 4.2 (b) of the question was very well answered. The majority of candidates identified four or more attributes of a reviewer and consequently scored maximum marks. The point most commonly overlooked was that the reviewer should have experience of listed companies.

5 Short form questions

5.1 Professional enquiry

- Unlawful acts or defaults by the client
- Serious doubts re client's integrity
- Information required by auditor being deliberately withheld by client
- Client's reasons for change not in accordance with the facts
- Important differences of principle or practice behind the proposed change
- A 'statement of circumstances' to be brought to attention of members/creditors

> **Tutorial note:**
>
> The existence of unpaid fees is not of itself a reason for not accepting nomination.

5.2 Rights on removal

- Copy of notice of resolution proposing removal
- Representations in writing notified to members
- Attendance at general meeting
- Hearing at general meeting

5.3 Points for inclusion in engagement letter and reason for inclusion

- To whom the report will be made available – to avoid reliance by unforeseen third parties

- The period covered by the forecast information and scope of work – to provide clarity on information that is subject to the review

- A clear statement of directors' and reporting accountant's responsibilities – to avoid any misunderstanding regarding responsibility for the forecast information

- A caveat warning that the forecast could be different to actual performance – to avoid over-reliance on any assurances provided regarding the forecast

- Any limitation of liability agreed with the directors for this engagement – to provide evidence of such an agreement should any issues arise in the future

- Agree the nature of any assurance provided and the form of any reports to directors – to avoid any misunderstanding regarding the output from the engagement

- The intended use of the cash flow information and any reports produced by firm – to reduce liability of firm where such information is used for means other than those identified

5.4 Senior

- Report to firm's Money Laundering Reporting Officer (MLRO)

- Money laundering reporting officer to decide whether to report to National Crime Agency (NCA)

- Avoid tipping off

- Consider the implications for:
    - understatement of revenue, taxation and VAT
    - auditor's report if figures materially understated

Reasons

- Represents benefits from criminal conduct
- Criminal offence if auditor does not report suspicions of money laundering
- Tipping off may prejudice subsequent investigation

5.5 **Payment not on Sole's ledger**

- Evidence that payment received after year end/early December
    - Remittance advice/bank statement details/cash receipts book

Discount

- Whether entitled to discount/compliance with terms
    - Terms of trading/contract/invoice

Wrong goods

- Evidence that goods returned/included in inventory
    - Copy of goods returned record/credit note

5.6 **Before audit assignment:**

- Assess juniors' skills and set out their areas of responsibility
- Brief juniors on the nature of the audit client, audit risks and issues which may arise during the engagement
- Explain the detailed approach to the engagement including relevant timings
- Hold a meeting to enable the juniors to discuss the assignment and ask questions
- Introduce team members to client staff

During audit assignment:

- Review specific pieces of juniors' work to ensure that:
    - sufficient and appropriate audit evidence is being obtained
    - the audit work supports the conclusions reached
    - appropriate consultations have been made and that the results of these have been documented
- Check that juniors are carrying out their work per the audit plan and that they understand the instructions given
- Provide feedback to juniors on the work reviewed
- Track the overall progress of the audit work against the audit plan and update the plan as and when necessary
- Address matters arising during the audit engagement and answer questions raised by juniors
- Consider the need to consult upwards, with manager or partner, on any issues raised during the audit engagement

5.7 **How planned procedures differ**

- The planned procedures for a review engagement will consist predominantly of:
    - analytical procedures; and
    - enquiry of management
- The planned procedures for an audit under the Companies Act 2006 will include:
    - additional substantive procedures (such as inspection of documentation); and
    - may also include tests of control.

Why planned procedures differ

- A lower level of assurance is usually provided for review engagements
- Therefore less evidence is required
- The level of assurance is usually agreed with whoever requests the review engagement
- It is not set out in law as with an audit required under the Companies Act 2006

5.8 Erica may continue in order to maintain audit quality

ES S3 permits when substantial change in the business provided:

- Only for additional period of up to two years/no longer than seven years in total
- Expanded review of work undertaken by Engagement QC Reviewer
- Fact and reasons disclosed to shareholders as early as practicable

If company not prepared to make such disclosures, should not accept

5.9 • Any indication that the entity misunderstands the objective and scope of the audit

- Any revised or special terms of the audit engagement

- A significant change in:
  - ownership
  - management
  - nature or size of the entity's business

- A change in:
  - legal or regulatory requirements
  - the financial reporting framework adopted in the preparation of the financial statements
  - other reporting requirements
  - engagement partner or structure/status of the audit firm

5.10 • Senior person/partner within the firm or a suitably qualified external person
- Experience of the pharmaceutical industry
- Experience of listed companies
- Independent of the engagement team
- Not connected to Pharma

5.11 Obtain the client's permission to contact the previous auditor for professional clearance.

- If the client refuses, it may be an indication that management has something to hide.

- The outgoing auditor may provide information in respect of unpaid fees, unlawful acts or disagreements.

Obtain references from reliable third parties such as professional advisors or credit agencies

- To identify deficiencies in the character or behaviour of the directors

Undertake searches of relevant databases including those at Companies House

- To ascertain whether the directors are listed as undesirable characters or disqualified directors

Undertake internet/press cuttings searches

- For evidence of scandals, adverse publicity, failed companies involving the directors which may provide evidence about unscrupulous behaviour

Hold discussions with the directors

- Which may provide evidence of a cavalier attitude towards business ethics or lack of social responsibility for example willingness to pay taxes

Undertake client identification procedures

- To establish that the directors are who they say they are

Inspect prior year auditor's reports

- For evidence of disagreements or inappropriate accounting policies

5.12 Fees should be determined with reference to the following:

- Seniority and professional experience of the members of the team
- Number of staff required/time expended by each
- Greater amount of time required in first year
- Risk which the work entails
- Inherent risk likely to be high in oil and gas sector
- Nature of the client's business and complexity of its operations
- Priority and importance of the work to the client
- Expenses properly incurred such as overseas travel
- Extent to which firm can rely on work of component auditors
- Extent to which reliance can be placed on internal audit
- Whether an auditor's expert is required

5.13
- Examine the profit and cash flow forecasts for the period specified by the directors

- Consider the reasonableness of the assumptions

- Provide limited/moderate assurance

- Conclusion expressed negatively

  - In the form of nothing has come to our attention

  - Which causes us to believe that these assumptions do not provide a reasonable basis for the forecast

- Providing an opinion as to whether the forecasts are properly prepared on the basis of the stated assumptions

- Whether the engagement is to be conducted in accordance with ISAE 3400

- Intended use/for the purpose of supporting the application for funding for use by bank and not general distribution

5.14 Affects engagement risk

- Ie, risk that the auditor expresses an inappropriate opinion
- Higher risk of misstatement

Affects reputational risk

- Firm's reputation may be tarnished by association with an unscrupulous character

May indicate a lack of integrity/honesty of the managing director

- Consideration of integrity of client's management required by ISA (UK) 220

A lack of integrity may be indicative of:

- aggressive interpretation of accounting standards
- window dressing
- poor control environment/tone at the top
- an inability to obtain sufficient appropriate audit evidence/intimidation
- money laundering/other criminal activities
- unreliable management representations

5.15 **Engagement quality control review (hot review)**

- Only for audits of listed clients and for those engagements the firm has determined an EQCR is required/high risk audits

- Objective/independent evaluation of the significant judgements the team has made and the conclusions it reached in forming the opinion

- EQCR takes place on or before date of auditor's report

- Not a review of all working papers

- Evaluation involves:

  - Discussion of significant matters with engagement partner
  - Review of financial statements and proposed auditor's report
  - Review of selected documentation
  - Evaluation of proposed auditor's report
  - Re-listed entities, consideration of:

    (a) The team's evaluation of firm's independence
    (b) Whether appropriate consultation regarding differences of opinion

Monitoring (cold review)

- Conducted after the date of the auditor's report
- On a sample of files
- Ensure compliance with firm's procedures and:

  - International Standards on Auditing
  - Ethical Standard
  - legislative requirements
  - UK Audit Regulations

- Identify areas requiring improvement
- Take remedial action/training

5.16 Internal controls (two only)

- Unopened mail kept securely
- **Dual** control over opening of mail/counting of receipts
- Immediate recording of amounts
- Prompt banking of cash/cheques
- Independent reconciliation of amount recorded with bank records
- Approval of bank reconciliation by responsible official
- Segregation of duties between opening/recording of mail and banking

Tests of controls (two only)

- Enquiry of relevant personnel re their responsibilities
- Observation of procedures
- Comparison of dates cash collected and cash banked
- Inspection of bank reconciliation for signature evidencing approval.

5.17 Points for inclusion in response

- Engagement letter is required by ISA (UK) 210
- Even where the law prescribes requirements the letter needs to:

  - state that the relevant law applies
  - indicate that management acknowledges its responsibilities, which include:

    (1) Preparation of financial statements
    (2) Internal controls
    (3) Providing auditor with access to information/persons
    (4) Providing written representations

- May wish to include other elements not prescribed by law such as:

  - Form of other communications
  - Practical arrangements, such as staffing, locations and timing
  - Basis of fees and billing arrangements

- Nature of the level of assurance should be explained
- Particularly important as first time Moose requires an audit

- Include any proposals to limit liability
- Helps to avoid any misunderstandings/expectations gap

5.18 Points for inclusion in tender document

- Firm adopts a system of internal control in accordance with ISA (UK) 220

- Specific requirements in relation to quality of work of engagement team include the following:

    - Assignment of staff with relevant competence, expertise and experience

    - Ensuring adequate resources and time available to complete work to an appropriate standard

    - Engagement meeting with team to brief it on relevant matters, such as:

        (1) objectives of work
        (2) nature of client
        (3) risks and potential issues

    - Supervision of junior staff by senior staff throughout the audit

    - Review of work by more senior staff and/or partner

    - Consultation by team on technical or contentious issues

    - Engagement quality control review if considered necessary

- Firm also has human resources policies in place to ensure quality of work, including the following:

    - Robust recruitment procedures
    - Training and CPD for all staff
    - Regular performance evaluation of staff
    - Performance based promotion and compensation

5.19
- Allocate work to juniors

    - In accordance with experience/competency

- Brief juniors to ensure they understand

    - Objectives of the work
    - Risks and nature of King's business
    - Materiality levels

- Track progress of engagement to ensure

    - Sufficient time available to complete work
    - Work is of an appropriate standard

- Answer questions from juniors to ensure

    - They understand instructions/responsibilities

    - Significant issues can be raised and the planned approach modified where necessary

- Review work of juniors to ensure

    - Performed properly/according to audit plan
    - Sufficient and appropriate audit evidence obtained
    - Evidence supports conclusions reached
    - Work appropriately documented
    - Identification of significant matters to raise with more senior staff
    - Juniors receive feedback on quality of their work

5.20 Conducted in accordance with ISRE 2400

- Limited assurance
- Procedures consist of making inquiries of management and analytical procedures
- Do not express an audit opinion/not an audit/express a conclusion
- Expressed negatively/'nothing has come to our attention....'
- Addressed to management/bank
- Not for general distribution
- Signed in name of assurance firm

Report for external audit

- Conducted in accordance with ISA's/CA06

- Obtain evidence about amounts and disclosures in FS

    - To give reasonable assurance

    - That FS are free from material misstatement whether caused by fraud or error, which includes assessment of:

        (1) whether accounting policies are appropriate/consistently applied/disclosed
        (2) reasonableness of significant accounting estimates
        (3) overall presentation of the FS

- Express an opinion

- Positively

- Report by exception/statement on consistency of directors' report

- Addressed to the shareholders

- Bannerman paragraph

- Signed by senior statutory auditor

5.21 Factors re resourcing

- Need engagement team members who:

    - understand the specific regulatory environment
    - have relevant technical/scientific skills/qualifications
    - have information systems expertise if systems are complex

- May require use of an external/auditor's expert

- Reasonable assurance engagement requires more work/resources
- May need:
  - an engagement quality control review
  - to plan site visits to the factories
  - to rely on the work of another firm in respect of the factory in Poland if the firm does not have representation in Poland
- Potential language issues

Examiner's comments:

This question was generally well answered as the majority of candidates identified the points relating to technical expertise, regulatory environment, geographical coverage and the use of an auditor's expert. However, the majority of candidates overlooked the information in the question regarding the fact that it was a reasonable assurance engagement and failed to consider whether the firm would be able to undertake the amount of work necessary to provide this high level of assurance. A significant number of candidates assumed, incorrectly, that it would be a limited assurance engagement and wasted time writing about the type of procedures undertaken on such engagements. Weaker candidates failed to relate the factors to the specific engagement and included only generic points that might be relevant to resourcing any engagement. Fewer marks were available for such generic points.

5.22 Procedures to address potential conflict of interest

- Separate engagement teams
- Brief staff/clear guidelines on confidentiality issues/procedures
- Information barriers:
  - Physical separation/use staff from different offices
  - Confidential/secure data filing
- Procedures in place for dealing with any need to disseminate information beyond barrier
- Staff to sign confidentiality agreements
- Regular review of the application of safeguards by a senior individual not involved in the engagements

Examiner's comments:

This question was generally well answered and many candidates scored full marks. Most candidates were able to provide a range of relevant points such as separate teams, information barriers and confidentiality agreements. A number of candidates appreciated that there should be an independent review but failed to specify that the review should cover the application of safeguards. A significant number of candidates wasted time citing the need to obtain informed consent from the respective clients, failing to appreciate that the scenario stated that this had already been obtained.

5.23 Reduce exposure

- Conduct the audit in accordance with International Standards on Auditing (ISAs)
- Quality control procedures such as:
    - Client due diligence before acceptance
    - Use of experienced and competent staff
    - Direction and planning
    - Supervision and review
    - Consultation on difficult or contentious matters
    - Documentation of work performed
    - Sufficient and appropriate evidence
    - Engagement quality control review
    - Having sufficient time to complete work
- Disclaimer of liability in auditor's report (a 'Bannerman' paragraph)
- Agree, with shareholder approval, a liability cap which is fair and reasonable
- Professional indemnity insurance
- Operate through a limited liability partnership

5.24 Purposes of the review of work performed by audit junior

- To consider if:

    - work performed in line with audit strategy/plan

    - work performed in accordance with professional standards/regulatory requirements

    - significant matters have been raised for further consideration

    - appropriate consultations have taken place

    - work adequately documented

    - there is a need to revise nature/timing/extent of audit procedures

    - work performed supports conclusions reached

    - sufficient and appropriate evidence obtained

    - objectives of audit procedures achieved

- To provide feedback for audit junior's development

Examiner's comments:

Answers to this question were of a mixed standard. Those candidates who were familiar with the contents of paragraph A17 of ISA (UK) 220 tended to score full marks. Candidates who did not make use of the Open Book struggled to identify more than two or three relevant points. The points most commonly identified were those relating to performance in accordance with professional standards, procedures carried out properly and sufficient appropriate evidence. The points most commonly overlooked were those relating to work carried out in line with the audit plan and the need to revise audit procedures. A minority of weaker candidates confused the review of an audit junior's work, which is required on every audit, with an engagement quality control review and consequently identified inappropriate purposes.

6 Sparkleen Ltd (June 2010)

			Marks
6.1	(a)	Management's responsibilities	3	
		Purpose and scope of work	5	
		Limiting liability	5	
	(b)	Reasons	3	
		Maximum		8
6.2		Identification of relevant receipt or payment (each)	½	
		Plausible matter to consider (each)	½	
		Maximum		12
	Total marks available			20

6.1 (a) The following points should be included in the letter of engagement for the examination of the cash flow forecasts:

Management's responsibilities

Management is responsible for the preparation and presentation of the forecasts and the identification and disclosure of assumptions on which the forecasts are based. Management should provide the reporting accountant with all relevant information and source data used in developing the assumptions.

Purpose and scope of work

The reporting accountant's responsibility is to examine the cash flow forecasts for the three years ending 31 March 20X3. This includes the consideration of the reasonableness of the assumptions underlying the forecast and whether the forecasts are properly prepared on the basis of the stated assumptions. The level of assurance provided on the reasonableness of the assumptions will be limited and expressed negatively in the form of 'nothing has come to our attention to indicate that the assumptions do not provide a reasonable basis for the forecasts'.

Limiting liability

The use and distribution of the forecasts should be restricted to management for the purpose of obtaining funding from its bankers. The report should not to be shown to any other party without the written permission of the reporting accountant. A liability cap, stating the maximum monetary amount of damages that can be claimed against the reporting accountant, may be included. In addition, there should be a caveat warning that there could be differences between the forecast and actual performance due to unforeseen circumstances.

(b) **Reasons**

These matters should be included to:

- bridge any expectation gap and avoid misunderstandings
- limit the amount of damages to which the firm is exposed
- avoid liability to unforeseen third parties

6.2 **Receipts**

The new loan should be sufficient to enable the company to expand the business and be included before expansion.

Customer receipts should take account of the following:

- The expected level of inflation and whether government contracts allow for price increases; and

- The timing of receipts which should reflect the early payment discount, slow payers and the terms of the new government contracts.

Proceeds from the sale of the premises which should be considered in light of similar properties in the locality.

Proceeds of sale/scrapping of current IT equipment, which should be included after the installation of the new system.

Rebate from suppliers should be calculated in accordance with the contract terms, consistent with the volume of goods purchased and reflected in the forecast quarterly in arrears.

Payments

Supplier payments should reflect the increased level of activity and the terms of trading agreed with suppliers.

Rent should include payments for the temporary premises until the agreement ceases and for the new premises quarterly in advance. Consideration should be given to whether the agreement for the new premises allows for rent reviews.

The purchase of IT infrastructure and vans should be based on quotes and supplier price lists. Consideration should be given to whether there will be staff training costs and an increase in vehicle running costs due to additional vehicles. Consideration should be given to the completeness of any other refurbishment costs such as shelving, fork-lift trucks etc.

Removal costs should be in line with any quotes and with scheduled moving date(s).

Wages and salaries should reflect the level of activity, the recruitment costs of extra staff and PAYE and NIC, which should be paid on due dates.

Corporation tax, including any tax on the sale of the warehouse should be consistent with the profit forecasts and paid on the due dates. VAT payments should be consistent with purchases and sales in the profit forecast and paid on the due dates.

Loan repayments should reflect the balance outstanding on the existing loan which should be repaid following the sale of the premises. The instalments relating to the new loan should be paid on the due dates.

Finance costs should be in line with market rates and reflect the level of borrowing and should reduce following the repayment of the existing loan.

Operating costs should reflect a higher amount while running old and new premises and consideration should be given to whether the new larger premises are likely to have higher running costs.

Professional fees should include fees for selling agents, reporting accountants and legal costs.

Sensitivity analysis should be undertaken on key variables such as the level of customer receipts, interest rates and exchange rates.

Part 6.1

This part of the question was very well answered and many candidates scored full marks. In respect of management's responsibilities, the point most commonly overlooked was that relating to its responsibilities regarding the underlying assumptions. Weaker candidates often drifted into management's responsibilities for financial statements, accounting records, prevention of fraud and error and internal controls. In respect of the purpose and scope of the reporting accountant's work, the points most commonly overlooked were those relating to the reasonableness of the assumptions and whether the forecasts were properly prepared on the basis of the assumptions. Weaker candidates confused the purpose of the examination with the purpose of an audit, often citing 'true and fair view' as part of the objective. In respect of limiting the firm's liability, the points most commonly overlooked were those relating to the caveat and the fact that permission would be needed to show the report to any other party. A common error was to state that the results of the firm's examination would be restricted entirely to the directors of Sparkleen Ltd, failing to appreciate that the bank would need to see the accountant's report. As for the reasons for inclusion of the above items, most candidates mentioned the expectation gap. However, only a minority identified the avoidance of liability to unforeseen third parties.

Part 6.2

The part of the question was generally well answered as most candidates were able to identify the key receipts and payments which would be included in the cash flow forecasts. The points most commonly overlooked in relation to receipts were the introduction of the loan and the proceeds from the disposal/scrapping of the current IT facilities. The points most commonly overlooked in respect of payments were wages and salaries, VAT and corporation tax. Weaker candidates incorrectly discussed non-cash related items such as accounting for depreciation and profit on sale of the warehouse. Another common error was to overlook the fact that the work involved examining a forecast and consequently cite verification procedures that would be undertaken on historical cost financial information such as checking amounts to invoices and bank statements. Some candidates, while identifying relevant receipts and payments, were unable to identify matters to be considered when reviewing the reasonableness of the assumptions underlying those receipts and payments and simply made comments such as 'check if reasonable.' This is too vague to be awarded any marks.

7 Bambi Ltd (December 2010)

Marking guide

			Marks
7.1	Revenue	7	
	Gross profit margin	7	
	Operating margin	8	
	Inventory days	5	
	Payables days	4	
	General	1	
	Marks available	32	
	Maximum		12

		Marks

7.2 Supporting schedules   1
       Management accounts   1
       Profit forecasts   1
       Segmental information   1
       Industry sector and competitor information   1
       Previous year full FS   1
       Cash flow statements   1
       Marks available   7
       Maximum   4

7.3 Assurance level – review of FS   2
       Assurance level – statutory audit   3½
       Scope of work is narrower   1
       Marks available   6½
       Maximum   4

Total marks available   20

7.1 Briefing notes on matters to be discussed with the management of Bambi

Revenue

Increase of 10.8% is out of line with previous years. How much of this increase is due to:

- the new retail outlet in Paris?
- the expansion of the product range?
- increases in selling prices?

The point at which revenue is recognised in respect of:

- The accessories which have to be ordered
- The internet sales of items which are subject to stockouts

Method used to translate sales made by the Paris retail outlet.

Gross profit margin

Increase of 2% is significant in light of significant increase in revenue. Would not have been surprised to see the margin fall. Is the increase due to:

- higher margin on accessories
- beneficial effect of movement in exchange rates
- cheaper goods from Portuguese suppliers
- possible understatement of purchases
- possible overstatement of inventory

Operating margin

The reason for the significant fall of 4%, which is surprising in light of increase in gross margin. Is the fall due to:

- misclassification of costs between cost of sales and operating expenses
- marketing costs of the new range and overseas expansion
- depreciation relating to the new IT infrastructure
- running expenses associated with the new Paris retail outlet
- leasing costs of the purpose-built warehouse facility (any up-front leasing costs accounted for incorrectly)
- misclassification of expenditure by expensing items which should have been capitalised

Inventory days

Inventory days have increased by 14 days which is surprising in view of the company's policy of holding limited inventory for the more expensive items. Is this increase due to:

- slow moving or obsolete items which need to be written down
- build up of new range of less expensive accessories
- translation errors in respect of items purchased from overseas suppliers
- whether the book figure is supported by a physical count

Payables days

Payables days have fallen by six days. Is the fall due to:

- understatement of payables due to unrecorded invoices
- tighter credit terms with new suppliers
- translation errors

General

The controls exercised over data transfer to the new IT system and whether the old and new systems were subject to parallel running.

7.2 The following financial information would be useful when undertaking analytical procedures:

- Schedules supporting the figures included in the financial statements for example, a breakdown in operating expenses

- Management accounts for the corresponding six-month period

- Profit forecasts for the corresponding six-month period

- Segmental information, including:

    - mail order v retail outlets
    - accessories v clothing
    - outlet by outlet basis

- Industry sector and competitor financial information

- The full financial statements for the whole previous year

- The cash flow statement for the corresponding six-month period

7.3 A review of the financial statements provides limited/moderate assurance as to the credibility of the financial information. A limited assurance engagement reduces the risk to a level that is acceptable in the circumstances. The conclusion is expressed negatively in the form of 'nothing has come to our attention that causes us to believe that the accompanying financial statements do not give a true and fair view'.

A statutory audit provides reasonable assurance as to the credibility of the financial statements. A reasonable assurance engagement reduces the risk to an acceptably low level. It provides a high, but not absolute, level of assurance that the financial statements are free from material misstatement. The conclusion is expressed positively in the form of 'in our opinion the financial statements give a true and fair view of the state of the company's affairs…'

A review provides less assurance than an audit because the scope of the work is less.

General comments

Answers to this question attained the second highest average mark on the written test section of the exam. In general, answers to parts 7.3 were better than answers to parts 7.1 and 7.2.

Part 7.1

Answers to this part were mixed. Those candidates who dealt with each of the given ratios in turn, stating a plausible matter to be discussed with management, tended to score high or full marks. However, many lost marks by being too vague and just stating 'obtain reason for the increase' instead of demonstrating an understanding of what might be the cause of the significant increase. The points most commonly overlooked were: in respect of gross profit margin, the possibility of understated purchases and cheaper suppliers, in respect of inventory days, the possibility of translation errors and in respect of payables days the possible understatement of payables. Furthermore, only a minority of candidates appreciated that an increase in gross margin coupled with a fall in operating margin may result from a misclassification of costs. Weaker candidates digressed into the consideration of the business risks such as failing to deliver goods or failing to comply with overseas laws and regulations.

Part 7.2

Answers to this part of the question were mixed. Strong candidates identified additional information such as management accounts, budgets and forecasts, industry information and full financial statements for the previous year. Some candidates ignored the requirement 'in addition to the interim financial information' and identified items that would be available in the interim statement of financial position. For example, many cited figures needed to calculate ratios such as the quick ratio and other liquidity ratios which would already be available in the interim statement of financial position. The points most commonly overlooked were those in respect of the segmental information.

Part 7.3

This part was very well answered by the majority of candidates with many scoring full marks. The point most commonly overlooked was that in respect of the scope of the work being less in an engagement to review financial information. A small minority of candidates stated, incorrectly, that the level of assurance provided by such a review engagement was low.

8 Paradise Ltd (March 2011)

Marking guide

			Marks
8.1	(1)	Practical implication	4
		Purpose	1½
	(2)	Practical implication	2
		Purpose	1
	(3)	Practical implication	2½
		Purpose	1
	(4)	Practical implication	1½
		Purpose	1
	(5)	Practical implication	½
		Purpose	1
	Maximum		8

		Marks
8.2 Communication with external auditor	4	
Maximum		2
8.3 General	6	
Reasonableness of assumptions	10	
Procedures regarding inclusion of Russell's figures	5	
Reasonableness of assumptions regarding Squirrel's investment	3	
Disclosure/presentation	4	
Written representations	1	
Maximum		10
Total marks available		20

8.1 (1) Practical implication

The firm cannot express an opinion as to whether the results contained in the business plan will be achieved. There will be a statement of negative assurance as to whether the assumptions provide a reasonable basis for the prospective financial information such as 'nothing has come to our attention which causes us to believe that these assumptions do not provide a reasonable basis for the forecast'. However, the firm will give an opinion as to whether the prospective financial information is properly prepared on the basis of the assumptions and if it is presented in accordance with the relevant financial reporting framework. This is not a statutory audit and therefore International Standards on Auditing will not be followed.

Purpose

This phrase makes clear the specific standards (criteria) that will be followed and ensures no misunderstandings arise over the nature of the examination to be undertaken or the nature of the conclusion expressed by the accountant. It also provides assurance to Paradise that the appropriate standards are being followed.

(2) Practical implication

The firm is unable to provide absolute or reasonable assurance due to the prospective nature of the information being examined. Less work will be undertaken than on a statutory audit engagement.

Purpose

This phrase ensures there is no misunderstanding regarding the level of assurance that can be given and hence reduces the expectation gap. It will prevent over-reliance on the conclusion expressed by the accountant.

(3) Practical implication

Management will need to sign a written representation regarding the intended use of the prospective financial information, the completeness of significant assumptions and management's acceptance of its responsibility for the prospective financial information.

Purpose

This phrase is included to avoid any misunderstanding regarding the firm's and management's respective responsibilities and also to avoid any misunderstandings arising in terms of explanations provided by management to the firm during the examination.

(4) **Practical implication**

Paradise's directors would have to discuss sharing the report, with anyone other than Squirrel, with the firm before making the information available. The firm may choose to decline the request for Paradise to circulate the report more widely. The report is intended to be private and not for public record.

Purpose

The phrase aims to prevent reliance by unknown third parties on the firm's opinion and reduces the liability of the firm to unforeseen third parties.

(5) **Practical implication**

A liability cap is placed on the amount of damages which may be payable by the firm to Paradise and Squirrel.

Purpose

The inclusion of a liability cap is aimed at protecting the firm from excessive claims against it and of any liability to any other parties.

8.2 The firm should notify the external auditor of the engagement to examine the prospective financial information as this allows the external auditor to communicate with the firm and provide any information that might help with the effectiveness of the examination. The firm may also wish to gain access to the external auditor's working papers in order to check opening balances and the examination may also affect the way the external auditor discharges his own responsibilities.

8.3 **General**

Consider the consistency between each of the elements of the prospective financial information and carry out recomputations based on the assumptions made by management to check arithmetical accuracy.

Undertake sensitivity analysis around key assumptions, such as sales volumes.

Assess the competency of those preparing the prospective financial information.

Consider the appropriateness and consistency of accounting policies adopted including any in respect of the consolidation of financial information relating to Russell.

Assumptions

The reasonableness of assumptions should be considered in light of historical information, the internal consistency of the assumptions and whether:

- the basis of assumptions reflects current political/economic situations

- inflation is appropriately anticipated

- seasonality is fairly reflected

- increases in interest rates are appropriately anticipated

- the impact of currency fluctuations is considered

- appropriate taxation has been fairly reflected

- plans are within Paradise's capabilities and where expansion is anticipated that associated costs are also included

Consideration should be given to the source and reliability of evidence supporting best-estimate assumptions.

Russell

Consider the extent and reliability of evidence available, for example, review Russell's audited financial statements.

Investigate the likelihood that Russell's shareholders will sell their shares to Paradise.

Examine the assumptions around the timing and cost of acquiring Russell and whether:

- appropriate costs of integration have been included
- potential future cost savings are appropriately recognised

Squirrel

Check that the investment from Squirrel included in the plan is in line with the terms currently being negotiated and that the financial return to Squirrel is in line with those terms and appears reasonable.

Check that the investment from, and the returns to Squirrel, are included at the appropriate time.

Disclosure/presentation

Assess whether:

- the presentation is informative and not misleading
- the disclosure of assumptions is adequate
- accounting policies are clearly and adequately disclosed
- the business plan shows a viable business and that debts can be met as they fall due

Management representations

Obtain written representations from management regarding the completeness of significant assumptions and that management accepts its responsibility for the prospective financial information.

Examiner's comments:

General comments

This was the least well answered written test question. Answers to part 8.1 and 8.2 were disappointing. Candidates demonstrated a lack of understanding of the purpose of specific phrases included in an engagement letter and a lack of knowledge around obligations to the external auditor of a client where the firm has accepted a non-audit engagement. It was pleasing therefore to see a number of strong answers to part 8.3 and candidates have clearly made use of similar past exam questions to improve their responses to the request for procedures in respect of the examination of prospective financial information.

Part 8.1

Answers to this part were disappointing. Many candidates failed to make any distinction between practical implications and purposes thereby providing answers that lacked structure.

Candidates that took each phrase in turn tended to score more highly than those who took a general or holistic approach to their answers.

Overall, candidates provided better answers for explaining phrases (3) to (5). Most candidates did not provide adequate explanations for phrases (1) and (2) and often simply repeated elements of the phrases given in the question rather than trying to explain what the implication or purpose of them was. A number of candidates failed to read the question requirement and dealt with phrases (1) and (5) only, overlooking phrases (2) to (4).

Part 8.2

Answers to this part were very disappointing. Many candidates stated that the firm should seek professional clearance from the previous auditors. They failed to appreciate that the appointment was to examine prospective financial information and so did not require professional clearance to be obtained, and that the engagement has already been accepted by the firm. Other candidates explained, inappropriately, the procedures that the firm should follow in order to place reliance on the work of the external auditors.

Part 8.3

There were a number of strong answers to this part with many candidates identifying appropriate procedures relating specifically to the information provided in the scenario.

However, there were some weak answers stemming from candidates' lack of understanding of what prospective financial information is and the procedures necessary to reach a conclusion on the examination of such information. These answers included, inappropriately, a large number of points relating to the audit of historical financial information such as detailed assessments of internal controls and the verification of account balances.

A number of candidates made use of ISAE 3400 *The Examination of Prospective Financial Information* in the open text but failed to apply the generic procedures from the standard to the specifics of the scenario presented in the question and consequently did not score as highly as they might have.

Weaker candidates lost marks by presenting vague procedures, for example, 'recompute calculations' or 'assess disclosure' without specifying the calculations that should be recomputed or the disclosure that should be assessed.

9 Pampered Pooches Ltd (December 2012)

Marking guide

				Marks
9.1	(a)	Purpose and scope	5	
	(b)	Limiting liability	4½	
		Marks available	9½	
		Maximum		5
9.2		Revenue	5½	
		Gross profit	10½	
		Profit from operations	4½	
		Inventory	8	
		Receivables	8	
		Payables	6	
		General documentary information	2½	
		Marks available	45	
		Maximum		15
Total marks available				20

9.1 The engagement letter should include statements on the following:

(a) **Purpose and scope**

The engagement is to review the financial information for the six months ended 31 October 20X2 and will involve enquiry of management and the application of analytical and other review procedures.

A reference to any relevant standards such as ISRE 2400 *Engagements to Review Historical Financial Statements* (or if applicable, ISRE 2410 *Review Of Interim Financial Information Performed By The Independent Auditor Of The Entity*).

The engagement is not an audit, is limited in scope and the assurance provider will not express an opinion on the financial information.

The level of assurance provided will be moderate/limited and expressed negatively in the form of 'nothing has come to our attention that causes us to believe that the accompanying financial statements do not give a true and fair view in accordance with International Financial Reporting Standards'.

(b) **Limiting liability**

The engagement cannot be relied upon to disclose whether fraud, errors or illegal acts exist.

The report is prepared for the sole use of the management for the purpose of providing assurance to the designated investor and should not be shown to any other third party without the express permission of the assurance firm.

A liability cap stating the maximum amount, which may be claimed in damages resulting from the negligence of the assurance firm.

9.2 **Revenue**

Enquiries

What are the procedures for recording sales and cash handling at the retail outlets?

How much of the sales to the public relate to the new retail outlets and has there been any impact on mail order or internet sales?

How much of the sales to the other retailers relates to AA?

Documentary information

Documented procedures and control processes

A schedule detailing a breakdown of sales between:

- internet and retail outlets for sales to the public
- independent retailers and AA

Gross profit

Enquiries

What is the reason for the fall in gross profit margin? Is it due to:

- a lower margin on AA sales or bulk discounts to customers?
- adverse exchange rates on overseas purchases?
- an increase in input costs such as direct labour, materials or carriage inwards?
- a change in sales mix towards lower margin items (eg, between manufactured and bought in items)?
- competitive pressures on selling prices?

Why have purchases increased disproportionately to sales (31.2% compared to 25.8%)?

What cut-off procedures were in place?

Documentary information

- Contract with AA
- Schedule detailing selling prices and costs for each product line
- Schedule detailing the costs included in cost of sales

Profit from operations

Enquiries

What is the reason for a fall in operating margin which is greater than the fall in gross margin? Is it due to:

- the additional cost of setting up and running the retail outlets?
- setup costs relating to the AA contract?
- an increase in distribution costs?

Documentary information

Schedule detailing the expenses included in operating expenses

Inventory

Enquiries

What is the reason for the increase in inventory days (fall in turnover), when revenue has increased significantly? Is it due to:

- any slow-moving, damaged or obsolete items?
- the need to hold items for AA (to call down on a just in time basis)?
- the level of inventory at the retail outlets?

Is the inventory figure supported by continuous records or was it subject to a full count at 31 October 20X2?

What is the policy regarding the translation of items bought from overseas suppliers?

Documentary information

- Aged inventory report/movements listing/breakdown by location
- Results of inventory counts
- Record of any adjustments to sales prices post year end

Receivables

Enquiries

What is the reason for the increase in receivables days outside the normal 30 day credit terms? Is it due to:

- extended credit terms under the AA contract?
- overdue balances?
- a change in/difficulties with credit control procedures?

Documentary information

- Contracts with AA and independent retailers
- Aged receivables listing
- Calculations re any allowances for doubtful debts
- Customer correspondence

Payables

Enquiries

What is the reason for the increase in payables days? Is it due to:

- new suppliers with extended credit terms or disputed balances?
- delayed payments to stay within overdraft facility/cash flow problems?

What is the policy regarding the translation of balances payable to overseas suppliers?

Documentary information

- Contracts with suppliers
- Aged payables listing
- Correspondence with suppliers/supplier statements

General documentary information

- Budgets/forecasts for the corresponding period
- Management accounts for the corresponding period
- Information regarding the loan from the managing director
- Bank correspondence/overdraft facility
- Board minutes

Examiner's comments:

Answers to both parts of this question attained the lowest average marks on the written test section of the exam. In part 9.1 a significant number of candidates demonstrated a lack of knowledge of the features of a review engagement and the existence of ISRE 2400 *Engagements To Review Historical Financial Statements*. Although there were many strong answers to part 9.2, a significant number of candidates failed to demonstrate the analytical skills required.

Candidates who were familiar with the contents of ISRE 2400 *Engagements to Review Historical Financial Statements* and/or ISRE 2410 *Review Of Interim Financial Information Performed By The Independent Auditor Of The Entity*, performed well on part 9.1 of the question and, in particular, in respect of the level of assurance and the manner in which the conclusion would be expressed. Weak candidates, who were not familiar with the features of a review engagement, often lapsed into the purpose and scope of an audit or an examination of prospective financial information for which they scored no marks. In respect of limiting liability, most candidates restricted the use of the report to management and to a lesser extent the designated investor. Furthermore, many candidates cited liability cap but few scored the additional mark for explaining what it meant. However, many wasted time writing about setting up limited liability partnerships and professional indemnity insurance. A number of candidates also wasted time writing about matters to be included in the letter of engagement, other than the purpose and scope of the engagement and limiting liability.

Although a significant number of candidates scored full marks on part 9.2 of the question, many answers were disappointing. Those candidates who scored high marks used the ratios provided in the question as a framework and listed plausible enquiries, which demonstrated that the candidate understood what might have caused a change in the ratio. Candidates who scored low marks tended to do so because they asked general or vague questions. (for example, 'why has gross profit margin fallen?') or restated information provided in the scenario (for example 'inventory days have increased') instead of directed questions that focused on actual reasons why changes in the ratios may have occurred (for example,' has the gross profit margin fallen because sales to AA are subject to lower margins?'). Candidates who performed poorly on this question often gave little thought to the layout of their answers which were presented as rambling and unstructured lists of questions in no particular order. A small number of students confused the years they were looking at and as a result analysed the ratios incorrectly ie, thinking a rise had occurred in a ratio between years when in fact it had been a fall. A small number of candidates wasted time by providing workings to calculate the ratios that had already been provided in the question.

10 Giza Science Group plc (March 2014)

Marking guide

		Marks
10.1	**Matters to consider**	
	½ mark per matter identified, 1 mark per explanation	
	Marks available	44
	Maximum		18
10.2	**Differences in scope and reasons for differences**	
	Marks available	10½
	Maximum		5
Total marks available		23

10.1 New audit client

- Although the firm has experience in the industry sector, it lacks cumulative audit knowledge of Giza and its directors, leading to increased risk.

- The firm will have limited comfort over opening balances.

Giza is a listed company operating in the scientific research sector.

- The firm must consider whether it has relevant experience in meeting the additional reporting requirements for listed companies. There will be higher risk due to the public interest nature of Giza and the potential for aggressive earnings management.

- The financial statements are likely to be complex, due to the size of the entity and also include high risk items such as intangible assets.

Breach of animal protection laws identified by a current affairs TV programme resulting in employees being suspended. The breaches may:

- give rise to reputational risk for the firm and may indicate a lack of director/management integrity; and

- indicate lack of internal controls or poor control environment which increases the risk of material misstatements and the issue of an inappropriate audit opinion.

Giza is subject to a number of laws and regulations.

- This increases the risk of non-compliance with laws and regulations which could result in closure, suspension of licences, fines or issues over the going concern status of the entity.

Giza owns subsidiaries worldwide.

- The firm must consider whether it:

    - will be required to audit Giza's subsidiaries;
    - has representation in the relevant countries; or
    - may be required to instruct component auditors.

- The firm is likely to require knowledge of laws and regulations in other countries and will need to be able to address any potential language barriers.

The firm already has a number of clients in the same industry including SciRay, a supplier to Giza.

- Potential conflicts of interest or confidentiality issues may arise when acting for competing audit clients and these clients may not be willing to provide written consent for the firm to act for Giza.

- The firm must consider whether it has the available employees/resources to implement appropriate safeguards to address any conflicts of interest.

- Marlena Sato may have an ulterior motive in recommending the firm (eg, access to confidential information).

The directors of Giza have requested help in valuing the shares of Minion.

- This engagement could give rise to a management threat if the firm is expected to make a decision whether to acquire Minion or make a judgement as to the value of the shares.

- The firm could be exposed to negligence claims if the acquisition is unsuccessful or if the shares in Minion prove to be overvalued.

- A self-review threat would arise, in the future, if items which are the subject of the examination of Minion's financial statements or the valuation services are included in Giza's future financial statements.

- Future audits may place too much reliance on the firm's valuation work and audit teams may be reluctant to identify errors or shortcomings in that work.

- A conflict of interest would arise if Minion is a client of the firm.

Fees relating to the on-going review of Giza's interim financial statements and the audit of its financial statements.

- A self-interest threat may arise if recurring fees for these engagements exceed 5% of the firm's income.

- Additional resources would be required to implement relevant safeguards and to monitor the proportion of the firm's fee income earned from Giza.

- If recurring fees are expected to exceed 10% of the firm's income the firm cannot accept all the engagements.

The previous auditor resigned.

- This may have been due to disagreements with management, intimidation, unpaid fees, illegal acts or an inability to obtain sufficient appropriate audit evidence giving rise to a modified audit opinion.

Adequacy of the firm's resources and expertise.

- The firm must ensure that sufficient personnel are available to perform the engagements competently and to conduct an engagement quality control review of the audit which is mandatory for the audit of a listed entity.

10.2 Scope of review of interim financial information

A review of interim financial information does not normally require corroboration of the information obtained as procedures are limited to inquiry, analytical and other review procedures. It is not necessary for the practitioner to perform procedures to identify events occurring after the date of the review report, other than enquiring of management about significant transactions occurring in the first several days of the next interim period. This is therefore less in scope than an audit.

Scope of external audit of financial statements

An external audit of financial statements will require the use of tests of detail and tests of control and will include inspection, observation and confirmation of accounting records.

An external audit will include a subsequent events review with proactive responsibility up to the date of the auditor's report requiring specific procedures.

Reasons for differences

A review of interim financial information provides moderate or limited assurance compared with reasonable assurance provided by an external audit. The conclusion is expressed negatively whereas an audit opinion is expressed positively.

A review is conducted in accordance with ISRE 2410 compared with an external audit which is conducted in accordance with the Companies Act 2006 and International Standards on Auditing.

The objective of a review is to reduce engagement risk to a level that is acceptable in the circumstances but where the risk is greater than for an audit. The objective of an external audit is to reduce engagement risk to an acceptably low level.

Examiner's comments:

This was the second best answered question on the exam with answers to part 10.1 being stronger than those to part 10.2. However, candidates' answers to part 10.1 were often disorganised meaning candidates wrote at length and repeated points already included in their answer.

Part 10.1

Although the majority of candidates covered a number of relevant matters to be considered, answers were often unstructured and repetitious. This was particularly the case in respect of threats to objectivity, which were often dealt with in very general terms and not linked to the circumstances of the scenario. Strong candidates linked the threats to the appropriate situation (ie, management and self-review to the service in respect of the acquisition target and the self-interest threat to the level of fees). However, a common error was to link the self-review threat to the work associated with the interim financial information. Many candidates strayed beyond the requirement to identify and explain the **matters to be considered** by the firm before deciding to tender for the services requested by the entity and wasted time describing the **procedures** to be undertaken. Some candidates wrote at length about the process of professional clearance and the checks undertaken to assess the integrity of management. There were no marks available for these procedures.

Part 10.2

Answers to this part of the question were disappointing. Generally, candidates' answers in respect of the reasons for the differences in scope were better than their descriptions of the differences in scope between the two types of engagement. Weaker candidates did not appreciate that a review of interim financial information is based on historical financial information and wrote about prospective financial information. The points most commonly overlooked were those in relation to the level of risk associated with each type of engagement.

11 Pytch Ltd (September 2014)

			Marks
11.1	Research and development	6½	
	Previous auditor	7	
	Withdrawal of new product	7	
	Aubrey Swanson's retirement	10½	
	Marks available	31	
	Maximum		13
11.2	List of questions, 1 mark per point		
	Marks available	10	
	Maximum		4
11.3	Advice on replacement costing system	4	
	Advice on valuation of shares	7½	
	Marks available	11½	
	Maximum		6
Total marks available			23

11.1 Research and development (R&D) involves estimates which are complex and subjective. This increases inherent risk including the risk of inappropriate capitalisation of R&D expenditure. The firm must have employees available with the relevant audit and industry experience and may need to consider the use of an auditor's expert. The high failure rate of R&D projects may result in Pytch failing to write off non-recoverable development costs and may give rise to cash flow issues and doubts over Pytch's ability to continue as a going concern.

The previous auditor qualified the prior year audit opinion due to an inability to obtain sufficient appropriate audit evidence. This may indicate there will be insufficient appropriate evidence over opening balances or for transactions and account balances in the year to 31 December 20X4. This is more likely to be the case as Pytch has not yet replaced its project costing system. The firm should not accept an audit engagement where there is a significant limitation on the scope of the audit. The failure of internal controls identified by the previous auditor indicates a weak control environment or a poor management attitude to internal controls and an increase in control risk. The firm may need to undertake a substantive approach with no reliance on internal controls. The resignation of the previous auditor may indicate issues such as disagreements with Pytch's directors, concerns over management integrity, intimidation, illegal acts or unpaid fees.

The withdrawal of the new hair colourant could result in legal claims from consumers or Perfect Ltd. There may also be fines arising if any laws or industry regulations were breached. The firm may need to audit a significant uncertainty resulting in higher inherent risk and large claims or fines may give rise to doubts over the going concern status. The adverse press may result in loss of business or confidence in Pytch's products which could also give rise to doubts over the going concern status. The reports of insufficient testing may raise concerns about management's integrity. The firm may not wish to be associated with Pytch due to the possible damage to the firm's own reputation.

Aubrey Swanson's retirement means that Pytch will lose its founder/leader and key finance provider which may result in a loss of strategic direction. Funding issues may arise if finance is not forthcoming from the new shareholders and it is unclear if the remaining board members have the skills to direct the company. This gives rise to further risk over the going concern status. New directors and management team, who would be unknown to the firm, may need to be brought in and the firm may not wish to be associated with them. The sale of Aubrey's shares to Club Ltd and the remaining directors of Pytch gives rise to a risk of management bias. Aubrey will have an incentive to inflate profits pending the sale. A potential conflict of interest also arises between the parties involved and the possible reliance by the future investors on the firm's audit opinion increases the engagement risk.

11.2 Are you willing for the firm to act for both Pytch and Club in light of the potential conflict of interest?

Why did the previous auditor resign?

Are the directors willing to grant permission for the firm to contact the previous auditor?

Have any adjustments or fixes been made to the project costing system to address the deficiencies in internal controls identified in the prior year?

What are the potential implications, eg, legal claims, of the hair colourant withdrawal for Pytch?

What has been the impact of the adverse press on the business?

How does management intend to deal with hair colourant issues/withdrawal?

What future sources of finance does Pytch have available after Aubrey's retirement?

What is the company's intention regarding the future structure of the board and senior management?

How far have the negotiations progressed for the sale of Aubrey's shares to Club?

11.3 Advise on replacement of Pytch's project costing system

The results of the new project costing system will be reflected in amounts included in Pytch's future financial statements giving rise to a self-review threat. The firm may need to place significant reliance on the project costing system in future audits. The audit team may rely too heavily on the work performed by the firm during its advice on the project costing system or may be reluctant to point out any deficiencies identified in the system.

The firm may be expected to make management decisions giving rise to a management threat. If management expects the firm to design, provide or implement a system or select an off-the-shelf package, the firm's views may become too closely aligned with those of management.

Advise on an appropriate valuation of the shares to be sold to the other directors and Club Ltd

A conflict of interest will arise between the firm and Aubrey and the other directors/Club Ltd as Aubrey will want to maximise the share value while the other directors/Club Ltd will want to the minimise the share value. The firm may not be able to act in the best interests of all parties.

A self-interest threat may arise as the firm would not wish to act against the interests of the other directors/Club Ltd for fear of losing future audit work.

A self-review threat arises as the shares purchased by Club Ltd may be material to Club Ltd's financial statements. The firm may not sufficiently scrutinise the valuation of Club's investment during the subsequent audit of Club Ltd's financial statements and it may be reluctant to highlight any errors in the valuation.

Examiner's comments:

This was the least well answered of the long-form questions. However, it was pleasing to note that many candidates did make a reasonable attempt at parts 11.1 and 11.2 which were presented in a different style to those questions previously used to examine engagement acceptance. Answers to part 11.3 were generally poor which is disappointing given this is an area in which candidates should be well rehearsed.

Part 11.1

Answers to this part of the question were of a mixed standard. Those candidates who systematically worked through each paragraph and explained the relevance of each item of information to the firm's decision whether to accept appointment as auditor scored higher marks. A number of candidates reiterated the information given in the scenario but failed to earn marks because they were unable to provide a plausible explanation as to its relevance with many candidates often stating that the information gave rise to 'high risk'. For example, statements such as 'research and development is high risk' were common. To earn marks elaboration was required, such as the need to exercise judgement in deciding whether to capitalise or expense research and development costs. Although the majority of candidates identified the need for the auditor to have expertise in the industry sector, surprisingly few candidates considered the use of an auditor's expert. Other points which were commonly overlooked were those in respect of not accepting an engagement where there was a known significant limitation on the scope of the audit, the loss of strategic direction following the retirement of the managing director and the higher engagement risk associated with reliance on the financial statements by potential investors. Weaker candidates wasted time writing about procedures to be performed and wrote at length about procedures such as professional clearance and client background checks for which no marks were awarded.

Part 11.2

This part of the question was very well answered with many candidates scoring full marks. The points most commonly identified were those in respect of the previous auditor, the deficiencies in the costing system and the effects of the adverse publicity. The points most commonly overlooked were those in relation to the succession arrangements and the future funding of the business. A small minority of candidates failed to score well because they did not tailor their answers to the circumstances of the scenario.

Part 11.3

Answers to this part of the question were disappointing, mainly due to poor performance in respect to the threats associated with the advice on the share valuation. The majority of candidates appreciated that the advice on the replacement of the costing system posed self-review and management threats and were able to provide plausible explanations of these threats. In relation to the share valuation, many candidates identified self-interest and self-review threats but were unable to provide plausible explanations. In respect of the self-interest threat, many candidates wasted time writing about fee dependency failing to appreciate that these engagements were one-off and would not impact on regular fee income. In respect of the self-review threat, the majority failed to appreciate that this would arise in respect of Club's financial statements after the acquisition had taken place and not in the financial statements of Pytch. A number of candidates incorrectly identified an advocacy threat in relation to the share valuation. A significant minority of candidates ignored the instruction, in the requirement, not to list safeguards and wasted time describing the safeguards to be applied in each of the two non-audit engagements.

12 University of Downtown (December 2014)

		Marks
12.1 Key receipts and matters to consider		
Funds received from bank	1½	
Sale proceeds of playing fields	2½	
Government grant	2½	
Student fees	3	
VAT receipts	2	
Key payments and matters to consider		
Interest on bank loan and repayments of capital	1½	
Demolition and clearance payments	1	
Building costs	4½	
Quantity surveyor (project management) payments	1½	
New equipment costs	1½	
Running costs of the new building	1	
Staff costs	2	
General	2	
Marks available	26½	
Maximum		12
12.2 (a) **General representations**		
The intended use of the forecast	1½	
The completeness of significant management assumptions	2	
Management's acceptance of its responsibility for the forecast	1½	
(b) **Level of assurance**		
Report on cash flow forecast	3	
Auditor's report on financial statements	2½	
Reasons for different levels of assurance	4½	
Marks available	15	
Maximum		8
Total marks available		20

12.1 Key receipts and matters to consider

Funds received from bank

The amount should be consistent with the amount needed to execute the expansion plan and the receipt should precede the start of the building work.

Sale proceeds of playing fields

This should be a prudent estimate and in line with the market value of similar land. The estimate should be checked to a valuer's report, if available. Enquire if planning permission has been obtained for the playing fields as this will affect the valuation and inspect the planning permission application. Inspect correspondence with the developer for evidence of likelihood of the sale proceeding and any indication of the sales value.

Government grant

The timing of the receipt in the cash flow forecast should be after the completion of the new workshop and classrooms. The feasibility of completion by September 20X6 should be assessed, referring to the grant letter where necessary for the detailed conditions of the grant. The size of the grant should be 40% of the building costs included in the cash flow forecast payments and this calculation should be checked.

Student fees

The receipt from student fees should be based on the number of students multiplied by the fee per student and this calculation should be checked. The number of students should be consistent with the capacity of new workshop and classrooms. The fee per student should be in line with current rates. Total fees should increase in September 20X6 when the new building is in use and these should be in excess of the additional running costs incurred for the new workshop and classrooms.

VAT receipts

Enquiries should be made as to the VAT status of the new building. An analytical procedure based on the VAT rate and the materials purchased should be performed. Repayments of VAT should be received at appropriate intervals, for example, quarterly or monthly.

Key payments and matters to consider

Interest on bank loan and repayments of capital

Prudent assumptions should be made regarding interest payments, for example, in line with market rates or consistent with those cited in correspondence with the bank and should be based on the principal outstanding. Repayments of capital should be consistent with those cited in correspondence with the bank.

Demolition and clearance payments

These payments should be based on the tenders received, which should be inspected.

Building costs

Enquiries should be made with the director of estates as to how he/she arrived at the estimate of building costs of £2,500 per square metre. The qualifications and experience of the director of estates should be considered and working papers, if available, reviewed. The estimate of £2,500 per square metre should be compared to building costs for other similar buildings and an independent surveyor or architect consulted to confirm whether this is a reasonable estimate.

The estimate should be checked to see if it is in line with design and architect's plans, if available. The calculation of £2,500 per square metre multiplied by the size of the new building should be checked for accuracy. The timing of any retention payments in the cash flow forecast should also be considered.

Quantity surveyor (project management) payments

These costs should be either fixed fee or a percentage of building costs and should be in line with market rates or the letter of engagement with Crawley and Co, if available.

New equipment costs

These costs should be as per quotes or catalogue prices and in line with number and size of the new workshop and classrooms.

Running costs of the new building

The running costs such as utility costs, insurance and maintenance should be consistent with the size of the new engineering workshop and classrooms.

Staff costs

The number of classes and the average class size should be considered when reviewing the reasonableness of staff costs and the timing of payments to HMRC should be monthly in arrears.

General

The timing of payments should be consistent with the progress of the building work. For example, the demolition payment should be at the start of the project, the payments for construction should be throughout the building phase of the contract and the payments for equipment should be in advance of the opening of the new workshop and classrooms in September 20X6. The increase in the running costs should be after September 20X6 once the workshop and classrooms are in use.

The assumptions should take into account inflation and key variables should be subjected to sensitivity analysis.

12.2 (a) **General representations**

The general representations that should be obtained are:

The intended use of the forecast

This is to ensure that the audit firm is aware of all users of the forecast and that there are no unforeseen users which could impact on the risk associated with the engagement. This representation reduces the extent of the reporting accountant's liability and exposure to potential claims.

The completeness of significant management assumptions

The knowledge of the assumptions used to compile the forecast is largely confined to management. The reporting accountant cannot undertake the examination of the forecast unless all assumptions are adequately disclosed. The reporting accountant reports on the 'reasonableness' of assumptions and therefore needs confirmation, via a representation, that they are complete and free from management bias.

Management's acceptance of its responsibility for the forecast

The reporting accountant is not responsible for preparation of the forecast and is only responsible for examining and providing an assurance report on the forecast. This representation reduces the expectation gap and any misunderstandings regarding the responsibilities of the respective parties.

(b) **Level of assurance**

A report on the cash flow forecast provides limited/moderate assurance as to the credibility of the financial information. The conclusion is expressed negatively in the form of 'nothing has come to our attention that causes us to believe that the assumptions do not provide a reasonable basis for the forecast ...'

An auditor's report on annual financial statements provides reasonable assurance as to their credibility. It provides a high, but not absolute, level of assurance that the financial statements are free from material misstatement. The conclusion is expressed positively in the form of 'in our opinion the financial statements give a true and fair view of the state of the company's affairs, have been properly prepared in accordance with the relevant reporting framework and have been prepared in accordance with the requirements of the Companies Act 2006'.

A review provides less assurance than an audit. The reason is that an audit is based on historical information which can be verified to a greater degree whereas the examination of a forecast is based on assumptions and judgements about the future which is subject to uncertainty.

Examiner's comments:

This was the least well answered long-form question particularly in respect of part 12.2 (a). A number of candidates presented incomplete answers to part 12.1.

Answers to part 12.1 of the question were good. As in previous sessions, candidates were better at identifying the key receipts and payments that would be included in the cash flow forecasts, but were weaker at identifying the specific matters to be considered when reviewing the reasonableness of the assumptions underlying the receipt or payment. Weaker candidates tended to identify a key receipt or payment but then stated that the firm should 'consider its reasonableness' but this explanation was insufficient to score any marks. Receipts for VAT and payments for staffing costs were the most commonly overlooked cash flows. Most candidates failed to consider inflation and sensitivity analysis in their answers. A minority of weaker candidates continued to confuse cash flow forecasts with profit forecasts and incorrectly included items such as depreciation, profit or loss on the disposal of the playing fields and spreading the government grant over the period covered by the forecast. Some candidates failed to recognise that the loan had yet to be agreed and incorrectly referred to the loan agreement as evidence for the interest rate. Some candidates included the payment for the acquisition of the disused factory in the cash flow forecast but did not score any marks as the acquisition predated the start of the cash flow forecast.

Answers to part 12.2 (a) were very disappointing as the majority of candidates answered in terms of the role of written representations in a statutory audit of financial statements or an engagement to review historical financial statements, instead of the examination of prospective financial information. Consequently, they listed the requirements of ISA (UK) 580 *Written Representations* or paragraph 62 of ISRE 2400 *Engagements to Review Historical Financial Statements* for which no marks were awarded. The minority of candidates who were familiar with the contents of paragraph 25 of ISAE 3400 *The Examination of Prospective Financial Information*, often scored full marks as once they listed the required representations they demonstrated an understanding of why they were needed particularly in respect of limiting the reporting accountant's liability and reducing the expectation gap. A number of candidates provided representations that were specific to the scenario. These answers scored no marks as the requirement was to list general representations.

Part 12.2 (b) was very well answered by the majority of candidates. The points most commonly overlooked were that an auditor's report refers to the financial statements being properly prepared in accordance with the relevant reporting framework and in accordance with the requirements of the Companies Act 2006.

13 Clymene Ltd, Dusky Ltd, Risso Ltd, Irrawaddy Ltd (September 2015)

Marking guide

	Marks
Clymene (½ mark per point)	
Matters to consider	13
Steps	6½
Dusky (½ mark per point)	
Matters to consider	7½
Steps	2½
Risso (1 mark per point)	
Matters to consider	9
Steps	4½

	Marks
Irrawaddy (1 mark per point)	
Matters to consider	11
Steps	3½
Marks available	57½
Total marks available	25

Clymene

Matters to consider

The reduction in the number of employees in Clymene's accounts department may make obtaining audit evidence more difficult, especially if key employees have left before any audit work commences. It may result in an increase in the risk of misstatement.

The additional engagement to prepare financial statements will require additional resources and may present a threat to objectivity due to:

Familiarity threat

- The firm has been acting for Clymene for a number of years and may be too trusting of the client's management.

Self-review threat

- The results of accounts preparation work will be reflected in the financial statements that are the subject of the external audit. The audit team may be insufficiently questioning of the work performed to prepare the financial statements or may be unwilling to highlight any deficiencies identified in that work.

Management threat

- The team preparing the financial statements may be expected to make decisions/judgements about the amounts included, whereas these should be made by management. Their views may become too closely aligned with the views of management.

Self-interest threat

- The firm may place too much reliance on the fee income generated from Clymene and may be unwilling to modify its opinion on the financial statements due to fear of losing the client.

- Fees will increase to £750,000 which may be on a recurring basis if the firm prepares the financial statements each year. The firm's gross income from Clymene will then be £7,150,000 which represents 10.5% of gross practice income. This is below the 15% threshold for unlisted companies but above the 10% threshold. Therefore, safeguards will be required.

As Clymene is not a listed company, an engagement to prepare financial statements is permitted.

Steps

Ensure that adequate resources and expertise are available within the firm.

The engagement partner should be rotated if necessary to mitigate any familiarity threat.

Determine if the firm is able to implement the following safeguards:

- Preparation of the financial statements to be performed by a separate team that is not involved in the external audit

- Arrangement of an external independent quality control review

Ensure the client understands that the firm cannot make management decisions and that the service to prepare the financial statements is of a technical and mechanical nature, ie:

- No authorisation/approval of transactions
- No preparing originating data
- No determining/changing journal entries

The firm must document the existence of informed management.

Ascertain if Clymene requires the firm to prepare the financial statements on an on-going basis and disclose the fact that fees are above the 10% threshold to the firm's ethics partner and to those charged with governance at Clymene.

Dusky

Matters to consider

Whether the level of assurance required is limited or reasonable. There may be a risk of an expectation gap given that any system has inherent limitations. The firm cannot provide absolute assurance that the system is free from control deficiencies. The system may include control deficiencies not identified in the firm's report to management and are therefore unlikely to have been addressed by the recent system changes.

The scope of engagement, including the period or point in time to be covered and nature of the report required.

There is a potential threat to objectivity due to a self-review threat as the assurance report on the systems may be used as part of the external audit. The audit team may be insufficiently questioning of the assurance work or may be unwilling to highlight deficiencies in the work.

Steps

Discuss the scope of the engagement and the level of assurance required with the directors to ensure their expectations are appropriate.

Determine if the firm is able to put appropriate safeguards in place, ie:

- A separate team for the assurance engagement whose members are not involved in the external audit
- An independent partner review to assess whether the systems are rigorously reviewed as part of external audit work

Ensure that adequate resources and expertise are available within the firm.

Risso

Matters to consider

There is a potential threat to professional competence and due care. Risso operates in the marine biology industry, a highly specialised sector, in which the firm may not have sufficient expertise. The firm may also be unaware of the same set of facts as the incumbent auditor.

The directors appear to be 'opinion shopping' which may call into question the integrity of management and the firm may not wish to be associated with the client due to reputational risk.

A self-interest threat exists if the firm is tempted to give the opinion the client desires in order to obtain future work from Risso.

Ethical issues, such as conflicts of interest, may exist and, if so, will need to be addressed.

Steps

Seek permission to contact the incumbent auditor. If the management of Risso refuses, the firm should consider declining the engagement. If permission is obtained, contact the incumbent auditor to ensure the firm is apprised of all the facts relevant to the issue at the time the opinion was modified.

Perform searches/background checks on Risso's management.

Ensure adequate resources and expertise are available within the firm.

Irrawaddy

Matters to consider

There is high engagement risk due to reliance by the bank on the firm's assurance report and the firm should consider the level of the liability cap it should put into place.

The firm lacks cumulative knowledge of the business and its management and it is unclear why the current auditor was not offered the assurance engagement. It may indicate a potential management integrity issue if management is hiding something from the external auditor. The firm may not wish to be associated with Irrawaddy due to reputational risk.

The current year audit is not complete and it is unclear whether the audited figures for the year to 30 June 20X5 will be available to provide opening balances for the prospective financial information.

Whether management accepts that it is responsible for the preparation of the prospective financial information and whether it understands that an engagement to examine prospective financial information provides a limited level of assurance.

Ethical issues, such as conflicts of interest, may exist and, if so, will need to be addressed.

Steps

Ascertain if permission will be given to communicate with/inform the incumbent auditor.

Ascertain from management why the incumbent auditor was not offered the engagement to examine the prospective financial information.

Perform searches/background checks on Irrawaddy's management.

Ensure adequate resources and expertise are available within the firm.

Examiner's comments:

General comments

This was the second best answered long-form question. However, the quality of candidates' answers varied significantly between the four scenarios presented. A number of candidates wasted time presenting information relevant to engagement performance whereas the requirement asked candidates for matters to consider and steps to take before acceptance.

Clymene

This part of the question was generally well answered as the majority of candidates identified the self-interest, self-review and, to a lesser extent, management threats and provided plausible explanations of each threat. The familiarity threat, arising from acting for a number of years, was often overlooked by many candidates. A small number of candidates wasted time discussing whether there were any going concern issues (due to the reduction in employee numbers) when there was no evidence of this. The most common omission was the failure to specify that the independent review should be an external review. Candidates generally cited appropriate steps in relation to the matters they identified. However, a significant minority of candidates continue to incorrectly cite information barriers in relation to a self-review threat when this is only appropriate where there are confidentiality issues. Some candidates also wasted time discussing fee monitoring procedures that should be in place when these would only be relevant after the engagement had been accepted.

Dusky

Answers to this part of the question were very disappointing. The vast majority of candidates failed to appreciate that an engagement to provide assurance on the effectiveness of internal controls could be a reasonable or limited assurance engagement. Most candidates assumed that it could only be a limited assurance engagement. However, a significant number of candidates did appreciate that absolute assurance could not be given and that there was an expectation gap on the part of management. A significant minority of candidates assumed, incorrectly, that the engagement was an internal audit engagement and consequently identified, incorrectly, a management threat. A number of candidates also identified a self-interest threat in relation to fee income. This was not appropriate as the engagement was likely to be non-recurring.

Risso

This part of the question was generally well answered as the majority of candidates identified that the prospective client was opinion shopping and that this had implications for management integrity and the fundamental principle of professional competence and due care. Many also identified the significant self-interest threat and the need to obtain client consent to discuss the reason for the modification with the incumbent auditor. The point most commonly overlooked was that relating to the need to be aware of the same facts as the incumbent auditor.

Irrawaddy

Answers to this part of the question were very disappointing. The points most commonly identified were those relating to the reason why the incumbent auditor was not offered the non-audit service and the implications for management integrity. The points most commonly overlooked were those relating to engagement risk associated with the bank's reliance on the assurance report. A number of candidates wasted time listing irrelevant threats to objectivity, such as an advocacy threat, or seeking clarification on the intended use of the information when this was clearly stated in the scenario. A small number of candidates wasted time discussing going concern, believing, incorrectly that a company seeking finance must be in financial difficulty.

14 Tasty Sauces Ltd

Marking guide

			Marks	
14.1	(a)	Management's responsibilities	3½	
		Purpose and scope of work	5	
		Limiting liability	3½	
	(b)	Explanation	5	
		Marks available	17	
		Maximum		8
14.2		Receipts from and payments to supermarkets	10½	
		Payments to Mixit	4	
		Proceeds from disposal of manufacturing unit	5	
		Payments for rented warehouse etc	3	
		Receipts from and payments to Denzil Dragon	4	
		General	1	
		Marks available	27½	
		Maximum		10

		Marks
14.3 Four key differences	8	
Marks available	8	
Maximum		4
Total marks available		22

14.1 (a) **Management's responsibilities**

The engagement letter should state that management:

- is responsible for the preparation of the cash flow forecast and for the identification and disclosure of the assumptions on which the forecast is based; and

- will provide the reporting accountant with all relevant information used in developing these assumptions and written representations specifically on:

    - intended use of the forecasts
    - completeness of significant assumptions; and
    - its acknowledgement of its responsibility for the forecasts.

Purpose and scope of your firm's work

The engagement letter should state:

- that the reporting accountant will examine the cash flow forecast for the three years ending 31 December 20X8

- that the examination will consider the reasonableness of assumptions and whether the forecast is properly prepared on the basis of those assumptions

- whether the engagement is to be conducted in accordance with the provisions of ISAE 3400

- that there could be differences between the forecast and actual performance due to unforeseen circumstances

- limited assurance will be provided by the reporting accountant expressed in a negative form ('nothing has come to our attention...') as to whether the assumptions provide a reasonable basis for the prospective financial information.

Limiting your firm's liability

The engagement letter should identify the intended users, that is, the management, bank and Denzil Dragon for the purpose of obtaining funding and that the report should not be shown to any other party without permission. A liability cap should be stated (that is the maximum monetary amount of damages payable by the reporting accountant).

(b) **Explanation**

The reasons why these matters should be included in the engagement letter are to reduce the risk of any misunderstandings (bridge the expectation gap) and to make it clear that the examination of the cash flow forecast does not constitute an audit. By including the matters in respect of limiting liability, the firm limits the amount of damages to which it is exposed. By identifying the intended users, the firm reduces the risk of claims for damages by unforeseen third parties.

14.2 (1) Receipts from and payments to supermarkets for the sale of products

The contract with Terose expires in June 20X6 so the final receipt for the sale of sauces should be reflected 75 days later. A rebate payable to Terose should be included in the cash flow forecast at the end of the contract only if the specified volume of sauces is forecast to be purchased by Terose. The contract with Terose should be examined to confirm the specified volume and the profit forecast checked to confirm the forecast volume sales of sauces to Terose.

The receipts from the new supermarkets should commence after June 20X6 with a credit period of 30 days following the sale. The likelihood of obtaining four-year contracts with five new supermarkets should be considered through examination of correspondence and discussion with TSL management. The 30 days credit period should be checked to ensure that it is consistent with current negotiations or draft contracts. For sales transacted in foreign currencies, the assumptions used for the exchange rates should be discussed with management.

An increase in receipts should be reflected in June 20X7 when soups are sold for the first time and, again, in June 20X8 when curries are sold for the first time. It should be considered as to whether the length of the research and development phase is consistent with other new product development periods.

The seasonality of receipts should be reflected in the cash flow forecast as sales of sauces are higher in warmer months.

(2) Payments to Mixit

The payments to Mixit should start in June 20X6 and should be consistent with the level of sales and purchases assumed in the profit forecast and should reflect a realistic and prudent gross margin. There should be cash payments in advance for the first 12 months and credit terms of 30 days thereafter. The terms should be checked to correspondence and any contract with Mixit.

The capacity of the Mixit facility should be considered to see that it is sufficient to fulfil the volume of orders assumed.

The financial position of Mixit should be ascertained to see if it can continue trading for the foreseeable future.

(3) Proceeds from the disposal of the manufacturing unit

This should be a prudent estimate and in line with the market value of similar properties in the locality. The estimate should be checked to a valuer's report, if available. Correspondence with the developer should be inspected for evidence of the likelihood that the sale will proceed and any indication of the sales value and whether the sale is contingent on obtaining planning permission. The planning permission application to change the use from industrial to residential should be inspected as this will affect the market value if the planning application is successful. The forecast should reflect the timescales involved in obtaining planning permission and the six months needed to decommission the manufacturing unit.

(4) Payments for the rented warehouse, office and research facility

These payments should reflect the six-month rent-free period followed by quarterly payments in advance. The rental payments will commence in 20X7. The amounts in the cash flow forecast should be in line with the rental agreement or market rates and reflect any future rent increases.

(5) Receipts from and payments to Denzil Dragon

The equity funding should be reflected in equal tranches in March and June 20X6 and the repayment of half of the equity funding should only be reflected in the cash flow forecast if the specified level of profit is reached in the forecast. The dates and amounts of the receipt and repayment of equity funding should be consistent with the shareholders' agreement and any correspondence. The profit forecast should be examined to check whether the specified level of profit is expected to be achieved. Dividends of one quarter of annual profits should be reflected in the cash flow forecast. Again, the profit forecast should be examined to see that dividends are one quarter of forecast profits.

General

The assumptions should take account of inflation and key variables should be subjected to sensitivity analysis.

14.3 Profit forecasts are prepared using the accruals principle whereas cash flow forecasts are prepared using the cash basis of accounting. The key differences in the case of the forecasts prepared by the directors of TSL are as follows:

- Items of expenditure such as purchases, rebates, rent, interest and tax are recorded in the profit forecast as costs when they are incurred. The cash flow forecast includes these transactions only when there is an expected outflow of cash.

- Revenue is recorded in the profit forecast as income once it is earned. The cash flow forecast includes revenue only when there is an expected inflow of cash. Allowances to reduce inventory to NRV for slow-moving inventories or for doubtful debts are included in the profit forecast but not in the cash flow forecast.

- Capital expenditure is included in the cash flow forecast when there is an expected outflow of cash. Depreciation of assets acquired is included in the profit forecast but would have no cash flow implication.

- Development expenditure is included in the cash flow forecast when there is an expected outflow of cash. Amortisation of development costs is included in the profit forecast but would have no cash flow implication.

- Proceeds from the disposal of the manufacturing unit are included in the cash flow forecast when there is an expected inflow of cash. The profit forecast records the profit or loss on the disposal of the manufacturing unit.

- The cash flow forecast includes the receipt and repayment of the equity finance from Denzil Dragon but this would have no impact on the profit forecast.

- Value added tax (VAT) is included within the receipts and payments in the cash flow forecast. The profit forecast includes income and expenditure net of VAT.

Examiner's comment

Part 14.1

This part of the question was generally well answered. The most common error was that many candidates failed to demonstrate an appreciation that an engagement letter in respect of an examination of cash flow forecast would differ from an engagement letter in respect of a statutory audit. Consequently, they wasted time covering the matters to be included in an engagement letter for a statutory audit (for example responsibility for the prevention and detection of fraud). Candidates who focussed on an engagement letter for the examination of a cash flow forecast generally earned marks from each of the three sections specified in the requirement and the majority correctly identified that narrowing the expectations gap was a primary reason for including those matters in the engagement letter. Other reasons, such as making it clear that the engagement was not an audit and limiting the amount of damages the firm may be exposed to, were frequently overlooked. Many candidates lost marks for failing to appreciate that the firm would owe a duty of care to the bank and incorrectly stated that a restriction on the distribution of the firm's report would limit the firm's liability to the bank. A minority of weaker candidates wasted time discussing other means of limiting a firm's liability such as limited liability partnerships and professional indemnity insurance which was outside the scope of the question as they would not be included in an engagement letter.

Part 14.2

Answers to this part of the question were disappointing and a number of candidates provided very brief answers that scored few marks. A significant number of candidates were unable to identify any matters to consider when reviewing the reasonableness of the assumptions underlying the receipt or payment. This matter has been identified by examiners in previous commentaries as an area where candidates struggle.

The following points were commonly overlooked:

- Consideration of the likelihood of obtaining contracts with the five new supermarkets
- Exchange rate considerations in respect of the new contracts
- Seasonality of receipts
- The growth in receipts from the sale of soups and curries
- The link between payments to Mixit and the volume of sales receipts
- The capacity and financial viability of Mixit
- Correspondence with the developer

Most candidates failed to consider inflation and sensitivity analysis in their answers.

A number of weaker candidates approached the question from the perspective of the firm conducting a financial statements audit, instead of consideration of the reasonableness of assumptions underlying receipts and payments in a cash flow forecast. For example, candidates discussed issues such as:

- removing assets from the asset register

- vouching the cost of the manufacturing unit

- ensuring the correct accounting treatment was followed for the rent free period and the rebate to Terose

- the audit of the rebate payment

- the need to identify related party transactions

- the audit procedures that should be performed at inventory count attendances.

None of these points was relevant to the answer.

A number of weaker candidates confused a cash flow forecast with a profit forecast and incorrectly discussed items such as depreciation and profit or loss on the disposal of the manufacturing unit. This matter has also been identified in previous examiners' commentaries on questions concerning the examination of cash flow forecast information.

Most candidates correctly commented on the timing of receipts and payments. Stronger candidates identified the terms of contracts, market value of properties similar to the manufacturing unit and the examination of the agreement or correspondence with Denzil Dragon to corroborate the equity funding receipt and its repayment.

Part 14.3

Answers to this part of the question were disappointing. Stronger candidates were able to identify, from the list above, four key differences between the items included in the profit forecasts and the receipts and payments included in the cash flow forecasts and scored maximum marks. However, weaker candidates appeared confused by the concepts of a cash flow forecast and a profit forecast. As a result, many candidates were unable to state any key differences between the items in a profit forecast and the items in a cash flow forecast. A large number of candidates restricted their answers to a general discussion of the accruals basis used in the preparation of financial statements without providing any specific examples and failed to score any marks. The most popular key differences identified were in relation to proceeds from the disposal of the manufacturing unit and the profit or loss on its disposal. Few candidates identified the VAT difference. A significant number of candidates did not attempt this part of the question.

Section 2: Planning engagements

15 Short form questions

15.1 Adequacy of the scope of the work and related programmes

Whether

- Assessment of the internal audit function remains appropriate
- Work is performed by persons having adequate technical training and proficiency
- Work of assistants is properly supervised, reviewed and documented
- Sufficient appropriate evidence is obtained to be able to draw reasonable conclusions
- Conclusions reached are appropriate in the circumstances
- Any reports prepared are consistent with the results of the work performed
- Any exceptions or unusual matters disclosed by internal audit are properly resolved

15.2 Matters

The nature and significance (materiality) of the matter which is the subject of the modification to the financial statements of Narberth Group plc.

Whether the matter which is the subject of the modification can be resolved when preparing the financial statements of Narberth Group plc.

15.3 Unexpected variations

Errors indicated

- Inventories, receivables, or cash and cash equivalents could be understated
- Payables or bank overdrafts could be overstated
- Revenue could be understated
- Purchases could be overstated

Areas re extra work

- Inventories, receivables and payables
- Particularly:
    - Cut off
    - Provisions/write downs

15.4 Audit work - 'advances'

- Item is material by nature

- Item needs to be disclosed regardless of value

- Director transactions if not disclosed in financial statements, must be disclosed in auditor's report

- Balance may indicate other related party transactions that need to be disclosed in financial statements

- May be tax liabilities not provided for in financial statements

- Item not quantitatively material

15.5 Audit risks and procedures to address

- **Audit risks**

    - Non disclosure
    - Transactions not at arm's length

- **Procedures to address**

    - Identify full list of related parties at commencement of audit from prior year working papers

    - Review minutes of meetings of shareholders and directors

    - List names from statutory books

    - Make enquiries with directors and staff during audit

    - Obtain written representations on completeness of disclosure

    - Review loan agreements for guarantors

    - Review transactions between the two parties to ensure arm's length basis

15.6 Using experts

Planning

Assess the experts':

- Competence
- Capabilities
- Objectivity

Assessing results of work

Assess appropriateness of audit evidence re financial statement assertions, especially:

- Source data – sufficient, relevant, reliable?
- Assumptions and methods – reasonable?
- Reasons for changes since prior period
- Results of work in light of auditors' own knowledge of business

15.7 Suspected fraud

- Look for evidence of deficiencies in the systems (eg, from previous management letter)

- Increase professional scepticism

- Evaluation/testing of controls over payroll system to identify deficiencies

- Increase substantive work/sample sizes on wages/payroll costs (eg, leavers deleted properly, existence checks on employees)

- Investigate any apparent override/circumvention of procedures

- Engage payroll clerk in conversation and query lifestyle

- Consider impact on other areas (eg, bank payment approvals)

15.8 Consideration re reduction in substantive procedures

- Reasons for deviations (eg, person responsible on holiday → isolated error)

- Whether deviation indicates

    - Lack of operation of control, ie, control failure; or
    - Just lack of evidence, eg, no initials evidencing check performed.

- Whether quantitative error(s) arose as a result of the deviations (confirming lack of operation of control)

- Whether extended tests prove satisfactory, ie, no further deviations found

- Whether compensating control exists – so monetary errors did not arise

15.9 Risks re payroll processing

Risk

- Misstatements of payroll costs and liabilities to HMRC

- Unrecorded interest for late payment

- Unrecorded provision for damages/breach of contract or disclosure as contingent liability for damages

How addressed

- Evaluate and test controls over payroll processing
- Detailed analytical review procedures
- Confirm payments in respect of PAYE and NIC made on time
- Confirmation of status of any litigation with legal advisers
- Inspect correspondence

15.10 Approach

- Substantive based approach
- Lack of internal controls (high control risk) due to:

    - lack of segregation of duties; and
    - the possibility of unreliable software.

- Higher detection risk associated with new audit
- Greater emphasis on tests of details
- Limited use of analytical procedures as:

    - no prior year comparisons; and
    - lack of cumulative knowledge.

15.11 Audit procedures for warranty provision

- Make enquiries of management as to the basis for the estimate of the warranty provision

- Compare the prior year provision with the actual warranty claims in the year to ascertain the accuracy of management estimates

- Compare the 'free warranty' provision as a proportion of revenue with the same calculation for the prior year and ascertain the reasons for any material variation

- Ascertain the level of provision by warranty type with the number of 'live' warranties in that category and compare to the same calculation for prior year

- Review the level of returns occurring after the year end and compare with the assumptions made about rates of returns

- Review the records of repair costs incurred after the year end and compare with the assumptions made

- Check that movement on provision has been recorded as credit/debit in the statement of profit or loss

- Compare the actual provision to the level forecast

- Review the financial statements for appropriate disclosure of provision

- Request that management provide a written representation regarding the reasonableness of the assumptions made

- Review the board minutes for evidence of any product recalls

- Re-perform management's calculations

- Agree the brought forward balance to prior year financial statements

15.12 **Key audit risks**

- High level of cash transactions
- Could lead to understatement or incomplete income due to error or misappropriation
- The cafés are run and staffed by volunteers
- They may be insufficiently trained or have insufficient experience leading to errors
- Donation income is likely to be unpredictable
- Auditor unlikely to be able to derive comfort from analytical procedures

15.13 **Reasons**

- May have material impact on the financial statements
- Failure to comply may result in penalties/fines
- Requiring provision (if probable) or disclosure (if possible)
- Serious breaches may have going concern implications
- Due to closure or inability to pay fines
- May be indicative of poor control environment/lack of management integrity
- Breaking the law to save costs may be considered to be money laundering

Examples

- Minimum wage and working time directives
- Health and safety at work regulations
- PAYE and NI compliance
- Pension scheme requirement

15.14 **Matters to be considered**

- Whether the component auditor:

    - Understands and will comply with the ethical requirements that are relevant to the group audit and in particular is independent and objective

    - Is willing to provide written confirmation of ability to comply with relevant ethical requirements

    - Operates in a regulatory environment that actively oversees auditors

- The component auditor's professional competence

- Whether the group engagement team will be able to be involved in the work of the component auditor to the extent necessary to obtain sufficient appropriate audit evidence

15.15 **Why necessary to have an understanding of laws and regulations**

- Having an understanding of the legal and regulatory framework applicable to the client and the industry sector in which it operates is required by ISA (UK) 250A *Consideration of Laws and Regulations in an Audit of Financial Statements* and ISA (UK) 315 *Identifying and Assessing the Risks of Material Misstatement through Understanding the Entity and its Environment.*

- The auditor is required to assess the controls in place at the client to manage its risk of non-compliance.

- Failure of the client to comply with laws and regulations could have a material impact on the financial statements by necessitating:

    - recognition of liabilities; or
    - disclosure of uncertainties resulting from fines and penalties.

- Large fines or revoking of licences by regulators could also affect the client's ability to continue as a going concern.

- Breaking laws and regulations in order to save costs may represent fraud or money laundering.
- Non-compliance may also indicate issues in respect of management's integrity.

15.16 Risks of misstatement

- The revaluation is a subjective measurement and may not have been carried out correctly, or may have been recorded inappropriately.
- The loss on the sale of plant may indicate that useful lives are not estimated reliably.
- The loss may have been calculated incorrectly, or disposed of assets may not have been correctly eliminated from the accounting records.
- The depreciation charge for the year seems inappropriately low compared to the prior year and the increased value of non-current assets, indicating a potential misstatement.
- Additions during the year may have been capitalised inappropriately, instead of being expensed; or
- Errors may have occurred in relation to cut-off, and the amounts recorded.
- Useful lives of new assets may be inappropriately estimated.

15.17 Effect on overall audit strategy

- Increased risk of window dressing/misstatement/bias
- In order to increase purchase consideration
- Reduce materiality thresholds
- Increase the level of testing

Emphasis on:

- Testing assets and income for overstatement
- Testing liabilities and expenses for understatement

- Increase the level of professional scepticism
- Look carefully at judgement areas
- Place less reliance on management representations
- Use more experienced staff
- Arrange a quality control review

15.18 Considerations for audit planning

Likely to have material impact on financial statements:

- Refunds for returns
- Allowance to reduce inventory to NRV for faulty inventory
- Increase in provisions for warranties
- Provisions/contingencies relating to legal claims

Adverse publicity may impact on going concern.

15.19 Analytical procedures

Comparisons with:

- Previous corresponding six months
- Month by month
- Industry sector data
- Budget/forecast

Relationships between figures/changes in ratios

Use of proofs in total

Obtain plausible explanations for significant movements

Limitations

- A good knowledge of the business is required to understand results

- Consistency of results may conceal an error

- May be a tendency to carry out procedures mechanically, without appropriate professional scepticism

- Requires an experienced member of staff to be done properly

- Reliable data may not be available

- Lack of comparability if business is growing/changing

15.20

- All boxes to be uniquely numbered
- Register of numbers and to whom distributed/where located
- Provision of means of securing boxes to counters (eg, chains)
- Sealing of boxes so that opening before collection by entity is apparent
- Regular collection of boxes from retail outlets and restaurants by trusted persons
- Dual control (ie, two people) over opening and counting of cash donated
- Immediate recording of amounts in boxes
- Prompt banking of cash
- Independent reconciliation of amount recorded with bank records

15.21 May be window dressing/cut off error

May be material misstatements in financial statements if:

- Excluded from inventory
- Included in sales and receivables
- Goods are faulty/no allowance for cost below NRV

May be indicative of:

- Need for further allowances to reduce inventory to NRV re additional returns/items in inventory

- Lack of management integrity/unreliable management representations

15.22 **Profit forecast**

Profit/loss on disposal of old equipment

- Prudent estimate of sales proceeds (alternative: estimate based on market value)
- Calculated using carrying amount at the expected time of sale

Depreciation of old and new equipment

- Appropriate estimate of useful life for new equipment
- New equipment depreciated from point available for use
- Old equipment depreciated up to point of sale

Interest on bank loan

- Accrued to the end of each year

Cash flow forecast

Cash proceeds from sale of old equipment

- Prudent estimate of sales proceeds (alternative: estimate based on market value)

Cash payments to acquire new equipment

- In line with expected cost of such equipment or quotes obtained

Bank loan

- Amount and timing in line with the application made to the bank

- Interest payments in line with anticipated loan agreement (alternative: at a realistic rate of interest)

General

- Timing of payments and receipts appear realistic and are consistent with items in the profit forecast

15.23 Planned procedures for review engagement will be limited primarily to inquiries of company personnel and analytical procedures whereas an audit will involve test of details and potentially tests of controls.

A review engagement plans to obtain less evidence than for an external audit engagement.

Bank reconciliations:

A review engagement would make inquiries of client personnel regarding old or unusual reconciling items whereas an external audit would trace a sample of reconciling items to supporting documentation.

An external audit would obtain evidence of items that should be included as reconciling to ensure they are included on the bank reconciliation.

A review engagement would make inquiries regarding transfers between bank accounts whereas an external audit would vouch transfers between bank accounts.

Bank confirmation letter:

A bank confirmation letter would be obtained as part of external audit procedures but not for a review engagement where any encumbrances or restrictions on accounts would be identified through inquiry.

15.24 The potential misstatements are not material in isolation:

- Disputed receivable: 3.8% of profit before tax
- Cut off error: 2.3% of profit before tax

However, potential misstatement in aggregate is £695,000 which is 6.1% of draft profit before tax

This could be material in aggregate as it falls into the 5-10% of profit range

Additional work is therefore required to ascertain:

- if any adjustment is required to the financial statements
- whether there are further errors in the financial statements that might be material

The impact on the audit opinion will need to be considered in light of further findings.

Disputed trade receivable

One relevant procedure such as: Review any additional correspondence up to date of auditor's report for indication of whether amount will be paid.

Cut-off error

One relevant procedure such as: Review year-end inventory count records to ascertain whether the inventory delivered post year end was correctly included in the inventory listing.

15.25 Payments to BuildaWeb for design and build

- In line with quote and any deposit/staged payments included in correct months

Payments to BuildaWeb for hosting and maintenance

- Included monthly and on the date per proposed maintenance agreement
- The fixed fee is in line with quote and included from June 20X3

Payments to BuildaWeb for charge per appointment

- In line with estimated number of appointments on website

- Which are realistic in relation to current appointment volumes

- Expected growth in appointments as customers adopt the online booking system appropriately reflected

All outflows in line with BuildaWeb credit terms

15.26 Factors in risk of misstatement in payroll

Average gross pay in 20X1 was £23,901 (£2,175,000/91)
Expected average gross pay for 20X2 is (£24,379 (£23,901 × 1.02)
Total expected payroll in 20X2 of £2,072,000 (£24,379 × 85)
Actual payroll is £117,000 higher than expectation (£2,189,000 – £2,072,000)
This is 10.8% of PBT and therefore material
May indicate **overstatement** of gross pay
Payroll taxes deducted in 20X1 were 30% of gross pay (£652/£2,175)
Payroll taxes deducted in 20X2 were 25% of gross pay (£548/£2,189)
Suggests either an **understatement** of amounts paid/due to HMRC
May indicate cut-off error at year end
Or may be **further evidence of overstatement** of gross pay

Note: Marks were awarded for alternative calculations.

15.27 Implications for the audit

Firm will need to audit the following:

- Payroll figures prepared by Canary for period 1 March to 31 May 20X2
- Payroll figures prepared by Cockatoo for period 1 June 20X2 to 28 February 20X3
- Accuracy of transfer of any payroll balances at 1 June to new system
- Accuracy of transfer of any standing data to new system

Firm will need to the following:

- Gain an understanding of services provided by Cockatoo

- Assess Cockatoo's reputation and competency

- Ascertain access to audit evidence from Cockatoo

- Including any assurance that can be obtained regarding effectiveness of internal controls

May need to place reliance on description of Cockatoo's systems and controls provided by its management and any report prepared by audit of Cockatoo on its opinion on management's description.

May be higher risk due to changes in process and transfers of data in the first year.

May need to allocate the following:

- More time to audit payrolls before and after changeover
- More experienced staff to mitigate higher risk

15.28 Business risks

- Legal claims by victims
- Statutory fines/penalties
- Rectification costs
- Adverse impact on profit
- Adverse impact on cash flow
- Loss of reputation
- Forced closure/going concern

Implications for financial statements

- Liabilities/provisions
- Contingencies/uncertainties/disclosures
- Impairment of assets
- Basis of preparation/break-up basis

Examiner's comments:

Answers to this question were generally good. However, candidates provided better answers in respect of identifying the business risks to which accidental breaches of regulations could expose Petro than they provided in respect of the implications for the financial statements. Most candidates correctly identified business risks such as legal claims, fines, loss of reputation and loss of licence. However, fewer candidates identified the adverse impact on profit and cash flow. The most commonly overlooked implications for the financial statements were the impairment of assets and the impact on the basis of preparation of the financial statements if Petro was not considered to be a going concern.

15.29 Budgetary control/comparison of actual to budget

On a store by store basis

Investigation of variances

Inter-store comparisons

Use of key performance indicators (KPIs)

Eg, margins, revenue per employee/floorspace

Store visits

On surprise basis:

- Checking compliance with standard procedures
- Confirm physical inventory agrees with records
- Differences investigated
- Cash counts
- To confirm amounts agree with point of sale (POS) records
- Differences investigated

Agree POS records to amounts banked:

- Differences between POS records and bankings investigated
- Delays in banking investigated

Review of exception reports:

- Slow moving inventory
- Difference between book and actual/review of inventory count results
- Level of refunds

Review of computer usage to monitor changing of passwords/failed access to system

Rigorous HR procedures/disciplinary procedures

Staff references/training/evaluation/employee verification procedures

Examiner's comments:

Answers to this question were very disappointing with very few candidates scoring maximum marks. Most candidates failed to outline internal control procedures that would be exercised by **head office** and instead cited internal control procedures that would be performed by staff and managers employed in the retail stores. Stronger candidates correctly identified that head office internal control procedures would include spot checks on stores, reconciliation of point of sale records to amounts banked, reconciliation of physical inventory with records and rigorous HR procedures. The points most commonly overlooked were budgetary control and inter-store comparisons using KPIs, use and review of exception reporting, review of computer usage and changing of passwords.

15.30 **Internal Control Procedures**

- Applications from students to be on standard forms

- Background checks to confirm that applicants are bona fide, for example, students are 18 to 21 year olds and are in full time education in London

- Adequate documentation is presented to the decision makers

- Any conflicts of interest are declared and recorded by decision makers

- Formal authorisation of the grant by decision makers or senior management

- Records of grant decisions are maintained

- Evidence that the grant is spent properly, eg, copies of invoices

- Segregation of duties between awarding and payment of the grant

- Limits on the amount payable to one student

- Comparison of bank payments to approved applications

- Monitoring of procedures to ensure compliance.

Examiner's comments:

Answers to this question were mixed. The majority of candidates were able to identify two or three controls to be exercised over the awarding and payment of grants. The controls most commonly identified were those relating to confirmation that the students were in full time education, the need for independent authorisation and segregation of duties between those responsible for awarding the grants and those responsible for payments. A common shortcoming was to cite segregation of duties as a control but then fail to specify the duties to be segregated. The points most commonly overlooked were those relating to declaration of conflicts of interest and the need to maintain records of decisions regarding the grants awarded.

15.31 Points to include in an engagement letter and an explanation as to why their inclusion is necessary

- Responsibilities of the firm
  - To review the claim
- Responsibilities of Madison
  - To prepare the claim
  - To provide written representations and access to information
- Limited level of assurance
  - Expressed negatively
- To avoid any misunderstanding and reduce expectations gap
- Identify the intended users of the report
  - Limit liability to unforeseen parties
- Agreement to limit liability
  - Reduce exposure to damages.

Examiner's comments:

This question was well answered as the majority of candidates were able to provide sufficient points to attain a pass on this question. The points most commonly identified were those relating to responsibilities of management and the assurance firm and the level of assurance provided by a review engagement. Weaker candidates strayed beyond the requirement and listed points to be included in an engagement letter for an audit conducted under ISAs, for example, the inherent limitations of an audit.

15.32 Walk-through tests

Designed to establish that internal controls exist and are as documented

Obtain an understanding of the audited entity's internal controls, accounting systems and processes

Will influence auditor's decision whether to plan to rely on internal controls or perform substantive procedures only

Cannot place reliance on walk-through for purpose of obtaining audit assurance

Tests of controls

Designed to obtain sufficient appropriate evidence as to the operating effectiveness of relevant internal controls where:

- Auditor intends to rely on operating effectiveness of controls in determining nature, timing and extent of substantive procedures and to gain assurance on which to base audit opinion
- Substantive procedures alone cannot provide sufficient appropriate audit evidence

May allow reduced substantive procedures to be undertaken

Answers to this question were disappointing as many candidates were unable to distinguish between the purpose of a walk-through test and a test of control. A significant number of candidates stated, incorrectly, that a walk-through test could be used to test the effectiveness of controls instead of confirming the auditor's understanding of an audited entity's system. Weaker candidates wasted time providing examples of how each of these tests should be conducted instead of focusing on the purpose of the tests.

15.33

- Is the revenue increase wholly due to new retail outlets?

- Have selling prices increased without a corresponding increase in input costs?

- Is increase in overall gross profit margin due to retail outlets having higher gross profit margin?

- What was the impact of exchange rates on revenue/selling prices?

- Have raw material costs reduced, eg, bulk purchase discounts or changes in suppliers?

- Has gross profit margin increased due to use of spare capacity in factory/economies of scale?

- The fall in operating margin is inconsistent with increase in gross profit margin – could costs have been misallocated between cost of sales and operating expenses?

- Have costs of opening and operating the retail outlets led to fall in operating margin?

- Were cut-off procedures in place for revenue and costs?

Examiner's comments:

Although there were some very good answers to this question, many answers were disappointing. Those candidates who scored high marks listed plausible enquiries which demonstrated that they understood what might have caused a change in the ratios presented. Candidates who scored low marks tended to do so because they asked general or vague questions, for example, 'why has gross profit increased?' instead of directed questions that focused on actual reasons why changes in the ratios may have occurred. In respect of the increase in gross margin a more directed enquiry would be 'is there a higher gross margin on sales through retail outlets' or 'has the company benefited from economies of scale'. Weaker candidates demonstrated a lack of understanding of the factors that impacted on each of the ratios and failed to use the information presented in the scenario to a sufficient extent. Some candidates enquired, incorrectly, whether the costs of running the retail outlets impacted on the gross margin, failing to appreciate that such costs would impact on the operating margin. In addition, comments such as 'the drop in operating margin indicates high operating costs' were too vague to be awarded a mark.

15.34 Whether reliance can be placed on an expert's valuation

- Perform background checks on the expert and consider:
    - Independence and objectivity
    - Qualifications
    - Experience/competence/expertise
    - Reputation/credibility
- Obtain a copy of the valuer's report
- Consider reasonableness of the basis of valuation/assumptions

---

- Review the valuer's letter of engagement and determine appropriateness of scope
- Compare valuation to the value of other similar properties in the locality
- Consider the use of an auditor's expert.

Examiner's comments:

The majority of candidates identified the need to consider the credentials of the management's expert, in particular, his/her experience, qualifications and objectivity and to research the valuation of other similar properties in the locality. The points most commonly overlooked were those relating to obtaining a copy of the expert's report and reviewing the terms of the engagement between the audited entity and the expert.

15.35 Further audit procedures

- Review report of health and safety regulator
- Ascertain if failure relates to events before the year-end
- Ascertain likely actions to be taken against Ice, such as:
  - Withdrawal of licence/closure and whether temporary or permanent
  - Fines and likely amounts
- Review the outcome of similar cases
- Discuss with directors how they propose to respond to the failed inspection
- Review press coverage for any adverse comment
- Review post year-end management accounts to assess impact on company performance
- Obtain and review updated cash flow forecasts and consider implications for Ice's ability to meet debts as they fall due
- Consider whether financial statements need amending

Examiner's comments:

Answers to this question were of a mixed standard. Those candidates who used the techniques of enquiry and inspection to generate audit procedures scored well. However, many candidates failed to focus on audit procedures. For example, the majority of candidates identified that going concern might be an issue if the breach resulted in large fines or the regulator closed the business, but failed to generate procedures to provide assurance about the going concern status. Consequently, the majority of candidates overlooked procedures in respect of cash flow forecasts and post year-end management accounts.

15.36 Audit procedures to address the risk of management override of internal controls

- Substantiate journal entries
- Investigate reconciling items
- Review significant accounting estimates and judgements for bias
- Investigate transactions outside the normal course of business
- Review 'whistle-blowing' arrangements
- Review internal auditor's reports
- Interview management to assess its attitude towards the control environment
- Review minutes of management meetings

15.37 Matters to consider

- Reasons why milk powder became contaminated
- Whether it resulted from breach of regulations, as may:
    - indicate inadequate internal controls/weak control environment
    - indicate lack of management integrity
    - result in fines/penalties from regulators
    - result in suspension of licence/closure
- Whether any other areas/items affected
- Whether any babies have been harmed by contamination which may result in:
    - legal claims against Squid
    - potential significant uncertainty
- Potential negative impact on Squid's reputation/bad publicity resulting in loss of revenue
- Increased risk of material misstatement:
    - Refunds for returns
    - Irrecoverable trade receivables
    - Inventory to be written off
    - Provisions/contingent liabilities for legal claims/fines
    - Squid may no longer be a going concern/doubts over going concern (GC):
        - GC basis of preparation may not be appropriate/break-up basis required
        - Uncertainty over GC may not be adequately disclosed

15.38 **Data analytics routines**

- Comparing the last time an item was bought with the last time it was sold, for cost/NRV purposes

- Inventory ageing and how many days inventory is in stock by item

- Analyses of revenue trends split by product or region

- Analyses of gross margins and sales, highlighting items with negative margins

- Matches of orders to cash and purchases to payments

- Three-way matches between purchases/sales orders, goods received/despatched documentation and invoices

15.39 **Data analytics on data extracted from information systems**

- Analyses of revenue trends split by product or region

- Analyses of gross margins and sales, highlighting items with negative margins

- 'Can do did do testing' of user codes to test whether segregation of duties is appropriate, and whether any inappropriate combinations of users have been involved in processing transactions

- Identify who is raising journals and when

- Compare the number of manual vs system-generated journals

- Year on year comparisons of journal entries

15.40 **Internal control deficiency**

- Novak does not have procedures in place to ensure that its anti-malware software is routinely updated

Possible consequences

- Hackers may be able to access Novak's system
- Deliberate sabotage could take place
- Malicious programs could be inserted into the system
- Loss, theft or misuse of data
- Reputational damage
- Failure to protect legally defined personal data

Recommendations

- Policy to be updated, implemented and communicated to staff

- Responsibility for updates to be allocated to a designated person who should sign off to confirm that updates have taken place

- Designated person should report compliance on a regular basis

- Monitoring of procedures and disciplinary action for breaches of policy

15.41 **Risks of outsourcing payroll function**

- Loss, theft or misuse of personal data
- Reputational damage
- Fines for late submission to the tax authorities
- Fines for breach of data protection legislation
- Potential material misstatements in the financial statements, such as:

  - Failure to recognise provisions
  - Failure to disclose contingent liabilities in respect of fines

15.42 Matters that should be considered by the audit committee to monitor the performance of the internal audit function

- Audit committee to consider the internal audit function's:
  - Planned programme of work
  - Arrangements for direction and supervision of work
  - Completed reports
  - Independence and objectivity

- Establishment of performance indicators such as:
  - Actual time compared to budget
  - Actual work completed compared to planned work
  - Number of recommendations accepted
  - Feedback from users
  - Numbers of qualified staff used

- Monitoring of performance indicators

Examiner's comment

Answers to this question were of a mixed standard. Those candidates who used their knowledge of internal audit and outsourcing to generate matters to be considered by the audit committee often scored full marks. The points most commonly identified were those relating to the objectivity of the internal audit function, the arrangements for planning, supervising and review of the function's work and, to a lesser extent, the review of completed reports. Few candidates appreciated the need for establishing and monitoring performance indicators and considering the planned programme of work. A minority of candidates did not attempt this question.

16 Styleco Ltd (June 2009)

Marking guide

			Marks
16.1	Receipts	6	
	Payments	20	
	Maximum		13
16.2	**Purpose**		
	Review of forecasts	4	
	Audit	5	
	Scope		
	Review of forecasts	3	
	Audit	3	
	Maximum		7
Total marks available			20

16.1 The following matters should be considered when reviewing the reasonableness of the assumptions underlying the receipts and payments:

Receipts

The loan from the bank is shown in the cash flow forecast as an inflow of cash before any major outflows of cash. The amount of the loan should be sufficient to fund the expansion and allow the company to pay its debts as they fall due while staying within any overdraft facility.

In respect of receipts from sales, whether:

- the inflows reflect a gradual increase in receipts (possibly causing a decline in internet and mail order receipts) as the retail outlets are opened and take into account seasonal fluctuations;

- growth expectations are feasible over the three years in light of the economic climate and are supported by market research; and

- the inflows have been subjected to sensitivity analysis.

Payments

- Payments for fixtures and fittings are complete (ie, include electronic point-of-sales systems CCTV etc), supported by quotes and are included before the opening of the outlets.

- Payments for advertising, recruitment and training are also reflected before the opening of the outlets.

- Payments to suppliers reflect the company's payments policy and the exchange rates used to translate payments have been subjected to sensitivity analysis.

- Refunds are reflected and recognise that the level of returns may be different for the retail outlets compared with mail order and the internet (ie, they may be lower than 8% as customers see the goods before purchasing).

- Commission in respect of credit card transactions is in accordance with the terms of the contract with the credit card companies.

- Rent is included quarterly in advance from the date of acquisition of the lease and rent reviews are taken into account.

- Payments to employees reflect the higher rate of remuneration and include bonuses which should be based on the company's formula and paid on the due dates.

- Payments relating to heat and light, waste disposal, insurance and servicing costs reflect the size of the outlet and, where relevant, the location of the outlet.

- Payments for professional fees such as architects, lawyers and reporting accountants have been included.

- Interest payments reflect the level of borrowings and are based on interest rates in line with market expectations and have been subjected to sensitivity analysis. In addition, interest and any loan instalments are paid on the due dates.

- Payments to HMRC include VAT, PAYE, NIC and corporation tax and are consistent with the profit forecast and are paid on the due dates.

- Payments reflect additional costs such as increased operating costs of head office and shipping costs from warehouse to outlets.

16.2 Comparison of review with statutory audit

Purpose

A review of the profit and cash flow forecasts provides limited assurance as to the credibility of the forecast financial information. A limited assurance engagement reduces the risk to a level that is acceptable in the circumstances. The conclusion is expressed negatively in the form of 'nothing has come to our attention which causes us to believe that these assumptions do not provide a reasonable basis for the forecasts'. In the case of Styleco, the report is solely for the management to support the application for funding.

A statutory audit provides reasonable assurance as to the credibility of the financial statements. A reasonable assurance engagement reduces the risk to an acceptably low level. It provides a high, but not absolute, level of assurance that the financial statements are free from material misstatement. The conclusion is expressed positively in the form of 'in our opinion the financial statements give a true and fair view of the state of the company's affairs…' An auditor's report is addressed to the shareholders of a company, but is available to the public once lodged at Companies House.

Scope

The work undertaken in examining the forecasts will be less in scope than that of the audit. It will involve checking the reasonableness of the assumptions and the calculations on the basis of the assumptions. It is likely to include analytical procedures, enquiry of management and computation. However, an audit will include a wider range of substantive procedures including transaction and balance testing. The terms of the review of the forecasts will be agreed by management but may include a reference to ISAE 3400 *The Examination of Prospective Financial Information*. The terms of an audit engagement are determined, in the UK, by the Companies Act and International Standards on Auditing.

Examiner's comments:

Answers to this question scored the lowest average on the written test section of the exam. Although there were some very good answers to part 16.1, many candidates scored low marks on this part of the question but managed to salvage the situation with strong performances on part 16.2.

Answers to part 16.1 of the question were mixed. The main problem stemmed from candidates' lack of understanding of what a cash flow forecast comprises. Many candidates included points relating to profit forecasts (eg, depreciation and inventory obsolescence) instead of cash inflows and outflows. Others wasted time describing internal controls that should be implemented to prevent fraud in a retail situation and listed controls over till operations and cash handling and banking. Of those who did consider the relevant receipts and payments, many failed to appreciate the importance of the timing of the cash flows. Only a minority identified that fixtures would be paid up front and that tax and interest should be paid on the due dates. Although many identified the uncertainties inherent in forecasting, only a minority considered sensitivity analysis on key variables such as sales receipts, interest payments and exchange rates.

Part 16.2 of the question was generally well answered as most candidates understood the differences between an audit of financial statements and an examination of forecast financial information. The points most commonly overlooked were those relating to the fact that the audited financial statements are available to the public whereas the forecast information is for private use. Although many candidates appreciated that the scope of the audit was wider than the review of the forecast information they did not develop the point by stating that the work would be restricted to checking the calculations on the basis of the assumptions and the reasonableness of the assumptions.

17 Dunlec Ltd (December 2009)

			Marks
17.1	Identification of relevant receipt or payment (each)	½	
	Plausible matter to consider (each)	½	
	Maximum		8
17.2 (a)	**Not a going concern**		
	FS prepared on break-up basis	2½	
	FS prepared on a going concern basis	3	
(b)	**Uncertainty regarding going concern**		
	Uncertainty adequately explained	2½	
	Uncertainty not adequately explained	3	
	Maximum		7
17.3	Sued by company	3	
	Sued by third parties	3	
	Bannerman	2	
	Maximum		5
Total marks available			20

17.1 The following matters should be considered when reviewing the reasonableness of the assumptions underlying the receipts and payments:

Receipts

Trading receipts reflect:

- the reduction in demand in the construction sector;

- potential loss of business following the closure of the two depots;

- ninety-five percent of the contract price is received on completion and 5% received six months later; and

- the fact that amounts due may not ultimately be paid.

Proceeds from the sale of the two depots are realistic and reflect local property values.

Payments

- Payments for components and raw materials reflect the 30 day credit terms

- Rent is paid on the due dates and takes into account any rent reviews

- Final instalment of the loan is paid in September 20X2

- PAYE, NIC and other taxes are paid on the due dates

- Redundancy payments are in accordance with legal/contractual obligations

- Ongoing wages reflect reduced workforce following the redundancies

- Interest on the loan and overdraft is paid in accordance with the terms

- Any extra costs (eg, transportation costs) involved in servicing contracts from distant depots and a fall in overheads after the sale of the two depots are reflected

- Professional costs (eg, legal and selling agent) involved with the sale of depots are included

Assess

- Impact of changes in key variables (sensitivity analysis) on receipts, interest rates and the proceeds on the sale of the two depots
- Consistency of items with related items in the profit forecast

17.2(a) **Not a going concern**

If the financial statements are prepared on the break-up basis and this is explained in the notes to the financial statements, an unmodified opinion can be given. The auditor's report will be modified with an emphasis of matter paragraph highlighting the issue and drawing the users' attention to the note in the financial statements. There should be a specific statement stating that the audit opinion is not qualified.

If the financial statements are prepared on the going concern basis, the report/opinion should be modified due to material misstatement. The opinion should be an adverse opinion (ie, 'do not give a true and fair view') as the issue is material and pervasive. The reasons for the adverse opinion and the effects on the financial statements should be explained in a paragraph immediately after the opinion paragraph.

(b) **Uncertainty about going concern status**

If the financial statements are prepared on the going concern basis and the uncertainty is adequately explained in the notes to the financial statements, an unqualified but modified report should be issued. There should be a paragraph headed 'material uncertainty related to going concern after the opinion paragraph drawing users' attention to the note in the financial statements. There should be a specific statement stating that the audit opinion is not qualified.

If the uncertainty is not, or inadequately, explained in the notes to the financial statements, the opinion should be modified due to material misstatement. The modification may be a qualified opinion/except for if considered material but not pervasive or an adverse opinion if considered material and pervasive.

17.3 The firm may be sued by the company and the shareholders as a body, (ie, the Dunlop family), for breach of contract if the auditor has been negligent in performing the audit.

Third parties (ie, parties with whom there is no contract), such as the company's bank may sue for damages under the Tort of Negligence. The third party must demonstrate that a duty of care was owed by the auditor and that a loss was suffered by relying on the financial statements with an unmodified auditor's report.

However, auditors may be protected from third party claims by the inclusion of a Bannerman paragraph in the auditor's report stating that the report is prepared for the company's members and no other party.

Examiner's comments:

General comments

Answers to this question scored the lowest average on the written test section of the exam. This was mainly due to a significant number of candidates failing to complete the question, possibly indicating that they had run out of time.

Part 17.1

There was a marked improvement in answers relating to reviewing the assumptions underlying the receipts and payments in a cash flow forecast compared to previous sessions, with an increased number of candidates appreciating the importance of the timing of cash flows and sensitivity analysis. However, there were a significant number of weak answers. The main problem stemmed from candidates' lack of understanding of what a cash flow forecast comprises. Many candidates included points relating to profit forecasts (eg, depreciation) instead of cash inflows and outflows. A significant number of candidates failed to consider future cash flows and wasted time dealing with past cash flows, such as the proceeds of the sale of the London freehold premises instead of the potential proceeds from the two regional depots. Some candidates wasted time considering general points such as the competency of those preparing the forecasts and the arithmetical accuracy and failed to restrict their answer to considering the specific assumptions underlying the receipts and payments.

Part 17.2

Pleasingly many candidates scored maximum marks on this part of the question. The vast majority of candidates recognised that this was a discursive question and that the implications for the auditor's report depended on whether or not the directors had prepared the financial statements on a break-up basis in 17.2 (a) and disclosed the uncertainty in 17.2 (b). The most common omissions related to the requirement for a disclosure of the break-up basis and the contents of any modification to the opinion in 17.2 (a). As in previous sessions, there was evidence of confusion over the terminology used in relation to modified auditor's reports. Some candidates did not appreciate that a report can be modified without the audit opinion being qualified. More worryingly, a number of candidates stated, incorrectly, that an 'except for' opinion is an unqualified opinion.

Part 17.3

Answers to this part of the question were mixed. Although many scored full marks, weaker candidates just cited a list of potential parties and failed to consider the circumstances under which those parties may be successful in claiming damages. A significant number did not appreciate that for third parties to be successful, a duty of care had to be demonstrated and that any loss needed to be as a result of relying on the audited financial statements. Some candidates did not attempt this part of the question, possibly due to running out of time.

18 Paravel Gardens Ltd (March 2012)

Marking guide

			Marks
18.1	First year audit	3½	
	Going concern	4½	
	Non-current tangible assets/Assets under construction	3½	
	Inventory	5	
	Liabilities	4½	
	Revenue	3½	
	Purchases and trade payables	4	
	Finance cost	3½	
	Wages and salaries and balances due to HMRC	1½	
	Sponsorship payment	4½	
	Control risk	3	
	Management bias	2½	
	Marks available	43½	
	Maximum		20
18.2	Receipts		
	New loan received from the bank	3½	
	Sales of gourmet food and gifts	3½	
	Payments		
	Interest payments on bank loan and repayments of capital	2½	
	Payments to acquire inventory	4½	
	Payments for additional staff	4½	

		Marks
Payments to acquire fridges and shelving	2½	
Payment to upgrade computerised tills	2½	
Payments of professional fees	2½	
Payments of VAT and Corporation Tax	1	
General	1	
Marks available	28	
Maximum		10
18.3 Explanation of difference	1	
Bank loan	2	
Payments for fridges and shelving	1	
Allowances against inventories	1	
Amortisation charge	1	
Marks available	6	
Maximum		4
18.4 (a) Responsibilities of the firm to include making recommendations		
ISAE 3400 guidelines	2½	
Edmund's proposal	3	
Advocacy threat	1	
Self-review threat	1½	
Future claims by Paravel	1	
(b) Payment of firm's fee		
Contingent fee not permitted	2	
Application to the bank	2½	
Marks available	13½	
Maximum		6
Total marks available		40

18.1 First year audit

Paravel is a new client and as such the firm will lack cumulative audit knowledge and experience. This will increase the risk that the firm's audit procedures do not detect material misstatements in the financial statements. It may be difficult to gain assurance over opening balances as the firm did not audit these in the prior year.

Going concern

Paravel has experienced significant growth in recent years leading to rapid expansion. The business is also seasonal in nature and both of these factors could lead to cash flow difficulties, particularly during the winter months when sales are lower and the company must continue to service its debts. Paravel is increasingly reliant on loans from the bank and has plans to increase debt further in order to finance its diversification plans which will put further strain on its cash flow. The bank may also be unaware that £2 million of the recent loan was used to pay for the sponsorship deal. If this falls outside the purpose of the loan the bank may require the loan to be repaid in full immediately. Paravel is also subject to import licence terms and is regularly inspected for compliance. Any non-compliance may result in the licence being withdrawn and impact on Paravel's ability to continue trading.

Non-current tangible assets/assets under construction

A programme of building works has been ongoing during the year. This may result in inappropriate capitalisation of costs associated with the building works or could lead to costs being included in the statement of profit or loss that should be capitalised. In addition, management's determination of useful lives may be inappropriate or depreciation may be charged in error while assets are still under construction.

Inventory

Inventory days has increased from 25 days to 35 days which may suggest obsolete or slow moving inventory particularly given the perishable nature of some of the inventory in question. Trees and plants are purchased from overseas and invoiced in suppliers' local currencies. This could lead to translation errors or an inappropriate exchange rate being applied. Certain species of plant may be difficult to recognise if those undertaking the inventory count are not specialists and consequently inappropriate values may be applied to the items counted.

Liabilities

The bank loan was obtained on 31 October 20X1 and is repayable over three years. There is a risk that the loan balance may not be correctly classified as current and medium-term liabilities. Were Paravel to fail an inspection as part of its requirement to have an import licence, this may lead to fines or penalties which may not be properly recorded or disclosed in the financial statements.

Revenue

Paravel's business is a cash-based retail business resulting in an increased risk that sales are made without some transactions being recorded, resulting in an understatement of revenue. However, revenue has increased by 34.2% on the prior year which indicates a possible overstatement of revenue.

Purchases and trade payables

Trade payables days have fallen from 36 days to 31 days and the gross profit margin has increased from 30% to 36% both of which may indicate an understatement of purchases and trade payables.

Finance cost

Interest on the loan is due quarterly in arrears which may result in a failure to accrue for the payment due in the last quarter of the year. In addition, finance costs in the draft financial statements have only increased by 3% on the prior year. The increase would be expected to be greater given that the directors obtained a new loan on 31 October 20X1.

Wages and salaries and balances due to HMRC

A large volume of temporary workers are employed in the peak sales season between April and September. This may result in errors in recording payroll costs and the associated PAYE and NIC payments due to HMRC.

Sponsorship payment

The sponsorship agreement covers a two-year period. The expense should be matched to the periods which benefit from the sponsorship arrangement. For example, matching 1/8th (3/24 months) to the current financial period and recognising 7/8ths as a prepayment. If there is any question as to whether there is any future benefit arising from the sponsorship arrangement then it may be necessary to recognise all of the cost in the current year's financial statements, increasing the risk of misstatement.

Control risk

Paravel employs a large volume of temporary staff across 45 garden centres which results in an increased risk of human error or failure to understand and apply internal control procedures. This may lead to an increased risk of misstatement in the financial statements.

Management bias

Paravel has applied for a further loan to finance its diversification plans. The bank has requested a copy of the audited financial statements before making a decision to provide Paravel with the loan requested. Such reliance by the bank increases the risk of management bias in the financial statements as management will be keen to reflect the financial status of the company in a way that will secure the additional finance sought. Furthermore, there may be loan covenants attached to the existing finance which further increases the likelihood of management bias where such covenants relate to items in the financial statements.

18.2 Receipts

New loan received from the bank

The loan received from the bank to finance the diversification plans should be in line with the application made to the bank and sufficient to cover the expected costs of the diversification. The loan should be received after the date on which it is expected that the audited financial statements would be available for the bank to review but before the expenses relating to the diversification are incurred.

Sales of gourmet food and gifts

The assumptions made around the level and growth of sales should be prudent and reflect the current state of the economy. They should also reflect the size of the available sales area for the goods in question as well as the anticipated seasonality, ie, a peak in the October to December period.

Payments

Interest payments on bank loan and repayments of capital

Interest payments and repayments of capital should be in line with existing loans and take account of any anticipated changes in interest rates. The timing of payments should be realistic, eg, quarterly and in line with any discussions already held with the bank.

Payments to acquire inventory

Cash outflows to acquire inventory should be consistent with the anticipated level of sales and consistent with the size of the sales area in each garden centre. An initial large outflow of cash will be required in order to purchase the inventory needed before the opening of the gift and food halls followed by regular replenishment of inventory as goods are sold. Payments should be consistent with credit terms of suppliers.

Payments for additional staff

Payments for additional staff should be included in the cash flow forecast from the time the food halls and gift shops are due to open. Wages should be in line with wages paid to current retail staff with realistic assumptions made regarding the level of wage increases. The number of staff included should be in line with the size of the food halls and gift shops. Payments to HMRC should be made on the due dates.

Payments to acquire fridges and shelving

Payments should be in line with any quotes received from suppliers or the market values of similar assets and should include the costs of installation and servicing where appropriate.

Payment to upgrade computerised tills

The payment to upgrade the computerised tills should be in line with the any quotes from Caspian or represent a realistic estimate of time and rates relevant for such an upgrade. The payment should include all stores which will hold the diversified product range.

Payments of professional fees

Payments should be paid when work is due to be completed and be in line with appropriate rates or agreed terms of engagement.

Payments of VAT and Corporation Tax

Additional payments of VAT and corporation tax resulting from the diversified product range should be in line with the relevant sales, purchases and profits generated by the new range.

General

Realistic assumptions should be made regarding the rate of inflation over the period of the forecast. Key figures, such as receipts from sales and interest payments, should be subjected to sensitivity analysis.

18.3 Profit forecasts will be prepared using the accruals principle whereby revenues are recorded when they are earned and costs are recorded when they are incurred whereas the cash flow forecast will include transactions only when cash has been paid or received. The key differences in the case of the forecasts prepared by the directors of Paravel would be the following:

- The cash flow forecast would record the receipt and repayment of the bank loan but this would have no impact on the profit forecast. The interest payments on the loan would be recorded in the profit forecast as they fall due but in the cash flow forecast when they are to be paid.

- Payments to acquire the required fridges and shelving would be shown in the cash flow forecast when paid but would not impact on the profit forecast. Depreciation of fridges and shelving would be shown in the profit forecast but would have no cash flow implication.

- Allowances against any inventories that are slow moving, or write-offs of inventory that are obsolete would be shown in the profit forecasts but not in the cash flow forecasts.

- If Paravel is able to capitalise the costs associated with the upgrade of the computerised tills, then an amortisation charge would be shown in the profit forecasts but the cash flow forecast would show a cash outflow of the full amount at the time it is paid.

18.4 (a) **Responsibilities of the firm to include making recommendations**

ISAE 3400 *The Examination of Prospective Financial Information*, sets out guidelines for firms undertaking engagements to review forecasts such as those prepared by the directors of Paravel. Responsibilities of the firm would include the following:

- Assessing the reasonableness of management's assumptions

- Consideration of whether the forecasts are properly prepared on the basis of the assumptions

- Consideration of whether the forecasts are properly presented

- Consideration of whether the forecasts are prepared on a consistent basis with the historical financial statements using appropriate accounting policies.

Edmund's proposal for the firm's responsibilities goes beyond the procedures that normally form part of such an engagement as set out by ISAE 3400. It is management's responsibility to prepare the forecasts and if the firm were to advise the directors of Paravel on the preparation of the forecasts this may threaten the objectivity and independence of the firm. A management threat is likely to arise as such work would involve making judgements and decisions about the content of the profit and cash flow forecasts.

An advocacy threat may also arise if the firm is seen to be supporting Paravel's position with regard to management's application to the bank with the risk that the firm's views become too closely aligned with those of management.

A self-review threat would be created if the firm were to advise the directors of Paravel on the preparation of the forecasts and then also undertake the independent examination of the forecasts as requested by the bank. It is unlikely the firm would criticise its own work or highlight issues in relation to the preparation of the forecasts in its report to the bank.

The firm may also be exposed to future claims by Paravel if, having advised on the content of the forecasts, the request to the bank for finance is then unsuccessful.

(b) **Payment of firm's fee**

The fee arrangement proposed by Edmund represents a contingent fee which is not permitted by the ICAEW Code of Ethics. The provision of non-audit services on such a basis threatens the auditor's objectivity and independence by creating a self-interest threat.

The firm would not be paid if the application to the bank was unsuccessful and the firm would be reluctant to reach a conclusion on the examination which may result in the application being declined by the bank. Consequently, the firm may reach an inappropriate conclusion. Such a threat is so significant that safeguards cannot adequately reduce the threat. It may also be perceived that the firm's interests become too closely aligned with those of the directors at Paravel.

Examiner's comments:

Answers to part 18.1 of the question were very good. Most candidates were able to identify, correctly, a range of audit risks and explain the factors leading to the identification of the risk. Candidates who planned their answer and clearly set out the audit risk with the explanation of the related factors tended to score higher marks. Going concern issues and risks associated with Paravel being a new client were well answered. The audit risks and explanations most commonly overlooked were in relation to payments for building works and the payment for sponsorship to Miraz, a gardening show event management company. Few candidates discussed the issues around appropriate capitalisation of building costs and very few candidates appreciated that the sponsorship payment covered a two-year period which may have required the payment to be recognised in the financial statements over two years. Some candidates did not use the figures provided in the scenario and so did not score the marks that were available for analytical procedures. A small number of candidates suggested audit procedures to be used to address the audit risk which were not required.

Answers to part 18.2 of the question were mixed. Candidates that focussed on identifying receipts and payments in respect of the diversification plans, as set out in the requirement, scored higher marks. These candidates worked systematically through the scenario identifying the receipt or payment and the specific matters to consider in the review of the assumptions used. However, a number of candidates wasted time by writing at length about the receipts and payments for the existing business, which was not required. Where candidates had identified receipts and payments relevant to the diversification plans many were then unable to identify appropriate specific matters to be considered when reviewing those receipts or payments. Answers such as 'check for reasonableness' are too vague to be awarded any marks. As noted in previous examiners' commentaries, a number of candidates identified and discussed items such as depreciation, amortisation and provisions, failing to appreciate that these items are not found in a cash flow forecast.

Answers to part 18.3 of the question were disappointing as many candidates were unable to state the key differences between the items in profit forecasts and the items in cash flow forecasts. A large number of candidates restricted their answers to a general discussion of the accruals concept without providing any specific examples and therefore failed to score highly. Candidates who did attempt to identify key differences relevant to the scenario mainly cited the differences in relation to payments for tangible non-current assets/depreciation and the receipt of the bank loan/interest payments. Few candidates discussed allowances against slow moving inventory or the sponsorship payment. A small number of candidates did not attempt this part of the question.

Answers to part 18.4 of the question were disappointing. Generally answers in respect of proposal (b) were better than those for proposal (a). A number of candidates wasted time explaining how the threats arising from each proposal could be mitigated, which was not required. In proposal (a) the management threat was the most frequently identified issue with most candidates offering a good explanation of this issue. Fewer candidates identified the advocacy threat. While a number of candidates identified a self-review threat, they failed to score any marks because their explanation was in the context of an external audit instead of the preparation of, and subsequent report on, the profit and cash flow forecasts. Very few candidates cited the guidelines set out in ISAE 3400 in respect of the firm's responsibilities on engagements to review prospective information. In proposal (b) many candidates correctly identified that the directors' proposal regarding payment of the fee amounted to a contingent fee and were able to explain the professional issues that this raised.

19 Luxstove Ltd (June 2012)

Marking guide

		Marks
19.1 **Revenue**		
Enquiries	4	
Documentary information	1½	
Gross profit margin		
Enquiries	8	
Documentary information	1	
Operating margin		
Enquiries	3	
Documentary information	½	
Inventory		
Enquiries	7½	
Documentary information	1	
Trade receivables		
Enquiries	3½	
Documentary information	1	
Trade payables		
Enquiries	4½	
Documentary information	1	
General documentary information	2½	
Marks available	39	
Maximum		15
19.2 Review engagement	1½	
Audit engagement	2½	
Reasons	3	
Marks available	7	
Maximum		5
Total marks available		20

19.1 Revenue

Enquiries

Why has the rate of growth doubled, which is surprising in light of the recession?

How much is due to the introduction of accessories and the new showroom?

Has there been a significant increase in selling prices?

At what stage is revenue recognised in respect of the showroom sales (recognised on order instead of despatch)?

Documentary information

Schedule with a breakdown of sales between the following:

- Stoves by type and accessories
- Showroom and retailers

Gross profit margin

How has an increase in gross profit margin been achieved with such a significant increase in revenue?

Is it due to:

- increased sales of higher margin items?
- accessories and or showroom items having a higher margin?
- beneficial effects of movements on exchange rate movements in respect of imports?
- availability of bulk discounts from suppliers?
- understatement of purchases?
- overstatement of closing inventory?
- more efficient use of direct labour/understatement of labour costs?

Documentary information

Schedule of selling prices and costs on a product basis

Breakdown of the cost of sales figure

Operating margin

Why has the operating margin fallen when gross profit margin has increased?

Is it due to:

- changes in classification of costs between cost of sales and operating expenses?
- operating costs of the showroom?

Documentary information

Breakdown of operating costs

Inventory

Why have inventory days increased when revenue has increased significantly?

Is it due to:

- a build-up of accessories and/or inventory for the showroom?
- any slow-moving items such as superseded models of stoves?

What is the policy regarding the translation of components bought from overseas suppliers?

Is the inventory supported by continuous records or was it subject to a full count at 31 May and what cut-off arrangements were in place?

Is the basis of valuation consistency with prior periods?

Documentary information

- Breakdown of inventory figure/aged inventory report
- Results of any inventory counting procedures/details of adjustments

Trade receivables

Why have receivables days increased when sales through the showroom are on a cash basis?

Is it due to:

- old outstanding debts which should be written off?
- relaxation in credit terms extended to retailers?

What cut-off arrangements were in place at 31 May?

Documentary information

Aged receivables listing

Correspondence with customers/lawyers/contracts with retailers

Trade payables

Why have payables days fallen when the business has expanded?

Is it due to:

- understatement due to unrecorded invoices?
- tighter credit terms imposed by suppliers?

What is the policy regarding the translation of payables?

What cut-off arrangements were in place at 31 May?

Documentary information

- Breakdown of trade payables/aged payables
- Main supplier agreements/contracts

General documentary information

Budgets/forecasts for the corresponding period

Management accounts for the corresponding period

Industry/competitor information

Board Minutes

Details of exchange rates used

19.2 Review engagement

The conclusion of the assurance report, following a review of financial information, provides limited/moderate assurance and is expressed negatively in the form of 'nothing has come to our attention that causes us to believe that the financial statements do not give a true and fair view'.

Audit engagement

The opinion in the auditor's report on financial statements is expressed positively and provides reasonable assurance that the financial statements:

- Give a true and fair view
- Have been properly prepared in accordance with relevant generally accepted accounting practice
- Have been prepared in accordance with the requirements of the Companies Act 2006

Reasons

The objective of a limited assurance engagement is to reduce risk to an acceptable level whereas the objective of reasonable assurance engagement is to reduce risk to a low level. As a result, the work undertaken on an audit engagement is wider in scope and includes tests of control and tests of details.

Examiner's comments:

Answers to this question attained the lowest overall average on the written test questions. Answers to part 19.1 were of a mixed standard whereas answers to part 19.2 were generally good.

Although there were some very good answers to part 19.1 of the question, many answers were disappointing. Those candidates who scored high marks used the ratios provided in the question as a framework and listed plausible enquiries which demonstrated that the candidate understood what might have caused a change in the ratio. A significant number of these candidate demonstrated higher skills by identifying that movements in some ratios were out of line with movements in others. For example, 'the fall in payables days was inconsistent with the significant increase in revenue'. Candidates who scored low marks tended to do so because they asked general or vague questions. (for example, 'why has gross profit increased?') or restated information provided in the scenario (for example 'inventory days have increased') instead of directed questions that focused on actual reasons why changes in the ratios may have occurred (for example, 'Have higher margins on showroom sales caused the gross profit margin to increase?'). Candidates who performed poorly on this question often gave little thought to the layout of their answers which were presented as rambling and unstructured lists of questions in no particular order. In respect of the documentary information that would be useful for review procedures, some candidates detailed any documentation that would help with audit procedures rather than documentation aimed specifically at justifying potential reasons for changes in the ratios.

Part 19.2 of the question was generally well answered, as the majority of candidates cited the basic points regarding the different levels of assurance provided by the conclusions within each report and gave an example of each. Many candidates cited, correctly, that the level of assurance was determined by the extent of the work, but few referred to the level of risk. Weaker candidates strayed beyond the requirement and wasted time writing about the differences between the reports as a whole, instead of focusing on the **conclusions** in each of the reports.

20 Pyramid Event Structures Ltd (March 2014)

Marking guide

			Marks
20.1	Principal threats	4½	
	How firm should respond	7	
	Marks available	11½	
	Maximum		5
20.2 (a)	Revenue		
	– Justification	5	
	– Audit procedures	8	
(b)	Intangible assets – development costs		
	– Justification	4	
	– Audit procedures	11	

			Marks
(c)	Property, plant and equipment		
	- Justification	8½	
	- Audit procedures	11½	
(d)	The contract with Nefario		
	- Justification	5	
	- Audit procedures	7	
	Marks available	60	
	Maximum		24

20.3 Additional area of audit risk

	Marks	
Identify and explain	15½	
Audit Procedures	20	
Marks available	35½	
Maximum		8
Total marks available		37

20.1 Principal threats

Self-review threat

The results of the secondment will be reflected in the financial statements and the audit team will be required to re-evaluate this work. The audit team may place too much reliance on the work or may be reluctant to identify errors in the work.

Management threat

The firm's view may become too closely aligned with the views of management and the firm may be expected to make management decisions in determining how to treat the research and development costs in the financial statements. This is likely to be the case as accounting for development costs requires the exercise of judgement, ie, to capitalise or expense costs.

How firm should respond

PES is not a listed company, therefore providing such services is permitted. However, the firm must have adequate safeguards in place and must not make management decisions regarding the accounting treatment. The secondment must be of a purely technical, mechanical and informative nature and should be for a short period of time.

The firm must establish that informed management exists. Management must agree that the seconded individual will not hold a managerial position and must acknowledge its responsibility for directing and supervising the work to be performed. The work must be performed by a member of the firm who is not involved in the external audit. Therefore the request to use a member of the audit team is inappropriate and must be refused.

A second partner review of the audit work undertaken on research and development costs should be performed to ensure the work has been properly assessed by the audit team.

The ethics partner should be consulted.

20.2 (a) Revenue

Justification

Recognition of revenue relating to events running over the year end may be inappropriate. If the full cash receipt is recognised as revenue at the start of an event, revenue will be overstated. If cash receipts are not recognised as revenue until the end of an event, revenue will be understated.

Revenue has fallen by 16.5% compared to the prior year and the mark-up on cost has fallen from 45% to 25%. This appears low compared to the standard mark-up of 60% and suggests revenue may be understated.

Procedures

Ascertain and test the controls over revenue recognition

For a sample of contracts completed in the year agree the contract price to revenue recognised. For a sample of contracts spanning the year end:

- Trace the receipt of 50% of the contract price to deferred income

- Agree the cash receipt to bank statement

- Recalculate the revenue to be recognised in the current year based on the number of weeks the event has run

- Trace the transfer from deferred revenue to revenue

Discuss with the directors the reason for the fall in revenue

Compare the average monthly event revenue with the prior year to identify any unexpected variations

(b) **Intangible assets – development costs**

Justification

Research costs may be capitalised inappropriately and capitalised development costs may not meet relevant capitalisation criteria. The accountant responsible for recording research and development costs has left PES and no one has filled this role since 31 December which may increase the risk of errors or omissions in recording and accounting for development costs.

Inappropriate useful life/amortisation rates may have been selected and MezzSpace may be incorrectly amortised for the full year.

PES constantly replaces and improves its structures therefore intangible assets relating to these items will be vulnerable to impairment.

Procedures

Obtain a schedule of costs included at 1 March 20X3:

- Consider whether they continue to meet the relevant criteria
- Ensure no research costs are included

Vouch a sample of MezzSpace costs to invoices/contracts and determine whether their inclusion is appropriate. Vouch any employee costs capitalised to timesheets/project records

Ascertain from management the basis for determining the useful life of MezzSpace and consider whether it is reasonable. Recalculate the amortisation charge for a sample of intangible assets. Ensure that amortisation for MezzSpace is pro-rated appropriately.

Discuss with management if structures which continue to have related development costs are still in use. Inspect management's impairment review. Review board minutes for any indications of problems with, or decisions to cease using, any structures.

(c) **Property, plant and equipment**

Justification

Overseas suppliers are paid in their local currency which may result in translation errors.

Estimates of useful lives may be inappropriate. Structures consist of component parts which may have different useful lives making depreciation calculations complex and more prone to error.

Estimates of residual values may be inappropriate.

PES regularly replaces its structures, therefore assets may become obsolete or impaired leading to an overstatement of property, plant and equipment if such assets are not written down or removed from the asset register. Components that are replaced may not be removed from the asset register.

The viewing platform that collapsed is likely to be impaired and may need to be written down. The faulty manufacture of the pillars may affect the other three platforms purchased which would then need to be written down.

The total cost of the four platforms was £360,000 which is 2.4% of revenue. Failure to write down impaired platforms would result in a material error.

Procedures

For additions in the year:

- Vouch amounts to purchase invoices

- For a sample of items purchased from overseas suppliers, reperform the foreign currency translation using a rate from a reliable independent source

- Ascertain from management the basis for estimating useful lives and consider whether these are reasonable.

- Physically inspect a sample of assets included in the asset register

- Recalculate the depreciation charge on a sample of assets

Compare the total depreciation charge as a percentage of cost/carrying amount to the same calculation in the prior year and obtain explanations for any significant variation.

For assets disposed of, compare residual value with disposal proceeds to ascertain if estimates of residual value are reliable.

Ascertain and test the controls in place for recording property, plant and equipment in the asset register. Enquire of management whether additions in the year replace existing components/structures and whether such items have been disposed of and removed from the asset register or written down.

Inspect management's impairment review.

Review correspondence with the platform supplier and results of any investigation into the platform collapse to ascertain the consequences for the platforms. Discuss with management its intentions regarding the valuation of the platforms.

As a general point, the firm did not audit the prior year financial statements and the opening balances for intangible assets and property, plant and equipment may be misstated. The prior year auditor's working papers/PES's prior year working papers should be reviewed.

Opening balances should be checked to make sure that they have been brought forward correctly, and consideration should be given as to whether substantive procedures on opening balances are required.

(d) **The contract with Nefario**

Justification

Revenue from Nefario may be understated by £200,000 (£1 million − £2 million × $^2/_5$) as this would be included in deferred income had the event continued. However, as no refund is due, this amount should be recognised as revenue. The contract is now loss-making and the £300,000 (£1 million – £1.3 million) loss may not be recognised in full. £300k is 2% of draft revenue and therefore material.

PES may fail to include the future costs of dismantling the structures.

Procedures

Review the contract with Nefario to ensure that no refund is due and that cancellation is permitted.

Review the financial statements to ensure that the loss is fully accounted for and that £1 million is recognised as revenue.

Vouch the £1 million cash receipt to the bank statement.

Discuss with management its intentions regarding any provision for dismantling costs.

20.3 Additional areas of risk

Claims may be made against PES by injured spectators or by customer(s) for refunds and loss of revenue. The collapse may also result in fines/penalties imposed by regulatory authorities.

A significant uncertainty exists. Provisions or disclosure of contingent liabilities may be necessary, each of which requires estimation and the exercise of judgement.

The going concern presumption may be in doubt if the platform collapse results in:

- bad publicity or loss of reputation for PES
- closure by the regulatory authorities
- removal of other platforms currently in use leading to losses/non-payment by customers
- cancellation of future events

The estimation and disclosure of a contingent asset may be required if PES has insurance to cover the platform collapse or if it can claim against the platform supplier.

Audit procedures

Ascertain from management whether any claims have been made against PES. Review correspondence with the following:

- Spectators and customer(s) to ascertain the extent of any claims
- PES's legal advisers to ascertain the likely outcome of any claims
- The relevant regulatory authorities to ascertain the action that might be taken against PES

Discuss with management how they intend to address the issues in the financial statements/review the financial statements for provisions or disclosure of contingent liabilities.

Review the press/internet for evidence of negative publicity.

Inspect the post year-end management accounts or order book for evidence of any decline in business.

For contracts commencing post year end ascertain if any were cancelled by customers after the collapse on 15 February.

Ascertain whether the other three platforms are currently in use and, if so, whether management intends to remove them.

Examine the cash flow forecast to ascertain whether PES can pay its debts as they fall due. Perform sensitivity analysis on the cash flow forecast in respect of the number of contracts.

Consider the reasonableness of assumptions underlying the figures in the forecast.

Inspect board minutes for indications of management's intentions/developments.

Discuss with management their future plans for the business and obtain a written representation on the feasibility of their plans.

Ascertain whether PES is insured and whether the directors intend to make an insurance claim.

Inspect the contract with the platform supplier for any clauses regarding faults or claims.

Ascertain from management whether it intends to take any legal action against the supplier.

Examiner's comments:

This was the best answered of the written test questions. However, candidates performed significantly better in parts 20.1 and 20.3 compared with part 20.2. In part 20.2 it was disappointing that many candidates failed to make use of the financial information provided in the scenario.

Part 20.1

This part of the question was very well answered with a significant number of candidates attaining maximum marks. Most candidates correctly identified self-review and management as the principal threats to independence and objectivity. However, some candidates adopted a scattergun approach and also incorrectly cited familiarity and intimidation threats. Most candidates provided a number of appropriate actions that the firm could take in response to the threats. The points most commonly overlooked were a second partner review of the audit work performed on research and development costs to ensure that this area had been effectively assessed and that management must take responsibility for directing and supervising the work to be performed by the seconded member of the audit firm's staff.

Part 20.2

Answers to this part of the question were mixed and many candidates failed to attain the marks available in respect of the Nefario contract.

Previous examiners' commentaries have noted that the audit procedures cited by candidates to address audit risks were often too vague or unrelated to the justification of the audit risk. This was again a feature of some candidate's answers in this examination.

Revenue

Most candidates correctly identified that issues around revenue recognition posed an audit risk. However, the majority of candidates failed to earn the marks available for identifying that revenue may be understated if cash receipts were not recognised as revenue until the end of the event or that revenue may be overstated if cash deposits were recognised as revenue immediately on receipt. Several candidates failed to appreciate that the payment of 50% of the contract price on the signing of the contract needed to be accounted for as deferred revenue.

Few candidates used the financial information provided and so failed to earn marks available for applying basic analytical procedures. A minority of candidates incorrectly stated that there could be foreign currency translation errors and therefore had failed to appreciate that it was only suppliers that invoice in their local currency.

Weaker candidates incorrectly digressed into areas such as whether the revenue recognition policy was appropriate, accounting for doubtful debts or the calculation of the mark-up on cost applied to the contract, none of which was relevant.

Intangible assets – development costs

The majority of candidates correctly identified that research costs may be inappropriately capitalised and that capitalised development costs may not meet the relevant criteria. The most commonly overlooked justification was that PES offers its customers the latest structures and constantly seeks to improve its range and therefore intangible assets associated with these structures will be vulnerable to impairment. Audit procedures most commonly overlooked were inspection of management's impairment reviews, the vouching of the cost of the intangible asset to invoices/contracts and vouching any staff costs to timesheets/project records.

Property, plant and equipment

Most candidates correctly identified that translation errors may occur when recording components purchased from overseas suppliers and that assets' useful lives and residual values may not be estimated appropriately. They were also able to cite appropriate audit procedures to address these audit risks. Stronger candidates correctly identified that PES offers customers the latest structures and seeks to improve or replace its structures increasing the risk that assets may become obsolete or impaired. The most commonly overlooked point was in relation to the platform collapse which may indicate that the collapsed platform and the other three platforms purchased at the same time had suffered impairment.

The contract with Nefario

This was the least well addressed area of audit risk. Few candidates correctly identified that the revenue on the contract may be understated given that no refund was due to be paid by Nefario, that the contract was now loss making and that there may be additional costs in respect of dismantling the equipment that required recognition. Most candidates failed to use the financial information provided in respect of the contract to help support their answers and consequently were unable to identify any procedures to address the risk. A number of candidates wasted time by digressing into the areas of going concern and trade receivables which were not relevant.

General

Most candidates overlooked that, because the firm had recently been appointed as external auditor, there was no comfort over opening balances. As a result, very few candidates gained the marks available in respect of the procedures for auditing opening balances.

Part 20.3

The majority of candidates identified several of the points available and scored well. In particular, most candidates correctly identified the points in relation to legal claims from injured spectators and the impact of bad publicity on PES's reputation and hence whether the business would be able to continue as a going concern. Appropriate audit procedures were then cited to address these risks. Only stronger candidates earned the marks available for identifying that a contingent asset may require disclosure if PES had adequate insurance cover or if it was able to make a successful claim against the supplier of the viewing platform. The points most commonly overlooked were the risks that other events may have to be cancelled or that the viewing platforms currently in use at other events may have to be removed.

21   Barden Metalwork Ltd (September 2014)

Marking guide

				Marks
21.1	(a)	Howard Ng	4	
	(b)	Capella LLP	3	
		Marks available	7	
		Maximum		4
21.2	(a)	**Work in Progress**		
		Justification	8½	
		Procedures	16½	
	(b)	**Trade receivables**		
		Justification	4	
		Procedures	8½	
	(c)	**Trade payables**		
		Justification	4	
		Procedures	10	
		General (any section, marks awarded once only)		
		Justification	½	
		Procedures	1	
		Marks available	53	
		Maximum		23
21.3		**Supplier statements not reconciled with the trade payables ledger**		
		Consequences	9½	
		Recommendations	5½	
		Work started before approval obtained		
		Consequences	7	
		Recommendations	7½	
		General (either section, marks awarded once only)		
		Recommendations	1	
		Marks available	30½	
		Maximum		13
		Total marks available		40

21.1 (a)   Howard Ng

The firm should consider the following:

- Howard's qualifications, competence, experience, professionalism and due care.

- Howard's objectivity – his work was directed by the finance director and therefore he was not independent of the finance function. Consequently, he may have been under undue influence which could have compromised his objectivity.

- Howard's audit procedures – they do not cover the full year as he was only in post for four/five months. As he left before the year end the firm will not be able to communicate with him. In addition, his report was not completed and his reasons for leaving are unclear. These matters may mean the firm is unable to obtain sufficient appropriate evidence from Howard's work.

(b)   Capella LLP

The firm should consider whether Capella:

- will cooperate with the firm, allowing involvement of the firm's engagement team in its work and following the group auditor's instructions

- adheres to ethical/independence requirements

-   is professionally competent

-   has a good reputation/previous dealings with Capella are positive

Whether Bellass is a material/significant component as this will affect the amount of reliance that may be necessary.

21.2(a) **Work in progress**

Justification

Inventory days have increased from 48.6 in 20X3 to 57.3 in 20X4 suggesting overstatement.

Written approval may not have been obtained for commissions where work has already started and the bespoke nature of the products means materials may not be separately realisable.

Quality issues with purchases from new suppliers and fluctuating metal prices could lead to cost overruns on fixed-price commissions resulting in WIP having a net realisable value lower than cost.

The manual transfer of material and payroll costs into the job costing system may result in errors and the increase in the volume of commissions may have led to a backlog in recording material and labour costs.

The 20% addition to cover overheads may not be appropriate as the estimate requires the exercise of judgement.

Some metals are invoiced in suppliers' local currencies and therefore translation errors may arise (alternatively awarded under trade payables).

Procedures

Discuss with management the reasons for the large increase in WIP compared to the prior year.

For commissions in progress at the year end:

-   Vouch to signed customer approval

-   Ascertain reasons for any commissions started without customer approval

-   Review correspondence with customers to identify any issues with approval

-   Inspect ageing of WIP to identify any unbilled/irrecoverable WIP

-   For delayed or unapproved commissions obtain direct confirmation from the customer that the commission will be accepted

Ascertain whether any WIP at the year end includes metals purchased from suppliers where quality issues have arisen.

Compare fixed price to total costs to date/estimated total costs to identify potential loss making contracts.

Evaluate and test the controls exercised over:

-   the recording of purchases and payroll costs; and
-   the transfer of purchase and payroll costs to the job costing system

For a sample of commissions included in WIP at the year end:

-   Vouch entries for labour to payroll/ timesheets
-   Vouch entries for metals/materials to suppliers' invoices

Ascertain the basis for the 20% addition to direct costs to cover overheads and consider its reasonableness. Ensure it is:

- based on production/attributable overheads only and
- consistent with prior years.

Re-perform the overhead calculation

For a sample of invoices in foreign currencies check the exchange rate to a reliable external source and recalculate the translation.

(b) **Trade receivables**

Justification

Trade receivables days have increased from 26.8 in 20X3 to 39.8 in 20X4, which exceeds the 30-day credit terms suggesting overstatement.

Failure to obtain written approval from customers may mean there is no contractual basis on which to commence proceedings for recovery of amounts incurred.

Quality issues with new suppliers have led to an increase in complaints from customers who may withhold payment increasing the risk of the allowance against trade receivables being understated.

Procedures

Perform direct confirmation of trade receivables balances and review the aged debt analysis for overdue receivables.

Inspect post year-end cash receipts for evidence of recoverability of year-end trade receivable balances.

Inspect post year-end credit notes for evidence of amounts not recoverable at the year end.

Review correspondence with customers/legal advisors for evidence of any issues over quality or non-payment.

Ascertain whether overdue or disputed balances have a signed customer approval and whether the related commission includes metals purchased from suppliers with quality issues.

Ascertain the basis of the allowance against trade receivables and consider its reasonableness. Recalculate the year-end allowance.

(c) **Trade payables**

Justification

Trade payables days have fallen from 39.9 in 20X3 to 32.2 in 20X4 suggesting understatement.

Supplier statements are not reconciled to the trade payables ledger which may result in errors or omissions in trade payables not being identified.

Amounts due to suppliers in respect of metals where quality is in dispute may have been omitted from the trade payables ledger.

Procedures

Inspect contracts with new suppliers to ascertain whether there are shorter credit terms in respect of new suppliers.

For a sample of goods received records in respect of materials received before the year end, trace to invoice to ascertain if the amount should be included in trade payables at the year end.

For payments made in the period after the year end trace to invoice and ascertain if amounts should be included in trade payables at the year end.

Where available, request supplier statements and perform a reconciliation with the amounts included in the year-end trade payables ledger.

Where supplier statements are not available, perform direct confirmation of trade payable balances and investigate any differences.

Review correspondence with suppliers to ascertain if there are any amounts in dispute, due to quality issues, that are not included in the payables ledger. Discuss with management the reasons for not including disputed amounts in year-end trade payables.

General point

Justification

Barden is a new audit client and it may be difficult to obtain assurance over opening balances.

Procedures

Review the prior year auditor's working papers for evidence regarding opening balances.

Evaluate whether procedures performed in current year provide evidence regarding opening balances.

21.3 (a) Supplier statements not retained or reconciled with the payables ledger

Consequences

Suppliers may be under paid or not paid on time which could result in the following:

- Loss of prompt payment discounts, interest charges or penalties for late payment

- Damage to supplier relationships, Barden's account being stopped or tighter credit terms

- Delays in receiving materials required. This may cause delays in starting work on commissions and an inability to complete customer orders on time, resulting in loss of reputation or cancelled orders

Suppliers may be overpaid in error.

Errors and fraud are not likely to be detected without supplier statement reconciliations.

All of the above may result in an adverse impact on Barden's cash flow and profits.

Recommendations

Reconciliations between supplier statements and the trade payables ledger should be undertaken on a regular basis by employees independent of the ordering and recording functions.

Reconciling items should be investigated and explained.

Reconciliations should be reviewed by a manager and signed as evidence of having been reviewed.

The new procedures should be communicated to employees who should be trained in the new procedures.

(b) **Metals ordered and work started before written approval of the design and price obtained from the customer**

Consequences

The customer may cancel or fail to approve a commission or may request a design change before approval.

Any specialist metals already ordered may not have a use in another commission and where work has been started metals and labour costs incurred may be wasted.

Where inappropriate work has been started this could result in delays to completing commissions and a loss of reputation and customer goodwill.

Without written customer approval there is no contractual basis on which to commence proceedings for recovery of any costs incurred.

All of the above may result in an adverse impact on cash flow and profits.

Recommendations

The policy of not ordering metals before customer approval should be re-communicated to employees who should be re-trained in the policy.

A standard document/quote form should be signed by each customer who should be made aware of the policy in Barden's terms of trading.

Details of commissions should not be passed to the production team until approval has been received from the customer. This may be achieved by:

- implementation of IT software that prevents ordering of materials without a job number which is only raised after customer approval is obtained, or

- authorisation by a manager to purchase materials and commence work.

Purchase orders should be matched to signed customer approvals before an order is sent to the supplier and the purchase order should be signed as evidence of having been matched.

High value orders should be approved by a senior manager or director after checking the order to the customer approval.

As a general point, there should be monitoring of compliance with procedures and disciplinary procedures for non-compliance.

Examiner's comments:

This was the second best answered long-form question on the exam with many candidates performing well on all three parts of the question. However, part 21.1 was the least well answered and weaker candidates failed to make use of the information in the scenario when outlining matters to consider in relation to reliance on the work of an internal auditor and component auditor. It was pleasing to note an improvement in the use of analytical procedures in part 21.2.

Part 21.1

Answers to this part of the question were of a mixed standard. While the majority of candidates were able to outline some relevant matters in respect of placing reliance on the work of internal audit these were often generic points and were not tailored to the information provided in the scenario. For example, candidates commonly identified that the firm should consider the experience and qualifications of the internal auditor but failed to consider the implications of the fact the internal auditor was not independent of the finance function or that the post had only been filled for part of the year. Answers in respect of reliance on Capella, a component auditor, were generally weaker with many candidates failing to state straightforward matters such as whether Capella would co-operate with the group auditor and whether the component is material to the group audit and the effect that this has on the amount of work to be performed by the group auditor.

Part 21.2

Answers to this part of the question were generally good. It was pleasing to note that the majority of candidates attempted to make use of the financial information provided in the scenario, which has been identified in previous examiner's reports as a deficiency in answers. It was also pleasing to note that many candidates cited procedures to address audit risks that were adequately explained and relevant to the justification of the audit risk.

A number of candidates incorrectly digressed into consideration of risks around going concern, citing cash flow issues and providing a number of associated audit procedures. Going concern was not identified as a key risk for consideration in this question and consequently there were no marks available for this.

Most candidates overlooked that the firm had recently been appointed as external auditor and that obtaining assurance over opening balances in each of the key areas of risk may be an issue.

Work in progress

Most candidates were able to provide some reasons to justify why work in progress was an area of audit risk and provided relevant audit procedures.

The most commonly overlooked justification points were that the increase in the volume of commissions may lead to a backlog in recording costs and cut-off issues and that fixed price commissions may result in cost overruns resulting in WIP with an NRV below cost. While many candidates correctly identified that the basis for covering overheads may be inappropriate, few candidates were able to describe audit procedures to establish whether the basis of the calculation was appropriate. For example, ascertaining whether the calculation was based only on production overheads or considering the consistency of the basis with prior years was rarely cited by candidates. Other commonly overlooked audit procedures were vouching year-end work in progress balances to customer approvals for commissions and ascertaining the reasons for any commissions in progress at the year end which did not have customer approval. Many candidates also failed to consider the direction of testing in tests of detail, for example, tracing amounts from payroll records and invoices to the job cost system instead of vouching items included in the year-end WIP balance to payroll records and invoices which is more appropriate given the identified risk of overstatement.

A number of candidates incorrectly digressed into providing audit procedures in respect of revenue recognition.

Trade receivables

There were a number of good answers to this part of the question. The justification point most commonly overlooked was that failure to obtain written approval from customers may mean that there is no contractual basis on which to commence proceedings for the recovery of debts. Consequently, the associated audit procedures for this point were not provided. Other audit procedures commonly overlooked were ascertaining whether disputed balances had a signed customer approval and whether these commissions included metals purchased from suppliers with quality issues.

Trade payables

There were a number of good answers to this part of the question with many candidates correctly identifying most of the justification points. Audit procedures were less well answered with commonly overlooked procedures being inspection of contracts with new suppliers to ascertain whether credit terms are shorter and discussing with management the reasons for not including disputed amounts in year-end trade payables. A number of candidates correctly identified that the fall in trade payables days may be an indication of cut-off issues. However, very few of these candidates were able to go on and cite procedures for testing cut-off, such as examination of payments made after the year end or goods received records just before the year end. Typically, candidates cited 'perform cut-off tests' for which only a ½ mark was available.

Part 21.3

There were a number of very good answers to this part of the question with the majority of candidates identifying several of the points available. Answers in respect of both the consequences and recommendations arising from the failure to reconcile supplier statements with the trade payables ledger were generally better than those in respect of work starting before written approval was obtained from the customer.

Weaker candidates failed to describe their recommendations and consequently lost marks. For example, many stated only the converse of the weakness, ie, 'perform supplier statement reconciliations', without going on to recommend the frequency with which the procedure should be performed or that there should be a management review evidenced by signature. Candidates commonly overlooked the fact that such reconciliations should be performed by employees independent of the ordering and recording functions. Some candidates strayed beyond the scope of the given control deficiency and recommended a number of improvements to the purchasing system, such as greater controls over new suppliers including the introduction of approved supplier lists. These points did not score any marks.

In respect of ordering materials before written approval is obtained from the customer, many candidates simply restated the existing company policy of requiring the customer to provide written approval before the design is passed to production. Since this company policy had clearly failed, marks were only awarded where candidates were able to identify procedures to remedy the situation, such as implementing a software system that would prevent ordering of materials on unapproved commissions or authorisation of purchase orders by management.

22 Hyena Ltd (December 2014)

Marking guide

			Marks
22.1	Obtain authority from the company	3½	
	Answer promptly any communication	3	
	Confirm any matters to be disclosed	4	
	Avoid tipping off	2	
	Transfer books and records	2	
	Marks available	14½	
	Maximum		6
22.2	**Revenue**		
	Justification	6½	
	Procedures	18½	
	Detailed analytical procedures	7	
	Payroll		
	Justification	5	
	Procedures	14	
	Detailed analytical procedures	15½	
	Fitness equipment		
	Justification	8	
	Procedures	11½	
	Detailed analytical procedures	4½	
	General		
	Justification	1	
	Procedures	1	
	Marks available (plus 28 marks for detailed analytical procedures)	64½	
	Maximum		26

22.3 **Engagement partner appointed as NED**

Threats	1½
Safeguards	3
Calculation of taxation amounts	
Threats	3½
Safeguards	3½
Fitness club package	
Threats	3
Safeguards	2½
Marks available	17
Maximum	8
Total marks available	40

22.1 Obtain authority from the company to discuss Hyena's affairs with the incoming auditor. This authority is required to comply with the fundamental principle of confidentiality. If Hyena refuses to grant permission to discuss the client's affairs, this should be reported to the incoming auditor to alert him/her that the client may be hiding information.

Answer promptly any communication from the incoming auditor about the client's affairs. A prompt response will avoid the perception of lack of professionalism and help in a smooth changeover. Record in writing any discussions with the incoming auditor to provide evidence if questioned in the future.

Confirm whether there are any matters about which the incoming auditor ought to know, explaining them meaningfully (honestly and unambiguously) or confirm there are no such matters. Matters to be disclosed may include the following:

- Unlawful acts by Hyena
- Unpaid fees
- Differences of opinion

This ensures that the incoming auditor is in full possession of the facts and can therefore make an informed decision.

If the outgoing auditor has made one or more suspicious activity reports relating to money laundering or terrorism, the outgoing auditor should not disclose that fact to avoid the offence of tipping off.

Transfer promptly all books and records belonging to the company (unless the outgoing auditor is exercising a lien for unpaid fees) so that the company can comply with statutory requirements regarding adequate accounting records.

22.2 (a) **Revenue**

Justification

Revenue has increased by 23.9% compared to the prior year. This is out of line with the revenue growth of 5% per annum in the previous five years and the increase in the number of fitness clubs of 11.1%. This is material and suggests an overstatement of revenue. The potential overstatement of revenue is supported by the detailed analytical procedures set out below.

As a result of systems issues, some monthly subscriptions were taken twice and revenue may be overstated if all refunds have not been paid or properly recorded.

The payment received in advance for annual subscriptions may lead to inappropriate revenue recognition if the full subscription is recognised as revenue in the year of receipt. Consequently revenue may be overstated.

Cash taken at club receptions may lead to an understatement of revenue if cash is misappropriated and not recorded.

Detailed analytical procedures (7 marks):

Revenue – expectation of revenue in 20X4

Average revenue per club in 20X3 = £562.5K (75,937/135)

Expected average revenue per club in 20X4 = £590.6K (562 × 1.05)

Total expected revenue = £88,593K (591 × 150)

Actual revenue is £5,530K above expectation (94,123 – 88,593)

This is 35.6% of profit before tax

Revenue – comparing revenue per club

Average revenue per club in 20X3 = £562.5K (75,937/135)

Average revenue per club in 20X4 = £627.5K (94,123/150)

Revenue up by 11.6% ((627.5 – 562.5)/562.5)

Note: Credit given for slightly different answers where figures have been rounded in the workings.

Procedures

- Discuss with directors the reasons for the rise in revenue
- Substantiate explanations given, for example, whether new clubs are busier
- Obtain breakdown of revenue by:
    - Pay-as-you go
    - Monthly subscriptions
    - Annual subscriptions
    - Fitness club
- Compare with previous year (where relevant)/budget
- investigate significant variances

Cash/debit cards taken at club receptions

- Evaluate and test controls over cash taken at receptions/review internal audit work in this area
- Compare records of takings/till records with bankings
- Investigate delays in banking

Monthly subscriptions

- Evaluate and test controls over system for recording monthly subscriptions
- Inspect workings regarding refunds and corresponding journals
- Discuss with management steps taken to prevent recurrence
- Analytical procedures, for example, number of members (per list of members) × annual subscription

Annual package

- Evaluate and test controls over revenue recognition/deferred revenue
- Agree cash received to bank statement
- Trace transfer of revenue from deferred revenue to revenue account
- For a sample of subscriptions, check correct amount of revenue/deferred revenue recognised

(b) **Payroll**

Justification

Payroll costs have risen by 6% but this is inconsistent with the 2% pay rise, the 11.1% increase in the number of clubs and the 10.2% increase in the number of employees. This is material and suggests an understatement of gross pay. The potential understatement of payroll is supported by the detailed analytical procedures set out below.

A number of deficiencies were highlighted by the internal audit function in the first half of the year. There is a risk that data may have been incorrectly transferred to the payroll system at Zebra. Furthermore, there may be issues obtaining access to systems at, and information produced by, Zebra.

Detailed analytical procedures (15½ marks):

Expectation of total payroll in 20X4

Average pay in 20X3 = £17,588 (47,225/2,685)

Expected average pay in 20X4 = £17,940 (17,588 × 1.02)

Total expected pay in 20X4 of £53,085k (17,940 × 2,959)

Actual pay is £2,935k lower than expectation (50,150 – 53,085)

This is 18.9% of profit before tax

Expectation of average pay in 20X4

Average pay in 20X3 = £17,588 (47,225/2,685)

Expected average pay in 20X4 = £17,940 (17,588 × 1.02)

Average pay in 20X4 = £16,948 (50,150/2,959)

Actual pay is £992 lower than expectation (17,940 – 16,948)

Average pay

Average pay in 20X3 = £17,588 (47,225/2,685)

Average pay in 20X4 = £16,948 (50,150/2,959)

Payroll costs down by 3.6% ((16,948 – 17,588)/17,588)

Pay per club

Pay per club in 20X3 = £349,814 (47,225/135)

Pay per club in 20X4 = £334,333 (50,150/150)

Pay down by 4.4% ((350 – 334)/350)

Average employees per club

Average number in 20X3 = 19.89 (2,685/135)

Average number in 20X4 = 19.73 (2,959/150)

Reduction of 0.16 or 0.8%

Procedures

- Evaluate and test controls over payroll processing
- Review the work of the internal audit function
- Sample check on calculations
- Review monthly breakdown of payroll and compare with budgets

- Audit procedures to cover:

  - Payroll figures prepared by Hyena for period 1 Dec 20X3 to 31 May 20X4 (old system)

  - Payroll figures prepared by Zebra for period 1 June 20X4 to 30 Nov 20X4 (new system)

  - Accuracy of transfer of data at 1 June to new system

  - Accuracy of transfer of any standing data to new system

- Obtain an understanding of services provided by Zebra
- Assess Zebra's reputation/competency
- Ascertain access to information held by Zebra
- Obtain payroll reports produced by Zebra
- Evaluate and test controls at Zebra

(c) **Fitness equipment**

Justification

The carrying amount of equipment has increased by 29.8%. This is inconsistent with the 11.1% increase in the number of clubs. This is material and suggests that equipment could be overstated or impaired. The potential overstatement of equipment is supported by the detailed analytical procedures set out below.

The depreciation charge for the year of 16.5% of the net book value of equipment compared to the previous year of 20.8% seems low, and this suggests an understatement of depreciation.

Equipping the clubs with the latest equipment may result in obsolete or impaired items which need to be written down.

The equipment is imported from manufacturers who invoice in US dollars which could result in translation errors.

The capitalisation of own employee costs for installation may be inappropriate.

The loss on sale of the equipment indicates that useful economic lives (UEL) may be too long or the estimate of residual values too high. The cost and accumulated depreciation on disposals may not be correctly eliminated from the non-current asset register.

Detailed analytical procedures (4½ marks):

Expectation of the book value of equipment

Book value in 20X3 = £9,049 (135 clubs)

Expected in 20X4 = £10,054 (9,049/135 × 150)

Actual equipment is £1,695 above expectation (11,749 - 10054)

Comparing equipment by club

Equipment per club in 20X3 = £67,030 (9,049/135)

Equipment per club in 20X4 = £78,327 (11,749/150)

16.8% increase

Note: Credit given for slightly different answers where figures have been rounded in the workings

Procedures

- For a sample of additions in the year vouch amounts to the purchase invoice
- Inspect the non-current asset register to check that items disposed of have been removed from the register
- For a sample of items purchased from overseas suppliers, recalculate the foreign exchange translation and trace the rate used to a reliable independent source
- Confirm with management its intention to continue to replace items after five years and that five years is a reasonable basis for estimating UEL
- Select a sample of fitness equipment on the asset register and physically inspect
- Confirm equipment is still in use and not impaired
- Recalculate depreciation charge
- Vouch capitalisation of employee costs to employee timesheets
- Ensure all costs capitalised meet the recognition criteria
- Inspect evidence of impairment reviews undertaken by management

General

The firm did not audit the prior year financial statements and opening balances, in relation to fitness equipment, may be misstated.

Procedures

Review outgoing auditor's working papers, if available

22.3 Engagement partner appointed as non-executive director

Threats

The appointment of the engagement partner as a non-executive director presents a management threat. The partner would be expected to make decisions as a non-executive director and the audit firm's position would become closely aligned with the views and interests of management.

Safeguards

The firm must refuse the request for the partner to join the board as a non-executive director while continuing as a partner in the firm. Dual employment is prohibited by Ethical Standard S2 and by the Companies Act 2006. As a non-executive director, the partner will be involved in taking decisions and, consequently, the management threat is insurmountable. The partner could attend meetings solely in connection with audit matters acting in his/her capacity as the engagement partner providing advice only and not voting when a decision is required.

Calculation of amounts to be included in respect of taxation in the financial statements

Threats

A self-review threat arises when the results of a non-audit service performed by the external auditors are reflected in the amounts included or disclosed in the financial statements, such as the tax charge in the statement of profit or loss or the tax liability included in the statement of financial position. Audit staff may be reluctant to identify shortcomings in their colleagues' work or may place too much reliance on that work without checking it. A management threat also arises if members of the firm are expected to make decisions on behalf of management.

Safeguards

The tax services should be provided by partners and staff who have no involvement in the external audit of the financial statements. In addition, the work should be reviewed by an independent partner or senior staff member with appropriate expertise. Alternatively, if the tax computations are prepared by the audit team they must be reviewed by a partner or senior tax employee, who is independent of the audit team. The firm should ensure that the management of Hyena is 'informed', ie, designated members of management have the capability to make management judgements and decisions on the basis of the information provided. However, if the management threat is too great, the work must be refused. The ethics partner should be consulted for his/her view as to whether objectivity has been compromised.

Free one-year package to a fitness club

Threats

The gift creates a self-interest threat, unless the value is clearly insignificant. There is an incentive not to upset the client by, for example, overlooking any errors for fear of losing the gift. Ethical Standard S4, *Fees, Remuneration and Evaluation Policies, Gifts and Hospitality, Litigation* states that those in a position to influence the conduct and outcome of an audit cannot accept such gifts. The firm should consider whether it is probable that a reasonable and informed third party would conclude that objectivity is likely to be impaired. This appears to be likely in the case of a full year's membership of a fitness club.

Safeguards

The firm should decline the offer of the free subscription. There are no safeguards that could be put in place to reduce the threat to objectivity. In addition, the firm should consider whether the offer has any impact on its assessment of management's integrity. The firm should have established policies in place on the nature and value of gifts that may be accepted and the ethics partner should be consulted to confirm that these policies are adequate.

Examiner's comments:

This was the highest scoring long-form question on the exam with a number of excellent answers to parts 22.2 and 22.3.

Part 22.1

Answers to this part of the question were of a mixed standard. A number of candidates incorrectly identified duties of the outgoing auditor required by Companies Act 2006, even though these were specifically excluded by the requirement. Stronger candidates were able to identify correctly a number of responsibilities of the outgoing firm such as seeking permission from Hyena to respond to the incoming auditor, answering communications promptly and confirming whether there are any matters which the prospective auditor ought to be aware. A significant proportion of stronger candidates also provided appropriate reasons why such responsibilities were necessary. However, some candidates failed to address this part of the requirement and therefore failed to earn the higher skills marks available for giving reasons. The most commonly overlooked points were those relating to the possibility of the client refusing permission to discuss its affairs with a prospective auditor and that this fact should be reported to the prospective auditor so that he/she is aware that the client may be hiding information and the importance of not disclosing suspicious activity reports.

Part 22.2

Answers to this part of the question were generally good and many candidates were able to provide a number of justifications as to why an item had been identified as a key area of audit risk. These candidates then cited a range of procedures to address audit risks that were both adequately explained and relevant to the justification of the audit risk. However, weaker candidates continue to cite vague audit procedures not linked to the audit risk.

While it was pleasing to note that the majority of candidates attempted to make some use of the financial information provided in the scenario, this was often restricted to a comparison of the 20X4 figures against the previous year. Only a small number of stronger candidates earned the higher skills marks available for performing more detailed analytical procedures by using the additional information given in the scenario to help with analysis. These candidates frequently scored maximum marks by, for example, calculating an expectation of revenue based on the prior year increase in revenue and the increase in the number of clubs or an expectation of payroll based on the average number of employees and the company-wide pay rise. A number of candidates did not present their workings for the detailed analytical procedures and consequently lost marks when the incorrect answer was given. Weaker candidates proposed performing analytical procedures, without elaboration, either to justify the audit risk or as a procedure to address the risk but failed to appreciate that the information was available in the scenario to enable them to do this.

Many candidates overlooked that the firm had recently been appointed as external auditor and that obtaining assurance over opening balances in respect of fitness equipment may be an issue.

Revenue

Most candidates were able to provide a number of reasons to justify why revenue was a key area of audit risk including making use of basic analytical procedures. The most commonly overlooked justification point was that misappropriation of cash from pay-per-session receipts might lead to an understatement of revenue.

The most commonly overlooked audit procedures were investigating delays in banking of cash takings and tracing the transfer of revenue from deferred revenue to the revenue account in respect of the annual membership packages.

Payroll

Most candidates were able to provide a number of reasons to justify why payroll was a key area of audit risk, including making use of basic analytical procedures such as comparing the increase in payroll costs with the increase in number of clubs and/or the increase in the number of employees and the fact this was inconsistent with the 2% annual pay increase. Most candidates also correctly identified that deficiencies in the payroll system, highlighted by the internal audit function, increased the risk of misstatement. A significant number of candidates also cited the outsourcing of payroll to a payroll service organisation as a justification of why payroll was a key area of audit risk. However, this was insufficient to earn the marks available since the payroll service organisation may have reduced risk in this area. To earn the marks available, candidates were required to identify that errors may have occurred when transferring payroll data part way through the year and that obtaining audit evidence from a third party may be more difficult.

Audit procedures in respect of payroll were the weakest of the three key areas identified. The majority of candidates earned the marks available for evaluating and testing the controls over payroll processing, reviewing the internal auditor's report and performing sample checks on calculations. However, there were a number of audit procedures that were commonly overlooked in respect of the outsourced payroll. These included testing the accuracy of the transfer of payroll data to Zebra, the service provider, obtaining an understanding of the competency of Zebra, ascertaining what evidence would be available from Zebra and reviewing reports on the payroll system by Zebra's auditor. The majority of candidates also failed to identify or explain that the firm's audit procedures would need to cover both the period to 31 May, when the payroll system was operated by the client, and the period from 31 May to 30 November, when the payroll had been outsourced.

Fitness equipment

Answers relating to the justification of audit risk for fitness equipment were generally good with the majority of candidates identifying a number of appropriate factors. The most commonly overlooked justification was that the company's policy of replacing equipment every five years may result in obsolete equipment. Candidates were also able to cite a number of appropriate audit procedures to address the risks. However, a number of candidates failed to consider the direction of testing between the physical asset and asset register, for example tracing physical assets to the items included in the asset register instead of tracing items in the asset register to the physical asset which is more appropriate given the identified risk of overstatement. The most commonly overlooked audit procedure was inspecting evidence of impairment reviews undertaken by management.

Part 22.3

Answers to this part of the question were good although there was evidence of a number of candidates who adopted a 'scatter-gun' approach to the threats to objectivity, resulting in identification of a number of inappropriate threats. The majority of candidates correctly identified that it was inappropriate for an engagement partner to be appointed as a non-executive director due to an insurmountable management threat and that dual employment is prohibited by Ethical Standard S2 and the Companies Act 2006. However, only stronger candidates earned the marks available for stating that the engagement partner could attend audit committee meetings providing it was in his/her capacity as engagement partner and of an advisory nature only.

The majority of candidates also correctly identified and explained the self-review and management threats with respect to the firm preparing tax calculations. However, a significant minority of candidates wasted time discussing self-interest and advocacy threats for which no marks were available. The most commonly overlooked safeguard in this scenario was the documentation of informed management.

The self-interest threat in relation to the gift of a free year's membership of a fitness club was correctly identified and explained by most candidates. However, very few candidates considered if it was probable that a reasonable and informed third party would conclude that objectivity was likely to be impaired or considered whether the offer of the gift impacted on the firm's assessment of management's integrity. A significant minority of weaker candidates either incorrectly concluded that the gift was not significant, and could be accepted, or failed to reach a conclusion on whether the gift was significant or not.

23 Weselton plc (March 2015)

Marking guide

			Marks
23.1	Matters that the firm should have considered	16½	
	Procedures	5½	
	Marks available	22	
	Maximum		10
23.2	(a) **Work in progress**		
	Justification	12	
	Procedures	17	
	(b) **Trade receivables**		
	Justification	10½	
	Procedures	15	
	Marks available	54½	
	Maximum		18
23.3	**Firm recently appointed**	4	
	High control risk	5	
	Marks available	9	
		18	
	Maximum		5
23.4	(a) **No written confirmation**		
	Consequences	4	
	Recommendations	2	
	(b) **No monitoring of actual costs**		
	Consequences	4½	
	Recommendations	3	
	General recommendations (awarded only once across a and b)	1½	
	Marks available	15	
	Maximum		7
Total marks available			40

23.1 Matters that the firm should have considered:

- Weselton is a new audit client which means the firm has a lack of cumulative audit knowledge and experience, resulting in increased detection risk and no comfort over opening balances.

- The reason the previous auditor didn't seek reappointment, such as disagreements, intimidation, unpaid fees or illegal acts.

- Management's integrity and whether there is any risk to the firm's reputation from association with Weselton.

- The level of fees as a self-interest threat may arise especially as Weselton is the firm's largest audit client. The firm should have established whether recurring fees earned from Weselton are below 10% of the firm's gross practice income. If fees are in excess of 5% of the firm's gross practice income the firm should have considered the resources required to implement additional safeguards, such as monitoring fees on a regular basis.

- Ethical issues including any threats to the firm's independence and objectivity, such as conflicts of interest, whether the firm's employees hold shares in Weselton and whether Weselton's management will try to influence the audit process by insisting on a controls approach. Where ethical issues were identified the firm should have considered its ability to implement appropriate safeguards.

- Adequacy of the firm's resources given the global nature of Weselton's business and whether the firm can undertake an engagement quality control review and meet the relevant reporting deadlines for a listed company.

- Adequacy of the firm's experience and knowledge of the overseas regulatory framework(s) to ensure the audit can be performed competently and reduce the risk of an inappropriate audit opinion.

- Level of audit risk, especially in light of the problems arising in the year with the job costing system.

- Level of engagement risk given Weselton is listed and is subject to public interest.

Procedures

The firm should have:

- enquired of management why the previous auditor did not seek reappointment

- obtained professional clearance to act by:

  (1) obtaining permission to contact the previous auditor

  (2) communicating with the previous auditor and considering any points raised in the response

- inspected the statement of circumstances deposited by the previous auditor

- performed a preliminary risk assessment to ascertain the extent of audit work required to reduce risk to an acceptable level

- held discussions with the directors to ascertain their attitude towards areas such as internal control and tax issues

- performed client identification procedures

- performed a Companies House search/reviewed press cuttings/internet for evidence regarding management's integrity

- reviewed Weselton's prior year's financial statements and the auditor's report

23.2(a) **Work in progress**

Justification

WIP appears to be overstated because of the following:

- Mark-up for 20X5 is 47.6% compared to 35% in 20X4 which is inconsistent with the policy of a 35% mark-up

- WIP days in 20X5 are 85 days compared to 60 days in 20X4

- Customers are likely to challenge any costs incorrectly allocated to their project, arising from the following:

  - Project managers managing multiple projects
  - Invoices for the cost of overseas packers covering multiple projects

- Customers are more likely to dispute future invoices for amounts included in WIP at 28 February:

  (1) Where they have already been invoiced for a project meaning any un-invoiced WIP may not be recoverable

  (2) As they are not required to confirm in writing changes to their requirements and there is no monitoring of actual costs compared to estimates

There is a potential for understatement of WIP at 28 February due to the following:

- Cut-off issues arising from invoices received from suppliers after the year end which relate to services received before the year end

- Unrecorded invoices resulting from the back log of recording costs

Overseas suppliers invoice in local currencies which may result in translation errors.

Errors may arise from the implementation of the new job costing system due to the following:

- Incorrect transfer of balances from the old to the new system
- Lack of parallel run to check the new system was operating correctly
- Delays in training

Errors may have arisen during the year due to the use of the outdated project costing system

Procedures

Ascertain from management the reasons for the increase in WIP.

Vouch a sample of temporary packer costs recorded in the job costing system to purchase invoices.

Trace hours recorded on a sample of project managers' timesheets to the job costing system.

Trace invoices for temporary packer costs to the job costing system.

Check that each is allocated to the correct unique code.

Inspect the aged WIP report to identify any unbilled/irrecoverable WIP.

Compare actuals to estimates to identify any projects with costs significantly above the initial estimate.

Ascertain whether WIP at the year end has been billed after the year end and subsequently settled by Weselton's customers.

Inspect supplier invoices received or recorded after the year end and trace to the job costing system/WIP balance at 28 February where they relate to pre year-end activity.

Ascertain from management whether the backlog has been cleared.

Inspect the additional customer invoices raised in March and ascertain if the related costs were included in WIP at 28 February.

Review correspondence with these customers to ascertain if there are any disputes.

Reperform the translation of a sample of foreign currency invoices using an exchange rate obtained from a reliable 3rd party.

Compare a sample of balances transferred to the new job costing system with the old job costing system for accuracy.

Enquire of Weselton's employees whether they have identified any issues with the functioning of the new system.

(b) **Trade receivables**

Justification

Trade receivables may be overstated because:

- trade receivables days in 20X5 are 44 days compared to 33 days in 20X4

- this appears to be inconsistent with the credit terms of 30 days

- customers may refuse to pay the additional invoices, relating to the unrecorded costs

- Bulda is refusing to pay an invoice for £1.8 million. This is 4% of revenue and therefore material. It may only be £0.5 million in dispute which is 1.1% of revenue and therefore also material

- there may be other disputed invoices at the year end where actual costs are significantly above those estimated

- the risk of disputes is higher due to the lack of written confirmations of changes and inadequate monitoring of costs

Sales invoices may be inaccurate due to:

- misallocation of project manager time/temporary packer costs between projects in the job costing system

- errors arising due to the implementation of the new system and the back log of recording costs both of which may result in customers refusing to pay or a high volume of credit notes being raised after the year end

- errors in calculating the 35% mark-up

Procedures

Undertake direct confirmation of trade receivables balances at the year end. Include the balance due from Bulda and customers who received additional invoices in February. Investigate any discrepancies.

Identify cash received from customers after 28 February which relates to trade receivables at the year end

Inspect correspondence with Bulda to ascertain the amount in dispute and review the contract with Bulda to ascertain whether it is contractually bound to pay the full amount invoiced.

Review the aged receivables analysis to identify any old outstanding amounts. Discuss with management the basis for any allowance against receivables or for any old balances for which an allowance is not included at the year end. Recalculate the allowance against receivables.

Inspect correspondence with customers other than Bulda for evidence of any disputes. Inspect credit notes raised after the year end for evidence of amounts disputed/errors at 28 February.

For a sample of invoices:

- Trace amounts to costs recorded in the job costing system
- Re-perform the mark-up calculation

23.3 The firm is recently appointed and it may therefore be difficult to obtain evidence that controls operated effectively throughout the year.

The new system was only in place for part of the year so controls over both systems would need to be tested which is unlikely to be efficient.

There is high control risk due to the problems with both the old and new job costing systems, in particular:

- the old system had become outdated and therefore may not have been operating effectively

- the lack of familiarity and delays in training on the new system

- there was a backlog in recording costs

- there was no parallel run

23.4 (a) **Customers are not required to provide written confirmation of changes to their requirements during a relocation project**

Consequences

Weselton will have no evidence that the customer requested the change or that the customer was aware of any implications of the change on costs/price. It will be more difficult to recover monies in the event of a dispute over requirements or a customer refusing to pay. This would lead to a negative impact on profit and cash flow.

Changes in requirements may be misunderstood leading to customer dissatisfaction and loss of future business as well as having a negative impact on Weselton's reputation in the market place.

Recommendations

All changes to customer requirements should be documented. The impact of changes on costs/price should be notified to the customer immediately. The customer should sign the document detailing the changes as evidence of acceptance of the changes before they are implemented.

(b) **Project managers do not monitor actual costs incurred to date compared with the estimated cost of each project**

Consequences

Errors in recording costs in the job costing system, such as incorrect allocation of costs between projects, may go undetected. Cost overruns on projects will not be identified in a timely manner and therefore customers cannot be informed of increases in the final price. It is therefore more likely that disputes with customers will arise where there are cost overruns. This will have a negative impact on profit and cash flow and lead to a loss of customer goodwill and a negative impact on Weselton's reputation.

The opportunity to improve the process for estimating costs will be missed.

Recommendations

Project managers should monitor project costs on a regular basis and should prepare a variance analysis to explain cost overruns/errors. Identified cost overruns should be notified to the customer immediately and written authority for cost overruns should be obtained.

Any errors identified should be corrected in a timely manner.

Project managers should produce regular reports for senior management to highlight any significant project cost issues.

General recommendations (awarded only once across (a) and (b)):

- Policies should be communicated to staff
- Disciplinary procedures should be in place for non-compliance with policies
- Monitoring of compliance by management

Examiner's comments:

This was the second best answered long-form question on the exam. However, part 23.3 was poorly answered by a significant number of candidates. In part 23.2 candidates' answers in respect of trade receivables generally scored more highly compared with their answers in respect of WIP.

Part 23.1 of the question was well answered with most candidates able to identify a number of relevant matters that the firm should have considered and a range of procedures that it should have performed before accepting appointment as external auditor. The points commonly identified were the reasons why the previous auditor resigned and the procedures associated with the professional clearance process, the level of fees and the adequacy of the firm's resources and its expertise. The points most commonly overlooked were those relating to the first-year audit ie, a lack of cumulative audit knowledge resulting in higher detection risk and no comfort over opening balances. A number of candidates wasted time citing procedures to be undertaken once the firm was appointed as auditor such as agreement of the engagement letter with the client and procedures to be undertaken during the audit. Candidates who followed the instruction to 'list' produced succinct answers which covered a wide range of points. These candidates generally scored more highly than those candidates who provided very detailed explanations of each point made in their answers.

Answers to part 23.2 of the question were of a mixed standard. In previous examiners' commentaries, it was noted that the procedures cited by candidates to address audit risks were often too vague or unrelated to the justification of the audit risk. This was again a feature of some candidates' answers in this examination. Most candidates made some use of the financial information provided but, disappointingly, a significant minority did not refer to this information in their answers and so lost the marks that were available for applying analytical procedures to illustrate why an item had been selected as an area of audit risk. Where candidates did make use of the financial information, many restricted their answers to simple percentage changes and therefore did not earn the higher skills marks available for considering the analysis of WIP days, trade receivable days or comparison of the mark-up with the company's stated policy. A number of weaker candidates suggested tests of control as part of audit procedures for both work in progress and trade receivables. Such procedures did not earn any marks as the internal control deficiencies highlighted in the scenario and the requirement in part 23.3 clearly indicated that reliance on internal controls was unlikely to be appropriate.

Work in progress

Most candidates were able to provide some points to justify why work in progress had been identified as a key area of audit risk and described a range of procedures to address the risk. The justification points commonly overlooked were those relating to the backlog of recording costs, the possibility that un-invoiced WIP may not be recoverable and that customers are not required to confirm in writing changes to their requirements. The procedures commonly overlooked were those relating to the inspection of aged work in progress reports, comparison of actual costs to estimates and consideration of whether any work in progress at the year end had subsequently been invoiced and settled by the customer.

A large number of candidates wasted time discussing issues associated with estimates such as the stage of completion of the project and allocation of overheads. Estimates are only relevant to the pricing of each project and not to the valuation of work in progress which is based on actual costs. A number of candidates confused the 35% mark-up with overhead absorption failing to appreciate that the mark-up is only applied once a customer is invoiced. Some candidates failed to appreciate that Weselton provided services rather than goods and wasted time covering points such as the physical verification of work in progress, attendance at the inventory count and the audit of goods in transit, none of which were relevant to the scenario. Some candidates digressed into areas of going concern and cash flow and scored no marks for these points.

Trade receivables

Answers in respect of the justification of audit risks and procedures to address each risk were of a higher standard for trade receivables than those for work in progress and candidates generally made better use of the draft financial information to justify the risk of overstatement of trade receivables. Many candidates also correctly identified the dispute with Bulda as a justification point. However, few candidates used the financial information provided in respect of the disputed invoice to demonstrate that it was material to the financial statements. The procedures commonly identified were those relating to the direct confirmation of balances, the review of cash receipts from customers after the year end, the review of aged receivables to identify old outstanding amounts and discussion with management of the reasons for unprovided old balances. The points commonly overlooked were that customers may refuse to pay additional invoices sent in February for unrecorded costs and the risk of disputes with customers due to cost overruns arising from the failure to monitor costs incurred against estimated costs. Consequently, few candidates considered associated audit procedures such as inspection of correspondence with customers or post year-end credit notes for evidence of disputes. A large number of candidates incorrectly cited the risk of translation errors and the related audit procedures to address that risk. This was not relevant to trade receivables as the scenario clearly stated all customers are invoiced in sterling.

Answers to part 23.3 of the question were of a mixed standard. The points commonly identified were those relating to the outdated system, delays in training, lack of parallel run and the backlog of costs. Most candidates failed to conclude that overall sufficient evidence of effectiveness was unlikely to be obtained. Other points commonly overlooked were those relating to the recent appointment ie, the difficulty of obtaining evidence that controls operated effectively throughout the year and that both systems would require testing which was unlikely to be efficient. Weaker candidates did not make use of the information provided in the scenario and made general points concerning inherent limitations of internal control systems and the need for both control and substantive audit procedures which did not score any marks.

Part 23.4 of the question was well answered with most candidates able to identify a range of relevant consequences and recommendations for each internal control deficiency. The recommendations commonly overlooked in respect of deficiency (1) were that the impact of changes on costs should be notified to the customer and that contracts should state that prices may change. The points most commonly overlooked in respect of deficiency (2) were that errors arising when recording costs in the job costing system may go undetected and that errors identified should be corrected in a timely manner. A number of candidates wasted time by explaining the impact of each weakness on the work in progress and trade receivable balances in the financial statements for which there were no marks available. A significant minority of candidates incorrectly identified susceptibility to fraud as consequences of both control deficiencies.

24 Arendelle Ltd (March 2015)

Marking guide

			Marks
24.1	Ethical issues		
	(a) Management threat	2	
	(b) Self-interest threat	3½	
	Marks available	5½	
	Maximum		3
24.2	(a) **Revenue**		
	Analytical procedures	5½	
	Questions for Elsa	6	
	(b) **Margins**		
	Analytical procedures	7	
	Questions for Elsa	14	

(c)	**Warehouse rent**		
	Analytical procedures	6½	
	Questions for Elsa	6	
(d)	**Depreciation: delivery vehicles**		
	Analytical procedures	2½	
	Questions for Elsa	2	
(e)	**Marketing expenses**		
	Analytical procedures	3½	
	Questions for Elsa	6	
(f)	**Trade receivables**		
	Analytical procedures	5½	
	Questions for Elsa	10	
(g)	**Trade payables**		
	Analytical procedures	5½	
	Questions for Elsa	6	
	Questions for Elsa: breakdown and budgets	2	
Marks available		88	
Maximum			17
Total marks available			20

24.1 Ethical issues

(a) A management threat arises as the firm may be expected to make judgements/decisions. The preparation and presentation of the interim financial information is management's responsibility. The firm's interests may be perceived to be too closely aligned with those of Arendelle.

(b) There is a self-interest threat to the firm's objectivity and its ability to perform the engagement with professional competence and due care. The firm may be reluctant to state in its conclusion that matters have come to its attention that causes the firm to believe the interim financial information is not true and fair. It will fear that the loan application will then be unsuccessful resulting in the firm not receiving its fee. The firm must not undertake an assurance engagement on a contingency fee basis.

24.2 (a) Revenue

Analytical procedures

Revenue has increased by 45% compared to the prior year and the six months to 31 January 20X5 represents 72.6% of the prior full year. Expected revenue for the interim period would be £3,470k being half of the prior year plus £220,000 in relation to six months of the new nursing home contracts ($22 \times £20k \times 6/12$). Therefore, revenue is £1,250k higher than expected and implies that revenue from non-care home contracts is 38% higher than in the prior year ($£1,250k/(6,500k \times 6/12)$).

Questions for Elsa

What are the sources of increased revenue other than that from the nursing home contracts?

How has nursing home revenue been recognised?

How has this additional demand been met given delivery vehicles are already fully utilised?

(b) **Margins**

Analytical procedures

Gross profit has increased by 84.6% and operating profit has increased by 68.2%. This is out of line with the increase in revenue.

Gross profit margin has increased from 21% to 27% and operating profit margin has increased from 11.4% to 13.2%. There may be a misallocation of costs between cost of sales and operating expenses.

Questions for Elsa

Is the margin on nursing home contracts/other new revenue significantly higher than on contracts in place last year?

Are costs charged by new suppliers lower than existing suppliers?

Have bulk purchase discounts been negotiated?

Has the proportion of business given to new suppliers increased beyond that needed to fulfil the nursing home contracts?

Has the product mix changed?

Have selling prices increased?

Have market prices of fruit/vegetables fallen significantly?

(c) **Warehouse rent**

Analytical procedures

Rent has increased by 39% compared to the prior year and the six months to 31 January 20X5 represents 69% of the prior full year. There appears to be an additional rental expense of £35k (£125k - (£180k × 6/12)). An increase in rental expense is expected given that an additional storage facility has been rented to fulfil the new nursing home contracts. However, these contracts only represent a 6.8% increase in revenue. Rent was 2.8% of revenue in 20X4 but the extra rental is 15.9% of the additional nursing home contract revenue (£35k/£220k). The increase in rental appears high compared to the extra revenue from nursing homes.

Questions for Elsa

Is the additional storage facility charged at a premium rental?

How much additional space is being rented compared to the existing storage space?

Is the storage space being used for purposes other than the nursing home contracts, such as the sources of other revenue?

(d) **Depreciation - delivery vehicles**

Analytical procedures

Depreciation is consistent with the prior year (ie, half year is 50% of full year). Expected depreciation would be £27.5k for the half year given 20 of the 40 delivery vehicles are now fully depreciated. Depreciation therefore appears overstated.

Questions for Elsa

Have the fully depreciated delivery vehicles continued to be depreciated in error?

(e) **Marketing expenses**

Analytical procedures

Marketing expenses have increased by 104% compared to the prior year and the six months to 31 January 20X5 represents 102% of the prior full year. Expected marketing expenses would be £96,000 (£192,000 × $^6/_{12}$). Marketing expenses therefore appear to be overstated.

Questions for Elsa

Marketing expenses

What marketing activity has taken place in the six months to 31 January 20X5 to cause the increase?

Are marketing expenses 'front loaded' in the year?

How has the £100,000 for marketing in the new delivery areas from April been accounted for?/Has it been expensed in error?

(f) **Trade receivables**

Analytical procedures

Trade receivables days are 2.4 days. Receivables days are expected due to the 30 day credit terms extended to the nursing homes. However, £62,000 represents 51 days of nursing home revenues (£62,000/£220,000 × 182.5 days). 30 days of revenue would be £36,000 (£220,000/six months). Therefore trade receivables days appear high compared to the 30 day credit terms extended to nursing homes. Trade receivables may be overstated or some debts may be irrecoverable

Questions for Elsa

Have credit terms been extended to any other customers?

Are nursing homes slow payers?

Have credit checks been run on nursing homes?

Are there any amounts in dispute which may be irrecoverable and therefore require an allowance against them?

Has Arendelle introduced any credit control procedures since extending credit?

(g) **Trade payables**

Analytical procedures

Trade payables have increased by 51.7% compared with the prior year. Trade payables days have increased from 31 days in 20X4 to 35 days. This is inconsistent with the fact that new suppliers have not extended credit terms to Arendelle. Consequently it is expected trade payables days would fall. Trade payables may be overstated.

Questions for Elsa

Have credit terms since been negotiated with the new suppliers?

Is Arendelle paying its creditors more slowly than in prior year due to disputes for example?

Are there cash flow difficulties resulting from paying new suppliers on delivery?

Request:

- Breakdown of amounts/balances
- Budget/forecasts for the period

Examiner's comments:

This was the least well answered of the long-form questions. Although the ethical issues in part 24.1 were adequately explained, many candidates wasted time writing more than was required to earn 3 marks. Answers to part 24.2 were of a very mixed standard and differentiated those candidates who have a good understanding of the purposes of analytical procedures from those who do not.

Part 24.1 of the question was generally well answered with most candidates correctly identifying and explaining the management threat in respect of the request to provide guidance on the presentation of the financial information and the self-interest threat in respect of the contingency fee. It was pleasing to note that the majority of candidates recognised that contingency fees were not appropriate for assurance work. The most commonly overlooked point was that self-interest posed a threat to the firm's objectivity and professional competence and due care. A significant minority of candidates wasted time providing safeguards, to mitigate each of the threats, which were not required. A number of candidates adopted a scattergun approach and wrote lengthy answers covering a number of ethical issues which were not relevant to the scenario. Such candidates would do well to make note of the mark allocation available for each part of a question when determining how much to include in their response.

Answers to part 24.2 of the question were of a mixed standard. Stronger candidates were able to calculate relevant ratios and perform sensible analysis which enabled them to produce a list of appropriate questions for the client's finance director. Such candidates related the information provided about the business to their analysis and identified issues where the analysis did not appear to support the circumstances of the business. These candidates scored highly. Weaker candidates failed to use the information provided about the business and performed only basic calculations, such as percentage changes, which then led to very basic questions, such as 'why has revenue gone up?'. There were no marks available for questions of this nature. A significant minority of candidates failed to appreciate that the review was in respect of a six-month period. Consequently, their calculations failed to take into account the fact that the prior year financial information was for a full year compared with the current financial information which was for six months. This led to these candidates performing some meaningless comparisons.

25 Hutton plc (June 2015)

Marking guide

				Marks
25.1	Benefits		4	
	Limitations		7	
	Marks available		11	
	Maximum			5
25.2	(a)	**Volume-based supplier rebates**		
		Justification	9	
		Procedures	14	
	(b)	**Inventory**		
		Justification	9	
		Procedures	21	

		Marks
(c)	**Intangible assets**	
	Justification	6½
	Procedures	14
	General	
	Justification	1½
	Procedures	1½
	Marks available	76½
	Maximum	30
Total marks available		35

25.1 Benefits

The benefits of using analytical procedures at the planning stage of an external audit are that they are used to:

- obtain an understanding on the audited entity and its environment
- identify risk areas or areas of potential material misstatement
- identify areas requiring more resources
- indicate areas where detailed testing can be kept to a minimum

Limitations

The limitations of using analytical procedures at the planning stage of an external audit are that:

- substantial knowledge and understanding of the business is required to interpret the results

- sufficient knowledge and understanding may be absent in the first year of an external audit

- an experienced member of staff is required to interpret the results

- the consistency of results from one year to another may hide a material error

- they may be performed mechanically without the application of professional scepticism

- they rely upon good quality information which may not always be available

- they are of limited use if a business is changing (such as rapid growth or decline)

25.2 (a) Volume-based supplier rebates

Justification

This is a complex area with 350 suppliers offering rebate terms ranging from 1% to 15% and contracts that straddle Hutton's accounting year end. The calculation of rebates involves many estimates and judgements.

At 7.9% of revenue the rebates are material.

They have increased from 7.1% to 12.9% of cost of sales. This is very close to the upper end of the rebate range, as only principal suppliers offer rebates. The increase in the level of rebates is inconsistent with the fall in cost of sales of 3.6% and the decline in revenue of 16.3% resulting from difficult trading conditions. All of this suggests a potential overstatement of rebates.

Spreadsheets are used to collate the information and these could be subject to manual error.

Note: Credit given for calculating the expected rebate figure based on the previous year's average rebate rate.

This is:

Expected 7.1% × 1,434 = 102

Actual = 185

Difference = 83

Procedures

- Obtain spreadsheets and sales forecasts used in the calculation of rebates

For a sample of calculations:

- Check calculations for accuracy
- Match details used in the calculations (such as rebate rate, length of contract) to signed supplier contracts

For a sample of sales forecasts:

- Discuss assumptions used in the forecast with sales and purchases managers
- Consider reasonableness of the assumptions used
- Consider whether assumptions are consistent with the expected decline in the number of stores
- Assess the reliability of forecasts by comparison with post year-end management accounts
- Compare rebates recognised to post year-end receipts from suppliers

Other procedures:

- Discuss with the directors the reasons for the increase in supplier rebates in the year
- Ascertain if Hutton is using more suppliers with higher rebates
- Test controls over the:
  - management of spreadsheets
  - preparation of sales forecast (such as any finance department input)
- Obtain management representations regarding the appropriateness of the assumptions used in preparing the sales forecast
- Obtain direct confirmation from suppliers of volumes and contract terms

(b) **Inventory**

Justification

Inventory days have increased from 53.9 to 77.8 (inventory is up by 39%). This is inconsistent with the planned reorganisation involving the closure of stores indicating a potential overstatement of inventory.

Inventory includes smartphones which are susceptible to rapid technological change and soft furnishings which are susceptible to changes in fashion. Trading conditions are difficult and planned store closures may mean inventory items need to be discounted in order to sell. There may be obsolete inventory requiring write down to net realisable value.

The smartphones are desirable items subject to pilferage and the loss may not be reflected in the inventory records.

The inventory system may be recording incorrect balances as a result of:

- website issues
- integration issues with the EPOS system
- inadequate controls over updates to the system for the results of inventory counts

The cost of inventory is adjusted to reflect any volume-based supplier rebates.

Foreign suppliers are paid in local currency and there is the potential for translation errors

Procedures

- Evaluate the work of the internal audit function to assess if its work can be relied upon

- Review reports of internal auditors' attendance at inventory counts:
    - Evaluate the level of discrepancies identified at inventory counts
    - Consider the implications for the reliability of the inventory system

- Plan to attend the 19 June 20X5 inventory counts:
    - Determine coverage of branches following evaluation of internal audit work
    - Evaluate and test controls over inventory count procedures
    - Perform two-way test counts of inventory
    - Identify slow-moving or obsolete items

- Follow up inventory count notes to ensure allowance to reduce inventory to NRV is made for slow-moving or obsolete inventory identified at the count

- Review and vouch key movements in inventory between 19 June and year end

- Evaluate and test controls over updates to the perpetual inventory records from feeder systems

- Match despatch and goods received records with entries in the inventory records to test cut off

- Evaluate and test controls over the preparation of aged-inventory analysis

- Review aged-inventory analysis to identify slow-moving or obsolete items

- For those items in inventory check post year-end selling prices to determine whether net realisable value is less than carrying value

- Discuss basis of allowance to reduce inventory to NRV for slow-moving or obsolete inventory with management

- Sample test cost of inventory to suppliers' invoices

- Review rebate adjustments and consider if they are consistent with spreadsheet calculations

- For a sample of items purchased from overseas suppliers, recalculate the foreign exchange translation and trace the rate used to a reliable independent source.

(c) **Intangible assets – website development costs**

Justification

Website development costs have increased 181.8%. At 1.3% of revenue, the costs are material.

Costs may be capitalised inappropriately resulting in overstatement of costs. For example, training costs associated with the new system or scrapped/abortive costs may be incorrectly included.

The cost of time spent by Hutton's own employees has been estimated by the IT director and there may be insufficient audit evidence to support the estimate. This indicates a potential misstatement of costs.

The determination of the useful life of intangible assets is an accounting estimate and susceptible to misstatement.

ICAEW 2019

Amortisation may not have commenced when the system was ready for use or may not have been appropriately pro-rated for part of the year leading to an incorrect amortisation charge.

The asset may be impaired due to issues with the replacement website.

The prior year balance of £11 million may not have been written down.

Procedures

- Obtain a breakdown of costs and ensure all costs capitalised meet recognition criteria
- Vouch capitalisation of external software costs to contract or purchase invoices
- Ascertain the basis of the IT director's estimate for internal staff costs and consider reasonableness
- Vouch capitalisation of employee costs to employee timesheets, if available
- Confirm with management that 10 years is a reasonable basis for estimated useful life
- Compare useful life to that used by other companies in the industry sector
- Recalculate amortisation charge and check that it has been correctly pro-rated
- Ensure the amortisation policy is correctly stated in the notes to the financial statements
- Discuss functionality of system with staff
- Review correspondence with Sweepweb and confirm whether issues were resolved
- Consider results of testing undertaken by IT auditors
- Inspect evidence of impairment reviews undertaken by management
- Check that any costs relating to the old website have been written off

General

The firm did not audit the prior year financial statements and opening balances may be misstated. Additionally, the figures in the financial statements may be deliberately misstated because of stock market pressure to maintain earnings.

Procedures

- Review outgoing auditor's working papers, if available
- Check opening balances have been brought forward correctly
- Consider if substantive procedures are required

Examiner's comments:

Answers to part 25.1 of this question were of a mixed standard. In respect of benefits, the points most commonly identified were those relating to risk and the targeting of resources to risk areas. In respect of limitations, the points most commonly identified were those relating to the requirement for knowledge of the business and experienced staff to interpret the results of analytical procedures. The points most commonly overlooked were those relating to areas where detailed testing can be minimised and mechanical performance without the applications of professional scepticism. A number of candidates focused on the benefits and limitations of analytical procedures as used at other stages of the audit, which did not address the question and therefore did not score marks. A small number of candidates restricted their answers to setting out the benefits of analytical procedures and did not provide any limitations.

Answers to part 25.2 of the question were generally good. It was pleasing to note that the majority of candidates attempted to make some use of the financial information provided in the scenario, which has been identified as a deficiency in answers in previous examiners' reports. It was also pleasing to note that many candidates cited procedures to address audit risks that were adequately described and relevant to the justification of the audit risk. However, weaker candidates continue to cite vague audit procedures not linked to the audit risk.

Many candidates overlooked that the firm had recently been appointed as external auditor and that obtaining assurance over opening balances may be an issue.

Volume-based supplier rebates

Answers to this part of the question were particularly pleasing as candidates had to consider the risk associated with supplier rebates using 'first principles' rather than listing justifications and procedures that had been rote learned from the learning materials. Most candidates were able to provide a number of reasons to justify why supplier rebates was a key area of audit risk, including making use of analytical procedures to identify that the increase in rebates was inconsistent with the decrease in revenue and cost of sales. Most candidates also correctly identified that it was a complex area (due to the volume of suppliers, range of rebate percentages and contracts straddling the year end), that it relied on estimations in forecasts and that the reliance on spreadsheets to calculate the rebates increased the risk of manual error.

Most candidates identified a number of plausible procedures such as testing the reasonableness of assumptions in the revenue forecasts, agreeing rebate percentages to contracts with suppliers, testing arithmetical accuracy of calculations and evaluating controls over spreadsheets. The most commonly overlooked procedures were:

- enquiring of management why the movement in rebates was inconsistent with the decrease in revenue and cost of sales

- obtaining a written representation from management regarding the appropriateness of the assumptions used in the calculations

- confirming purchase volumes with suppliers

- comparing rebates actually received after the year end to the estimates included in the year-end figure

Inventory

Again, most candidates identified a number of reasons to justify why inventory was a key area of audit risk, including making use of analytical procedures such as calculating inventory days. Most candidates also correctly identified that inventory may not be stated at the lower of cost and net realisable value due to factors increasing the risk of obsolescence, such as the nature of inventory (being technological and fashionable items), competitors undercutting sales prices and the planned store closures. The majority of candidates also correctly identified that the issues encountered with the integration between the systems may give rise to errors as would inappropriate translation of supplier invoices denominated in a foreign currency. A significant number of candidates also cited that the absence of a year-end inventory count increased the risk of misstatement, failing to appreciate that a perpetual inventory system may provide added assurance. These candidates frequently went on to suggest that the auditor demand that the client perform a year-end count, or that the audit firm perform one itself, which would not be appropriate.

The majority of candidates presented a range of relevant procedures. Commonly cited appropriate procedures included the following:

- Attending 19 June 20X5 inventory count and carrying out relevant procedures (such as testing the controls over the count procedures, performing test counts and inspection of inventory for potentially obsolete items)

- Obtaining the aged inventory analysis to identify slow-moving items

- Agreeing costs recorded in the inventory records to supplier invoices
- Performing cut-off procedures

The most commonly overlooked procedures included the following:

- Considering reliance on the work of the internal auditors who had attended a number of inventory counts during the year
- Reviewing post year-end selling prices to ascertain whether items included in inventory were subsequently sold below cost
- Following up items identified as potentially obsolete at the inventory count
- Vouching key movements in inventory between 19 June count and the year end

Intangible assets – website development costs

Answers relating to the justification of audit risk for website development costs were generally good with the majority of candidates identifying a number of appropriate reasons. The most commonly overlooked justifications were those relating to potential impairment resulting from the issues identified with the system during the year, and the prior year balance of £11 million.

Candidates were also able to cite a number of appropriate audit procedures to address the risks, such as vouching external costs to the Sweepweb contract, ascertaining the basis for the IT director's estimate of internal employee costs and obtaining a breakdown of the costs to ascertain whether they met the recognition criteria. The most commonly overlooked procedures were those relating to impairment, such as inspecting evidence relating to management's impairment review, considering the results of any testing undertaken by the internal auditors, discussing the functionality with employees and reviewing correspondence with Sweepweb.

The majority of candidates also appreciated that the determination of the useful life of the asset was subjective and that it would be appropriate to ascertain the basis for the estimate and compare this with that used by other companies in the sector.

26 Haskett Ltd (September 2015)

Marking guide

			Marks	
26.1	(a)	**Revenue**		
		Justification	10	
		Procedures	15	
	(b)	**Property, plant and equipment (PPE) – buses**		
		Justification	6	
		Procedures	19	
	(c)	**Legal claim**		
		Justification	5	
		Procedures	6½	
		Marks available	61½	
		Maximum		25
26.2	(a)	Ownership of Dolphin by Clay McCarthy	15	
	(b)	Haskett being a component of MT Group	13	
		Marks available	28	
		Maximum		10
	Total marks available			35

26.1 (a) **Revenue**

Justification

Draft revenue is 20.5% higher than budgeted revenue and draft gross profit is 20% higher than budgeted gross profit of 17%.

These results are inconsistent with delays in the start of the bus service and suggest revenue is overstated.

Cash:

There is a risk that revenue is understated due to:

- potential for misappropriation of cash receipts
- delays in banking receipts at year end

Contactless card:

There is a risk of misstatement of revenue due to:

- lack of experience in the use of such systems
- no checks on the amounts recorded/remitted by Dolphin
- revenue from Dolphin being incorrectly recorded net of the 12% commission
- internal control deficiencies in the newly-formed company, Dolphin
- potential delays in the transfer of funds from Dolphin at year end

There may be issues regarding obtaining sufficient appropriate evidence if there are problems gaining access to Dolphin's systems.

Season tickets:

There is a risk of inappropriate revenue recognition where season tickets span the year end due to:

- incorrect revenue recognition (ie, recognition in full on receipt)
- errors in calculating the proportion of revenue to defer

Procedures

Discuss with management the reasons for the variance between actual and budgeted figures

Obtain a breakdown of revenue by stream/month to identify any anomalies

Cash:

Ascertain and test controls over the collection and recording of cash on buses

Reconcile amounts recorded on the buses with cash book and bankings

Review after date bank statements for cash banked after year end which relates to pre year-end journeys and check such income is appropriately accrued

Contactless card:

For a sample of daily remittances from Dolphin:

- compare amounts received to journey volume data recorded by card reader/sales reports for reasonableness
- check that revenue is recorded before deduction of 12% commission.

Perform tests of controls at Dolphin or seek assurance from Dolphin's auditor.

Ascertain that any other auditor relied on is:

- independent of Dolphin and Haskett
- professionally competent

Ensure that remittances for journeys taken just before the year end are received and included in the accounting records

Inspect bank statements for remittances, which relate to pre year-end journeys, received from Dolphin after the year end

Season tickets:

Trace bank receipts to revenue/deferred revenue account

Ascertain the basis for calculation of revenue/deferred revenue and consider reasonableness

Re-perform the calculation

(b) **Property, plant and equipment – buses**

Justification

The PPE (buses) balance is 40% above budget suggesting PPE (buses) is overstated or depreciation is understated.

Refurbishment costs capitalised may not meet the relevant criteria, for example, repairs may be incorrectly capitalised.

The estimated useful life of buses may be inappropriate because:

- both refurbished and new buses are being depreciated over 10 years but new buses would be expected to have a longer useful life

- buses may have no use at the end of the eight-year contract.

Buses have not been owned by Haskett for the full year, therefore depreciation may not have been pro-rated correctly.

Buses may not have been depreciated when ready for use if they were ready before 1 February.

The residual value of buses may have been over- or under-estimated.

Procedures

New buses:

- Vouch costs capitalised to invoices/contract with EchoBus

- Ensure that any purchase costs that do not meet capitalisation criteria are excluded

Second hand buses:

- Vouch purchase cost to agreement with MT subsidiary/bank statement

- Vouch to ownership/registration documents

- Select a sample of buses from the asset register and physically inspect and assess their condition

- Inspect management's impairment reviews

Obtain a schedule of refurbishment costs:

- Ensure costs included are capital in nature/meet IAS 16 Criteria
- Vouch time spent on refurbishment by employees to timesheets
- Vouch materials costs to purchase invoices

Compare the value attributed by Haskett to second-hand buses with similar-aged buses on the market

Compare the useful life of buses to other buses in MT group/other similar companies

Consider whether significant profits/losses arise on disposal of buses in the group

Enquire of directors:

- The basis of estimated useful life
- The reason why refurbished buses have the same useful life as new buses
- Reasons the useful life extends beyond the length of the eight-year contract
- The basis of estimates of residual value.

Recalculate depreciation ensuring that charges are pro-rated correctly

(c) Legal claim against Haskett

Justification

The £250,000 claim represents 2.8% of revenue and 46.5% of profit before tax and is therefore material.

The absence of a provision or disclosure may be inappropriate. If the claim is probable to succeed a provision should be recognised. If the claim is possible to succeed a disclosure should be included in the financial statements.

A contingent asset may not be offset against a liability as this does not comply with IFRS.

Procedures

Ascertain from the directors of Haskett the reason for not including a provision/disclosure in the financial statements

Review the contracts between Haskett and the government body and EchoBus to ascertain the terms/penalties for any breach

Review correspondence with Haskett's legal advisers to determine the likely outcome of the claim(s)

Review correspondence with the Government body and EchoBus to determine the likelihood of settlement

Review board minutes regarding any developments surrounding the claims, such as an out of court settlement

Obtain a written representation from management regarding its intention to settle/fight the claim against Haskett

26.2(a) The ownership of Dolphin by Clay McCarthy

Dolphin appears to be a related party of Haskett as it is controlled by Clay McCarthy who is a key manager at Haskett. Transactions between Haskett and Dolphin are material by nature and therefore require disclosure in the financial statements. There may be a risk of non-disclosure if Haskett's management is unwilling to disclose such transactions. The 12% commission charge appears high and transactions may not be on an arm's length basis.

The auditor will require a written representation from management that disclosure of related party transactions is complete and it will need to include audit procedures in the audit plan to verify the adequacy of related party disclosures. The component auditor will need to disclose such transactions to the group auditor.

Sufficient, appropriate evidence over transactions may be difficult to obtain given the need to rely on information from Dolphin in light of Haskett's internal control deficiencies surrounding transactions with Dolphin.

There is an increased risk of fraudulent behaviour and consequently a need for increased scepticism which must be discussed by the engagement team during planning.

(b) **Haskett being a component of MT Group**

The component auditor will need to involve the group auditor in its risk assessment at the planning stage as there may be additional risks identified by the group auditor. Instructions will be issued by the group auditor setting out its requirements and the materiality thresholds relevant to the group audit. The component auditor may need to carry out additional audit procedures to address any risks identified by the group auditor and will need to confirm to the group auditor that its instructions have been followed.

The group engagement team may be involved in the work of the component auditor and the timing of audit procedures will need to take into account the timetable for reporting set by the group auditor.

The form of communications/report required by the group auditor must be confirmed and the component auditor will need to report significant issues/risks to the group auditor, such as:

- Evidence of management bias
- Any non-compliance with laws/regulations or suspected fraud
- Related party transactions (ie, amounts received from Dolphin)
- Intra-group transactions (ie, sale of buses to Haskett)
- Information regarding the legal claim(s)
- A list of uncorrected misstatements

The component auditor should also consider whether its subsequent events review will need to be extended to cover any gap between signing the auditor's report on Haskett's financial statements and the date of the auditor's report on the group financial statements.

Examiner's comments:

General comments

This was the least well answered of the long-form questions. Part 26.1 was generally well answered with the majority of candidates providing justifications of the key risks along with suitable audit procedures. However, a significant minority of candidates failed to appreciate that Haskett was a newly-formed company and wasted time citing procedures in relation to opening balances and obtaining prior year working papers from the previous auditor, which were not relevant. Answers to part 26.2 were disappointing, particularly in relation to the implications of Haskett being a component of the MT group.

Part 26.1

It was pleasing to note that the majority of candidates attempted to make use of the financial information provided in the scenario, appearing to have taken on board points raised in previous examiners' commentaries. While the majority of candidates appreciated that budgeted information was provided (in the absence of prior year figures) a significant minority of candidates wasted time citing procedures to test the accuracy of the budgeted figures.

Revenue

Most candidates provided a number of reasons to justify why revenue was a key area of audit risk, including making use of basic analytical procedures. However, only stronger candidates identified that the actual figures presented were inconsistent with the delay in starting the bus service. Candidates who structured their answers around the three revenue streams (cash, contactless cards and season tickets) tended to produce better answers than those who took a scattergun approach. The most commonly overlooked justifications were in relation to the contactless card – that there may be issues for the auditor in gaining access to Dolphin's system and that revenue may have been incorrectly recorded net of the 12% commission deducted by

Dolphin. The most commonly overlooked audit procedures were those relating to reliance on Dolphin's auditor to gain assurance over the contactless system and the independence and professional competence of that auditor. The majority of candidates correctly identified that revenue recognition issues may arise in relation to season tickets. However, fewer candidates appreciated that cut-off issues might arise in relation to cash and contactless payments if amounts were banked or remitted to Haskett after the year end.

Property, plant and equipment (PPE) – buses

Most candidates provided a number of reasons to justify why PPE – buses was a key area of audit risk and made use of basic analytical procedures. The most commonly overlooked justifications were:

- the risk of buses being assigned an inappropriate useful life given both refurbished and new buses were depreciated over the same 10-year period and that buses may not have any use at the end of the eight-year government contract

- The possible over- or under-estimation of residual values

The most commonly overlooked procedures were:

- vouching of ownership documents

- inspecting management's impairment reviews

- comparing the useful life of the buses to those used by similar companies and consideration of whether there were significant profits or losses on the disposal of buses in the group

- enquiring of management why refurbished buses have the same useful life as new buses and why the useful life of 10 years extended beyond the eight-year government contract

- enquiring of management the basis of the estimated residual values

In respect of the audit procedure for testing the existence of the buses, a number of candidates lost marks by incorrectly stating that the sample of physical buses should be selected and traced to the asset register instead of selecting a sample from the asset register and verifying the buses' existence.

The majority of candidates correctly identified that some costs may be inappropriately capitalised as part of the refurbishment of buses acquired from other MT subsidiaries. However, fewer candidates earned the marks for vouching the capitalised costs to invoices and timesheets.

Legal claim against Haskett

Most candidates recognised that the legal claim was material but only stronger candidates were able to provide further reasons to justify why the legal claim was a key area of audit risk. The most commonly overlooked justifications were relating to whether the claim should be disclosed or provided for depending on whether the outcome was either possible or probable. Generally, most candidates identified some appropriate audit procedures to address the risk. A number of candidates cited, in general terms, a relevant audit procedure (eg, review board minutes) but didn't earn the marks available for explaining the relevance of that procedure (ie, a review of board minutes would provide information on developments such as an out of court settlement). A number of candidates wasted significant amounts of time discussing the going concern implications of the legal claim which was outside the scope of the requirement.

Part 26.2

Answers to part 26.2 were disappointing with answers to section (a) being of a higher standard than section (b). A number of candidates did not attempt section (b) or presented very short or irrelevant answers and therefore failed to score any marks for this section.

In respect of section (a), those candidates who correctly identified that Dolphin was a related party of Haskett then went on to score reasonably well. However, a significant minority of candidates failed to identify the related party issue. The points most commonly cited, having identified Dolphin as a related party, were that related party transactions are material in nature and therefore disclosures are required in the financial statements. Stronger candidates were then able to set out some further matters to consider as part of the audit planning such as the need to obtain written representations. The points most commonly overlooked were those relating to the difficulty in obtaining evidence for related party transactions, the need for the audit team to increase professional scepticism and appropriate discussion of issues by the engagement team during audit planning.

In respect of section (b), the points most commonly identified by stronger candidates were those relating to risks identified by the group auditor, materiality thresholds, the timetable for the audit and the need to report significant issues to the group auditor. However, few candidates were able to provide examples of the significant matters that need to be reported to the group auditor. The point most commonly overlooked was that relating to the extension of the subsequent events review to cover any gap between signing the auditor's report on Haskett's financial statements and the auditor's report on the group financial statements. Weaker candidates were often unable to set out any matters to consider as part of audit planning arising from Haskett being a component of MT Group. A significant number of weaker candidates wasted time setting out irrelevant ethical threats (eg, conflict of interest, self-interest, familiarity and self-review) and safeguards to mitigate those threats (eg, information barriers) failing to appreciate the nature of the relationship between the component auditor and the group auditor, including the fact that the audit teams were part of the same audit firm. Candidates who had an awareness of the contents of ISA (UK) 600 produced significantly better answers to this part of the question.

Section 3: Concluding and reporting on engagements

27 Short form questions

27.1 Incorrect classification last year

- Comparatives form part of financial statements
- But no opinion on comparatives as such
- No effect on current year figures
- If comparatives not adjusted, should consider implications for report
- If comparatives adjusted and adequately disclosed, opinion not modified

27.2 Breach in company policy

Consequences

- Duplicate orders
- Use of unauthorised suppliers
- Terms/prices negotiated with unauthorised suppliers generally less favourable
- Purchase of unauthorised non-business goods and services
- Goods may not be to appropriate standards or requirements
- May result in breach of budgets and loss of control by buying department
- Invoices may not be entered in purchase ledger, resulting in understated liabilities

Recommendations

- All significant purchase orders over pre-determined limit to be placed by buying department except for small orders (say under £1,000)

- Employees in breach of company procedures to be informed in writing

- Circulate company policy to all staff, and staff to confirm in writing that they understand company policy

- All suppliers to be informed in writing of company policy

27.3 Matters to be considered

- Check opening balances correctly brought forward

- Review client working papers for prior year

- Check appropriateness of accounting policies/accounting policies consistently applied year to year

- Any changes appropriately accounted for/disclosed

- Substantive work on opening balances (where no alternative available)

- State in auditor's report that comparative figures not audited (ISA (UK) 710)

- Ensure disclosure of lack of audit in prior year in financial statements

- Integrity of accounting system/strength of control environment

27.4 Further information and why required

(1)
- Amount of cheque confirms balance outstanding
- Cheque received, banked and posted after year end
- To confirm as acceptable timing difference in conclusion

(2)
- Provided for at year end = acceptable timing difference
- Not provided for = error in conclusion of test
- Whether isolated occurrence or not
- For need to extrapolate or not in conclusion

27.5 **Effect on auditor's report**

Fletcher Ltd

- Qualified opinion
- 'Except for'
- Inability to obtain sufficient appropriate audit evidence

Dervish Ltd

- Disclaimer of opinion
- Unable to form opinion on true and fair

Both

- Description of circumstances/amounts

27.6 **Going concern**

- Going concern is fundamental underlying assumption
- Assumption that business can continue operating for foreseeable future

(1) • Disclosure of:

  - statement of relevant facts
  - nature of concern
  - assumptions made in using going concern basis
  - plans and actions taken

(2) • Statement that accounts not prepared on going concern basis ie, prepared on a break up basis

  - Assets written down to recoverable amounts

  - Liabilities re-assessed

  - And reclassified from long to short term

27.7 **Subsequent events review**

- Consider whether provision in place

- Whether any monies re amount outstanding received from Gamlec since reporting period date

- Correspondence from liquidator/likelihood of receipts

- Whether any additional goods despatched to Gamlec

- Whether liquidation of major customer will impact on going concern status of Beacon/provides evidence of problems in the industry

27.8 **Effect on auditor's report**

- Unmodified opinion if note considered adequate
- Material Uncertainty related to Going Concern paragraph
- Drawing users' attention to note
- Statement that opinion not modified in this respect
- If note inadequate or disagree with basis of preparation – modified opinion

27.9 **Whether to rely on written representation**

- Internal controls in place over cash sales/segregation of duties
- Whether independent analytical review of GP%/reconciliations
- Whether GP% in line with industry sector
- Integrity/attitude of MD/well informed
- Lifestyle of MD in relation to stated income
- Whether audit testing consistent with representations

27.10 Why investigate further

- Cash book may have been left open after year end (inappropriate cut-off)/overstatement of cash/impact on trade receivables collection period
- Management to be informed of delay in banking
  - Poor cash management/cash flow
  - Teeming and lading

27.11 Actions

- Discuss with directors the inconsistency between directors' report and auditor's understanding of the entity
- Ascertain if there is a legitimate reason for the inconsistency
- if the auditor's understanding is incomplete or incorrect, then consider whether further audit evidence needs to be obtained in relation to trade payables
- If there is no legitimate reason for the inconsistency, ask the directors to change the directors' report
- Bring the matter to the attention of the audit partner
- If issue cannot be resolved through discussion, ask directors to seek legal consultation
- Notify directors in writing of concerns/document reasons
- Obtain own legal advice
- Use right to be heard at AGM to notify shareholders of inconsistency
- In extreme, might consider resignation and circulation of statement of circumstances

Implications for auditor's report

- Auditors are required to include a section headed "Matters on which we are required to report by exception"
- The auditor should describe the misstatement regarding Bomburst's compliance with suppliers' payment terms in this section

27.12 Matters included

- Responsibility of management – to prepare the financial information
- Responsibilities of practitioner
  - To provide limited assurance
  - Financial information free from material misstatements
  - Limited to enquiries and analytical procedures
  - Not an audit
  - Do not express an audit opinion
  - Reference to standards/criteria (eg, ISRE 2400 *Engagements to Review Historical Financial Statements*)
- Conclusion
  - Expressed negatively
  - 'Nothing has come to our attention that causes us to believe that the accompanying financial statements do not give a true and fair view'
- Disclaimer of responsibility – do not accept or assume responsibility to anyone other than the company

27.13 Issues arising and actions regarding adjusting subsequent event

- Liquidation of customer is a material adjusting subsequent event
- The audit firm has no responsibility to search for subsequent events after the auditor's report is issued but needs to consider action where it becomes aware of material facts affecting the financial statements
- The firm should discuss with management its intentions regarding any amendments to the financial statements
- Perform procedures to ascertain if any amount is recoverable, eg, review correspondence with liquidators
- Carry out procedures to ascertain the impact of a loss of major customer on the going concern presumption
- If management amend the financial statements the firm should undertake audit procedures in respect of those amendments and reissue the auditor's report accordingly on the new financial statements
- If management refuse to amend the financial statements and auditor agrees then no further action is necessary
- If the auditors consider the financial statements are no longer true and fair in the absence of any amendments they should request that management do not issue the financial statements
- If management do issue the financial statements then the auditors need to prevent reliance by the shareholders on the audit opinion
- Auditors could use their right to speak at the company's AGM
- Or resign and have written representations circulated to shareholders
- Auditors should also obtain legal advice if the directors refuse to make necessary amendments

27.14 Auditor's responsibilities, in the UK, with respect to forming and reporting their opinion on the directors' report

- Auditor should read other information in annual report including the directors' report
- Both the Companies Act 2006 and ISA (UK) 720 *Other information* require the auditor to state in its report on the company's annual accounts whether, in its opinion, the information given in the directors' report is consistent with the financial statements
- Where the information given is consistent the auditor should state this in the 'Other information' section
- Where the auditor's opinion is that the directors' report contains an uncorrected material misstatement, then the auditor should explain the nature of the inconsistency in the 'Other information' section

27.15 Comments

Failure to disclose a material related party transaction results in a material misstatement in the preparation of the financial statements

Therefore, the audit opinion should be modified with a qualified (except for) opinion, and the reason for the material misstatement in the auditor's report should give details of the related party transaction

An emphasis of matter paragraph is used where the auditor considers it necessary to draw users' attention to a matter which is presented correctly in the financial statements but where the audit opinion would not be qualified in respect of the matter in the emphasis of matter paragraph

The audit junior's suggestion is therefore unsuitable, an emphasis of matter paragraph is not appropriate

27.16 Consequences

- Assets recorded in the register may not exist or may have been stolen
- Assets in existence, acquisitions or disposals may not be recorded
- Incorrect capital allowances may be claimed
- Assets may be fully written down but still in use and consequently undervalued
- Assets may be impaired or no longer in use and consequently overvalued
- Depreciation charges on assets may be inappropriate
- Resulting in misstatements in the financial statements

Recommendations

- Regular/monthly/quarterly reconciliation of register and assets

    - Physical to register to ensure completeness of recording
    - Register to physical to ensure existence and in good condition

- Reconciliation to be performed independent of custodian
- Differences to be reported and investigated
- Train staff on how to carry out procedures
- Monitoring of procedures to ensure checks undertaken

27.17 Consequences

Delays in invoicing weakens the cash flow of the business and may result in future cash flow difficulties or issues over going concern

There is an increased risk of non-payment by clients once invoicing has taken place or that invoicing will never take place

This will lead to reduced profitability and may damage the company's relationship with clients if invoicing is persistently late

Recommendations

Implement and communicate to all staff a company policy regarding the amount of time that is acceptable between handing over of a project to a client and the client being invoiced

Require that project managers notify the accounts department immediately when a project is handed over to a client

Introduce a system of stage payments throughout projects, particularly for long projects

Account managers should hold monthly meetings with the finance director to assess the level of unbilled work in progress

The finance director should review an analysis of aged work in progress on a monthly basis

Regular monitoring to ensure procedures are followed

27.18 Consequences

The quality of raw materials may be inappropriate
Dawn may not benefit from most favourable prices
Absence of an approved supplier list increases scope for fraudulent acts by staff ordering goods

Recommendations

Compile an approved supplier list by researching price lists of suppliers for best rates, quality of products from each supplier, availability of bulk purchase discounts, suppliers' ability to meet delivery requirements

Final supplier list to be approved by senior management

Communicate approved supplier list to staff responsible for ordering

Require that when orders are authorised the supplier is checked against the list and any instances of non-compliance are notified to management

Take disciplinary action where staff are found to have ordered from suppliers not on the list

Supplier performance to be monitored and the approved supplier list to be updated on a regular basis

27.19 Procedures

Assess whether warranty claims are consistent with management expectations by inspecting post year-end:

- Customer correspondence
- Board minutes
- Goods returned records
- Records of repair costs
- Amounts paid/refunds under warranty

Internet searches for evidence of issues with products

Obtain written representation from management

27.20 Consequences

- Loss of revenue/profits
- Adverse impact on cash flow
- Inconsistent pricing could lead to customer dissatisfaction
- Overpayment of sales staff if remuneration is target driven
- Collusion between customer and staff/kickbacks

Recommendations

- Employees to be made aware of the importance of adhering to company policy
- Any 'extra' discount (to clinch a sale) to be authorised by sales manager
- Monitoring of procedures to ensure adherence
- Breaches to be investigated and staff disciplined
- If relevant, limit controls on tills to prevent discounts above authorised levels

27.21 Highlight inconsistency to management/Chairman

- Ascertain reasons for inconsistency determining whether financial statements or Chairman's statement require revision

- If inconsistency due to error in financial statements firm may need to modify its audit opinion

- If inconsistency due to error in Chairman's statement should request client to amend Chairman's statement

- If client amends – no further action required

- If client refuses to amend:

    - Inform those charged with governance

    - Describe the misstatement of the Chairman's statement in the 'Other information' section of the auditor's report

    - Seek legal advice

    - If matter considered extreme, withdraw from engagement or withhold auditor's report

    - Speak to members at AGM

27.22 £50,000 difference between carrying amount and sale proceeds

    = 11.1% of profit before tax
    = 5.1% of total assets

therefore material

- Indicative of impairment at year end/conditions at year end therefore adjusting event
- Represents material misstatement
- Modified opinion/qualified/except for opinion
- Isolated to one area therefore matter is not pervasive

27.23 The difference of £25,000 between cost and net realisable value (NRV) is:

- 11% of PBT
- 5.1% of TA
- Therefore material
- Adjusting subsequent event
- Provides evidence of conditions at year end
- Material misstatement/overstated assets
- Modify/qualify audit opinion/except for
- Not pervasive
- Confined to specific elements of financial statements

Examiner's comments:

Answers to this question were generally good with many candidates scoring maximum marks. The majority of candidates correctly calculated that the inventory was overstated by £25,000, resulting in a material misstatement. They then correctly identified that as the matter was confined to a specific element of the financial statements, that is was not pervasive and therefore a qualified (except for) opinion was appropriate. The points most commonly overlooked were adjusting subsequent event and evidence of conditions at the year end.

27.24 **Intended use of prospective financial information (PFI)**

- To ensure there are no unforeseen users of the PFI

- Which could impact on the risk associated with the engagement or the extent of the reporting accountant's liability

Completeness of significant management assumptions

- Facts/knowledge regarding assumptions for PFI will be largely confined to management

- Reporting accountant cannot undertake examination of PFI unless all assumptions are adequately disclosed

- Reporting accountant reports on 'reasonableness' of assumptions and therefore needs confirmation they are complete

Management accepts responsibility for PFI

- Reduces expectation gap/avoids misunderstandings regarding responsibilities
- The reporting accountant is not responsible for preparation of PFI

Answers to this question were very disappointing as the majority of candidates misread the question and answered in terms of the role of written representations in a statutory audit of financial statements, instead of the examination of prospective financial information. Consequently, they listed the requirements of ISA (UK) 580 *Written Representations* for which no marks were awarded. The minority of candidates who were familiar with the contents of paragraph 25 of ISAE 3400 *The Examination of Prospective Financial Information*, often scored full marks as once they listed the required representations they generally demonstrated an understanding of why they were needed, particularly in respect of limiting the reporting accountant's liability and reducing the expectation gap.

27.25 Consequences

- Non-current assets may not be acquired on the most favourable terms
- Leading to negative impact on cash flow and profits
- Quality issues/may not be fit for purpose
- Use of suppliers who give kickbacks

Recommendations

- Independent review of quotes by senior management
- Approval of purchase order/expenditure by senior management not involved in acquisition of non-current assets
- Employees reminded of company policy/training of staff
- Disciplinary action for failure to adhere to company policy
- Monitor procedures to ensure compliance

Examiner's comments:

Many candidates scored maximum marks on this question. Most candidates appreciated that the failure to apply the company's policy of obtaining three quotes before acquisition of a non-current asset could result in overspending and as such would have an adverse impact on profits and cash flow. However, a significant number cited fraud as a risk but failed to explain how it could be perpetrated. No mark was awarded for identifying fraud as a risk if there was no elaboration. In respect of the recommendations, most candidates identified the need to remind employees of the company policy and disciplinary procedures for breaches. The most common shortcoming in respect of the recommendations was the tendency to cite the converse of the deficiency without any elaboration. For example, many cited 'Three quotes to be obtained' without specifying how the company could be assured that the procedure was being followed.

27.26 Auditor's report

- Addressed to members/shareholders
- Conducted in accordance with ISAs
- Reasonable/high assurance
- Positive opinion as to whether:

    - FS give true and fair view/free from material misstatement
    - prepared properly in accordance with relevant reporting framework
    - prepared in accordance with CA06

- Signed in name of senior statutory auditor
- Opinion as to whether directors' report consistent with FS

Report on examination of PFI

- Addressed to management
- Conducted in accordance with ISAE 3400
- Restricted distribution
- Limited/moderate assurance
- Negative expression of statement as to whether the assumptions provide a reasonable basis for PFI
- Opinion as to whether:
  - Forecast properly prepared on basis of assumptions
  - Presented in accordance with relevant financial reporting framework
- Caveat re achievability of results
- Signed in name of firm

Examiner's comments:

This question was generally well answered. The most common misunderstanding was to cite the differences between the two engagements instead of the reports. For example, many candidates cited that the audit is based on historical financial information and the examination of prospective financial information is based on forecasts. There were no marks for these points.

27.27 Actions firm should take

- Discuss reasons for inconsistency with directors
- Ascertain if error/material misstatement arises in FS or directors' report
- If material misstatement in FS consider whether further audit procedures required
- Request FS/directors' report corrected
- Document further audit procedures/resolution

Potential implications for auditor's report

- If error in directors' report and is:
  - Corrected, no impact on auditor's report
  - Not corrected:
    - (1) Include a section headed "Opinions on other matters prescribed by the Companies Act 2006" which describes the inconsistency between the directors' report and the financial statements
    - (2) If there is a misstatement in the directors' report, include a section headed "Matters on which we are required to report by exception" which describes the misstatement in the director's report
- If material misstatement in FS and is:
  - Corrected, no impact on auditor's report
  - Not corrected:
    - (1) Modify audit opinion on FS
    - (2) Consider if reporting by exception required under CA06

Answers to this question were very disappointing as most candidates failed to consider whether it was the directors' report or the financial statements that needed amending. The vast majority incorrectly assumed that failure to correct the inconsistency must result in a modified opinion on the financial statements. Candidates did not appreciate that if there is an error in the directors' report, the financial statements are not misstated and, consequently, there would be no need to modify the opinion on the financial statements. In such circumstances, the auditor's responsibility is discharged by reporting on the inconsistency between the directors' report and the financial statements. A significant number stated, incorrectly, that if the directors do not amend the directors' report the auditor should refer to the issue in an emphasis of matter paragraph. These candidates fail to appreciate that an emphasis of matter paragraph is only used to draw users' attention to a matter disclosed in the notes to the financial statements.

27.28 Consequences of an inappropriate audit opinion

- Professional negligence claims
    - From the bank
    - If a duty of care owed
    - Damages may be payable
    - Legal costs incurred
    - Firm may be protected by a Bannerman paragraph or
    - Material Uncertainty related to Going Concern paragraph
    - Professional indemnity insurance premiums may rise

- Subject to greater scrutiny by the regulators (eg, ICAEW)
    - Disciplinary procedures
    - Fines or withdrawal of registered auditor status

- Loss of reputation
    - Loss of clients and key staff
    - In extreme cases financial collapse of the firm

- Criminal proceedings if auditor's report was issued recklessly (Companies Act 2006)

This question was generally well answered with a significant number of candidates scoring full marks.

The majority of candidates identified the possibility of legal action by the bank and investigation by regulators. Most of these candidates then proceeded to list the possible outcomes relating to these actions such as damages awarded against the firm, disciplinary procedures and reputational issues. The points most commonly overlooked were those relating to increased costs of professional indemnity insurance and the inclusion of Material Uncertainty related to Going Concern paragraph in the auditor's report.

27.29 Actions to take, with reasons

- Report to Money Laundering Reporting Officer (MLRO) within the firm
- Money laundering reporting officer to report to National Crime Agency
    - Represents proceeds of crime
    - Criminal offence if auditor does not report
    - No *de minimis* limit with money laundering
    - Appears to be disguising within accounting records

- Do not tip off
    - As this might prejudice legal proceedings
    - Tipping off is a criminal offence
- Consider impact on other areas of the financial statements
- Reconsider assessment of management's integrity.

Examiner's comments:

This question was generally well answered as the majority of candidates identified that the situation described in the question represented money laundering. Consequently, most candidates proceeded to cite the reporting responsibilities of the audit junior and the firm. Only a minority of candidates identified that tipping off might prejudice legal proceedings and that there was no *de minimis* in respect of amounts relating to money laundering.

27.30 Actions firm should take

- Assess whether misstatements are material in aggregate/by nature
- Consider whether there are any other misstatements
- Revise audit plan/perform further procedures
- Communicate misstatements to management/request misstatements corrected
- Perform audit procedures on any changes made
- Document:
    - Amount below which misstatements considered trivial
    - Accumulated misstatements
    - Conclusion regarding materiality of uncorrected misstatements
- Obtain written representation from management that the effect of uncorrected misstatements is immaterial

Examiner's comments

This question was well answered as most candidates identified that the individually immaterial items should be aggregated to determine whether they were material in aggregate and that they should be communicated to management. However, few candidates considered whether this was indicative of other misstatements and whether the audit plan needed revision. Only a minority of candidates identified the need for a written representation that the effect of uncorrected misstatements is immaterial. A number of candidates strayed beyond the requirement and wasted time describing the various audit opinions that might be provided, failing to appreciate that the requirement related to actions to be taken before reaching the audit opinion.

27.31 Ascertain what explanations were obtained by audit team for GP% fall. Consider whether these are consistent with understanding of client/market. Inspect evidence indicating explanations were corroborated.

Ensure that risks of error were appropriately tested, such as:

- cut off errors
- misclassification of expenses
- overstatement of revenue/understatement of costs

27.32 External auditor's reports on the financial statements of listed companies (which are required to apply the UK Corporate Governance Code) have to provide additional information about the audit work performed in line with ISA (UK) 701 *Communicating Key Audit Matters in the Independent Auditor's Report*.

Auditors of listed companies are required to apply ISA (UK) 701 *Communicating Key Audit Matters in the Independent Auditor's Report*. ISA (UK) 701 requires them to make disclosures about the audit process.

Additional information

- Descriptions of the key audit matters. These are the matters of most significance to the audit. The description must include:

    - the overall audit strategy
    - the allocation of resources in the audit
    - directing the efforts of the engagement team (ISA (UK) 701: para. 11)

- Why the matter was considered a key audit matter, and how it was addressed (ISA (UK) 701: para. 13).

- The most significant assessed risks of material misstatement, and the auditor's responses and key observations in relation to these risks (ISA (UK) 701: para. 13R-1).

- An explanation of how the auditor applied the concept of materiality in planning and performing the audit (ISA (UK) 701: para. 16-1):

    - The materiality threshold for the financial statements as a whole
    - An overview of the audit scope

- A statement on the audited entity's compliance with the relevant provisions of the UK Corporate Governance Code.

Benefits to users

- Provides greater information, as the auditor's report is specific to each company

- Narrows the expectation gap by giving greater information about the work of the auditors

    - Eg, identifying areas where the auditor made critical judgements.

Examiner's comment

Answers to this question were disappointing with a number of candidates failing to score any marks because they either did not attempt an answer or presented incorrect answers. Many candidates just listed, incorrectly, the information that is included in all auditors' reports instead of the **additional information** required for listed companies applying the UK Corporate Governance Code and ISA (UK) 701. The disclosure requirements of auditor's reports on the financial statements of listed companies required to apply the UK Corporate Governance Code are covered in the Audit and Assurance Study Manual. A number of candidates did not attempt this question.

28 Progear Inc (December 2009)

			Marks
28.1	Increase in revenue	3	
	Fall in gross profit margin	4	
	Increase in operating expenses	4	
	Reduction in inventory days	4	
	Reduction in receivables days	5	
	Maximum		13
28.2	Title and addressee	1	
	Restriction on use	3	
	Subject matter	1	
	Respective responsibilities	2½	
	Scope of work	4	
	Level of assurance	1	
	Conclusion	1	
	Details of reporting accountant	½	
	Maximum		7
Total marks available			20

28.1 Matters to discuss with the financial controller include the following:

Reason for 9% increase in revenue and why this is out of line with previous years.

Whether due to:

- any new customers/marketing campaign/wider product range
- change in income recognition policy or cut off errors

Reason for fall in gross profit margin to 16.5% from 19% and why less than standard margin of 20%.

Whether due to:

- increase in number of customers entitled to discount
- understatement of inventory as inventory days have fallen

Reason for increase in operating expenses as a % of sales (13.9% from 13.2%) or alternatively the fall in operating margin to 2.5% from 5.8%.

Whether due to:

- more customers taking advantage of early payment discount
- higher selling costs to achieve revenue growth
- any new or one-off expenses

Reason for reduction in inventory days to 40.6 from 43.7 days.

Whether due to:

- more efficient management of inventory
- understated inventory/cut off errors

Reason for reduction in receivables days to 27.7 days from 29.9 days.

Whether due to:

- more customers taking advantage of early payment discount
- improved credit control procedures
- possible understatement of receivables/cut off errors (eg, after date cash treated as received in year)

28.2 **Main components of the report**

- Title and addressee: ie, *Independent Review Report* to Progear Inc

- Restriction on use: a statement to the effect that the report is made solely to the company, and to the fullest extent permitted by law the firm does not accept or assume responsibility to anyone other than the company

- Subject matter: ie, the financial information for the six months ended 30 September 20X9

- Respective responsibilities of management for preparing and the reporting accountant for reviewing the financial information

- Scope of the work: limited to enquiries of company personnel and applying analytical and other review procedures. There should be a statement that an audit has not been performed and that an audit opinion is not expressed. There may be a reference to any standards under which the review has been conducted for example, ISRE 2400 *Engagements to Review Historical Financial Statements* or ISRE 2410 *Review of Interim Financial Information Performed by the Independent Auditor of the Entity.*

- Level of assurance: moderate/limited assurance that financial statements are free from material misstatement

- Conclusion: expressed negatively in the form of 'nothing has come to our attention....'

- Details of reporting accountant including name, signature and address and the date of the report

Examiner's comments:

General comments

Answers to this question attained the second highest average mark on the written test section of the exam. On the whole, candidates performed better on part 28.1 of the question.

Part 28.1

This part of the question was generally well answered. Strong candidates calculated the change in revenue, profit margins and inventory and receivables days and then identified enquiries to be made of management. The inventory and receivables days were sometimes calculated for the full year instead of, more correctly, for the six-month period. Candidates who relied on the calculation of more straightforward percentage changes in the key financial data given in the question scored less well. Pleasingly, a number of candidates identified that the increase in revenue coupled with the fall in gross profit margin might be due to more customers taking advantage of discounts. A number of candidates identified that the inventory had increased over the previous year but failed to appreciate that inventory days had fallen and consequently wasted time writing about the possibility of slow-moving and obsolete inventory. Similarly, a number of candidates failed to appreciate that receivables days had fallen and failed to link the fact to the possibility that more customers might be taking advantage of the early payment discount.

Part 28.2

Answers to this part of the question were mixed. The best candidates laid out the framework or key headings of the report required and provided a description of the contents using information in the scenario. Lower scoring answers focussed on outlining the headings of the report without tailoring the contents to a review engagement. For example, many just cited management's responsibility without describing that its responsibility was to prepare the financial information. Furthermore, many just cited scope of work without referring to analytical procedures and enquiries of management. Many failed to specify that a review was not an audit and that an audit opinion was not expressed. A significant number of candidates were not

29 Gourmet Ltd (December 2011)

Marking guide

		Marks
29.1 Receipts		
Sales receipts	4	
Loan from bank	2	
Payments		
Expenditure on refurbishment and vehicles	2½	
Payments to suppliers	1½	
Vehicle running costs	1	
Premises running costs	2½	
Wages and salaries	2	
Sundry payments	2	
Loan repayments and finance costs	2½	
Tax payments	1½	
Dividend payments	1	
General	1	
Marks available	23½	
Maximum		10
29.2 Role of written representations	2	
Evidence provided	4	
Marks available	6	
Maximum		3
29.3 Forecast information	5	
Audit of financial statements	2½	
Reasons	3	
Marks available	10½	
Maximum		7
Total marks available		20

29.1 Receipts

Sales receipts

These should include sales from the new outlets and delivery service which should be staged to reflect the roll out. The inflow should reflect prior years' patterns and, in respect of the new outlets, commence after the completion of the refurbishment. Consideration should be given as to whether amounts are prudent in light of the economic conditions and whether the introduction of the delivery service may impact on take away sales.

Loan from bank

The amount should be consistent with any negotiations, as evidenced by bank correspondence, be sufficient to cover the expansion costs and the inflow should be included before commencement of the new business.

Payments

Expenditure on refurbishment and vehicles including logo painting

These should be based on suppliers' price lists or quotes and the outflow should be reflected before the commencement of the new business.

Payments to suppliers for ingredients and packaging

These should reflect the level of forecast sales and payments for items other than fruit and vegetables should reflect the suppliers' terms of trading.

Vehicle running costs

These should be based on the proposed number of vehicles and the anticipated usage following the introduction of the delivery service.

Premises running costs

These should include the extra costs (eg, rent and utility costs relating to the two new outlets). The rent should reflect the terms of any lease agreements such as up-front premiums and rental periods (eg, quarterly) and rent reviews.

Wages and salaries

These should reflect the increased number of staff for the new outlets, the drivers for the delivery service and rates above the industry sector. Any bonus should be based on the forecast profit.

Sundry payments

These should include advertising, training and recruitment costs relating to the new business and the outflow should be reflected before the commencement of the new business. Professional fees should include payments to the legal advisers and the reporting accountant.

Loan repayments and finance costs

Loan instalments should reflect the repayment terms being negotiated with the bank and finance costs should reflect market rates and the level of borrowings. All outflows in respect of these items should be reflected on the anticipated due dates.

Tax payments

PAYE, VAT and corporation tax should be consistent with the relevant figures in the profit forecast and paid on due dates.

Dividend payments

These should be in line with prior years' policies or take into account any anticipated changes in policy which should be confirmed by the directors.

General

Sensitivity analysis should be undertaken on key variables eg, customer receipts, finance costs and ingredients.

29.2 Role of written representations

When conducting an engagement to examine forecast information, written representations are obtained from management regarding:

- the intended use of the forecast information;
- the completeness of significant management assumptions; and
- management's responsibility for the forecast information.

The representations provide evidence that management accepts its responsibility regarding the assumptions and will reduce the risk of any misunderstanding regarding respective responsibilities (ie, narrow the expectation gap). The representation regarding the intended use of the forecasts may protect the reporting accountant from claims for damages from unforeseen third parties.

29.3 Forecast information

The conclusion of the assurance report on the forecast information will include a statement of negative assurance (ie, limited/moderate assurance) in the form of 'nothing has come to our attention which causes us to believe that the assumptions do not provide a reasonable basis for the forecast'. It will also include an opinion on whether the forecast information is properly prepared on the basis of the assumptions and is presented in accordance with the relevant financial reporting framework.

Audit of financial statements

The opinion in the auditor's report on financial statements will provide reasonable assurance that the financial statements:

- give a true and fair view;

- have been properly prepared in accordance with relevant generally accepted accounting practice; and

- have been prepared in accordance with the requirements of the Companies Act 2006.

Reasons

Financial statements are mainly based on historical information whereas forecast information is based on assumptions about future events. The historical information can be verified to a greater degree whereas the forecasts are subject to uncertainty.

Examiner's comments:

Answers to part 29.1 of the question were mixed. Weaker candidates incorrectly discussed non-cash related items such as accounting for depreciation, the distinction between capital and revenue items and cut-off issues. Another common error was to overlook the fact that the work involved examining a **forecast** and consequently cite verification procedures that would be undertaken on historical cost financial information such as checking amounts to invoices and bank statements. Some candidates, while identifying relevant receipts and payments, were unable to identify matters to be considered when reviewing the reasonableness of the assumptions underlying those receipts and payments and simply made comments such as 'check if reasonable' or 'check if they accounted for it correctly'. These points are too vague to be awarded any marks.

Answers to part 29.2 of the question were disappointing as many candidates were unaware of the requirement of ISAE 3400 *The Examination of Prospective Financial Information* to obtain such representations. Many candidates wasted time and wrote about the role of written representations in an audit of financial statements instead of their role in examining and reporting on forecast information. Although many identified management's responsibility for the forecast information, surprisingly few mentioned reduction of the risk of misunderstanding regarding respective responsibilities. A small number of candidates mistakenly thought that written representations were produced by the reporting accountant and tended to confuse them with the contents of a letter of engagement.

Part 29.3 of the question was generally well answered as the majority of candidates cited the basic points regarding the different levels of assurance provided by the conclusions within each report and gave an example of each. However, only a minority of candidates could provide plausible reasons why the conclusions were different. Many failed to indicate that audits of financial statements are based on historical information while forecasts are based on assumptions about future events and that consequently the figures in forecast information could not be corroborated to the same extent as with historical information. Weaker candidates strayed beyond the requirement and wasted time writing about the differences between the reports as a whole, instead of focusing on the **conclusions** in each of the reports.

30   Kipo Ltd (March 2013)

Marking guide

			Marks
30.1	Consequences	5½	
	Recommendations	9	
	Marks available	14½	
	Maximum		7
30.2	Management's explanation inadequate	5	
	Assurance provided	3	
	Assurance report	5	
	Marks available	13	
	Maximum		8
30.3	Quality of management representations	6	
	Addressing internal control deficiencies	6	
	Marks available	12	
	Maximum		5
Total marks available			20

30.1 Consequences

The control deficiencies identified give rise to potential loss of revenue and profits, a negative impact on cash flows of the Cambridge restaurant and the risk of inaccurate recording of revenue.

This arises from the opportunity for fraudulent conduct by staff through giving discounts when no voucher is presented or entering discounts on the cash till but charging customers full price and keeping the difference.

The manual calculation of the discounts increases the risk of incorrect amounts being deducted as discounts which could result in loss of customer goodwill if discounts given are too low.

Fraud or error when recording discounts may go undetected as a result of not reconciling discounts given with the vouchers presented each day.

Recommendations

The cash till should be programmed to automatically discount sales by 5% using a discount button.

The input of discounts into the till should be authorised by senior members of staff.

The cash till should record the level of discounts entered and authorised by each member of staff.

Discount vouchers presented by customers should be kept in the till and reconciled daily to the value of discounts recorded in the till.

The restaurant manager should review and sign the reconciliation.

The restaurant manager should regularly review the level of discounts given by each member of staff to identify any staff appearing to give excessive discounts.

Staff should be trained in new procedures which should also be monitored for compliance.

30.2 Management's explanation of the decrease in revenue at the Cambridge restaurant is inadequate as it does not explain the 12% decrease in the Cambridge restaurant net revenue given the vouchers only allowed a 5% discount.

The internal control deficiencies around the use of discount vouchers also give rise to doubts regarding the accuracy of the recording of net revenue at the Cambridge restaurant and means the firm is unable to obtain sufficient appropriate evidence (limitation on scope) regarding the level of revenue or any material misstatements that have arisen.

The firm is therefore unable to provide any assurance on the level of revenue for the Cambridge restaurant. However, it is able to provide assurance in respect of the other three restaurants and consequently the matter is not considered pervasive.

The assurance report should explain the circumstances in respect of the Cambridge restaurant and provide a qualified conclusion (except for). The conclusion will provide limited assurance which will be expressed negatively in the form:

'Except for the financial effects of any adjustments that might have been determined to be necessary had we been able to satisfy ourselves as to the revenue of the Cambridge restaurant, nothing has come to our attention that causes us to believe.'

30.3 The inability of management to explain adequately the 12% decrease in net revenue at the Cambridge restaurant raises questions over management competence and integrity as it may be deliberately understating revenue to achieve reduced lease rentals. The firm may not be able to rely on management representations or explanations and may no longer wish to be associated with the client due to the risk to its own reputation.

The firm should consider whether management intends to address the internal control deficiencies identified as a failure to address them could lead to an inability to obtain sufficient appropriate evidence (limitation on scope) during the 20X3 engagement. The firm should not accept an engagement where there is a known limitation on scope.

If management do intend to address the deficiencies identified, the firm should consider whether the internal controls implemented are effective.

The firm should also consider the impact on its relationship with the management of Kipo if it issues a qualified conclusion in respect of the 20X2 engagement.

Examiner's comments:

Answers to this question attained the lowest overall average in the written test section of the exam. However, answers to part 30.1 attained the highest average score for any part of the written test questions but answers to parts 30.2 and 30.3 significantly reduced candidates' overall performance in this question, particularly part 30.3 which attained the lowest overall average for any part of a question in the written test section of the exam.

Part 30.1 of the question was very well answered with many candidates being awarded maximum marks. Candidates were able to identify the consequences of the internal control deficiencies described in the scenario and make practical and relevant recommendations to remedy the deficiencies. Many candidates wasted time repeating the same consequences for each internal control deficiency which did not earn any extra marks. The most commonly overlooked consequence was regarding the failure to perform daily reconciliations between the vouchers presented and discounts recorded in the till meaning that any fraud or errors in discounts would go undetected. The most commonly overlooked recommendation was that relating to the review of reconciliations and the monitoring of compliance with the new procedures.

Answers to part 30.2 of the question were generally weak. Stronger candidates correctly identified that management's inability to offer an adequate explanation of the 12% decrease in revenue at the Cambridge restaurant represented an inability to obtain sufficient appropriate evidence (limitation on scope). These candidates scored highly by then correctly explaining the implications of this for the firm's assurance report and report conclusion. Weaker candidates did not identify this issue and therefore tended to earn marks only for explaining that the nature of the assurance engagement meant only limited assurance could be provided and that it would be expressed negatively.

Answers to part 30.3 of the question were very disappointing with only the very strongest candidates attempting to relate the issues directly to the scenario presented. Stronger candidates did correctly outline issues around management competence and integrity in light of their inability to explain the 12% decrease in the Cambridge restaurant revenue and also considered whether or not management intended to implement the recommended control procedures. However, few of even the strongest candidates appreciated that the firm should not accept an engagement where there is a known inability to obtain sufficient appropriate evidence (limitation of scope) or considered the impact on the firm's relationship with Kipo if a qualified conclusion was given in 20X2. Weaker candidates listed general engagement acceptance considerations, such as ethical issues, resourcing and fees, for which there were no marks available, as these matters would have been considered before accepting the 20X2 engagement.

31 Hattie Ltd, Moon plc (March 2014)

Marking guide

				Marks
31.1	(a)	Key purposes of obtaining written representations		
		1 mark per point		
		Marks available	9	
		Maximum		5
	(b)	Hattie	7	
		Vector	8	
		Marks available	15	
		Maximum		9
31.2	**Implications for audit opinion**			
		Significant uncertainty	2½	
		Claim is possible	2	
		Firm not satisfied with disclosure	3	
		Claim is probable	4	
		Marks available	11½	
		Maximum		6
Total marks available				20

31.1 (a) Written representations are a source of audit evidence required to be obtained by ISA (UK) 580 *Written Representations*. They provide evidence that management has fulfilled its responsibilities with respect to the financial statements and has made all relevant information available to the auditor. Written representations are also used to support other audit evidence. Failure to provide written representations may indicate the existence of significant issues such as lack of management integrity. Written representations are likely to be more reliable than oral representations from management and they help to avoid confusion or misunderstandings over matters discussed during the audit. They provide documentary evidence of management's plans or intentions and judgements that have an impact on the financial statements.

(b) **Hattie**

The audit opinion should be modified as the refusal to provide written representations means the auditor is unable to obtain sufficient appropriate audit evidence (limitation on scope). The issue is material and pervasive as the possible effects are not confined to specific elements, accounts or items in the financial statements.

ISA (UK) 580 *Written Representations*, requires the auditor to issue a disclaimer of opinion. The disclaimer will be headed up 'Disclaimer of opinion on financial statements....' and an explanation of the reasons for the disclaimer of opinion will be given immediately after the disclaimer paragraph in the 'Basis for disclaimer of opinion on the financial statements' paragraph.

Under the Companies Act 2006 the auditor is also required to report by exception that:

- not all information necessary for the audit was obtained; and

- the auditor was unable to determine whether adequate accounting records have been kept.

Vector

The audit opinion should be modified. The administration of Perkins is an adjusting subsequent event as it indicates conditions existing at year end. It is doubtful that Vector will receive payment and the amount should be provided for. The irrecoverable amount is 2.2% of total assets and 12.7% of profit before tax and is, therefore, material.

A material misstatement has arisen but it is not pervasive as it is confined to a specific element of the financial statements. The opinion will be qualified (except for) and headed up 'Qualified opinion due to material misstatement...'. The reasons and amounts involved will be included in the 'Basis of qualified opinion' paragraph, immediately after the opinion.

31.2 The claim represents a significant uncertainty. The amount is 1.2% of total assets and 10.5% of profit before tax and is therefore material. The implications for the audit opinion depend on the expected outcome of the claim and whether or not the accounting treatment is appropriate.

If the claim is only **possible** to succeed the issue should be disclosed in a note to the financial statements. If the firm is satisfied with the adequacy of the disclosures made by the directors then an unmodified opinion should be issued.

However, if the firm is not satisfied with the adequacy of the disclosures made, a material misstatement arises which is not pervasive as it is confined to a specific disclosure. The firm should modify the audit opinion with a qualified ('except for') opinion.

If the claim is **probable** to succeed the amount should be included as a provision in the financial statements. The directors have only included a note and therefore a material misstatement arises. The firm should modify the audit opinion. As the amount is not pervasive, because the issue is confined to a specific element of the financial statements, a qualified (except for) opinion should be issued.

Examiner's comments:

This was the least well answered of the written test questions due to generally poor performance by candidates in part 31.1 (a) and part 31.2. However, part 31.1 (b) was well answered. Candidates generally failed to make use of the open text in part 31.1 (a) and failed to **discuss** potential outcomes for the audit opinion in part 31.2.

Part 31.1

(a) Answers to this question were very disappointing as only a minority of candidates scored full marks. Many candidates did not appear to be familiar with the contents of ISA (UK) 580

Written Representations, which is available in the open text. Most candidates stated, correctly, that the purpose of obtaining written representations is to confirm that management has fulfilled its responsibilities with respect to the financial statements and the provision of information to the auditor. Only a minority of candidates were able to cite the purposes of obtaining documentary evidence of matters discussed during the audit particularly in respect of management's judgements and plans for the business. Weaker candidates confused the purpose of written representations with the role of the engagement letter and wasted time writing about the expectation gap.

(b) **Hattie**

The majority of candidates identified that the circumstances represented a limitation on scope and warranted a modified opinion. However, a significant number of candidates were unaware that paragraph 20 of ISA (UK) 580 *Written Representations*, requires a disclaimer of opinion to be issued in these circumstances and proceeded to hedge their opinions. A significant number of candidates overlooked the responsibility, under the Companies Act 2006, to report the matter by exception.

Vector

This part of the question was very well answered. Most candidates attained the marks available for identifying the issue of material misstatement, calculating and commenting on materiality and reaching a correct conclusion on whether or not the opinion should be modified. Disappointingly, a number of candidates continue to confuse the purposes of an emphasis of matter paragraph with the basis of a modified opinion paragraph.

Part 31.2

Answers to this part of the question were disappointing. Many candidates failed to **discuss** the types of opinion that could be issued depending on whether or not the auditor agreed with the accounting treatment. Furthermore, most candidates failed to consider whether the accounting treatment as a contingent liability was appropriate and, consequently, did not consider whether the liability should be recognised as a provision. The majority of candidates strayed beyond the requirement to discuss the implications for the audit **opinion** and wasted time describing the implications for the auditor's **report**.

32 Mansard plc, Gable Ltd, Hip Ltd (June 2014)

Marking guide

			Marks
32.1	(a)	**Bribery prevention policies**	
		Consequences	9
		Recommendations	5
	(b)	**Employee references**	
		Consequences	4½
		Recommendations	2½
	(c)	**Not following accounting policies**	
		Consequences	7
		Recommendations	5
		For all the above communication, confirmation, disciplinary action and monitoring	2
	Marks available		35
	Maximum		13

	Marks
32.2 Gable	
Disagreement over accounting treatment	2
Disagreement over recoverable receivables	2
Effect on audit opinion	6½
Hip	
Limitation of scope	3
Effect on audit opinion	4
Marks available	17½
Maximum	10
Total marks available	23

32.1 (a) **Bribery prevention policies**

Consequences

The Bribery Act 2010 makes bribery or failing to prevent bribery a criminal offence. The Bribery Act is global in scope and makes the company responsible for the actions of its employees. The company is liable if employees or persons associated with the company offer or accept or bribe a foreign public official. The absence of policies means that employees do not know what to do or how to proceed if they suspect bribery. The penalties for bribery or failing to prevent bribery are severe and include imprisonment.

The risk of bribery is heightened as new overseas offices are opening which require licences to trade and this may require interaction with foreign public officials. Additionally, office managers have a strong incentive to win business because of the bonus structure in place.

The financial results of the company may be adversely affected. There could be additional expenses arising through the payment of bribes, the cost of any fines or penalties imposed by the authorities and the cost of legal fees to resolve any bribery issues. There may be adverse publicity if bribes are offered or accepted leading to a reduction in sales. Ultimately, the going concern status may be threatened as the company may have its licence to trade revoked.

Furthermore, external auditors have a duty to report suspicions of bribery to NCA.

Recommendations

- Document and implement bribery prevention policies

- Introduce a whistleblowing policy and procedures for reporting bribery

- Appoint a designated person responsible for compliance

- Government (Ministry of Justice) guidelines which set out the principles on which policies should be based, ie:

  - Proportionate procedures to mitigate risks
  - Top level commitment/anti-bribery culture
  - Risk assessment to identify bribery
  - Due diligence procedures
  - Embedded culture of bribery prevention
  - Making improvements to procedures when necessary

(b) **Employee references**

Consequences

Employees that lack the appropriate skills or qualifications for the role leading to poor quality work may be hired. This may result in additional staff training and development costs.

Employees who lack integrity or have criminal backgrounds may be hired leading to the theft of assets.

Employees may have falsified information about past roles or their identity. For example, the company may be breaking the law by hiring employees who do not have the right to work in the UK and this could leave the company legally exposed and result in fines.

Recommendations

- Obtain references for all staff

- Ensure at least two references are obtained with at least one from a previous employer

- All offers of employment should be made subject to satisfactory references and formal approval by management

(c) **Not following accounting policies**

Consequences

Monthly returns and head office management accounts are unreliable and management may make decisions based on incorrect information. Furthermore, the year-end financial statements and published unaudited interim results could be materially misstated.

The company may pay bonuses that have not been earned and may overpay tax on profits resulting in lower profits and an adverse impact on cash flow.

Recommendations

- Standardised monthly returns to be completed which set out the basis of preparation

- The returns should be signed by the local office manager who should confirm compliance with company policies

- The returns should be reviewed by a designated member of staff at head office and significant variances against budget investigated

In all of the above scenarios the following recommendations apply:

- Communication of procedures and staff training
- Staff to sign to confirm that they will comply with the policy
- Disciplinary action if procedures are not followed
- Regular monitoring of procedures by senior management

32.2 Gable

There is a disagreement over accounting treatment in respect of the plant leading to an overstatement in the financial statements. The amount represents 2.89% of profit before tax and 0.52% of total assets and is not material.

There is a further disagreement over the level of recoverable receivables. The amount represents 4.14% of profit before tax and 0.74% of total assets and is not material.

The aggregate effect of the misstatements must be considered. The aggregated amount represents 7.03% of profit before tax and 1.26% of total assets which is above lower materiality thresholds but not pervasive as it is confined to specific elements in the financial statements. This represents a material misstatement. The audit opinion should be modified with a qualified 'except for' opinion and the opinion paragraph headed up 'qualified opinion on financial statements'. An explanation of the matter giving rise to the qualification should be included in the 'basis for qualified opinion' paragraph immediately after the opinion paragraph.

Hip

As a result of the managing director's refusal to give the firm permission to contact the customer to confirm the outstanding balance and as there are no alternative audit procedures available to establish the existence of the debt, the auditor is therefore unable to obtain sufficient, appropriate evidence (limitation on scope). The value of the unpaid balance is £170,000 being 11.33% of profit before tax and 3.26% of total assets. This is material but not pervasive as it is confined to specific elements in the financial statements and any error is unlikely to represent a substantial proportion of the financial statements.

The audit opinion should be modified with a qualified 'except for' opinion and the opinion paragraph headed up 'qualified opinion on financial statements'. An explanation of the matter giving rise to the qualification should be included in the 'basis for qualified opinion' paragraph immediately after the opinion paragraph. Following the opinion paragraph, the auditor should also report by exception under the Companies Act 2006 that all information required for the audit was not obtained.

Examiner's comments:

This was the second highest scoring question on the exam but was mainly due to a number of excellent answers on part 32.2.

Part 32.1

There was a range of answers to this question. Most candidates were able to outline a number of the consequences of failing to have bribery prevention policies in place (Scenario 1) and the lack of references (Scenario 2) and provide a number of suitable recommendations. However, generally, candidates did not cope as well with the failure to follow accounting policies (Scenario 3). The most common omission in Scenario 1 was in respect of the six principles relating to bribery prevention demonstrating a lack of knowledge of the contents of section 5.7 in Chapter 2 of the Audit and Assurance Study Manual. Other common omissions related to the heightened risk due to the opening of overseas offices and the bonus scheme in operation and the need for external auditors to report suspicions of bribery. A common omission in Scenario 2 was that formal approval to appoint a new employee is required and, in Scenario 3, common omissions were that returns should be standardised and should be reviewed with variances against budget investigated.

Part 32.2

It was pleasing to note that this part of the question was very well answered with a significant number of candidates scoring maximum marks. Those candidates that did not score well demonstrated either a disappointing lack of knowledge and understanding of how and when to modify audit opinions or displayed evidence of time pressure. Common errors on Gable included candidates incorrectly stating that the error would be considered pervasive on the grounds that more than one area of the financial statements was misstated or failing to aggregate the two issues and therefore concluding that no modification to the audit opinion was required. Common errors on Hip included recommending that an emphasis of matter paragraph was appropriate for the limitation on scope and failing to net off the amounts already received by Hip thereby incorrectly calculating the error on gross figures.

33 Speedy Shifters plc, Letterbox Group Ltd (December 2014)

			Marks
33.1 (a)	**No approved supplier list**		
	Consequences	2½	
	Recommendations	5	
(b)	**No business continuity plan**		
	Consequences	3½	
	Recommendations	5	
(c)	**Truck drivers exceed legal limit for driving hours**		
	Consequences	4	
	Recommendations	4	
(d)	**Internal audit plans and monitoring**		
	Consequences	5½	
	Recommendations	5	
	Marks available	34½	
	Maximum		14
33.2 (a)	Implications for the auditor's report	8	
(b)	Appropriate for firm to continue to act as external auditor	5	
	Marks available	13	
	Maximum		6
Total marks available			20

33.1 (a) No approved supplier list

Consequences

Poor quality parts may be purchased resulting in damage to trucks and long periods of downtime while trucks are repaired. The company may pay higher prices for parts and there is an increased scope for fraudulent acts by those ordering parts (for example, kickbacks from suppliers). The above points will lead to an adverse impact on profits and cash flow.

Recommendations

- Compile an approved supplier list by researching:
    - Suppliers' prices for best rates
    - Quality of products from each supplier
    - Availability of bulk purchase discounts
    - Suppliers' ability to meet delivery requirements

- The final list to be approved by senior management/directors
- Communicate the approved supplier list to those responsible for ordering
- When ordering, the supplier should be checked against the approved supplier list
- Suppliers' performance should be monitored
- Update approved supplier list regularly

(b) **No business continuity plan**

Consequences

A systems failure could result in the loss of accounting data and management information. Employees may not be aware of their responsibilities in the event of a systems failure. This will hinder the efficiency of operations such as payment of suppliers and the invoicing of customers. Customer and supplier goodwill will be damaged leading to a loss of reputation impacting on future trading. Furthermore, there will be additional costs involved in recovering data, thereby reducing profits. Ultimately, the going concern status may be at risk and the company could cease trading.

Recommendations

- Business continuity plans, specifying interim arrangements, should be as follows:
  - In place/fully documented
  - Communicated to employees
  - Approved by the audit committee
  - Periodically tested to ensure works as intended
  - Reviewed and updated as the needs of the business change

- Responsibility for every task to be assigned to an individual or outsourced to a service provider

- Computer files to be backed up on a regular basis

- Backup stored at a separate location

- Insurance should be sufficient to facilitate recovery and cover loss of profits

(c) **Truck drivers exceed legal limit for driving hours**

Consequences

This may result in accidents, fines and litigation. The company may be in breach of insurance terms and conditions. If the purpose of breaching the legal limit for driving hours was to save costs, the company could be considered to be involved in money laundering. The above could result in loss of reputation and an adverse impact on profits and cash flow. Ultimately going concern issues may arise if, for example, the company loses its license to trade.

Recommendations

- Make more driving resource available by recruiting more drivers or using a service provider

- Reports detailing drivers hours produced on a regular basis

- Monitoring of reports by Head Office

- Communicate policy to depot managers and drivers

- Make a whistleblowing facility available

- Disciplinary action for non-compliance

(d) **Internal audit plans and monitoring**

Consequences

The failure to approve internal audit plans means that there is no independent scrutiny in advance of planned internal audit work.

This may mean that the scope of internal audit work does not cover all of the company's operations or that inappropriate internal audit work is undertaken. There is an increased risk that deficiencies in internal control may not be identified resulting in a higher risk of fraud and error. All of these consequences may be indicative of a weak control environment.

The failure to monitor the effectiveness of the internal audit function may mean that the function is ineffective or represents poor value for money. The internal audit function may be under or over resourced and planned internal audit work may not be completed. External audit may not choose to rely on work completed by the internal audit function leading to increased costs.

Recommendations

- Annual work plan should be scrutinised and agreed by the audit committee, before the commencement of work

- Audit committee to monitor its own performance, for example, to see if it is complying with its own terms of reference

- Agree performance indicators for internal audit such as the following:

    - Work done compared with plan
    - Time spent compared with plan
    - Number of recommendations accepted by management
    - The number of qualified staff
    - Feedback forms for completion by the areas reviewed by internal audit

- Monitor performance indicators on a regular basis

- Feedback to the internal audit function on areas for improvement

33.2 (a) **Implications for the auditor's report**

The results of Pampas represent 12.5% of the consolidated profit before tax which is material. Management has imposed a limitation on scope of the audit by refusing to grant access to the accounting records of the South American subsidiary and disclose information about its activities. The auditor is therefore unable to obtain sufficient appropriate audit evidence about the subsidiary. The implications for the auditor's report depend on whether the matter is considered to be pervasive. If the matter is considered to be pervasive because it affects a substantial proportion of the consolidated financial statements, the auditor will disclaim an opinion as a qualification would be inadequate to communicate the gravity of the situation. However, if the matter is not considered to be pervasive as it is confined to specific elements of the consolidated financial statements, the audit opinion will be modified with an except for opinion. In both cases, the matter should be explained in a basis for (qualified or disclaimer of) opinion section after the opinion section. The auditor should report by exception under the Companies Act 2006 that all information required for the audit was not obtained.

(b) **Appropriate for your firm to continue to act as external auditor**

The group auditor is responsible for the audit opinion on the consolidated financial statements even though the component is not audited by the group auditor. The management imposed limitation on scope could cast doubt on the directors' integrity and if this persists then the firm should withdraw from the 20X4 audit. However, this may not be practical because the audit may be substantially complete as management imposed the limitation on scope sometime after Pampas was acquired on 1 November 20X4, eleven months after the start of the financial year. In this case the auditor would issue the auditor's report with a qualified or disclaimer of opinion. For the 20X5 audit, if the firm has representation in South America, the external auditors should ask the directors of Pampas if they are willing to appoint the firm as component auditors. If the directors refuse and the limitation on scope persists the firm should not seek re-appointment.

Examiner's comments:

This was the second highest scoring long-form question but was mainly due to a number of excellent answers on part 33.2. Disappointingly, a number of candidates presented incomplete answers to this question.

Part 33.1

Generally, candidates were better at identifying the consequences of the internal control deficiencies than providing recommendations. Most candidates were able to outline a broad range of possible consequences and provide some suitable recommendations for the absence of supplier lists (Scenario 1), no business continuity plans (Scenario 2) and exceeding the legal limit for driving (Scenario 3). However, the standard of answers in respect of the lack of approval of internal audit plans and monitoring of the internal audit function (Scenario 4) was disappointing.

The most common omissions in Scenario (1) were that preferred supplier lists should be compiled by researching suppliers' prices, suppliers' ability to meet delivery requirements and the quality of products. The most common omissions in Scenario (2) were that the continuity plan should be approved by the audit committee and be periodically tested. In Scenario (3) most candidates stated that driving hours should be monitored but did not identify who should undertake the monitoring and that the driving policy should be communicated to all employees, failing to appreciate that the driving policy is only relevant to drivers and their management. These answers were too vague to be awarded any marks. In Scenario (4) most candidates struggled to provide any consequences other than inappropriate work may be undertaken and that there was a weak internal control environment. Most candidates were unable to identify any relevant recommendations such as identifying suitable performance indicators for use by the audit committee to monitor the performance of the internal audit function. A significant number of candidates failed to appreciate the distinction between governance and management or understand the roles of an internal audit function and an audit committee and how they interact with each other. Consequently, there were a number of inappropriate recommendations such as management approving internal audit plans or management supervising and taking disciplinary action against the audit committee which did not score any marks.

Part 33.2

Part (a) of this question was very well answered by the majority of candidates. Most candidates correctly recognised that the results of the subsidiary were material to the consolidated financial statements, that management had imposed a limitation on scope and that the implications for the auditor's report depended on whether the matter was considered to be pervasive. These candidates then correctly stated that the auditor would report by exception because they would not have been able to obtain all the necessary information for the audit. A small number of candidates incorrectly recommended including an emphasis of matter paragraph in the auditor's report and some candidates incorrectly stated that as there had been a disagreement with the directors an adverse opinion was appropriate.

Answers to part (b) were of a mixed standard. The majority of candidates recognised that the imposed limitation on scope could cast doubt on the directors' integrity and that the firm should therefore resign from the audit. Only a small number of candidates were aware of paragraph A13 of ISA (UK) 705 *Modifications to the Opinion in the Independent Auditor's Report* which discusses the practicality of withdrawing from an audit that is substantially complete. A number of candidates digressed into the discussion of bribery or money laundering for which there were no marks available.

34 Rescue24 (September 2015)

			Marks
34.1 (a)	**Collection boxes**		
	Consequences	3	
	Recommendations	6½	
(b)	**Veterinary drugs**		
	Consequences	2½	
	Recommendations	3	
	Marks available	15	
	Maximum marks		7
34.2	Identify and explain status of Rescue24		
	Marks available	13½	
	Maximum marks		7
34.3 (a)	Make appropriate disclosures	4½	
(b)	Do not make disclosures	4	
	Marks available	8½	
	Maximum marks		6
Total marks available			20

34.1 (a) Collection boxes

Consequences

Cash donations are susceptible to misappropriation and errors in the counting proceeds may not be identified.

If a collection box is not returned, Rescue24 will be unable to determine which one is missing or to hold collectors accountable for specific collection boxes.

Rescue24 will be unable to identify which are the most effective collectors or collecting locations.

This will have a negative impact on revenue and cash flows

Recommendations

Collection boxes should be sealed with a tamper-proof seal and sequentially numbered.

Collectors should sign for a numbered collection box when taken. A record should be kept of which collector has which box and in which location and all collection boxes should be checked in when returned at the end of the collecting period.

Proceeds should not be counted by collectors but should be counted and recorded by two people in the presence of the collector who should be given a receipt for the amount collected.

Proceeds should be banked promptly and an independent reconciliation of amounts recorded and amounts banked should be undertaken.

(b) **Veterinary drugs**

Consequences

There is an increased risk of theft of drugs and Rescue24 may be unable to treat animals if drugs run out unexpectedly.

Contravention of the requirements of the VMD may lead to fines or disciplinary action including loss of licence or closure.

This will have a negative impact on profits and cash flows.

Recommendations

Install a lockable secure container which is fixed to the floor/wall.

Keys or security codes should only be made available to those with authority to use drugs and the keys should be stored securely or security code changed on regular a basis.

A record of drugs in/out should be maintained and any movements signed for.

Regular inventory checks should be performed comparing the quantity of drugs in the container with the records.

34.2 Rescue24 is in a net liability position posing the risk that it may be unable to meet debts as they fall due.

Expenditure exceeds income resulting in an inability to generate cash to cover Rescue24's activities.

Rescue24 has faced difficulties raising funds through traditional activities as well as suffering from a decline in government funding which means it is unlikely to be able to rely on these sources of funding in future.

The trustees failed to promote a crowdfunding campaign or recruit any employees with crowdfunding experience. Consequently, the campaign was unsuccessful and no funds were raised. It appears unlikely that new sources of funding will be identified quickly.

Rescue24 is reliant on its overdraft facility which is repayable on demand and could therefore be withdrawn. An overdraft is an expensive form of funding and interest payments will put a strain on cash flow.

The bank loan is secured on Rescue24's only premises. If Rescue24 defaults on the loan payments or breaches covenants the bank may call in the loan and seize the property. The charity will be left with no base for its operations.

Three of the five trustees and the fundraising manager resigned. There may be insufficient expertise to continue with Rescue24's activities and there may be a possible breach of its constitution. There is no fundraising expertise left in the organisation and it may be difficult to recruit new employees in view of the present difficulties.

As a result of non-compliance with the VMD requirements, Rescue24 may be at risk of losing its licence and any resulting fines will exacerbate its present cash flow issues.

34.3 (a) **Make appropriate disclosures**

There is no material misstatement and no limitation on scope, therefore an unmodified audit opinion with a modified auditor's report will be issued. A paragraph headed 'Material Uncertainty Related to Going Concern' will be included immediately after the opinion section to draw users' attention to the matter disclosed in the financial statements as the issue is fundamental to users' understanding of the financial statements. A statement that the opinion is not modified in respect of the uncertainty should be included.

(b) **Do not make any disclosures**

There is a material misstatement due to the lack of appropriate disclosure and therefore a modified opinion/report is required. If the matter is considered material (but not pervasive) a qualified opinion (except for) will be issued. If the matter is considered material and pervasive an adverse opinion will be issued. The auditor's report will include a section headed 'basis for qualified opinion'/'basis for adverse opinion', describing the matter giving rise to the modification.

Examiner's comments

General comments

This was the best answered long-form question with candidates scoring higher marks on parts 34.1 and 34.3 compared to part 34.2. A significant minority of candidates' answers for this question were very short suggesting that time management had been an issue for them.

Part 34.1

Deficiency (1)

This part of the question was generally well answered as most candidates identified that donations may be stolen or collection boxes could be lost and that these risks could be mitigated by sealing and numbering the buckets. It was pleasing to note that the majority of candidates appreciated the need for dual control during counting and segregation of duties between collecting and counting/recording. The points most commonly overlooked were those relating to the negative impact on revenue and cash flow and the need to reconcile amounts recorded with amounts banked.

Deficiency (2)

Most candidates identified that drugs could be stolen and that the entity could face fines or even lose its licence to operate as a result of the breach in regulatory requirements and that these risks could be mitigated by storing the drugs in a lockable container with restricted access. The points most commonly overlooked were those relating to the adverse impact on profits and stockouts. A number of candidates merely stated that Rescue24 should comply with VMD requirements and consequently failed to earn the marks available for describing how the procedures might work.

Part 34.2

This part of the question was generally well answered as the majority of candidates provided a range of factors that indicated uncertainty about the going concern status. However, many candidates were unable to provide plausible explanations as to why those factors indicated an uncertainty about the going concern status. For example, the vast majority of candidates identified the reliance on the overdraft facility as a factor but only a minority appreciated that this was an expensive form of funding which would have an adverse impact on cash flow and that the facility could be withdrawn at any time. A number of candidates incorrectly cited that the overdraft (rather than the bank loan) was secured on the premises.

Part 34.3

Although many candidates scored maximum marks on this part of the question, a significant number of candidates' answers were very disappointing. This stemmed from the fact that these candidates did not read the question carefully. The question was based on the assumption that the firm had concluded that there was an uncertainty about the going concern status. However, these candidates assumed that the financial statements had been prepared on an inappropriate basis and consequently reached inappropriate conclusions in respect of the audit opinion. In part (a), a significant minority of candidates demonstrated that they are not clear on the difference between a modified report and a modified opinion which meant they scored fewer marks. In addition, many candidates failed to point out that the uncertainty surrounding going concern was fundamental to the users' understanding of the financial statements and did not score the mark available for this point. In part (b), weaker candidates were not able to deal with the fact there were two potential options for the audit opinion depending on whether the absence of the disclosure was considered material or material and pervasive. Consequently, answers became muddled and difficult to follow resulting in fewer marks being awarded.

35 Mint Ltd, Coriander Ltd, Basil Ltd

Marking guide

		Marks
35.1 Mint	6	
Coriander	3½	
Basil	5½	
Marks available	15	
Maximum		11
35.2 **Consequences**		
Professional negligence claims	2½	
Investigation by regulatory bodies	1½	
Adverse publicity	3½	
Quality control procedures		
Recruitment and training	1	
Competent and experienced staff	1½	
Consultation	2	
Engagement quality control review	1½	
Due diligence	1	
Marks available	14½	
Maximum		7
Total marks available		18

35.1 Mint

A modified opinion should be issued which should be a qualified (except for) opinion due to inability to obtain sufficient appropriate audit evidence, as evidence reasonably expected to be available is not available. 7% of revenue is material but not pervasive as it is confined to specific elements in the financial statements. Reference to the inability to obtain sufficient appropriate audit evidence should be made in the 'basis for qualified opinion' section of the auditor's report which should explain the reasons and state the amounts involved. The auditor should also report by exception under the Companies Act 2006 that:

- adequate accounting records were not maintained; and
- all information required for the audit was not obtained.

Coriander

There will be no modification to the audit opinion. The liquidation of the customer and subsequent sale of inventory is an adjusting subsequent event, providing additional evidence of the value of inventory at the year end. The inventory should be valued at net realisable value (NRV), because it is lower than cost. However, the difference between the cost and NRV is £300,000 and is not material as it is only 2.3% of profit before tax and 0.77%

of total assets. Even if the directors refuse to amend the financial statements in respect of the misstatement over the accounting treatment, the audit opinion will not be modified.

Basil

A modified opinion should be issued which should be a qualified ('except for') opinion. As the managing director refuses to disclose the transaction there is a material misstatement. The amount of the transaction is not material by size as it is only 0.25% of gross assets. However, it is material by nature as it is a related party transaction because Saffron is owned and managed by the husband of Basil's managing director. It is not pervasive as it is confined to a specific item in the financial statements and is not fundamental to the users' understanding of the financial statements. There should be an explanation of the issue (reason and amount involved) in the 'basis for qualified opinion' section of the auditor's report.

35.2 Consequences

The firm may be subject to professional negligence claims from the audited entity and its shareholders and/or third parties where it can be demonstrated that the auditor owed the party a duty of care. Although damages awarded against the firm may be covered by professional indemnity insurance, the cost of future insurance will increase.

The firm may be investigated by the regulatory bodies, which may result in disciplinary action and penalties such as fines or withdrawal of registered auditor status.

The adverse publicity associated with legal claims and disciplinary procedures may result in the loss of clients and key staff may leave the firm. There will be an increase in costs for the firm as a result of greater scrutiny. In extreme cases this could lead to the financial collapse of the firm.

Quality control procedures

The firm should have robust procedures to ensure competent employees are recruited and subsequently trained.

The firm should allocate competent and experienced staff to each engagement team. Junior members of the team should be adequately briefed, before starting their work, and supervised throughout the audit. All team members' work should be subject to a review by a more senior member of the team.

Consultation should take place on contentious issues and all such matters, including their resolution, should be documented.

An engagement quality control review should be performed on audits of all listed companies and other audits where audit risk is considered higher than normal.

The firm should undertake due diligence procedures, including the assessment of management's integrity, before accepting new clients and deciding whether to continue with existing clients.

Examiner's comment

Part 35.1

This part of the question was very well answered with a significant number of candidates scoring maximum marks.

Mint

Most candidates correctly identified that this scenario represented an inability to obtain sufficient appropriate audit evidence and that it was unlikely to be pervasive. The points most commonly overlooked were those relating to the UK Companies Act requirement regarding proper accounting records and the availability of information required for the audit. A number of candidates incorrectly stated that the scenario represented a material misstatement rather than an inability to obtain sufficient appropriate audit evidence.

Coriander

The majority of candidates correctly identified that inventory should be included at its net realisable value (NRV) because it was lower than cost. However, some candidates failed to appreciate that it was the difference between the cost of inventory included in the financial statements and the NRV that should be considered for materiality purposes. Instead, they considered the materiality of the total inventory figure and consequently concluded that the amount was material when in fact the difference between cost and NRV was not material. As a result, these candidates reached the wrong conclusion in respect of the implications for the auditor's report.

Basil

Most candidates identified that the scenario represented the non-disclosure of a related party transaction (RPT) and that the RPT was material by nature but not by size. Most of these candidates identified that the matter was not pervasive and reached a correct conclusion on whether or not the opinion should be modified. Weaker candidates hedged their bets and discussed the possibility of the issue being pervasive, thereby demonstrating a lack of understanding of what constitutes a pervasive issue.

Part 35.2

The majority of candidates correctly identified a range of potential consequences for the audit firm. However, a significant number of candidates lacked an understanding of the quality control procedures required to reduce the risk of issuing an inappropriate audit opinion. Weaker candidates cited the objectives of quality control instead of the procedures to be exercised by the firm. A significant number of candidates stated, incorrectly, that forming limited liability partnerships, agreeing liability caps and including a Bannerman paragraph in the auditor's report would reduce the risk of issuing an inappropriate audit opinion. These candidates failed to appreciate that such actions would only reduce the auditor's exposure to damages in the event of an inappropriate opinion being issued and would not reduce the risk of issuing an inappropriate opinion.

March 2016 exam answers

36 Short form questions

36.1 Ethical issues

Raises doubts over integrity of FC

- May impact other areas of the financial statements/audit

Trainee has not acted with integrity

- Outcome of audit sample is likely to be misleading
- Adjusting sample to produce a 'better outcome' is not truthful

Objectivity compromised

Intimidation threat

- FC has pressurised trainee/exerted influence

Self-interest threat

- Fear of consequences if FC tells audit partner trainee is incompetent

Professional competence and due care compromised

- Trainee has not performed audit procedure correctly
- Trainee did not exercise sound judgement

Professional behaviour of trainee/FC compromised

- Reasonable and informed 3rd party would conclude actions would discredit firm/profession

Examiner's comments

Answers to this question were generally very good as the majority of candidates identified the intimidation and self-interest threats to objectivity. Many of these candidates then went on to identify the threats to the other fundamental principles of integrity, professional competence and due care and, to a lesser extent, professional behaviour. The minority of candidates who did not perform well on this question tended to focus on threats to objectivity and overlooked the other fundamental principles or focused on the trainee and ignored the fact that the financial controller was an ICAEW member.

36.2 Appropriateness of arrangement with audit client

Not appropriate/should decline offer

ES S2 states firms should not enter into business relationships with an audited entity unless clearly inconsequential

As Gruber expects to increase sales by 50% it does not appear inconsequential

Self-interest threat to firm's independence/objectivity as firm may:

- be reluctant to modify opinion/take actions during the audit of Gruber that adversely impact the commercial arrangement
- recommend software to clients, where it is not appropriate, to earn additional fees

Answers to this question were generally disappointing. The majority of candidates displayed a lack of knowledge of the provision in paragraph 29 of ES S2 *Financial, Business, Employment and Personal Relationships*, which only permits business relationships with audit clients if they are inconsequential to both parties. This was clearly not the case in the scenario as the arrangement could have a significant impact on the audit client's revenue. However, it was pleasing to note that the majority of candidates concluded that the arrangement was inappropriate, albeit for the wrong reasons.

36.3 Ethical issues

Proposal represents 'lowballing'

Threat to the fundamental principle of professional competence and due care

- Risk that audit quality is adversely affected

If non-audit services obtained objectivity/independence may be impaired:

- Self-interest threat
    - Fee dependency/fear of losing fee/extra work
    - May cause reluctance to report unfavourably/modify opinion
- Self-review threat
    - Over reliance on colleagues' work
    - Reluctance to notify firm's errors to client's management
- Management threat
    - May be expected to make decisions
    - Views too closely aligned with management

ES S4 states that audit fee must not be influenced by the provision of other services

Examiner's comments

This question was very well answered with a significant number of candidates scoring full marks. Most candidates appreciated that the firm's policy represented lowballing and that such a policy has associated risks in respect of audit quality thereby posing a threat to the fundamental principle of professional competence and due care. Additionally, many candidates identified and explained the self-interest threat and, to a lesser extent, the management and self-review threats to objectivity that could arise if the audit firm succeeded in winning the lucrative non-audit work. A minority of candidates confused lowballing with contingency fees whereby a fee is calculated on a pre-determined basis relating to the outcome or result of a transaction, or other event, or the result of the work performed.

36.4 Performance materiality

- An amount set at less than level(s) for the FS as a whole or particular classes of transactions, account balances or disclosures
- To reduce to an appropriately low level the probability that the aggregate of uncorrected and undetected misstatements exceeds materiality for the FS as whole

Reasons set by external auditors

- Individually immaterial misstatements which are material in aggregate have a greater chance of being detected
- Auditor will perform more audit work
- Provides a margin of safety
- Reduces detection risk
- Reduces risk of inappropriate audit opinion

Examiner's comments

Answers to this question were very disappointing as a significant number of candidates were unable to distinguish performance materiality from materiality for the financial statements as a whole and, consequently, scored no marks. Those candidates who did score marks tended to do so by providing the definition of performance materiality as set out in paragraph 9 of ISA (UK) 320 *Materiality in Planning and Performing an Audit*. Few of these candidates were able to provide plausible reasons as to why performance materiality is set by external auditors.

36.5 **Consequences**

- Oral instructions may be misunderstood
- Unauthorised/fraudulent changes
- Resulting in errors in changes/inaccurate standing data
- Fictitious employees could be recorded on system
- Incorrect payments made to employees
- Adverse impact on profit and cash flow
- Adverse impact on employee goodwill
- Cost/time spent to correct errors

Recommendations

- All changes must be made on written authority
- Signed by HR manager
- Periodic one-for-one checking of all standing data
- Regular exception reports of changes made

  - Checked back to written authority
  - Signature evidencing check

- Password protection on system
- Amendments processed independently of payroll staff

Examiner's comments

This question was well answered with a significant number of candidates scoring full marks. In general, candidates were more proficient at outlining the consequences than the recommendations, which tended to be vague. For example, many candidates cited that the amendments should be checked but failed to specify how they should be checked (ie, back to the document authorising the amendment). Very few candidates considered the need to undertake one-for-one checking of the standing data on a periodic basis.

36.6 Review report

- Addressee determined by the engagement
- Conducted in accordance with ISRE (2400)
- Work consists mainly of inquiries of management and analytical procedures
- Would state 'have not performed an audit'/less in scope than audit
- Moderate/limited assurance
- Negative opinion

  - 'Nothing has come to our attention'

- Signed by reporting accountant

External auditor's report

- Addressee is shareholders/members
- Conducted in accordance with relevant laws/CA06/ISAs
- Reasonable assurance
- Positive opinion

  - 'True and fair view'

- Signed by statutory auditor

Examiner's comments

This question was very well answered and the vast majority of candidates scored full marks. Most candidates obtained marks for differentiating between the level of assurance provided by the two types of engagement and the manner in which the assurance is expressed. The points most commonly overlooked were those relating to the addressees and signatories of the reports.

37 Marmalade Ltd

Marking guide

			Marks
37.1	When planning an external audit	4	
	When undertaking substantive procedures	4	
	Marks available	8	
	Maximum		4
37.2 (a)	**Revenue**		
	Justification	10½	
	Procedures	15½	
(b)	**Property, plant and equipment**		
	Justification	7½	
	Procedures	11½	
(c)	**Inventory**		
	Justification	8	
	Procedures	22½	

	Marks	
General		
Justification	1	
Procedures	1	
Marks available	77½	
Maximum		28
37.3 Key matters to be discussed	12	
Marks available	12	
Maximum		5
Total marks available		37

37.1 When planning an external audit

To obtain an understanding, or to identify aspects, of the entity of which the auditor was unaware.

To assess the risk of material misstatement and potential fraud through identifying unusual transactions, events, and amounts

To provide a basis for the firm's responses to assessed risks

When undertaking substantive audit procedures

To obtain relevant and reliable/sufficient appropriate audit evidence by identifying expected relationships or detecting material misstatements.

Analytical procedures may be used as a 'proof in total' which may reduce the need for tests of details.

37.2 (a) Revenue

Justification

Revenue appears to be overstated. Website sales increased by 35% which is inconsistent with the 25% increase in production capacity and the new production line only running for five months of the year.

Additionally, gross profit margin increased from 40% to 49.2%.

Revenue from the TaxiDair contract has not been recognised appropriately. 50% of the contract value has been recognised whereas only 27% of the contracted units of luggage have been completed and dispatched.

There is an overstatement of £262,733 as £300,267 should have been recognised as revenue. The overstatement is 2.6% of revenue and therefore material.

Sales are made to overseas customers in their local currency which could lead to translation errors.

The provision for returns is an estimate. In spite of an increased level of returns, due to dispatch problems at Pastuzo, there is no increase in the percentage applied which remains at 5% of sales made in December and January. The provision may be inadequate.

Procedures

Test the effectiveness of controls over the recording of website sales using CAATs/IT specialists.

Vouch the last sales recognised in the current year to despatch records before the year end.

Discuss with management the reasons for the increase in revenue, including how the volume of sales has been achieved in light of production capacity and timing of completion of the conversion.

Compare actual revenue to budgets/forecasts and obtain a breakdown of monthly revenues to identify any anomalies.

Perform a reconciliation of website sales with cash receipts.

Inspect the TaxiDair contract and ascertain the basis on which revenue is earned under the contract.

For a sample of sales in foreign currencies, agree the translation rate used to a reliable external source and reperform the calculation.

Discuss with the directors how the dispatch problems at Pastuzo were resolved.

Review the level of returns/refunds after the dispatch issues were resolved to ascertain if the rate of returns reduced.

Review the amount of returns/refunds after the year end and compare to the size of the provision.

Reperform the provision calculation.

(b) **Property, plant and equipment – freehold factory**

Justification

Factory cost may be overstated.

There is a risk of inappropriate capitalisation of costs if the costs of own employees do not meet the relevant criteria for capitalisation or if repairs are incorrectly included.

There is a 73% increase in the cost of the factory compared to a 25% increase in production capacity.

The depreciation charge is at the rate of 4% on cost in 20X5 which would indicate depreciation in 20X6 is expected to be approximately £312,000 (£7.8 million × 4%).

Therefore, the depreciation charge appears to be understated by £102,000. This is 1% of revenue and therefore material.

The freehold factory may be depreciated over an inappropriate period given the factory conversion was completed part way through the year.

Procedures

Obtain a schedule of capitalised costs and ascertain if they meet the relevant criteria.

Agree costs of the conversion to invoices from the contractor.

Ascertain whether any repair costs have been incorrectly included.

Agree employee time to timesheets and amounts to payroll records.

Ascertain the basis on which employee time has been capitalised.

Physically inspect the factory/conversion of warehouse.

Discuss with management the basis for depreciation and assess the reasonableness of this basis.

Reperform the depreciation calculation.

Ascertain the date the asset was ready for use and ensure depreciation is charged from this date.

(c) **Inventory – finished goods**

Justification

Inventory appears to be overstated. Inventory days increased from 72.5 to 126.9.

Product designs and colours are frequently updated which may result in older inventory being obsolete and having a net realisable value below cost.

Returned inventory may be damaged.

Marmalade must rely on Pastuzo's records to determine the quantity of inventory. Pastuzo's records may contain errors and it may be difficult to obtain evidence over inventory quantities and the effectiveness of controls over Pastuzo's inventory system.

Only one inventory count has taken place, in May 20X5. The firm's recent appointment as auditor means it will not have been able to physically inspect inventory or perform test counts at the year end.

Finished goods may be in-transit or still at Marmalade's factory on 31 January 20X6.

Returns may not be added back to inventory resulting in inventory being understated.

Procedures

Obtain direct confirmation of the year-end inventory balances from Pastuzo.

Obtain an aged inventory report and identify any slow-moving or obsolete items.

Review the post year-end sales of these items and ascertain their net realisable value.

Ascertain whether controls at Pastuzo over the recording of inventory movements are adequate by obtaining the assurance report from Pastuzo's auditor.

Evaluate whether:

- an appropriate period is covered by the report
- the controls identified/tested are relevant to the audit of Marmalade
- there were any exceptions identified or a modified opinion given

Ascertain that Pastuzo's auditor is:

- independent of Pastuzo
- professionally competent

Alternatively, directly test the effectiveness of controls over the recording of inventory at Pastuzo.

Obtain results of the inventory count in May 20X5 and compare the results of the count to records held by Pastuzo at that date to ascertain their accuracy.

Ascertain the procedures in place for amending records for discrepancies between physical inventory and the inventory records.

Ascertain from the factory manager whether any items were in the factory at the yearend or despatched to Pastuzo on 31 January 20X6.

Obtain copies of despatch records for these items and check that they are included in the year-end inventory report from Pastuzo.

Review records of inventory added by Pastuzo just after the year end and vouch to Marmalade's despatch records to ascertain if the items were despatched to Pastuzo before the year end.

Visit Pastuzo's premises to perform test counts after the year end and reconcile back to year-end inventory quantities using records of inventory movements.

Inspect inventory for any damage.

General

Being a first year audit it may be difficult to obtain assurance over opening balances.

Procedures

Review the prior year auditor's working papers.

Consider whether audit work for the current year provides evidence as to the reliability of opening balances.

37.3 Background information about the client and its industry, including any applicable laws and regulations

Relevant ethical requirements including the importance of independence and objectivity

The importance of professional scepticism

Areas of key audit risk, including any susceptibility to misstatement due to fraud and how fraud might occur

Business risks and how they impact on the financial statements

Objectives of the work to be performed and how the audit plan addresses the risks identified

Materiality/performance materiality thresholds

How the audit work is to be assigned to members of the audit team and how to raise issues arising

Requirements for documenting audit work and who will review junior team members' work

The timetable for completion of audit work

Logistics, such as locations and client contact details

Examiner's comments

Part 37.1

Answers to this part of the question were generally good. Candidates were more proficient in respect of analytical procedures when planning an external audit and some candidates overlooked the requirement in respect of substantive procedures. In respect of planning, the points most commonly identified were those relating to the understanding of the entity, risk assessment and the focusing of resources on risk areas. In respect of substantive procedures, the points most commonly identified were those relating to obtaining relevant and reliable audit evidence by identifying expected relationships. A number of candidates digressed into stating the benefits and limitations of performing analytical procedures, which was not required, or wasted time by giving detailed examples of several types of analytical procedures.

Part 37.2

Answers to this part of the question were generally good and many candidates were able to provide a number of justifications as to why an item had been identified as a key area of audit risk. These candidates then cited a range of procedures to address the audit risks that were both adequately described and relevant to the justification of the audit risk. It was pleasing to note that the majority of candidates attempted to make some use of the financial information provided in the scenario. However, as noted in previous examiners' commentaries, weaker candidates continue to cite vague audit procedures which were not awarded any marks. Many candidates overlooked that the firm had recently been appointed as external auditor and that obtaining assurance over opening balances may be an issue.

Revenue

Answers to this section of the question were good with the majority of candidates correctly identifying that:

- the increase in revenue was out of line with the smaller increase in production capacity;
- sales in overseas currencies may lead to foreign currency translation errors; and
- the provision for returns may be inadequate in light of increased level of returns.

Most candidates failed to calculate that revenue of £300,267 should be recognised in respect of the TaxiDair contract instead of the cash receipts of £563,000 and that this represented a material error.

Most candidates were able to cite credible audit procedures to address the identified risks, such as enquiring of management why revenue had increased, checking a sample of foreign currency calculations using exchange rates from a reliable external source and inspecting the TaxiDair contract.

The most commonly overlooked procedures included:

- the use of CAATs and IT specialists to test controls over the recording of website sales

- comparison of actual revenue to budget

- reconciliation of website sales with cash receipts

- discussion with the directors as to how dispatch problems were resolved

- reviewing the level of returns after the dispatch problems were resolved to ascertain if the rate of returns had fallen.

Property, plant and equipment – freehold factory

Answers to this section of the question were good. The most commonly overlooked justification was that depreciation appeared understated and that the understatement was potentially material. Few candidates used the financial information to form an expectation of the current year's depreciation charge.

Candidates were able to cite a number of appropriate audit procedures to address the risks. The most commonly overlooked procedures were those relating to the basis on which employee time was capitalised and physical inspection of the factory. A number of candidates referred to the risk that the factory cost was 'misstated' rather than overstated, that depreciation could be 'incorrect' rather than understated and that assets should be verified rather than the warehouse should be physically inspected. These points were too vague to be awarded any marks.

Inventory – finished goods

Answers to this part of the question were of a mixed standard. Most candidates identified a number of appropriate reasons to justify why inventory was a key area of audit risk, including making use of analytical procedures such as calculating inventory days. Most candidates also correctly identified that inventory may not be stated at the lower of cost and net realisable value as the luggage designs and colours are frequently updated and therefore could be obsolete. A significant number of candidates also correctly cited that only one inventory count in May increased the risk of misstatement and that Pastuzo's inventory system, used to determine year-end inventory quantities, may contain errors.

The majority of candidates presented some relevant procedures, including obtaining the aged inventory analysis to identify slow-moving items, reviewing post year-end selling prices to ascertain whether items included in inventory were subsequently sold below cost and performing cut-off procedures.

However, a number of candidates struggled to describe audit procedures to address the risk that Pastuzo's inventory system may contain errors. They failed to consider the procedures for amending the inventory records for discrepancies, between physical and records, identified at the inventory count and whether the controls over the movement of inventory were adequate.

In relation to the adequacy of controls over inventory at Pastuzo, a number of candidates correctly identified potential reliance on the assurance report prepared by Pastuzo's auditors. However, few candidates considered the period covered by the report, whether the controls tested by Pastuzo's auditors are relevant to the audit of Marmalade and whether Pastuzo's auditors are independent and professionally competent.

Only the strongest candidates were able to design appropriate audit procedures to obtain evidence as to the year-end inventory quantities. A number of candidates incorrectly suggested that the auditor demand that the client perform a year-end count (or perform their own year-end count) which was inappropriate as the yearend had already passed. Consequently, few candidates earned the marks available for obtaining records of goods despatched from Marmalade's factory on 31 January to check that these items were included in the year-end inventory report, or visiting Pastuzo's premises to perform test counts after the year end and then reconciling quantities back to year-end inventory amounts.

Very few candidates suggested obtaining direct confirmation, from Pastuzo, of the year-end inventory balance or inspecting inventory for slow moving or damaged items.

Part 37.3

Many candidates scored full marks on this part of the question because they were able to outline a range of relevant key matters that should be discussed with junior members of an audit team before performing the planned audit procedures. The points most commonly identified were those set out in paragraph A13 of ISA (UK) 220 *Quality Control for an Audit of Financial Statements* – compliance with ethical standards, the importance of professional scepticism, the objectives of the audit work, the nature of the entity's business, risk related issues, the audit approach and addressing any problems that may arise. A number of candidates wasted time by digressing into matters to consider when an engagement team is assigned to an audit, such as the competence and capabilities of the proposed team. A small number of candidates incorrectly outlined the matters to consider when reviewing the work of junior members of an audit team.

38 Underground Ltd

Marking guide

		Marks	
38.1	Incorporated	2	
	Trade asset transferred	8	
	Owner-managed	2	
	Notting contract	13½	
	Bank loan covenant	5½	
	Regulated industry	8½	
	Mechanical defect	5	
	Spreadsheets	6	
	Judy and Jonathan	3½	
	Marks available	54	
	Maximum		18

		Marks
38.2	Conflict of interest	4½
	Self-interest threat	3½
	Safeguards	5
	Marks available	13
	Maximum	7
Total marks available		25

38.1 Incorporated on 1 July 20X5

There is increased inherent and detection risk associated with a first year audit and there will be a lack of audited prior year figures for the performance of analytical procedures.

Trade and assets transferred from partnership/Goodwill arising on transfer

The valuation of the trade/assets/shares involves a high degree of judgement. There is likely to be only limited audit evidence to support the valuation. Judy and Jonathan may not have been objective in their valuation and goodwill of £1.8 million may be overstated. This is a high risk area with goodwill being vulnerable to impairment if the conditions in the Notting contract are not met or if there is any uncertainty over the going concern status of Underground.

Owner-managed business

There is a risk of management override and an increased risk associated with management's limited experience of running a business, having both previously been customer services managers.

Notting contract

Judy appears to have 'stolen' Notting as a customer while still working at Hill, which raises concerns about management integrity. A lack of management integrity results in an increased risk of fraud/money laundering and casts doubts on the reliability of management's representations. There is an increased risk of issuing an inappropriate audit opinion and the firm may not wish to be associated with Underground's management due to the risk of reputational damage to the firm.

Underground is heavily reliant on the Notting contract which provides 70% of its total revenue. It is unclear how Underground can cope with the increased volume of business and such rapid growth may place a strain on cash flow. There is a high risk of contract termination by Notting if required volumes are not met or if the refrigeration problems have affected the quality of sandwiches. The loss of the Notting contract would raise doubts about whether Underground can continue as a going concern.

Bank loan covenant

There is an increased risk of management bias due to the bank loan covenant resulting in an overstatement of assets/revenue and/or an understatement of liabilities/expenses. If the loan covenant is breached the bank may withdraw the funding resulting in an increased going concern risk. In addition, the reliance by the bank on the firm's auditor's report has liability implications for the firm.

Highly regulated industry/Issues found by regulator

The firm may have insufficient knowledge of the regulatory environment relevant to Underground. The failure to comply with regulation may result in fines requiring disclosure of a contingent liability in the financial statements at the year end. The regulator may have the power to close the business or revoke its licence resulting in an increased going concern risk.

Sandwiches already sold may have been inadequately refrigerated resulting in consumers suffering from food poisoning. This may result in legal claims against Underground and an increased risk of unrecorded liabilities if such claims are not recognised in the financial statements. The adverse publicity may also have a negative impact on Underground's reputation.

Mechanical defect in refrigerators

The mechanical defect identified by the regulator may indicate that management is not properly maintaining the refrigerators bringing management integrity into question. If tangible assets are not properly maintained an impairment may require recognition in the financial statements. Additionally, any repair costs already incurred to bring the refrigerators into line with regulatory standards may be incorrectly capitalised. Furthermore, the cost of repairs will put a strain on cash flow.

Spreadsheets for accounting records

It is likely that there are inadequate controls over accounting records increasing the risk of human error and material misstatements. Consequently, the firm is likely to adopt a substantive approach to the audit.

If the accounting records are inadequate there may be insufficient audit evidence. This would require the firm to issue a modified audit opinion, due to inability to obtain sufficient appropriate audit evidence, and to report by exception under CA06 that adequate accounting records have not been maintained.

Divorce of Judy and Jonathan/Exit of Judy from business

The divorce of Judy and Jonathan may make it difficult to obtain audit evidence if the directors are not co-operating with one another. The relationship with Notting, Underground's key customer, is through Judy and this may give rise to going concern issues when Judy leaves. Additionally, Judy may exhibit management bias in her preparation of the accounting records, eg, by overstating net assets, to achieve a higher valuation for her shares in Underground.

38.2 Conflict of interest

A conflict of interest arises between Judy and Jonathan. Judy will want to maximise the value of the shares whereas Jonathan will want to minimise the share value. There is a threat to the firm's objectivity as the firm may not be able to act in the best interests of both parties.

Self-interest threat

The firm may favour Jonathan's position as he will become the controlling shareholder in Underground after he acquires Judy's shares. There is a threat to the firm's objectivity as it may fear losing Underground as an external audit client.

Safeguards

The firm should explain the conflict of interest to Judy and Jonathan and obtain informed consent to act from both parties.

Separate personnel should be used which are physically separated. Additional information barriers, such as confidential and secure data filing, should be in place and there should be clear guidelines for staff who should also sign confidentiality agreements.

The ethics partner should be consulted and there should be regular review of the application of safeguards by a senior individual not involved in the engagements.

Part 38.1

Candidates who systematically worked through each paragraph and identified the issues specific to Underground and relevant to the firm's decision whether to accept appointment as auditor scored high marks on this part of the question. Strong candidates, having identified the issues then went on to explain why they were relevant. Weaker candidates cited generic points and failed to tailor their answers to the information presented in the scenario. For example, weaker candidates failed to appreciate that the financial statements had not been audited in the prior year and wasted time considering the outcome of professional clearance with non-existent auditors. The points most commonly overlooked were those relating to the lack of prior year audited figures for analytical procedures, the risk of overstated goodwill and management override.

Part 38.2

Candidates were more proficient at explaining the conflict of interest and the safeguards than they were at explaining the self-interest threat. In respect of the conflict of interest, most candidates identified that it would be difficult to act in the best interest of both parties because Judy would want a high share price and Jonathan would want a low share price. However, few candidates appreciated that the self-interest threat applied to the risk that the firm would favour Jonathan's position. Many candidates cited, incorrectly, that the self-interest threat would arise as a result of fee dependency arising from the non-audit engagement. These candidates failed to appreciate that this was a one-off engagement and would not give rise to regular income. In respect of the safeguards, most candidates were able to provide a number of steps to mitigate the threats to objectivity. However, the safeguard most commonly overlooked was in respect of the independent review of the application of the safeguards.

39 Brown Ltd, Bear Ltd, Windsor Ltd, Peru Ltd

Marking guide

			Marks
39.1	Brown	6½	
	Bear	10	
	Windsor	3	
	Peru	5	
	Marks available	24½	
	Maximum		10
39.2	Report	1½	
	Reasons for inclusion	7	
	Marks available	8½	
	Maximum		
39.3	Reduce exposure	5	
	Restrict distribution	1	
	Engagement letter	2	
	Marks available	8	
	Maximum		5
Total marks available			18

39.1 **Brown**

The receipt of a letter from the administrator of Duffel provides evidence of conditions existing at the year end and is therefore an adjusting subsequent event. The amount due from Duffel should be written off. The amount is 19.7% of profit before tax and 2.5% of total assets and is therefore material.

A modified auditor's report/opinion should be issued due to material misstatement. The matter is not pervasive as it only affects specific items in the financial statements and therefore a qualified ('except for') opinion should be issued. The auditor's report should include an explanation of the issue in the basis for modified/qualified opinion paragraph.

Bear

The Chairman's Statement is not part of the financial statements and the auditor is not required to express an opinion on the Chairman's Statement. However, the information relating to fair trade status in the Chairman's Statement is misleading and represents a material misstatement of fact. While this does not undermine information contained in the financial statements the auditor is required to take further action under ISA (UK) 720 *The Auditor's Responsibility Relating to Other Information*.

The auditor's report should be modified to include a description of the issue in the 'Other information' section, which is placed directly after the 'Basis for opinion' section and before 'Key audit matters'. The auditor's opinion on the financial statements is not modified.

Windsor

ISA (UK) 710 *Comparative Information – Corresponding Figures and Comparative Financial Statements* requires the auditor to state, in an Other Matter paragraph, that comparative financial statements are unaudited.

The audit opinion on the financial statements is not modified.

Peru

The assumptions over revenue do not provide a reasonable basis for the preparation of the prospective financial information. An adverse opinion should be issued in relation to the reasonableness of the basis for the assumptions. The report should describe the matters leading to this conclusion.

As the prospective financial information is properly prepared on the basis of the assumptions, the firm should express an unmodified opinion that the forecast is properly prepared.

39.2 The report should state that 'Actual results are likely to be different from the forecast since anticipated events frequently do not occur as expected and the variation may be material.'

Reasons for inclusion

The caveat is included to meet the requirements of ISAE 3400 *The Examination of Prospective Financial Information*. It warns users that prospective financial information may not be reliable because:

- assumptions made may not come to fruition

- unforeseen events may occur after completion of the prospective financial information/after the report is issued

The caveat aims to prevent over reliance on the firm's conclusion and seeks to narrow any expectations gap. It may protect the firm from legal action in the event that users of the prospective financial information incur losses as a result of relying on the information.

39.3 Firms can reduce their exposure to claims from unforeseen third parties by including the following in their audit and assurance reports:

- Specific addressee(s)/intended users of the report

- A clear statement of management's and the assurance provider's responsibilities

- Reference to the intended purpose(s) of the report

- In the case of external audits, a Bannerman paragraph which explicitly states the firm does not accept responsibility to anyone other than the company/members

Where possible the firm should seek to restrict the distribution of its report.

The engagement letter should state that the client must seek the firm's written consent before disclosing the firm's report to a third party. The firm should then refuse any requests to disclose to a third party where the risk of inappropriate reliance is considered too high.

Examiner's comments

Part 39.1

Brown

This scenario was well answered. The majority of candidates correctly identified that the issue was an adjusting subsequent event and that the directors' refusal to amend the financial statements represented a material misstatement. Most candidates also identified that the issue was not pervasive and consequently the modification should be a qualified opinion. Weaker candidates incorrectly stated that the explanation for the modified opinion should appear in the opinion section instead of the basis for qualified opinion section of the auditor's report.

Bear

A significant number of candidates confused the Chairman's Statement with the Directors' Report and stated, incorrectly, that there was a duty to report on the former. Many candidates stated, incorrectly, that there was an inconsistency between the Chairman's Statement and the financial statements. These candidates failed to appreciate that it was a misstatement of fact which had no impact on the financial statements. The candidates who understood that there was no misstatement in the financial statements identified, correctly, that the opinion would be unmodified but the report would be modified with an Other Matter paragraph.

Windsor

Although many candidates correctly identified that the opinion should be unmodified only stronger candidates appreciated that paragraph 19 of ISA (UK) 710 *Comparative Information – Corresponding Figures and Comparative Financial Statements* required the matter to be disclosed in an Other Matter paragraph. A significant number of candidates stated, incorrectly, that the issue should be disclosed in an Emphasis of Matter paragraph.

Peru

Answers to this part of the question were very disappointing and a significant number of candidates did not attempt it. Many candidates displayed a lack of knowledge of the requirement in paragraph 31 of ISAE 3400 *The Examination of Prospective Financial Information* to provide an adverse opinion in the circumstances described in the scenario. The points identified by candidates who scored marks on this part of the question were those relating to the expression of an adverse opinion and the inclusion of a description of the matter leading to the conclusion. Few candidates appreciated that the practitioner could express a conclusion that the prospective financial information was properly prepared on the basis of the assumptions, albeit one of those assumptions was highly unrealistic.

Part 39.2

Answers to this part of the question were generally disappointing as many candidates were unaware of the provisions of paragraphs 27-29 of ISAE 3400. Many wasted time writing about the level of assurance to be provided and cited examples of how this assurance should be expressed. There were no marks for these points.

Part 39.3

Answers to this part of the question were generally disappointing as many candidates strayed beyond the requirement which was focused on reducing exposure to legal claims by unforeseen parties. The majority of candidates identified, incorrectly, limited liability agreements such as liability caps, which would not protect against claims from third parties as these cover agreements between the practitioner and the client. However, most candidates earned the marks available for the inclusion of a Bannerman paragraph in the assurance report.

40 Short form questions

40.1 Actions to comply with the Money Laundering Regulations

- Appoint a Money Laundering Reporting Officer (MLRO) and a Money Laundering Compliance Principal (MLCP)
  - MLRO must be a senior member of the firm; MLCP must be on board of directors (or equivalent)
  - The roles of MLRO and MLCP may be performed by the same person
- Register with a supervisory body (eg, HMRC, ICAEW)
- Implement policies and procedures for:
  - Client due diligence
  - Record keeping of client identification
    - For five years after relationship ends
    - To cover identification of politically exposed persons
  - Reporting Money Laundering
    - Including no tipping off
- Introduce a staff training programme
- Monitor compliance with policies and procedures

Examiner's comments

This question was generally well answered as the majority of candidates identified the points relating to the appointment of a money laundering reporting officer, staff training and, to a lesser extent, client due diligence procedures. The points most commonly overlooked were those relating to the MLRO and MLCP; the maintenance of client identification records and the monitoring of compliance with money laundering procedures. A common error was to list the actions to be taken by individuals in the firm on suspecting or discovering money laundering instead of listing the **policies and procedures** to be implemented by the firm.

40.2 Audit procedures to address the risk of revenue misstatement

- Compare revenue with:
  - expectation (eg, sale of 2,400 boats pa)
  - prior year
- Discuss with management the reason for any changes in the number of boats sold and corroborate explanations
- Evaluate and test system for recording deferred income
  - Ensure 40% initial payment is accounted for as deferred revenue until delivered
- Match entries in the revenue account with invoices
- Match despatch records with invoices (cut off)
- Inspect post year-end credit notes which may relate to the year under review
- Inspect post year-end management accounts
  - Low level of sales may indicate inflation of pre year-end revenue

Answers to this question were of a mixed standard. Stronger candidates identified the need to check the revenue recognised with invoices and despatch records and used information in the question to apply analytical procedures, such as proof in total. Weaker candidates restricted their answers to making enquiries of management. The most common shortcoming was the failure to describe, as required by the question, the audit procedures to be undertaken. For example, many candidates identified the need to perform cut-off procedures but failed to **describe** how these procedures should be undertaken. Similarly, many identified the need to perform analytical procedures but did not specify which analytical procedures. Weaker candidates wasted time citing the procedures to address the risk of receivables misstatement instead of revenue misstatement. A number of candidates identified the risks facing the business instead of describing the audit procedures to address the risk of material misstatement.

40.3 Characteristics of journal entries that external auditors should select for testing to identify fraudulent activities

Journals that:

- relate to unusual or seldom used accounts
- are processed by individuals who do not normally make journal entries
- are recorded after closure of the financial statements
- have no explanation or have a vague description
- are in round numbers
- are made outside office hours
- are made to suspense accounts
- involve contra entries
- involve directors or related parties
- lack commercial rationale
- involve accounts prone to misstatement or were misstated in the prior year

Examiner's comments

Answers to this question were disappointing. This question was well answered by those candidates who were familiar with the contents of paragraph A43 of ISA (UK) 240, *The Auditor's Responsibilities Relating to Fraud in the Audit of Financial Statements*. These candidates provided sufficient characteristics to attain full marks. A common error was to cite the characteristics of routine journal entries, such as correction of errors, period-end accruals and depreciation adjustments instead of the characteristics of journal entries that might relate to fraudulent activities. A minority of candidates did not attempt this question.

40.4 Explain the factors which could indicate that the provision for warranty claims may be materially misstated

- Director's assessment is subject to uncertainty
- Non-current provision represents 1% (20X6) and 1% (20X5) of revenue
- Current provision represents 1.1% (20X6) and 1.25% (20X5) of revenue
- Inconsistent with the increase in extended warranty period from two to five years
- Possible understatement

Alternative calculations

Marks were awarded where candidates presented the following alternative calculations:

- Increase in non-current provision of 14.2%
- Increase in current provision of 1%
- Total of current and non-current provision 2.1% (20X6) and 2.25% (20X5)
- Increase in warranty provision of 6.9%
- Increase in revenue of 14.8%

Examiner's comments

Answers to this question attained the highest average mark in the SFQs. It was pleasing to note the majority of candidates applied analytical procedures to the data provided in the question. Stronger candidates then went on to specify that the provision appeared to be understated in light of the extended warranty cover. The point most commonly overlooked was that relating to the provision being an estimate and, as such, is susceptible to misstatement – deliberate or unintentional. A minority of candidates strayed beyond the question and wasted time describing audit procedures to be undertaken to verify the provision.

40.5 Rights and responsibilities, under the Companies Act 2006, relating to the change in appointment of an external auditor

Rights

- Outgoing auditors may:
    - make written representations
    - circulate these to members
    - attend and speak at the AGM

Responsibilities

- Prepare a statement of circumstances detailing the circumstances of resignation
    - To be deposited at Ash's registered office
    - And a copy sent to the Registrar of Companies

- As Ash is a listed company, there is no option to state there are no circumstances
- Obtain permission from Ash to reply to a prospective auditor's communication
- Return promptly all books and records of the company
- Maintain client confidentiality after ceasing to act
- Maintain client identification records
- Notify the audit authority of the change in appointment (eg, ICAEW/FRC)

Examiner's comments

This question was generally well answered. Most candidates were more knowledgeable about the auditor's responsibilities, in particular ethical responsibilities, than the auditor's rights. However, many candidates wasted time writing at length about communication with the incoming auditor. A number of candidates demonstrated a lack of knowledge of the Companies Act 2006 provisions. Many confused written representations (a right) with the statement of circumstances (a duty). Furthermore, a number of candidates cited the right to request the directors to convene an extraordinary general meeting. This right is only available if the auditor resigns before the term of office expires. Some candidates did not read the question properly and wasted time citing the auditor's right to receive notice, failing to appreciate that this had already been given to the auditor.

40.6 Outline the possible consequences of this internal control deficiency and provide recommendations to remedy this deficiency.

Consequences

- Staff may not have appropriate skills, leading to:
  - poor quality work
  - costs to rectify
  - adverse impact on reputation

- Staff may lack integrity, leading to:
  - theft

- Staff may have falsified information about identity or qualifications, leading to:
  - claims and legal action

- Staff may be breaking the law
  - Eg, right to work in UK, leading to:
    - fines

- Adverse impact on cash flow/going concern risk

Recommendations

- Communicate policy to staff
- Obtain two references
- At least one reference from a former employer
- Inspect proof of qualifications
- All offers of employment made subject to satisfactory references
- Formal approval to appoint new employees
- Monitoring of procedures
- Disciplinary procedures for failing to comply with the policy

Examiner's comments

This question was generally well answered with many candidates scoring full marks. In general, the consequences were dealt with better than the recommendations. In respect of consequences, most candidates cited the points relating to the risks of employing incompetent staff, poor quality work, customer dissatisfaction and the associated costs if these risks materialised. The points most commonly overlooked were those relating to the legal consequences of employing people who did not have the right to work in the UK. In respect of recommendations, the points most commonly cited were those relating to the communication of the policy to staff and disciplinary procedures for failing to apply the policy. Candidates commonly provided a recommendation to obtain references for all employees but failed to specify that it should be at least two references with one from a former employer. Points commonly overlooked included those relating to proof of qualifications, formal approval to appoint and offers of employment to be subject to satisfactory references.

41 Flint plc

			Marks
41.1	(a)	Those charged with governance	3½
		External auditors	4
	(b)	Risk factors	5
		Why a concern	6½
	Marks available		19
	Maximum		10
41.2	(a)	**Going concern**	
		Justification	12
		Procedures	18
	(b)	**Inventory**	
		Justification	9½
		Procedures	21½
		Marks available	61
		Maximum	20
41.3	(a)	Instructions	11
	(b)	Evaluation	9½
	Marks available		20½
	Maximum		10
Total marks available			40

41.1 (a)   Those charged with governance are primarily responsible for the prevention and detection of fraud. This responsibility is discharged by implementing and monitoring policies and procedures (including internal controls). The policies and procedures should include arrangements to deter and detect dishonest conduct. Such arrangements include training of staff, disciplinary action when fraud is discovered and whistleblowing facilities to report suspected fraud. There should be a culture of honesty and ethical behaviour reinforced by an active oversight by those charged with governance.

External auditors have no duty to prevent fraud. However, external auditors are responsible for obtaining reasonable assurance about whether the financial statements as a whole are free from material misstatement due to fraud. External auditors should therefore plan procedures around detecting material misstatements due to fraud and must respond if fraud is suspected or detected during the audit. External auditors must maintain professional scepticism and ensure all members of the audit team are briefed about how fraud might occur.

(b)   **Risks**

Risk posed by recent changes of subsidiary company auditors

- Results in higher detection risk as new auditors lack prior knowledge

Risk posed by autonomous subsidiaries

- Results in higher control risk as there is lack of supervision of subsidiaries

Risk posed by the application for increased bank facilities and stock market expectations

- Could lead to fraudulent reporting and management bias in the preparation of the financial statements

Risk associated with subsidiaries being responsible for maintaining customer relations and dealing with agents and governments

- Could lead to bribery which is a criminal offence, and there are serious implications for not reporting bribery to the NCA

Investigation by the UK Serious Fraud Office

- Could result in fines, unrecorded liabilities and going concern risk

- Uncertainties may not be disclosed or the financial statements may be prepared on an inappropriate basis

Internal audit function identified that payments were made before a contract was awarded

- Payments could have been bribes and the lack of internal controls raises doubts about management integrity

- Further unauthorised payments may not be identified or disclosed.

41.2(a) Going concern

Justification

Trading conditions are difficult as evidenced by a fall in revenue of 22.7%, a fall in gross margin from 26.2% to 19.6% and operating losses. Flint is facing strong competition as its engines are less efficient than those of its competitor. The fall in demand for current engines will have a knock on impact on the future sale of parts for a number of years. Flint's own range of more efficient engines will not be available until 20X8. There have been downward revisions to profit forecasts and falls in the share price.

All of this indicates an inability to generate cash from operations.

The statement of financial position indicates poor liquidity as the net current liabilities have increased and the bank loan is due for repayment in September 20X6. The overdraft has increased and is within £25 million of the facility limit. This facility is due for review and Flint may not be able to secure other finance if the facility is withdrawn. Flint requires finance to continue the development of its new engines. Flint may not be able to fund the development or pay its debts as they fall due.

Regulatory proceedings are pending and this may result in fines and legal expenses, reputational damage and ultimately the loss of Flint's trading licence.

Procedures

- Obtain profit and cash flow forecasts for at least one year from the date of the financial statements (per ISA (UK) 570) or from the date of approval of the financial statements (per ISA (UK) 570 (UK))

- Assess the assumptions for reasonableness, in particular the assumptions regarding:
    - future revenue
    - funds required for the development of the new engines
    - the outcome of the investigation

- Perform sensitivity analysis on key components of the forecast

- Review the forecasts to see if Flint can pay its debts as they fall due

- Consult experts on the feasibility of the new engines

- Review order book for new contracts

- Obtain written representation from management regarding the feasibility of future plans

- Ascertain management's contingency plans for alternative sources of finance should the bank overdraft be withdrawn

- Review bank correspondence for evidence of the banking relationship

- Review bank covenants and assess Flint's ability to comply with covenants and other terms and conditions

- Review post year-end management accounts to assess company performance

- Assess the impact of regulatory action by:

    - enquiry of legal advisers
    - consideration of the outcome of similar cases
    - review of subsequent events
    - inspection of correspondence with the regulator

(b) **Inventory of spare parts stored in the UK**

Justification

Inventory days have increased from 67.6 to 98.3. A fall in engine sales due to competition and difficult trading conditions have reduced the demand for parts. Fixed-price contracts could result in parts being sold at a loss. There may be obsolete inventory requiring write down and, consequently, inventory may be overstated.

The inventory system may be recording incorrect balances as a result of the following:

- Inadequate controls over the interface between inventory and cost accounting systems

- Some items may not be checked during the year

- Cut off errors due to goods in transit

The standard costing system may be inaccurate and may not reflect up to date costs of components and labour. Standard costs may not reflect the specification if parts have been modified over time. Production overheads may not reflect normal level of activity.

Foreign suppliers are paid in local currency and there is the potential for translation errors.

Procedures

- Evaluate and test controls over:

    - inventory count procedures
    - updates to the perpetual inventory records
    - updates to component costs
    - the interface between inventory and cost accounting systems

- Review reports of previous inventory counts, evaluate the level of discrepancies and consider the implications for the reliability of the inventory system

- Perform test counts of inventory at a periodic count

- Match despatch records with entries on the parts inventory system

- Identify slow-moving or obsolete items by reviewing the age analysis of inventory

- Compare fixed selling prices to costs of parts to determine whether NRV is less than carrying value

- Compare the inventory of parts with the number of engines still in use and assess whether the parts will be used

- Discuss the basis of allowance to reduce inventory to NRV with management

- Obtain standard cost specifications for each part and for a sample of parts:
    - Test cost of components to suppliers' invoices
    - Vouch labour costs to payroll
    - Ascertain the basis of overhead allocation
    - Ensure overhead allocation is based on normal level of activity
    - Reperform calculations

- Reperform a sample of foreign currency translations and check rates to a reliable source.

41.3 (a) Instructions to be sent to the subsidiaries' auditors

- Request confirmation that the component auditor will co-operate with the group audit team to ensure that sufficient appropriate evidence is likely to be available and that there is no inability to obtain sufficient appropriate audit evidence

- Timetable to allow component auditors to plan and project manage their work and meet deadlines

- Reporting requirements to ensure consistency across all component auditors and that group auditors get complete information

- Detail of the work to be performed and the use to be made of the work to ensure that nothing is overlooked and to allow the component auditor to plan audit procedures

- Ethical and independence requirements to ensure that the component auditor acts with objectivity and integrity and that the group auditor can rely on the work of the component auditor

- Materiality levels for the component to help with planning of work and ensure items material to the group are audited

- Significant risks that are relevant to the component auditor (such as bribery and going concern) to allow component auditors to focus work on areas assessed as high risk of misstatement

- A list of related parties and a request that component auditor notifies the group audit team of any other related parties to allow collation of related party transactions for disclosure and written representation purposes

- Work to be performed on intra-group transactions, unrealised profits and intra-group account balances to ensure no duplication or omission of transactions

- Instructions on subsequent events audit work to ensure that the component auditors extend subsequent events procedures beyond the normal period if there is a delay between completion of audit work in respect of the subsidiaries and signing of the group auditor's report

- A list of key contacts at Flint and at the group audit firm to facilitate communication

(b) Evaluation

The group auditor is responsible for the auditor's opinion on the consolidated financial statements. Consequently, the evaluation of the sufficiency and appropriateness of the audit evidence obtained by component auditors is mandatory under ISA (UK) 600 *Special Considerations – Audits of Group Financial Statements (Including the Work of*

Component Auditors). Any material misstatement in the subsidiaries' financial statements poses a risk of material misstatement in the group financial statements which, if undetected, could lead to an inappropriate opinion. Therefore, there is a need to determine whether the work undertaken by the subsidiaries' auditors is reliable and whether additional audit procedures are necessary.

The evaluation is undertaken by the use of questionnaires, visits to and discussions with the component auditors and a review of working papers and audit plans. The summary of the component auditors' conclusions should be reviewed and an evaluation of uncorrected misstatements made.

Examiner's comments

Part 41.1

Answers to this part of the question were of a mixed standard. In part (a) the majority of candidates were able to distinguish between the responsibilities of those charged with governance, for the prevention and detection of fraud, and the responsibilities of external auditors. Most candidates correctly identified that those charged with governance are primarily responsible for the prevention and detection of fraud and that their responsibility includes implementation of relevant policies and procedures, training of employees and demonstrating a culture of honesty. Most candidates also correctly identified that an external auditor's responsibility is to obtain reasonable assurance about whether the financial statements are, as a whole, free from material misstatement due to fraud. Fewer candidates went on to explicitly state that this excluded any responsibility for the prevention of fraud, that the auditor should plan procedures around detecting material misstatements due to fraud or that the auditor must respond if fraud is suspected during the audit. A number of stronger candidates correctly stated that the auditor must maintain professional scepticism and that audit team members should be appropriately briefed on the risk of misstatement due to fraud.

In part (b) candidates generally performed well when identifying factors in the scenario that increase the risk of material statement due to fraud. The most commonly identified factors were the following:

- The application for increased bank facilities
- Dealing with agents
- The regularity investigation
- The issues identified by internal audit

Factors less often identified were the following:

- The recent changes in subsidiary auditors
- The impact of stock market expectations
- Subsidiaries being responsible for maintaining customer relations

Candidates performed significantly less well when explaining why each factor was a concern. Many candidates were not able to relate the factor identified to its impact on material misstatement caused by fraud and many candidates failed to provide any explanations at all. A number of candidates cited that the perpetual inventory system was a deficiency and that the absence of a year-end inventory count would invariably lead to fraud. However, where a perpetual inventory system is operating effectively there is little risk of fraud. Translation errors in respect of foreign currency transactions were also cited as giving rise to fraud but there is no basis for this assertion.

Part 41.2

Answers to this part of the question were good with many candidates scoring the maximum 20 marks. Answers in respect of going concern tended to be better than those in respect of inventory. A number of candidates failed to make full use of the financial information given in the scenario. For example, they stated that gross profit had reduced but did not calculate the gross margin or that inventory had increased but did not calculate inventory days.

Going concern

Most candidates were able to identify a range of relevant factors justifying why going concern was a key area of audit risk. However, the points that were most commonly overlooked were that:

- additional finance is needed to continue the development of Flint's new engines;

- the new engines will not be available for sale until 20X8; and

- the fall in demand for current engines would have a knock on impact on the future sale of parts for a number of years.

Candidates were also able to identify a range of relevant procedures to address the going concern risk. However, the points most commonly overlooked were the following:

- Consultation with experts on the feasibility of the new engines

- Identification of the specific assumptions used in the cash flow and profit forecasts that particular attention should be paid to, including those in relation to future revenue, the level of funds required to continue development of the new engine and the outcome of the investigation by the UK Serious Fraud Office

- The review of the outcome of similar regulatory cases

A number of weaker candidates tended to over-rely on information from management when more reliable third party evidence should be available. For example relying on management views in respect of the following:

- Obtaining further funding from the bank, instead of correspondence with the bank

- The outcome of the investigation by the UK Serious Fraud Office, instead of Flint's legal advisors

- The feasibility of the new engines, instead of independent experts

No marks were awarded where candidates inappropriately relied on the opinion of management.

Inventory of parts stored in the UK

Candidates generally performed better on justifying why inventory of parts presented an audit risk but struggled to identify relevant audit procedures to address the risk of overstatement of inventory.

The points most commonly identified to justify why inventory was a key area of audit risk were the following:

- The fall in demand for engines may lead to obsolete parts, indicating a risk of overstatement of inventory

- That foreign currency transactions give rise to a risk of translation errors

The points most commonly overlooked related to the following:

- Reasons why the standard costing system might be inaccurate
- Potential cut-off errors due to goods in transit
- Fixed price contracts for the sale of parts could result in parts being sold at a loss

A number of candidates stated that the absence of a year-end inventory count gave rise to a risk of misstatement. However, no marks were awarded for repeating this point from the scenario as the presence of a perpetual inventory system could have mitigated such risks. To earn the marks related to this point candidates needed to state that the perpetual inventory system may not accurately reflect the actual quantities of inventory on hand at year end if, for example, some inventory is never counted as part of the periodic sample counts.

The most commonly identified procedures were the following:

- Undertaking test counts (with better candidates also stating that these then needed to be compared to the amounts recorded on the perpetual inventory system)

- Obtaining an aged inventory analysis to identify slow-moving items

- Re-performing translation of foreign currency transactions using an exchange rate from a reliable source

Many candidates also earned the half-mark available for correctly stating that the auditor should evaluate controls. However, most candidates failed to earn the further marks available for identifying the specific controls that should be evaluated, such as:

- Those over inventory sample counts
- Updates to the perpetual inventory system
- Those over the maintenance of the standard cost system

The procedures most commonly overlooked were the following:

- Comparing the fixed selling prices of parts to carrying value

- Comparing the amount of parts held with the number of engines still in use to assess whether the parts will be used

- Inspecting the specification costings, including vouching component costs to supplier invoices, labour costs to payroll records and ensuring the directors' basis for overhead allocation related to normal level of activity

Part 41.3

Answers to part (a) were of a mixed standard. Most candidates listed five appropriate items to be included in the instructions to component auditors. However, only stronger candidates provided plausible reasons as to why each item should be included. The most commonly overlooked points were instructions regarding work to be performed on intra-group transactions and subsequent events. A small minority of candidates did not read the requirement properly and incorrectly provided a list of items that should be included in the component auditors' correspondence to the group auditor. A number of candidates wasted time by providing more than five items as only the first five items were considered by markers.

Answers to part (b) were disappointing with few candidates specifically stating that the group auditor is responsible for the auditor's opinion on the consolidated financial statements and that the evaluation of the sufficiency and appropriateness of the audit evidence obtained by component auditors is mandatory under ISA (UK) 600. Stronger candidates correctly identified that the group auditor needs to consider whether the work undertaken by component auditors is reliable and to determine whether additional audit procedures are necessary. Candidates generally identified one or two relevant ways in which the firm could undertake the evaluation of the component auditors' audit evidence. The most commonly cited methods were through discussion with the component auditor and review of the component auditors' working papers. The most commonly overlooked methods were the use of questionnaires, review of audit plans and obtaining and evaluating the component auditors' documented conclusions or list of uncorrected misstatements identified during the audit of each subsidiary. A number of candidates did not attempt or provided very brief answers to part (b).

42 Shentan plc, Maxfield Ltd, Newbee Group plc

		Marks
42.1 Objectivity	1	
Independence	6½	
Marks available	7½	
Maximum		3
42.2 **Shentan plc**		
Threats	2	
Steps to take	1½	
Maxfield Ltd		
Threats	4½	
Steps to take – management threat	3½	
Steps to take – self-review threat	3	
Consult ethics partner	½	
Newbee Group plc		
Threats	4½	
Steps to take	3	
Marks available	22½	
Maximum		10
42.3 Ethical issues	2½	
Safeguards	4½	
Marks available	7	
Maximum		4
Total marks available		17

42.1 Objectivity is a state of mind that excludes bias, prejudice and compromise. Independence is freedom from situations and relationships which make it probable that a reasonable and informed third party would conclude that objectivity either is or could be impaired.

The primary objective of an audit is to provide assurance to the company's shareholders, who are often not involved in running the audited entity, that the directors have prepared the financial statements properly and without bias. The preparation of financial statements involves making judgements and the directors may wish to portray results which reflect favourably on their stewardship function. If auditors are not independent and objective, shareholders would not be able to rely on the auditor's opinion and the credibility of the financial statements would be at risk. The auditor also has a duty to act in the public interest and public confidence in the audit process depends on the perception of independence.

42.2 Shentan plc

Threats

There is a familiarity threat arising from the partner's long association with the audited entity. Continuing involvement with Shentan means the relationship partner can still directly influence the outcome of the audit. A reasonable and informed third party may consider the firm's independence and objectivity to be impaired.

Steps to take

ES S3 *Long Association with Engagements and With Entities Relevant to Engagements* requires that a relationship partner role would not be acceptable for a partner who has been rotated off the engagement team. Therefore, the relationship partner must be removed and must not return to the audit team within five years.

Maxfield Ltd

Threats

The work is not prohibited as the company is not listed. However, a management threat arises if the firm is expected to make judgements or decisions on behalf of management such as initiating transactions. Consequently, the firm may become too closely aligned with the views and interests of management. There is also a self-review threat, which arises when the results of a non-audit service are reflected in the amounts included or disclosed in the financial statements. External audit staff may be reluctant to identify shortcomings in their colleague's work or may place too much reliance on that work without checking it.

Steps to take

To protect against the management threat, the firm should limit the length of time for which help with the preparation of the financial statements is provided. Informed management should be in place to demonstrate that management is capable of making decisions. There should also be no initiating of transactions or making decisions. Services provided should be of a technical, mechanical or informative nature only, where management makes all decisions requiring the exercise of judgement and prepares the underlying accounting records.

To protect against the self-review threat, the loaned member of staff must have no involvement in the audit of the financial statements and audit documentation must demonstrate that Maxfield has made all management decisions. The agreed work should be set out in an engagement letter. There should be an independent review of both the audit work and the accounting services provided.

The ethics partner should be consulted about the work to be undertaken and the safeguards to be applied.

Newbee Group plc

Threats

There is a self-interest threat arising from fee dependency. The firm may be reluctant to issue a modified opinion due to the fear of losing the client and its fee income. Recurring fees amount to 9.35% ((95 + 47 + 45 = 187)/2010). ES S4 *Fees, Remuneration and Evaluation Policies* requires that fees from a listed company should not exceed 10% of a firm's annual fee income and that safeguards should be considered if fee income is expected to exceed 5% on a regular basis. Depending on the nature of the services, the tax and consultancy engagements may give rise to other threats such as self-review and management threats.

Steps to take

The level of fees should be disclosed to the ethics partner and to those charged with governance at Newbee. The fee levels should be monitored and consideration given to reducing the level of non-audit services provided.

42.3 Ethical issues

Acting for all three companies gives rise to a potential conflict of interest and threats to the fundamental principles of objectivity and confidentiality. The audit firm may not be able to act in the best interests of each client. There is the perceived threat that confidential information may be leaked.

Safeguards

Obtain consent to act from all three clients. Once obtained, separate teams should be used for each client with information barriers between the teams. There should be a system of confidential and secure data filing. The firm should have clear guidelines for members of each engagement team on issues of security and confidentiality and employees and partners of the firm should sign confidentiality agreements. The ethics partner should be consulted and there should be a regular review of safeguards by an independent person.

Examiner's comments

Part 42.1

Answers to this part of the question were of a mixed standard. Weaker candidates only provided definitions of independence and objectivity without explaining why they are important principles in the context of an external audit engagement. Few candidates identified the primary objective of an audit as being the provision of assurance to a company's shareholders regarding the preparation of the financial statements by the company's directors. Stronger candidates were able to explain the points around the preparation of financial statements involving judgement and public confidence being dependent on the perception of independence.

Part 42.2

It was pleasing to note that the standard of answers to this question was particularly high. Generally, most candidates identified the correct threats to objectivity in each scenario, explained the significance of the threats and correctly stated some of the steps the firm should take to address the issues arising. Weaker candidates, however, listed a number of threats in the hope of finding the correct threat, or listed a number of inappropriate steps to take.

Shentan

This was the least well answered of the three scenarios. Most candidates correctly identified the familiarity threat caused by long association. Fewer candidates identified that the relationship partner may still be able to influence the outcome of the audit or that the relationship partner must be removed from that role and must not return to the audit team within five years. Weaker candidates confused the roles of the engagement partner and the relationship partner. A number of candidates wasted time listing a number of inappropriate steps to take including identifying safeguards that should be in place, such as an independent partner review, were the relationship partner to continue in that role. These candidates failed to appreciate that there were no suitable safeguards in this situation.

Maxfield

The scenario was particularly well answered with most candidates correctly identifying and explaining the management and the self-review threats. These candidates listed a range of safeguards to mitigate the threats. The most commonly overlooked points were that the audit documentation should demonstrate that Maxfield has taken all management decisions, that there should be informed management and that the agreed work should be set out in an engagement letter.

Newbee Group

There were some excellent answers to this scenario. Most candidates identified and explained the self-interest threat and correctly calculated the level of recurring fees of 9.35%. These candidates also identified the fee thresholds set out in ES S4 and suggested a number of appropriate steps that the firm should take to address the issues arising. However, some candidates incorrectly calculated the fee percentage by including the one-off consultancy fees or excluding the annual taxation engagement in their calculation. Weaker candidates wasted time calculating every possible combination of annual fee percentages in the hope of finding the correct one. A significant minority of candidates confused the fee threshold limits for listed and unlisted companies. A number of candidates stated that there should be an independent quality control review but this did not score any marks because Newbee Group plc is a listed company and will already be subject to an engagement quality control review.

Part 42.3

It was pleasing to note that this question was very well answered with a significant number of candidates scoring maximum marks. Most candidates explained the ethical issues arising and suggested a range of safeguards. The ethical issue most commonly overlooked was the threat to objectivity. The safeguard most commonly overlooked was the regular review of safeguards by an independent person. Disappointingly, a minority of candidates did not submit an answer to this part of the question.

September 2016 exam answers

43 Short form questions

43.1 Use of separate teams

Firm provides non-audit services to external audit client

Mitigates the self-review threat

- To independence/objectivity arising from
- Results of non-audit services reflected in the financial statements

Reduces risk of:

- Over-reliance on non-audit work during audit
- Reluctance to highlight errors/omissions in non-audit work

Which may result in an inappropriate audit opinion

Firm acts for competing clients

Mitigates threat to firm's independence/objectivity arising from the potential conflict of interest between clients.

Where the firm may not be able to act in the best interests of both clients

Reduces risk of:

- Breach of duty of confidentiality
- Leakage of information
- Use of information regarding one client for benefit of another client

Supplemented by information barriers between the separate teams eg, physical separation and secure data failing

Examiner's comments

This question was generally well answered as most candidates identified the threats to objectivity in both circumstances. In respect of non-audit services, most candidates identified the self-review threat and provided a plausible explanation of the threat. However, a common error in respect of non-audit services was to identify a risk of confidentiality breaches. This is not generally an issue with non-audit services provided to the audited entity. In respect of acting for competing clients, most candidates identified the confidentiality and conflict of interest issues. The point most commonly overlooked was that relating to an inappropriate auditor's opinion when the firm provides audit and non-audit service.

43.2 Ethical issues

- Creates a self-interest threat to firm's objectivity/independence
- Influenced by introductory fee
- Conflict of interest between firm and client
- May not be acting in the best interests of Persow if firm makes inappropriate recommendation
- Advocacy threat as promoting client's product

Answers to this question were disappointing. Although the vast majority of candidates identified the self-interest threat to objectivity, only a minority identified the advocacy threat. A significant number of candidates wasted timed writing about a management threat which did not exist as there was no decision to be made by the audit firm. Most candidates identified that the receipt of a fee was an issue but few stated that it might influence the firm into making a recommendation that was not necessarily in the best interests of Persow.

43.3 Actions to be taken by audit manager

- Consider reliability of information provided by Bobby
- Advise Bobby to pass information onto senior management/advise senior management of the suspicions directly, but protect Bobby's identity
- Revise or extend procedures if necessary and advise the audit team
- Consider whether there is:
  - any material impact on the financial statements
  - risk of other fraud/management integrity issues
- Document findings
- Determine whether the issue is money laundering
- Report to the firm's MLRO
- Avoid tipping off

Examiner's comments

Answers to this question were generally disappointing. While the vast majority of candidates considered the action to be taken if the issue represented money laundering, few candidates considered the actions in respect of the audit of the current year's financial statements. Consequently, only a minority of candidates identified the potential need to revise planned audit procedures and to assess the impact on the financial statements. A significant number of candidates wasted time listing basic audit procedures undertaken on any payroll system irrespective of the matter discovered by the audit manager.

43.4 Factors affecting firm's fee calculation

- Whether Caul is an existing client and if the firm has cumulative knowledge and experience
- Experience of investments in India
- Scope of engagement/period covered
- Estimated time to complete engagement
- Timeframe for work/priority and importance to client
- Level of experience of staff required
- Whether external experts required
- Extent of partner reviews required
- Whether visits to India will be necessary and associated costs

- Whether firm has representation in India
- Degree of risk
- Whether the firm's report will be distributed outside of Caul, eg, reliance on the report by a provider of finance

Examiner's comments

This question was generally well answered with a significant number of candidates attaining full marks. The points most commonly identified were those relating to the scope of the work, the level of resources and the possibility of travel to India. The points most commonly overlooked were those relating to the degree of risk involved and the distribution of the report. A common error was to list the level of assurance required as a factor that would affect the fee for the engagement. However, these candidates failed to appreciate that only limited assurance is provided when reporting on cash flow forecasts.

43.5 Matters to consider when examining fee income for reasonableness

Breakdown of projected fee income over 25 offices

Higher receipts in April – September/lower receipts October – March

Fees consistent with:

- actual pattern of completions in previous years
- 2%/less than 2% of total projected sales value
- level of competition in market for local office
- rate of discounts in prior years

Sensitivity analysis re effect of different levels of discounts

Estimated sales values consistent with:

- market predictions about property prices in each locality

Realistic assumptions about:

- number of sales
- eg, sales reflect size of each office

average time to complete

Examiner's comments

This question was very well answered with many candidates attaining full marks. The points most commonly identified were those relating to seasonality, geographical location, discounts, consistency with previous years and property market conditions. The points most commonly overlooked were those relating to the breakdown of projected sales by office, sensitivity analysis and realistic assumptions in respect of the number of sales, size of each office and average time to complete a sale. Candidates who did not score well on this question failed to use information in the scenario to generate specific matters to consider. Statements such as "consider the reasonableness of assumptions made by management" or "consider inflation" without relating it to the specific circumstances in the scenario were not awarded any marks.

43.6 Impact of data analytics on conduct of an external audit

- Plan to monitor larger data sets/100% population, often on a continuous basis
- Identify anomalies for further investigation
- Planned audit evidence may include unstructured data sets
  - Eg, emails/social media
- Need to plan to extract data from client systems
- Inclusion of data/IT experts in the audit team

Examiner's comments

Answers to this question were very disappointing. This topic was added to learning outcomes 3i and 3j in the planning section of the syllabus. The minority of candidates who were familiar with the material in the Audit and Assurance Study Manual tended to score full marks. However, a significant majority of candidates did not demonstrate a knowledge of this part of the learning materials. The points most commonly identified were those relating to the examination of larger sets of data on an ongoing basis and the use of data analytics experts. Few candidates demonstrated knowledge of the use of new data sets.

44 Thought Train Ltd

Marking guide

			Marks
44.1	Benefits	4	
	Limitations	7	
	Marks available	11	
	Maximum		5
44.2	Materiality of office results	2	
	Source documents	5½	
	Internal controls	3½	
	Accounting systems	2½	
	Laws and regulations	1	
	Marks available	14½	
	Maximum		5
44.3 (a)	**Revenue**		
	Justification	11	
	Procedures	14	
(b)	**Employee costs and external consultants**		
	Justification	12	
	Procedures	8½	
(c)	**Trade receivables**		
	Justification	5½	
	Procedures	14	

General

Justification	3	
Procedures	2	
Marks available	70	
Maximum		25
Total marks available		35

44.1 **Benefits**

Analytical procedures are used to obtain an understanding of an entity and its environment or identify aspects of an entity of which the auditor was previously unaware. They identify areas at risk of misstatement and allow resources to be targeted to those risk areas. They also indicate areas where detailed testing can be kept to a minimum.

Limitations

Substantial knowledge of the business and experienced members of staff are required to interpret the results of analytical procedures. Consistency of results from one year to another may hide material errors and a high level of aggregation of data will only provide a broad indication of whether material misstatements may exist.

Analytical procedures may be performed mechanically and rely upon good quality information which may not be available. A lack of comparability arises if a business is changing, eg, growing or declining.

44.2 The materiality of the results of each TT office to the financial statements must be considered. Some offices, where figures are not material to the financial statements may be visited on a rotational basis.

Source documents are stored in each of TT's offices. It needs to be considered if the firm's overseas offices have appropriate resources and expertise to carry out work on the TT audit. If so, request them to perform work at TT's offices. Instructions will need to be provided to the firm's overseas offices, including timetables and the format for reporting.

TT's offices are run autonomously and, consequently, internal controls may be different in each location. Therefore, it may be more difficult to obtain assurance over the reliability of controls for TT as a whole and a substantive approach may be more efficient.

The accounting systems of each TT office are integrated with the accounting software used in the UK. The system will need to be tested and may require the use of an IT expert.

TT offices in different locations are likely to be subject to different laws and regulations, breaches of which may have implications for the financial statements.

44.3 (a) **Revenue**

Justification

There is a risk of overstatement because:

- revenue has increased by 18.9% compared to the prior year.
- gross profit has increased from 49.9% to 56.8%.
- revenue per employee has increased from £329k to £386k.
- average revenue per project has increased from £81k to £93.6k.
- TT offices are incentivised by bonus payments based on profit

Accrued revenue/percentage completion of projects in progress at the year end may be inappropriately estimated. Calculations are not checked by the UK financial controller and therefore misstatements may not be detected.

Procedures

Discuss with management the reason for the increase in revenue.

Review budgets/forecasts for the year to ascertain if revenue is higher than expected.

Obtain a breakdown of revenue by each TT office to identify any anomalies compared to the prior year.

For a sample of completed projects included in revenue in the year:

- agree the fee to the statement of work.
- vouch the fee to the cash receipt from the customer.
- perform cut-off testing.

Review post year-end management accounts for evidence of understated revenue indicating an overstatement of pre year-end revenue.

Review post year-end credit notes for evidence of the reversal of revenue recorded pre year-end.

Obtain accrued revenue calculations provided by the TT offices and for a sample of projects in progress, ascertain the basis of the estimate of percentage completion.

Inspect supporting documentation from the TT offices such as the statement of work and agree the fixed price.

(b) **Employee costs and external consultants' fees**

Justification

There is a risk of understatement because:

- costs are out of line with the increase in revenue.

- total employee/consultant costs have fallen by 2.3%.

- employee costs as percentage of cost of sales have fallen from 43.2% to 39.7% and external consultants' fees as percentage of cost of sales have remained static.

- the fall in employee costs is inconsistent with a 1.3% increase in employee numbers.

- the average cost per employee has fallen from £71.3k to £66.3k.

- the average employee/consultant cost per project has fallen from £33.5k to £31.6k.

- TT may fail to accrue for the employee bonus.

The accrual for consultants' fees at the year end may be understated because:

- consultant costs have remained stable whereas revenue has increased.

- no time records are kept by consultants.

- late invoices may be omitted from the accrual in error.

- TT offices are incentivised to understate costs due to the bonus being based on profit.

Procedures

Obtain a breakdown of salaries by month/office to identify any anomalies.

For a sample of employees, agree salary/bonus per payroll to HR records.

Reperform the bonus calculation ensuring it is based on the correct profit figure.

Review bank statements for payments made to consultants after 31 July 20X6 and inspect invoices received from consultants after 31 July 20X6. Identify if the amounts should be included in the year-end accrual.

Obtain a list of projects in progress at each TT office on 31 July 20X6. For a sample of these projects circularise the consultants who worked on the project to ascertain whether there are any outstanding amounts still to be invoiced.

(c) **Trade receivables**

Justification

There is a risk of overstatement of receivables and an understatement of the allowance against receivables because:

- trade receivables days have increased from 33.4 to 45. This is out of line with the 30-day credit period.

- Jangles is refusing to pay an invoice which represents 0.6% of revenue and is therefore material.

The poor quality work may have arisen due to the Hong Kong office reorganisation and may indicate that other dissatisfied customers will refuse to pay.

Procedures

Calculate trade receivables days on an office-by-office basis to identify any specific offices with slow-paying customers.

Ascertain and test credit control procedures.

Inspect bank statements for evidence of amounts received from customers after 31 July 20X6.

Perform direct confirmation of a sample of trade receivables balances at the year end.

Inspect correspondence between TT and Jangles and any legal correspondence to ascertain the basis for their refusal to pay.

Inspect the statement of work agreed with Jangles.

Discuss the issue with management to determine its intentions regarding the amount due from Jangles.

Review correspondence files to ascertain if any other customers are refusing to pay.

Ascertain Jangle's ability to pay by reviewing credit ratings/latest published financial statements.

Ascertain the basis for the allowance against receivables and:

- review aged receivables to identify overdue amounts.
- consider whether slow payers are adequately taken into account.
- reperform the calculation.

Obtain written representation regarding the completeness of the allowance against receivables.

General points

TT is a new audit client. The firm has a lack of cumulative audit knowledge and experience and, consequently, limited comfort over opening balances.

The accuracy of the accounting records at head office is reliant on the successful integration between the systems at TT offices and those in the UK. The system may not be working correctly.

Transactions are undertaken in foreign currencies which may result in translation errors.

Procedures

Obtain the previous auditor's working papers and assess the reliability of opening balances.

Test the integration of the systems using CAAT's or an IT expert.

For a sample of transactions and balances in foreign currencies, agree the exchange rate used to a reliable third party source and reperform the calculation.

Examiner's comments

The overall average mark on this question was the lowest on the long-form questions. This was largely due to poor performance by candidates in part 2 of the question as answers to part 3 of the question were of a good standard.

Part 44.1

Answers to this part of the question were of a mixed standard. In respect of benefits, the points most commonly identified were those relating to the identification of risk areas, targeting of resources to those areas and, to a lesser extent, an understanding of the business. In respect of limitations, the points most commonly identified were those relating to the requirement for knowledge of the business and experienced staff to interpret the results of analytical procedures. The points most commonly overlooked were those relating to areas where detailed testing can be minimised and mechanical performance of procedures. A small number of candidates restricted their answers to setting out the benefits of analytical procedures and did not provide any limitations. A number of candidates wasted time providing examples of the different types of analytical procedures. These points scored no marks.

Part 44.2

Answers to this part of the question were disappointing. Few candidates scored maximum marks and a number of candidates presented very short answers. Many candidates identified one or more of the relevant matters from the scenario, such as overseas storage of source documents, autonomous offices and integrated accounting systems. However, few candidates expanded their answers by setting out further considerations. For example, having identified that accounting systems were integrated very few candidates then set out the need for IT expertise to test that the integration is working appropriately. Few candidates considered the implications for the internal control system at each office as a result of offices operating autonomously. The point most commonly overlooked related to the materiality of each overseas office to the financial statements. Consequently, most candidates failed to consider whether all offices needed to be visited. A number of candidates wasted time discussing language barriers and different time zones which were not relevant as the firm had representation in each of the overseas locations.

Part 44.3

Answers to this part of the question were good and many candidates provided a number of justifications as to why each item had been identified as a key area of audit risk. These candidates then cited a range of procedures that were both adequately described and relevant to the justification of the audit risk. However, as noted in previous examiners' commentaries, weaker candidates continue to cite vague audit procedures (such as 'test balance for accuracy' or 'check item is recorded correctly') which were not awarded any marks.

Most candidates attempted to make some use of the financial information provided in the scenario although this was often restricted to a comparison of the 20X6 figures against the previous year. Only a minority of stronger candidates earned the higher skills marks available for performing more detailed analytical procedures by using the additional information given in the scenario such as the number of research projects in the year. Weaker candidates proposed performing analytical procedures, without elaboration, either to justify the audit risk or as a procedure to address the risk but failed to appreciate that the information was available in the scenario to enable them to do this.

Most candidates correctly identified that transactions in overseas currencies may lead to translation errors and identified that a sample of foreign currency calculations should be tested using exchange rates from a reliable external source. Many candidates overlooked that the firm had recently been appointed as external auditor and that obtaining assurance over opening balances may be an issue.

Revenue

Answers to this section of the question were good. Most candidates provided a number of reasons to justify why revenue was a key area of audit risk, including making use of basic analytical procedures. Most correctly stated that the 18.9% increase in revenue was out of line with the changes in the number of projects and number of employees which indicated a risk of overstatement. A significant number of candidates also correctly identified that overseas offices were incentivised to overstate revenue due to the bonus based on profit. Most candidates cited credible audit procedures to address the identified risks, such as enquiring of management why revenue had increased, obtaining accrued revenue calculations and for a sample of projects in progress ascertaining the basis of the calculations.

The most commonly overlooked procedures included:

- comparison of actual revenue to budgeted revenue

- obtaining a breakdown of revenue by local office to identify any anomalies compared to prior year

- inspecting supporting documentation from overseas offices such as statements of work

- reviewing post year-end credit notes for evidence of reversal of revenue recorded pre year end.

Employee costs and external consultants' fees

Answers to this section of the question were of a mixed standard. Most candidates provided a number of reasons to justify why payroll was a key area of audit risk. This included making use of basic analytical procedures to identify that there was a risk of understatement of payroll. Stronger candidates made use of the additional information to calculate the average cost per employee and the average cost per project. Most candidates also correctly identified that the accrual for consultants' fees at the year end may be understated and cited one or more reasons for this, such as the absence of time records and late invoicing leading to understatement of the accrual. Audit procedures in respect of payroll were the weakest of the three key areas identified. The majority of candidates earned some marks available but few candidates provided comprehensive answers. The most commonly overlooked procedures included:

- obtaining a breakdown of salaries by month or office to identify any anomalies

- checking salary or bonuses to HR records for a sample of employees

- inspecting invoices received from consultants after 31 July 20X6 to identify if any amounts should have been included in the year-end accrual

- obtaining a list of projects in progress at each TT office on 31 July 20X6 and circularising consultants who worked on those projects to ascertain whether there were any outstanding amounts to be invoiced.

Trade receivables

There were a number of good answers to this part of the question. Candidates that used the financial information provided correctly identified that there was a risk of overstatement and that the Jangles dispute was a contributory factor to this risk. These candidates went on to identify a number of relevant audit procedures and scored high marks. A number of candidates correctly concluded that the Jangles balance was material but failed to assess its materiality in the context of revenue to reach this conclusion. The procedures commonly identified were the direct confirmation of balances, the review of cash received from customers after the year end and the review of aged receivables to identify old outstanding amounts.

The most commonly overlooked procedures included:

- the calculation of trade receivable days on an office by office basis to identify any specific offices with slow-paying customers

- inspection of Jangles' statement of work

- obtaining written representations regarding the completion of allowances for doubtful debts

- the review of correspondence files to ascertain if any other customers are refusing to pay in light of the quality issues.

45 Byng LLP

Marking guide

		Marks
45.1 Responsibilities	$\frac{5}{5}$	
Marks available		
Maximum		2
45.2 Treats to objectivity and independence	½	
Fee income	8	
Non-audit services	7½	
Threats from Wagon's directors	4	
Bank loan	7	
Concealment of information	1½	
Departure of Rocket's financial controller	3	
Audit manager taking on FC role	$\frac{6}{37½}$	
Marks available		
Maximum		13
45.3 Parties	2	
Methods	$\frac{6}{8}$	
Marks available		
Maximum		$\frac{5}{\underline{20}}$
Total marks available		

45.1 Byng should deposit a statement of circumstances at Wagon's registered office. The statement should detail the circumstances connected with ceasing to hold office which Byng considers should be brought to attention of the members, or it should make a statement that there are no such circumstances.

Audit and money laundering documentation must be kept for the required number of years and any books and records belonging to Wagon should be returned.

Byng should maintain confidentiality after ceasing to hold office and it should co-operate with the incoming auditor.

45.2 Issues

There are a number of threats to the firm's objectivity and independence:

There is a risk that Byng fears losing fees from Wagon and Rocket which gives rise to a self-interest threat. If the firm ceases to be the auditor of Wagon, total fee income will fall to £13,945k. Regular fee income from Rocket is £1,430k, which is 10.3% of total fee income. This exceeds the threshold of 10% but is below the maximum threshold of 15%.

Currently, fee income from Rocket is 8.9% of total fee income and fee income from Wagon is 9.3% of total fee income. These are both quite close to the 10% threshold.

Byng performs tax services/non-audit services for its external audit clients. This gives rise to a self-review threat as the results of the work may be included in the financial statements. The audit team may place too much reliance on the non-audit work or be unwilling to highlight any errors identified.

A management threat arises if Byng is expected to make judgements.

Wagon's directors have threatened Byng that they may not recommend reappointment which represents an intimidation threat.

The firm may not perform the extra work required due to the pressure to sign the auditor's report on time. This is a threat to professional competence and due care. Furthermore, the audit procedures identified internal control issues with the new software at Wagon leading to an increased risk of material misstatement.

Byng was unaware of the reliance on the audited financial statements of Wagon by its bank. The directors appear to have concealed information from the firm. There is a risk of management bias when preparing the financial statements and an increased engagement risk because the bank may sue the firm if a duty of care is owed. The bank's reliance has not been taken into account when planning the audit work and the planned audit procedures may no longer be appropriate. This may represent a management imposed inability to obtain sufficient appropriate audit evidence.

The threatening behaviour of Wagon's directors and concealment of information raises concerns over management's integrity which could result in a reputational risk to the firm.

The audit manager has accepted the position of financial controller at Rocket. This gives rise to a self-interest threat. The audit manager is less likely to point out issues for fear of the job offer being withdrawn.

A familiarity threat may arise for future audits as the audit team may be too trusting of the new financial controller/previous audit manager.

Steps to be taken

Disclose the fee income from Rocket to the ethics partner and those charged with governance where it exceeds 10%.

Continue to monitor the proportion of fee income earned from Wagon and Rocket.

Undertake an independent quality control review, which must be external if fees represent more than 10% of total fee income.

Separate teams must be used for the audit and tax/non-audit work.

An independent partner review of the tax work should be undertaken to assess if it has been properly addressed in the audit.

Byng should document the existence of informed management.

The firm must not compromise on the audit work required to reach its opinion and should explain to Wagon's directors why the request is not possible.

The firm may consult the ICAEW helpline or seek legal advice.

Byng should discuss the nature and purposes of the bank loan with Wagon's directors and review the planned audit procedures to ascertain if they need to be extended.

The engagement letter should be re-issued to reflect the increased scope of the work.

Consult the firm's ethics partner.

Remove the audit manager from the audit engagement team immediately and re-evaluate any audit work performed by him. Reperform any procedures if necessary.

The composition of the audit team should be reconsidered in future years.

45.3 Parties

The firm may be liable to the shareholders of Wagon and to third parties to whom a duty of care is owed, for example Wagon's bank.

Methods

- A liability agreement which apportions the blame between the guilty parties (eg, directors and auditors)
- A liability cap of a fixed amount (eg, a multiple of the audit fee) which is fair and reasonable and approved by the shareholders
- A disclaimer of liability (Bannerman paragraph), inserted into the auditor's report, stating that the firm is not liable to third parties
- A limited liability partnership which limits claims to the assets in the firm and where no individual has responsibility for another's actions

Examiner's comments

Part 45.1

Those candidates who gained marks on this part of the question tended to do so by listing the professional responsibilities such as cooperating with the incoming auditor and maintaining confidentiality. A significant number of candidates failed to identify the legal responsibilities under the Companies Act 2006. Those candidates who did refer to the Companies Act 2006 provisions often referred to the auditor's rights (eg, written representations) instead of responsibilities (eg, statement of circumstances). There were no marks for rights as this was not required by the question.

Part 45.2

This part of the question was very well answered with many candidates scoring full marks. The vast majority of candidates identified the self-interest threat to objectivity arising out of fee dependency and the acceptance, by the audit manager, of the post of financial controller at the audited entity. A common error in respect of the fee dependency threat was the inclusion of the fees relating to one-off engagements when calculating the percentage of fee income as a proportion of total fee income. Candidates need to be aware that the fee thresholds only apply to regular income. A common error in respect of the audit manager joining the audited entity was to state that the firm should resign as auditor. Candidates need to be aware that resignation is only required when a partner joins an entity audited by the firm. The issues most commonly overlooked were the threats and related safeguards in respect of the provision of non-audit services and the implications of the sudden departure of the financial controller.

Part 45.3

Answers to this part of the question were disappointing given that this topic was examined in recent sessions. Although most candidates identified the shareholders and the bank as parties to whom the auditor may be liable, few identified that a duty of care to third parties such as the bank had to be established. The points most commonly identified in respect of the methods available to limit liability were a liability cap and Bannerman paragraph. However, many stated, incorrectly, that the inclusion of a Bannerman paragraph in the **engagement letter** would limit liability to third parties. These candidates failed to appreciate that third parties would not have access to the engagement letter. Only a minority of candidates identified proportional liability agreements.

46 Sednass Ltd, Gustdis Ltd, Raef Ltd

Marking guide

			Marks
46.1	Attributes of auditors' communications	7	
	Marks available	7	
	Maximum		4
46.2 (a)	Sednass	11	
	Gustdis	10	
	Raef	9½	
	General	1½	
	Marks available	32	
	Maximum		12
(b)	Sednass	6	
	Gustdis	4½	
	Raef	5½	
	Marks available	16	
	Maximum		9
Total marks available			25

46.1 Communications should be timely to allow management to act promptly. They should be made in writing with clear language to avoid any misunderstandings. They must be communicated to those in authority who are able to take corrective action and include a description of the deficiency, possible consequences and recommendations for improvement. This ensures there is sufficient information to understand and correct the deficiency. The extent, form and frequency should be appropriate to the size and nature of the organisation.

Points included should be of sufficient importance to ensure that information provided by the auditor is useful. Management comments should be included to indicate whether points are accepted by management and to aid the understanding of those charged with governance.

46.2 (a) Sednass

Anti-virus software is out of date and back-up data has not been stored. The IT manager's responsibilities were not covered during extended leave.

Consequences

Loss of data will result in additional costs to recover data. Systems may become corrupted and the business may not be able to operate. With no means to recover data to a previous position there will be a delay in the resumption of business. This results in a negative impact on profit/revenue and cash flows/going concern status.

Recommendations

Anti-virus software and back-ups must be maintained at all times. Back-ups should be stored off site.

Responsibility should be assigned to more than one individual. There should be clear, documented procedures, circulated to employees, for covering periods of absence.

Gustdis

Contracted service levels are not monitored.

Consequences

Breaches of service levels required by the contract are more likely to occur. Employees cannot focus on meeting the service levels required if they do not know which contracts are at risk of breach.

Loss of customer goodwill may result in termination of contracts, financial penalties or customers refusing to pay. Customers may sue Gustdis. This would result in a negative impact on revenue/profits and cash flows/going concern status.

Recommendations

Regular reviews of service levels should be performed by collecting data on performance against service levels required by the contract.

Performance against service levels should be regularly reported to senior management who should review the report for areas where service levels are 'at risk'.

Employees' objectives or job descriptions should include meeting contractual service levels.

Regular meetings should be held with key customers to review performance as well as regularly reviewing customer correspondence for potential issues.

Raef

Supplier statement reconciliations are not performed.

Consequences

Payments may be late or missed resulting in the loss of prompt payment discounts. A loss of supplier goodwill could result in Raef's account being put on hold by the supplier. This may mean Raef is unable to operate due to insufficient supplies or stock outs. Invoices may be paid twice.

There could be a negative impact on revenue/profit and cash flows and there may be misstatements in the financial statements due to unrecorded liabilities.

Recommendations

Supplier statement reconciliations should be performed on a regular basis by individual(s) not responsible for recording purchases/ payments. Any discrepancies identified should be investigated and resolved.

Senior management should review and sign off reconciliations.

General points

Training of employees in relevant procedures.

Disciplinary action for employees failing to follow procedures.

Monitoring of compliance with procedures.

(b) **Sednass**

The auditor's report and opinion should be modified due to inability to obtain sufficient appropriate evidence. The estimated value of the inventory is 11.1% of profit before tax and is therefore material. The issue is not pervasive as it is isolated to the inventory balance. The opinion will be qualified and an explanation provided in the basis for qualified opinion section of the auditor's report.

Under the Companies Act 2006, the firm should report by exception that the auditor did not receive all necessary information and explanations and that adequate accounting records were not maintained.

Gustdis

The auditor's report should be modified but the opinion unmodified, as there is no material misstatement and sufficient appropriate evidence has been obtained. However, a section headed 'Material uncertainty related to going concern' should be included after the 'Basis for...' section. The auditor's report should also include a statement that the opinion is not modified in respect of this matter.

Raef

The firm should issue a modified report with a modified conclusion due to a material misstatement. The exclusion of the payments amounts to 171% of profit before tax and is therefore material. Adjustment for the misstatement would turn the profit into a loss.

If the matter is considered material and pervasive an adverse conclusion should be issued. If the matter is not considered pervasive a qualified conclusion should be issued. In either case an explanation should be provided in the basis for qualified/adverse conclusion section.

Examiner's comments

Part 46.1

Answers to this part of the question were very disappointing given that this topic has been examined in recent sessions. The majority of candidates identified that the communication should be in writing, communicated on a timely basis and include a description of the deficiencies, their consequences and recommendations. The most common shortcoming was to list the attributes without an explanation. For example, the majority of candidates listed 'timely basis' but failed to explain that this would allow management to take corrective action promptly. The points most commonly overlooked were those relating to the nature of the organisation and the inclusion of management comments. A significant minority did not attempt this part of the question.

Part 46.2 (a)

A common shortcoming, in respect of each scenario, was to focus on the consequences for the auditor (eg, lack of audit evidence) and the impact on the auditor's report rather than the consequences for the audited entity.

Sednass

Candidates who focused on the IT issues relating to out-of-date antivirus software and failure to back-up data and related consequences of loss of data and file corruption scored well on this part of the question. However, weaker candidates failed to appreciate that the deficiencies related to the IT issues and identified, incorrectly, the lack of an inventory count as the deficiency. There was no evidence of this in the scenario. Consequently, these candidates wasted time describing internal control procedures within a perpetual inventory system. The points most commonly overlooked were those relating to the risks to the continuity of the business and the recovery costs.

Gustdis

This part of the question was generally well answered as most candidates correctly identified the deficiency as a failure to monitor service levels and that this deficiency increased the risk of breaches of contracts. Most of these candidates appreciated that such breaches might result in penalties, loss of reputation and termination of contracts. The points most commonly overlooked were those relating to reporting of performance to senior management and review of customer correspondence.

Raef

Answers to this part of the question were disappointing as many candidates failed to identify that the internal control deficiency was the failure to reconcile supplier statements with the payables ledger. Many cited the refusal to accrue for the invoices as the deficiency and then wasted time describing the controls exercised over the ordering and receipt of goods.

Part 46.2 (b)

Sednass

This part of the question was generally well answered as the vast majority of candidates correctly identified that due to lack of sufficient appropriate evidence, the opinion should be qualified on the basis that the issue was material but not pervasive. The points most commonly overlooked were those relating to the matters that should be reported by exception under the Companies Act 2006.

Gustdis

Although there were some excellent answers to this part of the question, weaker candidates failed to use information in the scenario. A number of candidates failed to appreciate that there was 'a significant uncertainty over going concern' and wasted time describing the effects on the auditor's report if the entity was not a going concern. Other candidates ignored the fact that the firm 'concluded that the note included in the financial statements is appropriate and adequate' and discussed the implications for the auditor's report if the note was not adequate or not disclosed. There were no marks awarded for these points.

Raef

The majority of candidates correctly identified that the situation represented a material misstatement. However, some candidates who concluded that the misstatement was pervasive stated, incorrectly, that the conclusion should be disclaimed. These candidates should note that a disclaimer is given when there is an inability to obtain sufficient appropriate audit evidence and that an adverse conclusion is given when there is a pervasive misstatement.

December 2016 exam answers

47 Short Form Questions

47.1 Benefits of the mandatory rotation of the appointment of audit firms

- Increased objectivity
- Increased independence
- Reduced familiarity threat
    - Greater professional scepticism
    - Reduced risk of inappropriate opinion
- Reduced self-interest threat
    - Auditors more likely to challenge their clients
    - No expectation of long-term relationship
- Increased competition
    - Opportunities for medium-sized firms to audit listed companies
    - May reduce cost to clients
- Greater confidence in the audit process

Examiner's comments

Most candidates focused on the mitigation of the familiarity and, to a lesser extent, the self-interest threats to objectivity and independence. Stronger candidates considered points other than objectivity, such as the beneficial effects of competition within the audit market. The point most commonly overlooked was that relating to greater confidence in the audit process. A minority of candidates misread the question and answered it in the context of engagement partner rotation. These candidates scored some marks for explaining the mitigation of the familiarity threat to objectivity and independence. However, they wasted time listing the *Ethical Standard* provisions relating to rotation periods for engagement partners for which they scored no marks.

47.2 Internal controls over cash donations received through the post and through collection boxes

Postal donations

- Unopened mail kept securely
- Dual control over the opening of mail
- Immediate recording of donations on opening of mail
- List of donations totalled and signed
- Independent reconciliation of amounts banked with the amounts recorded
- Designated funds highlighted

Collection boxes

- Sequential numbering of boxes
- Record kept of who has the boxes
- Sealed boxes
- Boxes secured in fixed locations
- Regular collection of collection boxes
- Dual control over counting of proceeds

General

- Prompt banking of cash
- Segregation of duties
    - Over collecting/recording/custody/banking
- Screening of volunteers
- Monitoring of controls

Examiner's comments

This question was generally well answered as most candidates provided a range of internal controls to be exercised over both types of donations. The points most commonly identified in respect of postal donations were those relating to dual control over the opening of the mail and prompt banking. The points most commonly identified in respect of the collection boxes were those relating to the sealing and sequential numbering of the boxes. The points most commonly overlooked were those relating to the immediate recording of donations and independent reconciliation of the amounts banked with the amounts recorded. Weaker candidates listed "segregation of duties" or "dual control" without specifying which duties should be split or have two people involved.

47.3 Threats to independence and objectivity

- Conflict of interest
    - Langdon wants to maximise share value
    - Portdean wants to minimise share value
    - firm may not be able to act in best interests of both parties

- Self-interest threat
    - May favour Portdean
    - In hope of retaining future audit work

- Self-review threat
    - Investment will be included in Portdean's financial statements
    - Firm may not sufficiently scrutinise it during Portdean's external audit or
    - May be reluctant to highlight errors with the valuation

- Management threat
    - Determining the valuation involves judgement

Examiner's comments

This question was very well answered with a significant number of candidates scoring full marks. The vast majority of candidates identified the conflict of interest and the self-review and management threats to objectivity. A minority of candidates strayed beyond the requirement and wasted time writing about confidentiality issues and listing safeguards despite the instruction in the question not to provide safeguards.

47.4 **Explain why this deficiency was identified and describe the actions that your firm should take**

- ISA (UK) 220 requirement
    - Review junior's work and
    - Record/document review (ISA (UK) 230)
        - What audit work was reviewed
        - Who reviewed the audit work
        - When it was reviewed
- Review may not have been undertaken
- Cannot demonstrate that firm has complied with ISAs
- Higher risk of material misstatement/inappropriate opinion if no review
- Adverse feedback following quality assurance review

Actions

- Staff training
- Disciplinary procedures
- Monitoring of policy
- Review of firm's procedures to ensure adequacy

Examiner's comments

Answers to this question were often disappointing. Although the majority of candidates correctly addressed the actions to be taken by the firm, many failed to explain why the deficiency had been identified. Consequently, the points most commonly identified were those relating to training of staff and disciplinary action. The points most commonly overlooked were those relating to the requirements in relation to the documentation of the review, ie, what, who and when. A significant number of candidates wasted time describing the purpose of a cold review.

47.5 **Explain why the managing director's expectation that the audit team should have discovered the fraud is unrealistic**

- The primary responsibility for the prevention and detection of fraud rests with management. This is discharged by:
    - promoting fraud prevention
    - creating a culture of honesty and ethical behaviour
    - implementing a system of control to reduce risk of fraud: and
    - monitoring of the system
- The auditor is responsible for obtaining assurance that the financial statements are free from material misstatement.
- Audit work must be planned so there is a reasonable expectation of discovering fraud which has a material impact on the financial statements.
- The amount involved is not material as:
    - 0.25% of revenue
    - 1.67% of profit before tax
- Audit involves sampling
- Fraud is often concealed and difficult to detect

This question was generally well answered. Most candidates identified that the amount of the fraudulent activity did not result in a material misstatement and, therefore, was beyond the scope of the auditor's responsibilities. However, a minority of candidates, whilst recognising that the amount involved was not material, lost marks by omitting their materiality calculations. The points most commonly overlooked were those relating to management's responsibility to create a culture of honesty and ethical behaviour and to implement and monitor the system of internal control.

47.6 Actions to be taken by the audit senior

- The amount is excessive in value
- May represent bribery
    - which is a criminal offence
    - under the Bribery Act 2010
    - and is global in scope
- Report to firm's MLRO or senior member of engagement team
- Required to be reported under Proceeds of Crime Act
    - benefiting from criminal conduct
- Avoid tipping off
    - so as not to prejudice subsequent investigation

Examiner's comments

Those candidates who appreciated that the issue gave rise to a suspicion of bribery and, as such, should be reported within the firm without tipping off the client scored good marks on this question. The points most commonly overlooked were those relating to the Bribery Act being global in scope and the reason for not tipping off (ie, so as not to prejudice any subsequent investigation). A significant number of candidates failed to appreciate the bribery implications and stated, incorrectly, that it was a related party transaction. These candidates wasted time writing about the implications of such transactions for the auditor's report.

48 United Cities Express plc

Marking guide

			Marks
48.1	(a)	**Going concern**	
		Justification	10
		Procedures	19
	(b)	**Provision for redundancy costs**	
		Justification	4
		Procedures	13½
	(c)	**Non-current assets – lorries**	
		Justification	6½
		Procedures	10
	Marks available		63
	Maximum		23

48.2 **Appointment of chief executive**

Threats	2½	
Response	3	
Internal audit		
Threats	5	
Response	3	
Alternative response	3	
Engagement partner		
Threats	1½	
Response	5½	
Marks available	20½	
Maximum		11

48.3 **Adequate disclosures**

Adequate disclosures	4	
No disclosures	4	
Marks available	8	
Maximum		6
Total marks available		40

48.1 (a) **Going concern**

Justification

Trading conditions are difficult as evidenced by a fall in revenue of 5.8% and an increase in the loss before tax of 3,269%.

UCEP is facing strong competition as it has lost business to its competitors who have invested in the latest technology to reduce costs and improve efficiency. There has been adverse media comment as UCEP is failing to meet its promise of delivering parcels within 24 hours. Additionally, the Whitenile contract, which generates 25% of UCEP's revenue, is due to expire in May 20X7 and may not be renewed. UCEP has recently announced a reorganisation and its chief executive is retiring.

The statement of financial position shows that UCEP is dependent on its overdraft, which has increased significantly, and is within £1.1million of the facility limit. There is insufficient headroom to pay redundancy costs and the bank loan, which is repayable in quarterly instalments of £1.5million. The overdraft facility is an expensive form of finance putting a strain on cash flow. It is due for review and UCEP may not be able to secure other finance if the facility is withdrawn. Additionally, UCEP may be in breach of bank loan covenants.

All of this indicates that UCEP may be unable to pay debts as they fall due.

Procedures

- Obtain profit and cash flow forecasts for at least one year from the date of the financial statements (per ISA (UK) 570) or from the date of approval of the financial statements (per ISA (UK) 570 (UK))

- Assess the assumptions for reasonableness, in particular, the assumptions regarding:

    - redundancy payments
    - loan repayments
    - replacement of old machinery

- Perform sensitivity analysis on key components of the forecast such as revenue and interest rates

- Review the cash flow forecasts to see if UCEP can pay its debts as they fall due

- Obtain the reorganisation plan and assess whether profit and cash flow forecasts are consistent with the plan

- Obtain written representation from management regarding the feasibility of future plans

- Ascertain management's contingency plans for alternative sources of finance should the bank overdraft be withdrawn

- Review bank correspondence for evidence of the relationship with the bank

- Review bank covenants and assess UCEP's ability to comply with covenants and other terms and conditions

- Ascertain whether quarterly loan repayments were made on due dates post year-end

- Inspect correspondence with Whitenile and assess the likelihood of the contract being renewed

- Ascertain management's contingency plans for alternative customers should Whitenile fail to renew the contract

- Review post year-end management accounts to assess company performance

- Review post year-end sales to assess whether sales have been affected by adverse publicity

(b) **Provision for redundancy costs**

Justification

The provision is 2.8% of revenue and is therefore material. It is estimated by management and may be deliberately understated due to the bank requiring financial statements for the overdraft review.

Redundancies are phased over one year and audit evidence may be limited due to few post year-end payments.

Procedures

- Obtain the schedule detailing the redundancy provision. Re-perform any calculations and confirm the provision reflects enhanced terms which are in excess of the rates set by the UK government.

- Discuss with the directors the basis for their estimate of the provision and consider its reasonableness.

- Multiply the expected number of employees to be made redundant by the average pay-out and compare to the provision. Obtain an explanation for any difference.

- For a sample of items on the schedule detailing the redundancy provision:
    - inspect employees' contracts for redundancy terms
    - check HR records to confirm length of service

- Inspect board minutes and ensure that the basis of the provision is consistent with what directors have authorised.

- Obtain copies of the public announcement and notices to employees and ensure that they were published before 30 November 20X6.

- Confirm that notices to employees offer enhanced terms.
- Review any post year-end payments.
- Obtain a written representation from management on whether the assumptions underlying the provision are reasonable.

(c) **Non-current assets – lorries**

Justification

The carrying amount of lorries has increased by 14.6%. Lorries may be overstated due to the bank requiring financial statements for the overdraft review.

The loss on sale of the lorries has increased by 37.1% and indicates that useful lives may be too long or the estimate of residual values too high. The cost and accumulated depreciation on disposals may not be correctly eliminated from the asset register.

The depreciation charge for the year of 14.8% of the net book value of lorries compared to the previous year of 17.2% seems low. This suggests an understatement of depreciation.

Lorries may be overstated due to capitalisation of inappropriate employee costs or routine maintenance costs.

Procedures

- Obtain a schedule of refurbishment costs and ensure all costs capitalised meet the recognition criteria
- For a sample of additions in the year vouch amounts to the purchase invoice
- Vouch capitalisation of employee costs to employee timesheets
- Inspect the asset register to check that lorries disposed of have been removed from the register
- Select a sample of lorries on the asset register and physically inspect
- Confirm lorries are still in use and not impaired
- Confirm with management its intention to continue to replace lorries after seven years
- Confirm with management how the residual value is assessed
- Recalculate depreciation charge
- Inspect evidence of impairment reviews undertaken by management

Examiner's comments

Answers to this part of the question were good with many candidates scoring the maximum 23 marks. Answers in respect of going concern and non-current assets – lorries tended to be better than those in respect of the provision for redundancy costs.

A number of candidates failed to make full use of the financial information given in the scenario. Although the majority of candidates used analytical procedures to justify the going concern risk, only stronger candidates applied analytical procedures to the financial information relating to the provision and lorries.

Going concern

Most candidates identified a range of relevant factors justifying why going concern was a key area of audit risk. However, the points most commonly overlooked were:

- additional funding may be needed to pay the bank loan and redundancy costs
- overdraft funding is expensive
- the chief executive is retiring.

Candidates also identified a range of relevant procedures to address the going concern risk. However, the points most commonly overlooked were:

- identification of the specific assumptions used in the cash flow and profit forecasts that particular attention should be paid to, including those in relation to redundancy costs and bank loan repayments

- whether sales had been affected by adverse publicity.

A number of weaker candidates relied heavily on information from management as a source of evidence when more reliable third party evidence should be available. For example, relying on management views in respect of:

- obtaining further funding from the bank, instead of correspondence with the bank

- likelihood of the Whitenile contract being renewed, instead of a review of the correspondence with Whitenile.

No marks were awarded where candidates inappropriately relied on the opinion of management.

Provision for redundancy costs

Answers to this part of the question were often disappointing. The majority of candidates struggled to justify why the provision for redundancy costs had been identified as a key area of risk other than to correctly state that it was an estimate. Very few candidates identified that:

- there was a risk of understatement due to the bank's reliance on the financial statements

- audit evidence would be limited due to a lack of redundancy payments in the period after the year end because the redundancies would be phased in over one year

- the provision represented 2.8% of revenue and was therefore material.

Stronger candidates identified relevant audit procedures including:

- obtaining management's estimate and reperforming the calculations,
- understanding the basis of the estimate and considering whether it was reasonable.

The most commonly overlooked procedures were:

- constructing a relevant proof-in-total calculation

- inspecting employees' contracts for redundancy terms

- checking that the public announcement was made before 30 November 20X6

- inspecting board minutes to ascertain whether the basis of the provision was consistent with what the directors had authorised.

A significant number of candidates correctly identified that the auditor should obtain a written representation from management but failed to state what the written representation would cover. Consequently, they failed to earn the additional mark available for stating it would cover the reasonableness of the assumptions underlying the provision.

Non-current assets - lorries

Answers relating to the justification of audit risk for lorries were generally good with the majority of candidates identifying a range of the justification points. Most candidates recognised that the depreciation charge was out of line with the overall increase in the net book value of lorries and that incorrect capitalisation of costs could overstate the net book value. Candidates cited a number of appropriate audit procedures to address the risks. However, a number of candidates failed to consider the direction of testing between the physical asset and asset register, for example tracing physical assets to the items included in the asset register instead of checking items in the asset register to the physical asset which is more appropriate given the identified risk of overstatement. The most commonly overlooked audit procedures were:

- vouching capitalisation of employee costs to timesheets

- confirming with management its intention to continue to replace lorries after seven years and how residual value is assessed

- inspecting evidence of impairment reviews undertaken by management.

48.2 Appointment of chief executive

Threats

A familiarity threat arises if the firm plays a significant role in the recruitment of the chief executive as the firm is less likely to be critical of information provided by the new chief executive. A management threat also arises as the firm may be required to select a candidate and, consequently, become too closely aligned with management.

Response

The firm must decline to assist with the recruitment of a new chief executive. The FRC's *Ethical Standard* (Part B5: para. 5.111) expressly prohibits audit firms undertaking an engagement to provide recruitment services in relation to a key management position of a listed company. However, a service can be provided in less formal ways such as the provision of salary surveys and interviewing and advising on a candidate's financial competence.

Internal audit

Threats

If the firm plans to rely on the work of internal audit, as part of its external audit, there is a self-review threat. The external audit team may be insufficiently questioning of the work performed by those undertaking the internal audit work or reluctant to highlight shortcomings in that work.

Providing an internal audit function could give rise to a management threat as the firm may be expected to make decisions in respect of the scope of the internal audit work, the design of internal controls or the implementation of changes thereto.

Response

As UCEP is a listed entity (and is not an SME listed entity), the self-review threat created by the provision of internal audit services is likely to be unacceptable. This is in line with the requirements of the FRC's *Ethical Standard* (FRC ES: para. 5.54).

The extent of the management threat would depend on whether the firm personnel take on decisions and judgements that are the proper responsibility of management. The point is, however, moot because the engagement is unacceptable on the grounds of the self-review threat that would be created.

Engagement partner

Threat

Julie Town has worked continuously as the audit partner for UCEP for five years. The long association of Julie represents a familiarity threat as she may be too trusting and insufficiently sceptical of the audited entity's point of view.

Response

FRC ES S3 allows that in circumstances where the audit committee decides that it is necessary to safeguard the quality of the audit, the engagement partner may continue for an additional period of up to two years. Examples of such circumstances include substantial changes to the nature or structure of the audited entity's business or where there are unexpected changes in the senior management. As UCEP has announced a reorganisation and the chief executive is retiring, Julie may continue in her role for a maximum of a further two years. However, there should be safeguards in place including an expanded review of audit work. The facts and reasons should be disclosed to shareholders and those charged with governance. If there is no disclosure the request for Julie to continue should be refused. The ethics partner should also be consulted.

Examiner's comments

Answers to this part of the question were of a mixed standard. There was evidence of a number of candidates who adopted a "scatter-gun" approach, resulting in identification of a number of inappropriate threats. This wasted time and did not earn any credit. A number of candidates, having correctly identified and explained the threats, failed to answer the second part of the requirement and did not state how the firm should respond to those threats.

Appointment of chief executive

Most candidates correctly identified and explained the familiarity threat but fewer candidates identified the management threat. Stronger candidates recognised that the work must be declined as FRC ES S5 prohibits recruitment services for listed companies. Weaker candidates hedged their bets and stated that the firm could only assist with the recruitment providing safeguards were in place and then wasted time by listing a number of inappropriate safeguards.

Internal audit

The majority of candidates correctly identified and explained the self-review and management threats with respect to the firm providing internal audit services. However, a significant minority of candidates wasted time discussing self-interest and advocacy threats for which no marks were available.

Engagement partner

Most candidates correctly identified and explained the familiarity threat. However, only the stronger candidates were familiar with the requirements of FRC ES S3. These candidates correctly identified that the reorganisation and the retirement of the chief executive were circumstances that would allow the engagement partner to continue for a further two years. These candidates were often able to identify the safeguards required such as an expanded review of audit work. Weaker candidates stated that the audit partner should be rotated as five years had elapsed and were unaware of the two-year extension that is allowed.

48.3 Adequate disclosures

There is no material misstatement and no inability to obtain sufficient, appropriate audit evidence. Therefore, an auditor's report with an unmodified opinion should be issued. The report will, however, include a section, headed "Material Uncertainty Related to Going Concern", to draw users' attention to the matter disclosed in the financial statements. A statement that the opinion is not modified in respect of the uncertainty should be included.

No disclosures

There is a material misstatement due to the lack of appropriate disclosure and therefore a modified opinion/report is required. If the matter is considered material (but not pervasive) a qualified opinion ('except for') should be issued. If the matter is considered material and pervasive an adverse opinion should be issued. The audit report will include a section headed "basis for qualified opinion"/"basis for adverse opinion", describing the matter giving rise to the modification.

This part of the question was generally well answered with a number of candidates scoring maximum or close to maximum marks. However, there were a number of very brief answers to this part of the question.

Adequate disclosures

The majority of candidates correctly identified that the opinion should be unmodified. However, a small minority failed to consider the use of a paragraph headed 'material uncertainty related to going concern' to direct the users' attention to the note in the financial statements. In addition, many candidates failed to point out that the uncertainty surrounding going concern was fundamental to the users' understanding of the financial statements and did not score the half mark available for this point.

No disclosures

The majority of candidates correctly identified that the opinion should be qualified or adverse depending on whether the absence of the disclosure was considered material or material and pervasive. Weaker candidates failed to deal with the fact that there were two potential options and presented unclear answers which did not earn any marks. A number of candidates incorrectly stated that if the absence of a disclosure was considered material and pervasive then a disclaimer of opinion, instead of an adverse opinion, should be given. A number of weaker candidates strayed beyond the requirement and wrote at length about the implications for the financial statements if the audited entity was not a going concern. These candidates failed to appreciate that the financial statements are still prepared on the going concern basis even if there is an uncertainty about the going concern status.

49 Speedy Pedals Ltd

Marking guide

		Marks
49.1	**Revenue**	
	Enquiries	4½
	Documentary information	1½
	Gross profit margin	
	Enquiries	5
	Documentary information	1
	Operating margin	
	Enquiries	4½
	Documentary information	1½
	Inventory	
	Enquiries	5½
	Documentary information	1
	Trade receivables	
	Enquiries	3
	Documentary information	1
	Trade payables	
	Enquiries	4½
	Documentary information	1
	General documentary information	4
	Marks available	38
	Maximum	15

		Marks
49.2	Review engagement	1½
	Audit engagement	2½
	Reasons	3
		7
	Marks available	
	Maximum	5
Total marks available		20

49.1 Revenue

Enquiries

Why has the rate of growth doubled and why is it out of line with recent growth rates? Is it due to:

- the launch of a new range of bicycles (the Super Speedy)?

- increased sales following the launch of the website?

- an increase in selling prices?

- the revenue recognition policy for the Super Speedy (for example, revenue recognised on order instead of despatch)?

Documentary information

- Breakdown of sales between components, for example, retailers and website sales
- Description of controls over the website ordering and payment facilities

Gross profit margin

Enquiries

Is the increase in gross margin due to:

- increased sales of higher margin items?
- beneficial effects of movements in exchange rates in respect of imports?
- availability of bulk discounts from suppliers?
- understatement of purchases?
- overstatement of closing inventory?
- understatement of labour costs?
- inappropriate cut-off arrangements?

Documentary information

- Schedule of selling prices and costs on a product basis
- Breakdown of the cost of sales figure

Operating margin

Enquiries

Why is the fall in operating margin out of line with the increase in the gross profit margin? Is it due to:

- changes in the classification of costs between cost of sales and operating expenses?
- provisions for damages and legal costs in respect of the patent infringement?
- amortisation and maintenance costs of the new website?
- advertising costs for the Super Speedy?

Documentary information

- Breakdown of operating costs
- Legal correspondence, for example correspondence from the patent lawyer

Inventory

Enquiries

Is the significant increase in inventory days due to:

- a build-up of inventory (raw materials, components) used in the production of Super Speedys?

- slow-moving items such as superseded models of bicycles?

What translation methods are used for components bought from China?

Is the inventory supported by continuous records or was it subject to a full count on 30 November 20X6?

How are differences between physical and recorded inventory accounted for?

Documentary information

- Breakdown of inventory figure/aged inventory report
- Results of any inventory counts

Trade receivables

Enquiries

Trade receivables collection period has increased and is 6 days greater than the credit terms offered. Is it due to:

- old outstanding debts which should be written off?
- a relaxation in credit terms extended to retailers?

What cut-off arrangements were in place at 30 November 20X6?

Documentary information

- Aged receivables listing
- Contracts and correspondence with customers

Trade payables

Enquiries

Is the fall in payable days due to:

- understatement due to unrecorded invoices?
- tighter credit terms imposed by suppliers?
- early payment to take advantage of discounts?

What translation methods are used in respect of the balance owed to the Chinese supplier?

What cut-off arrangements were in place at 30 November 20X6?

Documentary information

- Aged payables listing
- Contracts and correspondence with suppliers

General documentary information

- Budgets for the next period and the corresponding period
- Management accounts for the six months to 30 November 20X6
- Management accounts for periods after 30 November 20X6
- Industry information
- Board minutes
- List of exchange rates used
- Details of how the information is compiled

There were some very good answers to this part of the question. Those candidates who scored high marks used the ratios provided in the question as a framework and listed plausible enquiries which demonstrated that the candidate understood what may have caused a change in the ratio. Candidates who scored low marks tended to do so because they asked general questions (for example "why has operating margin decreased?") or restated information provided in the scenario (for example "inventory days have increased"). These candidates failed to ask questions that focused on reasons why changes in the ratios may have occurred (for example 'have website costs or advertising costs in respect of the Super Speedy caused the operating margin to fall?'). Candidates who performed poorly on this question often gave little thought to the layout of their answers which were presented as unstructured lists of questions in no particular order. In respect of the documentary information that would be useful for review procedures, some candidates detailed documentation that would assist with audit procedures rather than documentation aimed specifically at justifying potential reasons for changes in the ratios. The most commonly overlooked points related to cut-off arrangements for the gross profit margin, inventory, trade receivables and trade payables.

49.2 Review engagement

The conclusion of the assurance report following the review of the financial information provides limited/moderate assurance and is expressed negatively in the form of "nothing has come to our attention that causes us to believe that the financial statements do not give a true and fair view."

Audit engagement

The opinion in the auditor's report on financial statements is expressed positively and provides reasonable assurance that the financial statements:

- give a true and fair view of the state of the company's affairs;

- have been properly prepared in accordance with the applicable financial reporting framework; and

- have been prepared in accordance with the requirements of the Companies Act 2006.

Reasons

The objective of a limited assurance engagement is to reduce risk to an acceptable level whereas the objective of reasonable assurance engagement is to reduce risk to a low level. As a result the work undertaken on an audit engagement is wider in scope and includes tests of control and tests of details.

Examiner's comments

This part of the question was generally well answered as the majority of candidates cited the basic points regarding the different levels of assurance provided by the conclusions within each report and gave an example of each. Many candidates cited, correctly, that the level of assurance was determined by the extent of the work, but few referred to the level of risk. Weaker candidates strayed beyond the requirement and wasted time writing about the differences between the reports as a whole, instead of focusing on the **conclusions** in each of the reports.

50 Classy Cars plc

		Marks
50.1 **Higher risk of expressing an inappropriate opinion**	5½	
Mitigate risk	10	
Marks available	15½	
Maximum		8
50.2 **Excessive discounts**		
Consequences	2½	
Recommendations	2	
100 item checklist		
Consequences	6	
Recommendations	2	
General marks applicable to both scenarios	1½	
Marks available	14	
Maximum		8
50.3 In respect of the matter described in (c), state whether or not you would modify the audit opinion. Give reasons for your conclusion and outline the modifications, if any, to the auditor's report.	7	
Maximum		4
Total marks available		20

50.1 Higher risk of expressing an inappropriate opinion

There is an increased risk of expressing an inappropriate opinion in the first audit of Classy's financial statements because the firm has a limited understanding of the client's industry and operating environment. Specifically, the firm has no clients in the motor trade and no listed company clients, which have additional reporting requirements. The previous auditor resigned and the firm has no experience of management's integrity. Consequently, the auditor may fail to identify events and transactions, which impact on the financial statements. In addition, internal control weaknesses such as the absence of checks on cars prior to their sale might increase risk of future claims leading to unrecorded liabilities or undisclosed contingencies. Furthermore, there may be misstatements in the opening balances, which filter through to the current year's financial statements.

Mitigate risk

To mitigate the risk of expressing an inappropriate opinion, the firm should:

- exercise a higher degree of professional scepticism

- use (or recruit) senior audit staff with industry experience or experience in listed company audits

- spend time researching the motor industry

- exercise closer supervision over junior staff

- perform expanded reviews of audit work

- obtain more relevant and reliable audit evidence by placing more emphasis on third party evidence

- set lower materiality thresholds
- increase sample sizes to reduce sampling risk
- review previous auditor's working papers if available
- undertake substantive procedures on opening balances.

Examiner's comments

Answers to this question were often disappointing. Although most candidates cited a number of reasons why the risk of expressing an inappropriate opinion might be higher in the first year of an audit a significant number could only outline one or two ways to mitigate this risk. The reason most commonly overlooked was that relating to the risk of unrecorded liabilities or undisclosed contingencies arising from legal claims. Mitigations most commonly overlooked were:

- the need to exercise a higher degree of professional scepticism
- the expanded review of audit work
- lower materiality thresholds
- increased sample sizes to reduce sampling risk; and
- the need to obtain third party evidence.

A number of candidates wasted time by outlining methods to limit liability such as the use of a Bannerman paragraph, limited liability partnerships and liability caps. These points were not awarded any marks as the requirement was to outline how the firm should mitigate the risk of forming an inappropriate opinion.

50.2 (a) **Excessive discounts**

Consequences

Inconsistent pricing could lead to:

- customer dissatisfaction
- overpayment of sales staff if remuneration is target driven
- fraudulent acts by sales staff (for example, kickbacks from customers).

The above points will have an adverse impact on profits and cash flow.

Recommendations

- Any 'extra' discount (to clinch a sale) to be authorised by a manager
- Any bonuses to be linked to either margins or profits
- Discounts reviewed periodically
- Exceptions to be investigated

(b) **100 item checklist**

Consequences

Failure to complete the checks prior to the sale of cars could lead to:

- cars breaking down and/or accidents
- customers returning cars resulting in refunds and an increase in repair costs
- customers suing Classy resulting in compensation payments and legal fees
- customer dissatisfaction leading to a loss of reputation and a loss of future sales
- fines levied by regulators in respect of misleading claims and/or the selling of unsafe cars

The above points will have an adverse impact on profits and cash flow. Ultimately going concern issues may arise if, for example, the company loses its license to trade.

Recommendations

- Recruit more staff
- Reschedule existing staff workloads to allow checks to be completed
- Checklist to be reviewed and signed off by management prior to sale
- Remove 100 item claim until Classy complies

General points applicable to both scenarios

The following recommendations apply:

- Employees to be made aware of the importance of adhering to company policy
- Monitoring of procedures to ensure adherence
- Breaches to be investigated and staff disciplined.

Examiner's comments

Excessive discounts

Answers to this part of the question were generally good. Most candidates correctly identified that:

- the granting of customer discounts in excess of authorised levels would result in loss of revenue or reduced margins;

- inconsistent pricing may lead to customer dissatisfaction; and

- there was scope for collusion between staff and customers.

The most commonly overlooked consequence was the potential overpayment of sales staff if their remuneration was target driven. Weaker candidates incorrectly cited that excessive discounts would lead to an understatement of revenue. Most candidates were able to offer plausible recommendations such as recirculation of company policy or staff training, disciplinary action for breaches and authorisation to limit the level of discounts that staff could apply. Few candidates mentioned that bonuses should be linked to either margins or profits.

100 item checklist

Answers to this part of the question were generally good although a number of candidates provided brief answers. Most candidates correctly identified a range of consequences to score some marks. The most commonly overlooked consequences were that customers could return cars resulting in refunds and increases in repair costs and that action could be taken by regulators. Most candidates provided plausible recommendations such as management review and sign off of checklist prior to sale and the recruitment of more staff. Few candidates mentioned rescheduling existing staff workloads to allow checks to be completed.

A number of candidates wasted time by drafting points for inclusion in the firm's report in respect of the matter described in (c) which was not a requirement of the question and scored no marks.

50.3 The audit opinion will be modified. Inventory should be included at the lower of cost and net realisable value. The sale of the used cars in December 20X6 is an adjusting event which provides evidence of the net realisable value. Inventory is overstated by £1.5 million representing 1.24% of total assets and 6.55% of profit before tax, which is material. The matter also affects the calculation of the directors' bonuses. The matter is not pervasive as the material misstatement is confined to specific areas of the financial statements and therefore a qualified ('except for') opinion should be issued. The auditor's report will include a paragraph headed "basis for qualified opinion" describing the matter giving rise to the modification.

Examiner's comments

This part of the question was very well answered with the majority of candidates scoring full marks.

A minority of candidates incorrectly based their materiality calculations either on the book value of cars (£2.4 million) or the sale price of the cars (£0.9 million) instead of the difference of £1.5 million. Some candidates incorrectly stated that the misstatement was not material or thought that the misstatement was pervasive and would require an adverse opinion. Some candidate hedged their answers and incorrectly stated that an emphasis of matter paragraph was required.

March 2017 exam answers

51 Short Form Questions

51.1 Firm's response and reasons

Refuse the request

Not permitted by *Ethical Standard*

Investments are material to FS

Threat to independence/objectivity

Self-review threat, firm may:

- over rely on valuations during audit
- be reluctant to identify a misstatement in the valuation

Management threat:

- engagement may involve making decisions/subjective judgement
- firm's views may be too closely aligned with management's

Examiner's comments

This question was generally well answered as most candidates appreciated that the engagement should not be accepted because the threats to objectivity were insurmountable. The majority of candidates identified the self-review threat and, to a lesser extent, the management threat. The most common omissions were in relation to the explanations of the threats. Strong candidates provided plausible explanations of the threats, ie, over-reliance and reluctance to identify errors in the case of self-review threat and the use of judgement in respect of the management threat. Weaker candidates incorrectly stated it would be acceptable to take on the engagement as long as safeguards were in place and wasted time listing safeguards such as separate teams and an independent review. There were no marks for these points because the provision of valuation services, where the amount is material to the financial statements, to a listed entity is prohibited by the *Ethical Standard*.

51.2 Importance of professional scepticism

Professional scepticism is:

- having a questioning mind
- being aware of conditions which may lead to misstatement
- making a critical assessment of audit evidence

ISA (UK) 200 requires auditors to plan/perform audits with professional scepticism because:

- management may deliberately conceal fraud/error; and
- be biased in the preparation of the FS
- evidence may not be reliable
- items can be complex or involve judgement

Professional scepticism ensures:

- sufficient inquiry/challenge of management
- reliability of documents/responses is appraised
- contradictory evidence is followed up

- conditions that indicate possible fraud are identified/followed up
- alternative treatments in the FS are considered
- the risk of an inappropriate opinion is reduced

Examiner's comments

Answers to this question were disappointing. The points most commonly identified related to the definition of professional scepticism. However, a significant number of candidates failed to provide the full definition as set out in ISA (UK) 200 and only cited "a questioning mind". Other points commonly identified related to the importance of professional scepticism in recognising management bias and unreliable evidence. Few candidates identified the importance of exercising professional scepticism when dealing with judgemental areas in the financial statements. A number of candidates confused the concept of professional scepticism with the concepts of objectivity, independence and professional judgement. Furthermore, the vast majority of candidates failed to demonstrate an understanding that the exercise of professional scepticism is a requirement of ISA (UK) 200.

51.3 Key purposes of EQCR

For higher risk and listed clients, the EQCR provides an independent check:

- on significant judgements made by audit team
- that appropriate consultations have taken place
- that proposed audit report is appropriate
- that engagement team is independent

Key purposes of monitoring

A continuing part of quality control procedures designed to:

- ensure policies and procedures are operating effectively

- identify areas where changes to policies/procedures are needed or additional training is required

- assess effectiveness of review procedures

- assess compliance with ISAs and *Ethical Standard*

Examiner's comments

Answers to this question were of a mixed standard. Those candidates familiar with the contents of sections 20/21 and 23 of ISA (UK) 220 *Quality Control for an Audit of Financial Statements* tended to score full marks. The points most commonly identified in respect of the engagement quality control review (EQCR) were those relating to significant judgements made and conclusions reached by the audit team. The point most commonly overlooked in respect of the EQCR was that relating to appropriate consultations having taken place. Generally, candidates were more competent in dealing with the cold review as many identified that it was an ongoing process to ensure that quality control procedures were operating effectively and compliance with auditing and ethical standards. Some candidates confused the EQCR with that of the supervisory review that is required on all audit engagements. Weaker candidates did not distinguish between the two different reviews and it was difficult to award marks as it was not clear as to which one of reviews they were dealing with.

51.4 Why information should be considered as part of external audit

Increased risk of misstatement/increased inherent/control risk:

- Window dressing/manipulation of FS
- Jade will want to achieve highest possible valuation
- Likely to overstate assets/income/profit and understate liabilities/costs/ losses
- Jade may overly focus on negotiations rather than running the business

Increased detection risk:

- Jade may be motivated to conceal information from the auditor

Firm will need to reflect increased risk of misstatement in its audit approach:

- Lower materiality thresholds
- Larger sample sizes
- More experienced staff
- Increased level of professional scepticism
- Increased supervision/EQCR

Increased engagement risk:

- Possible reliance by prospective buyer on the FS for year ended 31 March 20X7
- Prospective buyer could sue the firm if they can prove a duty of care was owed

Examiner's comments

This question was well answered by candidates who identified the risk of window dressing to inflate the value of the business. These candidates often went on to specify the specific risks associated with this, eg, overstatement of assets and understatement of liabilities. The points most commonly overlooked were those relating to the management of detection risk and the duty of care to the prospective buyer. Weaker candidates overlooked the risk of window dressing and incorrectly assumed that the prospective buyer was also a client and, consequently, wasted time writing about confidentiality issues and conflicts of interest. A number of candidates incorrectly assumed that the shares were being sold because there were problems such as going concern issues with the business. There was nothing in the question to indicate this and consequently no marks were available for these points.

51.5 Relevance of letter

Further audit procedures are required due to:

- increased risk to going concern status

    - Artz accounts for a significant proportion of revenue
    - damage to Martial's reputation
    - issues with sales to other customers

- adjustments may be required for refunds/inventory write-downs

Break-up basis/disclosure of uncertainty may be appropriate

May result in a modified audit report

Examiner's comments

This question was well answered with many candidates scoring full marks. The vast majority of candidates identified that there was a potential going concern issue and that this had implications for the basis of preparation and disclosures in the financial statements. Many candidates also appreciated that the issue over the quality of goods could give rise to inventory write-downs. Weaker candidates wasted time writing, in general terms, about the auditor's responsibilities in respect of subsequent events.

51.6 **Audit junior's suggestion**

Emphasis of matter is only appropriate to draw users' attention to matters presented or disclosed in FS that are fundamental to users' understanding of the FS.

Audit junior's suggestion is inappropriate as situation does not meet these criteria.

Impact on auditor's report

- Auditor is unable to obtain sufficient appropriate evidence
- Matter is pervasive as it could impact FS as a whole
- Modified opinion
- ISA (UK) 580 requires a disclaimer of opinion
- Include explanation of matter in basis for disclaimer of opinion section
- Report by exception/not received all info and explanations

Examiner's comments

This question was generally well answered. Most candidates identified that an emphasis of matter paragraph was inappropriate because the situation represented an inability to obtain sufficient appropriate evidence and, as such, warranted a modified opinion. Although many candidates identified that the issue was pervasive, a significant minority of these candidates incorrectly stated that an adverse opinion should be given. These candidates failed to appreciate that an adverse opinion is given when there are pervasive misstatements. A significant minority of candidates incorrectly suggested that an 'Other Matters' paragraph should be used. The point most commonly overlooked related to the ISA (UK) 580 requirement for a disclaimer of opinion. Weaker candidates wasted time writing about the implications of the lack of management integrity instead of focusing on the impact on the auditor's report as required by the question.

52 Shifu Ltd

Marking guide

			Marks
52.1	(a)	**Revenue – user licence fees**	
		Justification	3½
		Procedures	12½
	(b)	**Revenue – set-up fees**	
		Justification	4½
		Procedures	7½
	(c)	**Intangible assets – software development costs**	
		Justification	7
		Procedures	14

			Marks
(d)	**Compensation payable and receivable**		
	Justification	5½	
	Procedures	10½	
General			
Justification		1	
Procedures		1	
Marks available		67	
Maximum			28

52.2 Identify and explain the audit risks that would arise if Shifu
failed to meet its responsibilities to protect their customers
from loss of data and breaches of data security.

Marks available	11	
Maximum		5

52.3 State, with reasons, the implications for the auditor's report if
Shifu's directors do not make any changes to the financial
statements for the year ended 31 January 20X7 in respect
of the £920,000 compensation payable to Shifu's customers.

Marks available	5	
Maximum		3
Total possible marks		36

52.1 (a) Revenue – user licence fees

Justification

Licence fees per user have risen from £73.75 in 20X6 to £92.72 in 20X7 suggesting
revenue is overstated.

Contracts straddle the year end and the full licence fee may have been incorrectly
recognised on receipt.

Over/under usage calculations are based on estimates.

Procedures

Enquire of management the reason for the increase in the licence revenue.

Ascertain whether there have been any price increases in the year.

Obtain a schedule of the user licence fee calculation and agree fees received to the
relevant contract and bank statements.

For contracts straddling the year end, recalculate the proportion of income to be
recognised in the year based on the number of months elapsed on the contract.

Obtain a schedule of adjustments made for over/under usage.

Ascertain the basis of the estimates for over/under usage.

For a sample of customers, compare estimated over/under usage with:

- actual users in usage reports
- expected users in the contract
- refunds paid/credit notes issued post year-end
- additional amounts invoiced to/received from customers post year end

Ascertain reasons for any discrepancies with the amount of revenue recognised in the
year.

(b) **Revenue - set-up fees**

Justification

Average set up fee has risen from £198.1K to £244.8K suggesting revenue is overstated. Revenue is recognised before receiving written confirmation, from the customer, of satisfactory set-up.

The customer may not be satisfied with the set-up.

Set-up activities may straddle the year end and revenue may not reflect the amount of work done or the full fee may have been incorrectly recognised on receipt

Procedures

Enquire of management the reasons for the increase in average set up fees.

Ascertain whether any rate increases occurred in the year.

For set-ups completed in the year:

- agree amounts to the relevant contract and bank statements
- inspect the customer's written confirmation

For set-ups in progress at year end:

- obtain a schedule of amounts to be recognised in the year

- ascertain the basis of revenue recognition and -compare this to the proportion of set-up activities that have been completed at year end

- reperform any calculations

(c) **Intangible assets - software development costs**

Justification

There is a risk of overstatement.

The carrying amount of software development costs has increased by 19.1% compared to the prior year.

Additions have increased by 69.5% but the cost of bug fixes has decreased by 46.4%.

Costs associated with bug fixes may have been capitalised inappropriately.

Shifu continuously improves Nodle which may result in an impairment of previously capitalised development costs.

The rate of amortisation has fallen from 35.6% to 28.4% suggesting that amortisation may be understated.

The determination of the useful life of software development costs involves judgement and may be inappropriate.

Procedures

Obtain a schedule of development costs capitalised in the year:

- agree to the head developer's monthly workings
- consider whether costs capitalised meet the relevant criteria for capitalisation
- vouch amounts to time and payroll records

Enquire of the head developer why bug fixes have fallen and capitalised costs increased.

Ascertain the nature of any major enhancements with reference to release notes/developers' documentation.

Request a demonstration of enhancements implemented on Nodle during the year.

Where enhancements replace existing features inspect write offs of previously capitalised development costs in the accounting records.

Inspect evidence of management's impairment review.

Ascertain the basis for the useful life of software development costs and assess the reasonableness of this basis by comparison to similar businesses.

Reperform the amortisation calculation.

(d) Compensation payable and receivable

Justification

Offsetting a liability against a contingent asset is not allowed.

The full liability to pay compensation to customers should be recognised. It represents 1.3% of revenue and is therefore material.

The large volume of customers may result in errors or omissions in the amount of compensation payable.

The claim against Mantis is unlikely to be settled before the audit report is signed and should only be recognised if the amount is virtually certain to be received.

There is a risk of overstatement of compensation receivable.

Shifu should disclose the compensation receivable if it is probable. There is a risk of inadequate disclosure.

Procedures

Obtain the calculation of the compensation due to Shifu's customers and check its arithmetical accuracy. For amounts included in the calculation:

- agree the basis of the amounts to a sample of contract terms
- agree to any amounts paid to customers after the year end

Select a sample of current contracts and check they have been included in the calculation.

Review the contract with Mantis and ascertain whether the terms support the basis of the compensation claim.

Review correspondence with Mantis and Shifu's legal advisors to ascertain the likely outcome of the claim.

Obtain a written representation from management that the significant assumptions used in making these accounting estimates are reasonable.

General points

This is a first year audit and it may be difficult to obtain assurance over opening balances.

Procedures

Review the prior year auditor's working papers and consider whether audit work in the current year provides evidence on the reliability of opening balances.

Examiner's comments

Answers to this part of the question were of a mixed standard with revenue being the least well addressed audit risk. A small number of candidates failed to follow the instructions to ensure that all responses are visible on screen and not hidden in cells. Candidates are reminded that their answers are presented to the examiner exactly as they appear on screen.

It was pleasing to note that the majority of candidates attempted to make some use of the financial and operational information provided in the scenario, which has been identified as a deficiency in answers in previous examiners' reports. However, the majority of candidates restricted their calculations to the percentage change in the financial information from 20X6 to 20X7. Stronger candidates provided more robust calculations such as gross margin, licence fee per user, average set-up fee, amortisation rates or attempted proof in total calculations, all of which attract higher marks than simple percentage change calculations.

Many candidates overlooked that the firm had recently been appointed as external auditor and that obtaining assurance over opening balances may be difficult.

Revenue – user licence fees and set-up fees

Answers to the section on revenue were of a mixed standard. A number of candidates did not distinguish between the two sources of revenue (user licence fees and set-up fees) which often resulted in confused, lengthy and overly-complicated answers. Those candidates that considered each source of revenue separately and made a number of valid points for each, tended to score higher marks.

User licence fees

Most candidates justified why user licence fees had been identified as a key area of audit risk and went on to cite relevant audit procedures to address the identified risks, such as:

- enquiring of management why user licence fee revenue had increased
- agreeing licence fees to contracts and bank statements
- re-calculating the proportion of revenue recognised for contracts straddling the year end.

Many candidates correctly identified that the adjustments for over/under usage at the year-end required judgement. However, many were unable to cite relevant audit procedures in respect of these adjustments other than obtaining a schedule of adjustments made for over/under usage and ascertaining the basis of the estimates. Very few candidates considered testing the reasonableness of the basis of the estimates by reference to actual users in usage reports, estimated users in contracts, refunds paid post year end or amounts invoiced/received post year end.

Set-up fees

Most candidates justified why user licence fees had been identified as a key area of audit risk. The most commonly overlooked justifications were that:

- 'evenly recognised' may not reflect the actual value of work done
- revenue is recognised before implementation is signed off by the customer
- the customer may not sign to confirm that set-up was satisfactory.

Candidates who concluded that set-up fees may be understated, based on their calculation that set-up fees had fallen by 3.9%, failed to take into account that the number of new customers (and hence set-ups) had fallen by 22% and therefore that the increase in the average set-up fee might actually indicate a risk of overstatement.

Candidates cited the more basic audit procedures to address the identified risks, such as:

- enquiring of management why set-up fees had increased
- agreeing set-up fees to contracts and bank statements
- re-calculating the proportion of revenue recognised for set-ups straddling the year end.

The most commonly overlooked procedures were:

- inspecting customers' written confirmations for set-ups completed in the year

- obtaining a schedule of revenue to be recognised for set-ups in progress at the year end

- ascertaining the basis of revenue recognition and comparing this to a relevant measure of actual progress through the set-up process, such as the proportion of set-up activities that have been completed at year end.

Intangible assets – software development costs

Answers relating to the justification of audit risk for software development costs were generally good with the majority of candidates identifying a number of appropriate justifications and audit procedures. The most commonly overlooked justification was that continuous improvement to Nodle may result in previously capitalised development costs being impaired.

The most commonly overlooked procedures were:

- ascertaining the nature of major enhancements with reference to release notes/developers' documentation

- requesting a demonstration of the features on Noddle

- inspecting write-offs in accounting records where new features replaced existing features

- inspecting evidence of management's impairment review.

A significant number of candidates failed to appreciate that the development costs being capitalised were in relation to developers' time and consequently suggested reviewing invoices as evidence of costs rather than the time records identified in the scenario.

Compensation payable and receivable

Many candidates did not distinguish between compensation payable and compensation receivable and presented muddled answers. Those candidates that considered each area separately tended to score higher marks. There was some evidence that candidates had not managed their time well resulting in short answers to this part of the question.

The majority of candidates correctly stated that compensation payable was material, as it represented 1.3% of revenue, and that it should be included in the financial statements. However, few candidates explicitly stated that the liability and contingent asset should not be offset. Few candidates identified that the large number of customers might lead to errors in estimating the compensation due to customers.

The justifications most commonly overlooked in relation to compensation receivable were that:

- the claim against Mantis was unlikely to be settled before the audit report was signed

- it should only be recognised if amounts due are virtually certain

- a disclosure would be required if the inflow of economic benefits is probable which might indicate a risk of inadequate disclosure.

Audit procedures identified in relation to compensation receivable were generally better than those in relation to compensation payable. A significant number of candidates correctly identified sources of evidence to support the compensation receivable such as the contract with Mantis, correspondence between Shifu and its legal advisor and obtaining a written representation from management. However, of those candidates stating a written representation should be obtained, very few earned the extra mark available for stating that it should cover the reasonableness of the significant assumptions used in making the accounting estimate.

The audit procedures most commonly overlooked in relation to compensation payable were:

- agreeing the basis of amounts included to a sample of contract terms
- agreeing the estimate to any amounts paid to customers after the year end.

A significant minority of candidates entered into lengthy discussions about legal claims from customers which was not relevant as Shifu was not disputing that compensation was due to its customers under the existing contractual arrangements.

52.2 • There is a risk of unrecognised provisions or undisclosed contingent liabilities arising from potential compensation claims from customers or regulatory fines.

- There is a going concern risk arising from a loss of reputation and subsequent loss of customers.

- Shifu may lose any certification that it meets established security standards.

- Shifu may incur significant rectification costs resulting in a negative impact on cash flow.

- Consequently, the basis of preparation of the financial statements may be inappropriate; or

- There may be inadequate disclosure relating to any uncertainty surrounding the going concern status of Shifu.

Examiner's comments

This part of the question was very well answered with a number of candidates scoring full marks. Most candidates identified and explained the risks of going concern and unrecognised provisions which might arise should Shifu fail to put measures in place to protect their customers from loss of data and breaches of data security. The points most commonly overlooked related to the risk of misstatement due to an inappropriate basis of preparation of the financial statements or inadequate disclosures. A minority of candidates wrote at length about the impact on the audit of data being lost and the fact it might result in a limitation on scope. These candidates had failed to appreciate that the question referred to data belonging to Shifu's customers rather than data that might be required as part of the firm's audit procedures. A small number of candidates identified and explained the risks that an audit firm would face if the firm failed to meet its responsibilities for protecting client data and scored no marks.

52.3 • The compensation is 1.3% of revenue and material to the financial statements.

- The liability should be recognised in the financial statements.

- Failure to do so results in a material misstatement.

- The misstatement is not pervasive as it only affects a specific item in the financial statements.

- The audit report should be modified with a qualified opinion.

- The reasons for the modification should be included in the Basis for Qualified Opinion section of the report.

53 Oogway, Dragoon, Pand, Dymsum

Marking guide

		Marks
53.1 **Oogway**		
Professional and ethical issues	5½	
Actions	4½	
Dragoon		
Professional and ethical issues	6½	
Actions	5½	
Pand		
Professional and ethical issues	6	
Actions	5½	
Dymsum		
Professional and ethical issues	10½	
Actions	7	
Marks available	51	
Maximum		22
53.2 List the specific matters, arising from the acquisition of Mei, that Shen LLP should consider when planning the audit of Dymsum.	7½	
		4
Total marks available		26

53.1 Oogway

Professional and ethical issues

There is a threat to the firm's objectivity and independence due to a familiarity threat:

- if Li Ping returns it will be less than one year since rotation

- this is less than the five years (of elapsed time before returning) that is required by the *Ethical Standard*

- Li Ping may have developed close relationships with Oogway's management and may be insufficiently questioning of management's point of view

However, the *Ethical Standard* allows an extension of up to two years to safeguard audit quality.

There is a risk to professional competence and due care if the audit planning is rushed in order to stay on schedule.

Actions

Ascertain if there is an alternative, sufficiently experienced partner to replace Sarah Bao. If no such partner exists and Li is reinstated as engagement partner the firm must:

- obtain agreement from Oogway's audit committee and disclose the facts to Oogway's shareholders

- perform an expanded review of the audit work.

The firm should also review the audit timetable and revise it if necessary to safeguard the quality of the audit.

The ethics partner should also be consulted.

Dragoon

Professional and ethical issues

This situation may indicate issues with management integrity and lack of management competency.

There is an increased risk of criminal and money laundering activities as well as breaches of laws and regulations.

There is an increased risk that the firm expresses an inappropriate opinion due to:

- error
- deliberate misstatement
- poor control environment
- unreliable management representations
- an inappropriate limitation on the scope of work.

This would expose the firm to:

- investigation by regulatory bodies
- claims from shareholders suffering a loss as a result of relying on the audit opinion
- loss of reputation.

Actions

Review the prior year audit report.

Undertake background checks on management and hold discussions with them to assess their philosophy and operating style.

If the appointment is accepted, additional work will be required on opening balances.

The firm should decline the engagement if the issues identified remain unresolved.

The ethics partner should also be consulted.

Pand

Professional and ethical issues

The double payment to the supplier may be an indication of fraud or money laundering.

The finance director appears to be offering Peony an incentive which raises doubts about his integrity.

The firm may not want to be associated with Pand due to the risk of reputational damage.

There is a threat to the firm's objectivity and independence due to:

Self-interest threat

- Peony may be tempted by the free holiday

Intimidation threat

- The finance director appears to be exerting pressure on Peony

There is a threat to professional competence and due care if Peony keeps quiet about the double payment.

Actions

Peony should inform a senior manager in the firm about the issues arising.

She should refuse the offer of the holiday.

The issue should also be raised with the firm's MLRO, who should report the suspicion of money laundering to the NCA.

Peony must avoid tipping off the client.

The engagement partner should consider whether it would be appropriate to resign from the engagement.

Dymsum

Professional and ethical issues

There is a threat to the firm's objectivity and independence due to:

Self-interest threat

- The regular fee income will be 13.9% of firm's annual fee income

- This is above the 10% threshold, but below the 15% threshold, set out in the *Ethical Standard*

- There is a risk of over-reliance on income from Dymsum

- The auditor may be reluctant to take actions adverse to the interests of the firm, such as modifying the audit report.

Management threat

- The engagement to review the internal controls at Mei may require the firm to make management decisions such as designing internal controls and implementing changes thereto

- The firm's views may become too closely aligned with management.

Self-review threat

- The results of the review of the internal controls at Mei may need to be re-evaluated as part of external audit

- The audit team may place too much reliance on the controls work and they may be reluctant to highlight any shortcomings identified in the controls work.

There is a risk to professional competence and due care as the firm may not:

- have the resources or experience to complete the audit of Mei
- have representation in China
- have sufficient knowledge of Chinese regulations.

Actions

The firm should undertake an external independent quality control review.

The expectation that fees from Dymsum Group will exceed 10% should be disclosed to the firm's ethics partner and to those charged with governance at Dymsum.

The proportion of the firm's income earned from Dymsum should continue to be monitored.

The firm should not make management decisions as part of the engagement to review internal controls at Mei and must ensure there is informed management.

Separate teams should be used for the audit and review of internal controls.

The firm must consider the appropriateness of its resources and experience before accepting either of the engagements at Mei.

Examiner's comments

Oogway

The majority of candidates identified the familiarity threat and provided a plausible explanation of it. Most of these candidates were aware of the provision in ES Section 3 which allows for an extension of up to two years to preserve audit quality. Although most of these candidates identified that an independent review was required many failed to specify that it should be an **expanded** review. Weaker candidates were unaware of the permitted extension and concluded, incorrectly, that the engagement partner must not be reinstated.

Dragon

Although the vast majority of candidates identified that there could be issues with management integrity, few candidates failed to explain fully the implications of this. Commonly overlooked implications included poor control environment, unreliable representations and limitation on the scope of audit work. A significant proportion of candidates wasted time discussing the impact on the firm's audit procedures when a decision had yet to be made regarding acceptance of the engagement.

Pand

The vast majority of candidates identified the self-interest and intimidation threats and provided plausible explanations of these threats. Most of these candidates also identified the possibility of money laundering and the actions to be taken in respect of such suspicions.

Dymsum

The majority of candidates identified the self-interest threat arising from fee dependency. Most candidates correctly included the recurring fee income in their fee percentage calculation. However, weaker candidates included the one-off fee in their calculation and, consequently, incorrectly concluded that the non-audit engagement should not be undertaken. Most candidates identified the self-review threat arising from the review engagement and the use of separate personnel to mitigate this threat. However, weaker candidates wasted time citing the need for information barriers which were not required in this situation. The points most commonly overlooked were those relating to the management threat and the threats to professional competence and due care.

53.2 The group engagement team needs to obtain an understanding of Mei to ascertain whether Mei is a significant component and assess the risks of material misstatement.

Materiality for the group financial statements as a whole and component materiality should be determined.

If Mei is not significant then only analytical procedures at group level need to be planned.

If reliance is to be placed on a local auditor, the firm must consider whether:

- they will comply with ethical requirements relevant to group audit
- they are competent
- the group audit team will be involved in their work to the extent necessary to obtain sufficient appropriate audit evidence
- they operate in a regulatory environment that actively oversees auditors.

Communication will be required with Mei's auditor on timely basis and will need to cover:

- the work to be performed
- the use to be made of the work
- the form and content of Mei auditor's communication with the group audit team.

Examiner's comments

Answers to this part of the question were very disappointing because the majority of candidates failed to consider the implications of using a component auditor. Many candidates wasted time citing issues to be considered prior to accepting the client (eg, independence issues) rather than the planning issues to be considered at the commencement of the group audit.

54 Viper Ltd

Marking guide

		Marks
54.1 **Journal entries are not authorised or reviewed.**		
Consequences		
Recommendations	6½	
There are no IT controls to prevent duplicate journal entries.		
Consequences		
Recommendations	4	
No evidence of goods dispatched is retained.		
Consequences		
Recommendations	9	
Marks available	19½	
Maximum		7
54.2 Engagement to review financial statements	4½	
External audit of unlisted company	5	
Marks available	9½	
Maximum		3
54.3 In respect of Warrior's overdue balance, state whether you would modify your firm's assurance report. Give reasons for your conclusion and describe the modifications, if any, to the assurance report.		
Marks available	7½	
Maximum		4

		Marks
54.4 Consequences	6	
Mitigation of financial consequences	3	
Marks available	9	
Maximum		4
Total marks available		18

54.1 Deficiency

Journal entries are not authorised or reviewed.

Consequences

- Errors may be made in journal entries which would go undetected.
- This might result in a misstatement in the financial statements.
- Fraudulent entries could be made.

Recommendations

- All journal entries should be authorised before being entered into the accounting records.

- A report of all journal entries posted should be regularly reviewed for accuracy and prior authorisation.

- Approval and review should be evidenced.

- Employees who are authorised to post journal entries should be restricted through the use of passwords.

Deficiency

There are no IT controls to prevent duplicate journal entries.

Consequences

- This may result in errors in the financial statements.
- Time and costs will be incurred to correct these errors.

Recommendations

- Journal entries should have a unique reference.

- IT controls should be introduced that alert users if they try to post a journal with a reference identical to an existing journal entry.

- If IT controls are not possible, an exception report of duplicate journal entries should be regularly reviewed and duplicates followed up and corrected.

Deficiency

No evidence of goods dispatched is retained.

Consequences

- Viper cannot keep track of customers' orders and orders may be dispatched twice in error.

- There is no means to prove goods were received by customer.

- This reduces the likelihood of enforcing payment from customers and increases the risk of disputes and bad debts.

- There will be a cost associated with attempting to recover receivables and a negative impact on profits and cash flow.

- Orders may not be dispatched at all resulting in loss of customer goodwill.

Recommendations

- A goods dispatched record should be created in the warehouse. These should be sequentially numbered and the sequence checked regularly for completeness.

- The customer should sign on delivery to acknowledge receipt of the goods and this record should be retained by Viper.

- Despatch records should be matched to customer orders and a regular review should be performed of customer orders to ensure goods have been dispatched.

- Customers should be provided with a copy of the signed despatch record in the event of a dispute.

Examiner's comments

Candidates were more competent in dealing with the journal entry deficiencies than they were with the lack of evidence in respect of goods despatched/delivered. In respect of the journal entries, most candidates identified the increased risk of fraud and errors, the importance of authorisation by senior management and the introduction of IT controls for restricting access and preventing duplication of entries. The point most commonly overlooked was that relating to the use of exception reports for highlighting duplicate journal entries. In respect of the lack of despatch records, a significant number of candidates incorrectly assumed that there were deficiencies in the entity's credit control system and wasted time describing credit control procedures.

54.2 Engagement to review financial statements

Addressee likely to be directors

Conducted in accordance with ISRE (2400)

Work limited to inquiries of management and analytical procedures

Would state "we do not express an audit opinion on these financial statements"
Moderate/limited assurance
Negative conclusion

"Nothing has come to our attention…."

Signed by practitioner/reporting accountant

External audit of unlisted company

Addressee is the shareholders

Conducted in accordance with relevant laws/auditing standards

Reasonable assurance
Positive opinion

"True and fair view"

Prepared in accordance with Companies Act

Conclusion on going concern

Opinion on other matters prescribed by Companies Act, such as the directors' report and matters on which the auditor is required to report by exception

Signed by statutory auditor

The majority of candidates attained full marks on this question. The points most commonly identified were those relating to the addressees, the level of assurance described in the reports and whether the opinion/conclusion was positive or negative. However, weaker candidates incorrectly stated that the level of assurance provided by a review engagement was low. The points most commonly overlooked were those relating to the additional information found in audit reports such as matters to be reported by exception. A significant minority of candidates confused the contents of a report following a review of financial information with the contents a report following an examination of prospective financial information. A number of candidates also wasted time describing the differences between the two types of engagement rather than the differences between the reports.

54.3 It is unlikely the amounts from Warrior can be recovered as there is no evidence to support the claim for the outstanding invoices.

The amounts should be written off.

They amount to 12.7% of profit before tax and are therefore material.

The firm should issue a modified report/conclusion due to a material misstatement.

The matter is not pervasive as it only affects one area of the financial statements.

The firm should express a qualified conclusion stating that "except for the effects of the matter described nothing has come to our attention…".

The reason for the qualification should be included in the basis for qualified conclusion section of the report.

Examiner's comments

Most candidates correctly identified that the situation represented a material misstatement and that the report should be modified with a qualification as the issue was not pervasive. However, many candidates failed to make their answers specific to a review engagement and stated incorrectly that the opinion would be modified. These candidates failed to appreciate that a practitioner expresses a conclusion, rather than an opinion, in the report following a review engagement.

54.4 **Consequences**

The firm may be sued for professional negligence by Viper's shareholders and by Po Bank if a duty of care is owed to the bank.

Disciplinary action may be taken and fines imposed by the regulator.

The firm is exposed to reputational risk which may result in the loss of:

- key clients
- key staff.

An increase in future professional indemnity insurance premiums may occur following a compensation payment by the insurance company.

Mitigation of financial consequences

Firms can mitigate financial consequences by:

- setting a liability cap for an agreed monetary amount or specified formula
- agreeing to share losses proportionately with clients
- structuring themselves as Limited Liability Partnerships
- ensuring they have adequate insurance cover in place
- restricting the use of the report by inserting a Bannerman clause in the assurance report.

Examiner's comments

The majority of candidates provided a range of relevant consequences of reaching an inappropriate conclusion and methods to mitigate the financial consequences. As a result, many candidates scored full marks. The most commonly overlooked consequence was that relating to the increase in insurance premiums. The most commonly overlooked method of mitigation was that relating to a proportional liability agreement. A number of candidates incorrectly stated that reliance on the report by third parties could be prevented by inclusion of restrictions in the engagement letter. Some candidates wasted time discussing caveats in relation to the review of prospective financial information, failing to appreciate that the review of Viper's financial statements was of historical information.

June 2017 exam answers

55 Short Form Questions

55.1 Actions

- Report to the money laundering officer within the firm (MLRO)
- MLRO to report to the National Crime Agency (NCA)
- Avoid tipping off the client
- Consider impact on financial statements
- Consider management's integrity

Reasons

- Suspicion of money laundering
- Transactions not consistent with trading history
- Not recorded in accounting records
- Activity may represent the proceeds of crime
- Criminal offence if auditor does not report
- Tipping off may prejudice legal proceedings.

Examiner's comment

Answers to this question were generally very good as the vast majority of candidates identified that the circumstances described in the question gave rise to suspected money laundering. Consequently, these candidates earned marks for identifying the issue, reporting it without tipping off and stating the legal obligations. The points most commonly overlooked were those relating to the reasons why suspicions should be aroused ie, no previous history of overseas trading and lack of entries in the accounting records. Weaker candidates did not consider money laundering and instead focused, incorrectly, on audit procedures in respect of related party transactions and translation of foreign currency transactions.

55.2 Journals that:

- relate to unusual or seldom used accounts
- are processed by individuals who do not normally make journal entries
- are recorded at the end of the period
- have no explanation or have a vague description
- are in round numbers
- are made outside of office hours
- are made to suspense accounts
- involve contra entries
- involve directors or related parties
- lack commercial rationale
- involve accounts prone to misstatement.

This question was well answered by those candidates who were familiar with the contents of paragraph A43 of ISA (UK) 240, *The Auditor's Responsibilities Relating to Fraud in an Audit of Financial Statements*. These candidates generally provided sufficient characteristics to attain full marks. A common error was to cite the characteristics of routine journal entries, such as correction of errors, period-end accruals and depreciation adjustments instead of the characteristics of journal entries that might relate to **fraudulent** activities.

55.3 Business risks

- Loss of data/breaches of data protection legislation
- Incorrect calculation of wages/taxes
- Loss of employee goodwill
- Reputational damage
- Late/incorrect submissions to the tax authorities
- Fines
- Increased costs
- Negative cash flow

Implications for financial statements

- Misstatement of wages/payroll taxes
- Unrecorded liabilities
- Undisclosed contingent liabilities.

Examiner's comment

Answers to this question were of a mixed standard. Those candidates who formatted their answers under the headings of business risk and implications for the financial statements tended to score higher marks. A significant number of candidates who did not use this format tended to produce muddled and often repetitive answers. Many of these candidates strayed beyond the requirement and wasted time listing potential internal control deficiencies that might exist within the service organisation. The business risks most commonly identified were those relating to payroll errors and late submission of returns to the tax authorities. The business risks most commonly overlooked were those relating to misuse of employee information and loss of employee goodwill. The most commonly cited financial statement implication related to the misstatement of payroll expenses and tax liabilities. The most commonly overlooked financial statement implication related to undisclosed contingent liabilities (which might arise from possible fines).

55.4
- Actual time compared to budget
- Actual work completed compared to planned work
- Number of reports produced within target dates
- Number of recommendations accepted
- Savings identified
- Feedback from users
- Results of third party reviews
- Number of staff in post against planned requirement/staff turnover rates
- Number of qualified staff.

Answers to this question were generally disappointing. It was evident that a significant number of candidates were not familiar with the contents of Chapter 10 Section 4.1.5 Monitoring of Internal Audit by the Audit Committee in the Audit and Assurance study manual. Those candidates familiar with this section tended to score full marks. The performance indicators most commonly identified were those relating to the number of recommendations accepted, actual time/cost v budget and the amount of planned work completed. The points most commonly overlooked were those relating to user feedback, results of third party reviews and staff turnover rates. A significant number of candidates demonstrated that they did not understand that a performance indicator by nature has to be a measurable value. For example, many candidates mentioned competencies but failed to present the point in the form of a performance indicator ie, number of qualified staff.

55.5 Threat to objectivity

- Self-interest threat

Explanation

- Senior employees may promote services not required by the client/exaggerate the benefits of non-audit services

- Audit quality may suffer/lack of scepticism.

Is arrangement appropriate?

- Not appropriate

- For each audited entity, ES4.57 states that the audit firm shall establish a policy to ensure that:

    - objectives of the members of the team do not include selling non-audit services

    - criteria for evaluating performance or promotion of the members of the audit team do not include success in selling non-audit services

    - no specific element of remuneration of the members of the audit team is based on success in selling non-audit services.

Examiner's comment

This question was well answered with many candidates scoring full marks. The majority of candidates identified the self-interest threat to the objectivity of the senior employees within the firm and that the arrangement was inappropriate. Many of these candidates also appreciated that there was a risk to audit quality. However, the points most commonly overlooked were those relating to the risk of exaggerating the claims regarding the benefit of non-audit services and the promotion of services not required by the client.

The requirement in the question was to identify "the threat" implying that only one threat was required. However, many candidates strayed beyond the requirement by listing a number of threats to the firm's objectivity in respect of the provision of non-audit services and the safeguards to such threats and scored no marks for these points. Disappointingly, a small number of candidates incorrectly stated that, with safeguards, the arrangement was appropriate.

55.6 • No work to be transferred that involves judgements/only work of mechanical nature
  • Recruitment of appropriately qualified/experienced overseas staff
  • Training of overseas staff/staff exchange with UK office
  • Direction/supervision of overseas staff
  • Review of work by overseas/UK office
  • Ensure instructions sent to overseas office followed
  • Ethical and independence declarations in place

Examiner's comment

Answers to this question were of a mixed standard. Those candidates who applied the basic principles of quality control applicable to engagement performance (ie, direction, supervision and review) coupled with the use of competent and trained employees scored higher marks. The most common shortcoming was to interpret "some external audit work relating to UK audited entities" as entire audits being transferred to an overseas office. Consequently, few candidates identified that only work of a mechanical nature should be transferred. Furthermore, a significant number of candidates wasted time listing points to be communicated to component auditors by a group auditor.

56 Top Hat and Boot Ltd

Marking guide

	Marks
56.1 Reasons why the previous auditor declined to tender and whether management gave permission to approach previous auditors	1½
Availability of staff resources and expertise, in particular	1½
Whether an appropriate audit opinion can be reached	1
Ethical issues	2½
Consider ability to implement safeguards	1
Whether the overall level of audit risk associated with the external audit is acceptable	2½
Management's integrity	4
Whether the engagement is commercially viable.	½
Marks available	14½
Maximum	7

56.2 (a) **Purchases and trade payables**	
Justification	6½
Procedures	12½
(b) **Inventory**	
Justification	6½
Procedures	26
General	
Justification	4
Procedures	2
Marks available	57½
Maximum	20

56.3 Assistance with the preparation of financial statements

Explanation of threats	4	
Response	7½	
Forensic specialist		
Explanation of threats	3½	
Response	1½	
Marks available	16½	
Maximum		9

56.4 Ethical issues

Ethical issues	5½	
Actions	2½	
Marks available	8	
Maximum		4
Total marks available		40

56.1 Reasons why the previous auditor declined to tender and whether management gave permission to approach previous auditors:

- this may indicate disagreements with management, unpaid fees, illegal acts or a limitation on scope of the audit.

Availability of staff resources and expertise, in particular:

- sufficient personnel and geographic coverage to perform the external audit competently access to personnel with e-commerce and IT skills.

Whether an appropriate audit opinion can be reached:

- the audit requires sign off by 31 August 20X7 to meet the bank deadline.

Ethical issues:

- Any threats to objectivity and independence
- Potential conflicts of interest or confidentiality issues as the firm already acts for competing clients in the retail sector.

Consider ability to implement safeguards:

- information barriers to protect against confidentiality breaches if acting for competing clients.

Whether the overall level of audit risk associated with the external audit is acceptable:

- although the firm has experience in the industry sector, it lacks cumulative audit knowledge of THB and its directors
- errors arising out of the inventory system and accounts payable issues
- an EQCR may be required to mitigate higher risk in the first year audit.

Management's integrity:

- Bank reliance increases the risk of fraudulent reporting
- Adverse publicity may indicate a lack of management integrity
- There may be a risk to the firm's reputation from association with THB
- The results of background checks on management and the risk of money laundering

Whether the engagement is commercially viable.

Examiner's comments

Answers to this question were of a mixed standard. Most candidates identified and explained a number of relevant matters that the firm should have considered before tendering for the external audit of THB. The most commonly cited matters were in relation to:

- the reasons for the previous auditor declining to tender

- the availability of staff resources

- whether any ethical issues would arise such as conflicts of interest

- the level of audit risk associated with the bank's reliance on the audited financial statements; and

- risk to the firm's reputation.

Fewer candidates considered the firm's ability to implement safeguards to address the ethical issues they had identified, the implications of the tight reporting deadline or whether the engagement was commercially viable.

56.2 (a) **Purchases and trade payables**

Justification

Purchases and trade payables may be understated because:

- trade payables days have fallen from 29.4 in 20X6 to 25.3 in 20X7
- trade payable days are lower than the 30 days payment terms
- the gross margin has increased from 45.6% in 20X6 to 48.1% in 20X7.

The failure to notify the accounts department of returns suggests overstatement of purchases and liabilities if credit notes are not recorded in the accounting records.

Procedures

- Evaluate and test controls over:

    - the recording of suppliers' invoices
    - payments to suppliers

- Inspect contracts with new suppliers to ascertain whether there are shorter credit terms which would explain the fall in payable days

- For a sample of goods received before the year end, trace the goods received record to the invoice entry in the ledger to ascertain if the amount is included in trade payables at the year end

- Vouch invoices recorded in the period after year end back to goods received records to ascertain if they are recorded in the correct period

- Inspect post year end payments to identify unrecorded liabilities at the year end

- Inspect credit notes received post year end to identify any relating to pre year-end purchases

- Where available request supplier statements and perform a reconciliation with the amounts included in the year-end trade payables ledger

- Where supplier statements are not available, perform direct confirmation of trade payables balances and investigate any differences

- Use data analytics to provide audit evidence or to identify items for further investigation, for example:

  - produce payables ageing analysis

  - three-way matches between purchase orders, goods received records and invoices

  (marks awarded for any relevant examples of data analytic routines which could be used as an audit procedure).

(b) **Inventory**

Justification

Inventory may be overstated because:

- inventory days have increased from 50.5 in 20X6 to 71.8 in 20X7

- designer clothing and accessories are susceptible to changes in fashion

- there has been media criticism about the quality of products sold

- a number of products will be heavily discounted in a promotion commencing after the year end

- obsolete inventory will require write down to net realisable value

- designer clothing is a desirable item subject to pilferage

- shortfalls have been identified at monthly counts

- the inventory system may be recording incorrect balances as losses may not be reflected in the records.

A firm of professional inventory counters will undertake a full inventory count at the year end. The counters may not be reliable.

Procedures

- Plan to attend the year-end inventory count:

  - Ensure that there is sufficient coverage of stores and the warehouse

  - Review count instructions for appropriateness

  - Evaluate and test controls over inventory count procedures

  - Note whether inventory is counted in pairs and the results appropriately recorded (for example on a hand held computer)

  - Note whether inventory movements are kept to a minimum

  - Perform two-way test counts of inventory

  - Identify slow-moving or obsolete items

  - Obtain details of last goods delivery and last despatch

- Obtain a copy of Whitechapel's report and test check that the inventory system is updated for the results of the count

- Follow up inventory count notes to ensure provision is made for slow- moving or obsolete inventory identified at the count

- Evaluate and test controls over updates to the perpetual inventory records for:

  - purchase prices
  - any differences identified during the monthly counts

- Evaluate and test controls over the preparation of aged-inventory analysis

- Review aged-inventory analysis to identify slow-moving or obsolete items

- Discuss the basis of the provision for slow-moving or obsolete inventory with management

- For those items in inventory check post year-end selling prices to determine whether net realisable value is less than carrying value

- Agree the cost of a sample of inventory items to suppliers' invoices

- Perform background checks on the firm of professional inventory counters and consider their:

    - independence and objectivity
    - experience and qualifications
    - reputation

- Review the letter of engagement with the firm of professional inventory counters to determine the scope of work

- Use data analytics to identify items for further investigation, for example, inventory items:

    - with negative margins (cost greater than selling price)
    - that are slow moving
    - with the highest discrepancies at inventory counts
    - with no recent cost price changes

    (marks were awarded for any relevant examples of data analytic routines which could be used as an audit procedure).

General points

- This is a first year audit and it may be difficult to obtain assurance over opening balances.

- Foreign suppliers are paid in local currency and there is the potential for translation errors.

- THB has applied for a bank loan and may seek to window dress the accounts.

- There is a tight reporting deadline and therefore a limited period for subsequent events review.

Procedures

- Review the prior year auditor's working papers and consider whether audit work in the current year provides evidence as to the reliability of opening balances.

- For a sample of items purchased from overseas suppliers, recalculate the foreign exchange translation and check the rate used to a reliable independent source.

Examiner's comments

Answers to this question were of a good standard. Most candidates justified why purchases and trade payables and inventory had been identified as key areas of audit risk and described relevant procedures to address the risks.

Purchases and trade payables

Most candidates correctly identified the risk of understatement of purchases and trade payables. However, many candidates lost marks by not attempting to calculate payables days or by incorrectly performing the calculation. The most commonly overlooked justification was in relation to the failure to notify the accounts department of returns to its largest supplier and that this indicated a risk of overstatement.

Many candidates correctly cited tests of controls as a procedure but few candidates earned the extra marks for describing these in any detail. Similarly, many candidates correctly cited that cut-off procedures should be undertaken but did not earn the additional marks available for describing how such procedures should be performed.

Other commonly cited relevant procedures were in relation to supplier statement reconciliations, direct confirmation of balances, and inspecting after date cash payments to identify unrecorded liabilities.

Fewer candidates considered procedures in relation to credit notes or reviewing contracts with suppliers to ascertain whether credit terms had been tightened.

Inventory

There were a number of good answers to this question. The majority of candidates correctly calculated inventory days and identified that the increase in days indicated a risk of overstatement. Many also correctly identified the deficiencies in the inventory system and that there were a number of factors, such as quality issues and fashion items, which contributed to a risk of obsolescence.

Fewer candidates earned the marks available for noting that certain items were to be heavily discounted after the year end or that the third party inventory counter may not be reliable.

Many candidates earned at least some of the marks available for the procedures around attendance at the year-end inventory count, such as performing test counts and inspecting the condition of inventory. Many candidates also correctly described relevant procedures such as reviewing the aged inventory analysis and ascertaining post year-end selling prices to establish whether NRV was below cost.

The procedures most commonly overlooked were in relation to ascertaining the reliability of the work performed by Whitechapel, the third party inventory counter. Few candidates considered obtaining a copy of Whitechapel's report or checking whether any of the findings during the inventory count had been addressed in the final inventory valuation. A number of candidates incorrectly stated that the external auditors should undertake an independent count of inventory.

General

There were a number of points available to candidates in either section of their answers. Those points most commonly cited were in relation to:

- THB being a new audit client and therefore additional procedures being required to test opening balances
- overseas suppliers invoicing in foreign currencies, and
- risk of management bias due to the bank's reliance on the financial statements.

Very few candidates earned the mark for noting that the tight timeframe for the audit work would limit the period available to review subsequent events.

In addition, candidates were required to include examples of data analytic routines in their answers. A large number of candidates overlooked this requirement whilst other candidates attempted to include such procedures with varying degrees of success. Candidates generally provided relevant data analytics procedures in relation to purchases and trade payables with many identifying ageing of trade payables and three-way matching of purchase orders/goods received records/invoices. Very few candidates identified any data analytics procedures in relation to inventory.

56.3 Assistance with the preparation of financial statements

Explanation of threats

The self-review threat arises when the results of a non-audit service performed by the engagement team, or others within the firm, are reflected in the amounts included, such as calculations, or disclosed in the financial statements. Audit staff may be reluctant to identify shortcomings in their colleagues' work or may place too much reliance on that work.

The management threat arises if members of the firm are expected to make decisions on behalf of management. The firm may become too closely aligned with the views and interests of management.

Response

THB is not a listed company, therefore providing assistance with the preparation of the financial statements is permitted, as long as appropriate safeguards are in place. However, the length of time for which assistance is provided should be limited and the ethics partner should be consulted about the request for assistance.

The staff member assisting with the preparation of the financial statements must have no involvement in the audit of the financial statements. In addition, the staff member should not be involved in initiating transactions, taking decisions or making judgements. Any such services should be of a technical, mechanical and informative nature. THB's management should take all decisions requiring the exercise of judgement and should have prepared the underlying accounting records.

The accounting services should be reviewed by a partner or other senior staff member, with appropriate expertise, who is not a member of the audit team. The audit work should be independently reviewed to ensure that the accounting services performed have been properly and effectively assessed in the context of the audit of the financial statements.

The firm should ensure that the management of THB are "informed", ie, designated members of the management have the capability to make management judgements and decisions on the basis of the information provided. Audit documentation should demonstrate that management has made all decisions. The respective responsibilities should be set out in a separate engagement letter.

Forensic specialist

Explanation of threats

Both the estimation of the loss by the forensic specialist and acting as an expert witness represent a litigation support service and this presents threats of self-review, management and advocacy.

The self-review threat arises because the specialist will provide estimates of inventory losses which will be reflected in the financial statements. The estimates will be examined during the external audit. Audit staff may be reluctant to identify shortcomings in their colleagues' work or may place too much reliance on that work.

The management threat arises because the audit firm will determine the estimate of inventory losses. This involves judgement and the amount may be material to the financial statements.

The advocacy threat arises because the firm will support management's position in legal proceedings and will be perceived as adopting a position too closely aligned to that of management.

Response

Litigation support services are prohibited by the *Ethical Standard* and must be declined. The work in respect of the quantification of the loss must also be declined because it would involve judgement by the audit firm and substantial losses imply that the amount could be material to the financial statements.

Examiner's comments

Answers to this question were of a mixed standard. Most candidates provided better answers on the provision of assistance with preparing the financial statements compared with those answers on the provision of a forensic specialist. Some candidates wasted time by adopting a scattergun approach and listed all of the ethical threats in the hope that some of the threats were correct. For example, a significant number of candidates incorrectly identified that the provision of non-audit services gave rise to the familiarity threat.

Assistance with preparation of the financial statements

Most candidates correctly identified and explained the self-review and management threats relating to this engagement. Many also correctly identified the firm could accept the engagement, as THB was not a listed entity, provided safeguards were put in place. Most candidates then went on to state appropriate safeguards such as the staff member providing the assistance should not be involved in the external audit, informed management, independent reviews of both the audit and assistance engagement, and referring the matter to the ethics partner.

Safeguards more commonly overlooked were:

- limiting the length of time for which the assistance was provided
- ensuring services were only of a technical, mechanical or informative nature
- not initiating transactions, and
- setting out the work in a separate engagement letter.

Forensic specialist

Answers to this part of the question were disappointing. A significant number of candidates concluded that the engagement could be accepted in spite of having already correctly identified a serious advocacy threat. Most candidates also correctly identified and explained the self-review and management threats. Many candidates wasted time recommending safeguards when the firm's response should have been to decline the engagement as it is prohibited by the *Ethical Standard*.

56.4 Ethical issues

There has been a breach of the fundamental principle of confidentiality due to the improper disclosure of information by the audit assistant to her family. Paragraph 140.1 ICAEW *Code of Ethics* requires that professional accountants refrain from disclosing, outside the firm, confidential information acquired as a result of professional relationships.

There has been improper use of information by the audit assistant as she has used confidential information to the advantage of third parties.

The audit assistant has solicited information by requesting details of any products to be discounted in the future. Paragraph 4.61D of the *Ethical Standard* requires that members of audit engagement teams should not solicit favours from clients.

The ethical issues arising raise concerns about the integrity and behaviour of the audit assistant.

Actions

- Remove the audit assistant from the engagement team immediately to prevent future breaches of confidentiality
- Notify the engagement partner or the ethics partner
- Disciplinary action/training of the audit assistant
- Obtain advice from ICAEW helpline
- Consider notifying the management of THB

Answers to this question were of a mixed standard. A large number of candidates correctly identified that there had been a breach of confidentiality and subsequently went on to earn the marks for correctly explaining improper disclosure and improper use of information. Very few candidates earned the marks available for discussing the ethical issue of soliciting information.

Candidates generally scored well in relation to the actions that the firm should take. Actions most commonly cited related to the removal of the junior from the engagement, notifying the engagement partner or ethics partner and disciplinary action/training. The actions most commonly overlooked related to obtaining advice through the ICAEW helpline and notifying management at THB. A number of candidates strayed beyond the requirement by discussing the ethical issues arising for the finance director of the client.

57 Ventnor Estates Ltd

Marking guide

			Marks	
57.1	**Explain the purpose of performing substantive analytical procedures.**			
	Marks available		3	
	Maximum		7	
				3
57.2	(a)	Expected rental income	5	
	(b)	Evidence to test reliability of data used	8	
	(c)	Enquiries based on the result of analytical procedures	8	
	Marks available		21	
	Maximum			10
57.3	(a)	**Asset verification**		
		Consequences	4½	
		Recommendations	6½	
	(b)	**Content of management accounting information**		
		Consequences	4½	
		Recommendations	3	
	Marks available		18½	
	Maximum			7
Total marks available				20

57.1 Explain the purpose of performing substantive analytical procedures.

Substantive analytical procedures assist the external auditor in forming an overall conclusion on the financial statements. The procedures are used to obtain relevant and reliable audit evidence by identifying expected relationships or detecting material misstatements and can be used as a 'proof in total'. The procedures assist audit efficiency as they can reduce the need for tests of details, reduce sample sizes and identify areas where further work is required.

Answers to this question were of a mixed standard. The points most commonly identified were those relating to obtaining relevant and reliable audit evidence by identifying expected relationships. A large number of candidates misread the question and explained the purpose of performing analytical procedures at the planning stage of an audit. A number of candidates digressed into stating the benefits and limitations of performing analytical procedures, which was not required, or wasted time by giving detailed examples of different types of analytical procedures.

57.2 (a) **Expected rental income**

	£'000
Rental income: based on prior year rental income and 2% increase (£15,687 × 1.02)	16,001
Tenant in administration: lost rental income (£100,000 × 3 quarters)	(300)
Vacant property: six months lost rental income on vacant property (£75,000 × 2 quarters)	(150)
Sold property: lost rental income (£400 × 2 quarters)	(800)
Total expected rental income	14,751

(b) **Evidence to test reliability of data used**

- Agree prior year rental income to prior year working papers/audited financial statements

- Agree rent increase to board minutes/correspondence/invoices

- Tenant in administration: Agree details to correspondence with the administrator

- Vacated property: Correspondence confirming dates of vacation

- Sale of property: Disposal/completion statement

- Agree current year rental income to the nominal ledger

- Agree amounts due to rental agreements

- Agree amounts received to bank statements

(c) **Enquiries based on the result of analytical procedures**

	£'000
Rental income recorded by Ventnor Estates	15,151
Expected rental income based on analytical procedures	14,751
Difference	400

The difference represents 2.64% of recorded rental income and is not acceptable as it exceeds the materiality threshold (ie, greater than 1%). Rental income therefore appears to be overstated.

Enquire of management as to what factors have affected rental income this year. For example:

- other sources of income or new properties that the auditor was not aware of

- change in revenue recognition leading to early rental income recognition or cut-off issues.

The auditor should request and review post year-end management accounts to see if rental income is lower than expected. A breakdown of rental income by property and month may help to identify why rental income is higher than expected.

Answers to this part of the question were of a good standard although a number of candidates did not attempt the question or presented very brief answers. The vast majority of candidates who attempted this question scored a very good mark on the calculation aspect and many calculated the correct figure of £14,751,000 for total expected rental income. Most candidates showed clear workings and, as a result, even where candidates didn't attain full marks for the calculation, they were still awarded method marks for calculating the total expected rental income. The most common mistake was the incorrect treatment of the rental increase of 2%.

Most candidates identified a range of appropriate audit evidence to test the reliability of the data used in their calculations. Bank statements and rental agreements were the most commonly identified sources of evidence. Fewer candidates, however, calculated the difference between the expected income and the actual income or assessed the materiality of this difference. A significant number of candidates failed to list the enquiries they would make based on the results of their analytical procedures. Many candidates failed to go beyond enquiring of management as to the reasons for actual rental income being higher than expected rental income. A number of candidates wasted time by digressing into business matters such as whether the annual rental income increase of 2% was appropriate, recommending credit checks on new tenants, suggesting the revaluation of properties and questioning why a property was sold.

57.3(a) Asset verification

Consequences

Assets may be overvalued because:

- assets recorded in the register may not exist or have been stolen
- assets may be impaired or no longer in use.

Assets may be undervalued because:

- acquisitions may not be recorded
- assets may still in use but fully written down.

Assets may not be available when required for use resulting in business disruption.

Additionally, incorrect capital allowances may be claimed and depreciation charges/useful life may be inappropriate.

Compliance with covenants may be affected by misstated assets/profits.

Recommendations

- Annual or more frequent reconciliations to be performed by a named person who is independent of the custodian of the assets
- Physical assets should be checked to the register to ensure completeness of records
- Entries in the register should be checked to the physical asset to ensure existence
- Inspections should include consideration of condition and appropriateness of useful life of the assets
- Differences to be reported to a responsible official who should investigate and resolve the differences
- Communication of policy to staff
- Monitoring to ensure that procedures are followed.
- Disciplinary action if procedures are not followed

(b) **Content of management accounting information**

Consequences

There may be cash flow issues and the business may be unable to pay its debts as they fall due.

The business could breach loan covenants resulting in the withdrawal of loans.

Extra costs may be incurred as a result of penalties imposed by the bank.

Ultimately the going concern status could be at risk.

The directors may be unable to take corrective action or may make poor decisions because of the lack of information.

The business may be trading illegally and the directors may be failing in their responsibility for maintaining solvency of the business.

Recommendations

- The agenda of directors' meetings should include a review of cash flow forecasts and compliance with bank covenants.

- Information presented at directors' meetings should include cash flow forecasts for at least the next 12 months (or the period of the bank loans), key assumptions used in their preparation, a sensitivity analysis and a commentary on compliance/non-compliance with covenants.

Examiner's comments

Answers to this part of the question were of a good standard. Most candidates outlined the possible consequences of the two internal control deficiencies and provided a number of suitable recommendations.

In respect of the asset verification, the points most commonly overlooked related to the lack of availability of assets resulting in business disruption, incorrect capital allowances and failure to comply with covenants. Most candidates provided a range of recommendations and scored well.

In respect of the content of management accounting information, the points most commonly overlooked related to the possibility of illegal trading due to the directors' failure to maintain solvency of the business. Few candidates mentioned that the cash flow forecasts should cover the next 12 months (or the period of the bank loans), or should include the key assumptions used in their preparation or be subjected to sensitivity analysis.

58 Bow, Euston, Oxford, Strand

Marking guide

			Marks
58.1	**Bow**	6½	
	Euston	6½	
	Oxford	7	
	Strand	4	
	Marks available	24	
	Maximum		13

		Marks
58.2 **Engagement to review financial statements**	4	
External audit of financial statements	4½	
Marks available	8½	
Maximum		4
58.3 **Additional information**	9	
Marks available	9	
Maximum		3
Total marks available		20

58.1 Bow

There are no records to substantiate the inventory held at the third party warehouse and therefore the auditor is unable to obtain sufficient, appropriate evidence (limitation on scope). The value of the inventory recorded by management is 2.5% total assets and 10.6% of profit before tax and therefore material but not pervasive as it is isolated to one area of the financial statements.

The audit opinion should be modified with a qualified/'except for' opinion and the opinion section of the report should be headed up "qualified opinion on the financial statements". A section, headed basis for qualified opinion, should describe the matter giving rise to the qualification.

The auditor should also report by exception under the Companies Act 2006 that:

- adequate accounting records were not maintained
- all information required for the audit was not obtained.

Euston

An unmodified opinion should be issued. The claim is 200% of profit before tax and represents a significant uncertainty. The auditor agrees with management's treatment and there is no limitation on scope. As a successful claim would turn Euston's profit into a loss, the existence of the claim is fundamental to the users understanding of the financial statements. Therefore, the audit report should be modified using an Emphasis of Matter paragraph and a brief description should draw the users' attention to the relevant disclosure note. This is included immediately after the opinion section and should indicate that the auditor's opinion is not modified in respect of this matter.

Oxford

The information relating to the company's expansion into China is inconsistent with the financial statements. The inconsistency is material, representing a difference of 10% between the figure for revenue in the strategic report and the figure given in the notes to the financial statements. The misstatement is in the strategic report and not the financial statements. The audit report should be modified to include a statement that the information in the strategic report is inconsistent with the financial statements. This should be headed 'Opinions on other matters prescribed by the Companies Act 2006'. The audit report should also include a section which describes the misstatement in the strategic report and is headed 'Matters on which we are required to report by exception'.

Strand

The report should be modified with an adverse conclusion because the financial statements are misstated as they have not been prepared in accordance with International Financial Reporting Standards. This matter is pervasive as it affects many elements of the financial statements. The matters leading to this conclusion should be described in the "basis for adverse conclusion" section.

Examiner's comments

This part of the question was generally very well answered with many candidates scoring maximum marks. There were some excellent answers in respect of the first two scenarios concerning audit reports. Candidates were less confident dealing with the final two scenarios and some candidates submitted vague or very brief answers. Some candidates lost marks by treating the final scenario as an audit.

Bow

The majority of candidates correctly identified that this scenario represented a material limitation on scope and that it was unlikely to be pervasive. Most candidates correctly identified the resulting impact on the audit report and that the auditor needed to report by exception regarding inadequate accounting records and lack of information.

Euston

The majority of candidates identified that the scenario required an unmodified opinion but modified report with an "Emphasis of Matter" paragraph. The points most commonly overlooked were that a successful claim would turn a profit into a loss, that the scenario represented a significant uncertainty and that the Emphasis of Matter paragraph is placed after the audit opinion. Some candidates having correctly identified that an unmodified opinion was required did not expand their answers any further and lost the marks available for emphasising the matter.

Oxford

Answers to this part of the question were of a mixed standard. Some candidates did not address the two issues separately and presented confused answers or only addressed one of the two issues limiting the marks they could achieve. Of those candidates who did separate out the two issues, a significant number correctly identified that the strategic report is not part of the financial statements and that a statement in the 'Other information' section was required. Common errors included candidates stating that an Emphasis of Matter paragraph or a qualified opinion was required.

Only a small number of candidates correctly identified that the non-disclosure of the floating charge in the financial statements is not considered pervasive and that a modified qualified ("except for") opinion should be issued. A large number of candidates incorrectly stated that the non-disclosure was a pervasive issue as it affected all of the assets and that this therefore required an adverse opinion. These candidates failed to realise that the misstatement is not considered pervasive as it is restricted to non-disclosure.

Strand

Most candidates, who attempted this part of the question, correctly identified that the situation represented a material misstatement and that the report should be modified with an adverse conclusion as the issue was pervasive. However, many candidates failed to make their answers specific to a review engagement and stated incorrectly that the opinion would be modified. These candidates failed to appreciate that a practitioner expresses a conclusion, rather than an opinion, in the report following a review engagement.

58.2 Engagement to review financial statements

A review provides limited/moderate assurance which is expressed negatively in the form of "Nothing has come to our attention".

Review procedures consist mainly of making inquiries of management and analytical procedures.

The objective of a limited assurance engagement is to reduce risk to an acceptable level.

The level of assurance is lower on a review engagement.

External audit of financial statements

An audit provides reasonable assurance which is expressed positively in the form of the financial statements give "a true and fair view".

An audit includes tests of control and tests of detail.

The objective of a reasonable assurance engagement is to reduce risk to a low level.

The scope of the work is more detailed on an audit.

Examiner's comments

This part of the question was generally very well answered with many candidates scoring maximum marks. The points most commonly identified were those relating to the description of the level of assurance provided by the reports and whether the opinion/conclusion was positive/negative. Some candidates then failed to provide reasons for the differences between the conclusion expressed following an engagement to review financial statements and the opinion expressed in an external auditor's report. A number of candidates incorrectly identified the users of the reports which was not required.

58.3 **Additional information**

- Key audit matters
    - Areas of higher assessed risk of material misstatement
    - Significant auditor judgments relating to areas in the financial statements that involved significant management judgement or estimates
    - The effect on the audit of significant events or transactions that occurred during the period
- How the auditor applied the concept of materiality
- An overview of the scope of the audit
- A statement that the auditor has complied with relevant ethical requirements regarding independence
- The name of the engagement partner
- Corporate governance statement issues.

Examiner's comments

Answers to this part of the question were of a mixed standard. The points most commonly identified were those concerning key audit matters and how the auditor applied the concept of materiality. Very few candidates identified that the name of the engagement partner should be included or mentioned compliance with relevant ethical requirements regarding independence. Disappointingly, a number of candidates did not present an answer to this part of the question or incorrectly discussed the various modifications that could be made to an auditor's report.

September 2017 exam answers

59 Short form questions

59.1 Firm's responsibilities

- Detection of material misstatements
- No obligation for the prevention of fraud
- Fraud not material to financial statements
- Therefore, firm not responsible for detection of it. Firm's responsibilities have been met.

Directors' responsibilities

Directors have primary responsibility for prevention and detection by:

- strong emphasis on fraud prevention/detection
- creating a culture of honesty and ethical behaviour
- active oversight by those charged with governance
- implementing a system of internal control
- monitoring control procedures

A policy was in place.

However, the system of controls failed.

Therefore, the directors' responsibilities were:

- not fulfilled regarding prevention
- fulfilled regarding detection

Examiner's comment

This question was generally well answered particularly by those candidates who formatted their answers under the headings of auditor's responsibilities, directors' responsibilities and a conclusion on whether those responsibilities had been met. Most candidates identified that it was the directors' responsibility to prevent and detect fraud and that this responsibility was discharged by implementing and monitoring a system of internal control. In addition, most candidates correctly identified that the auditor was only responsible for detecting material misstatements due to fraud. However, a significant number failed to state that the auditor had no responsibility for the prevention of fraud. Most candidates correctly concluded that the auditor's responsibility had been met as the fraud was not material to the financial statements. However, many failed to appreciate that the directors had met their responsibility in respect of detecting fraud but not preventing it. A significant number of candidates strayed beyond the requirement and cited the auditor's responsibilities in respect of reporting suspected money laundering.

59.2 Steps

- Establish amount of regular/recurring fees
- If exceed 5%: Safeguards required
- Disclose to ethics partner and those charged with governance
- Apply independent internal quality control review to audit
- Take steps to reduce work undertaken/fees if necessary
- Continue to monitor % of fee income to ensure recurring fees do not exceed 10% threshold

Reasons

- Potential self-interest threat to objectivity
- Over-reliant on fees from Dachshund/fear of losing client
- Reluctant to issue modified opinion

Examiner's comment

It was pleasing to note that most candidates scored maximum marks on this question. Many of these candidates identified that the level of fees posed a self-interest threat to objectivity and that because the fees were within the 5-10% thresholds, safeguards were required. Most of these candidates then proceeded to list the appropriate safeguards. The point most commonly overlooked was that relating to the consideration of the amount of fees that represented regular fees.

59.3 Procedures in relation to workplace accidents performance indicator

- Evaluate the system for collecting/recording accident data
- Review results of monitoring procedures
- Visit a sample of sites to review source data/accident books
- Compare accidents by:

  - location
  - month
  - prior year

- Perform media search/review of board minutes for any major accidents/incidents
- Inspect correspondence for evidence of claims
- Calculate expected total number of working hours based on number of employees
- Reperform KPI calculation

Examiner's comment

Answers to this question were of a mixed standard. Those candidates who focused on checking the accuracy of the safety performance indicator, specified in the question, often scored maximum marks. The points most commonly identified were those relating to inspection of the accident logs, analytical procedures and reperformance of the calculation. Few candidates considered the points in respect of evaluation and monitoring of the system for recording accidents, media searches and correspondence relating to compensation claims. A significant number of candidates listed more than three procedures. These candidates failed to appreciate that only the first three procedures were considered by markers. Weaker candidates wasted time writing about management's responsibility in respect of health and safety procedures and citing internal controls that should be in place to reduce the risk of accidents.

59.4 Additional audit procedures

- Inspect the contract with Pets to confirm credit terms are 60 days
- Inspect other contracts to confirm credit terms are 30 days
- Check date of contract with Pets
- Inspect records of goods despatched to Pets prior to year end
- Ascertain if amount was paid after year end

- Direct confirmation of balance with Pets
- Reperform trade receivables days' calculation excluding Pets and ascertain if:
    - days are in line with 30-day credit policy for other customers
    - days are in line with prior year

Examiner's comments

This question was generally well answered. The procedures most commonly cited were those relating to the inspection of contracts for credit terms, direct confirmation of the outstanding balance, after-date receipts and inspection of the aged receivables report. The point most commonly overlooked was that relating to the inspection of despatch records.

59.5 Actions before auditor's report is signed

Consider whether:

- errors indicate other misstatements might exist
- aggregate of misstatements is material
- audit strategy needs to be revised

Communicate all identified misstatements to management
Request management correct the misstatements
Reassess materiality
Request written representation from management that it believes any uncorrected misstatements are immaterial, individually and in aggregate

Document:

- amount below which misstatements regarded as trivial
- all misstatements accumulated
- whether corrected
- auditor's conclusion on whether uncorrected misstatements are material

Consider impact on audit opinion

Examiner's comment

Answers to this question were of a mixed standard. Those candidates who were familiar with the contents of ISA (UK) 450 *Evaluation of Misstatements Identified During the Audit* scored full marks. However, many candidates were unable to identify points other than considering the materiality of the misstatements in aggregate, reporting them to management and requesting management to amend the misstatements. Stronger candidates considered whether materiality needed to be reassessed and whether the audit plan needed to be revised. The points most commonly overlooked were those relating to written representations and the matters to be documented. A minority of candidates wasted time by discussing at length the various types of audit opinion that might be issued.

59.6 Implications for the auditor's report

- Misstatement
- £5.8 million impairment Which is 12.4% of PBT Material
- Auditor's report/opinion should be modified
- Not pervasive:
    - 0.7% of gross assets
    - not a substantial proportion/isolated to individual item in FS

- Qualified opinion/'except for'
- Explanation included in 'basis for qualified opinion' section

Examiner's comment

Many candidates scored maximum marks on this question. Most candidates scored marks for materiality calculations and concluding that the opinion should be qualified as the misstatement was material but not pervasive. Weaker candidates lost marks by using the gross amount of the investment in their calculations to determine whether the amount was material. However, they managed to salvage marks by correctly identifying the type of opinion that should be expressed. A minority of candidates wasted time considering the effect on the audit opinion if the directors recognised the impairment. These candidates failed to read the question properly. It was clearly stated that the directors had refused to recognise the reduction in value.

60 Gidget Ltd

Marking guide

			Marks
60.1	Scope of review of financial information	2½	
	Scope of external audit of financial statements	2	
	Reasons	6½	
	Marks available	11	
	Maximum		6
60.2	Data analytics routines		3
60.3 (a)	**Revenue**		
	Justification	10	
	Procedures	16	
(b)	**Rental expenses**		
	Justification	6	
	Procedures	13	
(c)	**Property, plant and equipment**		
	Justification	9½	
	Procedures	18½	
	General		
	Justification	1	
	Procedures	1	
	Marks available	75	
	Maximum		25
60.4	Identify and explain audit risks		
	Marks available	12	
	Maximum		5
Total marks available			39

60.1 Scope of review of financial information

- Procedures limited to inquiry, analytical and other review procedures
- Does not normally require corroboration of information obtained
- No responsibility to perform procedures to identify subsequent events
- Must enquire of management whether it identified/addressed subsequent events
- Less in scope than an audit

Scope of external audit of financial statements

Use of tests of details/tests of control

Includes obligation to:

- perform specific procedures re subsequent events/proactive responsibility
- up to the date of the auditor's report
- perform specific procedures such as reading minutes of meetings

Reasons

- A review provides limited assurance which is expressed negatively.

- An audit provides reasonable assurance which is expressed positively.

- A review is conducted in accordance with ISRE 2400 whereas an audit is conducted in accordance with Companies Act 2006 and ISAs.

- The objective of a review is to reduce engagement risk to a level that is acceptable in the circumstances, but where the risk is greater than for an audit.

- The objective of an audit is to reduce engagement risk to an acceptably low level.

Examiner's comments

This standard of answers to this part of the question were mixed. The points most commonly identified were those relating to the description of the level of assurance provided by each of the engagements and whether the opinion/conclusion was expressed positively/negatively. Most candidates also identified that the scope of the work is greater for an audit than for a review engagement. A significant minority of candidates incorrectly stated that an audit requires substantive procedures whereas a review does not. Many candidates wasted time identifying the addressees of the reports and to whom they were distributed which did not reflect a difference in scope. Few candidates referred to an external auditor's obligation with respect to subsequent events procedures and very few stated that the objective of the review is to reduce engagement risk to a level that is acceptable in the circumstances and that the objective of an external audit is to reduce engagement risk to an acceptably low level.

60.2 General

Identify unusual journal entries, such as those without authorisation or entered out of normal working hours. (Awarded once only under any of the key areas of audit risk.)

Revenue

Installation revenue cut off: extract data regarding installations occurring soon after the year end and match with receipts received before the year end and deferred income.

Charging point revenue proof: calculate the daily usage multiplied by the relevant hourly rate for each charging point.

Annual revenue for each charging point to identify outliers/anomalies. Matching each home installation with the OLEV receipt.

Rental expenses

Identify charging points where additional rentals will be payable based on total usage to date. Identify the number of rental payments recorded in year for each charging point.

Property, plant and equipment – charging points

Analyse the number of faults per charging point to identify charging points with high fault levels that may be impaired.

Identify charging points with few/no minutes used to identify those that may be impaired. Correlate usage and fault data to identify whether higher usage is related to increased faults. Detailed recalculation of depreciation.

Examiner's comments

Answers to this part of the question were of a mixed standard. Many candidates scored full marks but a minority of candidates scored zero. A number of candidates did not attempt this part. Most candidates described two or three relevant data analytics routines which made use of the data available in Gidget's accounting and business information systems. A small number of candidates cited basic analytical procedures such as the calculation of gross margin or the increase in revenue compared with the previous year. These calculations do not require the use of data analytics routines and did not score any marks. Very few candidates identified data analytics procedures in relation to journal entry routines.

60.3(a) Revenue

Justification

There is a risk of overstatement.

Total revenue has increased by 159% compared with the prior year and the gross margin has increased from 11.9% to 16.5%.

Revenue from home installations has risen by 138.6% which is out of line with the 52% growth in electric vehicle ownership.

Fees received before the year end in respect of installations due to occur after the year end may be included in the current year's revenue in error.

Claim forms are not checked for compliance with OLEV conditions.

OLEV will refuse payment on non-compliant claims.

There are no checks for gaps in the sequence of claim forms sent to OLEV. Revenue may be recognised in respect of claim forms that may not be submitted.

Revenue from public charging points has risen by 187.5% which is out of line with the 52% growth in electric vehicle ownership.

Revenue may be incorrectly recognised when funds are added to customers' accounts but not immediately used for charging.

The new mobile app and modifications to the charging points may increase the risk of errors. Data transmitted from charging points to the accounting system may be inaccurate.

Procedures

Evaluate and test the controls over deferred revenue. Inspect the management accounts for understatement of post year-end revenue. Compare actual revenue to budget.

Ascertain from management the reasons for the increase in installation revenue being out of line with the growth in electric vehicle ownership.

Calculate the total expected revenue from installations (number of installations x £800).

Obtain a schedule of receipts from customers close to the year end and ensure any installations occurring after the year end are excluded from the current year's revenue.

For a sample of claims recognised in revenue trace to cash receipts from OLEV.

Obtain a copy of OLEV conditions and for a sample of claims where the OLEV payment is outstanding:

- Review the claim form to see if the conditions have been met
- Check the claim was submitted to OLEV by Gidget.

Ascertain from management the reasons for the increase in public charging point revenue being out of line with the growth in electric vehicle ownership.

Select a sample of customers' accounts with credit balances and ensure these amounts are included in deferred revenue.

Test and evaluate the effectiveness of the controls around the mobile app and transmission of charging data.

(b) **Rental expenses relating to charging points in public car parks**

Justification

There is a risk of understatement.

Rental expenses have increased by 64.6% which is out of line with the 187.5% growth in charging point revenue.

Rental expenses represent 30.7% of cost of sales compared to 45.9% in the prior year.

Contracts straddle the year end, therefore rental expenses may be recorded in the incorrect period.

The accrual for additional rental is an estimate which is more difficult to predict in a rapidly growing market because it cannot be based on past experience.

Procedures

Ascertain from management why the increase in rental expenses is out of line with the increase in revenue/a smaller proportion of cost of sales.

Obtain the schedule of rentals.

For a sample of agreements that straddle the year end, calculate the rental that should be recognised in the year.

Agree the rentals to the rent agreement. Inspect post year-end payments/invoices to identify any rentals relating to the current year.

Obtain the calculation of the estimated additional rent accrual.

Agree the cost of additional rentals to the rent agreements and re-perform the calculation. Ascertain from management the basis of the estimated additional rental and consider the reasonableness of the assumptions.

Inspect records of actual usage post year- end and compare to the estimate.

For a sample of rental agreements, extrapolate usage to date for a full year and compare this to the number of standard minutes per the rental agreement.

Where additional rental appears likely to be payable ensure it is included in the year-end accrual.

(c) **Property, plant and equipment – charging points in public car parks**

Justification

There is a risk of overstatement.

Costs may be inappropriately capitalised and the overhead cost calculation is based on estimates.

Component suppliers invoice in their local currency which may lead to translation errors.

Depreciation may be understated. The depreciation charge was 22% of the carrying amount in 20X6 but is 19% in 20X7.

This is out of line with the policy of 25% pa. The depreciation policy of 25% may represent an inappropriate useful life.

The carrying amount of public charging points increased by 53% but depreciation only increased by 28%.

Depreciation on the modifications may be based over an inappropriate useful life or may be prorated incorrectly.

The increased usage of some charging points is likely to lead to increased damage or faults resulting in a higher risk of impairment.

Procedures

Obtain a schedule of costs capitalised in the year and ascertain if the costs meet the relevant criteria for capitalisation.

Agree capitalised labour costs to timesheets and payroll records.

Ascertain from management the basis for the inclusion of overheads and consider the reasonableness of the assumptions. Agree amounts used to the management accounts and reperform the calculation.

For a sample of components, vouch to invoices denominated in foreign currencies. Agree the exchange rate applied to a reliable external source and reperform the translation calculation.

Ascertain the basis for the 25% depreciation rate and consider whether this is reasonable. Ascertain why the rate of depreciation based on the carrying amount appears low. Reperform the depreciation calculation.

Ensure that modifications are depreciated over the assets' remaining useful life and are prorated correctly.

Review the results of any impairment reviews undertaken by management.

Identify whether any specific charging points have been replaced before the end of their useful life or whether any charging points have a high number of faults.

For a sample of charging points included in the asset register, physically verify the charging point and check they are in working order.

General

First year full audit may make it difficult to obtain assurance over opening balances.

Procedures

Review working papers from the prior year review engagement.

Consider whether audit work in the current year provides evidence on the reliability of opening balances.

Examiner's comments

Answers to this part of the question were generally good but the quality of answers across the three areas of audit risk were of a mixed standard. Rental expenses relating to charging points in public car parks was the least well addressed audit risk. A few candidates failed to follow the instructions to ensure that all responses are visible on screen and not hidden in cells. Candidates are reminded that their answers are presented to the examiner exactly as they appear on the screen and only visible responses are marked.

It was pleasing to note that most candidates attempted to make use of the financial information provided. However, a large proportion of candidates, restricted their calculations to comparing the percentage change in the financial information between 20X6 and 20X7. The examiners noted that many candidates expressed this calculation in the form of the 20X7 balance as a percentage of the 20X6 balance, for example, 20X7 revenue is 259% of 20X6 revenue. However, many candidates incorrectly described 259% as the increase in revenue and so did not score the marks available for the calculation as the actual increase in revenue from 20X6 to 20X7 was only 159%. Fewer candidates earned the higher skills marks for considering the relationship between different aspects of the financial statements. For example, many candidates correctly identified that rental expenses had increased by 65% but incorrectly concluded that this indicated a risk of overstatement. These candidates failed to appreciate that the increase was inconsistent with the much larger increase in revenue earned from public charging points and therefore that rental expenses were more likely to be understated.

Many candidates overlooked that this was the first audit of Gidget Ltd and that obtaining assurance over opening balances may be an issue. Those candidates that did identify this issue then went on to suggest contacting the previous auditor or review the previous auditor's working papers – thus failing to recognise that this was the first year Gidget was required to have an audit and that the firm had performed a review engagement in the prior year.

Revenue

Answers to the section on revenue were of a mixed standard. Many candidates did not distinguish between the two sources of revenue (installation fees and public charging point revenue) and presented confused, lengthy and overly complicated answers. Those candidates that considered each source of revenue separately and made a number of valid points for each source of revenue scored higher marks. Generally, candidates produced better answers in respect of installation fees than for public charging point revenue.

Installation fees

Most candidates correctly justified why user installation fees had been identified as a key area of audit risk. A significant minority of candidates incorrectly stated that revenue was overstated because the £500 contribution from OLEV should be only recognised as revenue on its receipt. Most candidates were able to cite relevant audit procedures to address the identified risks. The most commonly overlooked procedures were:

- obtain a schedule of receipts from customers close to the year end and for installations occurring after the year end, ensure these are excluded from revenue

- obtain a copy of OLEV conditions and review claims outstanding at the year-end for compliance.

Public charging point revenue

Most candidates correctly justified that (1) income from public charging points may be overstated due to the 187.5% increase which was out of line with the general growth in electric vehicle ownership, and (2) that unused credit on customers' accounts may be incorrectly included in revenue in the current year. The most commonly overlooked justification was that modifications for the new app for smartphones and the nature of the integrated system may increase the risk of data transmission errors.

The most commonly overlooked procedures were:

- select a sample of customer accounts with credit balances and ensure they are included in deferred revenue
- test and evaluate the effectiveness of controls around the new mobile app/transmission of data between systems.

Rental expenses

This was the least well answered area of audit risk with many candidates presenting very short answers to this part of the question. Some candidates presented answers which confused income from public charging points and the payment of rental expenses.

Some candidates incorrectly identified foreign currency translation errors as justification for this audit risk together with the associated audit procedures. This did not score any marks as it was unrelated to the payment of rental expenses. In respect of the rental accrual, a few candidates suggested direct confirmation of the estimated accrual with the car park owners as an audit procedure. However, this did not earn any marks as it is impractical. The estimates are calculated by Gidget and not the car park owner.

The most commonly overlooked justifications were:

- rental contracts straddle the year end and so rentals may be recorded in the incorrect period
- the calculation of rental expenses as a percentage of the cost of sales
- the additional rental expense is difficult to estimate because of the rapidly growing market.

The most commonly overlooked procedures were:

- inspect post year-end payments (or invoices) for rentals relating to the current year
- in respect of the additional rent accrual, agree the details to the rental agreement and inspect records of actual usage post year-end
- for a sample of rental agreements:
    - extrapolate usage to date for full year
    - compare to number of standard minutes per agreement
    - if additional rental is likely to be payable ensure it is included in the accrual.

Property, plant and equipment - charging points in public car parks

Answers relating to the justification of the audit risk for property, plant and equipment were generally good with most candidates identifying a number of appropriate justifications and relevant audit procedures. The most commonly overlooked justifications were:

- the calculation of depreciation charges for 20X7 and 20X6 as a percentage of carrying value
- depreciation on modifications may be calculated on inappropriate useful lives and prorated incorrectly
- the higher risk of impairment of some charging points due to increased usage.

The most commonly overlooked procedures were:

- check that modifications are depreciated over the assets remaining useful life
- review the results of management's impairment review
- identify whether any charging points have been replaced before the end of their useful life or have a high number of faults.

60.4 There is a risk that Gidget does not comply with data security legislation or that customers' personal data is stolen. This may result in unrecognised provisions/undisclosed contingent liabilities due to regulatory fines or compensation which may have to be paid to customers.

There is a going concern risk due to any resulting loss of reputation or loss of certificates that Gidget meets required security standards. This may lead to a loss of customers. Loss of personal data will result in significant costs associated with rectification and could result in a long period where charging points cannot be operated. These issues will have a negative impact on cash flow and profit.

Examiner's comments

This part of the question was well answered with many candidates scoring full marks. However, there was a small minority of candidates who failed to score any marks because they focused on the internal controls for data handling that should be implemented by Gidget rather than the audit risks.

Most candidates identified the loss of data and going concern risks but few candidates identified and explained the risks of non-compliance with data security legislation and unrecognised provisions/undisclosed contingent liabilities.

61 Terrier, Pug, Tabby

Marking guide

			Marks
61.1	**Terrier**		
	Threat	2	
	Steps	2	
	Pug		
	Threat	5½	
	Steps	7½	
	Tabby		
	Threat	3½	
	Steps	½	
	Marks available	21	
	Maximum		10
61.2	Listed company	4½	
	New audit client	3½	
	Pharmaceutical research company	3½	
	Planned major restructure/sale of subsidiaries	6½	
	Disagreement between the directors and previous auditors	1½	
	Overseas entities	4½	
	Marks available	24	
	Maximum		8
Total marks available			18

61.1 Terrier

A self-interest threat exists as the amount in dispute is significant. The firm may be more inclined to issue an unmodified audit opinion if it enhances its prospects of recovering the fee.

Steps

The ethics partner should be notified and a review of the audit work should be performed by a partner not involved in the audit. If the threat cannot be reduced to an acceptable level then the firm should resign.

Pug

The senior audit manager has been involved in the audit of Pug for more than seven years. This represents long association with a listed client and gives rise to:

- familiarity threat – the manager may have developed relationships with Pug's employees and become too trusting or insufficiently sceptical.

- self-interest threat – the manager may fail to identify or raise issues that have been missed in the past.

- self-review threat – the manager may place too much reliance on prior year figures.

Steps

The engagement partner should assess the extent of the threats, including the total period of time the manager has been involved, any changes in the nature of the work or role performed during the eight years and the portion of the manager's time spent on Pug engagements.

The engagement partner should discuss the situation with the engagement quality control reviewer and the ethics partner.

Consideration should be given to changing the role of the manager.

An additional review of the work performed by the manager should be undertaken by the engagement partner or other partners in the engagement team and additional procedures should be undertaken as part of the engagement quality control review.

Those charged with governance should be notified that an independence issue exists and that safeguards are in place to reduce the threats to an acceptable level.

If the threats cannot be mitigated the manager should be removed from the audit team.

Tabby

This represents lowballing. The FRC *Ethical Standard* specifies that fees for engagements should not be influenced by the provision of non-audit services. Therefore, the partner's proposal is not appropriate.

There is a self-interest threat because the firm may be reluctant to issue a modified opinion/report to enhance its prospects of obtaining the lucrative non-audit work.

Steps

The fee included in the tender should be based on the time, resources and level of experience required to complete the audit of Tabby to an acceptable standard.

Examiner's comments

Terrier

This part of the question was generally well answered as most candidates identified the self-interest threat and that the firm may be tempted to issue an unmodified opinion to enhance its prospects of recovering the fee. In respect of the steps to be taken, most candidates stated that the ethics partner should be consulted and that there should be an independent review of the audit work. The point most commonly overlooked was that relating to the significance of the fee.

Pug

Answers to this part of the question were of a mixed standard. Those candidates who were familiar with the provisions of paragraphs 3.21–3.23 of the FRC's *Ethical Standard* ES3 scored high marks. However, many candidates restricted their answers to the familiarity threat and failed to identify the self-interest and self-review threats. A significant number of candidates were unaware that it was possible for the manager to stay in post as long as safeguards were implemented. A common error was to cite the provisions of the FRC *Ethical Standard* (Part B, Section 3) which relate to an engagement partner instead of the senior audit manager.

Tabby

The points most commonly identified were those relating to the self-interest threat and lowballing. The points most commonly overlooked were those relating to the requirements of the FRC *Ethical Standard* (Part B, Section 4) ie:

- Paragraph 4.3D which specifies that fees shall not be influenced or determined by the provision of non-audit/additional services.

- Paragraph 4.4 which specifies that the engagement fee ordinarily reflects time spent, the skills and experience of the personnel performing the engagement and the competitive situation in the market.

A significant minority of candidates wasted time straying into issues not related to threats to independence and objectivity, such as the impact on audit quality if the firm were to cut corners due to the low audit fee.

61.2 Listed company

This will result in a higher level of engagement risk as Tabby is a public interest entity. There will be additional work associated with the audit of a listed company including performing a mandatory engagement quality control review. Reporting deadlines will be shorter compared with a non-listed entity.

New audit client

This will increase the level of detection risk and the amount of time needed to gain an understanding of the client. Additional time will be required to perform work in respect of opening balances.

Pharmaceutical research company

The firm may need to use an auditor's industry expert. There is likely to be significant development costs which involves the use of estimates.

Planned major restructure/sale of subsidiaries

The planned major restructure is likely to increase the risk of misstatement due to the complex nature of such transactions. There is also the risk of management bias in the preparation of the financial statements to achieve a higher sales price for the subsidiaries. The firm is likely to need staff with more relevant experience and may need experts in corporate restructures and valuations.

Disagreement between the directors and previous auditors

Any disagreements may extend the time and effort required to complete the audit.

Overseas entities

Additional time is required to audit the consolidated financial statements. The audit team may need to travel to the subsidiaries, incurring additional expenses or the firm may work with component auditors requiring time to communicate with them and review their work.

Answers to this question were of a mixed standard. Those candidates who identified the issues specific to the prospective client, such as a listed entity with overseas subsidiaries, operating in the pharmaceutical sector, scored high marks. A common shortcoming was to answer in very general terms how the fee would reflect the level of risk and expertise of the audit team without linking it to the specific circumstances of the entity. Such responses earned very few, if any, marks, as the requirement asked for 'specific factors relevant to …… the audit of Tabby.'

62   Redtail Ltd

Marking guide

			Marks
62.1	Reliance by bank on the audited financial statements	5	
	Request for early completion	3	
	Potential appointment as tax adviser	6	
	Marks available	14	
	Maximum		5
62.2	Reliance on Hawk	5	
	Purchasing components from Hawk at full list price	2	
	Fixed-price contracts and adverse movement in sterling	4	
	Customer contracts are negotiated years in advance	2½	
	Delays on the Tiberius contract	4½	
	Tiberius may invoke penalty clauses	3	
	Stock outs have occurred for some components	1½	
	Redtail is likely to exceed its overdraft limit	3	
	Adverse impact on Redtail's profitability	3	
	Marks available	28.5	
	Maximum		12
62.3 (a)	Make appropriate disclosures	5	
(b)	Do not make any disclosures	4	
	Marks available	9	
	Maximum		6
Total marks available			23

62.1 Reliance by Redtail's bank on the audited financial statements

There is a risk of management bias due to the need to secure funding. There is higher engagement risk as the bank could sue SLP if a duty of care is owed by the firm to the bank and the firm is found to be negligent.

There is a self-interest threat to objectivity and independence as SLP may be reluctant to issue a modified audit opinion for fear of the bank refusing to extend the facility. Without the facility, Redtail may not be able to continue to trade and consequently, SLP would lose its client.

The finance director has requested SLP complete the audit earlier than planned but resourcing for the audit is already scheduled

There is a threat to professional competence and due care and a higher risk of failing to identify material misstatements. The audit work may be completed too quickly and audit quality compromised. The firm may not be able to resource appropriately experienced staff.

The finance director's suggestion that SLP's support in meeting the new deadline will result in the firm being appointed as tax advisor

This appears to be an inducement and raises doubts about the finance director's integrity. A self-interest threat arises because the firm may be tempted to comply to obtain the additional tax work. A potential future self-review threat arises if the results of the tax engagement are reflected in the financial statements. The firm may be insufficiently questioning of the tax work and it may be reluctant to identify issues or errors in the tax work.

There is a potential future management threat if the firm is expected to make management decisions. Its views may become too closely aligned with those of management.

Examiner's comments

This part of the question was generally well answered as most candidates identified and explained the threats to objectivity and professional competence and due care arising from the finance director's request to complete the audit earlier than scheduled. A minority of candidates strayed beyond the requirement and wasted time citing safeguards to be applied to mitigate the threats. This was not within the scope of the requirement. The points most commonly overlooked were those relating to the engagement risk and management bias arising out of the bank's reliance on the audited financial statements.

62.2 Redtail is currently renegotiating its contract with Hawk and is reliant on Hawk for some components. Redtail may fail to renegotiate contract terms with Hawk which means it will be unable to continue with the assembly of turbines. It seems unlikely that Hawk will agree to further discounts as it is in a strong bargaining position.

Redtail is currently purchasing components from Hawk at full list price leading to an erosion of its gross profit margin from 23% to 18%. If this continues it may lead to an inability to generate cash from operations.

Redtail has fixed-price contracts with its customers and an adverse movement in sterling has made components more expensive. As Redtail invoices its customers in sterling, increases in import prices are not offset by changes in export prices. Contracts are likely to become unprofitable and any continued falls in sterling will exacerbate this issue.

Customer contracts are negotiated years in advance. It is unlikely that Redtail will be able to renegotiate non-profitable contracts without suffering significant penalties.

There have been significant delays on the Tiberius contract. This contract may be terminated and any work in progress may have a value below cost. Contract termination will impact adversely on Redtail's reputation and may result in the loss of future business.

Tiberius may invoke penalty clauses. There is likely to be a cash outflow to settle the penalty and to meet legal fees and expenses.

Stock outs have occurred for some components. This may result in delays on other contracts. Redtail is likely to exceed its overdraft limit by November 20X7 and the bank has requested to review the audited financial statements before approving an extension to the facility. An overdraft is an expensive form of finance and can be withdrawn at any time.

The above factors have an adverse impact on Redtail's profitability and cash flows increasing the likelihood that the company will be unable to pay its debts as they fall due.

Answers to this part of the question were generally very good as most candidates listed a range of factors that indicated uncertainty about the going concern status of the audited entity. Stronger candidates provided plausible explanations for each of the factors identified. However, weaker candidates often cited "this gives rise to going concern issues" by way of explanation. No mark was awarded for this generalisation.

62.3 (a) **Make appropriate disclosures**

SLP should issue an unmodified audit opinion. There is no misstatement as appropriate disclosures have been made and no limitation on scope as sufficient evidence is available.

The uncertainty is fundamental to the users' understanding of the financial statements and therefore SLP should issue a modified audit report with a 'Material uncertainty related to going concern' paragraph. This should be positioned after the 'Basis for opinion' section. It will draw users' attention to the matter disclosed in the financial statements and state that conditions indicate that a material uncertainty exists that may cast significant doubt on the entity's ability to continue as a going concern. It should also state that the opinion is not modified in respect of this matter.

(b) **Do not make any disclosures**

There is a misstatement due to the lack of appropriate disclosure. SLP should issue a modified audit report with a modified opinion.

If the matter is not considered to be pervasive a qualified opinion should be issued. If the matter is considered pervasive an adverse opinion should be issued.

A paragraph describing the matter giving rise to the modification should be included and headed "basis for qualified/adverse opinion".

Examiner's comments

(a) **Make appropriate disclosures**

Most candidates correctly identified that the opinion should be unmodified. It was pleasing to note that most candidates identified that a paragraph headed "Material Uncertainty Related to Going Concern" was required. However, a small minority of candidates were unaware of the fact that there had been a change in the requirements of ISA (UK) 570 and ISA (UK) 706 regarding the title of this paragraph and proposed an Emphasis of Matter paragraph.

(b) **Do not make any disclosures**

A significant number of candidates correctly identified that the opinion should be qualified or adverse depending on whether the absence of the disclosure was considered material or material and pervasive. However, many candidates failed to appreciate that ISA (UK) 570 Going Concern, paragraph 23 allows the expression of a qualified or adverse opinion. Consequently, these candidates restricted their answer to one of these options and limited the number of marks they could earn. Several candidates incorrectly stated that if the absence of a disclosure was considered pervasive then a disclaimer of opinion should be given. These candidates failed to appreciate that non-disclosure represents a misstatement. A few weaker candidates strayed beyond the requirement and wrote at length about the implications for the financial statements if the audited entity was not a going concern. These candidates failed to appreciate that the financial statements are still prepared on the going concern basis even if there is an uncertainty about the going concern status.

December 2017 exam answers

63 Short form questions

63.1 Failure to protect client data

Consequences

- Breach of legal requirements/confidentiality
- Reputational damage
- Loss of clients
- Litigation
- Fines
- Disciplinary procedures by professional body/loss of registered auditor status
- Increased insurance premiums
- Costs of reconstructing lost data
- Negative impact on cash flow/going concern

Internal controls

- Implement data security policy
- Procedures for reporting breaches of data security
- Monitoring of procedures
- Password protected laptops and files
- Passwords changed regularly
- Anti-malware/anti-virus software/firewalls
- Secure storage of files
- Staff training/disciplinary procedures.

Examiner's comments

This question was well answered, particularly by those candidates who formatted their answers under the headings consequences and internal controls. Candidates scored more marks in respect of consequences than they did on internal controls. The points most commonly overlooked in respect of consequences were those relating to increased insurance premiums and reconstruction costs following the loss of data. The points most commonly overlooked in respect of internal controls were those relating to IT controls such as anti-malware software and passwords.

63.2 Benefits of a voluntary external audit

- Better discipline over maintaining accounting records which:
    - reduces risks of material misstatement/errors
    - identifies fraud
    - reduces management bias
- May act as a deterrent to fraud:
    - eg, theft of cash, food and golf equipment
- More reliable business information:
    - leading to informed management decisions

- Enhances the credibility of the financial statements:
    - giving reassurance to third parties
    - eg, tax authorities, lenders and suppliers
- Business is scrutinised by a professional:
    - reduces business risk
    - improves controls/identies deficiencies
    - improves efficiency/performance.

Examiner's comments

Answers to this question were of a mixed standard. The points most commonly cited were those relating to credibility of the financial statements, assurance to third parties such as banks and recommendations in respect of internal controls. Surprisingly, only a minority of candidates identified the points relating to management bias, fraud and error. Few candidates considered the points relating to discipline over accounting records, more reliable business information and informed business decisions. A common error was to treat the entity as an incorporated body and cite irrelevant points such as ensuring that financial statements comply with the Companies Act provisions.

63.3 Audit procedures to address the risk of management override of internal controls

- Substantiate journal entries
- Investigate reconciling items
- Use of data analytics to identify exceptions
- Review significant accounting estimates and judgements for bias
- Investigate transactions outside the normal course of business
- Review 'whistle-blowing' arrangements
- Review internal audit reports
- Interview management to assess its attitude towards the control environment.

Examiner's comments

This question proved to be the most challenging of the short-form questions. A significant number of candidates did not attempt this question and many of those who did attempt it scored zero marks. The points most commonly identified were those relating to journal entries, management's estimates, transactions outside the normal course of business and management's attitude towards the control environment. Weaker candidates often cited discussing the risk of management override with management. No mark was awarded for such statements. Few candidates considered the use of data analytics, whistle-blowing arrangements or internal audit reports. A common shortcoming was to list more than three procedures as stated in the requirement. Candidates should be aware that only the first three points listed were considered by markers.

63.4 Request to provide a second opinion on a proposed auditor's report

Ethical issues

- Threat to professional behaviour
    - discredit the profession
    - may compromise/undermine the opinion of the existing auditor

- Client may be opinion shopping
  - may indicate lack of management integrity
- Threat to professional competence and due care
  - if firm is not in possession of all the facts
- Self-interest threat
  - to objectivity
  - firm may give the opinion the client desires to obtain future work

Response

- Obtain client's permission to contact the existing auditor
- Notify the auditor of the work to be undertaken
- If client refuses permission, consider whether it is appropriate to accept the engagement
  - must decline if ethical threats cannot be mitigated.

Examiner's comments

This question was well answered as most candidates identified that the prospective client was opinion shopping and that this had implications for management's integrity and the self-interest threat to objectivity. A significant number failed to consider the fundamental principles of professional behaviour and professional competence and due care. Many overlooked the fact that the prospective auditor needed to obtain client consent to discuss the reason for the modification with the incumbent auditor. The point most commonly overlooked was that relating to the need to be aware of the same facts as the incumbent auditor.

63.5 Reliability of an email as audit evidence and audit work that should be undertaken

Reliability

- The email:
  - should not be accepted at face value/must be critically challenged
  - does not provide sufficient evidence to support the going concern status
    - Sunwac may not have the funds to support Aire
    - Sunwac has not provided a timeframe for funding
  - was not sent directly to the auditors
  - could be forged
  - is not reliable
  - is not legally binding

Audit work that should be undertaken

- Request that a signed letter/direct confirmation/copy of Sunwac board minute pledging support is sent directly to auditors
- Consider whether Sunwac has the financial backing/resources to finance Aire
  - request access to and review the financial statements of Sunwac/undertake a credit check on Sunwac
  - request access to and review Sunwac's budgets/forecasts
  - confirm period of funding is for at least 12 months from the date the financial statements are approved.

Answers to this question were disappointing. Most candidates correctly identified that the email was not sufficient or reliable evidence in respect of the going concern status of the audited entity and that direct confirmation from the parent company was required. However, only a small minority of candidates appreciated that such confirmations are not legally binding. Stronger candidates appreciated the need to assess whether the parent company was able to provide the funding and consequently the importance of establishing whether the funds would be available. A minority of candidates strayed beyond the requirement and wasted time discussing the implications for the auditor's report.

63.6 Request that an engagement partner continues beyond rotation threshold

- Sue may continue as engagement partner:
  - to maintain audit quality
- ES permits when there are unexpected changes in the structure of the client's business:
  - such as the acquisition of competing business
  - only for an additional 2 years/no longer than 7 years
- Expanded review of audit work required:
  - to mitigate the familiarity threat
- Facts and reasons to be disclosed to:
  - shareholders
  - those charged with governance
- If no disclosure, should refuse the request
- Ethics partner should be consulted.

Examiner's comments

This question was well answered as most candidates identified that it was possible for the engagement partner to remain in post for an additional two years due to the change in business structure. Although most candidates appreciated that a review was required many of these failed to state that an **expanded** review was required under these circumstances. The points most commonly overlooked were those relating to the disclosures to shareholders. A small minority of candidates were unaware of the provisions of paragraphs 3.15/3.16 of the FRC *Ethical Standard* and, incorrectly, stated that the engagement partner must be rotated off the engagement immediately. These candidates scored no marks.

64 Lab Equipment Ltd

Marks

64.1 Process to obtain professional clearance   2½
Reasons for this process   7
Documentation   1
Marks available   10½
Maximum   6

64.2 Trade receivables
     Justification   6½
     Procedures   12
   Inventory
     Justification   9
     Procedures   19½
   General
     Justification   2
     Procedures   1½
   Marks available   50½
   Maximum   21

64.3 Catalogue update
     Consequences   3½
     Recommendations   3
   Bribery prevention policies
     Consequences   5½
     Recommendations   6
   Marks available   18
   Maximum   9

64.4 Self-interest threat   2
Intimidation threat   2
Threat to professional competence and due care   3
Marks available   7
Maximum   4

Total marks available   40

64.1 The firm should explain to LEL that it has a professional duty to communicate with the previous auditor. It should also obtain written authority from LEL to discuss LEL's affairs with the previous auditor. Once written authority is obtained, the firm should communicate with the previous auditor seeking any information relevant to its decision to accept the appointment as auditor. All discussions with the outgoing auditor should be documented.

Reasons

The process as set out by the ICAEW *Code of Ethics* is designed to maintain client confidentiality and mitigate reputational risk for the audit firm. It also ensures that the audit firm is in full possession of the facts and able to make an informed decision. The reason for the change in appointment could be due to disagreements with management or issues around management integrity that may not be easily overcome. The response may also highlight issues around unlawful acts or unpaid fees.

The documentation of discussions provides evidence of the process if the firm's acceptance is questioned at a later date.

Examiner's comments

Answers to this question were of a mixed standard. Most candidates correctly outlined the process set out by the ICAEW *Code of Ethics* relating to professional clearance from the previous auditors. This included identifying the need to obtain the client's permission to contact the previous auditors, communicating with them and identifying any reasons why the firm should not accept appointment. Candidates also identified a range of relevant reasons for this process including compliance with the principle of confidentiality, ensuring the firm was in full possession of the facts and alerting the firm to potential issues such as doubts about management integrity, disagreements, unlawful acts by the client and unpaid fees.

The most commonly overlooked points were:

- explaining the firm's professional duty to the prospective client
- recording discussions with the outgoing auditor in writing
- providing evidence of the process if questioned; and
- mitigating any reputational risk to the firm.

Several candidates wrote at length about the steps that should be taken if professional clearance was not obtained from the outgoing auditor or if issues were identified during the process. These did not earn any marks as the firm had already accepted the audit engagement and therefore these points were not relevant in this scenario.

64.2 Trade receivables

Justification

Trade receivables may be overstated because:

- trade receivables days have increased from 31.1 in 20X6 to 45.1 in 20X7

- REC is refusing to pay an invoice for £1.3 million. This is 1.04% of revenue and therefore material

- even if REC's balance is excluded, trade receivables days are 41.3 in 20X7

- this is inconsistent with the credit terms of 30 days

- issues with the quality of components may indicate potential disputes with other customers.

Procedures

- Inspect contracts to ascertain if credit terms have changed

- Obtain direct confirmation of trade receivables balances at the year end

- Identify cash received from customers after 31 December 20X7 which relates to trade receivables at the year end

- Review the aged trade receivables analysis to identify overdue balances

- Discuss with management the basis for any allowance against receivables. Recalculate the allowance against receivables

- Inspect correspondence with customers and solicitors and review board minutes for evidence of any disputes

- Inspect credit notes raised after the year end for evidence of amounts disputed at 31 December 20X7 or goods returned after 31 December 20X7

- Assess the financial position of key customers

- Vouch entries in the sales ledger with despatch documentation

- Perform cut-off procedures

- Use data analytics to identify items for further investigation, for example:

    - reproduce the receivables ageing analysis
    - three-way matches between sales orders, goods despatched records and invoices

(marks were awarded for any relevant examples of data analytic routines which could be used as an audit procedure).

Inventory

Justification

Inventory may be overstated because:

- inventory days have increased from 47.4 in 20X6 to 75.7 in 20X7

- the gross margin has increased from 40.8% in 20X6 to 45.4% in 20X7 which is inconsistent with higher prices charged by the new supplier

- the annual update of the product range may result in some instruments becoming obsolete

- there have been quality issues with components

- there was over purchasing by the chief buyer

- obsolete inventory will require write down to net realisable value

The standard costing system may be inaccurate and may not reflect up to date costs of components and labour.

Production overheads may not reflect the normal level of activity.

The inventory system may be recording incorrect balances due to inadequate controls over the interface between inventory and cost accounting systems.

Foreign suppliers are paid in local currency and there is the potential for translation errors.

Procedures

- Plan to attend an inventory count:

    - evaluate and test the controls over procedures
    - perform two-way test counts of inventory
    - identify slow-moving or obsolete items
    - obtain details of the last goods delivery and last despatch records

- Follow up inventory count notes:

    - ensure provision is made for slow-moving or obsolete inventory identified at the count

    - reconcile inventory at the count date to the year-end figure

- Review reports of previous inventory counts, evaluate the level of discrepancies and consider the implications for the reliability of the inventory system

- Evaluate and test controls over updates to the cost accounting and inventory systems

- Inspect aged-inventory analysis to identify slow-moving or obsolete items

- For those items in inventory at the year end, check post year-end selling prices to determine whether net realisable value is less than carrying value

- Review after date movements of over-ordered items

- Discuss with management the basis of the provision for slow-moving or obsolete inventory:

    - ensure there is appropriate provision for Partco inventory

    - obtain written representation that all defective items are identified and written down

- Obtain standard cost specifications for each instrument and for a sample of instruments:

    - discuss with management the basis of costings

    - agree the cost of components to suppliers' invoices

    - vouch labour costs to payroll

    - ascertain the basis of the overhead allocation

    - ensure the overhead allocation is based on normal levels of activity and that only production overheads are included

    - agree figures to management accounts

    - reperform calculations

- For a sample of items purchased from overseas suppliers, recalculate the foreign exchange translation and check the rate used to a reliable independent source

- Use data analytics to identify items for further investigation, for example, inventory items:

    - with negative margins (cost greater than selling price)
    - that are slow moving
    - with the highest discrepancies at inventory counts
    - with no recent cost price changes

(marks were awarded for any relevant examples of data analytic routines which could be used as an audit procedure).

General

Justification

This is a first-year audit and it may be difficult to obtain assurance over opening balances.

LEL has applied for a bank loan and may seek to window dress the financial statements.

Procedures

- Review the prior year auditor's working papers

- Consider whether audit work in the current year provides evidence as to the reliability of opening balances

- Consider whether opening balances reflect the application of appropriate accounting policies

Examiner's comments

Answers to this question were of a good standard. Most candidates justified why trade receivables and inventory had been identified as key areas of audit risk and described relevant procedures to be included in the audit plan. Both areas of audit risk were addressed equally well.

A significant proportion of candidates also correctly identified points relating to the fact this was a first-year audit, and therefore the risk associated with opening balances was greater and the review of the audited financial statements by the bank increased the risk of window dressing.

Very few candidates explicitly addressed the requirement to include data analytics routines to address either of the key areas of audit risk.

Trade receivables

Most candidates correctly identified the risk of overstatement of trade receivables and correctly calculated the increase in receivable days, identifying that this was out of line with the client's payment terms. Whilst most candidates identified the specific risk relating to the balance due from REC, few went on to state that this balance was material to the financial statements. The most commonly overlooked justification related to the issues with the quality of components which may give rise to disputes with other customers.

Most candidates cited relevant audit procedures including:

- review of the aged receivables analysis for overdue balances

- inspection of correspondence for evidence of disputes

- obtaining evidence of amounts received after the year end

- direct confirmation of balances with customers

- review of post year end credit notes and ascertaining the basis and reasonableness of the year end allowance.

The most commonly overlooked procedures were:

- assessing the financial position of key customers
- inspecting contracts to ascertain if credit terms had changed
- vouching entries in the sales ledger with despatch documentation.

A significant number of candidates incorrectly identified translation errors relating to the sale of instruments around the world. This was not relevant as the scenario stated that the company invoiced its customers in sterling.

Some candidates suggested one appropriate data analytics routine to produce the aged receivables analysis. However, few other variations of data analytics routines were identified and many candidates failed to state any data analytics routines at all.

Inventory

Most candidates correctly identified the risk of overstatement and correctly calculated the increase in inventory days. Relevant justifications relating to the risk of obsolete inventory were also commonly identified, including:

- the quality issues with components
- the annual update of the product range
- over purchasing by the chief buyer
- translations errors due to purchases in foreign currencies
- the integration between the costing and inventory systems.

The most commonly overlooked justification related to the increase in the gross margin being inconsistent with the higher prices charged by the new supplier.

Procedures relating to inventory was the least well answered of this part of the question. Several candidates incorrectly questioned the client's use of a perpetual inventory system and inappropriately recommended the firm carried out a full year-end count or insisted on the client doing so. Where candidates correctly recommended attendance at inventory counts during the year they then generally earned the marks relating to the procedures that would be carried out during the firm's attendance such as observing the count procedures, performing two-way test counts and identifying slow-moving or damaged inventory. Fewer candidates earned the marks available for following up on the inventory count notes or performing a reconciliation between the inventory at the count date and the year end.

Other commonly correctly cited procedures included:

- reviewing post year-end selling prices

- reviewing the aged inventory analysis for slow-moving items

- ascertaining the basis for writing down inventory, including that in relation to inventory purchased from the supplier with quality issues.

Few candidates earned the marks available for considering the movement of over-ordered items post year end or obtaining a written representation from management that all defective items had been written down.

Except for reperforming foreign currency translations and checking the rates used to a reliable external source, few candidates earned the marks available for procedures relating to the cost accounting system. Stronger candidates correctly cited agreeing the cost of components to purchase invoices and labour costs to payroll or timesheets. However, few candidates earned the marks relating to calculation of production overheads.

As with trade receivables, few candidates identified specific data analytic routines except for a minority of stronger candidates who correctly cited comparison of the cost of instruments to their selling price.

64.3 Catalogue update

Consequences

The sales staff may:

- misunderstand the oral instructions
- input incorrect prices
- make unauthorised amendments.

Instruments may be sold at sub-optimal prices leading to lower profits and an adverse effect on cash flow.

Instruments maybe overpriced leading to loss of customer goodwill and reduced demand for LEL's products.

Recommendations

- All amendments to be recorded on a standard form

- The standard form should be signed by the sales director

- A printout of amendments to be obtained and checked to the standard form and the printout should be signed as evidence of review

- Periodic checking of all prices to the authorised price list

Bribery prevention policies

Consequences

The Bribery Act 2010 makes bribery or failing to prevent bribery a criminal offence. The Bribery Act is global in scope and holds the company responsible for the actions of its employees. The company is liable if employees or persons associated with the company offer, accept or bribe a foreign public official. The absence of policies means that employees may offer or accept bribes without realising the consequences or do not know what to do if they suspect bribery. The penalties for bribery or failing to prevent bribery are severe and include fines and imprisonment.

The financial results of the company may be adversely affected. There could be additional expenses arising through the:

- payment of bribes
- cost of any fines or penalties imposed by the authorities
- cost of legal fees to resolve any bribery issues.

There may be regulatory investigations and adverse publicity leading to a reduction in sales. Ultimately, the going concern status may be threatened as the company may have its licence to trade revoked.

Furthermore, external auditors have a duty to report suspicions of bribery to the National Crime Agency as required by the Proceeds of Crime Act.

Recommendations

- Document and implement bribery prevention policies

- Introduce a whistle-blowing policy and procedures for reporting bribery

- Appoint a designated person responsible for compliance

- The bribery policies should be communicated to all employees

- Policies should be based on Government (Ministry of Justice) guidelines which set out the following principles:

    - Proportionate procedures to mitigate risks
    - Top level commitment/anti-bribery culture
    - Risk assessment to identify bribery
    - Due diligence procedures
    - Embedded culture of bribery prevention
    - Making improvements to procedures when necessary.

Examiner's comments

Answers to this question were of a mixed standard although candidates tended to perform better when outlining the consequences of each internal control deficiency compared with the recommendations to address them.

Amending prices in the online catalogue

Most candidates correctly identified that amending prices on the oral authority of the sales director might result in errors in pricing with customers being either over or under-charged and a subsequent negative impact on profit, cash flow and customer goodwill.

Most candidates correctly recommended that written authority should be obtained for any changes to catalogue prices. However, fewer candidates earned the marks available for extending their recommendations to include regular printouts of amendments, checking to the written authority and signing the printout as evidence that the review had taken place.

Bribery prevention policy

Most candidates correctly identified that the absence of a bribery prevention policy contravened the Bribery Act 2010 and increased the risk that bribery might take place. Most also went on to explain relevant consequences such as:

- regulatory investigation
- fines
- adverse impact on the company's reputation
- negative impact on profit and cash flow
- going concern risk.

Fewer candidates earned the marks for stating that:

- the Bribery Act 2010 is global in scope

- the company is responsible for the actions of its employees

- the auditors have a duty to report suspicions of bribery to the NCA under the Proceeds of Crime Act.

Most candidates earned marks for relevant recommendations such as documenting a bribery prevention policy, including whistle-blowing procedures that should be communicated to all employees.

The recommendations most commonly overlooked were:

- appointing a compliance officer
- Ministry of Justice guidelines.

64.4 There is a self-interest threat to objectivity and independence as the audit team may comply with the managing director's wishes to benefit from the hospitality offered. The offer is not trivial or inconsequential and is likely to be considered excessive by an independent third party.

There is a possible intimidation threat if the managing director exerts pressure on the audit team. The offer may represent an inducement and raises question over management integrity.

There is a threat to professional competence and due care and professional behaviour as the audit quality may be compromised to meet the deadline. Insufficient audit evidence may be obtained and an inappropriate opinion may be reached if a material misstatement is not highlighted.

Examiner's comments

Answers to this question were of a mixed standard although many candidates scored maximum marks. Most candidates correctly identified and explained the self-interest threat to objectivity as well as the fact that the offer may represent an inducement by the managing director which raised questions about management integrity.

A significant number of candidates also correctly identified the threat to professional competence and due care if the audit work was rushed and an inappropriate opinion issued because of the managing director exerting pressure on the audit team. Fewer candidates stated that insufficient audit evidence might be obtained.

Few candidates earned the marks for identifying that there was a risk of unprofessional behaviour which might discredit the profession. A significant number of candidates wasted time by stating the actions that the firm could take in response to the threats which was not required.

65 Crystal Diamond Screens Ltd

				Marks
65.1	(a)	General representations		
		Intended use of the forecast	3½	
		Completeness of significant management assumptions	3½	
		Management's acceptance of its responsibility	2½	
	(b)	Moderate assurance		
		Explanation	2	
		Why a higher level of assurance cannot be provided	4	
	Marks available		15½	
	Maximum			8
65.2	(1)	Receipts from ticket sales		
		Cinema numbers	2½	
		10% and 5% increases	1	
		Level of occupancy	2½	
	(2)	Payments for the conversion of cinemas, new seating and project management fees		
		Basis of payments	2	
		Estimate of cost per seat	1½	
		Project management payments	1	
	(3)	Proceeds from the sale of the two cinemas	5½	
	(4)	Payments to the film distribution company	2	
	(5)	Payments to employees	3	
	(6)	Receipts from and payments to the bank		
		Loan amount	1½	
		Assumptions	2	
	General – sensitivity analysis		1	
	Marks available		25½	
	Maximum			12
	Total marks available			20

65.1 (a) General representations

The general representations that should be obtained are:

The intended use of the forecast

This is to ensure that the audit firm is aware of all users of the forecast and that there are no unforeseen users which could impact on the risk associated with the engagement. This representation reduces the extent of the reporting accountant's liability and exposure to claims for damages.

The completeness of significant management assumptions

Knowledge of the assumptions used to compile the forecast is largely confined to management. The reporting accountant cannot undertake the examination of the forecast unless all assumptions are adequately disclosed. The reporting accountant reports on the 'reasonableness' of assumptions and therefore needs confirmation, via a representation, that they are complete.

Management's acceptance of its responsibility for the forecast

The reporting accountant is not responsible for preparation of the forecast and is only responsible for examining and providing an assurance report on the forecast. This representation reduces the expectation gap ie, any misunderstandings regarding the responsibilities of the respective parties.

(b) **Moderate assurance**

A report on the examination of the cash flow forecast is a limited assurance engagement which provides moderate assurance as to the credibility of the financial information. Engagement risk is reduced to a level that is acceptable in the circumstances. The conclusion is expressed negatively in the form of "nothing has come to our attention that causes us to believe that the assumptions do not provide a reasonable basis for the cash flow forecast ...."

The examination of the cash flow forecast is based on assumptions and judgments about the future which are subject to uncertainty. Procedures used in the examination are restricted due to the lack of corroborative evidence about future events. For a higher level of assurance to be provided, a greater degree of verification and corroboration of the financial information would be required.

Examiner's comments

Answers to part (a) were disappointing. Candidates who were familiar with the contents of paragraph 25 of ISAE 3400 *The Examination of Prospective Financial Information*, often scored full marks as once they listed the required representations they demonstrated an understanding of why they were needed, particularly in respect of limiting the reporting accountant's liability and reducing the expectation gap. Weaker candidates answered in terms of the role of written representations in a statutory audit of financial statements or an engagement to review historical financial statements, instead of the examination of prospective financial information. Consequently, they listed the requirements of ISA 580 *Written Representations* or paragraph 62 of ISRE 2400 *Engagements to Review Historical Financial Statements* for which no marks were awarded. Several candidates provided representations that were specific to the scenario. These answers scored no marks as the requirement was to list general representations.

Part (b) was well answered by most candidates who attempted this part of the question. Most candidates were able to explain the term moderate assurance and scored further marks for explaining why a higher level of assurance could not be provided. The points most commonly overlooked were those relating to engagement risk and the fact that forecasts were subject to uncertainty. Some candidates strayed into discussing reasonable assurance and the nature of testing, such as controls testing and tests of details that would be needed to achieve this.

65.2(1) **Receipts from ticket sales**

Receipts from ticket sales should reflect the number of operational cinemas, as follows:

- To June 20X8, there are 22 cinemas
- From July to December 20X8, there are 20 cinemas (two cinemas are closed for sale)
- In 20X9, there are 10 unconverted cinemas (10 cinemas are closed for conversion)
- In 20Y0, there are 10 converted cinemas (10 converted cinemas are operational but the remaining 10 cinemas are closed for conversion)
- In 20Y1, there are 20 converted cinemas.

Receipts therefore decline until the end of 20X9 and start increasing in 20Y0.

The receipts should reflect that tickets prices increase by 10% and the number of seats increase by 5% on completion of the conversions.

The level of occupancy of cinemas should be considered taking into account the capacity of each cinema before and after conversion, market trends and any variations from city to city. Market research reports should be inspected. Proof in total calculations, for example using number of seats, occupancy levels and price of tickets will provide added assurance.

(2) **Payments for the conversion of cinemas, new seating and project management fees**

Payments for the conversion of cinemas should be based on the tenders received, which should be inspected. The payments should commence in January 20X9 with the profile of the payments as set out in the tenders and should reflect any retentions (payments held back until a later date for any rectification work required).

Enquiries should be made of the directors as to how they arrived at the estimate of £150 for the cost of each cinema seat. The estimate should be compared to suppliers' price lists or quotes obtained for the new seating. The number of seats should be consistent with plans for the capacity of each cinema.

The project management payments should be either fixed fee or a percentage of building costs and should be in line with market rates or the letter of engagement with Monroe and Co, if available.

(3) **Proceeds from the sale of the two cinemas**

This should be a prudent estimate and in line with the market value of properties in the locality of each cinema. The estimate should be checked to a valuer's report, if available. Correspondence with the developer should be inspected for evidence of the likelihood that the sales will take place and any indication of the sales value and whether the sales are contingent on obtaining planning permission. The planning permission application to change the use from cinema to residential should be inspected as this will affect the market value if the planning application is successful. If the sale is contingent on obtaining planning permission and the proposed deal collapses, the ability to find another buyer should be considered. The forecast should reflect the timescales involved in obtaining planning permission. There should be consideration of whether the proceeds could be a lump sum or by instalments and should be net of selling costs.

(4) **Payments to the film distribution company**

The amounts in the cash flow forecast should reflect the level of ticket sales as shown in the profit forecast. The percentage fee should be as per the agreement with the film distribution company or market rates. The payments should reflect the three-month rent-free period followed by monthly payments in arrears.

(5) **Payments to employees**

The amounts in the cash flow forecast should be consistent with the number of cinemas in use and reflect an increase of 60 employees in each year after conversions are complete (six extra employees in each of the 10 cinemas converted). The cash flow forecast should include redundancy payments on closure of the cinemas for conversion and the sale of two cinemas. The minimum wage levels and statutory increases each year should be confirmed with government pronouncements. The profit forecast should be examined to see that bonuses shown in the cash flow forecast are consistent with the level of forecast profits.

(6) **Receipts from and payments to the bank**

The amount of the loan should be sufficient to fund the conversion of the cinemas into multiplexes and allow the company to pay its debts as they fall due while staying within any overdraft facility. The receipt should precede the start of the building work.

Prudent assumptions should be made regarding interest payments, for example, in line with market rates or consistent with those cited in any correspondence with the bank and should be based on the principal outstanding. Loan repayments should be consistent with those cited in any correspondence with the bank.

General

The assumptions should take account of inflation and key variables should be subjected to sensitivity analysis.

Examiner's comments

Answers to this part of the question were disappointing and many candidates provided very brief answers that scored few marks or failed to provide any answer in one or more of the six sections. The consideration of the reasonableness of assumptions in assurance engagements has been identified by examiners in previous commentaries as an area where candidates struggle.

The following points were commonly overlooked:

- Consideration of occupancy levels at cinemas

- Payment profile for the cost of conversions

- Examination of the correspondence with the developers

- Inspection of the planning permission documentation

- Consideration of redundancy payments

- Whether the loan would be received prior to the conversions or if it would be sufficient to fund the conversions.

Most candidates failed to consider inflation and sensitivity analysis in their answers.

Many weaker candidates approached the question from the perspective of the firm conducting a financial statements audit, instead of consideration of the reasonableness of assumptions underlying receipts and payments in a cash flow forecast. For example, candidates discussed issues such as:

- the internal controls in operation for ticket sales and payroll
- agreeing ticket sales receipts to bank statements or till records
- the risk of fraud when ticket sales are in cash
- the review of timesheets
- the risks associated with the manipulation of the profit forecast to ensure the bonus is paid.
- the review of bank statements and bank reconciliations.

None of these points was relevant to the answer.

A large number of candidates digressed into whether the points described in the scenario were valid, for example was it feasible to convert 10 cinemas a year or whether a film distribution company would allow a rent-free period of three months. Candidates also digressed into areas that were not part of the requirement, for example, the payment of running costs and the payment of taxes and dividends.

Weaker candidates confused a cash flow forecast with a profit forecast and incorrectly discussed items such as depreciation and profit or loss on the disposal of the two cinemas. This matter has also been identified in previous examiners' commentaries on questions concerning the examination of cash flow forecasts.

The points commonly identified by stronger candidates were the:

- increase in ticket prices and the number of seats following conversions

- timeframe for the payments

- review of contract tenders

- comparison of the costs of seating to supplier's price lists

- market value of properties in the locality of each cinema to be sold

- payments to the film distribution company should reflect the level of ticket sales with payment in arrears and include a three month rent-free period

- payment to employees should be consistent with the number of operational cinemas.

66 FOPT

Marking guide

		Marks
66.1 Auditor's report implications		
Foyle	3	
Ogmore	4	
Pattack	6	
Tyne	3	
Marks available	16	
Maximum		12
66.2 (a) Parties to whom your firm may be liable for damages	2	
(b) Methods available to your firm to limit its liability	6	
(c) Quality control procedures		
Procedures re. recruitment and training	1	
Engagement teams	2½	
EQCR	1½	
Client due diligence	1	
Marks available	14	
Maximum		8
Total marks available		20

66.1 Foyle

There will be no modification to the audit opinion. The loss of £0.2 million cannot be offset against profits on other contracts and a provision therefore should be made. However, the loss is not material as it is only 2.06% of profit before tax and 0.24% of total assets. Even if the directors refuse to amend the financial statements in respect of the misstatement, the audit opinion will not be modified.

Ogmore

As the disclosures in the financial statements regarding this matter are adequate, there is no material misstatement or limitation on scope. However, the firm has concluded that there are significant doubts as to whether Ogmore can continue as a going concern. Therefore, a modified auditor's report with an unmodified opinion will be issued. A paragraph headed 'Material Uncertainty related to Going Concern' will be included immediately after the opinion section. This should draw users' attention to the matter disclosed in the financial statements as the issue is fundamental to users' understanding of the financial statements. A statement that the opinion is not modified in respect of the uncertainty should be included.

Pattack

A modified opinion should be issued which should be a qualified ('except for') opinion. As the managing director refuses to disclose the transaction there is a material misstatement. The amount of the transaction is not material by size as it is only 3.54% of profit before tax and 0.45% of gross assets. However, it is material by nature as it is a related party transaction because Clyde Ltd is owned by the brother of the managing director. It is not pervasive as it is confined to a specific item in the financial statements and is not fundamental to the users' understanding of the financial statements. There should be an explanation of the issue (reason and amount involved) in the "basis for qualified opinion" section of the audit report.

Tyne

The audit report should disclose that the firm has taken advantage of the exemptions of the Provisions Available for Small Entities and that a former engagement partner has joined Tyne, unless the matter is disclosed in the financial statements. The disclosure should be set out in a separate paragraph. However, the matter does not affect the audit opinion which remains unmodified.

Examiner's comments

Answers to this part of the question were of a mixed standard. There were some excellent answers in respect of the first three scenarios with many candidates scoring maximum marks. Candidates were less confident dealing with the final scenario and some candidates did not attempt this scenario. However, disappointingly, a significant minority of candidates demonstrated only limited understanding of the implications for audit reports in each of the scenarios. These candidates wasted time by listing a number of different answers in the hope that one or other of their answers was correct. These candidates often failed to perform any materiality calculations, or if they were attempted, reached an incorrect conclusion as to whether an item was material.

Foyle

This part of the question was generally well answered with many candidates scoring maximum or close to maximum marks. The point most commonly overlooked was that a provision should be made for the loss. Disappointingly, several candidates having correctly calculated the percentage effect of the loss on profit before tax and total assets decided that the matter was material and therefore concluded, incorrectly, that a modified report was required.

Ogmore

This part of the question was generally well answered. However, there were some very brief answers to this part of the question. Most candidates correctly identified that the opinion should be unmodified. However, a minority failed to consider the use of a paragraph headed 'Material Uncertainty related to Going Concern' to direct the users' attention to the note in the financial statements. In addition, many candidates failed to point out that the uncertainty surrounding going concern was fundamental to the users' understanding of the financial statements.

Weaker candidates strayed beyond the requirement and wrote at length about the implications for the financial statements and the auditor's report if the audited entity was not a going concern. These candidates failed to appreciate that the financial statements are still prepared on the going concern basis even if there is an uncertainty about the going concern status.

Pattack

Most candidates identified that the scenario represented the non-disclosure of a related party transaction (RPT) and that the RPT was material by nature but not by size. Stronger candidates identified that the matter was not pervasive and reached a correct conclusion on whether or not the opinion should be modified. Weaker candidates hedged their answers and discussed the possibility of the issue being pervasive, thereby demonstrating a lack of understanding of what constitutes a pervasive issue. A number of candidates having correctly calculated the materiality percentages, incorrectly concluded that the matter was material by size.

Tyne

Answers to this part of the question were generally disappointing. Candidates that were familiar with paragraphs 6.15 to 6.17 of the FRC *Ethical Standard* or paragraph 3.16 of Chapter 4 in the 2017 Audit and Assurance study manual scored maximum marks. Most candidates, who attempted this part of the question, scored some marks by stating that the matter should be disclosed in the audit report and that the opinion should be unmodified. Weaker candidates incorrectly stated that the audit opinion should be qualified or that the firm should not offer any opinion as an audit was not required or that the firm should resign as auditors. Several candidates digressed into the ethical threats associated with engagement partners joining audit firms which was not required.

66.2 (a) **Parties to whom your firm may be liable for damages**

The firm may be subject to professional negligence claims from the audited entity and its shareholders and/or third parties where it can be demonstrated that the auditor owed the party a duty of care, such as the company's bankers.

(b) **Methods available to your firm to limit its liability**

The firm could agree a liability cap which would stipulate the maximum amount payable in damages, such as a fixed amount or based on a formula, eg. a multiple of the audit fee. The liability cap must be fair and reasonable and approved by the shareholders. A proportional liability agreement could be set up whereby there is an agreement to apportion blame between the guilty parties. The firm may be protected by the inclusion of a disclaimer of liability (a Bannerman clause) in the audit report stating that the report is prepared for the company's members and no other party. Trading as a LLP (limited liability partnership) means that liability is limited to assets in the partnership and there is no individual responsibility for the actions of other partners.

(c) **Quality control procedures**

The firm should have robust procedures to ensure competent employees are recruited and subsequently trained.

The firm should allocate competent and experienced staff to each engagement team. Junior members of the team should be adequately briefed, prior to starting their work, and supervised throughout the audit. All team members' work should be subject to a review by a more senior member of the team. Consultation should take place on contentious issues and all such matters, including their resolution, should be documented.

An engagement quality control review (EQCR) should be performed on audits of all listed companies and other audits where audit risk is considered higher than normal.

The firm should undertake due diligence procedures, including the assessment of management's integrity, prior to accepting new clients and deciding whether to continue with existing clients.

Examiner's comments

Answers to parts (a) and (b) were generally of a higher standard than part (c).

(a) **Parties to whom your firm may be liable for damages**

There were some good answers to this part of the question with many candidates scoring maximum marks. Most candidates correctly identified that the firm may be liable to the shareholders and the bank. Several candidates incorrectly stated that the audit firm would be liable to third parties who relied on the auditor's report. Audit firms are only liable where it can be demonstrated that the auditor owed the party a duty of care. Some candidates incorrectly cited that a duty was owed to organisations such as the Financial Reporting Council and the ICAEW.

(b) **Methods available to your firm to limit its liability**

Most candidates correctly identified relevant methods of limiting liability such as liability caps, disclaimer of liability in the audit report and limited liability partnerships. Several candidates stated that the disclaimer of liability should be included in the firm's engagement letter. This earned no mark as the parties in question would not have access to the engagement letter. A significant minority of candidates failed to mention that the liability cap could be a fixed amount or based on a formula. Most candidates identified trading as a LLP but lost marks as they did not explain that liability is limited to assets in the partnership and there is no individual responsibility for the actions of other partners.

(c) **Quality control procedures**

Answers to this part of the question were of a mixed standard. Most candidates identified review procedures including the use of an EQCR but did not expand their answers, for example, to explain that and EQCR should be performed on audits of all listed companies and other audits where audit risk is considered higher than normal. Few candidates identified due diligence or the consideration of management's integrity as a quality control procedure.

March 2018 exam answers

67 Short form questions

67.1 Steps

Evaluate whether the finding indicates:

- non-compliance with professional standards
- inappropriate audit opinion issued and if so seek legal advice
- systematic non-compliance with firm's policies
- firm's sampling policy is unclear

Communicate the finding to the engagement partner

Provide recommendations, such as:

- informing the training department
- making changes to quality control procedures
- taking disciplinary actions

Examiner's comments

Answers to this question were generally disappointing. The points most commonly identified were those relating to training and disciplinary actions. Stronger candidates identified the points relating to communicating with the engagement partner, the possibility of systematic errors and the need to address the firm's quality control procedures. However, few candidates identified the risks of non-compliance with professional standards and having expressed an inappropriate opinion. Weaker candidates misread the question and listed the features of a cold review instead of the steps to be taken following the discovery, during the cold review, of the failure to comply with the firm's policies in respect of sampling. Some candidates did not appreciate that a cold review is undertaken after the audit report is issued and wasted time stating that the audit team should be instructed to return to the client and redo the sampling.

67.2 Key factors and why important

Firm's experience in retail sector and online systems

Audit strategy, including reliance on controls/internal audit and use of data analytics

- would impact audit quality

Proposed approach regarding global stores

Whether the firm has overseas offices or would use a local auditor

- may impact cost/expenses

Proposed audit fee

- aim to get best value for money

Proposed personnel on the audit team

- whether Fantastic can work with senior team members
- experience/seniority of team will impact efficiency of audit

Proposed timetable

- whether firm can meet deadlines
- whether it will be disruptive/fall in busy periods

References

- assurance as to firm's reputation

Whether firm can offer any other services

- services may be more efficient and better quality if provided by same firm

Confidentiality arrangements

- conflicts of interest may arise/firm may act for competitors

Examiner's comments

This question was generally well answered as most candidates provided a range of factors that would be considered by the prospective client. The points most commonly overlooked were those in relation to audit strategy. However, it was pleasing to note that stronger candidates occasionally referred to the use of data analytics. A common misunderstanding was to answer the question in the context of what the audit firm should consider when tendering. Although these candidates salvaged some marks for the factors, they were not awarded any marks for the explanations. For example, in the case of proposed audit fee, those candidates who misread the question provided an explanation in the context of whether the fee would cover costs as opposed to providing value for money for the client.

67.3 Points for engagement letter and reason for inclusion

To whom the report is made available

Intended use

- avoid reliance by unforeseen third parties
- limit liability

Period covered by the forecast information

Nature of the assumptions (best-estimate/hypothetical)

- clarity on what is subject to review
- accountant reports on reasonableness of assumptions

Statement that management is responsible for assumptions, providing information and preparing forecasts

Performed in accordance with ISAE 3400

- not an audit
- avoid any misunderstandings / expectation gap

Caveat warning that forecast could be different to actual performance

- avoid over-reliance on forecast

Limitation of liability/liability cap

- evidence of agreement

Nature of assurance provided / limited assurance

Form of reports to be provided

- clarity about the output of the engagement

Answers to this question were of a mixed standard. Those candidates that listed points **specific** to the engagement to examine forecast information scored good marks by identifying a range of points to be included in the engagement letter. The points most commonly overlooked were those relating to ISAE 3400 and, in relation to the caveat, the prevention of overreliance on the forecast. The most common shortcoming was the failure to identify points "**specific to** the examination of the profit forecast". These candidates identified generic points, found in any engagement letter, such as management's responsibility without specifying what that responsibility is. Weaker candidates confused the examination of the forecast with a review of financial information and consequently, identified inappropriate criteria.

67.4 Key variables

Occupancy rates
Rate of inflation/prices of rooms
Variations in seasonality
Sales price of properties
Property selling costs
Time to achieve sale of properties
Number of employees taking redundancy vs transfer
Redundancy costs per employee
Exchange rates

Examiner's comments

Those candidates who understood what sensitivity analysis entails (ie, making alternative assumptions about the key variables) tended to score full marks. The key variables most commonly identified were, occupancy rates, proceeds of sale of properties and redundancy payments and, to a lesser extent, exchange rates. The key variables most commonly overlooked were those relating to the timing of the property sales and the selling costs. It was evident that a significant number of candidates did not understand what sensitivity analysis involves and these candidates tended to list the matters to consider when assessing the reasonableness of assumptions underlying the figures in the forecasts such as comparing the sale proceeds for properties to similar properties. No marks were awarded for these points.

67.5 Procedures in relation to cyber attack

Discuss with the directors/review board minutes for:

* reasons for/extent/nature of data lost
* plans to rectify situation/recover data

Review media for adverse commentary/reputational damage

Inspect correspondence with:

* regulators re: fines
* customers re: legal action
* lawyers re: outcome of legal action

Post year-end management accounts and revised cash flow forecasts:

* to ascertain impact on business performance and risk to going concern status

Inspect financial statements to ascertain if provisions/contingent liabilities are adequately provided/disclosed

Inspect after date payments for evidence of damages/fines

Examiner's comments

Answers to this question were of a mixed standard. Candidates who focused on **audit procedures** scored good marks. The audit procedures most commonly identified were those relating to discussion with the directors about the extent of the data loss and the remedial action, inspecting correspondence with regulators, customers and lawyers and consideration of the accounting treatment of fines and damages. The points most commonly overlooked were those relating to subsequent events review procedures such as inspection of management accounts and after date payments. However, many candidates missed the point of the question and wasted time listing the internal controls that should be exercised by the audited entity instead of the procedures to be undertaken by the audit team.

67.6 Analytical procedures

20X7 salary costs adjusted for:

- 2% pay rise
- 6% growth in employees

Average pay per employee compared:

- with prior year
- with budget
- by each office

Calculate expected PAYE/NI based on expected gross salaries

Average monthly wage bill per office to identify outliers

Examiner's comments

Answers to this question were generally disappointing. Many candidates listed tests of details such as checking payroll details to HR records and failed to list analytical procedures as required by the question. No marks were awarded for tests of details. The analytical procedures most commonly identified were those relating to comparisons with prior year and inter-office comparisons. Stronger candidates attempted a proof in total by taking the 20X7 figure and uplifting it for the annual pay rise and growth in number of employees. Few candidates listed any analytical procedures involving PAYE and NI and their relationship to gross salaries.

68 Barebones Ltd

Marking guide

		Marks
68.1 Going concern		
Justification	13½	
Procedures	21½	
Intangible assets – development costs of wearable technology		
Justification	9½	
Procedures	17½	
Trade payables		
Justification	4	
Procedures	13	
General		
Justification	3	
Procedures	3	
Marks available	85	
Maximum		28
68.2 Auditor's report implications of going concern uncertainties	7½	
Marks available	7½	
Maximum		4
68.3 Ethical issues	6	
Marks available	6	
Maximum		4
68.4 Component auditor communications	7	
Marks available	7	
Maximum		3
Total marks available		39

68.1 Going concern

Justification

- BB operates in a highly competitive market where retail customers have driven down prices resulting in a negative impact on BB's profitability.

- BB is reliant on two contracts with retail customers.

- BB may experience cash flow issues because:

    - retailers have negotiated extended credit periods which are longer than the credit terms BB receives from its suppliers

    - trade payables days are 45 days (or awarded under trade payables) which indicates BB may be delaying payment to suppliers. This could result in interest, penalties or accounts put on stop.

- BB operates in a high-tech industry where products might be superseded quickly.

- BB's directors wish to diversify into a new market, but the baby clothing market is unproven and the bank may refuse the additional loan.

- BB is reliant on a bank overdraft. This is an expensive form of finance and could be recalled at any time.

- Interest cover is 1.42. This is in breach of the bank loan covenant which requires interest cover of 1.5 or more. The bank may withdraw the loan.

- Nomaj has requested the firm accepts an engagement to review BB's five-year profit forecast which suggests Nomaj may not wish to support BB further.

Procedures

- Obtain BB's profit and cash flow forecasts for the 12-month period after the year end / date of approval of financial statements:
    - ascertain if BB can meet its debts as they fall due
    - assess BB's ability to meet the loan covenant
    - consider the reasonableness of the assumptions
    - ascertain the headroom available in the overdraft facility
    - perform sensitivity analysis on key variables, such as new contracts / exchange rates / interest rates.

- Obtain a written representation from management regarding the feasibility of BB's plans.

- Inspect post year-end management accounts.

- Ascertain the length of contracts negotiated with retailers to date and review post year-end events to identify whether any further contracts have been signed.

- Inspect correspondence with suppliers to ascertain whether any accounts have been put on stop, if so enquire of management how it will continue to manufacture.

- Inspect inventory balances to see if production schedules can be maintained.

- Review industry commentary and BB product reviews to ascertain if BB's products are rated favourably.

- Review the loan agreement to ascertain the loan terms and the consequences of a breach of the interest cover requirement.

- Inspect correspondence with the bank to ascertain the quality of BB's relationship with its bank.

- Obtain comfort letters from Nomaj and Macusa and assess their ability to continue to support BB.

Intangible assets – development costs of wearable technology

Justification

- The carrying amount has increased by 66% indicating a risk of overstatement.

- The costs capitalised may not meet the relevant criteria.

- If depreciation on equipment is incorrect this will result in a misstatement in development costs.

- Additions appear high given the product was ready in July 20X7. This may indicate that costs have been incorrectly capitalised after the development was completed.

- The high level of competition and technological change may indicate that the intangible asset is impaired.

- The estimate of attributable overheads may be inappropriate.

- The rate of amortisation has fallen from 16.3% to 11.3% indicating that it may be understated.

- This equates to approximately 6–9 years amortisation period which appears too long for a high-tech industry.

Procedures

- Obtain a schedule of development costs and check that costs meet the relevant capitalisation criteria and:
    - agree employee costs to payroll records
    - agree material costs to invoices
    - identify any items capitalised after July 20X7 and ascertain from management the reasons these costs were capitalised.
- Inspect the audit work performed on tangible assets to ascertain whether depreciation charges are reliable:
    - trace the depreciation capitalised to the accounting records for equipment
    - confirm the related asset is used in product development.
- Ascertain the basis for attributing overheads and:
    - consider the reasonableness of this basis
    - agree the overhead costs to the management accounts
    - reperform the calculations.
- Inspect evidence of management's impairment review.
- Ascertain the basis for the estimate of useful life and consider its reasonableness by:
    - comparing it to other similar companies
    - comparing it to the length of contracts negotiated with retail customers
    - obtaining expert advice on how long this type of technology is likely to last before being superseded.
- Reperform the amortisation calculation.

Trade payables

Justification

- There is a risk of understatement due to a backlog of invoices which may result in cut-off issues.
- Payables are managed on a spreadsheet which may result in errors due to inadequate controls.
- Trade payables days is 45 days (or awarded under going concern) which is inconsistent with suppliers' credit terms of 30 days.

Procedures

- Undertake direct confirmation with suppliers.
- Obtain or prepare supplier statement reconciliations and ensure that differences can be explained.
- Inspect correspondence with suppliers for evidence of overdue payments.
- Inspect post year-end bank statements for payments to suppliers and check that payments relating to purchases made before the year end are included in payables.
- Inspect purchase orders/delivery notes/goods received records/invoices for purchases made before the year end and trace to the payables listing.
- Perform data analytics routines for three-way matching of orders/goods received records/invoices.

- Inspect unprocessed invoices for items relating to goods received before the year end.
- Enquire of Henry Shaw whether the backlog of invoices was cleared before the year end.
- Identify invoices recorded after the year end and establish if they relate to goods received before the year end.

General (awarded anywhere but once only)

Justification

- It is a first-year audit and the prior year financial statements were not audited. There will be limited assurance over opening balances.
- Reliance by the bank on the financial statements may result in management bias.
- Materials are invoiced in local currencies which could result in translation errors.

Procedures

- Ascertain if the current year audit procedures provide evidence in respect of opening balances.
- Confirm opening balances are correctly brought forward and reflect appropriate accounting policies.
- Check the exchange rates used to an independent reliable source and reperform the calculations.

Examiner's comments

Answers to this question were of a good standard, particularly in respect of going concern. Most candidates provided relevant justifications and procedures for each of the three key areas of audit risk identified.

A small number of candidates failed to follow the instructions to ensure that all responses are visible on screen and not hidden in cells. Candidates are reminded that their answers are presented to the examiner exactly as they appear on screen.

Going concern

The points most commonly overlooked were that delayed payments to suppliers could result in additional interest or penalties and accounts put on stop. Few candidates identified that Nomaj had requested an engagement to review BB's five-year profit forecast indicating that Nomaj may not wish to invest further in BB.

Candidates also identified a range of relevant audit procedures to address the going concern risk. The points most commonly overlooked were:

- ascertaining the length or basis of contracts negotiated with retailers to date
- reviewing post year-end events to identify whether any further contracts had been signed
- inspecting correspondence with suppliers for evidence of issues, such as accounts have been put on stop, if so
- enquiring of management how it will continue to manufacture
- inspecting inventory balances to see if production schedules can be maintained.

Intangible assets – development costs of wearable technology

Answers in respect of the development costs were of a good standard. Very few candidates identified that if depreciation on equipment is incorrect this will result in misstatement of development costs. A significant minority incorrectly stated that the depreciation could not be included in development costs. Other points commonly overlooked were that:

- costs may have been capitalised after the development was completed
- a high level of competition/technological change may indicate that the intangible asset is impaired.

Candidates commonly identified relevant audit procedures which included:

- obtaining a schedule of development costs and:
    - checking costs meet the relevant capitalisation criteria
    - agreeing employee costs to payroll records
    - agreeing material costs to invoices.
- ascertaining the basis for amortisation and estimates in relation to attributable overheads and reperforming the related calculations.

As expected, the most commonly overlooked procedures were those relating to the most commonly overlooked justifications of risks, ie:

- identifying any items capitalised after July 20X7 and ascertaining from management the reasons these costs were capitalised
- inspecting the audit work performed on tangible assets to ascertain whether depreciation charges are reliable
- tracing the capitalised depreciation to the accounting records for equipment and confirming the related asset is used in product development.
- agreeing overheads to the management accounts
- inspecting management's impairment review.

Whilst several candidates correctly identified that the auditor should consider the reasonableness of amortisation few earned the marks for expanding on how the auditor would do this, ie:

- comparing to other similar companies
- comparing to the length of contracts negotiated with retailers
- obtaining expert advice on how long the technology is likely to last.

Trade payables

Most candidates correctly identified the risk of understatement of trade payables and cited a range of relevant justifications for this.

The relevant audit procedures most commonly identified were:

- direct confirmation with suppliers
- preparing supplier statement reconciliations
- inspecting post year-end bank statements for payments to suppliers to identify those relating to pre-year-end purchases which should be included in payables.

The most commonly overlooked procedures were:

- inspecting correspondence with suppliers for evidence of overdue paymentsdata analytics routines for three-way matching of orders/goods received records/invoices
- enquiring of management whether the backlog of invoices was cleared.

General

There were several points available to candidates in any section of their answers, but which were only awarded once in total. A significant number of candidates correctly cited points relating to:

- BB being a new audit client

- overseas suppliers invoicing in foreign currencies and the procedures for auditing these transactions

- the risk of management bias due to the bank's reliance on the financial statements.

Fewer candidates earned the marks for citing the additional procedures that should be undertaken to provide audit evidence over the opening balances.

68.2 • If the directors adequately disclose the uncertainty over going concern, the firm should issue a modified audit report with an unmodified opinion.

    • The report should include a section headed "Material Uncertainty Related to Going Concern" which:

        - draws users' attention to the note in the financial statements where the uncertainty is disclosed

        - states that a material uncertainty exists that may cast significant doubt on BB's ability to continue as a going concern

        - states the auditor's opinion is not modified in this respect.

    • If the directors do not disclose the uncertainty over going concern, there is a misstatement which may be material or pervasive.

    • The firm should issue a modified report with a qualified or adverse opinion.

    • The basis for qualified/adverse opinion should state that:

        - a material uncertainty exists that may cast significant doubt on BB's ability to continue as a going concern

        - the financial statements do not adequately disclose this matter.

Examiner's comments

This part of the question was generally well answered. Stronger candidates recognised that the implications for the auditor's report depended on whether the directors adequately disclosed the uncertainty over going concern or whether the directors failed to adequately disclose the uncertainty. These candidates often obtained full marks. In respect of where adequate disclosure had been made, it was pleasing to note that most candidates who considered this scenario correctly identified that a paragraph headed "Material Uncertainty Related to Going Concern" was required. However, there was a significant minority who incorrectly referred to an Emphasis of Matter paragraph. In respect of where there was no disclosure of the uncertainty, some candidates incorrectly stated that as this was considered pervasive then a disclaimer of opinion should be given. These candidates failed to appreciate that non-disclosure represents a material misstatement. Few candidates fully appreciated that the material misstatement might result in a qualified or adverse opinion. Some weaker candidates strayed beyond the requirement and wrote at length about the implications for the financial statements if BB was not a going concern and then went on to consider the implications for the auditor's report if the financial statements were not prepared on a break-up basis. These candidates failed to appreciate that the financial statements would be prepared on a going concern basis even if there is an uncertainty about the going concern status.

68.3 The request to review the profit and cash flow forecasts of BB raises doubts over Jacob's integrity because he has requested that the firm conceals this information from the directors of Macusa. This may have implications for BB's control environment and corporate culture and could indicate that information might be concealed from the auditor. It would also be difficult for the firm to act in the best interests of both Nomaj and Macusa.

There are threats to the firm's independence and objectivity as follows:

- Management threat: the recommendation over whether Nomaj should continue its investment in BB is a management decision.

- Self-interest threat: the firm may fear losing BB as an audit client if it recommends that Nomaj should dispose of its investment in BB.

- Self-review threat: the firm is likely to examine the forecasts as part of its going concern assessment in future audits.

Examiner's comments

Answers to this part of the question were disappointing. Most candidates were able to identify the ethical issues of self-interest, self-review and management threats to independence and objectivity and the conflict of interest arising in the scenario. However, weaker candidates did not earn the additional marks available for adequately explaining the reasons for the existence of these threats. Where an explanation was attempted, candidates often gave generic reasons for the existence of the threats rather than tailoring their answer to the circumstances set out in the scenario. Consequently, they scored no marks for the explanation. The points most commonly overlooked were:

- doubts over Jacob's and Nomaj's integrity

- the threat to the firm's integrity if it concealed information from Macusa

- implications for the control environment and corporate culture which may indicate that Jacob/Nomaj might conceal information from the auditor.

68.4
- Work to be performed, including work on subsequent events and intra-group transactions
  - Use to be made of the work
  - Form and content of the firm's communication with Macusa's auditor
  - A request for confirmation that the firm will cooperate with Macusa's auditor
  - Ethical / independence requirements
  - Component materiality
  - Significant risks identified
  - A request for communication of any other significant risks on a timely basis
  - List of related parties
  - Timetable
  - Dates of meetings
  - Key contacts

Answers to this part of the question were disappointing. Those candidates familiar with paragraph 40 and Appendix 5 of ISA 600, listed a range of requirements and information that the group auditor would include in its communication to your firm (the component auditor). Many candidates incorrectly listed items that would be sent to the group auditor at the conclusion of the work on the component audit and scored no marks. A significant number of candidates did not attempt this question or provided very brief answers.

69 NANN

Marking guide

		Marks
Niffler		
	Threats	7
	Actions	3½
Auror		
	Threats	5½
	Actions	1
Nundu		
	Threats	4½
	Actions	4
Newt		
	Threats	7
	Actions	5½
Marks available		38
Maximum		20
Total marks available		20

Niffler

There is a self-interest threat because the 20X8 fee income is 5.07% of the firm's total annual fee income.

Therefore, the fees from Niffler are expected to exceed the 5% threshold set by the Ethical Standard for listed entities but are below the 10% threshold.

There is a risk of over-reliance on the fees from Niffler.

The auditor may be reluctant to take actions adverse to the interests of the firm such as modifying the audit report/opinion.

There is a management threat because the firm may be expected to make management decisions during the engagements to perform non-audit services.

The firm's views may become too closely aligned with those of management.

A self-review threat arises because the results of the work performed during non-audit services may impact the financial statements.

The audit team may place too much reliance on the non-audit work and may be reluctant to highlight any errors.

Actions

Disclose the fee percentage to those charged with governance at Niffler and continue to monitor the proportion of fee income earned.

Separate teams should be in place for the performance of the audit and non-audit engagements.

The firm should document that there is informed management and ensure that it does not make management decisions when performing non-audit engagements.

The engagement quality control reviewer should ensure that independence is not impaired.

Auror

A self-interest threat arises because Frank, Mary's father, can influence the financial statements.

Mary may be reluctant to take actions adverse to the interests of Frank or Auror, such as identifying significant issues or modifying the audit report.

An intimidation threat may arise if Frank uses his relationship with Mary to influence the outcome of the audit.

A familiarity threat arises because Frank is a person closely associated with Mary. She may be too trusting or insufficiently questioning of Frank.

There is a risk to Mary's integrity if she is unable to be honest, fair and candid due to the close family relationship.

Actions

Mary must be removed from the audit engagement and the firm should assess whether there is an alternative partner to fill the role of engagement partner.

Nundu

There is a self-interest threat to objectivity and professional competence and due care.

An expensive watch is not inconsequential and the gift should not have been accepted.

The engagement team member may have overlooked issues identified during the audit resulting in the risk of an inappropriate opinion having been issued.

This represents a lack of professional behaviour by the member of the engagement team and raises doubts over management integrity.

The watch may have been an inducement.

Actions

The watch should be returned and the member of the engagement team should be disciplined.

The firm should ascertain if any other audit team members accepted gifts.

The work performed by the member of the engagement team should be reviewed again and the audit opinion issued should be reconsidered.

If the audit opinion is now in question the firm should seek legal advice.

The firm should ensure that its policies for accepting and declaring gifts are clear and properly communicated to the firm's employees.

Newt

There is a management threat because the firm may be expected to make management decisions and its views may become too closely aligned with management.

The preparation of the financial statements is management's responsibility.

A self-review threat will arise because the results of the accountancy service will be included in the financial statements.

The audit team may place too much reliance on the product of the accountancy service and may be reluctant to highlight any shortcomings.

There is a high level of engagement risk due to reliance by Newt's bank on the firm's audit report. The firm may owe a duty of care to the bank.

There is a risk to professional competence and due care if the firm does not have the required knowledge and experience of this specialised industry.

Actions

The firm should not assist with the preparation of the financial statements unless:

- it does not involve taking management decisions, and
- the services are of a technical, mechanical and informative nature only.

If the accountancy service is provided the work should be performed by a partner and staff not involved in the audit.

The accountancy service should be independently reviewed, and the audit work should be reviewed by a partner or senior staff member not involved in the audit to ensure the accountancy service has been properly and effectively assessed during the audit.

The firm should:

- ensure that there is informed management
- seek to agree a liability cap
- include a paragraph in its audit report to limit reliance by third parties
- consider its competencies and the resources available before accepting the engagement.

Examiner's comments

Niffler

This part of the question was generally well answered as most candidates correctly identified the self-interest threat arising from fee dependency. Many of these candidates also identified that the recurring fees fell within 5%–10% of the firm's fee income and consequently required the implementation of safeguards. Most candidates identified that the fee needed to be monitored. However, only a minority identified that the situation should be disclosed to those charge with governance. A significant number of candidates restricted their answers to the fee issue and omitted to consider the self-review and management threats arising from the provision of non-audit services.

Aurora

This part of the question was generally well answered. Most candidates identified that the close relationship between Frank and Mary gave rise to an insurmountable familiarity threat and that Mary should be removed from the audit team. Stronger candidates also identified that there were self-interest and intimidation threats. The points most commonly overlooked were those relating to Frank being in a position to influence the financial statements and the risk to Mary's integrity. Weaker candidates were insufficiently positive about removing Mary from the audit team. These candidates tended to only consider removing her alongside several other inappropriate safeguards, such as an additional independent review. These candidates did not earn any marks for their safeguards.

Nundu

This part of the question was generally well answered. Most candidates identified the self-interest threat to objectivity arising from the generous gift and that the integrity of management might be in doubt. These candidates also identified that the gift should not have been accepted as it could be construed as an inducement to overlook issues that should have been raised. Many candidates overlooked the threats to professional competency and professional behaviour and the possibility that an inappropriate opinion may have been issued.

Newt

Answers to this part of the question were generally disappointing. Most candidates focussed on the threats to objectivity arising out of the preparation of the financial statements. Many failed to consider the other professional issues such as those relating to professional competence arising from the specialist nature of the client and the engagement risk arising from bank reliance. Consequently, they failed to identify actions to be taken to mitigate those other professional issues. A significant minority of candidates wasted time citing the features of information barriers. These candidates failed to appreciate that these are only required where confidentiality is paramount.

70 Billywig Ltd

		Marks
70.1 Additional steps to be take		
(1) Gross profit margin	10	
(2) Depreciation of plant and equipment	5	
(3) Subsequent events – board minutes	14	
(4) Journals	5	
(5) Supplier statement reconciliations	6	
(6) Directors' report	5	
Marks available	45	
Maximum		16
70.2 Internal control deficiencies and recommendations		
Consequences	4½	
Recommendations	3	
Marks available	7½	
Maximum		3
70.3 Auditor's report implications	5½	
Marks available	5½	
Maximum		2
Total marks available		21

70.1(1) Gross profit margin

Steps to be taken

- Review the explanations obtained by the audit team for the increase in the gross profit margin, such as a change in the mix of government and non-government contracts.

- Ensure that management's explanations were adequately corroborated.

- Check that risks of misstatement were appropriately tested, such as:
    - cut off errors
    - misclassification of expenses
    - incorrect translation of foreign currency transactions.

Reasons

The increase in the gross profit margin is inconsistent with a fall in contract prices and the increase in the cost of pesticides due to weak sterling.

(2) **Depreciation of plant and equipment**

Steps to be taken

- Consider whether the errors identified are an indication of systematic errors.

- Ensure that the extrapolated error has been added to the list of uncorrected misstatements.

- Communicate the errors to management and request that they are corrected.

Reasons

There may be other errors which when aggregated with those identified result in a material misstatement.

It may also be an indication of similar errors in other classifications of asset.

(3) **Subsequent events – board minutes**

Steps to be taken

- Inspect the terms of the contract.

- Obtain an understanding of the nature and basis for the complaint and the potential implications in respect of the contract in question.

- Consider whether any amounts due from the customer are irrecoverable.

- Ascertain whether any other contracts could have similar issues.

- Consider the proportion of total revenue earned from this contract.

- Inspect board minutes since the end of the fieldwork.

Reasons

A breach of contract could result in:

- payment of fines/penalties/refunds
- legal action against Billywig
- termination of the contract.

The financial statements may need amending due to undisclosed provisions/contingent liabilities.

There may also be doubts about Billywig's going concern status.

(4) **Journals**

Steps to be taken

- Confirm that the journals posted outside hours were further investigated by the audit team and that management's explanations were adequately corroborated.

- Consider the materiality of the journals in question.

Reasons

The journals may indicate the existence of fraud and/or management override of controls. There may be internal control deficiencies.

(5) **Supplier statement reconciliations**

Steps to be taken

- Ascertain whether the audit strategy planned for reliance on supplier statement reconciliations.

- If so, ensure that alternative audit procedures were performed by the audit team, such as:

    - direct confirmation

    - supplier statement reconciliations

    - comparison of trade payable days based on the draft financial statements with the same ratio for the prior year.

Reasons

The absence of supplier statement reconciliations increases the risk of misstatement of trade payables.

(6) **Directors' report**

Steps to be taken

- Inform the directors of the inconsistency between the directors' report and the financial statements.

- Ask them to change the directors' report.

Reasons

There is an inconsistency between the directors' report and the financial statements and the firm has a responsibility to report on this.

If the discrepancy is deliberate it may bring the directors' integrity into question.

Examiner's comments

Whilst the overall marks for this part of the question were good, a significant number of candidates failed to appreciate the context of the scenario in that the audit fieldwork had already been completed and the engagement partner was undertaking a review of the working papers. Consequently, a recurring shortcoming across the scenarios was to state that the engagement partner should perform audit procedures that should have already been undertaken by the junior members of the audit team. Few candidates presented their answers using the headings 'Steps to be taken' and 'Reasons'. However, those that did tended to score full or close to full marks.

Gross profit margin

This part of the question was generally well answered. Most candidates identified that the increase in the gross profit margin was inconsistent with the fall in contract prices and the increase in the cost of pesticides and that explanations should have been sought in respect of this inconsistency. The points most commonly overlooked were those relating to what the engagement partner should be looking for in the working papers, ie, evidence that expenses were tested for misclassification and foreign currency transactions were tested for correct translation.

Depreciation

Answers to this part of the question were very disappointing with many candidates scoring zero. The point most commonly identified was that relating to the aggregation of errors. The points most commonly overlooked were those relating to the possibility of systematic errors and the communication of the misstatements to management. Several candidates misread the scenario and assumed the error related to the work of the audit junior. These candidates then wasted time discussing further reviews of the junior's work and the firm's training of audit juniors.

Subsequent events

This part of the question was generally well answered. Most candidates identified that the potential breach in contractual terms might result in the payment of compensation and that this would impact the financial statements by way of provision or contingent liability. Consequently, the points most commonly identified were those relating to the inspection of the contact and correspondence with the lawyers and customers. Stronger candidates also identified the possibility of breaches of contracts with other customers and the implications for the going concern status of the company. The points most commonly overlooked were those relating to the recoverability of the receivable and the inspection of the board minutes post fieldwork.

Journals

The point most commonly identified was that there was a risk that the journals involved fraudulent activity. Stronger candidates appreciated that there should have been evidence in the working papers that the journals were further investigated and substantiated. The points most commonly overlooked were those relating to the materiality of the journals and the possibility of internal control deficiencies.

Supplier statement reconciliations

This part of the question was generally well answered as most candidates identified the risk of misstated payables and the need for alternative audit procedures such as direct confirmation. The points most commonly overlooked related to consideration of whether the audit strategy planned for reliance on supplier statement reconciliations and the comparison of payables days with prior year.

Directors' report

This part of the question was generally well answered. Most candidates recognised that there was an inconsistency between the directors' report and the financial statements and that the directors should amend their report. Stronger candidates identified that it might indicate a lack of directors' integrity, but few followed up with the consideration of whether the firm should be associated with the client. The point most commonly overlooked was that relating to the auditor's responsibility to report on the consistency between the directors' report and the financial statements.

70.2 Consequences

The absence of any supplier statement reconciliations may result in unrecorded invoices. This could lead to the late payment of invoices, resulting in:

- penalties or loss of prompt payment discounts
- accounts put on stop
- poor relationships with suppliers.

Billywig may pay its suppliers twice in error or errors in suppliers' invoices may go undetected. This will have an adverse impact on cash flow and profits.

Recommendations

Supplier statement reconciliations should be completed once a month by a member of staff not responsible for the purchase ledger.

Any discrepancies identified should be followed up and resolved.

Reconciliations should be reviewed by the financial controller on a timely basis and evidenced as reviewed.

Examiner's comments

This part of the question was generally well answered with most candidates attaining full marks. Most of the consequences were identified by the majority of candidates. The point most commonly overlooked was that relating to the segregation of duties between the person responsible for posting to the purchase ledger and the person performing the reconciliations.

70.3 If the directors amend the directors' report there will be no inconsistency and the auditor can issue an unmodified report. The auditor should state that the information given in the directors' report is consistent with the financial statements.

If the directors refuse to amend the directors' report there is an inconsistency between the financial statements and the directors' report which is material. The auditor should modify the report stating that a material inconsistency exists and describe the inconsistency in a section headed "matters on which we are required to report by exception".

Examiner's comments

Answers to this part of the question were of a mixed standard. Those candidates who considered the two possible outcomes of whether or not the directors were prepared to amend their report tended to score full marks. However, most candidates assumed that the directors would refuse to change their report and consequently limited the pool of marks available to them. The points most commonly identified were those relating to the need to modify the report and the inclusion of an explanation. The point most commonly overlooked was that the explanation should be included in a section headed "matters on which we are required to report by exception".

71 Short form questions

71.1 Business risks

- Suspension of licence/closure
- Fines
- Litigation
- Rectification costs
- Loss of reputation
- Negative impact on:
    - cash flow
    - revenue/profits

Implications for financial statements

- Revenue overstated/refunds understated
- Irrecoverable trade receivables
- Inventory write-downs
- Provisions for fines/damages
- Going concern basis of preparation may not be appropriate
- Going concern uncertainty may not be disclosed.

Examiner's comments

This question was generally well answered, particularly by those candidates who formatted their answers under the headings business risks and implications for the financial statements. However, a significant minority of candidates restricted their answers to listing the business risks and failed to consider the impact on the financial statements. The most common shortcoming related to the failure to be specific about the financial statement implications. For example, many candidates identified that there may be going concern issues but failed to specify that it had implications for the basis of preparation or the disclosure of an uncertainty.

71.2 Actions

- Enquire of staff reason for the lack of evidence
- Extend sample used for controls testing
- Consider whether:
    - extended testing identifies further non-compliance
    - compensating controls are in place
    - management override
    - any monetary error
- If so, extrapolate monetary error across whole population
- If errors are isolated, rely on controls to reduce substantive procedures
- If controls can't be relied upon, increase substantive procedures
- Report deficiency to management.

This question was generally well answered with many candidates scoring full marks. The points most commonly identified were those relating to extending the sample, ascertaining the reason why the operation of the control was not evidenced and reporting the deficiency to management. The points most commonly overlooked related to consideration as to whether the lack of operation of the control resulted in a monetary error and if so, the need to extrapolate the error across the population.

71.3 Actions

- Inspect documents which have aroused suspicions
- Review previous report to management for any deficiencies allowing misappropriation
- Consider credit controller's integrity
- Consider chief accountant's integrity
- Investigate any apparent override of control procedures
- Reduce materiality
- Increase substantive testing/controls testing
- Detailed testing, for example:
    - tracing bank receipts to ledger
    - direct confirmation
    - review journal entries
    - inspect credit notes
- Consult engagement/ethics partner for advice.

Examiner's comments

Although there were a significant number of candidates who scored full marks on this question, many candidates scored zero marks. These candidates failed to read the question carefully and strayed down the money laundering route. The question was asking for the actions to take in respect of "assessing whether the credit controller's suspicions are valid" and as such required evidence to support the credit controller's allegation. The points most commonly identified by those candidates who understood the nature of the question related to consideration of the integrity of the credit controller and increasing the testing in the area of cash received from customers.

71.4 Procedures to address potential conflicts of interest

- Separate engagement teams
- Brief staff /clear guidelines on confidentiality issues
- Information barriers
    - physical separation of teams
    - such as using staff from different offices
    - confidential data filing
- Procedures for dealing with any need to disseminate information beyond barrier
- Staff to sign confidentiality agreements
- Regular review of the application of safeguards
    - by a senior individual not involved in the engagements.

This question was generally well answered with most candidates identifying a range of relevant points. Weaker candidates ignored the information in the question that informed consent had already been obtained and wasted time listing this as a procedure. Other candidates strayed beyond the requirement to "outline **the procedures** to address the conflict of interest" and wasted time explaining the threat to the fundamental principle of confidentiality. The points most commonly identified were those relating to separate teams, information barriers and confidentiality agreements. The points most commonly overlooked were those relating to the dissemination of information beyond the barrier and the independent review of the application of safeguards. Although many identified the need for an independent review, they failed to appreciate that it was the application of safeguards that had to be reviewed.

71.5 Explain why the levels of assurance differ

- Examination provides limited/moderate assurance
- Audit provides reasonable assurance
- Assurance lower on examination/higher on audit
- More work on audit/less work on examination
- Examination is on assumptions about the future:
  - which is subject to uncertainty
- Examination reduces risk to a level that is acceptable
- Audit is on historical information:
  - which can be verified to a greater degree
  - estimates can be corroborated by subsequent events
- Audit reduces risk to an acceptably low level.

Examiner's comments

Those candidates who focused on the reasons **why** the level of assurance was different tended to score full marks. However, weaker candidates wasted time describing, in detail, the differences between the level of assurance provided by each type of engagement and/or the differences between the contents of the reports. The points most commonly identified related to the fact that prospective financial information involved estimates based on assumptions about the future whereas audits of financial statements involved historical data. The points most commonly overlooked related to the level of risk associated with each type of engagement. A significant number of candidates stated, incorrectly, that the assurance provided by an assurance report on prospective financial information was a low level of assurance. No mark was awarded for "low level of assurance".

71.6 Audit procedures

- Review correspondence/consult with Dalton lawyers:
  - about the expected outcome
- Ascertain if covered by insurance
- Inspect Ron Osborne's contract of employment:
  - for terms and conditions

- Review correspondence from Ron Osborne or his lawyers:

    - for basis of claim

- Review any similar legal cases:

    - for indication of potential outcome

- Ascertain Dalton's intentions regarding accounting treatment:

    - if damages probable:

        - ensure a provision is recognised

    - if damages possible:

        - ensure disclosed as a contingent liability

- Inspect minutes/discuss with management

- Obtain written representation re:

    - management's intention to fight claim or settle out of court
    - assumptions used in accounting treatment.

Examiner's comments

Answers to this question were of a mixed standard. Strong candidates commonly identified inspection of legal correspondence in respect of the expected outcome and discussion with management about the accounting treatment. Many of these candidates also identified that the expected outcome would determine the accounting treatment. However, a number of candidates were unable to distinguish a provision from a contingent liability. The points most commonly overlooked were those relating to the written representation and subsequent events. Weaker candidates ignored the information given in the question that the going concern status would not be affected and proceeded to write about the implications for the audit report if the going concern status of the entity was an issue.

72 Puskas plc

Marking guide

		Marks
72.1	Work in progress (WIP)	
	Justification	11
	Procedures	22½
	Provision for warranty claims	
	Justification	8½
	Procedures	11
	General	
	Justification	2
	Procedures	½
	Marks available	55½
	Maximum	23

		Marks
72.2 Points for report to those charged with governance and management		
General recommendations	2	
No employee references		
Consequences	9½	
Recommendations	2½	
No routine update of anti-malware software		
Consequences	5	
Recommendations	2	
Marks available	21	
Maximum		10
72.3 Ethical issues		
Threat to integrity	2	
Familiarity threat	1½	
Threat to professional behaviour	2	
Actions	4	
Marks available	9½	
Maximum		4
72.4 Factors	7	
Marks available	7	
Maximum		3
Total marks available		40

72.1 Work in progress (WIP)

Justification

WIP appears to be overstated as:

- WIP days have increased from 50.0 days to 77.2 days (an increase of 64.7%)
- the gross margin has increased from 36.2% to 41.1%.

(Credit was given for alternative calculations).

Errors may have arisen during the year due to the unreliable contract costing system.

Errors may arise from the implementation of the new contract costing system due to:

- new system not functioning correctly
- incorrect transfer of data from the old system
- insufficient staff training.

Cost overruns on fixed-price contracts may result in losses. If losses are not provided for or WIP relates to an aborted contract, this will result in overstatement of WIP because the net realisable value of WIP will be lower than cost.

Judgement is involved in the calculation of WIP which may result in an inappropriate allocation of overheads.

Overseas suppliers invoice in euro and there is the potential for translation errors.

Procedures

For the contract costing system:

- discuss functionality issues with management
- ascertain controls over the transfer of data to new system

- test the transfer of a sample of balances from the old system to the new system
- evaluate and test the controls over
    - the interface between the purchases and payroll systems and the contract costing system
    - the initial recording of purchase and payroll costs.

For a sample of contracts underway at the year end:

- vouch entries for labour to payroll records
- vouch entries for components to suppliers' invoices
- physically inspect WIP.

To identify potential losses:

- compare actual costs to budget to identify cost overruns
- compare contract price to estimated total costs
- inspect ageing of WIP to identify any irrecoverable WIP
- inspect post year-end sales invoices to ascertain if WIP is invoiced soon after year end
- inspect post year-end receipts
- obtain a written representation from management confirming the adequacy of the provisions for losses.

For attributable overhead calculations:

- ascertain the basis of the assumptions
- reperform the calculation
- check that only attributable overheads are included
- agree the figures to the management accounts
- test the reliability of the management accounts
- assess the consistency of the valuation with previous years
- assess reasonableness of basis.

For a sample of items purchased from overseas suppliers:

- recalculate the foreign exchange translation
- check the rate used to a reliable independent source.

Agree the figure on the WIP schedule to the amount included in the financial statements.

Provision for warranty claims

Justification

Judgement is involved in the calculation of the provision for warranty claims which is based on the finance director's assessment of future claims.

Provisions appear to be understated because:

- the non-current provision represents 0.1% of revenue, the same as 20X7
- the current provision represents 0.08% of revenue lower than 0.1% in 20X7
- the warranty period has increased from 2 to 3 years
- there are no staff references for installation teams increasing the risk of sub-standard installations

(Credit was given for alternative calculations)

Procedures

- Inspect the terms of the warranty agreements
- Ascertain the basis of the assumptions used in the provision calculation
    - reperform any calculations
    - assess the reasonableness of the basis
- Compare the previous year's provision to actual claims made to establish the reliability of director's estimates
- Perform an analytical procedure based on the historical claim rate and the level of current year contracts
- Inspect post year-end claims and compare to the provision
- Inspect customer correspondence
    - identify complaints relating to any of the installations
    - trace claims back to their inclusion in the provision calculation
- Inspect board minutes
    - for an indication of problems with any of the company's installations
- Inspect records of rectification costs to assess the amounts involved
- Obtain a written representation from management regarding the assumptions underlying the provisions
- Agree the figures on the warranty schedule to the amounts included in the financial statements.

General

Justification

Errors may arise due to:

- possible window dressing of financial statements due to:
    - directors' remuneration scheme based on audited profit before tax
    - the bank requiring the audited financial statements in support of the loan application
- tight reporting deadline resulting in a limited period for subsequent events review
- the lack of regular anti-malware software updates
- the absence of staff references for finance team.

Procedure

Movements in balances to be discussed with the directors.

Examiner's comments

Answers to this question were of a good standard for both WIP and warranty provisions. Most candidates provided relevant justifications and procedures for each of the key areas of audit risk identified.

Candidates are reminded that their answers are presented to the examiner exactly as they appear on screen. A significant number of candidates did not adequately consider their presentation resulting in answers which lacked proper structure, such as paragraphs and bullet points.

WIP

Most candidates correctly identified the risk of overstatement by using the financial information in the question to perform some simple ratio analysis. Stronger candidates earned the higher marks available for calculating WIP days and the change in the gross margin. Weaker candidates tended to only calculate percentage increases in WIP and revenue/cost of sales. A minority of candidates failed to undertake any analytical procedures on the financial information.

Most candidates cited relevant justifications relating to the old and new contract costing systems, the use of estimates and the fact that suppliers invoice in euro. Fewer candidates were able to give an adequate explanation of the risk of cost overruns resulting from fixed-price contracts.

Procedures relating to the contract costing system were well explained by most candidates. The procedures most commonly overlooked were those relating to the identification of cost overruns, such as comparing actual costs to budget.

Most candidates correctly suggested considering the reasonableness of the assumptions underlying the overhead allocation calculation and testing its accuracy. However, very few candidates went as far as considering whether the calculations reflected the figures in the management accounts or whether the management accounts were reliable.

Provisions for warranties

Most candidates correctly identified a risk of understatement by comparing the percentage increase in the warranty provision with the percentage increase in revenue. Very few candidates earned the higher marks available for calculating the current and non-current portions of the provision as a percentage of revenue. Most candidates correctly recognised that the changes in the provision were out of line with the extension of the warranty period to three years.

The justification most commonly overlooked related to the absence of employee references which might lead to an increase in warranty claims due to sub-standard work performed by under-qualified employees.

Most students correctly identified procedures such as ascertaining the basis of the warranty provision calculation, assessing its reasonableness, inspecting customer correspondence for complaints and inspecting the terms of the warranty agreement.

The procedures most commonly overlooked were those relating to the reliability of management's estimate in the prior year, performing an analytical procedure based on the rate of claims in previous years, inspecting records of rectification costs and inspecting post year-end claims.

For both WIP and the provision for warranties, a large proportion of candidates correctly identified that a written representation should be sought from management. However, very few candidates went on to earn the additional mark available for giving an adequate explanation of what that representation should be.

72.2 General recommendations

Puskas should have policies and procedures in place for employee references and updating anti-malware software, which should be communicated to employees by way of training. Adherence to the policies and procedures should be monitored and there should be disciplinary procedures for employees who fail to comply.

No employee references

Consequences

Employees may be hired but lack appropriate skills or qualifications for the role. This could lead to:

- sub-standard work on electrical systems
- WIP that may not be recoverable; and
- an adverse impact on the reputation of Puskas.

In respect of finance employees, the accounting records may be unreliable.

This may result in additional costs to rectify the work which would have an adverse impact on profits and cash flow.

Employees who lack integrity or have criminal backgrounds may be hired leading to the theft of assets.

Employees may have falsified information about past roles or their identity. For example, the company may be breaking the law by hiring employees that do not have the right to work in the UK and this could leave the company legally exposed and result in fines.

Recommendations

- All offers of employment should be made subject to satisfactory references and formal approval by management.

- At least two references should be obtained with at least one from a previous employer.

- All formal qualifications claimed by potential employees should be verified.

No routine update of anti-malware software

Consequences

Systems are vulnerable to:

- hacking
- malicious programmes
- loss or theft of data leading to business interruption.

Damages may become payable and there could be an adverse impact on the reputation of Puskas.

Puskas could be in breach of data protection regulations leading to fines.

This may result in in additional costs which would have an adverse impact on profits and cash flow.

Recommendations

- Systems should be updated regularly for the latest anti-malware software
- Responsibility for updates should be allocated to a designated person
- Cover should be in place for holidays and absences
- The designated person should report compliance to senior management

Examiner's comments

Answers to this part of the question were of a high standard although candidates tended to perform better when outlining the consequences of each internal control deficiency compared with the recommendations to address them. Often recommendations were simply stated as the converse of the weakness identified, eg, obtain employee references, which was insufficient to earn any marks.

No employee references

In respect of consequences, most candidates cited the points relating to the risks of employing incompetent employees, poor quality work, customer dissatisfaction and the associated costs if these risks materialised. The points most commonly overlooked were those relating to the legal consequences of employing people who did not have the right to work in the UK.

In respect of recommendations, the points most commonly cited were those relating to the communication of the policy to employees and disciplinary procedures for failing to apply the policy. Candidates commonly provided a recommendation to obtain references for all employees but failed to specify that at least two references should be obtained, with one from a previous employer. Points commonly overlooked included those relating to proof of qualifications, formal approval to appoint and offers of employment being subject to satisfactory references.

No routine update of anti-malware software

Most candidates identified a range of consequences. In respect of recommendations, the point most commonly cited was that systems should be updated regularly for the latest anti-malware software. Very few candidates identified the need for holiday cover.

72.3 Ethical issues

There is a threat to the integrity of the partner. He is not acting in a transparent manner by attempting to gain an advantage in the tendering process through soliciting a favour from the audit committee member. Confidentiality could be breached by seeking inside information in advance of the tender.

There is a familiarity threat as the engagement partner has a close relationship with the audit committee member. She may be sympathetic towards the firm and comply with the request to meet with the audit manager.

There is a threat to professional behaviour as the actions of the partner, manager or audit committee member may discredit the profession. The audit engagement partner should follow the set procedure and present the firm's tender in front of the whole audit committee and should not contact or seek to influence members of the committee outside that process.

Actions

The audit manager should:

- consult with another partner in the firm or the ethics partner, and
  - document conversations held
- seek advice from ICAEW helpline
- decline the audit engagement partner's request to meet the audit committee member.

Examiner's comments

Answers to this part of the question were of a mixed standard although some candidates scored maximum marks. Candidates' answers in respect of actions were generally better than those in respect of the identification of the ethical issues. Most candidates correctly identified the familiarity threat but few candidates identified the threats to integrity, professional behaviour and confidentiality. The most commonly overlooked action was to document conversations held. Several incorrectly identified the ethical issues arising during the current year's audit or assumed that the firm had been successful in the audit tender. These candidates then went onto to describe actions that were not relevant such as the removal of the engagement partner and rotation of the audit team to address the familiarity threat.

72.4 The factors that an audit committee could use to monitor the effectiveness of the external auditor are:

- feedback from the audited entity's employees and audit committee members
- independence and objectivity
- audit planning and business understanding
- conduct and communication
- audit findings, deficiencies identified and quality of reports
- expertise, continuity and experience of personnel
- cost effectiveness including value for money and actual time compared to budget

Examiner's comments

Answers to this question were generally disappointing. It was evident that a significant number of candidates were not familiar with the contents of Chapter 5, Section 8 of the Audit and Assurance study manual which covers the role of audit committees in monitoring the effectiveness of the audit process. Those candidates familiar with this section tended to score full marks. The factors most commonly identified were those relating to audit findings, expertise and actual time compared to budget. The points most commonly overlooked were those relating to feedback, independence and objectivity and audit planning and business understanding. Some candidates provided impractical factors such as engaging another firm to review the external auditor's work or asking internal audit to reperform some of the testing. A common suggestion that scored no marks was the number of material misstatements identified by the external auditor. A number of candidates did not attempt this part of the question.

73 Alonso Ltd

Marking guide

			Marks
73.1	How ICAEW promotes improvements	10	
	Marks available	10	
	Maximum		5
73.2	Why matters reported to firm		
(1)	Commission paid to employees	4½	
	Actions	2	
(2)	No policies for holding shares in client companies	5	
	Actions	5½	
(3)	Senior manager seconded as head of internal audit	8	
	Actions	1½	
(4)	Communication of matters to those charged with governance	5½	
	Actions	2	
	Recommendations	3	
	Marks available	34	
	Maximum		12

73.3 Money Laundering Regulations
       Appoint a Money Laundering Reporting Officer   1½
       Implement money laundering policies and procedures   4
       Training programme and monitoring   1
       Marks available   6½
       Maximum   3
Total marks available   20

73.1 ICAEW promotes improvements in the quality of audit and assurance work by:

- influencing the development of ISAs and commissioning research of audit and assurance issues such as data analytics and cyber security

- publishing a Code of Ethics which requires members to comply with the fundamental principles of integrity, objectivity, professional competence and due care, confidentiality and professional behaviour

- offering a helpline to support members who are experiencing difficulties in the workplace

- monitoring compliance with standards through its Practice Assurance Scheme. The Quality Assurance Department undertakes inspections of audit firms and recommends improvements. It also publishes a summary of findings annually.

- investigating alleged misconduct and disciplining individual members and firms who fail to uphold the standards of the profession

- requiring trainees to pass rigorous exams and once qualified, members need to certify, annually, that they have undertaken CPD

- providing training via webinars and roadshows organised by the Audit and Assurance Faculty.

Examiner's comments

Answers to this part of the question were of a mixed standard. Many candidates described a range of ways in which ICAEW promotes improvements in the quality of the audit and assurance work performed by its members. Candidates correctly identified that ICAEW monitors compliance with standards through reviews of individual audit firms, its disciplinary powers, its helpline, its rigorous exams and research on audit and assurance issues. Fewer candidates identified the work of ICAEW in influencing the development of ISAs. A significant number of candidates confused the role of the FRC and ICAEW and incorrectly stated that ICAEW writes and issues ISAs and Ethical Standards. Some candidates who correctly identified that ICAEW has issued a Code of Ethics then wasted time by describing, in detail, the contents of the Code and the attributes required of an ICAEW chartered accountant. A few candidates failed to score any marks by listing quality control procedures implemented by individual audit firms. Some candidates incorrectly thought that the ICAEW performed hot reviews/engagement quality control reviews of audit files at audit firms.

73.2(1) **Commission paid to employees**

       There is a self-interest threat to independence and objectivity.

       Employees may promote services not required by the client or make exaggerated claims about the benefit of services to earn the commission.

Audit quality may suffer and employees may overlook errors or be reluctant to raise contentious issues.

Professional competence and due care is impaired and there may be a lack of scepticism.

The policy is not appropriate as it breaches FRC's Ethical Standard which requires that:

- objectives of the members of the audit team do not include selling non-audit services

- criteria for evaluating performance do not include success in selling non-audit services

- no specific element of remuneration of the members of the audit team is based on success in selling non-audit services.

Actions

The firm must remove the statement from its website. The policy should be changed so that commission is not paid for the successful generation of business from audit and assurance clients and this change must be communicated to employees. A review of completed audits should take place to ascertain if quality has suffered.

(2) **No policies for holding shares in client companies**

It is not appropriate for team members to hold shares in the audited entity as there is a self-interest threat to independence and objectivity.

Team members may be reluctant to take action that impacts adversely on the value of shares.

There is a self-interest threat to confidentiality if audit staff use information which is not in the public domain to deal in clients' shares. This is insider dealing which is illegal. It is also a threat to professional behaviour which could bring the profession into disrepute.

Actions

The firm should develop policies in respect of shareholdings in client companies.

Partners and employees should provide written confirmation of compliance with the firm's policies on independence on an annual or more frequent basis.

The firm should maintain an up-to-date list of all clients which should be available to all employees. Newly recruited partners and employees should be required to provide confirmations on joining the firm.

Procedures should be in place for prompt notification by partners and employees when circumstances change, for example if shares are inherited or if a new client engages the firm.

There should be regular training for partners and employees on the firm's policies and procedures on independence. Monitoring of compliance with the policy should be undertaken and disciplinary action should be taken for non-compliance with the policy.

(3) **Senior manager seconded as head of internal audit**

There are self-interest, self-review and familiarity threats to objectivity and professional competence and due care. If the firm plans to rely on the work of the internal audit function, as part of the external audit, the team may be insufficiently questioning of the work performed by the senior manager or reluctant to draw attention to errors or omissions in his work.

The head of internal audit is a management position and the senior manager should not have been seconded to this role. Acting as head of internal audit gives rise to a management threat as the senior manager may become too closely aligned with management and be expected to take decisions that are the responsibility of management.

If the firm plans to rely on the work of internal audit, as part of its external audit, there is a self-review threat as the audit team may be insufficiently questioning of work performed by the senior manager or reluctant to highlight errors or omissions in that work.

A familiarity threat also arises from the length of the secondment. Any secondment should be for a short period of time. A reasonable and informed third party may consider that the firm's independence is impaired if a secondment is for a long period such as 21 months.

Actions

The firm should remove the senior manager from the external audit team until a suitable time period has elapsed. The external audit work should be independently reviewed.

(4) **Communication of matters to those charged with governance**

The communication to those charged with governance of the planned audit approach and scope of the audit is required by ISA (UK) 260 *Communication with those Charged with Governance* (ISA (UK) 260). The communication of all significant facts and matters that may bear upon the integrity, objectivity and independence of the firm together with any safeguards adopted and an overall assessment of threats is required by FRC's *Ethical Standard*.

The communication promotes an effective working relationship and will assist those charged with governance in understanding the work of the auditor. Those charged with governance may assist the auditor to understand the entity, identify appropriate sources of evidence and provide information about specific transactions or events. Overall the quality and efficiency of the audit is improved.

Actions

The firm should establish a policy regarding communicating with those charged with governance and communicate this to employees. Monitoring of compliance with the policy should take place and disciplinary action taken for non-compliance with the policy.

Examiner's comments

This part of the question was generally well answered. Answers to the first three scenarios were of a higher standard than answers to the final scenario.

(1) **Commission paid to employees**

Most candidates identified the self-interest threat to the objectivity of employees and that the arrangement was inappropriate. Many of these candidates also appreciated that there was a risk to audit quality. The points most commonly overlooked were those relating to the risk of exaggerating the claims regarding the benefit of non-audit services and the promotion of services not required by the client. Disappointingly, a small number of candidates incorrectly stated that the arrangement was entirely appropriate. Other candidates wasted time by discussing lowballing, fee levels, employee recruitment and accepting high-risk clients, none of which was relevant.

(2) **No policies for holding shares in client companies**

Many candidates correctly identified that partners and employees should sign a declaration of compliance with the firm's policy and that the declaration should be made at least annually. In addition, most candidates identified the need for training, monitoring and disciplinary action for non-compliance. The points most commonly overlooked were those relating to the maintenance of an up-to-date list of clients, procedures for prompt notification of a change in circumstance in respect of share ownership and the points concerning insider trading.

(3) **Senior manager seconded as head of internal audit**

This part of the question was very well answered as most candidates cited a range of relevant threats and actions. The points most commonly overlooked were that the secondment to a management role should not have taken place, any secondment should be for short period of time, that 21 months was too long and the threat to professional competence and due care.

(4) **Communication of matters to those charged with governance**

Answers to this part of the question were disappointing. Many candidates were not familiar with the provisions of ISA (UK) 260 which requires the auditor to communicate an overview of the planned scope and timing of the audit nor with the FRC *Ethical Standard* which requires the auditor to communicate threats to integrity, objectivity and independence. Most candidates were unable to explain why these matters should be communicated other than stating that it would help the efficiency of the audit. Weaker candidates incorrectly discussed the reasons for and contents of letters of engagement. Some candidates provided a range of relevant action points, including establishing a policy, communicating this to employees and monitoring of the policy.

73.3 The firm must appoint a Money Laundering Reporting Officer (MLRO) who must be a senior member of the firm and must register with a supervisory body (such as HMRC, ICAEW). Firms must also appoint a Money Laundering Compliance Principal (MLCP), who must be on the board or of equivalent seniority; where the MLRO is already of this level of seniority then this person can act as MLCP as well.

The firm must implement money laundering policies and procedures in respect of:

- recognising money laundering
- client due diligence
- politically exposed persons
- record keeping of client identification procedures:
    - for five years after the relationship ends
- reporting money laundering:
    - without tipping off.

A training programme should be in place and cover any updates in money laundering regulations. The firm should monitor compliance with policies and procedures.

Examiner's comments

This part of the question was generally well answered as most candidates, who attempted the question, identified the points relating to the appointment of a money laundering reporting officer, training and monitoring compliance with money laundering procedures. The points most commonly overlooked were those relating to the fact that the MLRO should be a senior member of the firm, client due diligence and the maintenance of client identification records for five years. A common error was to list the actions to be taken by individuals in the firm on suspecting or discovering money laundering instead of listing the policies and procedures to be implemented by the firm. A number of candidates did not attempt this part of the question.

74 CKP

			Marks
74.1 (a)	Key purposes of obtaining written representations		
	Written representations as a source of audit evidence	2	
	Written representations used to support other audit evidence	3	
	Management's acceptance of its responsibility	2½	
(b)	Marks awarded for relevant examples of confirmations relating to specific items	$\underline{9}$	
	Marks available	14	
	Maximum		6
74.2	Auditor's report implications		
	Chobe	6	
	Kanye	4½	
	Pula	$\underline{5½}$	
	Marks available	16	
	Maximum		9
74.3	Why the behaviour of the directors of Kanye should be considered		
	ISA (UK) 220	1	
	Fraudulent reporting and lack of integrity	8	
	Intimidation threat/tarnished reputation	$\underline{3}$	
		12	
			$\underline{5}$
	Total marks available		$\underline{\underline{20}}$

74.1 (a) Written representations are a source of audit evidence required to be obtained by ISA (UK) 580 *Written Representations*. They provide evidence that management has fulfilled its responsibilities with respect to the financial statements. This includes the provision of all relevant information to the external auditor and the completeness of recording of transactions.

Written representations are also used to support other audit evidence. Written representations are likely to be more reliable than oral representations from management and they help to avoid confusion or misunderstandings over matters discussed during the audit.

(b) Marks were awarded for relevant examples of confirmations relating to specific items in the financial statements that could be included in a management representation letter. The list below is not exhaustive but items which may be included are:

- inventory: valued at the lower of cost and net realisable value

- trade receivables: stated at recoverable amounts

- tangible assets: assumptions used in determining useful lives

- related party transactions: fully disclosed in the financial statements

- subsequent events to the date of audit report: disclosed in the notes to the financial statements

- liabilities, actual or contingent: recognised or disclosed in the financial statements

- corresponding figures: restated to correct a material misstatement in the prior period's financial statements
- title over assets and assets pledged as collateral: disclosed in the financial statements.

Examiner's comments

Answers to part (a) were of a mixed standard. The points most commonly identified were those relating to audit evidence. The other points were rarely mentioned.

In respect of part (b), most candidates provided some examples of confirmations relating to specific items in the financial statements that could be included in a management representation letter. The most commonly cited were those relating to related party transactions and tangible assets. The confirmations about corresponding figures and title over assets were rarely mentioned. A number of candidates provided confirmations that did not relate to specific items in the financial statements such as management providing access to information, all transactions recorded in the accounting records and disclosure of information in relation to allegations of fraud and did not score any marks for these. Some candidates wasted time providing more than three examples of specific items for which they earned no marks.

74.2 Chobe

The opinion should be modified due to the limitation on scope imposed by the directors, as the auditor is unable to obtain sufficient appropriate evidence.

ISA (UK) 580 requires the auditor to disclaim an opinion on the financial statements when the directors refuse to provide representations regarding the fulfilment of their responsibilities in relation to the preparation of the financial statements.

The matter is material and pervasive as it could affect many items in the financial statements. The auditor should specify in the opinion section of the report that "we do not express an opinion". There should be an explanation of the reasons for the disclaimer of opinion in the "basis for disclaimer of opinion" section of the audit report.

The auditor should also report by exception under the Companies Act 2006 that:

- adequate accounting records were not maintained
- all information required for the audit was not obtained.

Kanye

The opinion should be modified due to the misstatement of the cash and trade receivables balances. The misstatement is material as both cash and trade receivables are each misstated by 5.9% of total assets. The opinion should be qualified (except for). It is not pervasive as it is confined to specific items (cash and trade receivables) in the financial statements. There should be an explanation of the issue (reason and amount involved) in the "basis for qualified opinion" section of the audit report.

Pula

The strategic report is not part of the financial statements and consequently, the opinion on the financial statements is not modified in respect of this matter. However, the Companies Act requires a specific statement on whether the strategic report has been prepared in accordance with applicable legal requirements. As the strategic report does not include a description of the risks and uncertainties facing the business, the audit report must be modified. The audit report should describe the matter in a section headed 'Opinion on other matters prescribed by the Companies Act 2006' and state:

- the strategic report has not been prepared in accordance with applicable legal requirements, and

- except for this matter, the information given in the strategic report for the financial year for which financial statements are prepared is consistent with the financial statements.

Examiner's comments

Answers to this part of the question were of a high standard. There were some excellent answers in respect of the first two scenarios with many candidates scoring maximum marks. Candidates were less confident dealing with the final scenario and some candidates did not attempt this part of the question. However, disappointingly, a significant minority of candidates demonstrated only limited understanding of the implications for audit reports in each of the scenarios. Some of these candidates wasted time by listing a number of different answers in the hope that one or other of their answers was correct.

Chobe

Most candidates correctly identified the situation as a limitation on scope and many of those appreciated that it required a disclaimer of opinion. Some candidates incorrectly stated that if the matter is considered material, but not pervasive, it would result in a qualified opinion (except for) or that the refusal to provide written representations represented a disagreement that was pervasive and an adverse opinion was appropriate. These candidates failed to appreciate that there was no choice regarding the type of modification, because ISA (UK) 580 paragraph 20(b) requires the auditor to disclaim the opinion on the financial statements if management refuses to provide written representations. Some candidates incorrectly concluded that the matter was not material and therefore the opinion was unmodified. Many candidates failed to identify the matters that are required to be reported on by exception by the Companies Act 2006. Where candidates did identify that there are items required to be reported by the Companies Act 2006 by exception many lost marks by failing to state what these were.

Kanye

Many candidates correctly identified that the situation represented a material misstatement and that it would warrant a qualified opinion (except for). Some candidates lost marks by stating that if the scenario was material and pervasive it would be an adverse opinion, failing to appreciate that the matter was not pervasive as the issue was confined to specific items and did not represent a substantial proportion of the financial statements. A number of candidates incorrectly stated that the errors on the overstated cash and understated trade receivables balance would net out to zero so there was no material misstatement.

Pula

Answers to this part of the question were of a mixed standard. A significant number correctly identified that the strategic report is not part of the financial statements and that an "other matters" paragraph was required. Common errors included candidates stating that an emphasis of matter paragraph or a qualified opinion or an "other information" paragraph was required. A number of candidates incorrectly stated the implications for an audit report if the strategic report was inconsistent with the financial statements. This was incorrect as it was not an inconsistency - it was an omission of information required by the Companies Act.

74.3 ISA (UK) 220 *Quality Control for an Audit of Financial Statements* (ISA (UK) 220) requires the engagement partner to consider the integrity of the principal owners, key management and those charged with governance when considering whether to continue acting for a client.

A willingness by the directors of Kanye to deliberately misstate the financial statements is fraudulent reporting. It demonstrates a lack of integrity and casts doubt on the reliability that can be placed on the representations of the directors. It may also be indicative of other misstatements in the financial statements, a weak control environment or criminal activities. This increases the risk of forming an inappropriate audit opinion.

The attitude of the directors may be indicative of an intimidation threat whereby the auditor's conduct may be influenced by fear or threats of removal from office. Association with cavalier directors could tarnish the reputation of the firm, resulting in the loss of clients. Furthermore, the audit may no longer be commercially viable due to the extra time and costs required.

Examiner's comments

This part of the question was generally well answered with many candidates scoring full marks. The points most commonly identified related to the integrity of the directors, the poor control environment, higher risk of forming an incorrect opinion and reputational risk of association with cavalier directors. The points most commonly overlooked were those relating to the requirement of ISA (UK) 220, the intimidation threat, and that the audit may no longer be commercially viable. A number of candidates provided very brief answers to this final question, possibly indicating time management issues.

September 2018 exam answers

75 Short form questions

75.1 Ethical issues

Conflict of interest
Threat to objectivity
Unable to act in best interest of both clients
Threat to confidentiality

- Risk of information leakage
- Which could benefit Flint/Island in the legal claim
- Should not be used in reaching an opinion on either audit

How to address

Consult ethics partner
Disclose conflict of interest to both clients
Obtain both clients' consent to continue to act
Separate audit teams
Confidentiality agreements
Clear guidelines for teams on security/confidentiality
Information barriers

- Physical separation of teams/separate offices
- Secure data filing
- Regular review of safeguards by senior individual not involved with clients

Examiner's comments

This question was generally well answered with many candidates scoring maximum marks. Strong candidates presented their answers under the headings "ethical issues" and "how to address". In respect of ethical issues, most candidates identified the conflict of interest and threats to the fundamental principles of objectivity and confidentiality. However, some candidates failed to provide explanations of the ethical issues. The points most commonly overlooked were those relating to how the leakage of confidential information could benefit one or other of the clients and how that might influence the audit opinion. In respect of addressing the issues, most candidates identified the need for information barriers and provided a range of examples of how these barriers should be implemented. Although many identified that an independent review was required, they failed to gain the extra mark for stating that the application of safeguards should be reviewed. A minority of candidates incorrectly assumed that the audit firm would be representing the client in litigation and wasted time identifying and explaining the threats associated with that work, ie. advocacy, management and self-review threats. No marks were awarded for these points.

75.2 Self-interest threat

Regular fees are 11.4% of firm's annual fee income
Fees should not exceed 15%
Over-reliance on client for fee income
Objectivity impaired
Firm reluctant to issue modified opinion/challenge management

How to address

Disclose to ethics partner and those charged with governance
At 10% safeguards are required
External independent quality control review
Regular review of fee income to ensure threshold not breached
Take steps to reduce work/fees if necessary

Examiner's comments

This question was generally well answered with many candidates scoring maximum marks. Almost all candidates identified that fee dependency was an issue and might give rise to an inappropriate audit opinion. However, a significant number of candidates calculated the fee % incorrectly either by including the fees for the one-off assignment or failing to include the recurring fees from the wholly-owned subsidiary. Many candidates identified that an independent review was required but few stated that such a review should be external. Weaker candidates strayed beyond the requirement which was confined to the self-interest threat and wasted time writing about the self-review and management threats that would arise from providing non-audit services. No marks were awarded for these points.

75.3 Inventory data analytics routines

Compare the last time an item was purchased to the last time it was sold
Compare the year-end value with the post year-end selling prices
Reproduce the inventory ageing analysis
Match purchase orders, GRNs and purchase invoices
Compare inventory held by each store with the square metre of retail space for that store
Recalculate currency translations using third party exchange rates
Identify journal entries impacting inventory

Examiner's comments

Answers to this question were of a mixed standard. Those candidates who were familiar with the content of Section 3.1.1 in Chapter 10 of the Audit and Assurance Study Manual provided valid examples of data analytic routines. The routines most commonly cited were those relating to the reproduction of the inventory ageing analysis, three-way checking, inter-store comparisons and retranslation of foreign currency transactions. Few candidates considered the identification of journal entries impacting inventory. A significant number of candidates demonstrated a lack of knowledge of the capabilities of data analytics routines and provided simplistic examples of procedures that could be undertaken manually such as comparing the inventory figure to the previous year. A significant minority did not attempt this question. Some candidates wasted time providing more than the required three routines.

75.4 Trade payables procedures

Inspect contracts/invoices for any changes to credit terms in the year

Review for evidence of prompt payment discounts

Direct confirmation of suppliers' balances to identify any unrecorded liabilities

Inspect/prepare supplier statement reconciliations

Inspect post-year end payments to suppliers to identify any relating to pre-year end purchases

Test/evaluate the controls over the recording of trade payables

Inspect any invoices not processed at year end to identify any relating to pre-year end purchases

Trace goods received records to entries in the payables ledger

Examiner's comments

Answers to this question were of a mixed standard. Those candidates who recognised that a fall in payables days posed a risk of understatement of payables provided more focused answers by listing procedures that would test the completeness and cut-off assertions. The points most commonly identified were the inspection of contracts for credit terms, supplier statement reconciliations and direct confirmation of payables balances. Although many identified that inappropriate cut-off might be an issue, only a minority listed procedures that would test for understatement such as tracing goods received records to invoice entries in the payables ledger.

75.5 Review of financial statements

Limited to inquiry, analytical and other review procedures
Less work than external audit (awarded once only)

External audit under CA06

Uses test of details/tests of control
Obligation to perform procedures re subsequent events
More work than review of financial statements (awarded once only)

Reasons

Review provides limited assurance and audit provides reasonable assurance
Review in accordance with ISRE 2400 and audit in accordance with ISAs
Engagement risk for review is higher/lower for audit

Examiner's comments

It was pleasing to note that many candidates scored full marks on this question. The points most commonly identified were those relating to the level of assurance and the amount of work carried out on each type of engagement. However, a minority of candidates stated, incorrectly, that a review would provide a low level of assurance. Weaker candidates confused an engagement to review financial statements with the examination of prospective financial information and listed irrelevant reasons for the differences, such as assumptions about the future and the problem of uncertainty.

75.6 Additional audit procedures

Obtain an understanding of Turner LLP

Ascertain:

- whether Turner is independent and will comply with ethical requirements

- Turner's professional competence

- if the firm will be involved in audit work of Turner or will need to plan its own audit procedures

Communicate with Turner:

- details of work to be performed
- form/content of communication
- materiality levels
- significant risks of fraud/error
- related parties

Request confirmation Turner will cooperate
Evaluate work of Turner
Determine impact of any errors on group financial statements

Examiner's comments

Answers to this question were of a mixed standard. The minority of candidates who were familiar with the contents of paragraphs 19–24 of ISA 600 *Special Considerations - Audits of Group Financial Statements*, scored high marks. The points most commonly identified were those relating to ethical issues, competency, materiality, risk and review of working papers. The points most commonly overlooked were those relating to the form of communication, related parties and impact of uncorrected errors on the group financial statements. A small minority of candidates stated, incorrectly, that the group auditor should limit their liability because of relying on other auditors. These candidates failed to appreciate that the group auditor is responsible for the opinion on the consolidated financial statements.

76 Ransome

		Marks
76.1 **General** (awarded once only)	3	
Revenue (awarded in either revenue section but only once)	4	
Justification – sales in local currency (translation errors)		
Procedures		
Revenue from retailers		
Justification	5	
Procedures	11	
Revenue from the premium service		
Justification	5½	
Procedures	6½	
Inventory		
Justification	12½	
Procedures	17½	
Going concern		
Justification	9½	
Procedures	11 ½	
Marks available	86	
Maximum		25
76.2 **Points for inclusion in report**		
Deficiency (a) – Movement of cameras occurred during the count	8	
Deficiency (b) – There is no review of the aged inventory report	6	
Deficiency (c) – There is no investigation of discrepancies		
between the count and inventory system	10	
General (awarded only once)	1½	
Marks available	25½	
Maximum		12
76.3 **Threats to independence and objectivity arising from offer**		
Self-interest, familiarity and intimidation threats	4	
Actions by the audit senior		
Inform the engagement/ethics partner of the offer immediately	½	
Actions by the engagement partner	2½	
Marks available	7	
Maximum		3
Total marks available		40

76.1 **General** (awarded once only)

The gross profit margin has increased from 38.7% to 45.9%.

The financial controller position has been vacant for many months which may result in insufficient oversight.

Revenue (awarded in either revenue section but only once)

Justification

Sales in local currency may result in translation errors.

Procedures

Re-perform the calculation for a sample of foreign currency transactions using a reliable third-party exchange rate.

Evaluate and test the internal controls over the recording of revenue.

Inspect post year-end management accounts for abnormally low sales.

Revenue from retailers

Justification

There is a risk of overstatement.

The average revenue per retailer has increased from £3.9 million to £4.1 million.

Contracted sales may have been incorrectly recorded if they were not despatched at year end.

Inferior quality components and complaints about malfunctions have led to refunds. The provision for refunds is an estimate and may not be accounted for in the appropriate period.

Procedures

Discuss with management the reasons for the increase in revenue from retailers such as whether new contracts were negotiated during the year or whether the company has benefitted from favourable exchange rate movements.

Inspect retailer contracts and ascertain if the terms stipulate increases in the number of cameras to be purchased by retailers during the year.

Vouch sales to invoices and despatch records.

Ascertain the basis for provisions relating to refunds. Consider the reasonableness of the basis by inspecting correspondence from retailers to assess the likely volume/value of refunds. Re-perform any related calculations.

Inspect post year-end credit notes/refunds and compare to the level of provision recorded at year end.

Revenue from the premium service

Justification

There is a risk of overstatement.

Revenue from the premium service has increased from 22.2% of total revenue to 27.3%.

Premium plans are paid for 12 months in advance. Advance payments may not be deferred correctly.

Refunds may need to be offered in respect of the premium service and these may not be correctly pro-rated.

Customers make payment via an app which may not be properly integrated with the accounting records or may be unreliable.

Procedures

Discuss with management the reasons for the increase in premium service revenue such as any marketing campaign for the premium service or favourable exchange rate movements.

Ascertain the basis for calculating deferred income on premium plans.

Re-perform the deferred income calculation.

Vouch recorded receipts to bank statements.

Ascertain the basis for any provisions relating to premium service refunds. Consider the reasonableness of the basis by inspecting a sample of premium service contracts to ascertain if refunds have been correctly pro-rated.

Re-perform any related calculations.

Inspect post year-end payments/bank statements for refunds and compare to the level of provision made at year end.

Inventory

Justification

There is a risk of overstatement.
Inventory days have increased from 39.2 days to 51.4 days.
This may indicate that some inventory is obsolete.
Issues were identified during the UK count, such as:

- inadequate procedures to check the aged inventory report

- movements of inventory during the count which may not have been accurately reflected in the count figures; and

- discrepancies between the quantities of physical inventory and the perpetual inventory records.

Each warehouse only has a physical count once in the year so at year end some warehouses will not have been counted for many months.

RG's products are high tech and the GrG-i model appeared old/damaged at the UK warehouse count, indicating an increased risk of obsolete inventory, especially if the GRG-i is also held at other warehouses at year end.

Quality issues have resulted in complaints from homeowners and may be due to Pemmican using cheaper components.

There is also a risk of understatement. Inventory may be in transit or held by the shipping company at year end. This inventory may be incorrectly omitted from the year-end inventory records.

Procedures

Review working papers from the firm's attendance at other warehouse counts held during the year to ascertain if similar control deficiencies were identified.

Arrange additional test counts at warehouses that were counted by RG towards the start of the year.

Review the results of RG's counts after the year end to identify whether there were any significant discrepancies between the physical inventory and the perpetual inventory system.

Inspect the year-end inventory listing for the other 11 warehouses to identify whether any held the GRG-i model. Discuss with management whether this model is obsolete.

Review the quantity/value of post year-end sales of the GRG-i model and check the GRG-i model has been written down if necessary.

Check the accuracy of any adjustments in the inventory records for discrepancies identified during the inventory counts.

Review the aged inventory analysis for any slow-moving items.

Ascertain the basis for inventory write downs, assess the reasonableness of the basis and re-perform any related calculations.

Agree the cost of cameras to the contract with Pemmican.

Compare post year-end selling prices to the carrying value of inventory at the year-end.

Inspect the findings of RG's quality control team to ascertain the reason for the camera malfunctions and determine whether this impacts any inventory held at year end.

Inspect shipping documents and goods received records soon after the year end to identify any inventory which may have been in transit at year end.

Going concern

Justification

RG has lower profit before tax compared to the prior year and inventory days are rising.

The company is dependent on a single supplier.

25% of contracts with retailers are due to expire and may not be renewed.

RG has experienced negative publicity due to quality issues and a cyber-attack. This may result in:

- a loss of reputation and customer goodwill
- termination of retailer contracts; and
- cancellations by customers using the premium services.

RG may be liable for fines if there were data protection breaches and customers may make claims against RG if customer data was stolen in the cyber-attack.

Refunds are payable to customers which will have a negative impact on cash flow and RG may not be able to pay its debts as they fall due.

Procedures

Examine forecasts for 12 months from date of/date of approval of the financial statements to see if RG can pay its debts as they fall due. Consider the reasonableness of the assumptions and perform sensitivity analysis on the key variables.

Inspect post year-end management accounts to ascertain the impact on revenue of the issues arising.

Ascertain whether the retail contracts due for renegotiation have been renewed.

Inspect any reports from RG's IT Security department to ascertain whether any data losses occurred.

Inspect customer correspondence to ascertain whether any claims have been made against RG and whether there is any evidence of contract terminations.

Inspect correspondence with RG's legal team to ascertain the likely outcome of any claims.

Inspect board minutes for reference to financing issues, contract issues or legal claims.

Obtain a written representation from management regarding their plans for future actions and the feasibility of those plans.

Examiner's comments

Answers to this part of the question were generally good with most candidates able to justify why each of the areas were key areas of audit risk and describe plausible audit procedures. Stronger candidates described audit procedures to specifically address their justification of the risks and scored more highly than candidates who took a scattergun approach to their audit procedures. Overall, candidates' answers covering inventory and going concern were better than those covering revenue from retailers and revenue from the premium service.

Revenue from retailers

Most candidates correctly identified the risk of overstatement. In addition, most candidates correctly explained the risks relating to invoices being denominated in foreign currencies and described appropriate procedures to address those risks, ie, reperforming the calculations using exchange rates obtained from a reliable external source. Most candidates also correctly identified that the complaints relating to the malfunction of cameras would lead to refunds and that these might not be accounted for correctly. Fewer candidates went on to explain that the provision for refunds was judgemental.

Many candidates correctly suggested that the reasons for the increase in revenue should be discussed with management but only a small minority earned the marks for considering what those reasons might be, such as the negotiation of new contracts during the year. Very few candidates suggested inspecting correspondence with retailers or reviewing post year-end payments as an indication of the appropriateness of the year-end provision for refunds.

Revenue from premium service

Most candidates correctly identified that advance payments for the premium service might lead to early revenue recognition and hence overstatement of premium service revenue. Most candidates also correctly calculated the 40% increase in revenue from the premium service. However, very few candidates considered that revenue from the premium service would be expected to be a consistent proportion of total revenue and therefore did not earn the higher marks for calculating that the premium service revenue had risen from 22.2% of total revenue in 2017 to 27.3% in 2018. Very few candidates identified that the quality issues might lead to refunds for the premium service if customers cancelled their agreements. Equally few candidates identified that there may be integration issues between the app and the accounting systems which might cause errors.

Many candidates correctly suggested discussing the reasons for the increase in revenue with management but most failed to expand on their answer by suggesting explanations such as additional marketing of the service to customers. Most candidates earned some marks for attempting to describe relevant procedures relating to the calculation of deferred income although some explanations were vague. Few candidates scored the mark available for vouching recorded receipts to bank statements. Very few candidates earned the marks available for describing procedures relating to refunds in respect of the premium service, primarily because refunds were not included in their justification.

Inventory

There were some good answers in relation to inventory. However, it was disappointing that fewer candidates used the data available to calculate inventory days. Most opted instead to calculate a simple percentage increase which attracted fewer marks. Most candidates justified why inventory was a key area of risk. The most commonly cited justifications were:

- internal control issues
- lack of reliability of the perpetual inventory system
- obsolescence issues including those related to the GRG-i model; and
- quality issues due to the cheaper components used by Pemmican.

The points most commonly overlooked were that the GRG-i model might be held at year end by other warehouses outside the UK and that there was also a risk of understatement of inventory if goods held by the shipping company at year end were not included in inventory. A small number of candidates incorrectly concluded that any goods in transit would lead to a risk of overstatement due to the risk of the inventory becoming lost or damaged.

Candidates' descriptions of audit procedures relating to inventory were not covered as well as their justifications. The most commonly cited procedures were those relating to the identification of aged inventory through a review of the aged inventory report and comparing post year-end selling prices to the carrying value at the year end. Points commonly overlooked included inspecting the findings of RG's quality control team to ascertain whether quality issues impacted inventory held at year end, checking the accuracy of adjustments to inventory records for discrepancies identified during the warehouse counts and reviewing working papers from other counts attended by the firm to ascertain if similar control issues occurred. A significant number of candidates suggested attending year-end inventory counts. These candidates failed to appreciate that counts were undertaken on a rolling basis and therefore the opportunity to attend these counts had already passed. Candidates going down this route then tended to waste time by describing in detail the audit procedures that would be performed during attendance at an inventory count. Some candidates incorrectly included foreign currency translation risks even though the scenario stated that invoices for cameras were denominated in sterling. Very few candidates identified any procedures to address the risk of understatement due to goods being in transit at the year end.

Going concern

This was the best answered area with most candidates able to provide well explained justifications as to why going concern had been identified as a key area of audit risk. Points commonly cited included:

- falling profit before tax
- contracts due for renegotiation
- negative publicity arising from the quality issues
- the impact on RG's cash flow of a high level of refunds
- risk of early termination of contracts; and
- the impact of fines and claims resulting from data security breaches.

The points most commonly overlooked were rising inventory days and RG's dependency on Pemmican. Candidates described a range of relevant procedures in relation to going concern including examination of RG's cash flow forecast to see if the company could pay its debts as they fall due and sensitivity analysis on the forecast. Candidates also often correctly described procedures relating to inspection of correspondence with customers and RG's legal team, inspection of board minutes and obtaining written representations from management. Very few candidates earned the additional marks available for describing the information they were looking for in the board minutes or the content of the written representation.

The most commonly overlooked procedure related to the inspection of post year-end management accounts to ascertain the impact on post year-end sales.

76.2 **Deficiency (a)**

Movement of cameras occurred during the count.

Consequences

Inventory might be counted and subsequently removed (double counted) or added after items have been counted (omitted).

This will result in discrepancies between the count and the inventory system.

Adjustments may be made to the inventory system incorrectly.

Errors in the inventory system may result in:

- stock outs; if the system records inventory which is not available, it may result in lost sales and damage to customer relationships.

- over-ordering; if the system records low levels of inventory but there is sufficient, it will have an adverse impact on cash flow and may result in obsolete inventory.

Recommendations

Freeze inventory movements during inventory counts.

Carry out counts when inventory movements are unlikely, eg, out of hours.

Implement procedures for recording necessary movements during the inventory count.

Ensure that any deliveries inwards on the day of the count are stored separately and counted at end of day.

Deficiency (b)

There is no review of the aged inventory report.

Consequences

Old or obsolete items will not be identified on a timely basis.

Inventory will be overvalued in the management accounts which may result in inappropriate management decisions.

Recommendations

Monthly reviews of the aged inventory report should be performed by a designated employee and signed as evidence of the review.

A report on slow moving items should be prepared for and reviewed by senior management.

Obsolete items should be communicated to RG's finance team so that write downs can be reflected in the accounting records.

Deficiency (c)

There is no investigation of discrepancies between the count and inventory system.

Consequences

Reasons for discrepancies will not be identified. Discrepancies could be due to:

- theft, resulting in an adverse impact on cash flow/profits.
- inadequate controls over count procedures.

Inventory records will be inaccurate resulting in:

- stock outs; if the system records inventory which is not available, it may result in lost sales and damage to customer relationships.
- over-ordering; if the system records low levels of inventory but there is sufficient, it will have an adverse impact on cash flow and may result in obsolete inventory.

Recommendations

Where discrepancies are identified:

- the inventory item should be recounted by a different counter.
- the reason for the discrepancy should be investigated.

Any adjustments to the inventory records should be reviewed and signed off by a senior employee.

A regular review of adjustments should be undertaken to identify any errors or unauthorised changes.

The level of discrepancies for each warehouse should be compared periodically to identify any warehouses that have an unusually high number of issues.

General recommendations (awarded only once)

Train employees in control procedures.
Monitor that procedures are properly performed.
Take disciplinary action for employees failing to adhere to procedures.

Examiner's comments

Answers to this part of the question were very disappointing. A large proportion of candidates gave very scant answers with many only citing recommendations that were the converse of the internal control deficiency. These answers do not score highly, and candidates need to consider how to 'add value' to their recommendations.

Deficiency (a)

This deficiency was the best addressed with many candidates correctly identifying the movement in inventory during the count as the internal control deficiency. Most candidates provided some relevant consequences such as inventory being double counted or omitted resulting in inaccurate inventory records. Only stronger candidates went on to earn the marks available for describing the consequences of inaccurate inventory records such as stock outs and over ordering. Most candidates earned a good proportion of the marks for recommendations. Freezing inventory movements and performing the count out of hours were the most commonly cited recommendations. Fewer candidates earned the marks for recommending RG put procedures in place for necessary movements of inventory during the count.

Deficiency (b)

This was the least well addressed deficiency. A large proportion of candidates failed to identify that the absence of a review of the aged inventory report was the internal control deficiency. Instead these candidates incorrectly stated that the presence of obsolete inventory was the deficiency, failing to appreciate that it was a consequence. Most candidates did earn the marks for identifying that inventory may be obsolete and hence overstated but very few earned the marks for considering that inaccurate information about inventory might result in inappropriate management decisions. Many candidates correctly identified that the aged inventory report should be reviewed on a regular basis by a designated employee. However, very few considered the reporting of slow-moving items to senior management.

Deficiency (c)

As with deficiency (b) weaker candidates failed to identify that the control deficiency was the lack of investigation of discrepancies before adjustment of the inventory system. These candidates tended to cite the discrepancies as the internal control deficiency. Many candidates correctly identified that the deficiency would result in inaccurate inventory records and leave RG exposed to the risk of theft. Few candidates identified that stock outs and over ordering might be consequences. Most candidates earned the marks available for recommending that discrepancies be investigated and that adjustments to the inventory system should be reviewed by a senior employee. However, few candidates went beyond these points. Very few considered that the inventory items should be re-counted by a different counter or that the level of discrepancies per warehouse should be monitored to identify warehouses with unusually high discrepancy rates.

76.3 Threats to independence and objectivity

There are self-interest, familiarity and intimidation threats:

- The audit senior may be unwilling to highlight errors or challenge the client for fear of losing the job offer.

- As a new financial controller pressure may be exerted over the audit team.

- Members of the audit team are likely to have a relationship with the audit senior and are therefore less likely to challenge a former colleague.

Actions by the audit senior

Inform the engagement/ethics partner of the offer immediately.

Actions by engagement partner

Remove the audit senior from the audit team immediately.

Review any work already completed by the audit senior.

Reconsider the composition of the audit team if the audit senior accepts the offer.

Appoint and brief a new audit senior to complete planning/audit work and explain the reasons for the change to RG's management.

Examiner's comments

Answers to this part of the question were very good with a high number of candidates earning full marks. Most candidates correctly identified and explained the self-interest and familiarity threats. Very few candidates identified the intimidation threat. Candidates also generally identified appropriate actions such as informing the engagement partner, removing the audit senior from the audit team and reviewing his/her work. Fewer candidates earned the marks for reconsidering the composition of the audit team if the audit senior were to take up the financial controller role.

77 Swallow

		Marks
77.1 Factors		
Firm may not have the relevant industry expertise and may need to use an industry expert	2½	
Swallow has three subsidiaries and manufacturing facilities in 20 countries	3½	
Swallow is a complex organisation – risk of management bias	6	
Swallow has recently been through a business reorganisation – inherent and control risk, possible going concern risk	3½	
New IT systems may include a new accounting system	5½	
Claims of compromised health and safety standards – risk relating to management integrity, potential risk to going concern, and risk to firm's reputation	7	
Changes to remuneration of the sales team may incentivise Swallow's employees to overstate sales	5½	
Dispute between Swallow's shareholders and the finance director has left	2	
Swallow's bank intends to place reliance on the financial statements and the auditor's report	4	
Requirement to complete the audit by 31 January 2019	3½	
Marks available	43	
Maximum		18
77.2 Ethical threats and safeguards		
Management of Swallow's payroll		
Threats	4½	
Safeguards	5½	
Assistance in recruiting a new finance director		
Threats	2½	
Safeguards	3	
Provision of advice in respect of a dispute with HMRC		
Threats	3	
Safeguards	½	
Marks available	19	
Maximum		8
Total marks available		26

77.1 Swallow is a specialist engineering company. The firm may not have the relevant industry expertise and may need to use an industry expert.

Swallow has three subsidiaries and manufacturing facilities in 20 countries. The firm may need to visit different locations or find local representation. There may be language barriers and differing local laws and regulations to address. The firm will have to work with component auditors. The audit plan would need to include any risks associated with currency or translation issues.

Swallow is a complex organisation with items in the financial statements requiring the exercise of judgement such as revenue recognition, provision for losses and development expenditure which is vulnerable to impairment. These areas may be subject to management bias and the firm will need to ensure it has sufficiently senior staff included in the audit team.

Swallow has recently been through a business reorganisation which increases inherent and control risk. It is also likely to limit the extent to which the firm can make use of analytical procedures. The challenging market conditions suggest an increased risk of going concern issues.

The new IT systems may include a new accounting system. There is an increased risk of error during the switch over and the firm may need to test any parallel running. The new system may not be reliable resulting in higher control risk. The firm may need to consider the use of IT experts.

There have been claims of compromised health and safety standards which may increase the risk of accidents and associated claims/fines which may not be adequately provided for or disclosed in the financial statements. Breaching health and safety regulations raises doubts about management integrity and there is a potential risk to going concern if Swallow is shut down by regulators or loses employees due to this issue. Swallow has received adverse publicity and there is a risk of reputational damage to the firm by association.

Changes to remuneration of the sales team may incentivise Swallow's employees to overstate sales. There has also been an increase in calls to the anti-bribery hotline which may indicate the presence of fraud/bribery. The firm may have a duty to report under the Proceeds of Crime/Bribery Acts.

There has been a dispute between Swallow's shareholders and the finance director has left. There may have been a lack of proper oversight leading to an increased risk of errors in the financial statements.

Swallow's bank intends to place reliance on the financial statements and the auditor's report. This increases the level of engagement risk. The firm may be liable to the bank if a duty of care is owed. The bank reliance also increases the risk of management bias when preparing the financial statements.

The invitation to tender document has requested that the firm demonstrates its ability to complete the audit by 31 January 2019. This leaves a very limited period to obtain audit evidence after the year end and may reduce audit quality. This increases the risk of the firm reaching an inappropriate audit opinion.

Examiner's comments

Candidates were generally strong at identifying the factors that should be considered when deciding to submit a tender. However, the explanation of the factor proved more challenging to many candidates. For example, although the vast majority of candidates identified that non-compliance with health and safety standards was a factor to consider, only a minority of candidates considered the risk of unrecognised or undisclosed liabilities arising from fines or legal claims. A significant minority of candidates strayed beyond the requirement to use "the information documented by the audit partner" and wasted time considering issues not referred to in the documentation such as professional clearance, due diligence procedures and conflicts of interest. A small minority ignored the instruction in the requirement not to consider the provision of non-audit services.

77.2 Management of Swallow's payroll

Threats

Self-review threat

- The results of the engagement are likely to be material to the financial statements.

- The audit team may be too trusting of the payroll work or reluctant to highlight any errors.

Management threat

- The firm may make decisions which are the responsibility of management.

Self-interest threat

- Management of Swallow's payroll will represent recurring income.
- This may result in fee dependency.

Safeguards

Ensure there is informed management.

Any services provided must be purely of a technical or mechanical nature.

The firm must not:

- authorise or approve transactions
- prepare originating data
- determine or change journal entries/classifications without management approval

The payroll work should be performed by staff not involved in the audit engagement.

The firm should undertake an independent partner review of the payroll services and the audit engagement to ensure the payroll services have been properly and effectively assessed during the audit.

There should be regular monitoring of the fee income from Swallow to ensure that fee thresholds are not breached.

Assistance in recruiting a new finance director

Threats

Management threat

- The firm may adopt a position too closely aligned with management.

Familiarity threat

- If the firm plays a significant role in the recruitment of a new finance director, the engagement team may be less critical of information and explanations provided by the individual.

Safeguards

The firm must not:

- decide on whom to appoint.
- provide advice on the quantum of the remuneration package.

The firm can contribute to the process in less formal ways by:

- interviewing the prospective director or advising on their technical competence.
- providing information gathered by the firm, eg, salary surveys.
- applying proven methodologies using given data.

Provision of advice in respect of a dispute with HMRC

Threats

Advocacy threat

- The engagement involves supporting the position of management in a dispute.

Self-review threat

- The outcome of the dispute with HMRC is likely to have a material impact on the financial statements.

Management threat

- The firm may be expected to make decisions on behalf of management.

Safeguards

The firm should not undertake this engagement.

Examiner's comments

Payroll services

Most candidates identified the self-review and management threats but only a minority identified that it was likely to give rise to recurring fees and possible fee dependency. Weaker candidates incorrectly stated that the Ethical Standard prohibited the provision of such services. These candidates failed to appreciate that it is possible to provide these services for an unlisted client if safeguards are in place. The safeguards most commonly identified were the use of separate teams, informed management and independent review. The points most commonly overlooked were those relating to the prohibited tasks such as approving transactions, preparing originating data and journal entries.

Recruitment services

Most candidates identified the management and familiarity threats and provided plausible explanations of the threats. Many candidates assumed that the service just related to the decision regarding who should be appointed as finance director and correctly stated that this service should not be provided. However, only a minority of candidates scored the extra marks available for demonstrating an understanding of how the firm could provide the service in less formal ways.

Dispute with HMRC

Most candidates identified the advocacy threat and correctly concluded that the service should not be provided. Fewer candidates identified the self-review and management threats.

	Marks
78 **Implications for audit or assurance reports**	
AMA	6½
Modified opinion	
Unable to obtain sufficient appropriate audit evidence over cash sales	
Material but not pervasive	
Also report by exception in accordance with Companies Act 2006	
Wild	4½
Modified opinion	
Related party transaction which is material by nature	
Material but not pervasive	
Opinion qualified and details of related party transaction included in section headed "basis for qualified opinion"	
Lake	5
Assurance report should be modified	
Adverse modification	
Report should state that the assumptions do not provide a reasonable basis	
Paragraph describing the matter giving rise to the modification should also be included and headed "basis for adverse conclusion"	
Sail	4
Assurance report should be modified but opinion should not be modified	
No misstatement or inability to obtain evidence	
Include an emphasis of matter paragraph in its report	
State that the opinion on the Greenhouse Gas Statement is not modified	
Marks available	20
Total marks available	14

AMA

The firm's audit report and audit opinion should be modified.

The firm was unable to obtain sufficient appropriate audit evidence over cash sales. Cash sales amount to 2% of revenue and 11.6% of profit before tax. This is material but not pervasive as the issue is isolated to cash sales.

The firm's opinion should be qualified. The report should include a paragraph, headed "basis for qualified opinion", describing the matter giving rise to the modification.

The firm should also report by exception in accordance with Companies Act 2006 that:

- adequate accounting records were not maintained; and
- not all information and explanations were received.

Wild

The firm's audit report and audit opinion should be modified.

The sale of the property to the managing director is a related party transaction which is material by nature and must be disclosed in the notes to the financial statements.

The misstatement is not pervasive as it is isolated to the related party disclosure.

The firm's opinion should be qualified and the details of the related party transaction should be included in a section headed "basis for qualified opinion".

Lake

The firm's assurance report should be modified.

Lake has made an inappropriate assumption with respect to revenue in its cash flow forecast which is significant.

ISAE 3400 requires the firm to issue an adverse modification.

The report should state that the assumptions do not provide a reasonable basis for the cash flow forecast and a paragraph describing the matter giving rise to the modification should also be included and headed "basis for adverse conclusion".

The firm may still be able to give an unmodified opinion that the cash flow forecast is properly prepared on the basis of the assumptions.

Sail

The firm's assurance report should be modified but the opinion should not be modified.

There is no misstatement or inability to obtain sufficient appropriate evidence.

The estimation of the emission figures for the period February to June is fundamental to the users' understanding of the Greenhouse Gas Statement. The firm should include an emphasis of matter paragraph in its report to draw users' attention to the disclosure in the Greenhouse Gas Statement.

The report should also state that the opinion on the Greenhouse Gas Statement is not modified in respect of this matter.

Examiner's comments

AMA

This scenario was generally well answered as most candidates identified that the auditor was unable to obtain sufficient appropriate evidence about cash sales which were material to the financial statements. Most of these candidates also correctly concluded that the issue was not pervasive and consequently warranted a qualified opinion. However, a small minority of candidates stated, incorrectly, that there should be a disclaimer of opinion. Some candidates also stated, incorrectly, that cash sales were misstated - there was insufficient evidence to reach such a conclusion. The most common omissions were the points relating to reporting by exception.

Wild

This scenario was generally well answered as most candidates identified that the transaction involved related parties and should have been disclosed in the financial statements. Most of these candidates also appreciated that it was not pervasive as it only related to a disclosure. However, a small minority of candidates stated, incorrectly, that it was pervasive and as such warranted an adverse opinion.

A significant minority of candidates wasted time discussing the implications for the audit arising from the possible lack of integrity of management. This was beyond the scope of the question and no marks were awarded for these points.

Lake

Those candidates familiar with paragraph 32 of ISAE 3400 The Examination of Prospective Financial Information scored good marks on this part of the question. Most candidates identified that the assumption regarding revenue growth was unrealistic but many stated, incorrectly, that because it related only to revenue, the modification should take the form of a qualification instead of an adverse modification. These candidates failed to appreciate that it was a significant assumption and as a result required an adverse modification. Few candidates identified that the reporting accountant may still be able to give an unmodified opinion that the forecast is properly prepared on the basis of the assumptions.

Sail

Strong candidates appreciated that because the matter had been appropriately disclosed in the GHG Statement and was fundamental to users' understanding of the statement it warranted the use of an emphasis of matter paragraph. A significant minority appreciated that it should be brought to the attention of users but stated, incorrectly, that it should be included in the Other Matters or Key Matters section of the assurance report.

REVIEW FORM – AUDIT AND ASSURANCE QUESTION BANK

Your ratings, comments and suggestions would be appreciated on the following areas of this Question Bank

	Very useful	Useful	Not useful
Number of questions in each section	☐	☐	☐
Standard of answers	☐	☐	☐
Amount of guidance on exam technique	☐	☐	☐
Quality of marking guides	☐	☐	☐

	Excellent	Good	Adequate	Poor
Overall opinion of this Question Bank	☐	☐	☐	☐

Please return completed form to:

The Learning Team
Learning and Professional Department
ICAEW
Metropolitan House
321 Avebury Boulevard
Milton Keynes
MK9 2FZ
E learning@icaew.com

For space to add further comments please see overleaf.

REVIEW FORM (continued)

TELL US WHAT YOU THINK

Please note any further comments and suggestions/errors below.